The Soldiers of the Flanders Field American Military Cemetery

Written and Published by Christopher Sims and Patrick Lernout

ISBN 978-1-908345-41-7

Christopher Sims was born in Nottingham, UK on 8 November 1953. Son of a British father and Belgian mother he emigrated to Belgium in 1965 where he graduated high school at the St. Vincentius College, Ypres in 1972. Although studying at the Higher Institute for Paramedic Studies in Gent, he continued in the footsteps of his father and was assigned as Cemetery Associate to the Flanders Field American Cemetery in 1974. He retired in January 2015 after more than 40 years of service with the American Battle Monuments Commission. During his tenure he acquired an in depth knowledge of the military campaigns and U.S. involvement in the Flanders region and researched many stories of the individual soldiers buried in the cemetery. He has also given presentations on the US soldiers of Flanders Fields in Belgium, France and in the USA. Through his friendship with John Giles, Founder of the Western Front Association in 1980, he became one of the contacts in Belgium of this renowned association in 1983. In 1989 he established the Belgian Branch of the Western Front Association and became its first area chairman. His lifelong friendship with Patrick Lernout encouraged them both to embark on a 12 year research project and completing this historical work.

Patrick Lernout was born in Roeselare on 6 December 1953. He graduated with a degree in textile engineering from the HRITK in Gent, and for quite some time worked as a human resources director. His interest in WWI began as a young child, when he would walk pass an old German war cemetery daily. At age 14 he visited the American cemetery at Omaha Beach and became fascinated and intrigued with what he saw. This encouraged him to learn more about the boys who were buried so far from home. Patrick researched many of these men for 12 years, finding relatives, photographs, and additional biographical information on them. During the search he also made many friends in the USA. In gratitude for the sacrifices that were made, his curiosity to know more about the lives and strife of these young men and his growing friendship with Christopher Sims resulted in the definite start and completion of this project.

ACKNOWLEDGEMENTS

We owe our sincere gratitude and appreciation to numerous people who supported and assisted us during our long journey of research towards the completion of this book. In the first place our families and especially our spouses, Katrien and Hilde, who spent many lonesome evenings during the 12 years of our research.

The rewarding bonds of friendship arising from these efforts were emphasized in 2008 during our tour in the United States. The whole-hearted support and encouragement by our American friends in New York and Washington, the presence of many family members of casualties buried or memorialized at Flanders Field, was simply inspiring. Assistance was provided from all corners of the world. Academically we are indebted to Dr. Mitchell Yockelson, Investigative Archivist at the National Archives, College Park, Maryland, who during our research at the National Archives ensured everything in his power for us to obtain the burial files. I owe particular thanks to my good friend Dr. Lisa M. Budreau, MA, Dphil., Historian and Senior Curator of Military History, Tennessee State Museum, for her encouragement, professional advice and support in providing details of her personal research from the diplomatic archives of the Ministry of Foreign Affairs, Quai d'Orsay, Paris, France. Dr. Benjamin A. Hill, Lt.Col., U.S. Army Physician Scientist, Medical Institute of Chemical Defense, Aberdeen Proving Ground, MD for his insight on WWI gas attacks and providing pertinent information on the Spencer reports.
Holly S. Fenelon, Gold Star Mother historian, inspired us for many years and provided a wealth of information on the history of the Gold Star Mothers. Closer to home, Dr. Jeroen Huygelier, Historian at the Historical Documentation Centre of the Belgian Army in Brussels and Sandrin Coorevits, who at the time was archivist at the city of Waregem. The assistance of librarians, genealogical societies and archivists in the United States and Europe were very rewarding.

Countless other people provided assistance. Patty Mackey from Anderson, SC provided information on several soldiers and was able to locate family members and relatives. Darren Peterson from Dothan, AL gave tips on how to conduct some specific research and provided many stories and photographs of soldiers. Scott Graczyk, Vonnie Pryor and Jim Green also assisted in retrieving pertinent information.
The many relatives who provided assistance and the many good friends we made over the years but cannot name out of fear that we might forget someone.

Jef Bogaert and Roger Verbeke who encouraged us and provided professional assistance in using the correct military terminology. Paul Foster, FSRA, author, speaker and tour guide for his assistance and guidance relating to this publication.

And finally: the 393 men documented in this book to which we owe our freedom. To quote with the words of one of them: "*to make this place a better world.*"

CONTENTS

REMEMBER THEM

If you are able,
save for them a place
inside of you
and save one backward glance
when you are leaving,
for the places they can no longer go.

Be not ashamed to say
you loved them,
though you may
or may not always have.

Take what they have left
and what they have taught you
with their dying
and keep it with your own.

And in that time
when men decide and feel safe
to call the war insane,
take one moment to embrace
those gentle heroes
you left behind.

An immortal poem, written by Major Michael Davis O'Donnel* on 1 January 1970 in Dak To, Vietnam. He wrote this poem in almost identical circumstances and conditions as John McCrae did 55 years earlier during the second battle of Ypres, with his poem "In Flanders Fields".
And history repeats itself...
The American engagement in World War I was short but violent and aggressive. Many American families lost a son, daughter or spouse in a far an unknown land.
This book does not specifically cover or emphasize on military operations in Flanders. We have tried to present a unique document with original photography which has never been published before. This way we have taken it a step further than most authors who mainly concentrate on strategy and battlefields.

* *Major* O'Donnell was a helicopter pilot killed in action on 24 March 1970 in Cambodia. He was listed as missing in action. His remains were found on 12 April 1995 and positively identified on 20 June 2001. He was given a final resting place at Arlington National Cemetery on 16 August 2001.

1

THE BEGINNING

"The surly drums beat terrible afar. With all the dreadful music of the war."

William Broome
"The seat of war in Flanders" 1710

The assassination of Archduke Ferdinand of Austria on 28 June 1914 is generally accepted as being the cause of the outbreak of World War I. One month after his assassination Austria-Hungary declared war on Serbia. This would be the start of a chain reaction and further declarations of war which finally erupted in a global conflict of which the dimensions could never have been envisaged beforehand.

The assassination of Prince Ferdinand and his wife, the Duchess of Hohenberg, is generally accepted as the stepping stone to cover the outbreak of "The Great War". Many authors have used this introduction to announce their vision of this dark period of the war to end all wars.

However, after careful historical research one can only come to the conclusion that the assassination of Prince Ferdinand was just the tip of the iceberg and that the origins of this world conflict were far more complex. As Voltaire once said: *"All is revealed at the end of the day, and everything is revealed when all the days are over."*

Our introduction to these origins is merely an attempt on our part to bring the reader in the general atmosphere on what the underlying causes of this world conflict were. By no means is this a complete version or based on all the facts encompassing the European parties concerned. Our main goal is to clarify in its simplicity and with pertinent details the cause of this global conflict.

As in every war, power and greed lie at its base. And as history repeats itself, in war there are no winners, only losers. If we make a comparison with recent conflicts, we can only come to the conclusion that the political situation has remained unchanged. Power and greed are still the main causes and factors in today's world. Only now, with the communication capabilities of the 21st century, it isn't so easy to pull wool over the eyes of the general public.

Europe was restless for more than a hundred years before it exploded into what is known as the First World War. The assassination of Archduke Ferdinand was only the fuse that set off the powder keg. At the start of the 20th century, the general public was unaware on how the world was evolving. Eventually they were startled to see how the world had technically made so much progress. Unfortunately not all for the good cause.

The urge for colonization by the Imperialistic Powers in the century leading up to the World War was immense. Not only Germany, but also Great Britain and France were eager to possess a piece of the pie. Enviousness and distrust caused dissension, intimidation and signing of secret treaties. By 1823, the urge for colonization could be felt in the United States. John Quincey Adams, Secretary of State to President James Monroe, informed the President: "*It is to be clearly understood that the American continents are not to be considered as subjects for future colonization by any European Powers.*" Europe, was now compelled to search elsewhere and so they turned their interests towards the African continent. It is here that the seeds of evil were sewn, their crop being agony, death and destruction.

One doesn't need to conduct intensive research to find the sources of differing opinions and arguments between France and Germany. A new chapter in the life of European history commenced at the Palais de Versailles with the German declaration of Unity on 18 January 1871. The annexation of Alsace - Lorraine was a persistent thorn of annoyance and irritation for France. Germany was very determined. Von Moltke declared: " *What we have now achieved, we must retain with all our power for the next fifty years.*"

Plans to expand the German fleet in 1900 caused tension and mistrust within the British Admiralty. Germany justified their plans by emphasizing that they needed to expand their fleet to protect and control their colonies. The British had their doubts and were wondering if Germany wasn't planning a future war. In any case, the expansion of the German fleet was seen as threat to their own substantial and well organized fleet.

Although Kaiser Wilhelm had proposed a treaty with Britain, its government later changed its views as the Kaiser was under the impression that the British were too eager to comply to his propositions. Wilhelm was confident that once his great fleet was ready, Britain would have no other option than to agree to his demands and sign a treaty based on Germany's propositions. Great Britain's future attempts to bring the two nations closer together in 1899 and 1901 were promptly denied.

As a safety precaution, Great-Britain decided to seek a closer relationship with France. Quarrelling nations for centuries, it was time to play safe and bury the hatchet. Their first attempt was in 1903 when King Edward VII paid a visit to Paris. Although at first, the French were in denial and showed him the cold shoulder, towards the end of his visit King Edward, widely known as the *"Roi Charmeur"*, was accepted and received with much praise and credibility. This visit resulted in a closer bond between the two nations and the signing of the British-French Entente the following year in 1904. In secrecy this meant that Great Britain would continue to have a free hand in Egypt while Britain turned a blind eye when France took steps in Morocco.

When France attempted to bring Morocco under its wings as a protectorate in 1905, the Sultan of Morocco turned to Germany for advice. Germany immediately took drastic measures. Kaiser Wilhelm travelled to the capital Tangiers to confront the French and declared the independence of Morocco (first Moroccan crisis). This was the beginning of an international argument that would last until 1911 (second Moroccan crisis) which ended with Germany, against their will finally accepting France's terms under certain conditions.

Part of Morocco became protectorate of France in exchange for the French districts that Germany had annexed in equatorial Africa. Many Germans were far from happy with this arrangement. They felt they had been dubiously swindled into this agreement and that the British and French had taken a run with the best part of the deal and so further dividing the continents.

This crisis, together with the conflicts in Bosnia and Herzegovina (Balkan wars of 1912-1913) and countless other religious conflicts and incidents resulted in Europe being brought to the boiling point. The totality of these incidents is known as being the underlying causes towards the outbreak of World War I.

We can only conclude, due to the evidence provided above, that Germany really could not have been the sole guilty party resulting in this disastrous war. Consequently, after the war, during the signing of the Treaty of Versailles, there was much doubt concerning the validity of article 231 condemning Germany as only nation causing this war. The Americans being in the front line, objected to its terms, specifically, the high price that Germany was to pay for its role as aggressor. Congress also had serious concerns that the League of Nations would pull the U.S. into further wars that were not in its interest. In the end, Congress refused to ratify the Treaty of Versailles and the U.S.A. negotiated its own settlement with Germany in 1921.

Many renowned American historians of which one in particular, Sydney Fay, publicized amazing facts and materials which resulted in this treaty being vehemently criticized and condemned.

2

1914 - 1917

"Hell vomited forth her legions of destruction and the stars around us stopped in their flight to watch a world gone mad with savagery and hate."

George V. Hobart,
The Washington Post - 4 July 1915

The further Europe evolved in this war, the more Wilson's policies came under pressure during his strife for power in the U.S. In a tribute in Washington on 28 September 1915 he declared: "*Democracy is the most difficult form of government, because it is the form under which you have to persuade the largest number of persons to do anything in particular.*" The first group opting for durable peace, the opposition demanding expansion of military forces in case of a conflict involving the United States. William Jennings Bryan (1860-1925) was a passionate pacifist. Wilson assigned him as Secretary of State in 1912. However Bryan resigned due to Wilson's indecisiveness after the sinking of the Lusitania. When the United States declared war on Germany in 1917, Bryan returned to office and fully supported Wilsons' government. In the meantime Wilson's opponent, the progressive Theodore Roosevelt, demanded the immediate expansion of Army and Naval Forces.

Wilson's opinion was that both parties were overreacting. As a humanitarian, he avoided pouring oil on the fire. His preference was inevitably leaning against the side of the pacifists but as head of State he of course could not show. Consequently, as a result, he gambled on both parties to sustain a state of balance in the U.S.

Although the supporters for expansion of military forces as a defensive measure would eventually win the battle, the indecisiveness and continuing dispute remained. The fact was that they were not prepared for a possible military confrontation. "*No man should draw a pistol who dares not shoot. A government that shakes his fist first and its finger afterwards falls in contempt. Our diplomacy has lost its authority and influence because we have been brave in words but irresolute in action.*", according to Elihu Root (1845-1937), who received the Nobel prize for Peace in 1912.

Wilson ignored all allegations and rebuked with a counter offensive. When a certain General Wood prompted that the U.S. should be prepared for military action in case of an attack,

Wilson simply responded that he did not believe that there was a necessity for immediate action. He feared that the general public would be shocked. He stated; *"No matter how the great war ended, there would be complete exhaustion, and even if Germany won, she would not be in a condition to seriously menace our country for many years to come."*

In the meantime many Americans were impatient and would not wait. By the end of October 1914 many travelled to Europe at their own expense to fight or provide humanitarian aid. They joined the French Army (as Alan Seeger, known poet - photo), Red Cross or one of the many organizations providing aid such as the *Young Men's Christian Association* (*YMCA*) or *Friends of France*, with their own ambulance service (*American Ambulance Service*). Others, who could not afford to make the trip travelled to Canada and joined the Canadian Expeditionary Forces. By the end of 1914 over two thousand had joined to fight against the German aggressor. In 1915 the number  had reached six thousand, June 1916 sixteen thousand and by February 1917 to fifty thousand. Eighty percent fought either with the British or Canadian Commonwealth Forces.*

It goes without saying that this caused certain embarrassment to Wilson's neutral politics. On 19 August 1914 Wilson declared to the Senate: *"The people of the United States are drawn from many nations, and chiefly from the nations now at war."* This could be no surprise. Between 1890 and 1914, 15 million people had emigrated to the United States. At that time the population in the U.S. was 76 million (US Census population estimates indicate 99,111,000). 10 million were born in Europe and another 26 million were first generation born in the United States. It goes without saying that these people still had a strong bond with their country of origin. Additionally Wilson explained: *"It is natural and inevitable that there should be the utmost variety of sympathy and desire among them with regard to the issues and circumstances of the conflict. Some will wish one nation, others another, to succeed in the momentous struggle. It will be easy to excite passion and difficult to allay it ."*

Notwithstanding his sympathy in this awkward situation, Wilson needed to clarify his position with dignity and authority. 1916 would be an important year for him with the upcoming presidential elections. A definitive decision was made based on the fact that Americans joining the Commonwealth Forces needed to make a political statement: *"I will be faithful and bear true allegiance to his Majesty King George V and I will defend his Majesty in person, Crown and dignity against all enemies, and will observe and obey all orders of his Majesty ..."*

On 3 November 1916 the *New York Times* announced: *"Took Foreign Oath, Loses Citizenship"*. Anyone who pledged allegiance to King George V, relinquished his U.S. citizenship. These Americans who, between 1914 and 1917, were killed in action, died of wounds or disease were buried in one of the many Commonwealth War Graves Commission cemeteries (see also A.G.R.S.)

*On 11 November 1927, Canada inaugurated a Cross of Sacrifice at Arlington National Cemetery, VA, in remembrance of the Americans who died whilst serving with the Canadian armies during World War I.

In spite the fact that Woodrow Wilson received an enormous amount of adverse critique during his political term in office (the irresolute action after the German submarine attack of 7 May 1915 on the Lusitania when 128 American lives were lost), he was still able to persuade the American people to vote for him and win the elections with the slogan *"He kept us out of the war."* His second term of office commenced on 5 March 1917.

In an attempt to keep the U.S. out of the war, Wilson changed his tactics. He would do everything in his power to find a short term solution to end the war in Europe. Unfortunately, notwithstanding his promise that during his second term of office he would provide a *"peace ticket"* within a month of his re-election, the escalation of attacks on shipping with American losses became untenable. The United States could no longer stay out of the war. The day after the sinking of three American cargo ships, he reluctantly made the decision to declare war on Germany. With this approach, he would also secure the U.S. a place at the peace conference after the war.

On 2 April 1917, President Wilson called a special session of Congress. He had prepared his opening remarks with great care: *"Vessels of every kind, whatever their flag, their character, their cargo, their destination, their errand, have been ruthlessly sent to the bottom without warning and without thought of help or mercy for those on board, the vessels of friendly neutrals along those of belligerents. Even hospital ships and ships carrying relief to the sorely bereaved and stricken people of Belgium, though the latter were provided with safe conduct through the proscribed areas by the German Government itself, and were distinguished with unmistakable marks of identity, have been sunk with the same reckless lack of compassion or of principle...The peace of the world is involved and its peoples and the menace to that peace and freedom lies in the existence of autocratic governments backed by organized force which is controlled wholly by their will, not by the will of their people... The world must be made safe for Democracy ... The right is more precious than peace, and we shall fight for the things we have always carried nearest to our hearts – for Democracy, for the rights of those who submit to authority to have a voice in their own governments, for the rights and liberties of small nations, for a universal dominion of right by such a concert of free people as shall bring peace and safety to all nations and make the world itself at last free."*
In addition President Wilson declared: *" We have no selfish ends to serve. We desire no conquest, no dominion. We seek no indemnities for ourselves, no material compensation for the sacrifice we shall freely make. We are but the champions of the rights of mankind. We enter this war only where we are clearly forced into it, because there are no other means of defending our rights."* He proposed Congress to share his views and declare war on Germany. With the exception of a few abstentions, Congress unanimously voted in favor of the proposal and on 6 April 1917, war was declared on Germany.

AMERICA WAS AT WAR

The United States decision to enter the war at such a late stage was not accepted with gratitude by the allies. Winston Churchill declared in the House of Commons : *"What he did in April 1917, could have been done in May 1915 (sinking of the Lusitania). And if done then what abridgement of the slaughter, what sparing of the agony, what ruin, what catastrophe's would have been prevented; in how many millions of homes would an empty chair be occupied today."*

3

1917 - 1918

"Listen, young heroes ! Your country is calling !
Time strikes the hour for the brave and the true !
Now, while the foremost are fighting and falling,
Fill up the ranks that have opened for you ! "

Oliver Wendell Holmes, 1862

The establishment of the American Expeditionary Forces (A.E.F.) was a slow process. When General Pershing was assigned as General of the Armies on 26 May, the National Army only consisted of 135,000 men. Although different sources provide different figures, one month after the declaration of war only 1,300 American soldiers had landed in France. In June, front page newspaper headlines showed *"General Pershing Landing at Boulogne"* (13 June - photo), a few weeks later: "*The First American Troops Arriving at St. Nazaire*" (26 June). This brought a total of 16,000 American troops in France. By the end of 1917, the number had reached 180,000. The majority of the troops still needed extensive training. Pershing's first priority was to establish training schools for his officers and respective divisions. Afterwards these officers would provide the basic principles of machine guns, mortars and chemical warfare to their men. The officers also trained their men in

digging and maintaining trenches that by then could be found all along the Western Front. By the end of May 1918, the AEF had expanded considerably. During that particular month 245,945 men had landed in France. From there on procedures were expedited and the following months showed great numbers of troops disembarking in France:

June: 278,664
July: 306,350
August: 285,974
September: 257,457

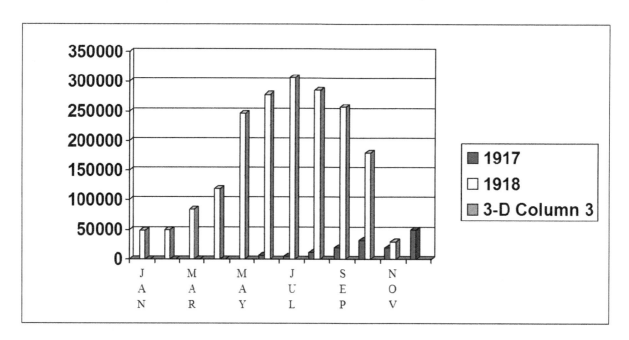

New York City would be one of the most important assembly points for all these troop movements. A total of 1,656,000 men, of which 368,000 New Yorkers, embarked and sailed from New York harbor to Europe. Manhattan was not only the center for storage depots and warehouses stocking general supplies and provisions but there were also depots for storing all kinds of medical supplies. Emergency hospitals were established wherever

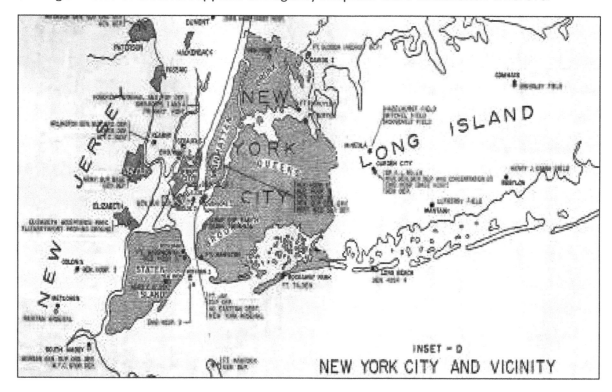

INSET - D

NEW YORK CITY AND VICINITY

feasible. Military equipment was shipped through the most important terminal: Brooklyn. On 11 November 1918 more than 2,000,000 American soldiers were stationed in Europe. Participation of American troops in this conflict was an enormous moral boost and support to the allies. One must also realize, that at that time, an American division, on an average, amounted to 25,500 men, a lot more than the British (11,800), French (11,400), German (12,300) and Belgian (10,000).

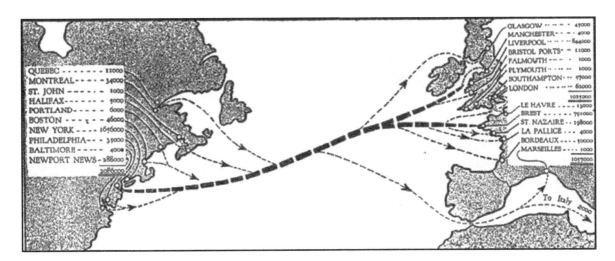

General Pershing was very much aware of the procedures that had taken place during the period 1914-1917. More than 55,000 Americans had joined the Canadian Expeditionary Forces and were now fighting with the Commonwealth. One example was Gunner Orville George Moyer from Columbus, IN (photo). He served with the 3rd Trench Mortar Bn., Canadian Field Artillery and was killed in action on 3 November 1917. He is interred at Vlamertinge New Military Cemetery, grave location XII.E.7.

Pershing not only found that it was logical but also a necessity that these Americans should now be transferred to his army. There had already been a number who had voluntarily solicited to that effect. On 31 August 1917, Pershing wrote a letter from his headquarters in Chaumont, Haute-Marne, France, to Field Marshal Sir Douglas Haig, Commander-in-Chief of the British Expeditionary Forces:

Dear Sir Douglas,

Applications have been received at these headquarters from a number of officers and soldiers (American citizens) in the Canadian and British armies, who desire to transfer for service with the American army. It is, of course, quite natural that these men should wish to join the American army and to serve with their own countrymen. Moreover, such of them as may be competent to instruct troops would really be of much use to us. These applications have been filed without action until the matter could be taken up with your headquarters.

I should like to suggest that, if entirely agreeable with you, some arrangement be made to enable these applicants to obtain release and enter our service. Possibly such men as your officers could recommend could be authorized to take a few days leave of absence to visit Paris for examination. After completion of their examination, they could return to their stations in your service, and I could advise you in due time as to the names of those found qualified, so that the necessary steps could be taken to discharge them from the British service.

A list of the names of the officers and men who have made an application is enclosed (List omitted). If you approve of this, perhaps these men could be granted permission to visit these headquarters for the purpose indicated. This subject is taken up in this manner in the hope of thus resolving the situation in the interest of both services. If this plan meets with your approval, perhaps you would kindly turn the matter over to the proper staff officer for action. I may add that our War Department has ruled that all men who have entered the British or Canadian Service and have hence taken the oath of allegiance to the British Government have lost their American citizenship. Applicants for appointment as officers in our service should, therefore, produce an authenticated copy of obligation they have assumed, in order that their status may be determined. Those men who desire to enlist as soldiers in the American army may do so without submitting evidence of citizenship.

With great respect and high esteem, I remain
Very sincerely,
John J. Pershing

With this letter Pershing firmly indicates that he is in command. In the first paragraph he already emphasizes the fact that these are American citizens. Furthermore he makes it quite clear that this will be their free choice seeing as they renounced their US citizenship by joining the Commonwealth Forces.
The rivalry between Generals has always been a common fact (especially between Pershing and Haig), so it was no surprise that a reaction to his letter was somewhat delayed.
Haig replied, or I should say a member of his senior staff did, on 19 September:

Dear General Pershing,

Field Marshal Sir Douglas Haig has transferred your letter of August 31 to me for action.
While readily appreciating your desire to collect such of your own countrymen as would be useful to you from a military point of view, yet, I am not sure that your proposal to have the applicants mentioned in your letter sent to Paris for examination is feasible. In the first place the majority of officers and a considerable proportion of the men are in England, and it would not be expedient to fill up shipping space with men whose retention out here was not assured.
It might hence be equally as convenient to you to send one or two officers to see these officers and men concerned who are serving out here. I do not anticipate any difficulty in getting them collected at their respective army headquarters, those on the L of C. being arranged separately.
So far as we are concerned, we are only too anxious to help you in every possible way, but I believe the arrangement that has been entered into by the two War Departments concerned is to the effect that the American Embassy in London will take any necessary executive action as regards applying for the release of any individuals whose services are required by the American Government.
On receipt of a reply from you, I will inform our War Office of your desire in respect to the men noted on the lists accompanying your letter of August 31, but I think it would be convenient to be able to state that arrangements for any examination of the men will be such as to enable the examination to take place near where the men are serving.

Yours sincerely,
George Henry Fowke
Adjutant General

The ball had been thrown back in his court and in this particular case, Fowke had every reason to do so. He makes it very clear to Pershing that their respective War Departments were already working on this issue through the American Embassy in London. This could indicate that Pershing was ignorant to the fact of what was going on or on the other hand, knowing Pershing, by his intervention he could expedite the negotiations and consequently the future transfers. It is a fact that many who had solicited to make the transfer to an American division actually succeeded. However, there were many more who decided to remain with the British and Canadian Forces. Evidence of this can still be found in different Commonwealth cemeteries to this day:

Private J.W.T. Petch of the 1st/5th Bn. York and Lancaster Regiment. He was 23 when he died on 10 March 1918. Hometown address: 21 Depot Street, Greenwich, NY, U.S.A. Petch is one

of 48 other American soldiers interred at Lyssenthoek cemetery, Poperinge. (grave location XXVII.EE.7), who preferred to fight next to their British and Canadian comrades versus re-obtaining their U.S. citizenship.

Another example is Private Ernest Clifford Davies (photo) from Gary, IN. He was killed on 30 September 1918. Born in Wales in 1899, he served with the Canadian Central Ontario Regiment (102nd Regiment). He is interred at Canada Cemetery in Tilloy-Les-Cambrai, France (grave location II.B.27).

When Pershing arrived in France in 1917, he was already known to be a stubborn individual, and to some even very obstinate and pertinacious. One example was the fact that he would not allow any allied General take command of an American division. On 10 December 1917, during a visit with King Albert I of Belgium, the French General Pétain gave his personal and severe opinion on Pershing: *"Les Américains n'ont aucune discipline et ne savent rien. Pershing est un vaniteux, très insuffisant. Ils devront recevoir de l'ennemi quelques leçons qui leur coûteront très cher."* (The Americans have no discipline whatsoever and know nothing. Pershing is worthless, very unsatisfactory. He will be taught hard and very costly lessons by the enemy.)

Hard lessons were definitely learned with the mass slaughter and carnage of the Meuse-Argonne campaign. The highest loss of American life ever during World War I.

As was already evident in King Albert's report on the meeting of 10 July 1918 at the Ministry of War, unfortunately the general opinion on Pershing had not improved. Arthur Balfour, Minister of Foreign Affairs under the Conservative Lloyd George declared: *"M. Balfour parle des difficultés que le gouvernement a avec les Américains et particulièrement avec le général Pershing. On a beaucoup de peine à se mettre d'accord avec eux. Les Anglais ont des canons sans artilleurs et des Américains ont des artilleurs sans canons; une entente rendrait de grands services."* (Mr. Balfour explains the difficulties his government is experiencing with the Americans, especially with General Pershing. We are encountering many difficulties in reaching an agreement with him. The British have artillery but no artillery units, the Americans have artillery units but no artillery. An entente and consensus would benefit all.)

King Albert would also personally experience that Pershing would not adhere to his requests:

La Panne, 14 August 1918

Dear General Pershing,

When general Gillain, the chief of my staff, went to see you at your headquarters, he expressed to you the wish of the Belgian nation and Army to obtain close cooperation of some American troops with our soldiers.
We understood quite well the difficulties of realizing immediately that project.
I come now to ask you this: the Americans are training an immense number of pilots. No doubt the American aviation will have a great share in the future operations. American pilots are attached to French and British squadrons.
For us it would be a special pleasure to receive some of your pilots. Having spoken over the matter with the commander of the Belgian air service, he proposes 35 as the right number, it will not be necessary to bring machines.
The growing importance of the aviation and the decisive action of American help on the Western Front would give a great signification to the arrival on our aviation grounds of some of your daring young men.
The moral effect on the army and public would be most excellent.
For our aviation, it would be a great encouragement and our pilots, who have proofed a gallant behavior and high professional knowledge, would very much appreciate it.
Personally, I would be extremely grateful if you would consider this question and give us a favorable answer.

I remain always, dear General Pershing,
Your sincerely affectionate
Albert

The fact that Pershing never replied to King Albert may be found in the reasoning that he had previously given in to the demands of the allies. As of 5 July, the 27th and 30th U.S. Divisions were under the general command of the Second British Army and would be actively engaged in fighting from 18 August through 4 September during the Ypres-Lys offensive near Vierstraat and Kemmel. A second, separate engagement leading up to the Armistice would take place during the final offensive of the 37th and 91st US Divisions in Flanders under the general command of King Albert of Belgium.

4

THE FOUR DIVISIONS

27th NEW YORK DIVISION

30th OLD HICKORY DIVISION

37th BUCKEYE DIVISION

91st WILD WEST DIVISION

27th NEW YORK DIVISION

MAJOR GENERAL JOHN F. O'RYAN

Commander 27th Division, A.E.F.

MOBILIZATION

The 27th Division, better known as the New York Division, consisted of men from the New York National Guard. The insignia "N.Y." in monogram with the seven major stars of the constellation Orion represents, according to the Greek mythology, a hunter with belt and sword. This was chosen for its phonetic resemblance to the Division's Commander Maj. Gen. John F. O' Ryan. These men were mustered at Camp Wadsworth, South Carolina, in September 1917. The Division was formed from the following units:

1st – 2nd – 3rd – 7th – 12th – 14th – 23rd – 71st and 74th New York Infantry
Squadron A, 1st New York Cavalry
1st – 3rd New York Field Artillery
22nd New York Engineers
1st Battalion New York Signal Corps
New York Ammunition Train
New York Supply Train
New York Sanitary Train
New York Headquarters and Military Police
6th New York Division Headquarters Troop

These units were transformed to:

Headquarters Troop

53rd Infantry Brigade
105th Infantry Regiment
106th Infantry Regiment
105th Machine Gun Battalion

54th Infantry Brigade
107th Infantry Regiment
108th Infantry Regiment
106th Machine Gun Battalion

52nd Field Artillery Brigade
104th Field Artillery Regiment (75mm)
105th Field Artillery Regiment (75mm)
106th Field Artillery Regiment (155mm howitzers)
102nd Trench Mortar Battery

Divisional Troops
104th Machine Gun Battalion
102nd Engineer Regiment
102nd Field Signal Battalion
Trains

The men received their basic training from French, British and American instructors. Part of their training was to march many long hours under the hot South Carolina sun.

On 28 April 1918, the first units received their orders to embark. They sailed from Newport News and Hoboken (New Jersey). They disembarked eight days later in Brest and Saint-Nazaire, France. All units of the division would arrive in France by 7 July.

Arrivals of the first units of the division, with exception of the 52nd Field Artillery Brigade, were sent to a British training camp on 28 May in the *Rue Buigny* area, 20 kilometers north of Abbeville. They were assigned to the British 66th Division. On 16 June they were transferred to the British Third Army and between 18 and 21 June settled in the areas of Beauval and Doullens, approximately 25 kilometers north of Amiens.

On 30 June they were attached to the British Second Army. Two days later they moved southwest of Ypres and attached to the British XIX Corps. On 9 July they received orders to proceed to a defensive sector east of Poperinge, the third defensive sector near Dikkebus and Mount Scherpenberg, a front of approximately 4 kilometers. (photo: dugouts in the flank of Mount Scherpenberg). During this period, a selected group were able to participate and gain their first frontline experience.  Corporal William (Billy) Leonard (Plot B - Row 2 - Grave 14) was one of the volunteers who took on this challenge on 14 July.

Billy Leonard was a member of the 107th Infantry Regiment. He wrote to his friend in Flushing (near Queens, NY) : *"We have hiked across a mighty section of France and I've seen a lot the censor won't let me tell. You bet someday I'll give you the story between puffs of your excellent cigars."*

Leonard had a nose for new stories and he could always manage to add a humoristic twist. As ex-editor of the *Flushing Daily Times* military experiences were always worth writing down. As Stephen Harris (Duty-Honor-Privilege, Brassey's Inc. 2001) so eloquently stated: "He could not wait to write about the times he was peeling potatoes and onions in boot camp, catching pneumonia, being admitted into hospital at Camp Wadsworth and falling in love with a nurse. Or the happy moments when children were cheering as they marched through France. But now he was ready for action at the front. Although it wasn't scheduled for the 107th Infantry Regiment to enter the trenches before 10 August, Billy informed his friend Sergeant Neely, that he had volunteered *"just to see how it goes"*. To another friend he wrote: *"The reason I am writing now is because one must grasp the opportunity when it comes. One never knows from day to day what will happen next."* He also described the sleepless nights due to heavy artillery fire. *"Every night the shells go whining over our heads. Sometimes they seem so close. Then "Jerry" comes over to drop a few bombs and we open up on him with anti-aircraft and machine gun fire and there's a very hell of a racket. It's devilish hard getting to sleep again."* To another friend he wrote : *"The nearer we get to the trenches the less we think about the war in its larger aspects. I imagine it's because we're cut off from the world, in a sense, rarely see a newspaper and our own particular job fills our time and thoughts."*

It was a cold, miserably wet day in Flanders on 14 July, especially for the French who were attempting to celebrate their national holiday. Billy was preparing himself for the trenches. The British had shown the Americans how to play cricket and in turn the Americans were teaching the British their famous game of baseball. Billy, dressed in full field pack was ready to go. He turned his head, smiled and waved to his comrades of second platoon and he was gone.

Later that night Billy was escorted to the trenches by a British guide. The mission was situated near Mount Scherpenberg. Together with a few men of the 26th Bn. Royal Fusiliers they were tasked to repair barbed wire in no man's land which had been damaged by artillery fire. No sooner had they left their trench, the British artillery opened fire towards the German lines which immediately triggered a counter artillery barrage. The British sergeant ordered the men back to their trench but before they could move an artillery shell burst in their midst. A British soldier was killed instantly and at the same time shell fragments had lodged into Billy's stomach. He was carried 100 yards back to safety but unfortunately Billy had already died. When news of his death reached his regiment, they were struck in awe and disbelief. His brother Eugene, who was serving with the Headquarters Company of the same regiment, was devastated. He wrote home saying *"The English did everything possible for him and brought up a chaplain from ten miles behind the lines and buried him with all the honors of a brave soldier."*

Billy Leonard was buried with the British soldier at Wedge Wood Bank, on the right slope of Mount Scherpenberg. His remains were later moved to Lyssenthoek British Cemetery. Congressman Chas Pope Caldwell was greatly interested in this case and requested his body be buried in an American cemetery as soon as possible.

Elements of the 27th Division gradually entered the front lines near Dikkebus Lake and Mount Scherpenberg on 25 July. There was little or no activity until 19 August, the day that the Ypres-Lys offensive commenced.

RELIEVED BY BRITISH FORCES

On 15 August, the 27th Division received orders from the British XIX Corps to relieve the British 6th Division during the nights of 22 - 23 and 23 - 24 August. The 53rd Infantry Brigade replaced two British brigades. The men entered the lines east of Dikkebus Lake. The 53rd Infantry Brigade were in the second line of defense. The front line covered an area of approximately 2 kilometers north of Mount Kemmel in the vicinity of Elzenwalle. There was hardly any activity and it was only on 30 August that the British XIX Corps had strong suspicions that the Germans were retreating. The 27th Division was ordered to check out enemy resistance and patrols of the 53rd Infantry Brigade executed a night reconnaissance mission reporting that they had hardly experienced any enemy resistance. On 31 August it was evident that the enemy had retreated from Mount Kemmel. The 53rd Infantry Brigade consolidated their line with the British 34th Division successfully connecting Lindehoek - Vierstraat. Consequently the 34th British Division followed up and took in their positions beyond Mount Kemmel and on 1 September continued the advance together with the U.S. 106th Infantry Regiment towards the edge of the village of Wytschaete, reconnoitering with the U.S. 30th Division.

It soon became evident that the Germans had halted their retreat, taking in strong positions in and around the town of Wytschaete. The front line was held by the 27th Division on 2 September and on 3 September they were relieved by the British 41st Division. The following day they were transferred in reserve to British headquarters in Doullens, France. On 24 September the 27th Division took part in the battle of the Somme.

Mount Kemmel 1919

30th OLD HICKORY DIVISION

MAJOR GENERAL EDWARD M. LEWIS

Commander 30th Division, A.E.F.

The popular nickname given to the division was Old Hickory, also derived from Andrew Jackson, seventh president of the USA. He was born in 1767 in South Carolina and as a child, during the War of Independence, was taken prisoner by the British. He became famous through his important victory against the British in 1812 (Battle of New Orleans) and his attitude towards the Native Indians. He died in Tennessee in 1845.

MOBILIZATION

One month after the U.S. declaration of war on Germany Congress passed the Selective Service Act. There were three registrations. The first being on 5 June 1917 for all men between the ages of 21 and 31. One year later on 5 June 1918, for those men who had attained the age of 21 after 5 June 1917 and finally on 12 September 1918 for all men aged 18 through 45. This was no issue for the Carolina National Guard as they had experienced their baptism of fire together with Tennessee units during the Pancho Villa uprising along the Mexican border in 1916 and 1917. North Carolina, South Carolina and Tennessee National Guards were the first units to arrive at Camp Sevier in Greenville, SC on 10 July 1917. General Orders No. 95, issued by the War Department on 18 July, announced that that from now on these units would become elements of the 30th Division. Men of all official and unofficial militias would become a part of this division. For example: units such as the Charleston Light Dragoons, Irish Volunteers, Washington Light Infantry Fusiliers and Sumter Guards were all part of the volunteer Militia Corps of Charleston. The 30th Division would finally comprise of the following units [1]:

Headquarters Troop   (Troop A, South Carolina Cavalry)

59th Infantry Brigade
117th Infantry Regiment   (former 3rd Tennessee Infantry)
118th Infantry Regiment   (former 1st South Carolina Infantry)
114th Machine Gun Battalion   (former 1st Squadron Tennessee Cavalry, Co. A,B and C)

60th Infantry Brigade
119th Infantry Regiment   (former 1st South Carolina Infantry)
120th Infantry Regiment   (former 3rd North Carolina Infantry)
115th Machine Gun Battalion   (former 1st Squadron N.C. Cavalry – Co. A,B and C)

55th Artillery Brigade
113th Field Artillery Regiment   (former 1st North Carolina Field Artillery)
114th Field Artillery Regiment   (former 1st Tennessee Field Artillery)
115th Field Artillery Regiment   (former 1st Tennessee Infantry)
105th Trench Mortar Battery   (former 1st Separate Squadron Tennessee Cavalry)

Divisional Troops
113th Machine Gun Battalion - Companies A, B, C, D (former 1st and 2[nd]Tennessee Infantry – former 1st North Carolina Infantry and 2nd South Carolina Infantry).
105th Engineer Regiment – 1st Battalion (North Carolina Engineers - Companies A, B and C) – 2nd Battalion (1st Battalion First North Carolina Infantry – Co. D, E and F).
105th Field Signal Battalion, Sanitary Detachment and Trains.

---

[1] *All these units, with exception of the Field Artillery, would serve in Belgium during the Ypres-Lys Offensive.*

To the great annoyance of all these men, it would be May 1918 before embarkation orders were received for Europe. Departing from various ports, they finally crossed the Atlantic on 25 British cargo ships between 7 May and 2 July. Their ports of entry being Glasgow, Liverpool, London in the U.K. and Brest in France.

The 119th Infantry Regiment embarked on 11 May 1918. The men were divided to sail on three different vessels. The Ascania (Cunard Line) sailed from New York City on 11 May. The Haverford from Philadelphia, PA and the Loamedon from Boston, MA. They joined the convoy at Halifax, Nova Scotia from where they crossed the Atlantic on 16 May. They arrived in Liverpool on 27 May from where they continued their journey by train to Dover, crossing the Channel and disembarking at Calais on the 29th. The men were immediately taken to British rest camps around the city. As it seemed they had become part of the British Army as to their astonishment they were ordered to exchange their American rifles for British Enfield's, campaign hats were replaced by helmets as were miscellaneous articles for less accustomed and awkward like type items. The Chinese Labor Corps were tasked to sort the American materials resulting in a few major incidents with disgruntled Americans. In one case Chinese were executed by American sentries. A special restraining order had to be issued to keep Americans at bay and ignore the Chinese. However these incidents were far and between and presumably caused by prejudice opinions.

On 31 May, the 119th Infantry was transferred by train to Audrique in northern France.

TRAINING IN EUROPE

The men of the 30th U.S. Division were divided under units of the 39th British division. For example the 119th Infantry Regiment was attached to the 9th Bn. Black Watch and the 9th and 10th Bn. Gordon Highlanders. These men were under the command of Brigadier General Hubbard. There were two training periods: phase A (Northern-France) and phase B (Poperinge, Belgium). The first phase comprised of extensive training on specific techniques and disciplines of trench warfare with 36 hours during the first week ending with 20 hours during the fourth week.

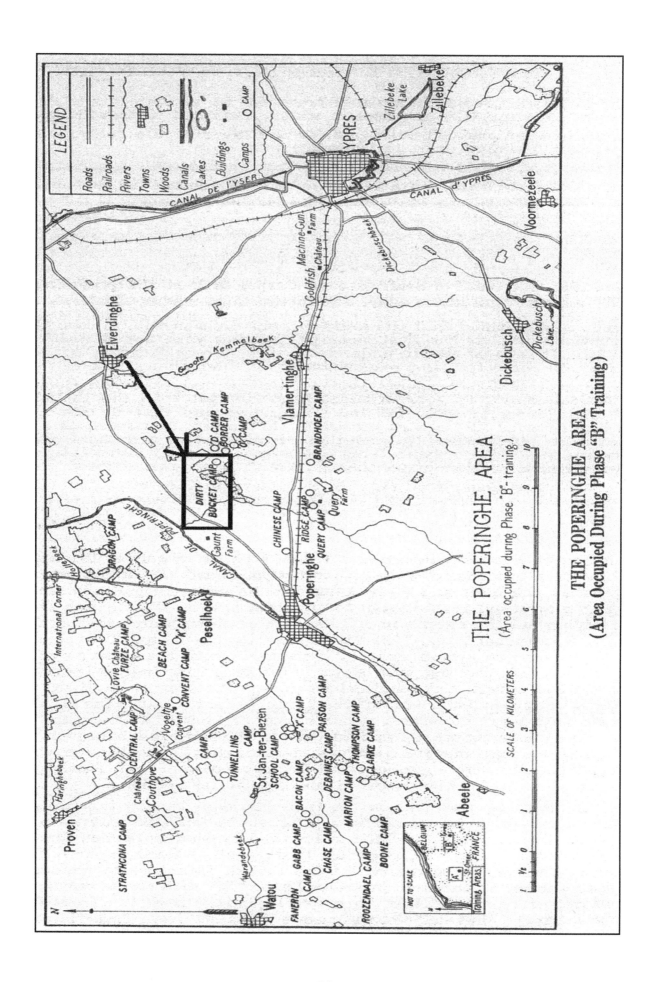

THE POPERINGHE AREA

(Area Occupied During Phase "B" Training)

Officers of the 119th Infantry Regiment were given separate training and the opportunity to experience the practical techniques of trench warfare in the vicinity east of Ypres. Here they also received their baptism of fire, earning battle experience that no doubt would become essential when leading their own men into battle.

On 15 June rumors were heard that the Germans were massing divisions for an attack east of Cassel, France. General Herbert Plumer, commanding the Second British Army requested that the 30th U.S. Division be set as his disposal in case of a hostile attack and proposed the division to occupy a sector (Winnezeele Line) east of Cassel. However final orders never materialized. It would be 2 July when unexpectedly orders were received to move the division to the *Roozendael- and Road Camp* area near Watou (Poperinge), Belgium. They remained under the command of the British Second Army, now located in the Ypres Sector. Their hike brought them to the village of Herzele on 4 July where they remained for five days before crossing the French-Belgian border. They were welcomed by the villagers who had decorated their homes with French and American flags for the occasion of Independence Day.

Although Watou was located in the so called "quiet sector", it was within range of German artillery. In his memoirs, 1st Lieutenant John Francis Williams[2] reported that, shortly after their arrival at Watou, their headquarters received a direct hit by an artillery shell killing one officer and severely injuring three other men.

During their training period they were honored and surprised by esteemed and high ranking visits. On 6 August they were honored by King George V of England and on 7 August by King Albert and Queen Elisabeth of Belgium. A more informal visit and a pleasant surprise for all the troops was a performance by Elsie Janis[3], known as "Little Elsie" and "Sweetheart of the A.E.F." (photo insert).

---

[2] *William John Francis II was 1st Lieutenant and later Captain of the 120th Infantry Regiment. Besides being awarded the Distinguished Service Cross and British Military Cross for his actions during the liberation of Voormezele on 1 and 2 August. He was also awarded the Belgian "Knight of the Order of the Crown " for meritorious services rendered in the common cause.*

[3] *Elsie Janis was born as Elsie Jane Bierbower in Columbus, OH on 16 March 1889. She was a born artist performing on the steps of her local church at the age of two. She became famous at the age of ten and was invited to the White House by President McKinley to perform during the Blue Room Gala. She made her debute in New York as youngest star on Broadway in 1905. At 18 she changed her name to Elsie Janis. Then came World War I.*

At the peak of her career she entertained the soldiers of the A.E.F. and was sent to France. With her mother as chaperone she gave 610 performances during the 15 months the U.S. was engaged at war. She became the first American singer to perform on foreign soil along the front. After the war she became writer/producer of stage productions and movies. In her first musical production, "Elsie and her Gang", she performed with veterans. Janis also wrote books. Her war memoires "The Big Show: My Six Months with the American Expeditionary Forces" was published in 1919. After a successful film career, Elsie continued to support war veterans mainly performing in VA hospitals. Her last movie in an active role was the 1940 wartime production "Women in War". Elsie Janis was nearly 67 when she died in in Beverly Hills on 27 February 1956.

After their training period they were attached to the 33rd and 49th British divisions. At first they assisted in improving the defense systems, installing and repairing barbed wire entanglements along the trenches. Later they fought side by side with their British counterparts in the front lines.

RELIEVED BY BRITISH FORCES

In the mean time we were mid-August and the time had come for the 30th Division to be reassigned as an independent fighting force. On 17 August they received orders to replace the 33rd British Division along their front line. This particular sector was known as the "Canal Sector" and reached from the southern outskirts of Ypres to the village of Voormezele which was approximately 2,400 meters. The British had long planned this attack. By 30 August it was confirmed that the Germans were retreating from Mount Kemmel and on 31 August and 1 September the 30th U.S. Division would have the opportunity to prove their battle worthiness.

In preparation of the attack, during the night of 26 - 27 August at 01:30 hours, a gas attack was executed by the 30th U.S. Division in the Canal Sector with a platoon of the 105th Engineer Regiment and three hundred men of the 120th Infantry Regiment. 2,517 gas cylinders (chlorine and phosgene) were pushed forward on cars and set off by electricity on a front of about 600 yards. The front lines had been evacuated. When the cylinders were discharged, the labor party was stationed 50 yards directly to windward with masks adjusted. As the gas was discharged, a downward current of air caught the edge of the cloud and blew it back on the members of the working party who were on the extreme left. The concentration to which these men were subjected to was tremendous and resulted in 34 casualties including three deaths. The latter due to the men trying to get out of the affected area and getting caught in barbed wire, thus disarranging their masks. These three gas victims are buried close together in plot B at Flanders Field: William Barlow, Ray Stroman and Dave Lee.

That the men were exposed to a tremendous concentration is shown by the fact that the clips of cartridges taken from their belts were heavily corroded. The strength of the gas was also shown by its effect on the fabric of the face piece, which, in some cases, was caused to shrink to three quarters of its original size. Tests made by the British had shown that 1 in every 15 or nearly 7% broke down within the first 6 minutes.

The major attack was launched on 31 August. Together with the British 14th Division on the left, the 27th U.S. Division on the right flank, the 119th and the 120th Infantry Regiment went over the top. They succeeded in achieving their objectives: Lock #8 (Lankhof farm) and the liberation of the village of Voormezele. Afterwards the 30th Division was assigned to different positions along the front line.

During the nights of 3-4 and 4-5 September, the 30th Division was relieved by the 35th British Division. On 6 September they were placed in reserve with British General Headquarters in the St. Pol area, approximately fifty kilometers north of Amiens. Not long after they were engaged in the battle of the Hindenburg Line in the Somme, France.

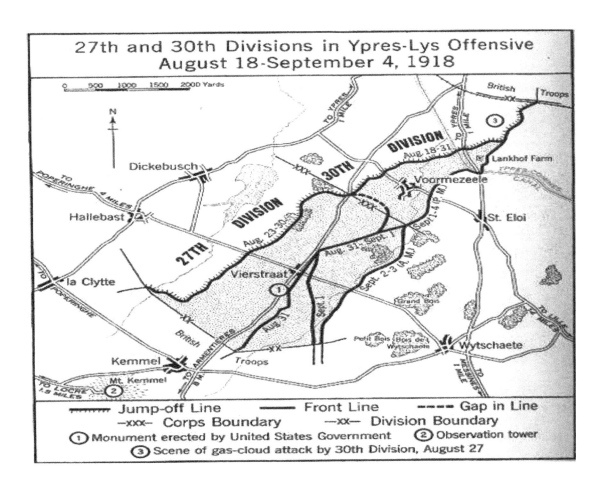

27th and 30th Divisions in Ypres-Lys Offensive August 18-September 4, 1918

Jump-off Line ———— Front Line ----- Gap in Line
-xxx- Corps Boundary —xx— Division Boundary
① Monument erected by United States Government ② Observation tower
③ Scene of gas-cloud attack by 30th Division, August 27

Lankhof Farm and Canal in 1918 – area of 30th Division gas attack marked "3" on map.

The 119th Infantry Regiment made history as being the first American unit occupying a section of the front line in Belgium, the first to be engaged in an attack, the first to take prisoners and the first to liberate a village (Voormezele).

During their engagements in Belgium (11 July - 6 September 1918) a total of 777 casualties were listed. 113 doughboys were killed in action and 43 died of wounds. 621 were lightly wounded.

There are 24 soldiers of the 30th Division interred at Flanders Field American Cemetery. Memorialized on the Wall of Missing are the names of four who were listed as missing on 31 August.

After the war, in December 1918, the 30th Division were issued their distinctive insignia shoulder patch. For reasons unknown, the patch was worn horizontally. Yet when held vertically one can clearly distinguish the O (of Old) and the H (of Hickory) with the Roman numerals 30.

Voormezele, liberated by the 30th Division on 1 September 1918 (photo 1915)

THE 37th AND 91st DIVISIONS IN FLANDERS

Monday 14 October 1918: Marshal Ferdinand Foch sends an urgent telegram to General John J. Pershing (Message Center, First Army, No. 4779):

"The action that has been taken today by the Belgian, French and British troops in Belgium has made sufficient progress to enable us to expect important results if it is pushed through, and with that object, followed up with sufficient forces.
Under those conditions and to that effect, I order that two American divisions chosen among those that have taken part in offensive operations, be sent to that region. The first of these divisions will be ready to entrain by October 16 by noon, the second on October 17. One of these divisions could be sent without artillery.
Please let me know by telegram on October 15 before noon the numbers of these divisions, which, it seems, ought to be chosen among the 26th, 89th, 90th or 78th Divisions.
It is always understood that this reduction of American forces will to no extent change the mission assigned to the American Army especially between the Meuse and the Aisne."

Pershing, already known for his stubborn attitude when it came to complying with the allies, felt he was forced into a difficult position. Although he complied with Foch's initial request, he completely ignored his propositions and designated the 37th and 91st Divisions to take part on this mission. The following coded message was eventually sent to King Albert of Belgium: *"Deux Divisions américaines sont désignées pour être mises à disposition du Roi. La 91ème avec artillerie, la 37ème sans artillerie"*

Le Lt.Col. chef mission belge G.Q.G. Fr. à Chef Q.G. belge le 17/10/18

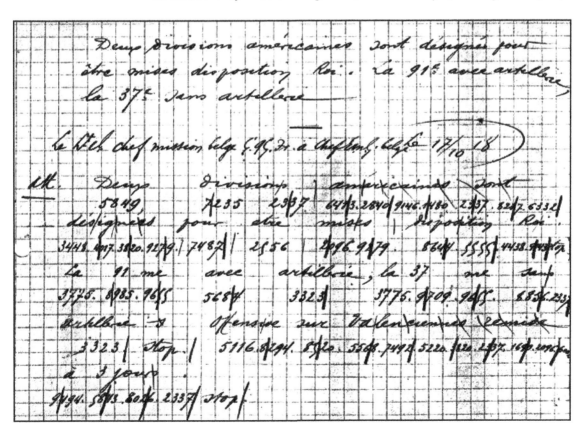

The divisions entrained and after a long train journey arrived in the vicinity of Ypres and Poperinge on 20 October, where they were encamped to rest for a few days.

Private Robert Dwight, Company D, 147th Infantry Regiment, 37th Division describes his arrival at *"Dirty Bucket Camp"* in his journal (see map location *"The Poperinghe Area-Phase B Training"* page 22): *" The camp is a construction of dugouts with corrugated iron roofs and concrete floors. In each compartment there are sleeping bunks available for 25 men. After two nights we are treated with a generous portion of cooties."*
He continues: *"After a breakfast of hard biscuits and corned beef we continue our march through No Man's Land. The depressing surroundings are only enhanced by the drizzly rainfall. Through Poelkappelle, Langemark, Westrozebeke and Hooglede we finally arrive in the village of Gits around noon on 25 October."*

In the diary of Private 1st Class W.E. Petersen of the 91st Division he describes his arrival at Izegem on 7 November: *"After marching a few miles we arrive at Iseghem. Cobblestone roads with mud on both sides. We scout the city and visit the church with the adjacent cemetery. There are 1500 soldiers buried here, Germans and other nationalities. There is little damage to buildings. French soldiers tell us that the war is over, "Fini", but I don't believe them."*

In Belgian literature one finds sporadic details on the arrival of the Americans, although seen from the civilian point of view and from quite a different perspective.

In the village of Hooglede, Edward Vermeulen's diary entry of 21 October documents: *"Slush and mud lie as weak dough along the streets. An American soldier named Cotner approaches me and enquires in French: "who provides you with food?" When I reply that no one cares about us and that we have to walk more than 2 hours to find bread he looks quite astonished. He probably thinks that this could never happen in America. He gave me a packet of biscuits."*

Gustave Vuylsteke from Meulebeke writes for 28 October: *"Many Americans have arrived today. Mostly infantry. Many of them speak German or French so that we understand them."*
His entry for 6 November: *"The American soldiers have lots of cash. When we give them bread or milk they reach in their pockets and easily pay 1,2,5 or 10 francs. They also buy a lot of chocolate in the local shops and distribute everything to the children in the streets. They drink vast amounts of schnapps and wine and pay well. Many soldiers who sleep in billets will easily pay 10 franks. They give away clothes and everything you can think of to the local population. When they have dirty washing they just throw away and when they move on they leave everything behind such as shoes, clothing, socks, etc."*

It was a fact, the Americans had arrived. The last offensive of the war documented in the annals of the 37th and 91st divisions and known as *"The Turnip Drive"* could begin.

37th BUCKEYE DIVISION

MAJOR GENERAL CHARLES S. FARNSWORTH

Commander 37th Division, A.E.F.

Popular nickname of the division was Buckeye: a species of the chestnut tree (Aesculus glabra) commonly seen in Ohio. Also a native of Ohio named after the "The Buckeye State".

MOBILIZATION

The 37th Division, known as the "BUCKEYE" Division, composed of men from the Ohio National Guard. They were mustered in Camp Sheridan, Montgomery, AL in August 1917. The division was composed from the following units:

Headquarters of Trains   (Columbus)
Military Police
        Company A   (Cincinnati)
        Company B   (Columbus)
Headquarters Ammunition Trains   (Columbus)
        Engineer Train   (Cleveland)
        Companies E en F   (Cleveland)
Headquarters 1st Infantry Brigade   (Toledo)
        2nd Regiment Infantry   (Lima)
Headquarters 2nd Infantry Brigade   (Columbus)
        4th Regiment Infantry   (Columbus)
        5th Regiment Infantry   (Cleveland)
        8th Regiment Infantry   (Bucyrus)
Headquarters 3rd Infantry Brigade   (Cleveland)
        1st Regiment Infantry   (Cincinnati)
        7th Regiment Infantry   (New Lexington)
        9th Regiment Infantry   (Columbus)
        10th Regiment Infantry   (Youngstown)
Headquarters Company 1st Field Artillery (Akron)
Supply Company, 1st Field Artillery   (Bellefontaine)
Battery A, 1st Field Artillery   (Cleveland)
Battery B, 1st Field Artillery   (Akron)
Battery C, 1st Field Artillery   (Columbus)
Battery D, 1st Field Artillery   (Dayton)
Battery E, 1st Field Artillery   (Mount Vernon)
Battery F, 1st Field Artillery   (Jackson)
2nd Regiment Field Artillery   (Cleveland)
3rd Regiment Field Artillery   (Cincinnati)
Outpost Company, Signal Battalion   (Toledo)
Sanitary Trains   (Columbus)

All these units were ordered to muster at their local bases on 15 July. Upon arrival the units were redeployed in units comprising the division.

Headquarters Troop

73rd Infantry Brigade
145th Infantry Regiment
146th Infantry Regiment
135th Machine Gun Battalion

74th Infantry Brigade
147th Infantry Regiment
148th Infantry Regiment
136th Machine Gun Battalion

62nd Field Artillery Brigade
134th Field Artillery Regiment (75mm)
135th Field Artillery Regiment (75mm)
136th Field Artillery Regiment (155mm howitzers)
112th Trench Mortar Battery

Division Troops
134th Machine Gun Battalion
112th Engineer Regiment
112th Field Signal Battalion
Trains

In May 1918, upon completion of their training in Camp Sheridan, they entrained for Camp Lee, VA and Upton, NY. From here they continued to the ports of Baltimore, Brooklyn, Hoboken, Montreal, Newport News, New York and Philadelphia, where the majority embarked for Europe on 6 June. They disembarked in Brest (France), Liverpool, Birkenhead (England) and Glasgow (Scotland). The troops arriving in England and Scotland were allowed a short rest period before continuing on to France where they disembarked at Cherbourg and Le Havre.

TRAINING IN EUROPE

The first units arriving, less artillery, were sent to the Bourmont training area (Department Haute-Marne) on 25 June. The artillery was sent for specific training to *Camp de Souge*, southwest of Bordeaux, on 15 July. The division was finally sent to the Baccarat sector (Vosges) on 4 August where they were attached to the de 77th Division to gain battle experience. They were relieved by the French on 16 September and transferred to the Meuse-Argonne front the following day.

THE DIVISION IS SENT TO FLANDERS

"Our vigilance must not relax and our aggressiveness become undermined by peace talks that is reaching us. The Boche is being run out of France by fighting, not by peace talk. The moment we stop fighting he will stop going. Leave all expectation and talk of peace. Keep up your training, your vigilance, your activity and your aggressiveness."

The role of American divisions in the Waregem – Oudenaarde area is not well known. Contrary to the other American divisions fighting in their own sector and under their own American commanders, the 37th Division was attached to XXX Corps of the French Sixth Army (General Degoutte) under the high command of King Albert I of Belgium.

Field Orders No. 32 of 17 October, General Farnsworth informed the 37th Division that they were engaged in the Ypres-Lys offensive. On 18, 19 and 20 October units traveled by train to Flanders. Headquarters was established in Hooglede on 22 October. (photo below - US Signal Corps III-SC-42260)

Field Orders No. 33 of 25 October, the divisional zone was extended to include the zone of Lichtervelde and Koolskamp. Division headquarters closed at Hooglede at 16:00 hours on 26 October and opened at Lichtervelde same hour and date. The same day at 19:00 hours Special Orders No. 8 was issued by General de Boissoudy (French Army in Flanders). By 28 October the 37th Division was moved to the zone Tielt – Meulebeke – Pittem. The 73rd Brigade to the Tielt area and the 74th Brigade in the zone Pittem. Headquarters were moved to Meulebeke and became operational by 14:00 hours. Special Orders No. 10 of 27 October placed the 37th and 91st Divisions at the disposal of the General commanding the French Army of Belgium effective midnight.

The French 132nd Division was relieved by the 37th Division southwest of the town Olsene during the night of 30 and 31 October. A general attack with main objective to reach the river Scheldt was planned for 31 October. The 37th Division attacked with the French 128th Division on her right flank and the French 12th Division on her left.

Olsene railroad station where the attack commenced. *(US Signal Corps III-SC-78282)*

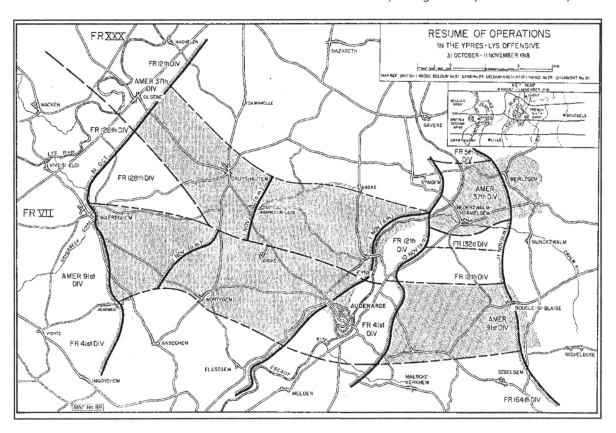

Résumé of operations 31 October – 11 November 1918

Thursday 31 October was a grey miserable day with light rainfall. The 37th US Division commenced the attack at 05:30 hours. By noon the men had advanced approximately 4 km and had reached the heights of Kruishoutem. The continued advance of American troops was however delayed due to the French 12th Division on their left flank not being able to advance accordingly due to enemy machinegun fire. Consequently the American flank was also exposed to enfilade fire. The men were ordered to dig in for the night. German resistance was mainly caused by machinegun nests. Infantry was sporadic however heavy artillery was prominent with a high number of gas shells being used. The chateau in Olsene received quite a few direct hits (see photo next page). In the meantime the Germans had commenced their retreat to approximately 1 km west of Kruishoutem.

During the attack of 31 October, the Medical Department with Ambulance Companies #145, #147 and #148 were stationed in the zones 1 km east of the river Lys. The following day the 146th Ambulance Company became active in Olsene and the 145th and 147th were moved to a more advanced position ten kilometers from the front. They had lost contact with the advancing troops during the night. It became a hazardous task for search parties to sweep the area. Farms were common shelters for the wounded to take cover. Here allied wounded, civilians and enemy soldiers were found. Field Hospital #145 was used as a triage post near the village of Dentergem. Surgical cases were moved to Field Hospital #146 in Tielt and #147 in Meulebeke. These were located approximately 10 kilometers behind the front lines. Evacuation Hospital #5 was located in Staden 40 kilometers behind the front line.

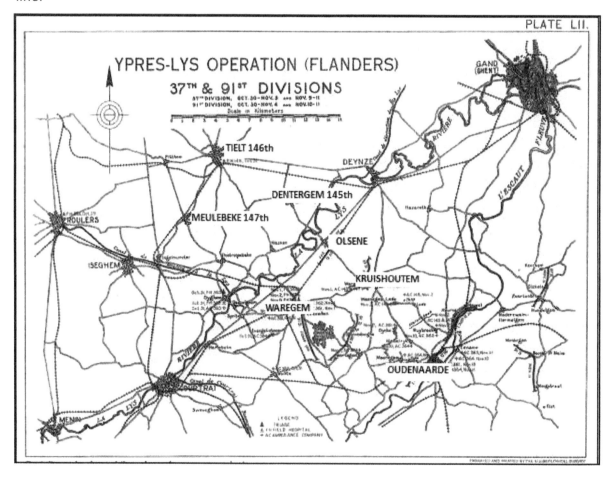

Location of Field Hospitals

Americans were also billeted in the convent in Tielt. This was confirmed by the Sisters of the Holy Family in Tielt. In 1913 the congregation of nuns were in the process of moving their school to a different location. The new building being completed in 1914, the pupils had already moved their desks and benches to their new location. Other new furniture was ready to be picked up at the railroad station when war broke out. As a result the move was cancelled and the Germans occupied the area until the liberation in October 1918.

On Thursday 31 October, Mother Superior requested three nuns to inspect the buildings and report the state and potential damages. Their journal revealed: "... *les locaux sont dans un état de grande malpropreté. Des prisonniers allemands y sont de corvée et balayent maintenant les corridors. Des troupes françaises et américaines y sont cantonnées."*

(The classes are in a filthy state. German prisoners are being tasked to sweep the corridors. French and American troops are currently billeted in the building.)

For Private Harold P. Boak of the 136th Machine Gun Battalion, 37th Division, 31 October would remained stamped in his collective memory. On 27 May 1979 he visited the Flanders

Field American Cemetery accompanied by his wife and shared his war experiences with the author. At 81, it was his first trip back to Europe and the area where he had lost so many of his comrades in arms. His lifelong dream had become reality. He was on a special mission. During his short stay at the chateau in Olsene (photo insert), during the night of 30 and 31 October 1918, he had taken as souvenir a miniature painting of the chateau. It had become time to return it to the rightful owner. Harold was received in style by the last direct descendant of the chateau, Lady Solange Piers de Raveschoot (1909-2002) who was 9 years of age at the time of the armistice.

Harold P. Boak with his wife
Christmas 1979

In the *Regimentsgeschichte* of the *Kurassier Regiment Von Seydlitz Nr. 7 (Magdeburgisches)*, one can read how the Germans experienced the attack of 31 October: "*At 06:30 hours, near our positions Lys, Waregem-Anzegem, all hell is breaking loose and a deadly rolling barrage is engulfing our lines.*"

A soldier of the 239th Reserve Infantry Regiment (RIR) who had been taken prisoner near the railroad station admitted that the Germans were planning to retreat beyond the river Scheldt. From the results of the interrogation it was also clear that the battle strength of these German units were only half their original strength as many had deserted and were trying to reach the Belgian border in civilian clothes.

Field Order No. 37 (31 October-22:00hours): the attack was resumed on 1 November at 06:30 hours supported by a rolling barrage advancing 100 meters at three minute intervals. The attack progressed according to plan and at 07:20 hours, the third battalion of the 148th Infantry Regiment had reached the town center of Kruishoutem. Their second objective, the village of Wannegem-Lede, was taken at 07:40 hours. Attempts to verify the advance along the front from the air were virtually impossible as civilians were waving everywhere with their handkerchiefs.

As all objectives had been taken earlier than planned it was decided to continue the rapid advance. However transmitting messages to and from headquarters and the troops in line were difficult. Witness statements from civilians confirmed that at 11:00 hours the troops were only 1 km away from the river Scheldt. By 18:00 hours it was evident that the division had reached the west bank of the river and immediately wheels were set in motion to plan a crossing of the river that same night. In the meantime, Divisional Headquarters had moved from Dentergem to Kruishoutem.

Kruishoutem 2 November 1918

37th Division HQ – Kruishoutem (US Signal Corps III-SC-78291)

74th Infantry Brigade Post Command – Kruishoutem (1919 and 2015 next page)

On 2 November, small units commenced the crossing of the river Scheldt at 08:25 hours. The 148th Infantry Regiment had improvised and constructed bridges from fallen trees and timber from the ruins of demolished homes from the village of Heurne. The second and third battalions succeeded in moving three hundred men to the east bank of the river.

The Germans, now in defensive positions along the east bank, counterattacked with heavy artillery and machine gun fire in the direction of Heurne. As such, the 112th Engineer Regiment was encountering major difficulties in bringing up timber and other materials to construct their bridges. Enemy artillery had intensified so much during the afternoon practically reducing the towns of Heurne and Heuvel to rubble and making all troop movements impossible. Orders were given to the French 128th and U.S. 91st Division to provide artillery support to the three hundred men now isolated on the east bank.
As a result the German artillery intensified even more changing their tactics and using gas shells in addition. For the Engineers the situation became untenable and impossible to safely transport their bridge materials to Heurne. As such they were ordered in the direction of Eine where at 18:00 hours an attempt was made to establish a pontoon bridge over the river. Notwithstanding the continuing German artillery the Engineers, working under darkness, succeeded in building one pontoon bridge close to Heuvel and two foot bridges at Eine.

Ruins at Heuvel *(US Signal Corps III-SC-42271)*

New attempts to cross the river Scheldt under fire were carried out on 3 November. The French 12th Division commenced their crossing on a pontoon bridge constructed by the 148th Infantry Regiment at 06:30 hours. Two companies and one machinegun company successfully reached the east bank. Other units made additional attempts. Ten German aircraft and intense artillery fire were directing their fire towards the troops in an attempt to prevent the crossing. The allied counterattack proofed successful along the whole line and by 18:00 hours three and a half companies of the 148th Infantry Regiment, four machinegun companies, six companies of the 145th Infantry Regiment including four machinegun companies of the French 12th Division had achieved a bridgehead on the east bank of the river Scheldt.

Operation Orders No. 43, XXX Corps, ordered the relief of the 37th Division being replaced by the French 12th Division during the night of 4 and 5 November. Headquarters of the 37th Division moved from Kruishoutem to Tielt. During the advance 3 German officers and 314 other men were taken prisoner.

Point where the 37th Division made the crossing at Eine *(US Signal Corps III-SC-42269)*

Company F, 146th Infantry, crossing under fire at Nederzwalm *(US Signal Corps III-SC-40614)*

Stories of the Belgium Drive

Back in Tielt the first priority for the men was getting deloused. The *"Cooties"*, as they were known, had made their own major invasion during the Belgian drive. A gift from the Germans, as it was generally said. The hasty delousing procedure proved to be unsatisfactory and it was not until after the armistice at the major delousing plant in Le Mans, France, that they finally got rid of these persistent little creatures. Until then, the *"shirt readings"* were a continuing evening and nightly pass time.

It had become evident that the Germans were retreating in the direction of Brussels. Small German units had been positioned in isolated defensive locations. On 2 November elements of the German 9th Reserve Division were encountered near the village of Heurne and on 5 November they had been relieved by the 21st Infantry Division. Their morale was very low; regiments had been reduced to 2 battalions of 3 companies. 2,400 of these men had been prisoner of war at the Somme between August and October. On 3 November elements of the 13th Reserve Division had been seen near the village of Nazareth.

Special Operations Order No. 470, the 37th Division was ordered to prepare themselves to re-enter the lines on 7 November. Chateau Huysse was their new Headquarters on 9 November effective 09:00 hours. Special Order No. 472 of 9 November indicated that the 37th Division would relieve the French 11th division during the night of 10 - 11 November. Their mission was to make a rapid advance in pursuit of the enemy on 11. The width of the Scheldt river in the 37th Division sector was between 24 and 26 meters. Their German opponents were elements of the 21st Infantry Division (80th, 81st and 87th Regiments) and the 207th Infantry Division.

It had come to the point that the Germans were retreating in disorder along the entire front. Machinegun nests hiding behind hedgerows and ruins were sporadic in delaying the allied advance. German infantry units were scattered to the rear in the event a counterattack was expected of them. At 11:00 hours the Armistice became effective and the Ohio men had reached their furthest point in the line Dickele – Zwartenbroeck beyond Oudenaarde.

De 37th Buckeye Division had played their role in the Great War. During their Flanders offensive (25 October – 11 November 1918) they had encountered 1648 casualties. 297 men had been killed in action and another 104 died of wounds. In addition 1,247 were lightly wounded. At Flanders Field American Cemetery 152 men of the 37th Division are buried. The mortal remains of ten were never found. Their names are memorialized on the Wall of Missing inside the chapel.

WE'RE COMING BACK TO YOU

Many months ago we left you,
Dear friends of Buckeye state,
To come to France and Belgium
To show Germany her fate.
We left you with our hearts bowed down,
For you're folks we love most,
Then too -- the trail which we came
Was marked by Death's Mile Posts.

We arrived in sunny France at Brest
Our voyage o'er quite "tame"
But six weeks from the time we sailed
Found us in the trenches -- in Lorraine
For five weeks we held the lines
Schooling ourselves at war
Proving to "Fritzie" his opinion of us
Was entirely wrong by far!

Then from Lorraine we "shouldered arms"
Our faces toward Verdun
To a front that was proclaimed by all--
Impossible -- Advance means doom.
The great advance in the Argonne,
Don't you remember the time,
'T was in the end of September
And your friends were there and mine.

Six days of rain, filth, shells and blood
Days lived in Hell's own gates;

With your friends "going west" and mine
To save the good old states.
But you just bet your last good cent

42

That for each chap " gone down"
There were three of "Fritzie's" comrades
Strewn on the shell swept ground

And "Jerry" could not stop us,
Though tired we kept step,
And when at last relief came
He had learned of Yankees pep
From the Argonne we went eastward
Up into St. Mihiel
When the boche again were promptly taught
An Ohioan won't keep still!!

Then little Belgium called us
To come to her at once,
To help her and the Poilus
Show up Germany a dunce.
At Olsene – in Belgium
We revived the spirit of yore.
Till on the fields of Flanders
Lay a thousand boche or more.

"Kamerad Kamerad Kamerad!"
Came each of "Jerry's" men
And a second drive was needless
For they knew 't was their Amen.
It was then that the news of peace came,
The words that meant so much
To all the allied nations
As well as those the "Dutch"

And now we're coming back to you--
Those of us who are left--
To share with you the happiness,
Of a world to live in rest.
We know you're glad we're coming
For we've tried our best to show
Just what we think in arms and deeds
Of our mother state Ohio

We love dear France and Belgium
But now the war is thru
We're returning to the state of states
Ohio, the Buckeye--and you.

Prior World War I, the towns of Eine and Nederename were connected by an iron bridge over the river Scheldt. With the German invasion the bridge was destroyed by the Belgian engineering corps in 1914. During the German occupation a wooden bridge was constructed which in turn was demolished upon their retreat in 1918.

Engineers of the 37th Division constructed a temporary wooden bridge with materials provided by the French Army. After the war, the State of Ohio financed the construction of a new bridge to commemorate the actions of the 37th Division during the offensive. The construction commenced in September 1928 under the supervision of the architects Walker and Weeks from Cleveland, Ohio. The project was followed up by the Parisian architects Lahalle and Levard. The 37th Ohio Bridge was inaugurated on 26 September 1929.

The original bridge in 1929 showed the inscription *"In Memory of the Crossing of the Scheldt by the 37th Division A.E.F."* The buffalo's facing each other at 37 meter distance.

Location where the 37th Division crossed the Scheldt river

General view of the grandstand and tribute during the inauguration ceremony on
26 September 1929

American delegation of the 37th Division with General Jackson and Governor of East-Flanders

The bridge was demolished by British engineers on 19 May 1940 in a desperate attempt to slow down the German invasion of World War II.

The current Ohio-bridge is but a shadow of the original architectural masterpiece. The buffaloes are now 250 meter apart and the original dedication plaques are the only surviving witnesses of the American participation during World War I. Photo insert shows Brigadier General John W.  Donaldson, Director European Region (now Overseas Operations), American Battle Monuments Commission, during an inspection visit in 1984.

91st WILD WEST DIVISION

MAJOR GENERAL WILLIAM H. JOHNSTON

Commander 91st Division, A.E.F.

MOBILIZATION

De 91st Division, with the popular nickname WILD WEST Division, was a National Army Division. All men originated from the States of Montana, Nevada, Wyoming, Utah, Washington, Oregon, California and Idaho.

The first men arrived for basic training at Camp Lewis, WA on 5 September 1917.

"Liberty Gate" entrance to Camp Lewis 1918

Camp Lewis 1917

The division was formed with the following units:

Headquarters Troops

181st Infantry Brigade

361st Infantry Regiment	(Washington)
362nd Infantry Regiment	(Montana)
347th Machine Gun Battalion	(Idaho)

182nd Infantry Brigade

363rd Infantry Regiment	(California)
364th Infantry Regiment	(California)
348th Machine Gun Battalion	(California)

166th Field Artillery Brigade

346th Field Artillery Regiment
347th Field Artillery Regiment
348th Field Artillery Regiment
316th Trench Mortar Battery

Divisional Troops

346th Machine Gun Battalion	(Montana)
316th Engineer Regiment	(California)
316th Field Signal Battalion	
Trains and Military Police	(California)

French military instructors arrived at Camp Lewis in November 1917. The French having had more than three years of experience in tactical warfare were more than welcome. By the end of December, 40,000 troops had received intensive training and were deemed ready to be sent to France.

After ten months of intensive training the first units were entrained for Camp Merritt, NJ between 19 and 21 June 1918 where they arrived six days later. The whole division made the transfer between 24 and 30 June and remained there until 5 July. The following day they embarked for Europe where the majority arrived at Liverpool (England) and Glasgow (Scotland) on 17 July. From there they entrained for Southampton, crossing the channel where first units arrived at Le Havre, France on 23 July.

TRAINING IN EUROPE

After a short rest period the troops moved by train to the Department of the Haute Marne, France where they received additional intensive training during the month of August. Major General William H. Johnston assumed command of the division on 29 August. On 7 September the training area moved closer to the front line where the division was placed in reserve of the First American Army during the St. Mihiel offensive. As of 24 September final preparations were made for the 91st Division to participate in their baptism of fire during the Meuse-Argonne offensive on 26 September.

To everyone's surprise their first engagement against the German armies was a great success. General Cameron, Commander V Corps, immediately sent a memo to General Johnston expressing his praise: *"At a time when the divisions on its flanks were faltering and even falling back, the 91st pushed ahead and steadfastly clung to every yard gained. In its initial performance, your division has established itself firmly in the list of the Commander-in-Chief's reliable units. Please extend to your officers and men my appreciation of their splendid behavior and my hearty congratulations on the brilliant record they have made."*

The 91st Division remained in the Meuse-Argonne sector until 4 October when it was relieved by the U.S. 32nd Division.

The 91st DIVISION IN FLANDERS

Field Orders No. 16 of 15 October issued orders for General Johnston to prepare the division's transfer to the Ypres sector in Belgium. Special Orders No. 439 of 22 October ordered the transfer of the 53rd Artillery Brigade (US 28th Division) to the 91st Division. The first units of the division entrained at Revigny on 16 October, arriving in the Ypres sector on 18 October. Sunday 20 October the division commenced their march towards the front establishing their headquarters in the town of Oostnieuwkerke. Many of the men took shelter in the church that night. On Thursday 24 October

their zone of occupation was extended to the Roeselare (Roulers) area moving their headquarters to Rumbeke on Saturday 26th (photo insert: HQ 91st Division - Chateau Rumbeke). Here King Albert of the Belgians expressed his welcome to the Americans followed by General Degoutte of the French Army the following day.

Field Orders No. 20 of 27 October designated the 91st Division as part of the French VII Army Corps and headquarters was moved to the town of Izegem the following day.

The "Turnip Drive" was just around the corner and as we were getting closer to the front additional precautions were taken during telephone conversations and transmitting of messages. Different codes were used not only to create a more homely atmosphere but also to prevent the Germans intercepting and decoding these messages.

The following codes were used to indicate place names:

Izegem - *Rosedale*
Ooike - *Highland*
Wortegem - *Oaklawn*
Moregem - *Clover*
Schelde rivier - *Defiance*
Oudenaarde - *Lakewood*
Eine - *Cliff*
Heurne - *Volunteer*

Units and officers were also designated with codes. The Commanding General became Raccoon #1, his Aide de Camp, Raccoon #2, etc... Raccoon #25 was the last in the sequence being the liaison officer.

The codes used for units of the 91st Division during the offensive were:

181st Infantry Brigade HQ - *Regard*
361st Inf. HQ - *Regatta* (1st Bn. - *Regent,* 2nd Bn. - *Register,* 3rd Bn. - *Regulator*)
362nd Inf. HQ - *Relay* (1st Bn. - *Relic,* 2nd Bn. - *Remark,* 3rd Bn. - *Remedy)*
347th Machine Gun Bn. HQ - *Renegade*

182nd Infantry Brigade HQ - *Republic*
363rd Inf. HQ - *Reptile* (1st Bn. - *Replica,* 2nd Bn. - *Repast,* 3rd Bn. - *Retainer*)
364th Inf. HQ - *Retort* (1st Bn. - *Return,* 2nd Bn. - *Reunion,* 3rd Bn. - *Reveille*)
348th Machine Gun Bn. HQ - *Revenge*

53rd Field Artillery Brigade HQ - *Radiant*
107th Field Artillery Regiment HQ - *Redeem*
108th Field Artillery Regiment HQ - *Rebel*
109th Field Artillery Regiment HQ - *Remodel*

These codes were strictly used for all Field Messages being delivered by courier. However sometimes attention to detail on place names were neglected. U.S. Army Field Message of 30 October 19:15 hours, delivered by courier from Regard 8 (Adjutant 181st Inf. Brig.) to Raccoon 3 (Major General HQ 91st Div.), is a relevant example.

U. S. A.

TIME FILED	N.J.	SENT BY	TIME	RECEIVED BY	TIME	CHECK

THESE SPACES FOR SIGNAL OPERATORS ONLY

From _Regard 8 - 181st Inf, Brig.t_

At _P.C._

Date _30 Oct_ Hour _19.15_ No._16_ HOW SENT _Courier_

To _Racoon 3_

P.C. established in white faced
1 story building on S. side of main
road in EVANGELIE BOOM. F.O.
Plans of liaison, maps, etc. rec'd.
Extra copy returned herewith. Liaison
established with both infantry regiments
Sketch showing their location follows.

Regard 8

In personal diaries, such as that of Private William Nielsen, one could follow the war from the soldiers point of view. One of the entries while he was marching with his unit gave the first indications of the "Turnip Drive": *"30 October: ready to move forward, beautiful countryside. We are marching through Rumbeke, Izegem, Ingelmunster. In comparison the buildings here are far less damaged. All runs smoothly until we reach Ooigem and dig in for the night. The Germans are bombing us and we flee in all directions hiding in a turnip field."*

With Field Orders No. 21 directives on troop locations are provided for the attack of 31 October. Zone of action 91st Division : Northern boundary Waregem - chateau Nokere - Ooike – Eine exclusive. Southern boundary Steenbrugge - Wortegem - exclusive Petegem - Schapendries. Division Headquarters at Desselgem. Post Commands 181st Brigade (Brigadier General John B. McDonald) and the 182nd (Brigadier General V.A. Caldwell) were at Evangelieboom and Gaverken respectively.

The 53rd Artillery Brigade (Brigadier General William H. Price Jr.) supported the 91st Division from Desselgem. The 59th and 264st French Artillery out of Gaverken and Nieuwenhove.

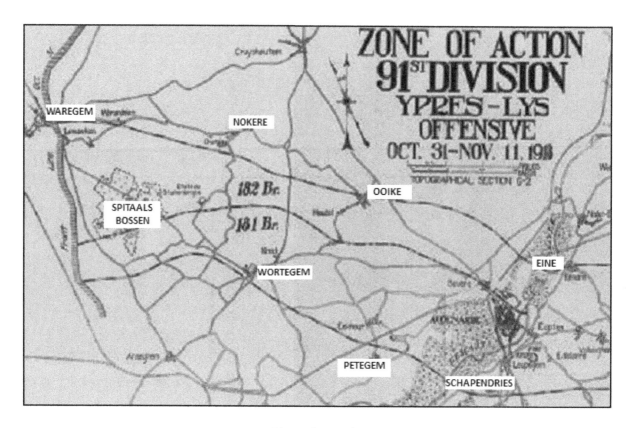

Plan of attack

On 15 October Field Hospital #362, supporting the British Casualty Clearing Station Nr. 36 in the village of Boezinge near Ypres, was moving towards Roeselare (Roulers) temporarily setting up their facilities in Oostnieuwkerke. During the night of 30-31 October ambulances of the 316th Sanitary Train were being transferred from Marseille, France. Evacuation of the Field Hospitals were effectively carried out using 15 ambulances moving the wounded to Evacuation Hospital #5 located near the village of Staden. (see plate LII chapter 37th Division: Location of Field Hospitals).

As mentioned earlier, 31 October was a grey miserable day with drizzly rain. The attack commenced at 05:30 as planned. Enemy artillery fire coming from the direction of Anzegem, machinegun nests securely dug in in the Spitaalsbossen and farms in the vicinity were a major hindrance to the troops in attempting to continue the advance. The French 41st Division on their right flank were experiencing even harder opposition. Because of this it was decided to modify the plan of attack. On 1 November the French 128th Division (advancing between the 37th and 91st Divisions) were ordered to continue the advance with Eine as objective instead of retreating and being placed in reserve.

Aerial photograph of the Spitaalsbossen taken by a French reconnaissance plane on 26 October. From the intersection (B.185) towards the group of buildings is where the Flanders Field Cemetery is now located (see comparison next page).

Photo courtesy 1st Tactical Reconnaissance Squadron U.S. Air Force Europe – 1 March 1946

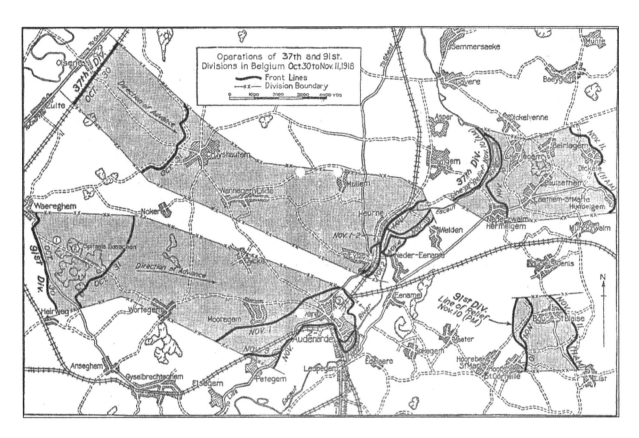

Plan of attack *(courtesy American Battle Monuments Commission)*

After interrogating the first German prisoners of war it was determined that they were soldiers of the 98th and the 209th Reserve Infantry Regiment of the 207th Infantry Division fighting around Waregem and the 49th Reserve Infantry Division scattered in the Spitaalsbossen.

Waregem was liberated by the end of the day. German artillery had inflicted considerable damage to the town as also to its inhabitants.

By the end of October morale of the German troops was low and in most cases indifferent. The number of men comprising a unit had declined considerably and they were only assigned defensive missions. By 1 November it had become evident that the Germans were retreating from the Spitaalsbossen. The 181st Brigade made a rapid advance towards the village of Wortegem and by late afternoon they had reached the outskirts of Oudenaarde. In the evening they patrolled the western part of the town. As all bridges had been demolished by the retreating Germans no further attempts to advance were made that day. Reconnaissance patrols along the banks in search of potential areas to make a crossing were carried out and materials were on the way to construct temporary pontoon bridges.

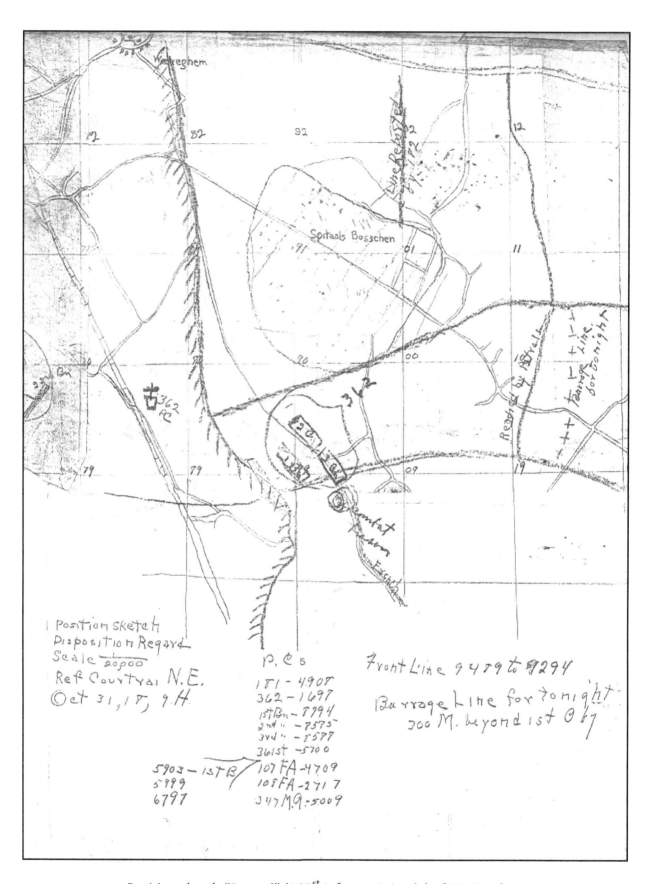

Position sketch "Regard" (181ˢᵗ Infantry Brigade) of 31 October

364th Infantry Regiment at the church of Waregem on 1 November 1918

Company A, 316th Engineers Regiment repairing tracks at the Waregem railroad station

Not all details of attacks were reported accurately and these examples were used for tactical training of infantry officers between the World Wars. One example is the attack of 2 November carried out by the 364th Infantry Regiment. Still being used to this day by the Infantry School, it is just one of the fine examples on how rules of combat can be influenced and changed by external factors (mission situation, terrain, weather, etc.).

On 2 November, the 364th Infantry Regiment was placed in reserve in the Spitaalsbosschen. That same evening their Commander received verbal orders to advance during the night. When he returned to his command post at 21:40 his officers were ready and waiting and

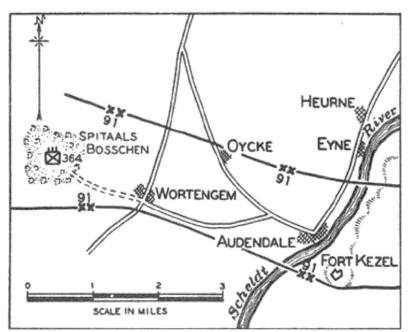

the verbal orders were immediately passed on to them. Twenty minutes later the 364th Infantry were on their way direction Wortegem. A written confirmation of the orders were only received at midnight. In addition, the 364th received orders to pursue their advance towards the footbridges over the river Scheldt between the villages of Eine and Heurne. After crossing the river they were to take a southerly direction towards Fort Kezel and then reconnoiter with the rest of the 91st Division who had already settled on the west bank of the river.

To succeed in their mission two major factors had to be taken into consideration. Firstly, the regiment would have to march ten miles, cross the river Scheldt, prepare for the attack which was situated yet another two and a half miles from the river and all of this under cover of darkness. Secondly, to ensure the element of surprise towards the enemy, the troops would have to reach Fort Kezel before sunrise.

At 04:00 hours, the 364th Infantry Regiment were 3 km beyond where they were met by guides. Here the troops were delayed by a message directing the colonel to proceed to an artillery command post supporting the upcoming attack.

At 04:45 hours, thirty minutes before sunrise, the men were still 3 km away from the footbridges. Enemy artillery had concentrated their fire on all the roads. Under pressure of these heavy bombardments the commander had no alternative than to order his troops to seek shelter east of Ooike and to cancel the attempt to cross the river Scheldt (personal experience of Captain Frederick W. Rote, Infantry).

German officers at Fort Kezel (winter 1915)

It is evident that the 364th Infantry Regiment received their orders too late. Their mission was practically impossible. The distance to the river being 10 miles, then after crossing another 4 miles towards Fort Kezel was stretching the limits. Even under normal circumstances of marching by night on normal roads at 2 miles per hour, one would need five hours to reach the river. After crossing the river the terrain was cross country at the rate of 1 mile per hour resulting in an additional two and a half hours. The whole operation would need seven and a half hours of constant marching, not counting the time needed to cross the river or other delays.

Theoretically, the plan could have succeeded. However based on practical issues it was not possible as the calculation of time and space factors had been too optimistic. Delays such as enemy artillery, time needed to cross the river and finally formation of the troops in preparation of the attack, had not been taken into account.

On 3 November, Oudenaarde was liberated by the 361st Infantry Regiment, 91st Division and was relieved by the French 41st Division on that day. With the 53rd Artillery Brigade the 91st Division moved to Oostrozebeke where they remained in reserve until 10 November.

Refugees returning to their homes near Oudenaarde

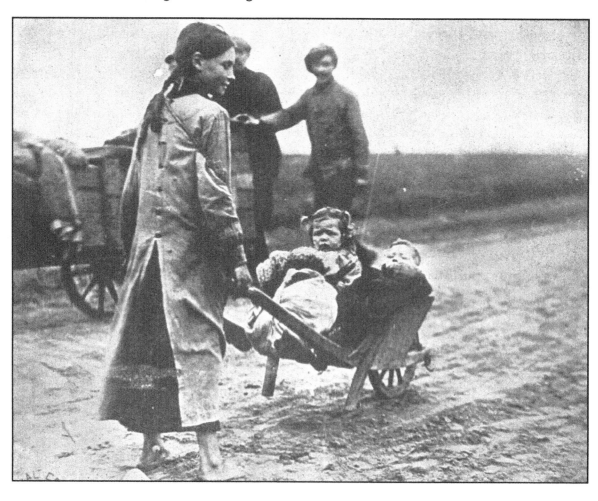

Field Orders No. 27 of 8 November ordered the 91st Division back to active duty with Headquarters being established in the Chateau of Nokere by midday on 10 November. Troops would advance in northerly direction from the train station at Ename and in southerly direction from Fort Kezel. They would follow the retreating Germans at close range.

At 15:00 hours headquarters were established in Oudenaarde. The Germans continued their rapid retreat. The war was coming to an end.

At 08:30 hours, 11 November 1918, Major General William H. Johnston issued the orders (Field Orders No. 33) that at 11:00 hours the "War to End all Wars" would finally be over.

St. Blasius-Boekel was the furthest point reached by the 91st Division.

91st Division in front of City Hall - Oudenaarde 12 November 1918

Homeward Bound

On March the tenth the orders came
To send us to the States again
This time it was a battle ship
On which to make the ocean trip
We cleaned her up from stern to bow
And on the trip we served some chow
March twenty-fourth we all could see
The face of Lady Liberty
We're back once more from toil and death
A bunch of Vets from the A.E.F.

E.L.T.
103rd Trench Mortar Battery

5

THE POEM "IN FLANDERS FIELDS"

Lieutenant Colonel John McCrae
Canadian Army Medical Corps

Lieutenant Colonel John D. McCrae was born in Guelph, Ontario, Canada, on 30 November 1872. He was the son of Colonel David McCrae and Janet Simpson Eckford McCrae. John was a doctor who started writing poems after his graduation from the University of Toronto in 1900 and joining the McGill faculty. John McCrae had already gained experience of war as he had served as an artillery subaltern in the Canadian Army during the Boer War in South Africa (1899-1901). When World War I broke out on 4 August 1914, John was at sea traveling to England. He immediately returned to Canada where he enlisted on 22 September. He arrived in Plymouth, England on 14 October as a doctor (Major) attached to the First Brigade of the Canadian Field Artillery. When he arrived in Flanders on 17 April 1915 he was promoted to Lieutenant-Colonel of the Canadian Army Medical Corps. On 5 January 1918 he was the first Canadian ever appointed as Consultant Physician to the British Armies in the field. Unfortunately John McCrae succumbed to pneumonia and meningitis on 28 January 1918. He was 45 years of age. Colonel McCrae was buried in Wimereux Communal Cemetery, Plot IV, Row H, Grave 3, Wimereux (Pas de Calais, France), a few miles north of Boulogne-sur-Mer.

McCrae's funeral procession, 29 January 1918 (*National Archives Canada - C18550*)

John McCrae had been very busy tending the wounded and performing surgery in the Ypres Salient for seventeen consecutive days. He was deeply troubled by the atrocities and miseries of war around him. When the shattered remains of his close friend and former student Lieutenant Alexis Helmer (photo insert) was brought in to his aid station on 2 May 1915, he was devastated.

After sunset on the same day, McCrae led a simple burial ceremony and recited a passage from the Order of Burial for the Dead near his aid station (now Essex Farm cemetery).

The following day, while staring at Helmer's grave, he wrote the unforgettable words to the poem "In Flanders Fields" which were first anonymously published in Punch Magazine on 8

December 1915. The Advanced Medical Dressing Station where John McCrae wrote the poem during the second battle of Ypres has now been restored adjacent the Essex Farm cemetery and has become a pilgrimage site to the many battlefield tourists.

The American cemetery in Waregem was also named Flanders Field and has always been associated with the poem.

Inspired by McCrae's poem, the American professor Moina Michael (1869-1944) from Georgia wrote an answer: "We Shall Keep the Faith". For her humanitarian efforts she would become known as the "Poppy Lady" as she was the first to use the poppy as a means of raising funds for disabled veterans and their families. She received numerous awards for her achievements. The Georgia General Assembly named a section of the U.S. Highway 78 the Moina Michael Highway in 1969.

John McCrae site 2015

In Flanders Fields

—

In Flanders fields the poppies blow
Between the crosses, row on row,
That mark our place; and in the sky
The larks, still bravely singing, fly
Scarce heard amid the guns below.

We are the Dead. Short days ago
We lived, felt dawn, saw sunset glow,
Loved, and were loved, and now we lie
        In Flanders fields.

Take up our quarrel with the foe:
To you from failing hands we throw
 The torch; be yours to hold it high.
 If ye break faith with us who die
We shall not sleep, though poppies grow
        In Flanders fields

Punch
Dec 8·1915

John McCrae

We shall keep the faith

Oh! You who sleep in Flanders' Fields
Sleep sweet - to rise anew;
We caught the torch you threw,
And holding high we kept
The faith with those who died.

We cherish, too, the Poppy red
That grows on fields where valor led.
It seems to signal to the skies
That blood of heroes never dies.
But lends a lustre to the red
On the flower that blooms above the dead
In Flanders' fields.

And now the torch and Poppy red
Wear in honour of our dead.
Fear not that ye have died for naught:
We've learned the lesson that ye taught
In Flanders' fields.

Moina Bell Michael – 8 November 1918

6

AMERICAN GRAVES REGISTRATION SERVICE

The task of the American Graves Registration Service (A.G.R.S) was an enormous project. Thousands of human remains were exhumed and repatriated to the U.S.A. or another country of the next of kin's choice. The final resting place of all others was in one of the eight permanent American military cemeteries in Europe. There was only one goal: to meet and execute the last wishes of the next of kin with respect and dignity. This is an attempt to provide a short sketch on the magnitude of this gruesome project, from the chaos of the Armistice on 11 November 1918 through 31 August 1920. The numerous problems that occurred in order to make this all happen, details of sensitive cases and illustrating the commitment of all personnel tasked to carry out this delicate and memorable project.

The inhuman conditions of the battlefields in many cases resulted in burial parties not being able to carry out their assigned task of performing dignified temporary burials and

consequently securing the identity of the individual for future disposition of the remains. A hasty burial would be marked by a rifle or improvised cross and even sometimes only with a stick in the ground. Bodies were more likely to be buried in shallow graves by comrades in arms without chaplains being able to perform the last rites.

There were also trench burials where soldiers were buried side by side, but in many cases this was an exception to rule under battlefield conditions. It was essential for the A.G.R.S. to follow up on these temporary burials as they were reported and as soon as it was safe enough to move forward in these specified areas. Individual graves would then be secured with a wooden "V" shaped peg with a metal plate attached indicating the soldier's identity. After hostilities these "V" type pegs were replaced with a wooden crosses and attached with an aluminum G.R.S. identity disc.

THE GRAVES REGISTRATION SERVICE BEFORE 1919

On 31 May 1917 the War Department approached Charles C. Pierce, a retired Major, tasking him to establish the Overseas Graves Registration (as it then was called) and supervise the operations in Europe. Major, later Colonel Pierce had organized and executed similar activities in the Philippine Islands (1899-1902) where he was able to positively identify and repatriate all 4,234 American victims of the conflict within two years. By 7 August he had assembled a qualified team of two high ranking officers and fifty men and was ready to sail for Europe. They were known as Advance Group #1 Graves Registration Service. Considering the magnitude of the project in supervising more than 73,000 graves, and as the work progressed, the Unit soon became a Department with 150 officers and 7,000 employees. Their first assignment was to identify the remains and register the exact location in each zone of action.

After the Unit arrived in Europe in October 1917, the Chief was responsible for the supervision and overview of all operations until September 1918. One must bear in mind that hostilities were still intense and ongoing which caused much pressure and stress for all those concerned during these operations. After September 1918, three zones with headquarters were established in France: one in Neufchateau, one in Soissons and one in Amiens.

After the Armistice it became much easier to regroup and consolidate graves and commence the construction of temporary cemeteries. By a provision in French law dated 29 December 1915, lands necessary for burial of American and allied soldiers were acquired by the French War Department and all costs borne by the French government. Belgium followed with a similar agreement on 5 September 1917.

As mentioned before, during hostilities burial was taken care of by the army. It was however required that a form, in duplicate, with all the details of the soldier killed in action be completed and forwarded to the G.R.S. The report also required that details of the grave be documented, either name, identity disc, cross, personal belongings in a bottle, etc. Every possible measure was taken to secure that the grave would be found for positive identification of the remains after hostilities had ended.

Instructions were also issued for burial of foreign soldiers. Indians were not to be buried in Christian cemeteries and Chinese were to be given a burial according to the customs of their country. Jewish graves were to be marked with a headboard of significant dimensions which later would be modified to carry a Star of David.

No grave was registered until a representative of the G.R.S. was fully satisfied of the identification procedure. Markers received a metal plate with the letters "G.R.S." as evidence that the registration had been completed.

The Statistical Department of the Adjutant General's office was responsible for the details of the inscription on the grave marker. This sometimes caused friction and discussions with family members. If a soldier or officer died on the day on which he received a promotion and had not yet accepted that promotion then the Adjutant General's office would decide on holding the lower rank. Families who had been notified of the promotion would frequently request a correction be made to the marker. An investigation would follow and would reveal the circumstances of the Adjutant General's final decision and the Graves Registration Service was forced to adhere to this decision. However, there were exceptions to this rule such as in the Flanders Field case of Sergeant Paul Gusler (A-02-18).

Until it was possible to install permanent wooden markers, smaller temporary markers were used. The dimensions were: height 1.04 meter, spread of cross 0.35 meter, width 0.05 meter. These temporary crosses were painted in olive green. The permanent wooden markers would later be twice the size and painted white. The first requisition of five thousand permanent markers could not be delivered by the French due to shortage of wood. However there was sufficient wood in stock to provide the smaller version of markers.

Even during hostilities, there were families requesting permission to erect a private monument at the grave of their loved ones. Their request was denied to prevent discrimination and to ensure uniformity of these military cemeteries. After the Armistice the rule was ignored and mostly wealthy families commissioned the construction and installment of private monuments. This all resulting in additional problems during future exhumations for the final disposition of remains.

The G.R.S. were also assisted by various voluntary organizations such as the "American Red Cross", "Young Men's Christian Association", "Knights of Columbus" etc. The motivation and commitment of these groups was phenomenal although in some cases individuals did cause major disruption. In one case a man had removed both identity discs from the body and sending them to the G.R.S. official instead of one identity disc remaining with the body.

For Flanders Field it is assumed that this was the case for Jessie Silcox (Wall of Missing). During our research both identity discs were found in his burial file at the National Archives.

The only systematical and professional approach was provided by the American Red Cross. As of November 1918, twenty-five professional photographers were assigned as permanent staff members for the G.R.S. They searched and systematically photographed individual graves and secured contacts with family members of the deceased.

After the Armistice the necessity of centralizing and maintaining the graves became an urgent issue. In April 1919 the Graves Registration Service was informed to end all operations of the Advance Section by 1 July. Their top priority would now be establishing and centralizing military cemeteries, also continuing the identification and registration of graves. Keeping accurate counts and registration of graves outside the zones of action was no problem. In zones of action it was clearly a nightmare as was experienced by the British and French. Their initial count of losses were more than 50,000 graves due to the continuous upheaval of the ground by heavy artillery.

A fine example of a successful operation in centralizing graves is no doubt Meuse-Argonne. The Graves Registration Service had anticipated this site to contain 26,000 graves (today it contains 14,246 permanent burials).

The process of double-checking and registering graves in France commenced in 1919. All personnel, including the men of the former Advance Section, were assigned for the task. One Grave Registration Unit and 100 labor troops were assigned to 640 square kilometers of combat territory. Twenty men per group would operate in skirmish line at fifty meter intervals. This covered 1 kilometer of front line. With sufficient men per G.R.S. unit, 8 kilometers of front line was covered. This included fields, woods and isolated areas. Working eight hour per day shifts an area of 64 square kilometers were covered. Twenty five surveying groups were assigned to cover certain map sections locating graves.

By 11 February it was evident that progress had been made. Adverse weather conditions had however thrown a wrench in the works. The banks of rivers and canals overflowed making sections of the terrain inaccessible. In some of the flooded areas the water was waist deep. Notwithstanding the major setbacks, 20,480 square kilometers had been covered by 21 February. In one sector covering 640 square kilometers more than 12,000 graves had been registered. This clearly illustrates the magnitude of the project and the great number of graves. It was also evident that many of the graves were too shallow resulting in remains in need of reburial.

Three areas in the Verdun sector were selected for centralizing graves: Beaumont, Pont-à-Mousson and Romagne (where the permanent cemetery of Meuse-Argonne is now located). By 11 March the centralization of remains had commenced at Romagne (photo next page).

It was hard work under wretched weather conditions. Working conditions were also hampered by the lack of transportation vehicles and the men were accommodated in war barracks as improvised housing.

The progress of the project is illustrated by the figures below. Total number of interments ending in the week of:
- 11 April: 1,525
- 30 April: 4,268
- 10 May: 6,573
- 20 May: 8,293
- 30 May: 9,527
- 10 June: 1,.933
- 20 June: 17,143

When finally complete, Romagne contained 21,000 graves. During the same period, temporary centralized burials were ongoing at the cemeteries in Suresnes, Belleau and Bony.

It is no coincidence that the heavy digging was performed by a battalion of Afro-American troops while the technical and searching work was taken care of by men selected from other units of the Grave Registration Service. In Volume I, page 35 of the History of the American Graves Registration it states: "*The handling of the bodies was entirely new work to the colored men but after witnessing the manner in which the white personnel performed the various operations, they proved to be efficient in the disagreeable task.*"

The general desire to complete the cemeteries as soon as possible and to designate them as being ready for general maintenance resulted in the premature decision of the American Expeditionary Forces to withdraw the majority of its men. Means of transport was removed and sold and records were moved to Washington DC. This decision was justifiably criticized as the remaining men had insufficient equipment to continue this enormous task. Nonetheless the heavy work was continued and regardless of the delays cemeteries were ready for routine maintenance in the summer of 1920.

When Colonel Pierce and his staff arrived in Washington DC they received a warm welcome and were praised for their achievements General Pershing wrote:

"It is a pleasure for me to express my thanks and the thanks of officers and men of the American Expeditionary Forces to you and your personnel, for the efficient work of the Graves Registration Service throughout the war.

You arrived in France, a lone advance agent of a branch of service which had still to be organized and which war's exigencies and hazards made imperative. You and your first handful of workers labored unceasingly, overcame obstacles, taxed your brains and hands to the utmost and finally achieved an organization worthy of the highest praise.

On every battlefield where Americans were engaged, and, having made the supreme sacrifice, were laid to their final rest, the results of your service were seen.

Your personnel toiled, often exposed to the same dangers as front line troops, and performed their duties there diligently, conscientiously and sympathetically. The liaison they maintained with our Allies was admirable.

The consecrated service you rendered to the kinsfolk of our soldiers conveying information and allaying undue anxiety and fears, the part you played in acting as personal representative of thousands of soldiers' relatives, meets not only with appreciation of the entire American Expeditionary Forces, but the gratitude of the American people.

A work, so comprehensive in its scope, yet characterized by an humanitarianism that is indeed laudable, stands forth in bold relief as a labor of duty and sympathy that will be credit to our country forever."

Sincerely yours
(signed) John. J. Pershing

REPATRIATION

These hearts were woven of human joys and cares
Washed marvelously with sorrow, swift to mirth.
The years had given them kindness. Dawn was theirs,
And sunset, and the colours of the earth.

"The Dead"
Rupert Brooke

It became evident that the American government, who in 1917 had promised to repatriate all dead to the U.S., had greatly underestimated the numbers involved. Two years had passed since the Armistice with no progress in sight and public opinion was not favorable towards the government. Propaganda made by American undertakers reached the ears of Congress. An editorial note in their magazine "The Casket" advertising methods in bringing home the dead and the fact that this would be secured by American undertakers resulted in a debate in Congress. Furthermore, in January 1920 Congress was awakened by news from across the Atlantic. A Paris undertaker circulated a letter, which was received by many relatives in the States, declaring that he was supported by an organization called "The Purple Cross" and that he had already secured a number of commissions returning bodies to New York at an average price of $605.

The American public was deeply shocked and the government was held guilty without trial. Statements were made as *"It looks like, if the French can get them out for money, the United States could get them out for loyalty to its citizens"*. The Secretary of War replied that this undertaker was making statements without legitimate grounds and promises in which he was in no position to keep.*

These incidents were very painful experiences , not only for the families concerned but also for the American government. However, this also resulted in the War Department finally appropriating $8,451,000 for the fiscal year 1919-1920 of which $2,500,000 was immediately allocated to commence the work in Europe.

* However during our research we came across one case that had slipped through the net and there could be more. (courtesy Denise Fransaer Corke, genealogist, Watseka Public Library and Iroquois County Genealogy Society, MT)
- ID 115227
- Name: Harold A. CLARK
- Sex: M
- Birth: 1 October 1889 in Great Falls, Montana
- Death: 10 October 1918 in Argonne, France
- Burial: 31 July 1919 in Malta, Montana, USA

The official closing date for next of kin to make the decision on the final disposition of remains was 1 April 1922.

On that day, exhumation and repatriation statistics showed that for the Flanders Field cemetery 1,027 men had been centralized. Theoretically 365 would receive a permanent burial at Flanders Field. These figures would fluctuate as family members revoked their initial decision. Field Section #7 in Soissons (Aisne, France) assigned one of her detachments to Belgium to commence exhumations. A total of 1,043 soldiers were accounted for in Belgium of which 675 were repatriated via the port of Antwerp. The total amount of burials for Flanders Field American Cemetery in Waregem would amount to 368.

FLANDERS FIELD AMERICAN CEMETERY #1252.
(Waereghem, Belgium).

CEMETERY NAME.	COMMUNE.	DEPART-MENT.	NUMBER OF BODIES.	
			Concen-trated.	Repatria-ted.
Military.	Motor Car Corner.	Belgium.	1	–
Communal.	Namur.	Belgium.	3	2
Lijssenthoek British Military Cemetery.	Poperinghe.	Belgium.	53	67
Nine Elms British Military Cemetery.	Poperinghe.	Belgium.	18	77
Abeele British Military Cemetery.	Poperinghe.	Belgium.	32	50
Hagle Dump British Military Cemetery.	Poperinghe.	Belgium.	10	15
Local Cemetery, American Plot.	Schoolselhof, Antwerp.	Belgium.	1	1
TOTALS.	7 Cemeteries.		118	212
From Waereghem Cemetery.			245	450
New Locations, (Unrecorded Burials).			2	
AGGREGATE.			365	662

This A.G.R.S. preliminary report indicates the temporary sites in Belgium from where remains were concentrated in Waregem.

By 15 May 1922, a total number of 45,149 remains had been repatriated to the United States. 30,260 had been shipped via the port of Antwerp. Antwerp became the largest port in Europe executing these operations. The other ports in France and England were St. Nazaire (3,538), Cherbourg (2,794), Brest (2,244), Calais (2,222), Bordeaux (2,111), Liverpool (1,106), Southampton (711), Toulon (145) and Portsmouth (18).

Not all remains were repatriated to the United States. By 31 August 1922 there were 454 men whose families had received permission to repatriate within Europe. The majority were transported to Italy (301), followed by Ireland (64), Greece (25), England (19), Poland (17),

Denmark (14), Sweden (6), Scotland (4) and Czechoslovakia (4). Due to the "German decree" of 22 July 1920 prohibiting the exportation or importation of remains of deceased soldiers it was considered inadvisable to communicate with the next of kin living in Germany as prospects of Germany reversing its decision was not to be expected in the near future. As such, it was recommended, as a policy, that in cases of next of kin of an American soldier residing in Germany, the remains of these dead would receive a permanent burial in one of the national cemeteries in France. It was also decided that no correspondence be initiated with relatives in which the U.S. government agrees to send the remains to that country as the Government then accepted an obligation that could not be carried out for an indefinite time.

Antwerp: arrival of caskets to be processed for repatriation

The final honors

Antwerp mortuary

Nine Elms Cemetery where 95 American soldiers were exhumed.

Lyssenthoek Cemetery, where 117 soldiers were exhumed. There were 3 "DND" – Do Not Disturb cases (Lieutenant James Pigue - Sergeant David Beattie - Private Harry King)

Abeele Cemetery, where 82 American soldiers were exhumed.

The furthest locations were Namur (Wilbert Lyons A-3-1, Roscoe Stubbs C-1-16, Lionel Anderson D-1-2) and the Schoonselhof cemetery in Antwerp (Bertram Horner C-1-1)

FLANDERS FIELD CEMETERY #1252

On 20 November 1920, the Commission of Fine Arts and the War Memorials Council designated the Minister of War to find a solution in coordinating the options for permanent cemeteries in Europe. As a follow-up, the Battle Monuments Board (later to become the American Battle Monuments Commission) was established on 11 June 1921. Waregem became a kind of terminal during the identification process and subsequent repatriation of remains. Those remains that were designated to be permanently interred in Europe would later be transported to the Flanders Field Cemetery in Bony, France, where a high number of permanent graves had already been concentrated. However, in August 1921 it was decided, for practical reasons, to develop a number of additional permanent sites. The number of permanent cemeteries in Europe were extended from six to eight, one additional cemetery in France (Oise-Aisne American Cemetery, Fère-en-Tardenois) and one in Belgium (Flanders Field, Waregem). The site in Bony became the Somme American Cemetery.

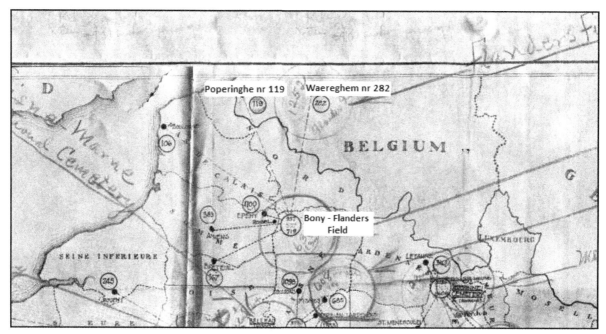

On the original map you can see the arrows pointing from the temporary cemeteries around Poperinge (number 119) and Waregem (number 282) in the direction of Bony (earmarked as Flanders Field). In Augustus 1921, Flanders Field, Waregem is marked in pencil as cemetery 1252. Bony, also in pencil, as the Somme American Cemetery.

Flanders had already taken steps much earlier to establish a temporary site in Waregem. A brief outline of the chronological steps taken are documented below:

9 January 1919: the district commissioner of Kortrijk informs the town of Waregem that he has no objections that the remains of French, British and American soldiers, currently scattered in isolated graves around different villages, to concentrate them in one designated area.

Field graves of 21 American near the village of Kruishoutem

Exhumations near the village of Olsene

MASSAGRAF 1918
AMERIKAANSE SOLDATEN OLSENE

Left insert: mass grave near Olsene: note Afro-American troops designated to carry out this task.

22 May 1919: the Mayor replies: *"A certain parcel of land on the road between Waereghem and Worteghem, belonging to Mademoiselle Melvina Delespaul, is judged to be the best option as a cemetery for the American soldiers who died for their country"*

18 June 1919: (insert below). During an inspection of the battlefields, President Woodrow Wilson and King Albert of Belgium, in Roeselare (Roulers). It is highly probable that President Wilson visited the graves of his fallen countrymen in the area of Poperinge (Lyssenthoek or Nine Elms British Cemetery) and maybe even Waregem. Unfortunately no details or photographic evidence was found during our research to confirm this assumption.

4 July 1919: the town of Waregem receives a letter from a Mr. Gabriel Bouckaert in which he specifies that the American cemetery in Waregem is in need *"of a man who is eloquent in at least three languages. His annual salary would be ten thousand Belgian francs, quarters and utilities free of charge."*

5 October 1921: one month after the A.G.R.S. decision to establish a permanent site in Waregem, an official statement in the Belgian Department of Orders and Decrees announces that permission is granted for the Ministry of Defense to dispossess the necessary parcels of land.

31 December 1921: the town of Waregem received notification from the Belgian Army Cemeterial Division in Bruges, to appropriate the parcels of land that have been selected for the establishment of the American Cemetery. The Mayor is to notify Miss Delespaul of their intent by registered letter.

10 January 1922: Appropriation of land belonging to Miss Malvina Delespaul. Miss Delespaul opposed the procedures. In her letter dated 18 February 1922 to the Provincial Health Commission she complained that the exhumations and reburial during the establishment of a cemetery would contaminate the well water on the farm located adjacent to the cemetery and also cause a serious hazard to public health.

6 March 1922: the town receives the results of a survey with section plan depicting the circumference of the site of the American cemetery from the Ministry of Defense.

23 March 1922: all appropriations were finalized. The 6 acre site would now become the Flanders Field American Cemetery.
The site being donated by the Belgian government in perpetuity for the use of a military cemetery did not mean that there were no financial expenditures necessary to secure the site. By the end of 1923, the American Government had spent a total of $111,000 for land

and landscaping of the cemeteries in France, England and Belgium. For Flanders Field the acquired amount was $ 5.000. (Joint Resolution 263, Public Res. #44, 67, U.S. Congress)

The earliest photographs of the Flanders Field American Cemetery. The photo above right, far left is the original wooden marker of Lieutenant Kearney. Photo below was taken on 2 November 1919 (courtesy Waregem City Archives).

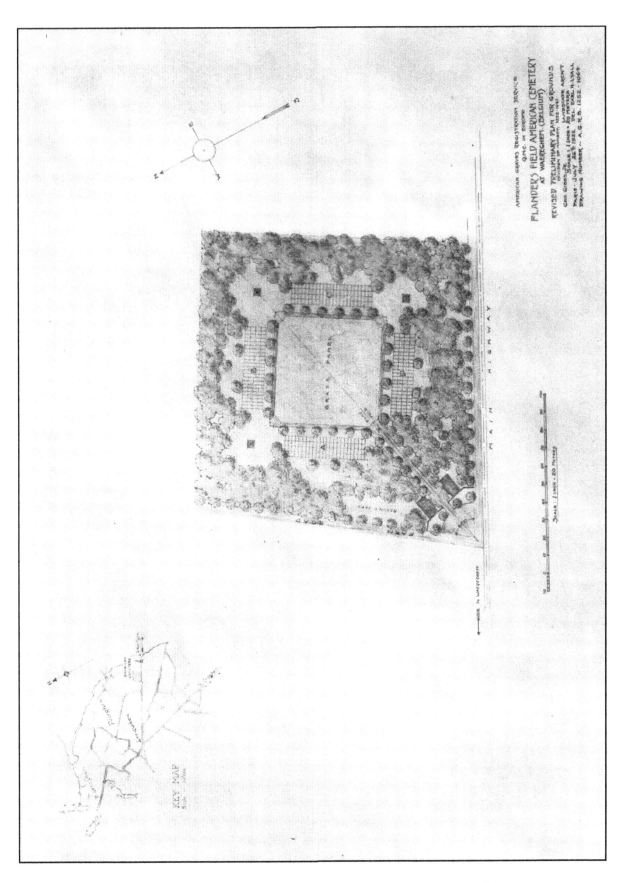

First draft by the American Graves Registration Service - 26 July 1922.

8

AMERICAN BATTLE MONUMENTS COMMISSION

The American Battle Monuments Commission (A.B.M.C.) was established by Congress in March 1923. The Commission of Fine Arts, under the leadership of Charles Moore, was the only official authority to approve the plans of these permanent sites.

President Harding appointed seven members to the Commission. General Pershing, Commander in Chief of the American Expeditionary Forces, became its chairman. Three representatives of veterans organizations, one delegate from the Gold Star Mothers, one Senator and one member of Congress were also designated. Major X.J.Price, Army Corps of Engineers was appointed Secretary.

The Ministry of War assigned two specific tasks to the Commission: construction of military cemeteries and erecting orientation tables on the major battlefields depicting where American troops fought. In an attempt to make these cemeteries more impressive, a chapel was added to the lay-outs of the Ministry of War. According to Elisabeth Grossman, Associate Professor of Art and Architectural History at the Rhode Island School of Design, A.B.M.C. had changed the original concepts of these projects in an attempt to enhance the historical achievements of military operations. This being the main reason to build chapels and monuments instead of modest orientation tables in stone or bronze. It was also a fact that A.B.M.C. ignored the recommendations made by the Ministry of War resulting in many conflicts and delays of these projects.

According to Moore, even before the Armistice, the original concept of these overseas cemeteries were destined to be "little Arlingtons". His vision was that of the Ministry of War, identical grave markers as in Arlington National Cemetery, VA. The emphasis was laid on grass and trees. This gave the impression that these cemeteries were larger. The emphasis with the British was stone, grass and plantations having a secondary role. The reasoning behind the Arlington model was mainly to establish a typical American symbol on European soil.

The Ministry of War completed their preliminary drafts for eight military cemeteries: six in France, one in England and one in Belgium. They contained approximately 31,000 graves. However these cemeteries would never resemble the little Arlington's of the National Cemetery in Virginia.

A.B.M.C. was also interested in the British concepts of their overseas cemeteries. In 1924 they decided it was time to arrange a meeting with Sir Fabian Ware of the Imperial War Graves Commission (now known as the Commonwealth War Graves Commission). During this meeting they learned about the War Graves Commission's plans of erecting monuments to the memory of their missing. The first monument was already under construction: the Menin Gate in Ypres.

The delegation continued their trip through Belgium. When they arrived in Ostend they were treated by the Mayor to a *Champagne d'Honneur* and in the evening they were guests and dined with King Albert and Queen Elisabeth.

On 21 June, the Governor of West Flanders informed the Mayor of Waregem that he would be receiving an important delegation on 26 June. He emphasized the fact that these were distinguished visitors and that he counted on every courtesy towards these honorable visitors.

ABMC delegation in Plot C during their visit on 26 June 1924. The Jewish marker in the front row is that of Lieutenant Colonel Morris Liebmann
(Signal Corps, photo III, No 86513, RG92, NARA)

It became evident that the Ministry of War was unable to oppose and object to A.B.M.C.'s new ideas. They were also under a lot of pressure from a private construction company who were at the point of erecting three impressive monuments in France. The architect Paul P. Cret (who later designed the chapel at Flanders Field) had already proven his professional skills. Commemorative architecture was in demand and Cret had already been hired by Mrs. Theodore Roosevelt in 1919 to design a memorial to her son Quentin at Chambéry, France. It is a fact that Cret's professionalism resulted in A.B.M.C. hiring him as a consulting architect in 1925. On 31 December 1924, Price wrote to Pershing that in his opinion, Cret was the most suitable architect to work out a couple of their plans. Cret was 48 at the time and although being a French citizen he had been living in the United States for more than 21 years.

General view 1925 – U.S. Signal Corps III-SC-86269

Flanders Field in 1925. There was no chapel and the wooden markers still needed to be replaced with Carrara marble headstones. There were only 367 graves. In the 1930's the remains of an American soldier were found in the river Scheldt, bringing the total to 368.

The chapel was dedicated on Memorial Day 1930. Little is found in the local archives relating to this event.

Because of the small size of the cemetery, Paul Cret had ensured that the chapel received a central implantation which gave it a dominating effect as a whole. Designed in Florentine art style, it is said that Cret was inspired by the "Tower of Winds" (right insert). This tower stands in the Roman Agora in Athens, Greece (J. Buhlmann's *"Die Architektur der Klassischen Altertums und der Renaissance"* - Stuttgart 1904).

The Flanders Field cemetery as we know it today was inaugurated on 8 August 1937 at 11:00 a.m.

DEDICATION

OF THE CHAPEL

IN THE AMERICAN CEMETERY

AT WAEREGHEM

AUGUST 8, 1937

DEDICATION OF THE CHAPEL
IN THE AMERICAN CEMETERY AT WAEREGHEM
At 11 A. M.
August 8, 1937

ARRIVAL of Official Belgian and American Delegations.

Playing of " LA BRABANÇONNE " and " THE STAR-SPAN-GLED BANNER " by the Band of the 2nd Belgian Infantry Regiment.

REVIEW OF GUARD OF HONOR.

SERVICES OF THE CHAPLAINS :
  Reverend Perry Smith,
  Father William P. O'Connor,
  Rabbi Michael Aaronsohn.

HYMN by the Band of the 2nd Belgian Infantry Regiment.

INTRODUCTORY ADDRESS : The Honorable Hugh Gibson, American Ambassador.

WELCOME : The Honorable H. Baels, Governor of the Province West Flanders.

ADDRESS : Mr. H. W. Colmery, National Commander of the American Legion.

ADDRESS : Lieutenant General Denis, Minister of National Defense of Belgium.

DEDICATORY ADDRESS : The Honorable F. Ryan Duffy, United States Senator.

RAISING OF THE AMERICAN FLAG : " The Star Spangled Banner ", sung by the school children of Waereghem.

ADDRESS : His Excellency Mr. Paul van Zeeland, Prime Minister of Belgium.

MILITARY MARCHES by the Band of the 2nd Belgian Infantry Regiment.

Senator F. Ryan Duffy gives a tribute.

Prime Minister of Belgium Paul van Zeeland

The Waregem school children

Pass in Review (courtesy – A.B.M.C. Overseas Operations, Paris, France)

On the same day the American Federal monuments were inaugurated. Oudenaarde at 2.30 p.m. and Kemmel at 3.30 p.m. The American monument in Oudenaarde was dedicated to the memory of the 37th, 91st Divisions and the 53rd Artillery Brigade of the 28th Division. The Kemmel monument in memory of the American soldiers of the 27th and 30th Divisions who were engaged in the region.

Oudenaarde

Kemmel

Kemmel

When World War II broke out, William Mozes, the American superintendent remained at his duty station until 13 May 1941. Mozes, together with 21 other American citizens working for the Commission were then advised to return to Washington and their respective families. His first attempt to escape from Paris, after the German invasion of Belgium on 10 May 1940, failed and on 12 June he returned to his duty station. Shortly after he wrote a letter to the headquarters in Washington with eye witness accounts of his employees on 23 May confirming that the Germans had entered the cemetery and had rampaged his quarters. Upon their departure they had stolen two bicycles belonging to the employees. During the absence of the superintendent the foreman, Achiel Adams, became the supervisor ad interim. William Mozes returned to his duty station on 8 January 1946 and remained superintendent at Flanders Field until the end of 1950.

Achiel Adams (photo's next page) moved into the government quarters for the duration of the war. He continued to maintain the site and acted as general caretaker for the cemetery. Assisting in the maintenance of the grounds were Camiel Verplancke and Camiel Amerlynck. Temporary employees were also hired when funds were available.

The administrative responsibility of the cemetery was taken over by a Belgian organization called *"Nos Tombes"* (Our Graves) on 19 July 1941. This way the salaries and any expenses incurred were secured for the employees. The United States government transferred funds through the Swiss Delegation for Foreign Affairs in Berlin.

SCHWEIZERISCHE GESANDTSCHAFT

IN DEUTSCHLAND

ABTEILUNG: SCHUTZMACHTANGELEGENHEITEN

BERLIN W 8
Parker Platz 2

January 15, 1942.

Mr. Achiel Adams,
Acting Superintendent,
W a r e g e m , Belgium

Sir:

On December 12, 1941, the Swiss Legation in Berlin has been entrusted with the representation of the interests of the U. S. Government in Germany and German-occupied territories.

To-day, we received your letter of Dec 11, 1941, addressed to the Special Disbursing Officer of the former American Embassy, Berlin, and we have pleasure in advising you that the Dresdner Bank, Berlin, has received instructions to remit to you the amount of bfrs 4352.00. You are requested to use this amount as follows:

Payroll December 1941:
Achiel Adams	frs 1500.00
Camiel Verplancke	1200.00
Camiel Amerlynck	360.00
Marcel Bruneel	192.00
	frs 3252.00
Enclosed coal bill	1100.00
	frs 4352.00

The December payroll has already been signed by the various payees and was taken into the files of this office. With regard to the coal bill, you are requested to have it receipted, stamped and signed by the dealer and to return it by registered mail to this office as soon as possible. Kindly address your letter "for the attention of Mr. Charles Knuchel".

Future business can be dealt with in exactly the same way as you did it so far with the American Embassy, Berlin.

Very truly yours,

Charles Knuchel

EM.

97

SCHWEIZERISCHE GESANDTSCHAFT

IN DEUTSCHLAND

ABTEILUNG: SCHUTZMACHTANGELEGENHEITEN

BERLIN W8, den 13. Februar 1942
Pariser Platz 2

USA 40 - CO/ke

Herrn

Achiel Adams,

Verwalter der Amerikanischen Kriegsgräber,

Military Cemetery,

Wareghem (Belgien)

     Unter Bezugnahme auf unser Schreiben vom gestrigen
Tage behändigen wir Ihnen beiliegend einige Quittungsformulare,
die Sie in Zukunft bitte anstelle der bisher gebrauchten,
amerikanischen Formulare benutzen wollen. Die anliegenden
Quittungen wären in Duplikat für jeden einzelnen Lohnempfänger
auszustellen und, mit Unterschrift versehen, an unsere Abteilung
für Schutzmachtangelegenheiten einzusenden, worauf die fälligen
Beträge sofort überwiesen werden, erstmalig also für den Monat
Februar 1942.

     Gleichzeitig behändigen wir Ihnen einige Fragebogen
mit der Bitte, dieselben freundlichst ausfüllen und wieder
einsenden zu wollen.

Mit vorzüglicher Hochachtung

SCHWEIZERISCHE GESANDTSCHAFT
Abteilung Schutzmachtangelegenheiten

i. a.

Beilagen

Shortly after the liberation of Waregem in September 1944, the remains of 28 American servicemen (pilots and crew members) buried in the vicinity of Waregem were interred at Flanders Field. During the final disposition of World War II dead (1945 – 1951), they were exhumed, repatriated or buried at Ardennes American Cemetery in Neupré (Luik).

Over the years, Flanders Field would become a pilgrimage site for the famous and less famous, civilian and military. Mrs. Theodore Roosevelt visited the cemetery in 1953 and 1955. William F. Clarke, author of *"Over there with O'Ryan's Roughnecks"*, visited Flanders Field with his wife on 5 June 1953.

| Wm T Clarke | June 5, 1953 | Altamont NY USA | Co A 104 M.G. BN. 27ᵗʰ Div. |
| Dorothy B. Clarke | " | " " " | |

Former President George Bush Sr. signs the visitors register – 26 July 1999

In the 1970's, John Eisenhower, son of General Dwight D. Eisenhower, became the U.S. Ambassador to Belgium and was guest speaker for the Memorial Day ceremonies. From the Vatican, Cardinal Schotte visited the grave of Private Ole Olson (D-01-03) upon his family's request. Former President George Bush Sr. visited Flanders Field in July 1999. President Barack Obama paid his respects in March 2014.

"GREET THEM EVER WITH GRATEFUL HEARTS"

Unfortunately, the most important visitors are usually lost out of sight: the veterans. Many American veterans visited Flanders Field in the 1950's. *"God bless the souls of my buddies"* and *"Paying respects to my comrades"* are common remarks found in the archives at Flanders Field. Holger Wilfred Roder wrote: *"Thank the USA for the beautiful memorial for my dear brother"* (Private William A. Roder, B–04-09).

It remains a fact, Flanders Field cemetery is unique in Belgium and will always remain to be a memorable place to visit.

Tribute President Barack Obama during his visit to Flanders Field - 26 March 2014
(Private collection Christopher Sims)

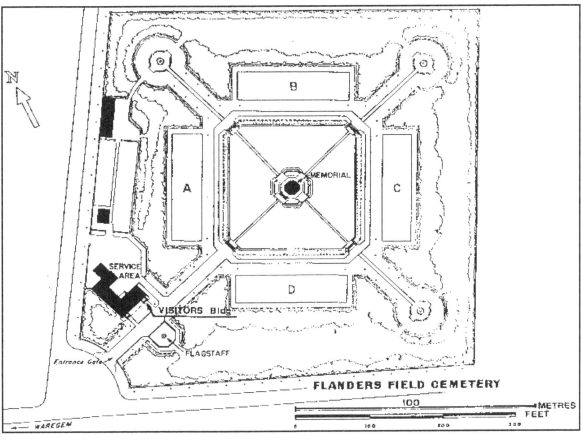

FLANDERS FIELD CEMETERY

METRES
FEET

WAREGEM

103

9

MEMORIAL DAY

There have always been discussions on the origins of Memorial Day, also known as Decoration Day. In general, everyone agrees that the roots lie with the aftermath of the Civil War. Decorating the graves of the fallen with flowers would become a common practice.

Local ceremonies mostly took place in the southern states as the majority of the soldiers were buried there. One of the first ceremonies to be registered was in Columbus, Mississippi on 25 April 1866. Macon in Georgia, Richmond in Virginia and many other towns carried out similar remembrance ceremonies on different days. The small town of Carbondale in Illinois even erected a memorial as evidence that Memorial Day took place on 29 April 1866. Afterwards as many as 25 towns claimed to be the first to celebrate Memorial Day. Three years after the Civil War had ended, on 5 May 1868, the Commander in Chief of the Grand Army of the Republic, Major General John A. Logan, announced that in the future Memorial Day would take place on 30 May of each year. Consequently the first major ceremony took place at Arlington National Cemetery in 1868.

The disputes and quarrels on who claimed to be the first would continue until 1966. The final decision was then made by Congress. Notwithstanding that the date was 5 May 1866, President Lyndon B. Johnson chose Waterloo, NY as the official birthplace of Memorial Day. He substantiated his preference based on the fact that there were detailed reports available documenting the procedures of the ceremony. Stores and private businesses remained closed, flags were flown at half-staff. For him that was sufficient evidence to claim a formal Memorial Day. However it would be 1971 before this day was recognized as an official holiday.

Notwithstanding the official holiday being 30 May, a number of southern states still remember their soldiers on different dates. Mississippi decided that their Decoration Day would take place on the last Monday in April, Alabama the fourth Monday in April, Georgia on 26 April, North and South Carolina on 10 May, Louisiana and Tennessee on 3 June.

After World War I it was decided that Memorial Day ceremonies would be held for all soldiers killed in war and not just the victims of the Civil War. On 13 May 1919, General Pershing issued an official memorandum to the American army in the field that on 30 May appropriate ceremonies would be held at the graves of their fallen comrades. The Graves Registration Service would assist in providing a list of locations of cemeteries and isolated graves. Steps had already been taken to ensure a sufficient number of American flags were available to decorate the graves.

GENERAL HEADQUARTERS, A. E. F.,
France, May 13, 1919.

OBSERVANCE OF MEMORIAL DAY.

1. The Commander in Chief desires that appropriate observance of Memorial Day be had so far as possible at all cemeteries in which American soldiers are buried in Europe. In view of the large number and scattered location of these cemeteries, it is necessary that the responsibility for such observance be assumed by commanding officers of American units, whatever their size or character, who may be stationed in the vicinity of such cemeteries on May 30th. All commanding officers are therefore directed to ascertain the location and number of American graves in their neighborhood and to make arrangements in advance for Memorial Day ceremonies. In case their units are ordered away from their present stations before May 30th, they will turn over all information on the subject to the senior American officer remaining on duty in the neighborhood. Inasmuch as most of the areas in which graves are located will be occupied only by S. O. S. troops on that date, commanding officers of such troops are particularly enjoined to assume responsibility in this matter.

2. The Graves Registration Service has complete records of American cemeteries. It also has available an ample supply of small American flags for the decoration of graves, which may be obtained for that purpose on application to the G. R. S. officers of advanced areas, base and intermediate sections. Commanding officers should confer, wherever possible, with local G. R. S. officers and the representatives of such authorized organizations as may desire to participate in the observance of the day.

By command of General Pershing:

JAMES W. McANDREW,
Chief of Staff.

GEMEENTEBESTUUR
VAN
WAEREGHEM

Waereghem, 28 Mei 1920.

M

Ter gelegenheid van den HERINNERINGS-DAG ingericht door het Amerikaansch Leger, en waaraan Afgevaardigden der Verbondene Legers zullen tegenwoordig zijn, wordt gij uitgenoodigd, met de leden uwer maatschappij en met vaandel of kartel, aan die plechtigheid te willen deelnemen, die zal plaats hebben op ZONDAG 30 MEI 1920.

Een stoet zal gevormd worden op het Statieplein om 2 ure namiddag, die zich vandaar naar het Amerikaansch Kerkhof zal begeven.

Wij rekenen op uwe tegenwoordigheid om aldus een blijk van erkentelijkheid en genegenheid te geven aan het Amerikaansch Leger dat zoo heldhaftig voor onze vrijheid heeft gestreden, en tevens om eene welverdiende hulde te brengen aan zijne heldhaftige dapperen, die alhier rusten.

DE BURGEMEESTER,
Jean BOUCKAERT.

The first formal Memorial Day ceremony was held at Flanders Field American Cemetery in 1920. The United States Army of occupation and the town of Waregem coordinated this major event. Invitations were sent by the local veteran's organizations and the Mayor, Mr. Jean Bouckaert (courtesy Waregem City Archives).

The first photographic evidence of Memorial Day ceremonies being held at isolated graves and in British cemeteries where American soldiers were temporarily interred in Belgium dates from 1921. At the same time, ceremonies were also held at the morgue in Antwerp

Photo's courtesy of American Graves Registration Service in Belgium – 1921

Memorial Day ceremonies at the morgue in Antwerp 1921

First photographic evidence of Memorial Day Ceremony at Flanders Field in 1922
(American Graves Registration Service – 1922)

The American Overseas Memorial Day Association (A.O.M.D.A.) was established in Paris in 1920. The Belgian branch would follow in 1923. The ceremony at Flanders Field took place on 3 June. The large crowds would become a typical phenomenon for all future Memorial Day ceremonies.

1923 (J. Vanthuyne collection – courtesy Waregem City Archives)

1923 (J. Vanthuyne collection – courtesy Waregem City Archives)

Also as of 1923, the Waregem school children sang the American National Anthem during the ceremony. In 1940 the ceremony was postponed due to the outbreak of World War II. The following ceremony would take place on 30 May 1945.

Waregem school children sing the Star Spangled Banner

Honor Guard, wreath bearers and firing platoon

U.S. Color Guard during the bi-centenary Memorial Day ceremony in 1976

The Memorial Day ceremonies of today have evolved due to the more professional involvement and organizational approach. The American Embassy in Brussels coordinate all procedures with the local cemetery administration and the Belgian Provincial Army Commando. The main task of the American Overseas Memorial Day Association - Belgium is to secure financial support. Not only the soldiers of Flanders Field but also the World War II cemeteries in the Ardennes and Henri-Chapelle are supported.

The ceremonies at Flanders Field are officially opened by the President of the American Overseas Memorial Day Association honoring the victims buried at Flanders Field but also the next of kin who are present for the ceremony. This is followed by a fly-over, traditionally by the U.S. Air Force. When engaged in global missions, the Belgian Air Force provide the honors. Invocation and benediction are provided by a chaplain of the U.S. Forces in Europe.

Tributes are given by the U.S. Ambassador to Belgium, U.S. Military Representative to N.A.T.O., a Belgian government official and the Mayor of Waregem.

The American Ambassador and U.S. and U.S. Military Representative to N.A.T.O. greet
veterans and flagbearers at the main gate

Honor Guard

F-15's from the U.S. Airforce base Ramstein, Germany, perform the Missing Man Salute.

2008 from left to right: Mayor, Governor of West-Flanders, Belgian Government Minister, Ambassador and Mrs. Sam Fox and the Belgian Prime Minister

Waregem school children sing the American and Belgian National anthems and decorate the graves with flowers and flags. The dignitaries commence with the wreath laying ceremony.

The last wreath is laid by representatives of the American Overseas Memorial Day Association - Belgium followed by firing of volleys and taps.

Taps

General view

The ceremony concludes with the poem by John McCrae, *"In Flanders Fields"* read by a student of an American school in Belgium followed by the Dutch version read by a Belgian high school student. The Belgian military band play host and U.S. National anthems. Troops march off.

U.S. Ambassador Sam Fox and Prime Minister Yves Leterme (2008)

Group photo in 2008

117

Memorial Day and "The Spirit of St Louis"

On 30 May 1927, nine days after his solo Trans-Atlantic flight, Charles Lindbergh flew over Flanders Field American Cemetery in his Spirit of St. Louis and dropped a bouquet of flowers in his silk flying scarf in honor of his fallen countrymen. He was flying from Brussels, where he had been a guest at the palace with King Albert I and Queen Elisabeth of Belgium, to London where on 31 May he was received by King George V. The King found him to be *a very nice boy and quite modest*. Lindbergh was always a little nervous when with Royalty but King George was known for his social skills and Lindbergh was soon at ease, enthusiastically providing details on his experiences during the historic flight. Later that Day Charles flew from Croydon to Gosport near Southampton where the Spirit of St. Louis was dismantled and shipped back to the States.

(J. Vanthuyne collection – courtesy Waregem City Archives)

10

THE GOLD STAR MOTHERS PILGRIMAGES
1930 – 1933

"Show me the manner in which a nation or community cares for its dead and I will measure with mathematical exactness the tender sympathies of its people, their respect for the laws of the land and their loyalty to high ideals".

William Ewart Gladstone (1809-1898)

The first Gold Star Mothers Pilgrimage financed by the U.S. Government sailed from New York on the "SS America" on 6 May 1930 with 231 mothers and widows on board. On 21 June of the same year, the first Flanders Field Gold Star Mothers sailed for Europe on the "Roosevelt".

Many hurdles had to be cleared before the U.S. government approved the pilgrimages with the general consensus of the nation being to forget the war as soon as possible.
By the end of 1919 the American Graves Registration Service had counted more than 2,400 cemeteries and approximately 15,000 isolated graves. 34,063 had been killed in action on the battlefields, 14,215 died of wounds, 23,210 of disease and 4,588 others due to other reasons. There were also 4,102 missing in action. The total number of Americans who died in Europe were 80,178 (NARA archive, Box 26, RG 92 Cemeterial Files).

In 1917 the American government's intentions were to repatriate all remains to be either interred in a National cemetery or a local cemetery of the next of kin's choice. When in 1919 the War Department sent out a questionnaire on the final disposition of remains to the next of kin it provided four options:

  Repatriation and interment at Arlington National Cemetery.
  Repatriation to the home town of the deceased with interment in the local cemetery.
  Repatriation and burial in one of the National Cemeteries in the U.S.
  Interment in one of the American overseas military cemeteries yet to be established.

With repatriation and upon arrival of the remains in New York, the next of kin were given an extra two weeks to make their final decision on the place of permanent burial. If this didn't happen within the given period the remains were automatically interred at Arlington. In cases where the next of kin, after numerous appeals by the War Department, failed to provide a response, the remains were interred in one of the permanent military cemeteries in Europe.

Unpardonable

SEVERAL months ago Owen Wister, an American novelist, issued a statement in Paris criticising the manner in which bodies of American soldiers were being exhumed for return to this country for reburial. He dwelt in almost sickening detail on the way duties which are in their very nature unpleasant were being performed by employes of the Graves Registration Service. His description was characterized by extreme bad taste and a touch of snobbishness—a reference to former soldiers engaged in cemetery work as products of the slums. Wister's statement disgusted many former members of the A. E. F., and was condemned by them on the ground that it was purposeless, its only effect being to aggravate the grief of parents in the United States who were awaiting the arrival of their sons' bodies from overseas. Ex-service men's organizations in Paris passed resolutions deploring the novelist's statements. Graves Registration Service employes denied the accuracy of his observations and charged that Wister was trying to obtain revenge because he had been excluded from a cemetery where exhumations were being made.

Wister is now back in the United States, preparing to write a book about his recent visit to France. In a newspaper interview he is credited with having said recently that it was extremely improbable that the families receiving bodies of soldiers actually got the remains of their own sons.

This is more than an outrageous innuendo. If Wister is quoted correctly he is guilty of making a palpable misstatement which insults the men who have been responsible for the return of our war dead and inexcusably distresses bereft mothers.

This was no easy task. Frequent remarks were made in the press "that is was highly unlikely that the repatriated remains were the identified bodies of their loved ones". This malicious assumption caused more than 13,000 families to revoke their original decision resulting in final permanent burial in Europe. (left insert: American Legion Weekly of 9 September 1921). Approximately 70% of the remains were repatriated to the U.S.

For those who had chosen for repatriation it seemed that a grave closer to home was the more appropriate manner to deal with one's grief and obtain closure. Yet even after their final decision it would sometimes take years before the remains reached their final destination (1921-1922). For those who had chosen permanent burial in Europe it was not so evident. No funeral services, no grave marker to stand and grieve at in a local cemetery (although in some cases a symbolic marker was placed in the family plot (example Ernest White and George Zellers), no immediate sense of closure. In many cases it wasn't feasible to travel to Europe and visit the grave of their loved ones.

ORIGINS AND PURPOSE OF THE GOLD STAR MOTHERS

A red bordered white flag centered by a blue star was known as a service flag. Each star represented a family member in service of his or her country. Multiple blue stars indicated that more than one family member was serving under arms, as was the case of Russell Swain, (C-01-19). When a service member was killed or died of wounds, the blue star was over sewn with a gold star. Hence the origins of the Gold Star Mothers.

With the American involvement in the war and as early as November 1917, the general consensus was to emphasize on the glorious dead rather than grief or loss. Consequently it soon became a custom to replace the traditional dress or mourning with everyday clothing and an armband with golden star was worn as a sign of mourning (below: Gold Star Mothers in Grant Park, Chicago, 1918, Chicago Daily News, negatives collection, BN 0070.73, reproduced with kind permission of the Chicago Historical Society). As of 1920 there were already movements and unofficial organizations such as the "American War Mothers" and "Gold Star Association", to name but a few. In 1928 a group of women living in Washington DC made an appeal to establish the Gold Star Mothers Incorporated.

They soon received federal recognition and the organization evolved in one of the largest politically influenced Gold Star Mothers organization in the United States.

Shortly after the Armistice voices were already heard on organizing a trip to Europe for all mothers and widows. The New York Congressman Fiorello La Guardia had already presented a bill to that effect in May 1919, but his proposal was rejected. His proposal covered government subsidized travel for fathers, mothers and widows.

An identical bill was submitted to Congress by Samuel Dickstein, a Democrat, in December 1923. His proposal supported that a budget be set aside for the purpose. This again was put on the back burner.

Shortly before the American Battle Monuments Commission was established in 1923, tensions and interests were so high that a pilgrimage was organized by the Gold Star Association of America in May 1925. The pilgrimage was funded by non-governmental institutions and the first pilgrimage became a fact for nine hundred mothers and widows, sailing for Europe and visiting the American cemeteries in France.

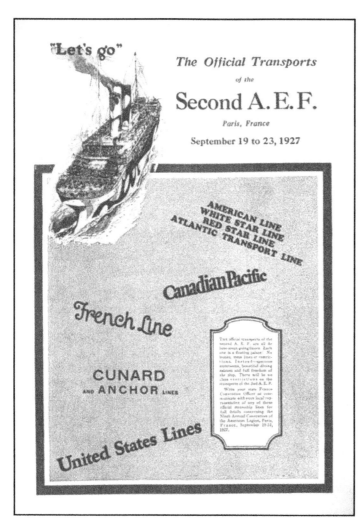

The opinion of the average American citizen was however that enough had been done to salve the conscience of America. Repatriation had already cost the American government many millions of dollars. As such, many Americans were of the opinion that these funds, instead of supporting the Gold Star Mothers pilgrimages, would be put to better use in aid of the many disabled veterans. These men were unable to find a job due to their disabilities and had become a constant financial burden to their families.

The American Legion (founded in Paris in 1919) organized their own affordable pilgrimages to Europe in the 1920's. This was a relief for those who decided not to wait on the government's decision to subsidize their trip.

In 1927, the tenth anniversary of the U.S. declaration of war on Germany, a large scale pilgrimage was organized by the Legion which was known as the "Second American Expeditionary Force".

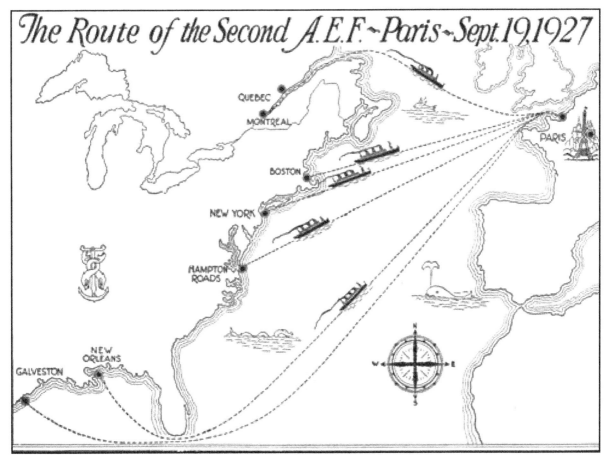

The Route of the Second A.E.F. ~ Paris ~ Sept. 19, 1927

QUEBEC
MONTREAL
PARIS
BOSTON
NEW YORK
HAMPTON ROADS
NEW ORLEANS
GALVESTON

American Legion Magazine – May 1927

President Calvin Coolidge, notwithstanding his initial strong views against the bill, officially approved the Gold Star Mothers Pilgrimages on 2 March 1929. The reasoning behind Coolidge's decision, just a few weeks before the end of his Presidential career, remains a mystery. Politically he had nothing more to gain. One must also bear in mind that this was practically on the eve of the Wall Street crash (24 October). It is said that, due to his wife's immense grief when their son died in 1924, that this geared him towards his decision. The enormous support Grace Coolidge provided to the Gold Star Mothers program is documented by the poem she wrote after her son's death, *"The Open Door"* which was read as a tribute during the Gold Star Mothers ceremony at Arlington National Cemetery in 1930.

Contrary to La Guardia's original proposition, fathers were not allowed to take part. Widows who had not yet remarried could take part. Stepmothers and mothers who had adopted children, were permitted under specific conditions only in the case when they had raised the children.

The logistics were of top priority. At first the Army opposed the idea of acting as escorts. The Red Cross was approached and then again this didn't seem to be the right way forward. Finally the Quarter Master Corps was tasked to prepare the pilgrimages.
Of all decisions made by the War Department, one was seen as beyond human dignity, the segregation of Afro-American mothers. As during World War I with the segregation of black troops, the same conditions were forced upon Afro-American mothers and widows in which they were denied to travel to Europe with their Caucasian counterparts. The decision

caused a major issue. The War Department shielded themselves and blamed the U.S. State Shipping

Lines. They had claimed that if Afro-American mothers were allowed to sail during the tourist season, Caucasians would refuse traveling with them resulting in a major financial loss to the companies. As such, Afro-Americans sailed for Europe on cargo ships. It did not end here. Many of them also had to make the long train journey to New York. Upon arrival they were given accommodation at YMCA (Young Men's Christian Association) youth hostels, a large contrast to the luxury hotels Pennsylvania and Commodore, where their counterparts were staying.

Party K, 1931, Afro-American mothers and widows *(National Archives, RG92)*

Statistics vary on the number of participants taking part. Of the 1.593 Afro-American mothers and widows entitled to make the trip only 233 accepted the invitation. Others had died, remarried or their health conditions prevented them

from taking part. Only 55 Afro-American mothers and widows took part in the first pilgrimage.

THE VOYAGE

Administrative preparations for the Pilgrimage was gigantic. A variety of documents had to be submitted to mothers and widows who, in turn, were required to complete the paperwork in order to obtain the necessary travel passes, luggage labels, train tickets, special ID cards, etc. Before their departure all mothers and widows were presented with a commemorative medal and a small American flag in a leather case holder.

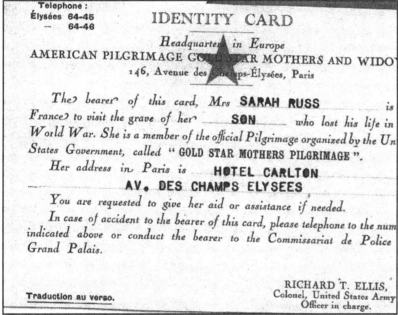

Gold Star Mother Pilgrimage documents (courtesy Holly Fenelon collection - GSM Historian)

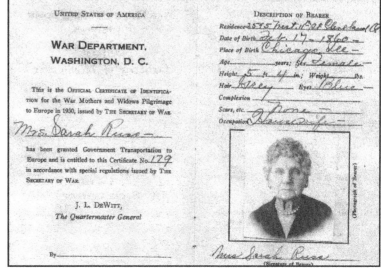

Gold Star Mother medal and American flag (Christopher Sims collection)

On 21 June 1930 the first Flanders Field group of mothers and widows sailed from New York for Europe on the SS Roosevelt. Most of them had already experienced a two-day train journey prior their arrival in New York.

Party "H", Group 7 arrived at the *Gare des Invalides* in Paris on Sunday 29 June and were escorted to the Paris Hotel Carlton, on the *Avenue des Champs Elysées*. The following morning they were free and in the afternoon the escort officer took them on a sightseeing tour of Paris at which time they also visited the *Arc de Triomphe*.

Tuesday 1 July bags were packed for the next part of their trip with destination Flanders Field Cemetery. Lille, 28 miles from Waregem, would become their base camp. They left their Paris hotel at 7.15 a.m. with a first stop at Compiègne and the *Carrefour de l'Armistice*, followed by short breaks at St. Quentin and Cambrai.

The French Army Memorial at Compiègne (courtesy Kearney & Stech families)

Wednesday 2 July was the first of a three day visit to the graves of their loved ones arriving at 09.00 a.m. Lunch was served at *Hotel de Flandres* in Waregem.

Flanders Field Gold Star Mothers in Waregem on 2 July 1930.
Superintendent John Blain served from 12/08/1926 - 31/12/1937 (courtesy Kearney family)

Superintendent John Blain standing center in uniform. Inscription on the back: *"Mr. Blain and his family, care-taker Flanders Field where my dear boy rests. He is an American married to a darling French girl and has two lovely girls. We spent three mornings at the cemetery – July 1930."*
In John W. Graham's *"The Gold Star Mother Pilgrimages of the 1930's"*, he refers to Superintendent Blain's remarks published in the Chicago Tribune, Paris edition on 30 May

1930: *"I have welcomed many a Gold Star Mother here in the past years. I know that for an hour or more they want to stay quietly beside the grave. I hope that the Gold Star Mothers who visit Flanders Field tomorrow will cry. Tears are consoling. I dread mothers who don't cry. Those mothers stand speechless and tearless at the grave of their sons I have sometimes carried as though lifeless from the cemetery after a few minutes."*

On the group photo taken at the American monument in Oudenaarde in 1931 one can see, standing in the middle of the front row Mrs. Flora Wattelet, widow of Captain Leonard Wattelet (A-02-22), to her right Mrs. Russia Barlow, mother of William C. Barlow (B-02-20), front row far left, Minnie Elrose, stepmother of Ralph Elrose (Wall of Missing) and back row second from right, Catherine Stech, mother of James Stech (B-02-03).

Photo next page one can see Mrs. Katie Gusler, mother of Paul Gusler (A-02-18). For each participant a floral wreath was ordered which was placed at the grave of their loved one. There were also wreaths available for mothers and widows who's loved one was missing in action or had no known grave. They became part of the pilgrimages as of 1931. Their wreath was placed at a grave Known but to God. (see A-04-05: Emily Elrose, stepmother of Ralph Elrose – Wall of Missing, at the grave of an unknown in 1931).

128

On 5 July it was time to start their return trip to Paris via Amiens and Beauvais. Once back in Paris they were free to take the time to visit the many places of interest in and around Paris. Photo insert right; entrance ticket to Emperor Napoleon's tomb.

The group disembarked in de New York on 22 July.

Regardless the many political differences prior the official approval of the pilgrimages, the Gold

Star Mother program can be seen as a great success. The average age being 65, one was 88 and even another 91 years of age, the predictions of a high number of deaths during the trip proofed to be unfounded. During these pilgrimages there were only four. One in New York before their departure; one during the return voyage and two in France. Mrs. Grace Kingsbury from Kansas died in her hotel room after visiting her son's grave. Mrs. Harriet Bates from Pennsylvania died of a stroke in Verdun before she had a chance to visit her son's grave. As for Flanders Field we can only mention the mother of Louis Landgraf (D-02-19), who shortly after visiting her son's grave had a heart attack and never fully recovered. She died five months later on 16 November 1930.

Only 6,000 of the 30,000 mothers and widows accepted the invitation by the U.S. Government entitled to take part in the Gold Star Mothers program. After the last ship had moored in New York, only memories survived as they were overshadowed by other conflicts and wars. The United States Government would never embark on another Gold Star Mother Pilgrimage again.

THE SOLDIERS OF FLANDERS FIELD

PLOT A

FLYNN Charles J.
Private, Co. G, 145th Infantry Regiment, 37th Division
DOW 2 November 1918
Plot A – Row 01 – Grave 01
Army Serial Number 2956617

Charles Flynn was born on 4 March 1890 in Philadelphia, PA. He was the son of Miles and Mary Flynn. Mary died prior to the outbreak of World War I. He had one brother James and three sisters: Catherine, Lizzie and Annie. Charles was a laborer in a yarn factory in Philadelphia.

On 2 November at 16:30 in the vicinity of Eine, Charles was wounded by shell fragments. He also suffered from a shattered foot. He was rushed to the nearest field dressing station but died the same day. He was buried in the village of Dentergem on 3 November.

no photograph available

CONDON Edward J.
Private 1st Class, HQ Co. 363rd Infantry Regiment, 91st Division
DOD 31 October 1918
Plot A – Row 01 – Grave 02
Army Serial Number 2779959

Edward Joseph Condon was born on 30 May 1887 in Dobbs Ferry, NY. His parents, Patrick and Mary, had four other children: William, John, Katherine and Mary. Edward moved to Seattle, WA, where he was employed as a longshoreman with the Owen Co., Shake River.

As so many others, Edward caught the Spanish flu. He was taken to Mobile Hospital #5 in Staden where he died from bronchial pneumonia, a common complication of the Spanish flu, on 31 October. He was interred at the American plot Staden row 1, grave #7. Both his parents passed away in 1920 and it was Mary, as next of kin, who decided that his remains be buried in Europe.

THOMPSON John
Corporal, Co. C, 112th Field Signal Battalion, 37th Division
KIA 1 November 1918
Plot A – Row 01 – Grave 03
Army Serial Number 1539567

John Thompson was born in New York City on 9 August 1888. His family moved to Ohio where John became a painter/decorator. On 12 June 1917 he joined the 8th Infantry Regiment National Guard, which later became the 146th Infantry Regiment, in Ashland, OH. In October 1917 he was transferred to the 112th Field Signal Battalion. He was promoted to Corporal in June 1918.

He was officialy listed as missing on 6 November. On 11 November it was confirmed that three men of the 112th Field Signal Battalion had been killed on 1 November. A search was made the following day and John's body was found 220 yards north of the road between the villages of Dentergem and Kruishoutem. He was buried near the town of Olsene, alongside the road to Gent, close to where his remains had been found. His emergency address was with his brother William in Elyria, OH.

TRAFKA Orine L.

Private, Co. K, 148th Infantry Regiment, 37th Division
KIA 31 October 1918
Plot A – Row 01 – Grave 04
Army Serial Number 2824685

Orine Lee Trafka was born on 3 December 1889 in Beaver Dam, WI. Son of Lawrence (Lorenz) and Annie Trafka who had three sons and four daughters. The family photo was taken in 1900. Back row from left to right: sister Ida, brother Walter with spouse. In the second row father Frank, mother Annie and another sister (name unknown). Front row: sister Marthe, Orine and his brother Frank. Orine lived in Beaver Dam his whole life. He was employed at the Monarch Range plant and during his days off was an ardent game hunter.

On 27 May 1918, Orine was called to arms. He was sent to Camp Grant, IL to train with the 161st Depot Brigade. After a month of intense training he was assigned to the 344th Infantry Regiment, 86th Black Hawk Division. Upon arrival in Europe he was transferred to the 148th Infantry Regiment.

Orine was killed in Olsene at the start of the attack. He was buried in a temporary American cemetery along the road to Gent, grave 11. On 4 June 1919 his remains were transferred to Waregem and temporarily buried in Plot B, grave #108.

2824685

TRAJEKA, ORINE LEO

B10294

Left: Orine Trafka's original wooden marker at Cemetery #1252.
Below: telegram announcing Orine's death.

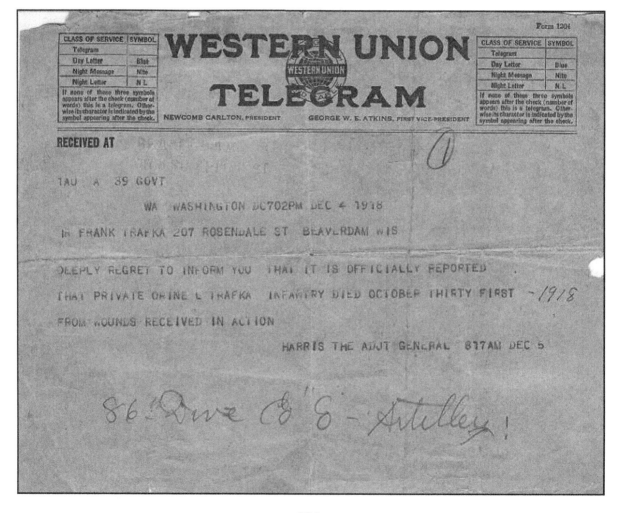

MIX Arthur J.
Private 1st Class, Co. B, 347th MG Battalion, 91st Division
DOW 3 November 1918
Plot A – Row 01 – Grave 05
Army Serial Number 2256082

Arthur Jay Mix was the son of Orson Mix and Leila Mae Moore, two pioneer farmers in the Northwest of Minnesota. Their land, once the settlement of the Chippewa Indians, was located in a dense woodland and waterways area. Arthur was born on 7 February 1887 as fifth in row of eleven children. Leila was an exceptional pianist and so the passion for music was passed on to her children. Arthur chose to play the guitar. He was a somewhat bashful and a quiet young man, who besides his passion for music, was also interested in mechanics.

The farmers in the area would bring their defective machinery to him for repairs. Arthur made the headlines of the local newspaper when, at 19 years of age, he was kicked in the face by a wild horse. His face was severely disfigured. In the spring of 1912, Arthur moved to Idaho seeking a temporary job (or so he thought) in a garage in Ashton. He remained there until 1916. Returning to visit his family he drove more than 2.000 miles in a vehicle that was nothing more than a motor on four wheels, a seat and a steering wheel (photo). After one month he returned to Idaho. This was the last time he saw his family.

Arthur was called to arms and, from the start of his training and all through the war, he was assigned to the 91st Division: Camp Lewis, St Mihiel and the Argonne. He also had two brothers on active duty: Archibald (left) and Oliver (right). On 3 November, Arthur was mortally wounded when a shell fragment struck his leg and bled to death. He was buried within the grounds of a chateau north of Oudenaarde (Isolated Grave Bevere). On 4 June 1919 his remains were interred in Waregem.

KEARNEY Thomas E.
1st Lieutenant, Signal Corps
KIA 14 August 1918
Plot A – Row 01 – Grave 06

Thomas Emmett Kearney was the son of Thomas Kearney Sr. and Anna (Anna Stastia) Dwyer from Memphis, TN. He was born on 1 July 1895 in Paducah, KY. He had two brothers (Joseph

Hugh and Arthur Raymond) and two sisters (Helen Mildred and Mary Katherine). He was an exemplary student and after completing his higher education he worked in the cotton industry.

In May 1917 he decided to volunteer, but for reasons unknown, he was rejected. Determined to become a pilot he crossed the border into Canada and joined the Commonwealth Forces. He was accepted and by 16 December he had earned his

wings. On 13 January 1918 he returned to the United States to join the American Air Service. Almost immediately he was sent to Europe serving with the British 22nd Aero Squadron until 12 August, when he was transferred to the 18th Squadron. He was shot down two days later.

On the evening of 14 August, Thomas and his observer Sergeant John Harvey Hammond (Royal Air Force) were part of a bombing raid. On their return flight above enemy lines, their DH4 A7856 was hit by anti-aircraft (commonly known as Archies). The aircraft took an uncontrollable spin and plummeted towards the earth. There was absolutely no hope of survival. Thomas was buried along the Estevelles - Meurchin road in Pont à Vendin in the Departement Pas de Calais, France (area of La Bassée). The remains of his observer Sergeant John Harvey Hammond were never found and he is memorialized on the Arras Flying Services Memorial.

Thomas' mother visited his grave with the Gold Star Mothers Pilgrimage in 1930. Eighty years later, Thomas' great-nephew Michael Kearney from Dallas, TX paid his respects during the Memorial Day ceremony on 30 May 2010.

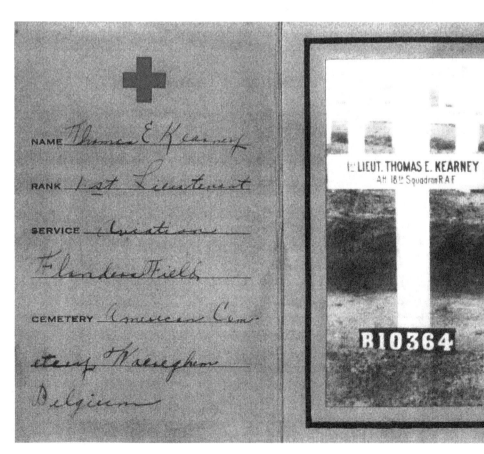

NAME Thomas E Kearney

RANK 1st Lieutenant

SERVICE Aviation

Flanders Field

CEMETERY American Cemetery

etery Waereghem

Belgium

1st LIEUT. THOMAS E. KEARNEY
AH 18th SquadronR.A.F

B10364

CLARK Harold E.
Private, Co. I, 361st Infantry Regiment, 91st Division
KIA 2 November 1918
Plot A – Row 01 – Grave 07
Army Serial Number 3960355

Harold Earl Clark was born in Sheldon, IL on 31 July 1892. Both his parents, Orman Rial Clark and Matilda Elizabeth Julien, died when he was fourteen. Harold then lived with his sister, Della Clark Young, in Kankakee, IL. He also had another sister, Ida Geraldine Clark Light. She would later name her son Harold.

Harold moved to Montana in search of better prospects in life. Pioneers could obtain their land after five years if they were willing to perform the hard labor and settle down there. Harold made an attempt in Ashland, Rosebud County. Unfortunately he was unable to own the property as he was called to arms on 24 July 1918 (this being before the five year term of lease expired). His second major disappointment was the fact that he was engaged to be married. On 25 July, he left for basic training with destination Camp Dodge in Iowa. On 15 September he had already arrived in France with the 335th Infantry Regiment, 84th Lincoln Division. Shortly after arrival this division was disbanded and the men filled the ranks of other divisions. Consequently, on 6 October, Harold was reassigned as a runner to the 361st Infantry Regiment. On 26 October he wrote home saying that he was serving in Belgium. The day after his sister Della received his letter, she received notice that Harold had been killed in action on 2 November. The cause of death within the family was known as: *"Harold left his shelter to light a cigarette. He was killed instantly by a shell fragment"*.

A stone marker was placed at Sheldon cemetery in Harold's memory (photo insert). His nephew Harold Light (Ida's son), who kindly provided us with this information, passed away on 15 June 2006. Traditionally, he would place flowers at his uncle's marker on Memorial Day every year.

BRIGGS Lewis A.
Private, Co. G, 145th Infantry Regiment, 37th Division
DOD 31 October 1918
Plot A – Row 01 – Grave 08
Army Serial Number 1519879

Lewis Arden Briggs was born in Painesville, OH on 5 January 1896. He was the son of Lincoln Lee and Emma Briggs (née Evans). He volunteered with the Ohio National Guard on 29 May 1917 and was assigned to Co. M of the 5th Infantry Regiment.

On 25 September he was sent to Camp Sheridan in Alabama for additional training. He embarked for Europe on 14 June 1918 with Co. G of the 145th Infantry Regiment, 37th Division in Hoboken, NJ. He disembarked seven days later in Brest, France. His only concern was not being able to fight the Germans. In one of his letters home he wrote: *"I am right up here where I can do my part when the time comes."* On 19 October, he wrote to his brother Paul, who was also serving with the A.E.F. in France: *"I was up the front three times, each time from a different direction. Our boys fell all around me and one dropped dead in my arms. My raincoat was shot full of holes."* On that same day he also wrote his last letter home to his parents: *"We are away back behind the lines, out of sound of the big guns. Yes I was in the big drive, I did my part."*

On 31 October 1918 Private Lewis Arden Briggs died of pneumonia, which was a common complication of the Spanish flu.

VOLZ Harry
Private, Co. M, 148th Infantry Regiment, 37th Division
KIA 10 November 1918
Plot A – Row 01 – Grave 09
Army Serial Number 3749083

Harry Volz was born in Westfield, WI on 16 February 1888. He was the son of August Volz and Rosine Rothaker (German immigrants). They had six sons: Robert, Charles, Harry, Frank, Walter and Fred. He grew up in Ableman later moving to Reedsburg, WI where he had found work on a farm as an agricultural laborer.

Harry was called to arms on 22 June. On 15 August he was assigned to the 344th Infantry Regiment, 86th Black Hawk Division. This division, mainly mustered with men from Illinois and Wisconsin, was disbanded upon arrival in Europe and Harry was reassigned to the 148th Infantry Regiment on 6 October.

He was killed in action along the banks of the river Scheldt on 10 November, the day before the Armistice. Killed by machinegun fire he was laid to rest in Ename, together with William Fossum (A-2-15) and Otto Madary (C-3-23). When their remains were transferred to Waregem on 10 June 1919, there was uncertainty on the identity of these men. Harry was positively identified and then temporarily buried in plot B, grave #136.

His brother Frank, also with the A.E.F. in Europe, returned home with a severe case of shell-shock. He never recovered and died in a military psychiatric hospital in 1950. He was buried next to his parents at Greenwood Cemetery in Reedsburg.

no photograph available

O'CONNOR Clement
Cook, Co. L, 361st Infantry Regiment, 91st Division
KIA 2 November 1918
Plot A – Row 01 – Grave 10
Army Serial Number 2258406

Clement O'Connor was born in Menominee, MI (as was Peter Lentz, C-4-23) on 22 March 1896. His parents were William and Rose O'Connor. According to the 1910 census they had 3 other children: Harry, Clement and Alma. Rose had another son from a previous marriage, William Lauzon. The family lived in Grays Harbor, WA and William worked as a lumber inspector for a company in Aberdeen. Clement worked on a steamboat with Aberdeen being port of registry.

On 2 November, in the vicinity of Wortegem, Clement became the victim of a heavy artillery bombardment. His head was struck by a dud 77 shell which shattered his skull. He was buried in the village churchyard of Wortegem.

no photograph available

MLEKO Stanley
Private, Co. H, 145th Infantry Regiment, 37th Division
KIA 2 November 1918
Plot A – Row 01 – Grave 11
Army Serial Number 1518978

Stanislas Mleko was born to Antoni and Marya Mleko of Pińczów (Poland, former Russia) on 24 January 1894. At eighteen he decided to emigrate to the U.S.A. He arrived in New York on 24 April 1913. From his immigration documents we note the following: he was single, height 5 foot 4 inches, blond hair and blue eyes. As so many Russian immigrants he worked as an agricultural laborer and he never learned to read or write. He immediately traveled to Cleveland, OH, where on 16 July 1917, he joined the National Guard.

He was assigned to the 145th Infantry Regiment, 37th Division and disembarked in Europe on 15 June 1918. Stanley was killed in action on 2 November. He was buried alongside the road towards the heights of Kruishoutem.

no photograph available

PERONE John
Private, Co. B, 148th Infantry Regiment, 37th Division
KIA 1 November 1918
Plot A – Row 01 – Grave 12
Army Serial Number 3339599

John Perone (Giovanni Peirone) was born in Rifreddo, fifty kilometers SW of Turin, (Italy) on 11 January 1890. He was the son of Domenico Peirone (a widower), who lived with his children (John, Joe, Paul and Constance) in Eveleth, MN. Dom had emigrated to the U.S.A. from Italy in 1899 and four years later his children followed in his footsteps. John lived in Duluth, MN where he worked as laborer for the Universal Portland Cement Co. It was from there that he was called to arms on 28 June 1918. His request to be exempted from military service to take care of his father, brother and sister was rejected.

He completed his training with the 161st Depot Brigade and less than two weeks later he was assigned to the 344th Infantry Regiment, 86th Black Hawk Division. Upon his arrival in Europe he was reassigned to the 148th Infantry Regiment. He was killed in action near the village of Heurne. This research came as a surprise to his family. They were unaware that a certain "John Perone" was related to them. John's name is also inscribed on the War Memorial in Chisholm, MN.

no photograph available

BASTL Tony

Private, Co. H, 145th Infantry Regiment, 37th Division
KIA 2 November 1918
Plot A – Row 01 – Grave 13
Army Serial Number 1519021

Tony Bastl (°1889) originated from Myto, Bohemia (Austria-Hungary) and was born as Antonin Basl. He was the son of Josef Basl and Maria Wocacowa. He had three brothers (Joseph, Vaclav and Karel) and three sisters (Anna, Frantiska and Marie). Another son, also named Vlacav, died in infancy. Tony left Myto from Bremerhaven, Germany and embarked on the liner *"Kaiser Wilhelm II"* arriving in New York on 28 August 1907. Personal details reveal that his height was 5 foot 8 inches and that he had grey eyes.

Tony's name "Basl" was changed to "Bastl" due to a clerical error. The name is common in Myto. In Cleveland he joined the 5th Regiment Ohio National Guard on 15 May 1917. This regiment was later transformed to the 145th Infantry Regiment. He was killed in action on 2 November. According to one source he was married. However his emergency address was with his brother Joseph in Chicago, IL. He is memorialized on the War Memorial in front of the church in Myto, currently located in the Czech Republic, with the inscription: *"Americky Legionar."*

144

no photograph available

FERRARO Francesco S.
Private, Co. A, 148th Infantry Regiment, 37th Division
KIA 1 November 1918
Plot A – Row 01 – Grave 14
Army Serial Number 1848786

Francesco Sabatino Ferraro was born on 9 March 1895 in Rivisondoli, Province of Aquila, Italy. His father was Pasquale Ferraro. The family was very poor and Francesco decided to emigrate to the U.S.A. where his uncle Ottavio already resided. They lived together in Pittsburgh, PA. Francesco worked as crane man for the Duquesne Steel Foundation.

He was called to arms and after his basic training assigned to the 148th Infantry Regiment. He died of wounds near the town of Olsene and was buried along the road to Gent (grave #33).

no photograph available

MEKONIS William
Private, Co. I, 145th Infantry Regiment, 37th Division
DOW 4 November 1918
Plot A – Row 01 – Grave 15
Army Serial Number 1851769

Wladislaw (William) Mekionen (Mekonis) was born in Lithuania on 19 July 1890. He was the son of Tamosin Mekionen. He settled in Braddock, PA, together with his brother Stanley and wife Roza. William emigrated to the U.S.A. in 1911. Stanislaw (Stanley) followed his footsteps two years later.

William was severely wounded and transported to Mobile Hospital #5 in the village of Staden where he later died. He was still a Lithuanian citizen at the time of his death.

His remains were moved to Waregem on 12 June 1922. Hospital bandages were still found on his remains.

GARWOOD Roy F.
Private, Co. K, 148th Infantry Regiment, 37th Division
KIA 2 November 1918
Plot A – Row 01 – Grave 16
Army Serial Number 1750082

Roy Francis Garwood was born in Salisbury, NC on 31 May 1895. Son of James Franklin Garwood and Louella Victoria Walser (photo insert), he was part of a large farming family consisting of 10 children: John, Daisy, Ila, Herman, Thomas, Roy, Carl, Gracie, Dorothy and Esther. At the age of twelve Roy started working at a weaving mill in Salisbury.

He later moved to Baltimore, MD where he joined the Regular Army on 23 June 1917. He was assigned to a Sanitary Detachment of the 312th Infantry Regiment, 78th Lightning Division. After a training period with the 153rd Depot Brigade he was transferred to Co. K of the 148th Infantry Regiment on 10 June 1918. He sailed for Europe on the 22nd of June.

Roy was killed in action near the village of Kruishoutem and was buried at the intersection on the ridge north of the village. One source mentions that Roy was awarded a high Serbian decoration: the Order of St. Sava. This is unlikely and no evidence was found to support this statement.

no photograph available

NEUHAUS Norman C.

Private, Co. A, 148th Infantry Regiment, 37th Division
KIA 2 November 1918
Plot A – Row 01 – Grave 17
Army Serial Number 3329775

Norman Clyde Neuhaus (°20 May 1888) was the youngest son of Frederick and Susanna Neuhaus (née Hirth.) They were German immigrants living in Toledo, OH. He had three older brothers: Edward, Carl and George. As of 1913 he lived together with Anna. At first she explained that she could not marry him as long as her parents were alive. Eventually Anna agreed in cohabitation and they both took care of her parents. She had told her parents, who were very religious, that they were married. This was probably the reason for their domestic problems as Norman became a heavy drinker and finally left Anna in December of that year. Until then he was working as a waiter at the Plankinton Hotel in Milwaukee, WI.

He was called to arms on 27 May 1918 and sent to the 161st Brigade for training. On 27 June he was assigned to Co. L of the 344th Infantry Regiment, 86th Black Hawk Division. Upon arrival on European soil, the division was disbanded and Norman was reassigned to the 148th Infantry Regiment on 7 October.

He was killed in action on 2 November near the town of Olsene (witness report states the date of death being 31 October which is more likely). With other men from his company, he was trying to find shelter from enfilade machinegun fire when a shell fell near Norman, fragments wounding him in his face. As he jumped up from the pain, machinegun fire killed him instantaneously. He was buried on the spot (Isolated Grave Olsene #3) and his remains were transferred to Waregem on 7 June 1919.

A son of his brother Edward (Edward Jr), was a member of a bomber crew flying missions over France and Germany during World War II.

SCHNELL Paul A.

Supply Sergeant, Co. C, 148th Infantry Regiment, 37th Division
KIA 31 October 1918
Plot A – Row 01 – Grave 18
Army Serial Number 1528980

Paul Schnell was born in Piqua, OH in December 1887. Parents were Urban and Mary Catherine Schnell (née Sarger). He had three brothers (Joseph, Carl and Ernst) and three sisters (Anna, Caroline and Marie). He grew up in Piqua and with two of his brothers he opened a café on North Main Street: *"Schnell's Sample Room"*. On 2 June 1917 he joined the 3rd Infantry Regiment Ohio National Guard, which later became the 148th Infantry Regiment. Within two months he had climbed the ranks to Supply Sergeant. In February 1918 he married Agnes (née Kipp???) Schnell, also a resident of Piqua.

He was one of the first to be killed in action on 31 October near the town of Olsene. The division commenced the attack along the railroad and as soon as he had crossed the rail track he was mortally wounded. A witness report by Sgt. Charles Henry of his company states: *"While advancing across the railroad at Olsene, Sgt. Schnell was about 20 yards in front of company main body. While on embankment of railroad he was struck by machine gun bullets and shell fragments."* He was buried at Olsene along the road to Gent (grave #15) and on 4 June 1919 his remains were transferred to Waregem.

In October 1919 the American Legion Post in Piqua was established. The Post was called Schnell-Westfall. His mother was eager to visit the grave with the Gold Star Mothers Pilgrimage but every time she had to postpone due to health issues. She had reached the age of 83 in 1931.

Business Card - Schnell's Sample Room with photos of Joe and Carl

WILSON John L.

Private, Co. M, 148th Infantry Regiment, 37th Division
DOW 1 November 1918
Plot A – Row 01 – Grave 19
Army Serial Number 2084634

John Louis Wilson was born on 5 June 1891. He was the son of Thorkel Wilson (a Norwegian immigrant) and Josephine Lindstad from St Paul, MN. (photo insert) Josephine was only fifteen years of age when she married Thorkel, who already had a daughter, Grunvar (Gunvor), from a previous marriage. Josephine and Thorkel had seven children: William, Mathilda, John, Josephine, Thorkel, Samuel and Hardis. John married Gladys Abbett on 21 November 1917.

John was called to arms on 24 June 1918 and received his basic training with the 161st Depot Brigade. On 18 July he was assigned to Company K of the 344th Infantry Regiment 86th Black Hawk Division. The Division was disbanded upon arrival in Europe and John became part of the 148th Infantry, 37th Division.

John was severely wounded during the attack near the village of Heurne. Shell fragments had lodged in his back and upper legs. He was taken to hospital but succumbed to his wounds. He was originally buried in the American section of the cemetery in Staden (row 4, grave #52) on 3 November. On 9 June 1922 his remains were moved to his final resting place in Waregem .

Gladys remarried in 1920 and as immediate next of kin made the choice for John's remains to remain in Belgium. As she had remarried she was not eligible to take part in Gold Star Mothers Pilgrimage. Josephine (photo) did join the pilgrimage to Flanders Field Cemetery. She crossed the Atlantic on the SS Roosevelt arriving at Cherbourg, France on 29 June 1930. She visited her son's grave at Flanders Field on 2, 3 and 4 July.

John's family suspected that Gladys was pregnant at the time of John's death. Their wedding photograph and that of Josephine's visit to his grave in 1930 on the following pages.

HORRELL Andrew B.

Corporal, Co. F, 147th Infantry Regiment, 37th Division
KIA 11 November 1918
Plot A – Row 01 – Grave 20
Army Serial Number 1757898

Barney Horrell and Mary Whitthoff were the parents of Andrew Horrell. They lived with their children Laura, Anna, Roselia, Andrew, Molly and Joseph Kozlik on a farm in Modoc, IL. Joseph was Mary's child from a previous relationship. Andrew was a happy and cheerful young man. Andrew as a child (left insert) and standing left with two friends. (insert right)

He was killed in action on the last day of the war: his face was severely disfigured from the impact of shell fragments. He was buried in Zingem (New Cemetery Zinghem, Grave #3, American Plot). Bernard and Mary initially requested that the remains of their son be repatriated to the US but later they reconsidered and withdrew their request.

Front row: Bernard and Mary; from the rear from left to right: Joseph (Joe), Anna, Laura, Molly, Rose(lia) and Andrew.

no photograph available

DI GIACOMO Pasquale - D.S.C – Silver Star

Corporal, Co. F, 145th Infantry Regiment, 37th Division
KIA 4 November 1918
Plot A – Row 01 – Grave 21
Army Serial Number 1518469

Pasquale Di Giacomo was born in Castel di Sangro (Italy) on 5 April 1896. He was one of five children raised in the family of Giacomo di Giacomo and Nicolina Tristani. In 1914 he departed Naples with his younger sister Filomena, and sailed on the SS Europa hoping to find a more prosperous life in the U.S.A. Brothers Guiseppe and Salvatore had taken this step five years earlier. Pasquale joined his brother Salvatore in Akron, OH where he found a job at the Benjamin Franklin Goodrich Company. Filomena joined her brother Guiseppe in Chicago, Illinois.

In June 1917, Pasquale was required to register for the draft. However he did not wait to be called to arms and volunteered to join the army in early October. He received his basic training with the 158th Depot Brigade until 27 October 1917 when he was assigned to Co. F of the 145th Infantry Regiment. He sailed for Europe on the Leviathan, a confiscated German cruise liner, on 15 June 1918.

Pasquale was the first man of the division (together with Corporal Hadnett - DSC #641 & #642), to be awarded the Distinguished Service Cross for actions in the Baccarat sector, in the Vosges, France. He also received a Divisional Citation resulting in a Silver Star. This decoration was originally a small silver star worn on the ribbon of a service medal until it was replaced by a separate medal in 1932. He was promoted to Corporal on 18 October 1918. Less than three weeks later, on 4 November, he was mortally wounded by machinegun fire. He was buried along the east bank of the river Scheldt.

The citation for his Distinguished Service Cross reads:

For extraordinary heroism in action east of Baccarat, France, August 15, 1918. He was one of four men who successfully held a small advanced post against a raid of 80 of the enemy. Two of the defenders were killed, but the staunch work of the others drove off the raiders. He engaged in a hand-to-hand encounter with the assailants with hand grenades and his rifle. Residence at enlistment: 58 Cuyahoga Street, Akron, Ohio.

LISTER Edward L.– Silver Star

Sergeant, Co. B, 347th MG Battalion, 91st Division
DOW 5 November 1918
Plot A – Row 01 – Grave 22
Army Serial Number 2280199

Edward Lee Lister was born in Louisville, KY on 14 June 1895. He was the son of Edward Hillon Lee and Minnie Bertha Richards. His mother remarried with Joseph Byron Lister in 1896, hence that Edward became a Lister. In her first marriage she also had a daughter: Culu Viola Lee. With Joseph Byron Lister, Minnie had two other children: Franklin Byron and Minnie Leora. In the meantime the family had moved to Idaho and Edward lived and worked in Montpelier with the Oregon Shortline Railroad Company until he was called to arms.

Edward was an exemplary soldier and he soon moved up the ranks to Sergeant. During his service in the Argonne and the Ypres-Lys offensive, Edward was mentioned in dispatches and in both cases awarded Divisional Citations (which after 1932 became the Silver Star) for his courage and exemplary behavior under fire. He was preparing to cross a street in Oudenaarde, covered by a German sniper, when he was shot in the abdomen. The Belgian family, from whose house he was emerging, dragged him inside attempting to render first aid. He was taken to a first aid station and later to the American hospital in Staden where he died of his wounds. His remains were transferred to Waregem on 6 June 1919.

His brother Frank also served with the Armed Forces. He had joined the Navy. His mother visited Flanders Field Cemetery with the Gold Star Mothers Pilgrimage in 1930. At that time she was 57 years of age.

NILSEN Karl

Private 1st Class, Co. C, 348th MG Battalion, 91st Division
DOW 31 October 1918
Plot A – Row 01 – Grave 23
Army Serial Number 2277937

(Hans) Karl Nilsen was born in Norway on 15 September 1889. He was the fourth child and second son of Nils Elias Nilsen Haugland (a fisherman) and Nicoline Andrea Korneliusdatter (photo insert). His siblings were Nilda, Kornelia, Nikolai (died in infancy), Nikolai Andreas, Nils, Johan, Elise and Emma. The family lived on a small farm close to the sea in Flekkefjord (where Christian Urdahl also lived). He emigrated to the U.S.A. with his two elder brothers in 1907 and settled in

Eureka, Humboldt County, CA, where he worked as a lumberman. One brother later settled in Marseilles, IL.

Karl registered fort the draft in June 1917. He was called to arms in February 1918 and sent to Camp Lewis for his basic training.

Karl was hit in the buttocks by shell fragments. This happened a short distance from battalion post command. He also complained of his stomach causing nausea. He was transferred to a first aid station but died of his wounds two hours later. He had signed a Petition for Naturalization while in Camp Lewis, Washington on 4 June 1918. However at the time of death he was still a Norwegian citizen. His emergency address was with his friend Knute Tellofron in Eureka, CA.

Right: Family home in Norway

KNOWLES FRANK A.
2nd Lieutenant, Co. E, 108th Infantry Regiment, 27th Division
DOW 1 September 1918
Plot A – Row 02 – Grave 01

Frank Augustus Knowles was the son of Augustus and Anna Knowles. His parents had emigrated from Sweden in 1882 and settled in Niagara Falls, Niagara County, NY in 1900. Frank was born in San Antonio, TX on 15 April 1891. The family raised five children: William, Frank, Ores, George and Margaret. Frank worked as a clerk with Erie Railway in North Tonawanda, NY. He volunteered for the National Guard on 9 November 1915 and in 1916 was assigned as 1st Sergeant with Company E of the 3rd Infantry Regiment along the Mexican border (the photo was taken during this period). During his training at Camp Wadsworth, SC in 1917, Frank decided to register for officers training school. His Army serial number at the time was 1225521. Just before his departure for Europe he married Helena Patterson.

Upon arrival in Europe, Frank was promoted to 2nd Lieutenant (15 July). He was severely wounded during the attack of 1 September and died of his wounds shortly afterwards. He was buried at Lyssenthoek Military Cemetery in Poperinge, Grave location XXXII.C.16. His parents only received the official notification of his death long after other sources had already revealed the circumstances of his death. 2nd Lieutenant Knowles was very much admired by his men for being an exemplary officer. He always remained friendly, fair and competent in his judgements.

His remains were moved to Waregem on 14 April 1921. In his burial file one can read that the features of his remains were still recognizable. This was because he had been buried in a coffin.

Only two men of the 108th Infantry Regiment are interred at Flanders Field Cemetery. Louis Herman (Plot C –Row 02 – Grave 11) also resided in Niagara County.

MONK Robert
Private, Co. M, 362nd Infantry Regiment, 91st Division
DOW 31 October 1918
Plot A – Row 02 – Grave 02
Army Serial Number 1995917

no photograph available

Robert Monk was born in Graysville, IN on 27 April 1895. He was the son of William Monk and Eliza Cox, both of farming stock. He had four brothers (Thomas, Ira, Frederick and Jesse) and one sister (Anna). The family later moved to West Union, IL.

Robert arrived in Europe with the 84th Lincoln Division but was transferred to the 362nd Infantry Regiment. He was killed in action during the battle of the Spitaalsbossen (a dense wooded area). He was hit by machine gun fire at approximately 12:30. Stretcher bearers had difficulties reaching him and when they did it was too late. He had already succumbed to the severity of his wounds. It was his first engagement in battle. He was buried along the Heirweg near the village of Anzegem (grave 4) on 3 November. His remains were moved to Cemetery #1252 on 3 June 1919 and buried in plot C, grave #54.

no photograph available

HASSETT John S.
Private, Co. L, 362nd Infantry Regiment, 91st Division
KIA 31 October 1918
Plot A – Row 02 – Grave 03
Army Serial Number 3536212

John Sullivan Hassett was born in Saint Louis, MO on 23 July 1889. He was the son of Jacob Hassett and Margaret Sullivan. He was married to Ethel Wolfe and they had a son John W. (°1909). However the marriage was short lived and they divorced.

John was called to arms in Lynchburg, VA on 29 July 1918. At the time he was foreman in a shoe factory. His emergency address was with his mother Margaret in De Soto, MO. He received his basic training with the 158th Depot Brigade and on 7 August 1918 was transferred to Co. D of the 336th Infantry Regiment, 84th Lincoln Division, which was a National Army Division comprising of men from Illinois, Wisconsin and Kentucky. Upon their arrival in Europe, these men were reassigned to other units.

Private John Hassett was killed by machinegun fire. He was struck in the left breast and judging from his position in which he lay on the ground, was apparently killed instantaneously. Corporal Charles McElheny of Middleport, Ohio arrived at the scene a few minutes afterwards and found him dead. This happened near the train station at Anzegem on 31 October. He was originally buried in a small American burial plot along the *Kleine Leiestraat* (Cemetery #1250, grave #8). His remains were moved to Waregem and buried in plot C, grave #56 on 3 June 1919 (photo insert).

no photograph available

GRZYWACZ Steve
Private 1st Class, Co. E, 148th Infantry Regiment, 37th Division
KIA 31 October 1918
Plot A – Row 02 – Grave 04
Army Serial Number 1529585

Steve Grzywacz was born in Gruszka, Poland (now Russia) on 16 August 1886. He was the son of Wawrzyniec and Josefa Grzywacz. They had a second son (Jozef) and a daughter (Maryanna). He was called to arms on 3 October 1917. At that time he was working in an iron foundry in Cleveland, OH. He had also submitted a request to obtain his U.S. citizenship.

Basic training was at Camp Sherman. One month later he was assigned to Co. E, 148th Infantry Regiment. Shortly after his arrival in Europe he was promoted to Private 1st Class. Steve was a gunner attached to a machine gun unit. He was killed in action together with the other members of his unit near Olsene: a bullet had lodged in his right temple. When he was found, he was still sitting upright, hands clenched to the trigger, machine gun pointing in the direction of a farm where the Germans had taken shelter. He was first buried with his comrades in arms close to where they fell. His remains were reinterred in Waregem on 3 June 1919 (Plot C, grave #59).

WILDFIER Joseph
Private 1st Class, Co. F, 148th Infantry Regiment, 37th Division
KIA 31 October 1918
Plot A – Row 02 – Grave 05
Army Serial Number 1905719

Joseph (Joe) Wildfier was born on 11 July 1888. He was the son of Joseph Wildfier (German immigrant from Bavaria) and Mary Scheider. They had nine children (of which Katie, Robert, Peter, Teresa, Annie, Joseph and Aloise). The family lived in Kersey, PA. Mary died when Joseph was only 5 years of age. He was raised and provided for by his six year older sister Teresa. He enlisted with the Ohio National Guard on 20 September 1917.

Joseph was shot through the head by machinegun fire and killed instantly. His remains were interred in Waregem on 3 June 1919 (Plot C, grave #61).

no photograph available

WIGNEL Frank M.

Private, Co. H, 362nd Infantry Regiment, 91st Division
KIA 31 October 1918
Plot A – Row 02 – Grave 06
Army Serial Number 3535319

Frank Marion Wignel was born on 11 January 1893. He was the son of Frank Wignel and Alice Conklin living in Chillicothe, OH. They had six other children: Lettie, William, Annie , Minnie, Gertrude and Bannem. Frank worked as a farmer in Huntingdon.

He was called to arms in Chillicothe on 26 July 1918. After a brief training period with the 158th Depot Brigade, he was assigned to the 338th Infantry Regiment, 85th Custer Division on 11 August. This division was disbanded upon arrival in Europe and Frank was reassigned to the 362nd Infantry Regiment on 5 October. He was killed instantly when a shell fragment lodged in his head. This happened during his very first engagement in battle, just 1000 feet south of Steenbrugge (Anzegem).

no photograph available

CHRISTY Angelo

Private, Co. H, 145th Infantry Regiment, 37th Division
KIA 2 November 1918
Plot A – Row 02 – Grave 07
Army Serial Number 2663572

Angelo Cristanziani was born in Acquasanta, Province of Ascoli, Italy on 26 May 1896. He was the son of Filippo Cristanziani and Celesta Lupini. Filippo departed for the U.S.A. in 1902. In 1909, Angelo and his sister Filomena (°1903), joined their father. They settled in Fayette, PA.

He was drafted in July 1917. His registration card indicates that he was illiterate and as occupation worked in a mine. He was called to arms in Uniontown, PA on 4 April 1918 and received his basic training with the 155th Depot Brigade until 16 April (less than two weeks). He embarked for Europe on 15 June, 1918, just 6 weeks after he was called to arms.
Angelo was killed by machinegun fire on 2 November. He was buried together with Stanley Mleko on the farm of Napoleon Rogge between the villages of Olsene and Kruishoutem. At the time of death he was still an Italian citizen. His emergency address was with his friend Carlo Emilio in Brownsville, PA.

GROVE Walter E.

Private 1st Class, Co. C, 145th Infantry Regiment, 37th Division
KIA 4 November 1918
Plot A – Row 02 – Grave 08
Army Serial Number 2708145

Walter E. Grove, son of John and Alice Grove (née Geesey) was born in Yoe, PA on 26 November 1893. He had two sisters: Alverna (°1895) and Viola (°1897). In 1902, Walter lost his mother following complications during child birth of his sister, Celestia. John remarried with Clara Belle with whom he had four more children: Vinarda (1906), Arthur (1907), Leola (1909) and Neva (1926, who died at the age of two). By that time Walter was working as an agricultural laborer and lived on the farm. Photo insert right is Walter with his father.

He was shot through the mouth by machinegun fire near the railroad at Eine. He was buried on the spot (Isolated Grave #2). Howard and Katherine Geesey (Alice's parents who were listed as contact in case of emergency) expressed their wishes for

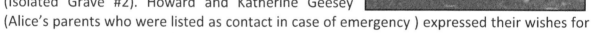

the remains to be returned to the U.S.A. His father Walter however made the final decision for his remains to be interred in Europe. On 10 June 1919, Walter's remains were moved to Waregem (Plot A, grave #83).

His stepmother, Clara Belle, visited his grave with the Gold Star Mothers Pilgrimage in 1932 (11, 12 and 13 August). She was 44 years of age. On her passenger questionnaire she indicated that she could speak Penna Dutch.

KINDER Ira M.
Private 1st Class, Co. A, 145th Infantry Regiment, 37th Division
DOD 18 November 1918
Plot A – Row 02 – Grave 09
Army Serial Number 1517266

Ira Milton Kinder was born on 1 November 1898. He was the son of John and Ida Kinder residing in Ladd, IL. The 1900 census indicates that he had three sisters (Emma, Pearl and Emilia) and an older brother (John). Ira was called to arms on 12 October 1917 and embarked for Europe on 28 May 1918. He served with Co. A of the 145th Infantry Regiment, 37th Division.

Ira was constantly in the front line, and yet he survived hostilities. Just 20 years of age, he died of lobar pneumonia (complication of the Spanish flu) on 18 November 1918, one week after the armistice. He was buried in the cemetery adjacent to the Evacuation Hospital in Staden.

Ira is mentioned on the Honor Roll of Bureau County, IL. On 4 October 1919, a monument was erected in Ladd City Park in honor of those who died during the world war. Five of the victims originated from Ladd.

World War I Memorial in Ladd City Park (dated 1919)

FORTIN Archie J.

Private 1st Class, Co. H, 148th Infantry Regiment, 37th Division
KIA 31 October 1918
Plot A – Row 02 – Grave 10
Army Serial Number 1910521

Archie Joseph Fortin was born in Gray, ME on 16 August 1893. He was the son of Arthur Fortin and Annie Sirois, both born in Canada. They lived with their eight sons (Philias, Arthur, Frederick, Joseph, Rosario, Homer, Edgar and Archie) and four daughters (Alice, Emilia, Grace and Alexandria) in Bridgeport, CT. Archie was employed by the Bryant Electric Co. in Hancock.

Archie was called to arms on 19 September 1917. He was first assigned to the 304th Infantry Regiment, 76th Division. This division was formed with draftees from New England. Two months later he was assigned to the 328th Infantry Regiment. This regiment was part of the 82nd Division. He remained with the regiment until April 1918. He then received further training with the 157th Depot Brigade and was finally assigned to the 148th Infantry Regiment in June.

On 31 October, at the start of the attack and while crossing the river Lys near Olsene, Archie was shot and died instantly. He was buried in the communal cemetery in Olsene (grave #1). His remains were transferred to Cemetery #1252 in Waregem on 14 June 1919. His mother expressed her desire for the remains to be repatriated to the U.S.A. However, in a letter dated 26 Aril 1920, the family had apparently decided that his remains be interred in a cemetery on European soil. He received his final resting place on 13 June 1922. His rank (Private 1st Class) is not inscribed on his headstone. (see Chapter 6 - American Graves Registration Service - page 72, paragraph 2).

His brothers Arthur, Frederick and Joseph also served their country on European soil. They all returned unscathed. After the war, Frederick named his son Archie in honor of his brother.

Annie had accepted the invitation to join the Gold Star Mothers Pilgrimage and she was looking forward to the trip. All preparations had been settled. Unfortunately Annie died on 26 December 1929, a few months before the date of departure overseas. Her husband Arthur, died just five days later on 31 December.

Seated: Frederick, Arthur Sr., Arthur Jr.
Standing: Joseph and Archie

DECKARD Isaiah

Private, Co. F, 362nd Infantry Regiment, 91st Division
DOW 7 November 1918
Plot A – Row 02 – Grave 11
Army Serial Number 3440517

Isaiah Deckard was born in Raeftown, IL on 27 December 1892. He was the son of John Elias Deckard and Ella Wetreau. They also had two daughters, Ina and Nora. He lost his mother at the age of three and his father when he was eight. His sister Nora also died within a year after her birth.

At the time he was called to arms Isaiah was working as a mechanic specializing in farm machinery. After his basic training he was assigned to the 335th Infantry Regiment, 84th Division. The division was disbanded upon arrival in Europe and Isiah was reassigned to the 362nd Infantry Regiment.

He was wounded on 31 October and transferred to the Evacuation Hospital #5 in Staden. He succumbed to his wounds on 7 November and was buried in the cemetery adjacent to the hospital on 9 November (row 7, grave #93). His remains were interred in Waregem: Plot A, grave #120 on 6 June 1919.

no photograph available

HUOVINEN JACOB

Private, Co. L, 148th Infantry Regiment, 37th Division
KIA 2 November 1918
Plot A – Row 02 – Grave 12
Army Serial Number 3336854

Jacob Huovinen was born in Väyrylä near Puolanka, Finland on 27 May 1888. His parents were Enoki Huovinen and Vappu Heikkinen, who also had two other children: Henry and Alma. Jacob emigrated to the U.S.A. in 1906 and lived with his uncle Henry Heikkinen in Brainerd, MN. He worked as an interior decorator in Duluth.

As so many other young men he was called to register for the draft. Strangely enough, his registry card indicates that he was a Russian citizen and claimed exemption on account of a lame leg. After his basic training with the 161st Depot Brigade he was assigned to Co. D of the 344th Infantry Regiment, 86th Black Hawk Division and sailed for Europe on 9 September. The division was disbanded upon arrival in Europe and as of 6 October he was reassigned to Co. L of the 148th Infantry Regiment.

He was killed in action on 2 November while attempting to cross the river Scheldt. His remains were only found six months later and on 9 May 1919 he was buried in the communal cemetery in the small town of Eke. At the time of death he had still not obtained his U.S. citizenship.

no photograph available

DINGEE Harry J.
Wagoner, HQ Co. 136th MG Battalion, 37th Division
KIA 3 November 1918
Plot A – Row 02 – Grave 13
Army Serial Number 1515153

Harry Dingee was born in Newburgh, NY in 1880. He spent most of his childhood living in Tarrytown, NY. He had three sisters (Laura, Edith and Gertrude) and two brothers (John and George). His father died in 1899. As such his mother, Mary Scott Dingee, became a single parent raising the family.

Harry moved to Youngstown, OH where he married and later divorced. He was a career army soldier and had already served under Captain Pershing for fifteen years. First in the Philippines (1899-1902) and then in Mexico. He was wounded at Vera Cruz and lay in a state of coma for six months at the American Hospital. His life was finally saved by inserting a silver plate in his head. After being found unfit for further military service he was medically discharged. Nonetheless, on 12 June 1916 he enlisted with the Ohio National Guard. Eventually he was assigned as wagoner and attached to Headquarters Company of the 136th Machine Gun Battalion, 37th Division.

The following witness statement was made by Wagoner Sardis White: *"On 3 November at 16:30 hours en route to Olsene, Belgium, Wagoner Dingee was driving Company B's kitchen. The kitchen was between the ration cart and the Combat Wagon. It was very dark that night and about a kilometer out of Cruyshautem (Kruishoutem), a shell burst on the right hand side of the road between the front and the rear wheels of the kitchen, about four feet of being a direct hit. On account of the direction the shell came most of the shrapnel was thrown into the front limber. Shrapnel very near tore off Dingee's right leg and hitting him in the back, disemboweled him. He was killed instantly"*.
He was buried in the communal cemetery of Wannegem-Lede and on 10 June 1919 moved to Cemetery #1252 in Waregem where on 13 June 1922 he received his final resting place.

One of his brothers was also serving in Europe. Not hearing anything from him in months, Mary feared the worst. It was a great relief when she received the good news that he had survived and was coming home.

As the Government only financed the repatriation of the remains to the town closest to the residence and did not cover the additional costs of the funeral, Mary decided for Harry's remains to be interred in Europe.

In 1921, a monument was inaugurated in North Tarrytown with the names of 334 men from the town who had served their country. Nine names were engraved separately: the names of those who hadn't survived, one of them being Harry.

GOMSEY Isaac Jr.

Private, Co. I, 148th Infantry Regiment, 37th Division
KIA 30 October 1918
Plot A – Row 02 – Grave 14
Army Serial Number 1916546

Isaac Gomsey, born on 28 December 1892 in Jalasjarvi, Finland, was the son of Isaac Urho "Gomsi" and Mary Lustila. He had four brothers: William, Vernon, Jacob and Toimi Emil. Isaac worked in a local mine in Nanty Glo, PA at the time he was called to arms. He signed a Petition for Naturalization on 26 October 1917.

On 30 October, the day before the great push, an artillery shell demolished the house in Olsene where Isaac was billeted. He was severely wounded to his head and died instantly. He was buried in the garden of the presbytery in Olsene. At the time of death he still retained the Finnish citizenship. A clerical error indicates the date of death on his headstone being 1 November. His remains were moved to Waregem on 10 June 1919 and buried in plot A, grave 93.

Mary visited the Flanders Field Cemetery in 1933. She was 67 at the time. Her trip started out as a nightmare as there was no sleeping compartment reserved for her during the train voyage from Warren, OH to New York.

Gomsey was the Americanized name for the Finnish name Gomsi. This name was also recorded as Gumsey, Gamsey and Gumay.

Murheella ilmotamme, että elämän ja kuoleman Herra katsoi hyväksi kutsua luoksensa sodan kauhuista rakkaan poikamme sotilaan

Isaac Gomsin,

Saimme surusanoman, että hän on kaatunut urhoollisesti taistellen Yhdysvaltain armeijassa Ranskan sotarintamalla marraskuun 1 päivä, 1918. Hän kutsuttiin Yhdysvaltain armeijaan syyskuun 22 p. 1917. Hän oli syntynyt Suomessa Jalasjärvellä, V. I. Oli kuollessaan 25 v. 10 kk. ja 11 päivän vanha. Ikävällä kaipaamaan jäimme isä, äiti, 4 veljeä sekä yksi veljen vaimo ja muita sukulaisia ja tuttavia tässä maassa sekä Suomessa.

Isaac ja Maria Gomsi,
Box 172, Nanty Glo, Pa.

Ei löydy siellä surua, ahdistus katosi. Ei kuulu siellä itkua, valitus vaikeni; Vaan rauha, riemu, rakkaus ja taivaallinen rikkaus On Herran tykönä.
Arpa lankesi minulle ja arvan kautta kruunu.
Emme kuitenkaan murehdi niin kuin ne murehtivat, joilla ei ole toivoa, sillä hänen kirjeensä Ranskan sotarintamalta tulkitsi elävää uskoa armon Herran, joka on suuri lohdutuksemme.

With sorrow we announce, that the Lord of life and death has seen it good to receive into his presence, out of the horrors of war, our beloved son soldier,

Isaac Gomsi

We received the sad news that he has fallen heroically while fighting with the United States Army on the battlefront in France November 1, 1918. He was conscripted into the United States Army September 22, 1917. He was born in Jalasjarvi, Finland. At the time of his death he was 25 years, 10 months and 11 days of age. Grieving survivors are his father, mother, 4 brothers, one sister-in-law, as well as other relatives and friends in this country and Finland.

Isaac and Maria Gomsi
Box 172, Nanty Glo, Pa.

"There is found no sorrow; suffering is perished,
There is heard no sound of crying, lamentation is silenced;
Only peace, rejoicing, love, and the richness of heaven in the presence of the Lord."

"The lot fell to me, and because of that lot, the Crown."

However, we do not grieve as they grieve who have no hope, for his letters from the battlefront in France conveyed a lively faith in the Lord of grace. That is our great consolation.

FOSSUM William T.
Private, Co. M, 148th Infantry Regiment, 37th Division
KIA 11 November 1918
Plot A – Row 02 – Grave 15
Army Serial Number 2816334

William (Bill) Theodore Fossum was born in Dassel, MN on 8 September 1893. He was the son of Edwin and Sofia Fossum. William had four brothers (Charles, Arthur, Henry and Richard) and three sisters (Augusta, Esther and Ruth). When he wasn't attending class or working on the farm, he was out hunting or fishing with one of his many friends.

Front: father Edwin with Richard on his lap, Esther and mother Sofia with Ruth on her lap.
Back: Henry, Arthur, Augusta, Charles and William

William was working as an agricultural laborer in Crystal Bay, MN at the time he was called to arms. On 24 June 1918 he was requested to report in Hopkins, MN where he was sent to Camp Grant, IL for basic training. (14th Training Co, 161st Depot Brigade). William wrote many letters home. From these letters it was evident that he was well read and an intelligent, sensitive young man. He gave a detailed picture of how life was at the training camp. On 30 June he wrote to his brother Charles informing him that he had finally received his uniform and was pretty sure he would be heading for France soon. His letter of 17 July: he was relieved that his mother wasn't aware how sad he was when he received his orders to embark: *"If I ever come back from over there, there sure is going to be something different and if I don't, forgive me for everything I have done and take good care of mother."* In a July letter he describes the experiences of a Lieutenant returning from the front: rats and lice would be their additional challenges. Soon after, William was reassigned to Co. D of the 344th Infantry Regiment, 86th Black Hawk Division. On 6 August he wrote from Camp Grant how exhausting the training was. His feet were bleeding but he wouldn't give up: *"Will be a better man than I was when I left"*. He received a new uniform and went to Rockford to have his picture taken to send home. He was promoted to Corporal but declined on the grounds that this would cause frictions from two sides, between him and the soldiers on the one hand and officers on the other. *"The financial advantages aren't worth it."* One week later rumors were that his unit would be sent to Russia; however *"the 86th Division could take care of a few of the Huns…. So you are planning on having a service flag …hope there won't be any more gold stars to add to it…. When I get home I will take care of mother …"*. On 22 August he wrote his last letter from Camp Grant.

The 86th Division was not sent to Russia, but to Europe where it was disbanded upon arrival. One month later (6 October) William was reassigned to the 148th Infantry Regiment. On 18 October he wrote home that he was with *"a nice bunch of fellows from Ohio"*. He requested candy for his *"Christmas box"* and further… *"Do not worry about me mother dear as He will take good care of me and bring me back to you in all safety."* A few weeks later he was killed in the village of Ename along the east bank of the river Scheldt on Armistice Day. He was buried where he fell. On 10 June 1919 his remains were moved to Waregem and temporarily buried in Cemetery #1252 plot B, grave #150. On 13 June 1922 he received his final resting place. Sofia was eager to join the Gold Star Mothers Pilgrimage, but because no one of her family was allowed to accompany her, she declined the invitation.

MOOREHOUSE Harold A.

Corporal, Co. F, 148th Infantry Regiment, 37th Division
KIA 31 October 1918
Plot A – Row 02 – Grave 16
Army Serial Number 1529822

Harold Ashmun Moorehouse was born on 8 April 1895 in Cleveland, OH. He was the only son of Herbert S. Moorehouse and Martha Quigley. He joined the Ohio National Guard on 8 October 1917. He was promoted to Corporal on 13 June 1918.

The eyewitness report by Mechanic Raymond Smith revealed that both of them were wounded and laying side by side near the town of Olsene. Harold was hit by machine gun bullets in left arm and later again right arm, throat and chest. He was buried in Olsene on 3 November. When his body was moved to Waregem it was also found that he had an upper fractured skull and bullet hole in forehead above the right eye. One pipe and one plug of STAR chewing tobacco were found on his remains.

no photograph available

READY Joseph F.

Private, Co. E, 363rd Infantry Regiment, 91st Division
DOW 1 November 1918
Plot A – Row 02 – Grave 17
Army Serial Number 2930755

Joseph Ready was born in Cincinnati, OH on 20 March 1896. His parents were Aloysius and Annie Ready (née Frazee). There were seven other children: Gertrude, William, Mary, Grover, Terrence, Beatrice and Sally Ann. Joseph was called to arms on 27 June 1918 and received his basic training with the 158th Depot Brigade. Less than one month later he was assigned to the 333rd Infantry Regiment, 84th Lincoln Division.

Upon arrival in France the division was disbanded and John was reassigned to the 363rd Infantry Regiment. He was mortally wounded by machine gun fire near Spitaalsbossen in Waregem. He was transported to the American Evacuation Hospital #5 in Staden, but all was in vain.

GUSLER Paul P. – Silver Star

Sergeant, MG. Co. 145th Infantry Regiment, 37th Division
KIA 31 October 1918
Plot A – Row 02 – Grave 18
Army Serial Number 1516824

Paul Philander Gusler was the son of Simon and Catherine (Katie) Gusler (née Gilbert) from Grover Hill, OH. He was born in Haviland, OH on 29 June 1895. In 1917 he was working as an agricultural laborer.

He joined the Ohio National Guard with Co. B of the 2nd Infantry Regiment on 17 June 1917. This later became the Machine Gun Company of the 145th Infantry Regiment. He crossed the Atlantic with his division on 15 June 1918. He was promoted to Corporal during the Meuse-Argonne campaign. On 16 October he wrote home: *"Do not grieve if anything should happen to me, because I am dedicated to this cause."* Two weeks later, on 31 October 1918, at 08:00 hours, he was killed instantly by an artillery shell (headstone indicates 1 November). He was buried the next day close to where he fell, on the right side of the Olsene-Gent road, where other men of his division had also been interred. On 24 December 1918 he was posthumously awarded a citation signed by the Divisional Commander, Major General Farnsworth, for *"his devotion to duty and his contributions during the operations of the 37th Division in France and Belgium"*.

His remains were moved to Cemetery #1252: plot B, grave 114 on 11 June 1919. On 17 March 1920 his parents expressed the desire for his remains to repatriated to his home town. However, on 20 July the Ministry of War received a second letter revoking their initial request: *"remains of our son be left to rest in peace where now buried"*. Paul Gusler received his final resting place at Flanders Field American Cemetery on 13 June 1922.

On 8 February 1924, the family received a standard letter from the Quartermaster General with the details of the permanent cemetery location of Paul's grave and the details of the inscription on his white marble headstone. They assured that *"in effecting the removal of the dead, the utmost reverential care was exercised and more than willingly accorded by those who performed this sacred duty. For the future these graves will be perpetually maintained by the Government in a manner befitting the last resting place of our heroes."* Reference was made to Corporal Gusler. His father replied to the letter indicating the fact that his son had been promoted to Sergeant a few days before being killed and requested that the records be set straight accordingly, consequently indicating the correct rank on his headstone. He immediately received confirmation that his request had been accepted and that the headstone would reflect the correct inscriptions. (Details in the burial file do indicate that during exhumation Sergeant stripes were found on the right sleeve of his tunic.)

In 1929, Katie received a letter which contained information regarding a pilgrimage to the cemeteries in Europe, giving her the opportunity to visit the grave of her loved one. She replied on 12 September that she was unable to participate as her husband was very ill. However, her children and husband urged her to make the trip and so in February 1930, Mrs. Gusler sent in a request to participate in the 1930 pilgrimage. At the time Katie E. Gusler was 68 years of age. She visited her son's grave on 2, 3 and 4 July 1930.

Paul (standing far left) with family and friends in Grover Hill.

SONVILLE Ernest A.
Private, Co. B, 347th MG Battalion 91st Division
DOW 2 November 1918
Plot A – Row 02 – Grave 19
Army Serial Number 2291560

E(a)rnest Arnold Sonville was born in Milwaukee, WI on 21 June 1892. In 1888 his parents, Abram and Jennie Sonville (née Desmith), had moved from the Netherlands and settled in Milwaukee, WI. Later they relocated to Minneapolis, MN. Ernest had one sister (Johanna, who had been born in the Netherlands) and two brothers (David and Lester). Their father died before 1910. In 1910 the children lived in Seattle, WA with their mother and step father, Richard Shapp, also a Dutch immigrant.

Earnest married Katie Mills (°1897 – photo insert) on 3 March 1911. Their son Arnold Frederick was born on 5 February 1912. Their happiness was short lived when Katie died on 11 August 1916 . She was buried in Evergreen-Washelli Memorial Park in Seattle, WA. When Ernest was called to register for the draft in 1917, he was working as a plasterer in the building trade for Dines & Son. Being a widower with a son five years of age, he requested exemption of military service. However this was rejected.

He died on 2 November. Seeking cover from German artillery in a private dwelling, a gas shell hit the shelter and Ernest was blinded by smoke and dust. He was unable to secure his gas mask in time. He was transferred to the American hospital in Staden but succumbed to his injuries the same day. His remains were interred in Waregem, plot B, grave #164 on 5 June 1919. Katie's mother Anna, took care and raised Arnold Frederick through childhood. She applied for permission to travel with the Gold star Mothers Pilgrimage to Flanders Field Cemetery but her request was denied.

BROKAW Charles S.

Corporal, Co. F, 148th Infantry Regiment, 37th Division
KIA 31 October 1918
Plot A – Row 02 – Grave 20
Army Serial Number 1529792

Charles Shivery Brokaw was born in 1898 as son of William H. Brokaw and Bertha Shivery of Phillipsburg, NJ. He spent most of his youth in Colton, CA. He had one brother (John Raymond) and a sister (Dorothy). He was known to be a friendly, optimistic, ambitious, religious young man who valued family life. He attended Colton High School where he was admired by all. He became a committee member of the *"German Club"*, an association where young people of a like mind gathered to learn about German culture and at the same time also learning and speaking the German language during these meetings. He was also co-editor of the school magazine: *"Crimson and Gold"* and active member of the basketball and baseball school teams. He was a wizard in mathematics. He graduated from High School in 1916, moved to Ohio where he attended the Adelbert College of the Western Reserve University. When the United States declared war he was one of the first (17 May) to volunteer and join the National Guard in Cleveland, OH. Via the 3rd Infantry Regiment he became part of Co. F of the 148th Infantry Regiment, 37th Division. On 1 September 1917 he became Private 1st Class and on 1 May 1918 he was promoted to Corporal.

Charles arrived in France on 22 June. He was in the thick of the Meuse-Argonne offensive near Verdun and survived unscathed. He was killed in action near Olsene, Belgium on 31 October. The day after his parents received the tragic news of his death, they received a cheerful letter from Charles from the front. He had enclosed a label to secure the safe arrival of his *"Christmas box"*. The letter was dated 31 October.
His brother John Raymond also served with the A.E.F. in Europe. He was one of the survivors of the famous "Lost Battalion". He died on 9 January 1990.

The roots of the Brokaw's can be found in Moeskroen (Mouscron), Belgium. Their ancestors were named Broucard. One ancestor, a certain Bourgon Broucard, was found in records of the French Congregation at Mannheim, Germany indicating that he and his family were from Mouscron in the Low Country (Belgium). The County of Flanders was included in the 1579 Union of Arras which only recognized Catholicism, abolishing all other religions. Bourgon fled the religious persecutions and married in Mannheim in 1663 and again in 1666 losing his first wife to the plaque. They then emigrated to the Netherlands in 1672 and to America in 1675 where they finally found peace and freedom of religion.

Graduation photo Colton High School (1916): Charles is in the back row second from right.

Basketball team: Charles seated first from right

Baseball team: Charles standing second from right.

no photograph available

DILUGI Patrick
Private, Co. I, 145th Infantry Regiment, 37th Division
DOW 2 November 1918
Plot A – Row 02 – Grave 21
Army Serial Number 2668368

Pasquale Di Luigi was born on 17 September 1891 in Montefino, Teramo, Abruzzo, Italy. He was the son of Antonio Di Luigi and Marina Prosperi. Seeking better prospects in life he emigrated to the U.S.A. in September 1909.

He settled in Philadelphia, PA when in 1917 he was requested to register for the draft. He was eventually called to arms on 27 April 1918. On 10 June 1918, during his last days at boot camp with the 37th Division in Camp Lee, VA, he was notified that his application for U.S. citizenship had been approved.
He died of wounds and was initially buried in the town of Dentergem, Belgium. His remains were moved to Waregem on 4 June 1919.

When the U.S. government sent out the questionnaire on final disposition of Patrick's remains they never received a reply. The language barrier was evidently the cause of misunderstanding. The letters to his mother were repeatedly sent in English.

In November 2009, Patrick finally received the first visit to his grave by his great nephew Ferrucio Di Luigi, who was unaware at the time that he had a great uncle buried in Belgium.

WATTELET Leonard A.

Captain, Co. A, 364th Infantry Regiment, 91st Division
KIA 31 October 1918
Plot A – Row 02 – Grave 22

Leonard Wattelet was born in Seattle, WA on 21 November 1886. He married Florence Handley of Victoria on 4 June 1913 and they had one son: Thomas Roswell (°1915).

In 1906, the 19 year old Wattelet played in two late-season games for the Seattle Siwashes of the Class A Pacific Coast League. He was hitless in five at-bats and although that marked the conclusion of his playing days in professional baseball, his affiliation with the minors was far from over.

In 1911, Wattelet joined the newly formed Victoria Bees (British Columbia) of the Class B Northwestern League, serving as business manager, secretary and treasurer. He became president of the club in December 1912. He remained with the Victoria Club through 1915, the team's last season in pro ball. He later entered military service with the U.S. Army, earned a commission as a captain at the first officers training school and was placed in charge of baseball operations at Camp Lewis near Tacoma, Washington.

After the U.S. declaration of war he obtained command of Company A of the 364th Infantry Regiment, 91st Division. During the Meuse-Argonne offensive he suffered from the effects of mustard gas. Although the seriousness of his injuries warranted him a ticket home, he refused stating that he preferred to be with his men who by then had been transferred to Flanders.

During the battle of the Spitaalsbossen, on 31 October 1918, he lost both his legs above the knees during a mortar attack. He was killed instantly. His body had been brought to a farm located adjacent the cemetery and buried NE of the Spitaalsbossen, a stone's throw from where the Flanders Field cemetery is now located, on 3 November. Among the personal effects sent back to the Wattelet family was a piece of shell fragment which had caused Leonard's tragic end. The piece is still in the possession of his granddaughter (Mrs. Kay Wood). These were trying times for Florence who, only two weeks later (12 November) also lost her father.

On 3 June 1919, Leonard's remains were reburied in plot A, grave #3 of what was then still American Cemetery #1252. In the meantime, his widow Mrs. Florence M. Wattelet had moved to Long Beach, CA where she had taken residence with Captain Wattelet's mother and sister. Her last wish was not to have his remains repatriated to the U.S. but permanently interred in Europe. On the 8th of March 1921, Leonard's remains were again disinterred as there was evidence that errors had occurred during the burial procedures within that particular row. He was positively identified and reinterred in the same grave.

In June 1922 he received his final resting place at Flanders Field American Cemetery.

In 1929, his widow (photo insert) was given the opportunity to visit the grave of her husband. She accepted the invitation and in 1931 departed on the long trip to Europe. At the time she was 40 years of age. The amount of $40 was provided to cover any expenses she might incur during her inland trip. On 18 June she departed on a 64 hour train journey to Chicago. She had been informed that every assistance would be provided during the trip. However, unfortunately she missed her connection in Chicago. On 24 June she boarded the SS Roosevelt and sailed for Europe with the Gold Star Mothers group. Upon their arrival in France (2 July) the group was escorted to the Hotel Lutetia in Paris where they stayed for three days to recuperate from their journey. On 6 July, Florence started on her trip towards Waregem where she visited her husband's grave on 7, 8 and 9 July. During this period the group stayed at the Hotel Royal in Lille. On 10 July they returned to Paris where they were able to spend the rest of their time sightseeing. On 16 July they commenced their return journey and traveled by train to Cherbourg. They arrived back in New York on 24 July.

Officers of the 1st Battalion, 364th Infantry Regiment, Camp Lewis
(Wattelet front row far left)

WILLIAMS Ringius

Corporal, Co. I, 106th Infantry Regiment, 27th Division
KIA 2 September 1918
Plot A – Row 02 – Grave 23
Army Serial Number 1208441

Ringius Wilhelmson was born in Blekinge, Sweden in December 1892. His father was Wilhelm Johansson. At eighteen he emigrated to the U.S.A. and lived with his mother in Brooklyn. In 1916 he had served with the 23rd Infantry Regiment along the Mexican border. In October 1917 he volunteered and joined the National Guard. At the time he left for Europe he was engaged and living together with his fiancée Alice Johnson.

He was killed in action near Vierstraat and buried by the British in Bedford House Military Cemetery . His remains were recovered by the American Graves Registration Service in 1922.

LYONS Wilbert E.
Sergeant, Co I, 106th Infantry Regiment, 27th Division
DOD 27 October 1918
Plot A – Row 03 – Grave 01
Army Serial Number 1208233

Wilbert E. Lyons was born in Boston, Massachusetts but lived in Brooklyn, NY. On 1 November 1915 he registered with the New York National Guard (23rd Infantry Regiment). He was only eighteen years of age. He was promoted to Sergeant in 1917.

He was taken prisoner of war and moved to Namur, Belgium. He died of influenza and was buried in Cemetery #1836. After the war, the American Graves Registration could not positively identify his remains. It was later confirmed by the Mayor of Namur that he was one of five buried at that location. However, due to details provided by his mother (X-ray of left arm fracture earlier in life), the supervisor of exhumations was satisfied and confirmed that Unknown #2801 was Wilbert Lyons. After the war, a letter from a certain Mr.

Calembert from Gembloux reached the military authorities. In this letter he depicted the deplorable conditions in the German military hospital in Namur. Priorities for treatment were given to the German casualties at all times. Others were treated on a case by case basis even if their condition were more critical.

His mother Ida visited his grave with the Gold Star Mothers Pilgrimage in 1930.

KNOWN BUT TO GOD
Plot A - Row 03 - Grave 02

Trees

I think that I shall never see
A poem lovely as a tree.

A tree whose hungry mouth is prest
Against the sweet earth's flowing breast;

A tree that looks at God all day,
And lifts her leafy arms to pray;

A tree that may in summer wear
A nest of robins in her hair;

Upon whose bosom snow has lain;
Who intimately lives with rain.

Poems are made by fools like me,
But only God can make a tree.

Sergeant Joyce Kilmer
165th Infantry Regiment, 42nd Rainbow Division
Killed in action on 30 July 1918
French Croix de Guerre

Oise-Aisne American Cemetery
Plot B – Row 9 – Grave 15

KNOWN BUT TO GOD
Plot A - Row 03 - Grave 03

The Anxious Dead

O guns, fall silent till the dead men hear
Above their heads the legions pressing on:
(These fought their fight in time of bitter fear,
And died not knowing how the day had gone.)

O flashing muzzles, pause, and let them see
The coming dawn that streaks the sky afar;
Then let your mighty chorus witness be
To them, and Caesar, that we still make war.

Tell them, O guns, that we have heard their call,
That we have sworn, and will not turn aside,
That we will onward till we win or fall,
That we will keep the faith for which they died.

Bid them be patient, and some day, anon,
They shall feel earth enwrapt in silence deep;
Shall greet, in wonderment, the quiet dawn,
And in content may turn them to their sleep.

John McCrae

SCHMITT Max S.
Private, Co. D, 147th Infantry Regiment, 37th Division
KIA 31 October 1918
Plot A – Row 03 – Grave 04
Army Serial Number 1754500

Max Stepin (Stephen) Schmitt was born on 22 May 1896. His parents were John and Katherine Schmitt from Buffalo, NY (both German immigrants). He was the youngest of four: Lena, John and Richard were his brothers and sister. He was a truck driver at the time he was called to arms on 29 April 1918. He completed his basic training with the 153rd Depot Brigade and within one month reassigned to the 147th Infantry Regiment as a messenger.

The last town he was in was Marialoop near the town of Olsene where he was killed and buried in an isolated grave. When he was disinterred on 6 June 1919, no positive identification could be made as his head was missing. Shoulders, arms and legs were fractured. As such he was initially registered as Unknown #2802. Later, during the identification process for permanent reburial in Waregem, a positive identification was eventually made. He is still buried between three "Known but to God" graves.

KNOWN BUT TO GOD
Plot A – Row 03 - Grave 05

Rendezvous

I have a rendezvous with Death
At some disputed barricade,
When Spring comes back with rustling shade
And apple-blossoms fill the air--
I have a rendezvous with Death
When Spring brings back blue days and fair.

It may be he shall take my hand
And lead me into his dark land
And close my eyes and quench my breath--
It may be I shall pass him still.
I have a rendezvous with Death
On some scarred slope of battered hill,
When Spring comes round again this year
And the first meadow-flowers appear.

God knows 'twere better to be deep
Pillowed in silk and scented down,
Where love throbs out in blissful sleep,
Pulse nigh to pulse, and breath to breath,
Where hushed awakenings are dear . . .
But I've a rendezvous with Death
At midnight in some flaming town,
When Spring trips north again this year,
And I to my pledged word am true,
I shall not fail that rendezvous

Alan Seeger [1886-1916]

The American poet Alan Seeger (uncle of Pete Seeger - died 2014 - the well-known folk singer with hits as *"Where have all the flowers gone"* and *"We shall overcome"*) was of prominent descent and graduated at Harvard in 1910. He joined the French Foreign Legion on 24 August 1914. He was killed in action on 4 July (Independence Day) 1916 in Belloy-en-Santerre, France.

no photograph available

JORGENSEN Louis.
Private, Co. A, 136th MG Battalion, 37th Division
DOD 24 October 1918
Plot A – Row 03 – Grave 06
Army Serial Number 3747254

Louis Jorgensen was born in Lockport, IL on 7 March 1890. He moved out west seeking a more prosperous living and landed in Big Sandy, MT. There he married Tina Jacobsen in October 1911. One year later he became a father of a fine daughter Louise. In 1916 he moved to Tomahawk, WI where he opened a saloon. He was an impressive individual: very tall and strong and it was said that he wasn't afraid of anything or anyone. He was very indecisive whether or not he should volunteer as at the time he was exempt of military service due to his domestic situation. Nonetheless he decided to shut down his saloon and volunteer. On 23 June 1918 he left Tomahawk together with 107 conscripts for basic training at Camp Grant. It was said that he was the happiest man on earth.

Louis was assigned to the 86th Black Hawk Division and arrived in France on 27 September. Later he was reassigned to the 37th Division. Unfortunately only one month later he died of pneumonia, one of the complications of the Spanish flu.

Louis' remains were not repatriated to the U.S.A. despite Tina's initial request and unsuccessful efforts. The reason for this was that Louis was registered as being buried in the American Plot at Lyssenthoek cemetery in Poperinge. During the disinterment process it was determined that a British soldier was buried under his marker: Thomas Halligan of the 9th Bn. Irish Fusiliers. On the other hand Halligan was also registered as being buried at

Duhallow Cemetery in Ypres (grave IV.1.27). When this grave location was investigated no remains were found and so they reburied Halligan where he was originally registered to be buried at Duhallow. However, in December 1927 during a refurbishing project at Duhallow Cemetery, two sets of remains were found at Thomas Halligan's burial location. Louis Jorgensen had been buried one meter below the remains of Halligan. The closing date for repatriation being 1 April 1922, all hope for Tina to have his remains returned to the U.S.A. were lost.

Tina visited his grave on 2, 3 and 4 June 1930 during the Gold Star Mothers Pilgrimage. She was 37 years of age. Private Halligan's remains is still buried at IV.1.27 at Duhallow Military Cemetery.

BEYERS Bernard
Private, Hq Co. 362nd Infantry Regiment, 91st Division
DOW 3 November 1918
Plot A – Row 03 – Grave 07
Army Serial Number 1994974

The roots of the Beyers family lie in Germany (Baden Baden). In 1845, John, Bernard's grandfather emigrated to the U.S.A. His grandfather on the maternal side of the family was a veteran of the American Civil War. Bernard, born on 18 March 1888, was the second child of Joseph and Wilhelmina (Minnie) Beyers (née Eckholt). Besides Bernard they had seven children: Elizabeth, John, Clara, Wilford, Loretta, Leo and Francis. Loretta died in 2002 at the age of 101.

Bernard was an agricultural laborer on a farm in Pana, IL when he was called to arms on 23 February. He received his basic training at Camp Taylor, Louisville, KY, at Camp Sherman, Chillicothe, OH and at Camp Mills, Long Island, NY. He embarked for Europe on 4 September 1918 with his original unit: Co. C, 335th Infantry Regiment, 84th Division. They disembarked in Liverpool on 16 September. Upon arrival in Europe the division was disbanded and the men were reassigned to other divisions. Bernard was finally reassigned to Headquarters Company of the 362nd Infantry Regiment, 91st Division.

He volunteered to be a messenger for his Captain and on 1 November, while performing his duties, was severely wounded at the head and chest. He was taken to the 3rd Australian Casualty Clearing Station located near Ledegem where he died two days later. He was buried in the Commonwealth Kezelberg Military Cemetery in Moorsele, West Flanders (II.A.17).

It was 1973 before the family realized that Bernard was buried at Flanders Field Cemetery. Quite an extraordinary story. Shortly after Cemetery #1252 was established, they received a Red Cross photograph of his grave (plot B, grave #126 - insert). In the official records of the American Graves Registration Service, Bernard Beyers was registered as *"Unlocated"*. Confusion all around.

When he was disinterred on 11 June 1919, no identification tag was found on his remains. As no positive identification could be made he was officially registered as unknown. On 12 October 1929, Bernard's parents were notified that his name would be inscribed on the Wall of Missing of the chapel of which the construction was still in its planning stages. When a family member visited Flanders Field in 1973, he was astonished to find the grave of Bernard Beyers.

One source (Gold Star Boys) claims that he was posthumously awarded a medal for extraordinary heroism, however this could not be confirmed with any official records. It is also claimed that his family received a certificate from Raymond Poincaré, the President of the Republic of France. Part of the inscription taken from Victor Hugo's famous poem was: *"For those who devotedly died for their country. It is right that the people come and pray at their graves."*

Bernard with friends. Far left, back row.

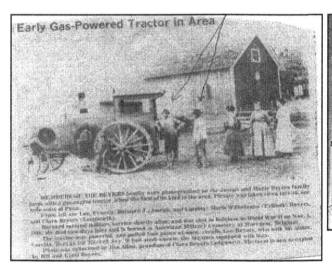

Memorial for the soldiers of Pana.

Photo 1915 or 1916; The Beyers family, the first farmers acquiring a gasoline driven tractor. Bernard is the man leaning against the tractor.

GUARINO Antonio

Private, Co. B, 148th Infantry Regiment, 37th Division
DOW 1 November 1918
Plot A – Row 03 – Grave 08
Army Serial Number 2414091

Antonio Guarino was the son of Donato Guarino and Angela Maio (photo inserts) who lived in Montella , Province of Avellino in Italy. They were blessed with ten children: Nicola (°1886), Guiseppe (°1889), Maria Luigia (°1891), Antonio (°6 januari 1894), Giuseppe (°1896), Guiseppine (°1899), Salvatore (°1904), Maddalena (°1905), Anna (°1907) and Pasquale (°1911). Maria Luigia and the two Guiseppes died at a young age. Angela, who was very emotional and sensitive , could not accept the loss. Their oldest son

Nicola, whose ambition was to become a monk at the monastery *"Monastero della Neve"* in Montella, was disillusioned when the monastery came to close, and decided to move to the United States. For many years there was no news from him which drove Angela into a depression. The family decided to send Antonio to the U.S.A. in an attempt to find Nicola and so alleviate the mental pressure on their mother. Antonio found him and wrote home that everything was fine with Nicola. Antonio decided to remain in the U.S.A. and found a job as a weaver in Paterson, NJ.

When the United States declared war in 1917, all young men were required to register for the draft. Antonio registered on 5 June 1917. Eventually he was drafted on 1 April 1918. He was immediately sent for basic training to Camp Dix, NJ and assigned to the 153rd Depot Brigade where he remained until 10 June. From there he was reassigned to Co. B of the 148th Infantry Regiment, at that time training in Camp Lee, VA. On 22 June he embarked for Europe. Antonio died of wounds and was originally buried in the American plot in the cemetery in Dentergem (grave #12). His remains were transferred to Cemetery #1252 in Waregem on 4 June 1919 where he received his final resting place on 17 March 1921.

As Angela spent most of her time in the cemetery, crying at the graves of her deceased children, Antonio's brothers and sisters decided not to have his remains repatriated to Italy. Nonetheless, Angela never could get over Antonio's death. The family recalls her praying continuously at his photograph.

Nicola was also serving with the A.E.F. in Europe but survived unscathed. Unfortunately a few years later he was killed and burnt alive by an explosion in the iron foundry where he was working at the time. This news was never passed on to Angela as the family feared the worst if this terrible news ever reached her. Consequently, Pasquale wrote letters to her with Nicola's signature, reassuring her that he was in good health and that all was fine.

On 23 November 1980, a major earthquake reduced Montella to a pile of rubble. One of the few precious mementoes that survived the Guarino family's home was Antonio's photograph.

SMEDLEY Clarence T.
Private, Co. I, 148th Infantry Regiment, 37th Division
DOW 1 November 1918
Plot A – Row 03 – Grave 09
Army Serial Number 1530525

Clarence Tack Smedley (° February 1897) was the youngest child in the agricultural family of John and Margaret Smedley. He had three brothers (Robert, Fred and Arthur), two sisters (Florence and Guila) and four half-brothers (Jef, Edward, Charles and John). He evidently had a difficult youth as he was detained for a short period of time in an institute for juvenile delinquents. There he learned to play the trumpet. He joined the 3rd Infantry Regiment, Ohio National Guard in Xenia, OH on 19 June 1916. During his basic training at Camp Sherman he was awarded a medal for marksmanship for his shooting skills and in May he won a competition for best bugler in the A.E.F.

He died of wounds received in action during the first day of the offensive. He was buried in the American Cemetery Olsene Grave #5. His remains were moved to Waregem on 4 June 1919 where he was laid to rest in plot B, grave #116. On 22 June 1922 he received his current and final resting place.

The whole family had fallen apart and they had no further contact with each other. As such his emergency address was with a friend in Yellow Springs, OH. Guila, who had raised Clarence from when he was an 18 month old baby, was the only point of contact known to the Graves Registration. She informed them that no one else in the family was interested in him and as such requested permanent burial in Europe. Florence, with whom Clarence had invariable arguments, had found and claimed his war insurance. She received payment in full although she had not contacted or spoke with him in sixteen years. This came as a major blow to Guila.

KISTNER Ray A.
1st Sergeant, Co. D, 147th Infantry Regiment, 37th Division
KIA 11 November 1918
Plot A – Row 03 – Grave 10
Army Serial Number 1525256

Ray Kistner was the son of Albert Kistner and Susie May Morgan. He was born in Fostoria, OH on 5 December 1891. He had one sister, Bessie. His grandfather, Christian Kistner, was a veteran of the Civil War. Ray spent his youth in Fostoria where he joined the 6th Infantry Regiment, Ohio National Guard on 25 August 1914. He served during the punitive campaign along the Mexican border with the 6th Infantry Regiment from July 1916 through March 1917. His uncle, Rawson Kistner, was also a member of the same National Guard Regiment and served in Cuba during the Spanish-American war. When Rawson returned home he was very ill and later died in Knoxville, TN.

On 30 April 1918, during his training period in Camp Sheridan, AL, Ray married Fay Stahl. She had traveled from Ohio as she expected he would not be able to take leave before he was sent to Europe. Unfortunately her premonition came true. Ray was mortally wounded by shell fragments on 11 November (at 10:20, just 40 minutes before cessation of hostilities). His friend, David Hogan, who was next to him enquired if he was wounded but there was no response. Nothing could be done. He was buried in the communal cemetery at Zingem. At the time of Ray's death announcement, cessation of hostilities had been signed just five hours earlier.

His sister Bessie had no happy life. Besides losing her only brother Ray, her husband Clyde Hildreth passed away just one month later (12 December 1918). Her daughter Martha died in 1940 and two years later her son (second marriage) Robert D. Loveless, was killed during WWII. Fay, Ray's widow, remarried and so was not eligible to join the Gold Star Mothers Pilgrimage.

MILLER James G.

Private, Co. I, 362nd Infantry Regiment, 91st Division
KIA 31 October 1918
Plot A – Row 03 – Grave 11
Army Serial Number 2480945

James "Poke" Miller was the oldest son of John and Isabelle Miller, Scottish immigrants. He was born on 30 January 1889 in Buckingham, OH and had three brothers and four sisters. The whole family moved to Luddington near Hemlock, OH, a small mining community with only a few hundred inhabitants.

James was called for the draft on 26 May 1918. In the photograph: James (far left) with three friends from Hemlock, ready to board the train. He received his basic training with the 158th Depot Brigade until 2 July. From there he was transferred to the 335th Infantry Regiment, 84th Lincoln Division. On 3 September he embarked for Europe. Upon arrival in France, the division was disbanded and James was attached to the 362nd Infantry Regiment.

James was hit by shell fragments and killed instantly during the advance into the Spitaalsbossen in Waregem. Also Frank Osborn, Angelo Mazzarella and William Garner were mortally wounded during the same action. He was buried where he fell and on 4 June 1919 his remains were transferred to Cemetery #1252 (plot B, grave #10 – photo).

In 1919 Isabelle decided that her son be interred in Europe: *"I want my son buried with the rest of the boys."* Shortly after the war she wanted to visit James' grave but was unable to do so due to financial setbacks. When the invitation was sent by the government to join the Gold Star Mothers Pilgrimage she had to decline for health reasons. She added that she regretted not having the remains of her son repatriated when she first had the opportunity and that she would meet him again in a place with no tears, only happiness.

no photograph available

DROBICHEVSKY Mitro
Private, Co. L, 145th Infantry Regiment, 37th Division
KIA 2 November 1918
Plot A – Row 03 – Grave 12
Army Serial Number 2967300

Dimitri (Mitro) Drobichevski was the son of Anton Raphaailovich Drobichevski and Anna Augustinova from Gomelskaya, Minsk Province, Belarus. He was born on 20 August 1895. Seeking a more prosperous life he emigrated to the U.S.A. and found employment in one of the many steel plants in Pittsburgh, PA.

Mitro was killed in action near the village of Heurne during an attack on a German machine gun nest. He was buried to the northwest of the village: American Cemetery grave #5. His remains were transferred to Cemetery #1252 on 4 June 1919 and laid to rest in plot B, grave #12. At the time of death he was still a Russian citizen.

In 1929, Anton wrote to the U.S. Government enquiring at what point in time he would receive the compensation of his son's war insurance. Times were desperate as he claimed: *"I will soon need to slaughter my cattle so that I can buy food for my family."* Evidence of any war insurance was never found.

In the NARA archives one can find his name spelled in seven different ways: Drobichevsky, Droaiachenski, Drobiachevski (as on his ID tags), Drobitevski, Drabitelskoii, Drobizcheuski, Drebiehevsky.

no photograph available

DAGLIS TONY
Private, Co. F, 148th Infantry Regiment, 37th Division
KIA 31 October 1918
Plot A – Row 03 – Grave 13
Army Serial Number 2418967

Antony Daglis was born on 1 May 1891 in Wilna, Poland. He was the son of Marjanna Jusszys and he had one sister, Maria. It is unknown when he emigrated to the U.S.A. He took residence with a friend (Peter Romanoffsky) in Central Falls, RI.

He was drafted on 27 April 1918. He received his basic training with the 153rd Depot Brigade and was assigned to Co. F of the 148th Infantry Regiment. He was killed instantly when he was shot through the head on 31 October near the town of Olsene. Tony Daglis is the only individual from Rhode Island buried in the cemetery.

WIESNEWSKI John J.
Private, Co. E, 148th Infantry Regiment, 37th Division
KIA 31 October 1918
Plot A – Row 03 – Grave 14
Army Serial Number 1907955

John Joseph Wiesnewski was born on 14 February 1896. According to the NY Abstracts of WWI Military Service, he was born in Germany. However on his WWI Draft Registration Card he is registered as being born in Russia. He was the son of Frank and Katherine Wiesnewski. He had three brothers: Benjamin, Frank and Joseph. The family emigrated to the U.S.A. and settled in Albany, NY. John was a machine assembler at the Consolidated Car Co.

John was the first to be drafted: he was called to arms on 21 September 1917 and was assigned to the 303rd Infantry Regiment, 76th New England Division. On 14 November 1917 he was transferred to the 327th Infantry Regiment, 82nd "All American" Division. It goes without saying that he experienced an extraordinary training period. On 9 April 1918 he was again reassigned to the 157th Depot Brigade. On 9 June he was finally assigned to the 148th Infantry Regiment.

Two weeks later John embarked for Europe. He lost his life near the town of Olsene when he was shot through the head. He was buried in the *"American Cemetery Olsene"*, grave #9. On 3 June 1919 his remains were transferred to Waregem plot C, grave #61.

GLENN George P.
1st Lieutenant, 17th Aero Squadron
KIA 20 July 1918
Plot A – Row 03 – Grave 15

George Preston Glenn was the son of Walter Glenn and Mary Black. He had an older brother (Walter) and sister (Annie). He was born in Lynchburg, VA on 21 June 1894 where he lived until 1917. He graduated from High School and became a salesman for the Guggenheimer Department Store. In the meantime he had also joined the National Guard. On 5 June 1916 he joined the Officer Reserve Corps at Fort Myer, VA and decided to become a pilot. He was commissioned Lieutenant in Fort Worth, TX.

It was on 20 July 1918 a black day for the 17th Aero Squadron when tragedy struck for the inexperienced 1st Lieutenant George Preston Glenn.

On the morning of 20 July, the 17th received their orders to escort a number of British DH-9 bombers. The targets were in the vicinity of Bruges, in German occupied territory. The DH-9's dropped their bombs without any major problems and returned to base. In other words, a successful mission. The 17th, itching for additional action decided to do a reconnaissance flight. At 10:00 a.m., they encountered five Fokkers over Ostend. The 17th were at 18,000 feet, the Fokkers at 19,500 feet. The Camels immediately went into action, whereupon one Fokker left the formation and dived towards Glenn. He fired at a short distance and disappeared in the clouds. In the confusion that followed it was witnessed that Glenn, at 5,000 feet, dived until he also disappeared in the clouds. Although at first they thought that their comrade in arms was safe, unfortunately turned out that it was the last time they would see George Preston Glenn. 1st Lieutenant Glenn crashed with his Camel D1938 behind German lines. He was the first pilot of the 17th Aero Squadron to be killed in action.

The man who downed George Glenn was Ober Lieutenant Theo Osterkamp (photo insert). Osterkamp was a German "Ace" with 32 victories. Glenn was his 17th kill. At first, Osterkamp was rejected for military duty with the Prussian Army due to health problems. As such he joined the *"Freiwilliges Marine Flieger Corps"*. He turned out to be one of the best World War I pilots. After the war he chose to fight the Bolsheviks. At 43 he was again in uniform and flying with the *Luftwaffe*. He flew missions over France and Italy, achieved six victories and was promoted to *Generalleutenant*. He personally received the Iron Cross from Adolf Hitler.

Lt. Glenn was originally buried at the Navy cemetery in the town of Gistel, near Ostend: grave #458. His remains were interred at Flanders Field on 23 June 1922.

In 1920, twenty trees were planted in Lynchburg and a Memorial Plaque inaugurated for the twenty casualties of the city who had given their lives for their country. A bronze plaque was inaugurated by his niece at the Lynchburg airport in 1931. It became the Preston Glenn Field.

TENNEY Levi S. Jr.
Private 1st Class, Co. L, 107th Infantry Regt., 27th Division
KIA 20 August 1918
Plot A – Row 03 – Grave 16
Army Serial Number 1212011

Levi Sanderson Tenney Jr. was born in Glen Ridge, NJ on 15 June 1897. He was the son of Levi Tenney (an attorney at law) and Louise Todd (attorney's daughter). They were blessed with seven children: Dwight, Malcolm, Grace, Helen, Levi Jr., George and Elizabeth. Photo insert right standing from left to right: Dwight, Helen and Malcolm; below George, Elizabeth en Levi.

Levi Jr. lived with his mother in New Jersey (Montclair) but joined the New York National Guard (7th Infantry Regiment) in

New York City on 11 April 1917. The fact that his father lived on Broadway will have played a major role in his decision. At that time he was a junior at Yale.

Levi was killed during a daylight raid near Dikkebus on 20 August. His squad was holding an advanced observation post which was raided by the Germans. He was shot in the stomach and died almost instantly. He was buried at Abeele Aerodrome Military Cemetery.

Levi's original marker on Cemetery #1252

WESTMORELAND Haymore O.
Private, Co. L, 120th Infantry Regiment, 30th Division
KIA 31 August 1918
Plot A – Row 03 – Grave 17
Army Serial Number 1321897

Haymore Oliver Westmoreland was the son of Arelius Layfette and Frances Westmoreland. He was born in December 1897 in Forsyth County, NC. His mother and sister died of measles in 1901. His father later remarried Susan Artansia (Tannie) Sapp. Haymore spent his youth in Thomasville, NC.

He joined the 3rd Infantry Regiment North Carolina National Guard, which later became the 120th Infantry Regiment, on 9 April 1917.

Haymore was killed by a sniper while carrying a message to a platoon commander near Lankhof Farm, Ypres. After the war his remains were found by a farmer in 1923, too late to fulfill his father's wishes of his remains being returned to the U.S. Haymore was first interred at Poelkapelle British Cemetery before final burial at Flanders Field on 23 October 1923.

Two other men from Thomasville are also buried at Flanders Field: Carl Link and Bennett Cornelius. Their names are also memorialized on the World War One Memorial in Lexington, NC.

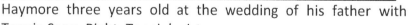

Haymore three years old at the wedding of his father with Tannie Sapp. Right: Tannie's sister.
Above right: Haymore 11 years of age
Below right: Haymore in 1918.

no photograph available

MUNCH Emil A.
Private, Co. K, 106th Infantry Regiment, 27th Division
KIA 2 September 1918
Plot A – Row 03 – Grave 18
Army Serial Number 2665956

Emil Munch was born on 10 March 1892. He was the son of Thibaut and Theresa Munch (French immigrants) from Closter, NJ. He lived and worked for Goseler Bros. in New York City.

There are no details on his training, his service in Europe or the circumstances of his death. He was first registered as missing in action. During the summer of 1923 two sets of remains were accidently found by Belgian laborers who were digging clay for a brickyard in the area of York Road (between Vierstraat and Kemmel). The remains had been buried in a trench which later apparently had been leveled with stone debris. Part of an ID tag was found and the workers had given it as a souvenir to the bartender of a café close by. The remains were first interred in the Poelkapelle British Cemetery. However, after inspecting the bone fragments it was determined that skeletal remains of a third soldier were evident. Returning to the area where they were originally disinterred and excavating further, additional remains and a skull were recovered. More importantly, another piece of an ID tag was found which after investigation matched the other part previously given to the bartender. The ID tag was that of Emil Munch. In October of the same year his lower skeletal remains were also found.

The repatriation program to the U.S. had been terminated in April 1922. As such there was no other alternative than to transfer the three remains to the Flanders Field Cemetery. The three men: Ayers, Hickton and Emil Munch are once again buried side by side.

no photograph available

AYERS Frederick A. Jr.

Private, Co. K, 106th Infantry Regiment, 27th Division
KIA 5 November 1918
Plot A – Row 3 – Grave 19
Army serial number 2451419

Frederick Ayers was born on 3 December 1894. He was the son of Frederick (°1858 in England) and Josephine Ayers (°1876) from Mount Vernon, NY. They had two other children, William (°1897) and Annie (°1908).

Frederick worked as an electrician at the time he was called to arms on 1 April 1918. He proceeded to Camp Upton, NY. He received his basic training with the 152nd Depot Brigade until 21 April when he was transferred to the 106th Infantry Regiment, 27th Division at Camp Wadsworth, SC serving at the Headquarters Company. Co. K eventually became his permanent unit.

Officially, he was slightly wounded on 27 September 1918 during the battle of the Hindenburg line (France) and later died under obscure circumstances on 5 November.
There is no doubt that this statement is based on a clerical error. A case of mistaken identity with a soldier bearing the same name. If it had been true, then his remains would have been interred in France, not Belgium.

The correct version is that in the summer of 1923 his remains were found by the same two Belgian workers under the same circumstances as Emil Munch (A-3-18). Ayers and Hickton were positively identified by their ID tags and dental records. As previously stated, the repatriation of remains program being terminated, they were buried side by side at Flanders Field. As Hickton and Munch were officially killed in action on 2 September, it is safe to say that Ayers was also killed on that same day. Their remains being found in the same location.

Josephine passed away on 28 August 1925. Frederick Sr. requested permission to take her place during the Gold Star Mothers Pilgrimage (1930-1933) but his request was denied.

HICKTON William T.

Private 1st Class, Co. K, 106th Infantry Regiment, 27th Division
KIA 2 September 1918
Plot A – Row 03 – Grave 20
Army Serial Number 1208507

William Thomas Hickton, born 27 May 1892 in Cohoes, NY, was the only son of Thomas Hickton and Henrietta Rivenburgh. The family moved to Brooklyn when William was 3 years of age. He was a mailman for the Wall Street Post Office in Manhattan at the time he volunteered with the 23rd Infantry Regiment New York National Guard on 30 July 1917. He was promoted to Private 1st Class on 12 October 1917.

William's mother requested that his remains be returned to the U.S.A. Unfortunately he had been listed as missing for too long, the closing date for repatriation having expired. (see Ayers and Munch).

HAMM Anthony J.
Private 1st Class, Co. C, 105th Infantry Regiment, 27th Division
KIA 2 September 1918
Plot A – Row 03 – Grave 21
Army Serial Number 1203753

Anthony Hamm, son of Henry and Fredricka Hamm (née Eich), was born in February 1896. He had one brother (Henry Jr.) and two sisters (Freda and Frances). The family lived in Brooklyn, NY.

At 21, Anthony volunteered for the New York National Guard. He was assigned to Co. C of the 71st Infantry Regiment on 9 February 1917 and promoted to Private 1st Class on 21 September 1918.

Anthony was killed at Dikkebus Lake during the battle for Mount Kemmel. While in a supporting trench, he was mortally wounded to the head by shell fragments. He was buried in an isolated grave near the village of Hollebeke. After the war, the British disinterred his remains and buried him at Oosttaverne Wood Cemetery, Wytschaete. From there his remains were moved to Waregem in 1926.

His mother visited her son's grave during the Gold Star Mothers Pilgri-mage in 1930 (party B). On 13 May she departed on the SS Republic, first sailing to the U.K. where she disembarked in Southampton on 24 May. On 26 May, while in London, she laid a wreath at the grave of the Unknown Soldier and at the Cenotaph. On the same day she visited the American cemetery in Brookwood and on 27 May she took the night ferry to Antwerp. At the Brussels Palace Hotel, she was received by the U.S. Ambassador Hugh Gibson on the 28th. The reason for this exceptional visit is unknown. Henry visited Flanders Field on 3 November 1956 with his son Joseph (photo). The visitor's register was signed by Robert and Joseph Hamm with the remarks " *We came to see our uncle's grave.*"

KNOWN BUT TO GOD
Plot A - Row 03 - Grave 22

KNOWN BUT TO GOD
Plot A - Row 03 - Grave 23

The Messages

"I cannot quite remember... There were five
Dropt dead beside me in the trench - and three
Whispered their last messages to me..."

Back from the trenches, more dead than alive,
Stone-deaf and dazed, and with a broken knee,
He hobbled slowly, muttering vacantly:

"I cannot quite remember... There were five
Dropt dead beside me in the trench, and three
Whispered their dying messages to me...

"Their friends are waiting, wondering how they thrive -
Waiting a word in silence patiently...
But what they said, or who their friends may be

"I cannot quite remember... There where five
Dropt dead beside me in the trench - and three
Whispered their dying messages to me..."

Wilfrid Wilson Gibson (1878-1962)

KNOWN BUT TO GOD
Plot A – Row 04 – Grave 01

Wirers

'Pass it along, the wiring party's going out' -
And yawning sentries mumble, 'Wirers going out.'
Unravelling; twisting; hammering stakes with muffled thud,
They toil with stealthy haste and anger in their blood.

The Boche sends up a flare. Black forms stand rigid there,
Stock-still like posts; then darkness, and the clumsy ghosts
Stride hither and thither, whispering, tripped by clutching snare
Of snags and tangles. Ghastly dawn with vaporous coasts
Gleams desolate along the sky, night's misery ended.

Young Hughes was badly hit; I heard him carried away,
Moaning at every lurch; no doubt he'll die to-day.
But we can say the front-line wire's been safely mended.

Siegfried Sassoon (1886-1967)

GIUNCHI Orlindo
Corporal, Co. M, 363rd Infantry Regiment, 91st Division
KIA 31 October 1918
Plot A – Row 04 – Grave 02
Army Serial Number 2265343

Orlindo Giunchi was born in Coreglia Ligure in the province of Genua, Italy on 29 November 1887. Seeking a more prosperous life, he emigrated to the U.S.A. in 1904. His father, Fedele, also emigrated to the U.S.A. while his mother, two brothers and his sister remained in Italy. Orlindo had already served with the Italian Army (photograph in Italian uniform).

He immediately took residence in Nevada City, CA. Although a miner by profession (Nevada City being known for its gold mines), he assisted his uncle (Anacleto Agostini) running the Sacramento Street Hotel. He had an energetic and pleasant "can do" personality and so made many friends.

Orlindo was drafted and left for Camp Lewis on 6 October 1917 where the 91st Division was formed. It was his intention that he would return after the war to help run the hotel again. He was assigned to Co. M of the 363rd Infantry Regiment. His previous experience in the Italian Army was no doubt the reason why he immediately obtained the rank of Corporal.

From letters sent to his mother one can learn how much he hated the war and how he longed for peace. However, during the first day of the attack, he was part of a 13 man detail who had halted at a farmhouse to inquire where the Germans were located. The day after, the Belgian farmer found five American bodies between even more German dead and buried them. The five American soldiers were George Bulaich, Alva Diver, Edward Smith, Jessie Silcox (later classified as unidentified) and Orlindo.

He had obtained his American citizenship on 1 June 1918. Apparently his name was omitted on the Memorial Wall in Grass Valley's Memorial Park, Nevada City. As a result of this publication, the local community gathered the necessary funds to set the records straight. Orlindo Giunchi will have his name inscribed on the Memorial Wall.

no photograph available

BULAICH George

Sergeant, Co. M, 363rd Infantry Regiment, 91st Division
KIA 2 November 1918
Plot A – Row 04 – Grave 03
Army Serial Number 2265301

George Bulaich was born in Grahovo, Montenegro on 28 August 1894. He emigrated to the U.S.A. in 1913 and found work in the mines at the Original Amador Mining Co., a goldmine located in Amador City, CA. Here he is commemorated on the World War I Memorial inside the courthouse.

On his registration card it is mentioned that he had two years of military experience with the infantry. This could explain why he achieved the rank of Sergeant in a short period of time.
He had filed a petition for naturalization whilst at Camp Lewis, WA on 30 May 1918. His emergency address was listed in Seattle and the city also mentions him in their Honor Roll.

As in the case of Orlindo Giunchi, during the first day of the attack he was also part of the 13 man detail who had halted at a farmhouse to inquire about the Germans. The day after, said farmer found five American bodies between even more German dead and buried them. The five American soldiers were Orlindo Giunchi, Alva Diver, Edward Smith, Jessie Silcox (later classified as unidentified) and George. At the time of death his application for American citizenship had not been finalized.

George is remembered on the WWI memorial of Amador County.

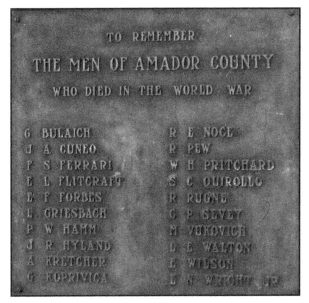

WILKENSON Reuben M.
Private, Co. D, 364th Infantry Regiment, 91st Division
KIA 2 November 1918
Plot A – Row 04 – Grave 04
Army Serial Number 2779299

Reuben Wilkenson was the son of Albert Wilkenson (an accountant) and Lottie (Charlotte) Cave, who lived in Santa Cruz, CA. He also had a younger brother: Leon. Reuben was born on 8 April 1894 in Los Angeles and graduated from Santa Cruz High School (photo taken from the 1914 annals). In school as in the community he was regarded as a man of distinction who joined in all kinds of sports and cultural activities. After leaving school he lived in Needles where he obtained a key position in the Claypool Company, a large grocery concern.

It was from here that, two years later, he was called to arms. He left for Camp Lewis, WA and received his basic training with the 91st Division. He became acting Corporal where his main task was drilling new recruits. On the day of his warrant for Corporal, sixteen volunteers were requested to fill the 91st Division for future embarkation to Europe. Reuben was the first to volunteer. He was assigned to Co. D of the 364th (California) Infantry Regiment. He left Camp Lewis at the end of June and traveled via Canada to Chicago, arriving 3 July. On 11 July he sailed with the Division to Europe.

In September he was severely wounded by shell fragments on two separate occasions during the Meuse-Argonne offensive. He lost consciousness for a long period of time being confined to hospital. During his recuperation process he wrote the following letter to his parents.

Sept. 30, 1918

"Dear Mother and Father

Well, I have a little blighty at last, but it is nothing serious, so if you have received word that I am a casualty do not be worried, as everything is O.K. I was in the first wave of our advance for two days and two nights and then I had to get bumped off. I sure would have liked to stay with the bunch and chased those boches clear off the map.

We were advancing in the face of the German rear guard action which consists mostly of machine gun and artillery fire when one of their high explosive shells broke so close to me that the man who was behind me was blown to pieces and the man in front was knocked down and I do not know if he was killed or not; I hope not, because we have been pals from the time we started.

Just before the explosion a machine gun bullet passed through the cuff on my shirt sleeve and when the explosion of the big shell came something hit me on the mouth and in the back of the head and I was thrown about ten or twelve feet and I struck on my knees. Then I got to my feet and went about 450 or 500 yards and then fell to be picked up later, which I do not remember, by the first aid men and here I am now.

Will close for the present hoping all are well, and with love to both, I remain
Your son,
REUBEN M WILKINSON"

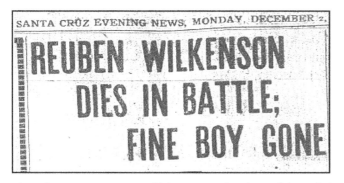

SANTA CRUZ EVENING NEWS, MONDAY, DECEMBER 2.

REUBEN WILKENSON DIES IN BATTLE; FINE BOY GONE

Shortly after he rejoined the Division Reuben was killed by a machinegun bullet while carrying messages as a runner on 2 November 1918. On 18 March 1921, close to the Santa Cruz High School, eleven Californian chestnut trees were planted to commemorate the eleven boys who lost their lives during the war. To this day these trees can still be seen. In the midst of these trees, a small monument was erected and on each tree a plaque bearing a name. Reuben was also designated a Memorial Tree.

KNOWN BUT TO GOD
Plot A - Row 04 - Grave 05

Emily Elrose, Ralph's stepmother, visited Flanders Field with the Gold Star Mothers in 1931. As she had no gravesite to visit, (Ralph Elrose – Wall of Missing) she laid her flowers at the grave of a soldier " Known but to God". The photograph was taken at this gravesite.

KNOWN BUT TO GOD
Plot A – Row 04 - Grave 06

The Stars shine bright in a field of blue;

They light the way where row on row

Is marked the resting place of you

Who peaceful sleep where poppies grow.

The fight is o'er; your faith we've kept;

The torch you flung burns brighter still

And though in Flanders field you slept

It led to victory – God's will.

Adam D. Bowman, Southport, IN, 1920

YATES Clement P.
Private, Co. M, 106th Infantry Regiment, 27th Division
KIA 2 September 1918
Plot A – Row 04 – Grave 07
Army Serial Number 1209115

Clement Putnam Yates was the son of George and Kate Yates from Saratoga Springs, NY. They also had two daughters: Mary and Hubertie. Kate was killed in a vehicle accident in 1911. George died in January 1918 while Clement was still training at Camp Wadsworth, SC.

Clement was shot through the head by a sniper and was killed instantly. Witness statements indicate that after his death his body had been mutilated by the enemy. His friends were able to retrieve his remains from the battlefield and he was buried in Kemmel by a burial party of the British 34th Division, who had relieved the U.S. 27th Division on that day.
His remains were moved to Lyssenthoek British Cemetery on 4 June 1919 and consequently to Waregem in 1922. At first there was uncertainty on the identity of these remains and he was buried with other unknowns. After further investigation a positive identification was achieved and "Unknown #2833" became Clement Yates.

KNOWN BUT TO GOD
Plot A - Row 04 - Grave 08

Come To Say Good-Bye

I'm here by your grave, at last my friend.
I hear the angels cry.
I see your smile. I hear your voice.
I come to say good-bye
Memories come of that time long ago.
I watch you as you die.
I hear you cry. I feel your pain.
I come to say good-bye.
You're not alone in this foreign field.
Your friends are here, close by.
The birds still sing, the flowers bloom.
I come to say good-bye
I slowly kneel by your grave in prayer.
You speak, and I reply.
I touch your stone, and shed my tears.
It's time to say good-bye.
So rest in peace, my boy-hood friend
As angels sing on high.
My prayers and thoughts are here with you.
I've said my last good-bye

Isabelle McBride

KNOWN BUT TO GOD

Plot A - Row 04 - Grave 09

Taps

Day is done, gone the sun,
From the hills, from the lake,
From the skies.
All is well, safely rest,
God is nigh.

Go to sleep, peaceful sleep,
May the soldier or sailor,
God keep.
On the land or the deep,
Safe in sleep.

Love, good night, Must thou go,
When the day, And the night
Need thee so?
All is well. Speedeth all
To their rest.

Fades the light; And afar
Goeth day, And the stars
Shineth bright,
Fare thee well; Day has gone,
Night is on.

Thanks and praise, For our days,
'Neath the sun, Neath the stars,
'Neath the sky,
As we go, This we know,
God is nigh.

KNOWN BUT TO GOD
Plot A – Row 04 - Grave 10

The Unknown Soldier

You need not ever know my name
This unknown soldier seeks no fame

I'm here to bring out thought from you
May your heart see more than your view

America, we marched with pride
We gave our life, for you we died

How well we knew the time might come
When life could sound that final drum

Please think of us as life moves on
We tried so hard till that last dawn

Do let our spirit fill the land
Pass treasured freedom, hand to hand

God blessed this country with such love
Hold in your heart, abundance of

And when you stand before my grave
Think not of one, but each who gave

Roger J. Robicheau
New Port Richley, FL 34656

US

KNOWN BUT TO GOD
Plot A - Row 04 - Grave 11

When You Go Home,

Tell Them Of Us And Say,

For Your Tomorrow,

We Gave Our Today

Kohima Epitaph by John Maxwell Edmonds (1875 – 1958)

DOHERTY William J.
1st Sergeant, Co. K, 106th Infantry Regiment, 27th Division
KIA 2 September 1918
Plot A – Row 04 – Grave 12
Army Serial Number 1208476

William J. Doherty was born in Brooklyn in 1896 and lived there all his life. He worked in a shipyard at the time he joined the New York National Guard in July 1917. He was assigned to the 14th Infantry Regiment and when the 27th Division was formed to Co. K of the 106th Infantry Regiment.

William Doherty was killed, as so many others of his unit, on 2 September. He had two brothers and one sister. He had four cousins who were also serving with the A.E.F. in Europe. John wrote home explaining that the dugout where William was sheltered was obliterated by a German mining company. The person notified of his death was his sister, Miss M. Doherty.

KNOWN BUT TO GOD
Plot A – Row 04 - Grave 13

Flanders Fields

Flanders Fields is where you go,
to see the many rows and rows,
of crosses, graves and many more
soldiers that went to fight in war.
Beautiful Flanders Fields.

So go there on Remembrance Day
to show your love in a loving way.
I will go, and so will you
to see the graves of soldiers
who did what they had to do
Lovely Flanders Fields.

by Natalie Sullivan (Aged 10)
Charlottetown, Prince Edward Island, Canada

KNOWN BUT TO GOD
Plot A - Row 04 - Grave 14

Ye Are Not Dead

In Flanders still the poppies grow
Among the crosses, bending low,
On fragile stems, their cups of red
Like censers swinging o'er the dead
That fell short days ago.

Ye are not dead! If it were so
We that abide could never go
As blithely marching by your bed
In Flanders fields.

Because your bodies lie below,
Above, with an intenser glow
The Torch moves on: in your brave stead
Men dare to bleed as ye have bled-
That larks may sing, and poppies blow
In Flanders fields.

Frank E. Hering, South Bend, Indiana (1920)

no photograph available

WILLIAMS Sherman H.
Private, Co. D, 135th MG Battalion, 37th Division
KIA 31 October 1918
Plot A – Row 04 – Grave 15
Army Serial Number 2713427

Sherman Williams was the son of George and Alice Williams from Bluefield, WV. They had five other children of which four sons: Ralph, Bruce, Frank and Phil and one daughter: Ada. Sherman was born on 16 August 1891 and lived his childhood and youth in Bluefield. Although professionally trained as a butcher he initially found a job as a clerk with the local Crystal Coal & Coke Company and later with the American Coal Company in McComas. On 26 April 1918 he left Bluefield, together with 13 other young men from this town, and headed for Camp Meade, MD. Later they were transferred to Camp Lee, VA and assigned to the 135th Machine Gun Battalion. Three weeks later Sherman was on his way to Europe.

Sherman was a victim of friendly fire. Shell fragments had lodged in his chest during an artillery barrage. He was buried together with Robert Tovsrud five hundred meters west of the village of Kruishoutem and 1 km off the road near the town of Olsene. His remains were interred in Europe which was contrary to his parents final wishes on the permanent disposition of his remains. Identification problems occurred after his remains had been interred in Waregem. Total confusion was caused due to the fact that the remains of Anthony Durand were found under the marker of Ira Matthews. Consequently, someone else had been buried under the marker of Durand. The remains were designated as Unknown #257. So in 1921, Sherman was reinterred at Flanders Field as an unknown. In 1926, four years after the repatriation program had been concluded, an in depth investigation resulted in a positive identification of Sherman Williams.

As such it was no surprise that his mother, regardless her age (77), was eager to visit her son's grave with the Gold Star Mothers Pilgrimage in 1930. She visited Flanders Field on 2, 3 and 4 July.

226

KNOWN BUT TO GOD
Plot A - Row 04 – Grave 16

Do Not Stand At My Grave and Weep

Do not stand at my grave and weep
I am not there. I do not sleep.
I am a thousand winds that blow.
I am the diamond glints on snow.
I am the sunlight on ripened grain.
I am the gentle autumn rain.
When you awaken in the morning's hush
I am the swift uplifting rush
Of quiet birds in circled flight.
I am the soft stars that shine at night.
Do not stand at my grave and cry;
I am not there, I did not die.

Mary Elzabeth Frye (1905-2004)

no photograph available

MUNDES William H.
Private 1st Class, Co. K, 148th Infantry Regt., 37th Division
DOW 6 November 1918
Plot A – Row 04 – Grave 17
Army Serial Number 2404405

William Henry Mundes was born in Marion, NJ on 18 July 1889. He was the son of Charles (Chas) F. Mundes and Frida Timms (both German immigrants). He was married to Grace and had one son William Jr. (born in 1912) and a second child of which the name is unknown. William was a very tall man: 6 foot 2 inches, with blue eyes and brown hair. He lived in Hoboken, NJ where he worked as a foreman for the American Lead Pencil Company. He was called to register for military service on 5 June 1917. He did not request exemption from military service although he was supporting his wife Grace and two small children. He was called to arms on 21 November 1917. He received his basic training with the 153rd Depot Brigade and on 9 June 1918 he was assigned to the 37th Division.

Details of his burial file indicated that he died of wounds received in action. However he had sustained a shattered skull, both arms fractured and shoulder was missing. He was temporarily buried in a French cemetery in the village of Mullem under the name of Charles St. John. The reason for this is that personal effects belonging to Charles St. John were found on his remains. However, Charles St John survived the war (honorary discharge in December 1918). That is why when the remains were moved to Waregem on 9 June 1919, he was interred as Unknown #2834 in Plot D, grave #42 and with the permanent landscaping of Flanders Field Cemetery in Plot A - Row 4 - grave 17 between other "Known but to God". A positive identification was only established at a later date.

KNOWN BUT TO GOD
Plot A - Row 04 – Grave 18

That Special Place

Take my hand, and come with me
To a special place across the sea
A sacred place in hallowed ground,
A place where love and sorrow's found.

It's not a church you'll understand.
Just a part of home in another land.
A place where gravestones stand arrayed
Like a phantom army on parade.

Stand close by me, and patience keep
And soon you'll see a brave man weep.
He cries for his comrade beneath the stone

And I tell you friend he's not alone.
Scenes like this are commonplace
In this our special meeting place.
So as you stroll down memory lane
Think of us who must remain.

And now it's time to say adieu
But remember friend, we died for you.

Cyril Crain

KNOWN BUT TO GOD
Plot A - Row 04 – Grave 19

Sleeping alone, so quiet and still,
Because of a War and because
Of God's Will;

They fought and they died
As Americans can,
Some barely old enough
To be called a man;

They were all Americans,
But not by birth,
For they all knew
Of Freedom's worth;

They went and they fought,
And all stood tall,
Some would survive
And some had to fall.

They rest forever
In a foreign land,
Never more knowing
A soft, warm hand;

And without the love
Of Mother or child,
Just with the poppies
That grow so wild.

They have the flowers
And birds that sing;
Perhaps if they listen,
They'll hear Freedom's Ring;

The Freedom that was
So dearly won...
Sleep well, my Soldiers,
Sleep well, my Sons.

Patty Mackey, 2006

no photograph available

SMITH Edward R.

Private 1st Class, Co. M, 363rd Infantry Regiment, 91st Division
KIA 31 October 1918
Plot A – Row 04 – Grave 20
Army Serial Number 2784052

Edward Robert Smith was born in St. Louis, MO on 25 January 1888. As a young man he moved to Nevada and took residence in Humboldt County. He worked for the Miller and Lux Company, a large ranch specializing in agriculture and stock breeding. When he was called to arms on 26 April, he gave his place of residence as: Amos, Humboldt County, NV. Before joining he had already served three years with the cavalry. He is the only individual buried in Flanders Field cemetery from Nevada.

He received his basic training at Camp Lewis, WA with the 166th Depot Brigade. He was later assigned to Company M, 363rd Infantry Regiment, 91st Division. He embarked for Europe on 7 July. He was promoted to Private 1st Class on 30 August.

He was in the thick of it from the time the 91st Division arrived in Europe; in reserve in St. Mihiel mid-September, heavy fighting in the Argonne near Cheppy and Gesnes end of September and beginning of October, finally being transferred to Flanders. On the first day of the attack in Waregem, he was part of the 13-man detail inquiring at a farm where the Germans were located. As previously mentioned, the farmer found five American bodies and many more Germans the following day and buried them. The five Americans being George Bulaich, Alva Diver, Orlindo Giunchi, Jessie Silcox (unidentified) and Edward.

No information or links could be found to family members. His emergency address was registered with his best friend, Harry Wilson, who lived in Cedarville, CA.

DIVER Alva E.

Private, Co. M, 363rd Infantry Regiment, 91st Division
KIA 31 October 1918
Plot A – Row 04 – Grave 21
Army Serial Number 2784431

Alva Edison Diver was the son of George Diver and Sarah Foglesong (photo insert) from Logansport, IN. He was born on 3 December 1888 and lived most of his life in Logansport where he found a job as an ice cream mixer. He also had three sisters, Sylvah (Sarah's daughter from a previous marriage to a James Devlin), Florence and Mary Anna, and two brothers, Levi and Herbert. In the Spring of 1917 he moved west and became a fruit farmer in Wenatchee, WA.

He enlisted on 30 April 1918. He received his basic training at Camp Lewis and was assigned to the 8th Battalion, 166th Depot Brigade. At the end of his training he wrote a letter home to his mother informing her how pleased he was that his unit was traveling via Canada to the east coast to finally make the crossing to Europe. He described his daily activities in which it became evident that their Canadian venture was mainly a publicity stunt. Parades were held everywhere and everyone was enthusiastic. They finally embarked for Europe on 20 June.

Alva wrote another letter to his mother on 2 August. He described the crossing: the sea was calm and he slept on the deck (*"safety first"*) and *"the moonlight was glistening on the water making it very pretty"*. An Italian quartet would sing until late at night making it a pleasant voyage. Upon arrival in France, he was surprised to see well dressed and well educated people and on the other hand the old fashioned way agricultural laborers worked on the land. He must have loved horses as most of the letter was explaining how the horses were used by the farmers, totally different than in the U.S.A. He also made references to Holland and continues: *"I'm sitting on the bank of a small river and it is so difficult to comprehend that a short distance away there's a war on. And yet it's true. I sure hope I can do my part before it is all over."* He concluded his letter asking that they keep all the newspapers so that, upon his return, he could show them all the places he had been.

In his letter of 26 August he mentioned receiving lots of mail but nothing from home. He promised he would send some gifts to his mother and sisters and mentioned how he had helped an old lady with her cart and how she, in gratitude, kissed his hand : *"quite contrary to the way they do in the States"*. He admired the courage of the French and their zest for work: *"a person can see what kind of people have backed up France in this big struggle, much similar to our hardy pioneers."*

Alva wrote many wonderful letters. It was evident that he was passionate about the safety of fellow human beings and that he also loved nature.

During the first day of the attack near Waregem, he was part of a 13 man detail who had halted at a farmhouse to inquire where the Germans were located. The day after, said farmer found five American bodies between even more dead Germans and buried them. The five American soldiers were George Bulaich, Orlindo Giunchi, Edward Smith, Jessie Silcox (later classified as unidentified) and Alva (official cause of death: gunshot wound).

They are all interred in plot A, row 4, with the exception of Jessie Silcox, who strangely enough is memorialized on the Wall of the Missing.

The devastating news of Alva's death nearly proved fatal to his mother. That was the main reason why she made the decision not to have his remains repatriated to the U.S.A. She wished she could have joined the 1930 Gold Star Mothers Pilgrimage to Flanders Field Cemetery, but she was too fragile. She was 76 years of age and practically blind.

Alva with horse and cart

SCELZO Anthony – Silver Star
Private, Co. I, 106th Infantry Regiment, 27th Division
KIA 2 September 1918
Plot A – Row 04 – Grave 22
Army Serial Number 1208414

Anthony (Antonio) Scelzo was born in May 1898 in Castellamare di Stabia, Napoli province, Italy. On 24 April 1917, shortly after the U.S. declaration of war, he volunteered with the New York National Guard in Brooklyn (14th Infantry Regiment). At that time he was still living at home with his parents Frank and Matilda (née Trevisan).

He received a Divisional Citation (see also Di Giacomo A-1-21) for his acts of courage and self-sacrifice. The advance of his platoon was delayed by enfilade machinegun fire. Anthony left his shelter, which was located near Vierstraat, in an attempt to silence the machineguns. He was killed during this action. His body was not found until a farmer stumbled across skeletal remains while ploughing his field. Between the skeletal remains a religious medallion was also found. Identification was difficult as no skull or major bone fragments were found. It is not clear how a positive identification was finally made. The religious medallion could have been the link, ultimately confirmed by his parents, which provided the evidence of his identity.

KNOWN BUT TO GOD
Plot A - Row 04 – Grave 23

A - 04 - 01 and A - 04 - 23 are unknown of the Jewish faith.

PLOT B

KLINGENSMITH Russell
Private, HQ Co. 145th Infantry Regiment, 37th Division
DOW 1 November 1918
Plot B – Row 01 – Grave 01
Army Serial Number 1519716

Russell Klingensmith was the son of Isaac and Mary Alice Klingensmith (née Hare). His ancestors emigrated to America as early as 1738. He was born in March 1898 as only son in a family of ten children. His sisters were Olive, Louise, Mary, Katherine, Beatrice, Elisabeth, Lenor, Adela and Phyllis. He was taken care of by his sister Louise as their mother was paralytic and unable to take care of routine domestic tasks. His father died in 1910 followed by his mother in 1912.

Russel died of wounds sustained in action on the first day of the advance and was buried in the village of Dentergem. During the permanent reburial procedure at Flanders Field

in March 1921, it was found that Russel was buried under the marker of Alex Henley (in Plot C, grave 118). There could be no mistake about his true identity as a bottle record was found with his remains.

Louise was granted permission by the government to join the Gold Star Mothers Pilgrimage. She departed with party H on the SS Roosevelt on 24 June 1931. She visited her brother's grave on 7, 8 and 9 July.

Photo insert left: Russell's original marker in 1919.

BALL Clayton O.

Corporal, Co. L, 145th Infantry Regiment, 37th Division
KIA 2 November 1918
Plot B – Row 01 – Grave 02
Army Serial number 1519664

Clayton Owen Ball was born in Albion, Erie, PA on 13 August 1888. He was the son of George Francis Ball (1861-1937) and Kitt Alzina Bush (1864-1920). They had five other sons: Levi Amos (°1884), William Henry (°1886), Kenneth Willard (°1894), Ralph Milton (°1897) and finally Bert Franklin (°1906).

The exact date when Clayton joined the forces is unknown, but it was evident that he was receiving basic training by the end of 1917. There is a letter to his mother dated November 1917 where he is grateful for her keeping in contact. He also wrote that he was feeling better, however: *"I am having difficulties, not only physically but also financially. I can hardly afford anything because I bought two liberty loans"*. In another letter dated April 1918 he describes his training in the trenches.

Corporal Clayton Owen Ball was killed near the village of Kruishoutem on 2 November; he was the victim of friendly fire. The VFW Post in Albion, PA is named after him and they placed a replica of his original headstone in Hope cemetery between his mother's and father's headstone.

ROSS Karl E. - D.S.C.
Sergeant, MG Co. 363rd Infantry Regiment, 91st Division
KIA 31 October 1918
Plot B – Row 01 – Grave 03
Army Serial Number 2262839

Karl Erskine Ross was born in Petaluma, CA on 27 June 1894. He was the youngest son of David and Carrie May Wilbur Ross. His three brothers were Arthur, Neil and Tindel Alan. Karl Ross was known as a man of many talents. Before he was called to arms he was working as office manager for the Shell Oil Company in Stockton, CA.

He was called to arms on 9 September 1917 and assigned to the Machine Gun Company of the 363rd Infantry Regiment, 91st Wild West Division. He became the best marksman of his company. In a letter to his brother Neil (26 October) he described the scenes and fighting at the Meuse-Argonne front. He also mentioned that he had been wounded on 5 October and in the confusion which followed lost his wallet, valuables and dog tags. The seriousness of his injuries warranted him some time behind the lines but he refused. For this act of courage he was promoted to Sergeant. Joking with his friends he would say that there was no German bullet with his name on it, however on a more serious note, he also expressed his worries about his mother. In his last letter home he mentioned that where he was now (Waregem), there was hardly any damage to buildings in the area.

He was killed in Waregem during the attack of 31 October as he encountered severe enfilade machine gun fire from five different directions. With his machine gun and standing in an upright position he disengaged one German machinegun nest. He was killed while attempting to disengage a second machinegun nest sheltered in a building. Five other members of his unit were also killed during this action. For his exceptional courage and perseverance in action he was awarded the Distinguished Service Cross. The official citation for his DSC is the following:

"For extraordinary heroism near Waereghem, Belgium, October 31st 1918. At a distance of less than 200 meters from the enemy, he set up and directed the fire of his guns, exposed during the whole operations to direct enemy fire. He killed one gunner and, while searching for the gun on his flank, was himself killed."

The following eyewitness accounts were provided by John Quinn and Eugene Fitzsimmons, his friends at the Anteros Club, where he was a member. The letter clearly describes the details on how Karl Ross was killed.

Watou, Belgium, Dec. 27, 1918

Gentlemen,

We feel that it is only our duty as friends and comrades to inform you of the death of one of your members, Karl E. Ross, who paid the supreme sacrifice of laying down his life for his country. The departure of this brave comrade fills us with sorrow, but at the same time he has left with us a memory that we treasure with pride.

Being, as we were, pals of his, we wish to let you know how Karl met his death. On September 26, 1918, our division the 91st made its initial trip "over the top". This was in the Argonne woods in France. Karl was one of the machine gunners when we went into action. Let us state here, through the commanding officer's own words, that Karl was beyond a doubt far superior to the average machine gunner, which in itself is an asset to be proud of. Through this bravery and good judgment during those ten days of hell, Karl was promoted to the rank of sergeant.

On October 31st we again went over the top – this time at Waereghem, Belgium. On this trip Karl was a leader of a section – and a leader to be proud of to. We went over the top at 5:30 a.m. and immediately we were confronted by heavy direct machine gun and sniper's fire. Karl, without hesitation, had one of his guns set up in the open near the enemy's wire. Instantly he was a target for two German machineguns – one directly in front and one on the right flank. This perilous position did not daunt Karl's courage. He directed the fire of his gun standing up. He killed the German gunner in front, and while searching for the gun on the flank he himself was struck by an enemy bullet and died almost instantaneously. He received a soldier's burial by the regimental chaplain in the vicinity of Waereghem, Belgium.

Although he has departed from our rank in person, he will ever remain present in our memories.

In conclusion we offer our humble condolence to all of Karl's relatives and friends.

Sincerely yours
John J. Quinn
Eugene S. Fitzsimmons
363rd Inf. M.G. Co., Amer. E.F.

There was a postscript to the letter by his platoon leader.

Postscript to above letter by censor:
As sergeant Ross' platoon leader at Waereghem, I would like his friends to know that his work there was all the above and more, too. I never saw a braver stunt than that duel of the two Huns against one of ours at less than 150 yards. Ross won the scrap but lost his life. I recommended him for the D.S.C. and sincerely hope he will get it, for no man was ever more entitled to it than our friend.
Sincerely
1st LT. JAS. BOYD JR. - O.K. Censored

Karl Ross left a fiancée behind. After the war the San Joaquin American Legion Post was named after him.

SCHAIRER James V. - D.S.C. - Croix de Guerre (F)
Private, Med. Det. 147th Infantry Regiment, 37th Division
KIA 30 October 1918
Plot B – Row 01 – Grave 04
Army Serial Number 1543536

 Private James (Jimmy) Vincent Schairer was born in Benton Harbor, MI on 14 August 1894. He was the youngest of ten (Dora, George, John Jr, Carrie, Joe, Jennie, Olive, Elizabeth, Anna and James). His parents were John and Olive Herman Schairer. Before he was sent to Europe he was working as a clerk for his brother George who was owner of a cigar factory. He was loved and appreciated by all. On 24 July 1917 he volunteered with the National Guard in Toledo, Ohio (6th Infantry Regiment) where he resided at the time. After his basic training at Camp Sheridan, AL, James was assigned to the Medical Detachment of the 147th Infantry Regiment.

In a letter home dated 26 October he wrote that all was well. On 30 October, the shelter where he and his unit were located received a direct hit. James was severely wounded (fractured skull). He was taken to a field hospital but succumbed to his wounds the same day. He was buried with full military honors in the village of Dentergem.

For his exceptional courage and self-sacrifice, James Schairer was awarded the Distinguished Service Cross and French *Croix de Guerre* for actions carried out on 26 September 1918 during the Meuse-Argonne offensive near Montfaucon: " *Seeing two men fall wounded, Pvt. Schairer immediately went to their assistance, unmindful of the extreme danger that he was exposed to and after dragging the men to a shell hole administered effective first aid.*"
The *Croix de Guerre* is not inscribed on his headstone. It is assumed that at the time they

were working on the permanent outline and landscaping of the cemetery that the American authorities were not aware of his foreign award.

In February 1919, a film real by *Pathé News* was run in a theatre where his family recognized a laughing James during a pillow fight in a Red Cross hospital a few months before his death.

At the family gravesite of his parents and sister, a star has been added in memory of James.

At the Crystal Springs Cemetery in Benton Harbor, the James V. Schairer Circle was inaugurated in November 1934. This cemetery is dedicated to all those who died in foreign wars. A monument with memorial plaque (donated by his brothers and sisters) and a British 5-inch artillery piece dominate the circle as a major focal point. The Veterans of Foreign Wars Post in Benton Harbor was named after him.

Memorial plaque donated by his brothers and sisters.

no photograph available

ZAISS Adolph O.

Private, Co. I, 363rd Infantry Regiment, 91st Division
KIA 31 October 1918
Plot B – Row 01 – Grave 05
Army Serial Number 2779786

Adolph Otto Zaiss was born in Denver, CO on 16 November 1887. He was the son of Christian Zaiss and Franzisca Yele, both German immigrants. Christian and Franzisca were blessed with fourteen children of which by 1910 only eight survived. Five sons (Adolph, Fred, Otto, Jacob, George) and two daughters (Sophie and Lulu); the gender and name of the eighth child is unknown. Christian was a brewer. He died in 1908. Franzisca later remarried with John Decker. Adolph also had two half-brothers (John and Charles Decker) and one half-sister (Olga Decker). Adolph was married to Bertha Estella Haak in Denver, CO on 30 August 1908. When he was called to register for the draft in 1917 he lived in Colton, CA where he worked as a car inspector for the Southern Pacific Railway Company. He was called to arms and sent to Camp Lewis for his basic training. His brother George was also called to arms.

Adolph was killed in Waregem during the first minutes of the attack. Before sunrise (05:40) his unit made a rapid advance and was caught by enemy enfilade machinegun fire. He was killed instantly. As it was still dark, no one had noticed Adolph being hit. He was buried in a field close to a pond SW of Waregem (American Cemetery #1 Waregem, Grave 8).

MOHLER Allen L.

Private, Co. L, 362nd Infantry Regiment, 91st Division
KIA 31 October 1918
Plot B – Row 01 – Grave 06
Army Serial Number 3526588

Allen Leonard Mohler was born in Middle Point, OH on 23 November 1895. He was the son of Allen Mohler and Lois Annetta Sites, of farming stock with six sons and one daughter. Charles David (°1882), Francis Irvin (°1883), Howard Luther (°1886), William Everitt (°1890), Jonas Ernest (°1894), Allen Leonard(°1895) and Myrtle Lois (°1903)). He was married to Annetta Eleanor Upp on 15 July 1918. One week later he was called to arms. He was sent to Camp Sherman, OH and received his basic training with the 158th Infantry Brigade. He was then assigned to the 336th Infantry Regiment, 84th Lincoln Division. Upon arrival in Europe the division was disbanded and the men were reassigned to the 362nd Infantry Regiment.

He was killed during his first engagement in battle near the Spitaalsbossen. On 3 November he was buried in the American Cemetery 1250 in Anzegem (grave 4) and his remains were moved to Waregem on 3 June 1919.

ADAMS Ralph W.
Private, Co. L, 148th Infantry Regiment, 37th Division
KIA 31 October 1918
Plot B – Row 01 – Grave 07
Army serial number 2943020

Ralph Winthom Adams was born in Rochester, NY on 26 November 1895. His parents, John Q. and Elizabeth Adams and their seven children resided at 324 Federal Street.

He enlisted on 30 April 1918 in Detroit, MI and was assigned to the 45th Company, 12th Battalion, 153rd Depot Brigade. Upon his own request Ralph was transferred to the 310th Infantry Regiment, 78th Division, a National Army division comprising of men from New York and the north of Pennsylvania. He received additional training at Camp Dix, Wrightsville, NJ. and subsequently transferred to the 37th Division (Company L, 148th Infantry Regiment), who were finalizing their training period at Camp Lee, Virginia. He embarked for Europe on 22 June 1918 and disembarked at Brest, France on 5 July. He served during the Meuse-Argonne offensive before being sent with his division to Belgium. During the first day of the battle near the town of Olsene, Ralph was mortally wounded and died almost instantly.

Stanford Dettmann from Langhorne, PA visited his uncle's grave on 15 April 2007.

Adams family picnic 1916 next page - Ralph back row second from left.

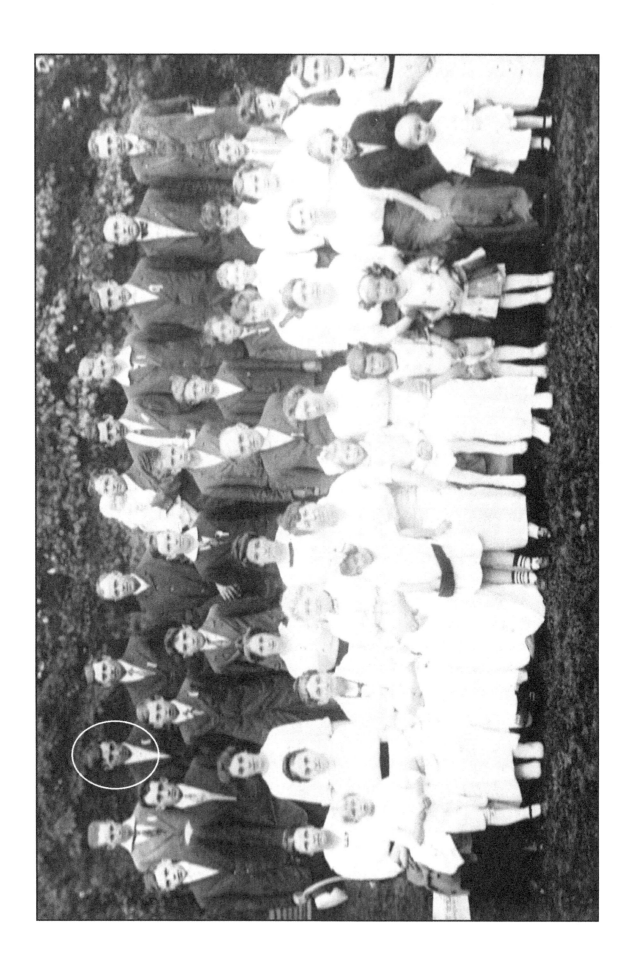

248

no photograph available

COMINA Albert

Private, Co. D, 363rd Infantry Regiment, 91st Division
DOD 20 November 1918
Plot B – Row 01 – Grave 08
Army Serial Number 2779645

Albert(o) Comina was born in Voltago, Belluno, Italy on 1 September 1894. His father, Sisto, died while still a young child so his mother, Redenta Miano, was alone to raise her children: Louis, Alberto, Teodoro and Amelia. In October 1911, at the age of seventeen, Albert emigrated to the U.S.A. He sailed from Le Havre, France, on the SS Rochambeau. His nephew and a friend, Giovanni Conedera and Abiano Casera, of same age and from the same town, accompanied him. Upon their arrival in New York they gave as final destination the Ohio Copper Company in Bingham, Utah. This mine, close to Salt Lake City, was originally a gold mine. Exploitation of copper only commenced in 1903. Albert was still working at the mine when he was called to arms on 25 April 1918. He embarked for Europe on 6 July and took part in the St. Mihiel and Meuse-Argonne campaigns.

Albert survived the hostilities of war but died of pneumonia, a common complication of the Spanish flu, nine days after the armistice. At the time of death he was still an Italian citizen.

He was first buried at the temporary American cemetery in the town of Staden and his remains were moved to Waregem on 5 June 1919. His friend, Umberto Conedera was from Rivamonte Agordino, a village close by, and is also interred at Flanders Field.

Louis (Luigi) Comina, his brother and two years his senior, worked in a mine in Arizona and was also called to arms. He served with the 28th Division. Louis was killed on 5 October after distinguishing himself during battle on 26 September. During the Meuse-Argonne offensive, close to Varennes, he volunteered together with two other men to penetrate and capture a German stronghold. Although under continuous enfilade machinegun fire, they succeeded in their mission. They killed four men and took eleven prisoners. Louis was awarded the Distinguished Service Cross. He is buried in Plot H Row 8 Grave 3 at the Meuse-Argonne American Cemetery in France (photo insert).

HENLEY Alex P.E.
Sergeant, Co M, 361st Infantry Regiment, 91st Division
KIA 3 November 1918
Plot B – Row 01 – Grave 09
Army Serial Number 2258526

Alexander Perewal Ewllen Henley was born in Lindsay, Canada on 20 September 1896. He was the son of Albert Henley and Jane (Jennie) Menzies, also both born in Canada and who emigrated to the USA in 1908. His brother, Lewis Arnold was born on 14 December 1909. Jane passed away in 1910 and Albert married Minnie in 1912. Albert died in 1915 so Minnie was left to raise Lewis as a single parent. Albert worked at a shipyard in Seattle, WA, which at that time did not have the current potential as a harbor.

Sometime later he moved to Grass Valley, OR. He was called to arms and sent to Camp Lewis for his basic training on 9 September 1917. At that time his request for U.S. citizenship was still ongoing. The photograph depicts the men of Sherman County who are waiting to entrain in Wasco, OR for Camp Lewis. (Alex is standing second from left).

Alex Henley was killed instantly by the impact of shell fragments on 3 November. He was buried in Bevere (Isolated Grave #1) along the main road to Oudenaarde. He was still a Canadian citizen at the time of death. At the time of permanent reburial, there was confusion on where his remains were interred in Cemetery #1252. They finally recovered his remains (with identification tags) under the marker of James Schairer. After the war, the Henley-Baker American Legion Post was established in Grass Valley. Minnie, aged 55, visited his grave with the Gold Star Mothers Pilgrimage in 1931.

GUTH Fred C.
Private, HQ. Co. 119th Infantry Regiment, 30th Division
KIA 31 August 1918
Plot B – Row 01 – Grave 10
Army Serial Number 1317519

Fred Clute Guth was born to a large farming family. Jacob Guth and Annie Loretta Northrup were blessed with twelve children: Mary, George, John, Emma, Gertrude, Harry, Fred, Albert, Mabel, James, Archie and Charles. Fred was born in Glenmary, TN on 12 August 1899. In the 1900 and 1910 census his father declared that he was a German immigrant. However, the 1920 census indicated he was a French immigrant. He was actually born in Haguenau in the department of the Alsace, which at the time of war was German territory and after the war returned as part of France.

Fred volunteered with the Tennessee National Guard (2nd Infantry Regiment) on 22 August 1917. He was assigned to Company H, which later became Headquarters Company of the 119th Infantry Regiment. He was accidently killed due to a malfunction of a trench mortar that he was operating during the attack.

His mother visited his grave with the Gold Star Mothers Pilgrimage in 1930. A number of articles were printed in the local newspapers describing her trip. She sailed together with 233 other mothers on the SS Roosevelt. From this group 29 were destined to visit Flanders Field. During the crossing she befriended Minnie Knaus from Minnesota whose son, Ludwig, was interred at Brookwood Military Cemetery, United Kingdom. She spoke very highly about the organization of the pilgrimage, the friendly assistance at all times and the beautiful landscapes of France and Belgium. She described her visit to the Ohio Bridge in Ename and the Menin Gate in Ypres. She was irritated by the fact that she constantly needed to change currency between France and Belgium. She was very perceptive and full of admiration for the tens of thousands of Belgian laborers who crossed the border every day to work in the factories of Northern France and the thousands of acres of sugar beet and flax, emphasizing on the abundance of beautiful flowers. It was evident that she was a very special lady.

no photograph available

McWALTERS James
Private 1st Class, Co. C, 106th Infantry Regiment, 27th Division
KIA 31 August 1918
Plot B – Row 01 – Grave 11
Army Serial Number 1206943

James McWalters was originally from Brooklyn, NY. He was the son of James and Annie McWalters, who were Irish immigrants. They also had two daughters: Helen and Kathryn.

The circumstances of his death are unknown. He was temporarily buried at the Abeele Aerodrome Military Cemetery on 3 September and his remains were reinterred at Flanders Field on 20 June 1922.

As both his parents had died in 1920, all correspondence in regards to the permanent disposition of his remains were sent to his sister Kathryn.

DE FOREST Walter – Silver Star – C.S.C.
Sergeant, Co. G, 105th Infantry Regiment, 27th Division
KIA 1 September 1918
Plot B – Row 01 – Grave 12
Army Serial Number 1204520

Walter De Forest was born in New York City on 3 August 1883. He was the son of Theodore De Forest and Charlotte Gardner Day and spent his youth living in Mahopac, NY together with his two sisters Mary and Helen and brother Edgar. He later went into partnership running a garage. He was a well-respected citizen of the community.

As a veteran of the 71st NY National Guard Regiment, he had served during the punitive campaign along the Mexican border but was later medically discharged as he was suffering from acute rheumatism. When the U.S. declared war on Germany he was readmitted regardless the fact that he failed his medical. The 71st Infantry Regiment later became part of the 27th Division.

Walter De Forest was awarded a Divisional Citation (Silver Star in 1932). He was also posthumously awarded the Conspicuous Service Cross (No.1685) on 13 January 1923.

"For exceptional courage and marked qualities of leadership in leading his platoon in an attack upon the enemy. Later after being relieved and returning to reserve under heavy shell fire, he showed extraordinary bravery and presence of mind in keeping his men in formation. He was killed by a direct hit of an enemy shell. This near Dikkebusch Lake, Belgium, August 30 to September 2, 1918."

Several men were killed during this incident. Captain Henry Maslin described how he went out to look for him and eventually found him in agony. When he asked him what he could do to help he replied: *"Make me fit to drill"*. Shortly afterwards he succumbed to his wounds. He was buried at Abeele Aerodrome Military Cemetery.

HYLAND William J.
Private, Co. G, 105th Infantry Regiment, 27th Division
KIA 2 September 1918
Plot B – Row 01 – Grave 13
Army Serial Number 1204763

William J. Hyland was the son of William Hyland and Mary Sloan. He was born in Gloversville, NY in September 1898. He had a younger sister Mary Claire and a younger brother Francis, who later became a doctor in the same town.

William joined the 2nd Infantry Regiment New York National Guard on 27 March 1917, which later became part of the 105th Infantry Regiment. He was killed during a German artillery bombardment when a shell obliterated his tent. He was buried at Lyssenthoek Military Cemetery in Poperinge.

BRINDZA Frank S.

Private 1st Class, Co. L, 105th Infantry Regiment, 27th Division
KIA 31 August 1918
Plot B – Row 01 – Grave 14
Army Serial Number 1205442

Frank Steve Brindza (°13 May 1895) was the son of William and Mary Brindza, both born in Germany. They lived with their four daughters (Annie, Fannis, Mary and Elisabeth) and a second son (William) in Astoria, NY.

Frank worked as a mechanic in New York and was engaged to L.V. Johnson. It is uncertain if he volunteered for the National Guard or if he was inducted. On 18 May 1918 he wrote a letter to his sisters while still in Camp Stuart, VA. He concluded with: *"We will end the war in no time when they ship this 27th division over. That consists of all New York troops."*

He was killed by concussion when a shell fell in his trench on 31 August. This occurred near Vierstraat. He was buried at Abeele British Cemetery near Poperinge (III.E.I).

FRANK S. BRINDZA
PVT I CL. 105 INF. 27 DIV.
NEW YORK. AUG. 31 1918

QUIGLEY Arthur
Private, Co. M, 106th Infantry Regiment, 27th Division
KIA 7 September 1918
Plot B – Row 01 – Grave 15
Army Serial Number 1209091

Arthur Quigley was born on 3 October 1899 and spent his youth in Brooklyn, NY. His parents were Irish immigrants and he had two brothers (Joseph and Patrick) and two sisters (Mrs. William Delehanty and Mrs. Frederick Douglas). He joined the local National Guard (23rd Infantry Regiment) on 6 September 1917.

He was originally interred at Abeele Aerodrome Military Cemetery. Due to health issues his mother, Mary, decided not to take part with the Gold Star Mothers Pilgrimage.

HARVEY Alfred R.
1st Lieutenant, Co. F, 120th Infantry Regiment, 30th Division
KIA 22 August 1918
Plot B – Row 01 – Grave 16

Alfred Rorer (Tub) Harvey was the son of Lewis Harvey (photo insert right) and Bettie Trollinger from Radford, VA. He was born in Pulaski County, VA on 15 August 1893. He was an example to all the young men of Radford: polite, friendly, never sarcastic or pretentious, etc. Alfred attended the State University in Blacksburg and graduated as a civil engineer at the Virginia Polytechnic Institute (now Virginia Tech) in 1915.

He joined the Virginia National Guard on 14 September 1914. In June 1916 he was sent with the 2nd Infantry Regiment to the Mexican border as a result of the of the riots caused by the uprising of Pancho Villa. They returned in February 1917. After the U.S. declaration of war, he received orders to train new recruits. "*Tub*", as he was called, was more ambitious and applied for officer's training. He was commissioned as 1st Lieutenant on 9 July 1918 and assigned to the 120th Infantry Regiment. He also had two brothers, Mack and Robert, who were serving their country. A younger brother (Henry) was still at home.

Alfred was shot in the head by a German sniper during a night patrol in no man's land. Also with him that night was a certain Richard Evelyn Byrd, who later was better known as Admiral Byrd. He was the first to fly over the North Pole in 1926 and consequently lead the first American expedition (since 1840) to Antarctica.

Alfred was first buried at Nine Elms British Military Cemetery. His mother wore black garments for the rest of her life and she had a memorial marker erected in memory of her son in Westview Cemetery, Radford, VA, which to this day is still there. On 3 September 1919, the Harvey-Howe American Legion Post was established in Radford.

On 22 August 2008, James Bertelson, great-nephew from, France visited his great-uncle's grave.

no photograph available

DE MARCO Louis P.
Private, Co. L, 105th Infantry Regiment, 27th Division
KIA 31 August 1918
Plot B – Row 01 – Grave 17
Army Serial Number 2671340

Louis P. De Marco was born in Salerno, Italy on 12 January 1890. He was married to Rose Manzo and had three daughters: Ida, Nancy and Carmella. His father was deceased and his mother and sisters lived in Italy. His draft registration card indicates that he was a New York City employee (Sweeper Dept. - street cleanup).

He was first interred at Abeele Aerodrome Military Cemetery. Rose would have joined the Gold Star Mothers Pilgrimage but unfortunately she had no one to take care of her children.

McGRATH Joseph H.
Private 1st Class, Co. D, 105th Infantry Regiment, 27th Division
KIA 24 August 1918
Plot B – Row 01 – Grave 18
Army Serial Number 1204059

Joseph McGrath lived in Troy, NY with his brother and sister. He was 5 foot 7 inches tall and had brown hair and grey eyes. His occupation was box maker at the time he enlisted with the 2nd Infantry Regiment New York National Guard on 23 June 1916 and consequently served during the punitive campaign along the Mexican border as of 1 July 1916.

He was 24 years of age when he was killed near Dikkebus. A shell fragment had lodged in the left side of his skull. He was interred at Abeele Aerodrome Military Cemetery.

His emergency address was with his sister Mary Courchaine in Troy.

CLEAR Francis J.
Private, Co. K, 105th Infantry Regiment, 27th Division
KIA 1 September 1918
Plot B – Row 01 – Grave 19
Army Serial Number 1205284

Francis Clear lived in Glenn Falls, Warren County, NY. He was born at Lake Luzerne in February 1897. His parents were Patrick G. Clear and Mary Agnes Champagne. The family was additionally blessed with Therese, Catherine, James, Rachel, John, Maurice, Edward, Thomas and Bernard.

In 1917, together with his two year younger brother Maurice (photo insert), he joined the 2nd Infantry Regiment New York National Guard. Both young men were High School students and first class baseball players. When the 27th Division was formed, the 2nd Infantry Regiment became the 105th Infantry Regiment. Francis, being an experienced baseball player became a runner. They arrived in France at the end of May. On 1 September, during the battle for Mount Kemmel, Francis

was hit by a shell fragment and killed instantly. He was buried at Abeele Aerodrome Military Cemetery the following day. Maurice had been shot in the arm by a sniper two days earlier. On his way to an aid station he was wounded again in the leg by shell fragments. He was then shipped to England for treatment. Maurice received his Purple Heart in 1986. He passed away in 1988. He had always dreamed to visit his brother's grave at Flanders Field but never made it.

no photograph available

McMAHON Walter F.

Private, Co. L, 107th Infantry Regiment, 27th Division
KIA 22 August 1918
Plot B – Row 01 – Grave 20
Army Serial Number 2671975

Walter McMahon, was born in Chelsea, MA on 17 June 1888 and lived in New York City. He was the son of John and Abby McMahon residing in Newtonville, MA and he also had two elder brothers (Joseph and John Jr.-who died young) and a younger brother Harold. He was a born artist and earned his living with his hobby. He worked for a company where he could draw and paint until his heart was content. He was called to arms on 5 April 1918 and attached to the 107th Infantry Regiment during the last period of its training at Camp Wadsworth. His friends claimed that one could always count on him whatever the circumstances.

"Walt" was killed by a German sniper on 22 August while performing his duties at an observation post near Dikkebus Lake. He was buried at Abeele Aerodrome Military Cemetery.

TODD Theodore W. – Silver Star

1st Sergeant, Co. L, 107th Infantry Regiment, 27th Division
KIA 22 August 1918
Plot B – Row 01 – Grave 21
Army Serial Number 1211828

Theodore Wallace Todd was born in Bedford Park, NY on 5 February 1889. He was the son of Perry and Margaret Todd. The family were proprietors of the Todd Salt Company, at the time one of the oldest businesses in New York. According to Stephen Harris' *Duty, Honor, Privilege* (published by Brassey's Inc. 2006), the Todd's were related to Teddy Roosevelt. Eleanor Roosevelt visited Todd's

grave at Flanders Field during her tenure as Commissioner A.B.M.C. in 1953 and 1956.

Theodore joined the 7th Infantry Regiment of the New York National Guard on 21 December 1915 and was promoted to Sergeant on 24 January 1916. In 1916 and 1917 he served along the Mexican border. He married Margaret Burr on 30 May 1917 and was promoted to 1st Sergeant on 30 July 1918.

In a letter from him dated 9 August 1918, he said: " *What you say about the unity of nations is no more clearly shown than the spirit exhibited among the soldiers I have met from all parts of the world. It is very gratifying to know that our people and nation in general are giving us their support as we are the human breakwater which harbors the peace of our homes."*

Theodore Todd received a Divisional Citation *: "For qualities of leadership, courage, and determination. This gallant soldier was killed in action while defending his post against an enemy raid. This in the vicinity of Mount Kemmel, Belgium, August 22, 1918."* He was killed by a mortar shell while he and Captain Nicoll were trying to reorganize their men after the Germans had succeeded in breaking through their lines. Everyone was aware that Theodore had been killed but after the battle they could not find his remains. A man from his company requested permission to search no man's land during broad daylight. His remains were found and recovered by a patrol that same night. He was admired and respected by all for his exceptional qualities in leadership. He was buried at Abeele Aerodrome Military Cemetery. His father replied on the preference of repatriation or not: *"prefer buried with his comrades".* There was an error in rank on his original marker. This was corrected upon his parents request.

Theodore was the youngest of five children. However, with the exception of Theodore, all died very young. His parents were informed of Theodore's death in a letter sent by his best friend Sergeant Breusch. The official government telegram arrived days later. Sergeant Breusch later named his son Theodore Todd Breusch and consequently his son repeated the act of honor.

His parents and widow sailed for Europe and visited his grave in 1923. His mother returned with the Gold Star Mothers Pilgrimage and visited his grave on 7, 8 and 9 July 1931. Margaret had since remarried and so had become ineligible for the trip.

Theodore's original marker at Cemetery #1252 and Memorial Plaque at Mount Hebron cemetery, Upper Montclair, Essex County, New Jersey.

BISSETT Wiley Clifton
1st Lieutenant, Co. D, 119th Infantry Regiment, 30th Division
KIA 18 July 1918
Plot B – Row 01 – Grave 22

Wiley Clifton Bissett was born in Wilson County, NC on 5 February 1896. He was the second of six children (Charles Thomas, Wiley, Gladys Mae, Frank, Herbert and Jesse Lawrence) of Charles Harris Bissett and Lucinda Batts. The family described Clifton (as he was called) as an adventurous, intelligent, lovable and romantic young man.

After his graduation Wiley moved to New Bern, NC, where he first worked in a cigar store and later for an insurance company. It was in New Bern that he met Christine Thomas.

By 1913 he had already joined the North Carolina National Guard and in 1916 he was sent to the Mexican border for a period of six months. Serving with Co. K, 2nd North Carolina Infantry Regiment, he was promoted to Sergeant. Upon their return they were sent to Camp Sevier, SC, for additional training. In September 1917 the 2nd North Carolina Infantry Regiment became the 119th Infantry Regiment of the 30th Division. At that time the regiment comprised of about 1,800 men from North Carolina, 900 from Tennessee and 700 from other States. Wiley was promoted to 2nd Lieutenant on 27 December.

In the Spring of 1918 he was granted leave. He rushed back to New Bern where he married Christine Thomas on 13 April. When he returned to Camp Sevier, he was promoted to 1st Lieutenant and on 30 April assigned to Company D, 1st Battalion, 119th Infantry Regiment. In the meantime his older brother Thomas (photo insert) had also joined the service and was a Sergeant with Company A in the same battalion. The first men of the regiment left Camp Sevier on 8 May in preparation of the voyage to Europe. At that time Wiley had only been married four weeks.

Lieutenant Wiley Clifton Bissett was killed on 18 July 1918 (the date of 17 June on his marker is a clerical error) at 05:00 hours during a fierce battle near Voormezele. He was killed instantly when a shell exploded close by. A Private next to him was also severely wounded losing an arm. Wiley was the first officer of the 119th Infantry Regiment to be killed in action. In an official document, the regimental chaplain declared that Clifton was buried at Nine Elms British Cemetery in the village of Elverdinge on 19 July between John Huffman (C-04-08) and Robert Porcelli (B-02-11).

They were the first Americans to be buried in this cemetery. Ironically, the cemetery is close to where the unit marched by on their way to the front a few days earlier. Thomas was on sick leave from 18 through 22 July but was able to attend the funeral. On 23 July he wrote a letter home informing that "*Clifton*" died in hospital and was buried the following Friday.

After Christine was notified of Wiley's death, she stayed with his parents for a few days, left and then never returned. She later claimed and received his war insurance. At first, she had requested that Wiley's remains be repatriated and returned to his parents in Wilson. However, in January 1921 she informed the military authorities that she had changed her mind. Wiley would remain in Flanders Field. Wiley's parents were devastated and did everything in their power to reverse the decision. However they were told that the widow's wishes were final. Christine remarried in 1922 and moved to Virginia. As such she became ineligible to take part in the Gold Star Mothers Pilgrimage although she did intend to. Wiley's mother never replied to the invitation to visit Flanders Field. She died in 1969 at the age of 99.

In January 2009, Wiley did finally receive a visit. His great-niece Lou An Cozart from North Carolina visited his grave accompanied by her husband.

NOONAN John E.
Private, Co. B, 107th Infantry Regiment, 27th Division
DOW 13 August 1918
Plot B – Row 01 – Grave 23
Army Serial Number 1210010

John Noonan was born in Kingston, NY. He was the son of Dominick and Mary Noonan. He had three brothers (Francis, Thomas and Edward) and four sisters (Mary, Agnes, Helen and Jeanette). Shortly after the U.S. declaration of war he joined the 10th Infantry Regiment New York National Guard. He apparently lied about his age claiming that he was 19 at time of enlistment. He was actually only sixteen when he joined the service. If this is true then he is one of the youngest soldiers buried in the cemetery, not even 18 years of age.

On 15 June he wrote a letter to his aunt Mary Noonan Brennan saying he was feeling good. He also wrote that he was safe and that there was absolutely no reason to worry: *"I am as safe here as I ever was"*. He described the nightly air raids and how they all stood and looked up to the sky.

He died of wounds sustained in action and was originally buried at the Abeele Aerodrome Military Cemetery.

Mary, although only 55, declined the invitation to the Gold Star Mothers Pilgrimage due to ill health. The main reason however was that her husband Dominick had suffered a stroke and had become permanently disabled.

On Memorial Day 2008, Constance Brennan Barone visited her great uncle's grave.

no photograph available

JOHNSON George H.
Corporal, Co. I, 363rd Infantry Regiment, 91st Division
KIA 31 October 1918
Plot B – Row 02 – Grave 01
Army Serial Number 2264661

George Henry Johnson was born in Oakland, CA on 22 September 1894. He was the son of William Johnson (a Norwegian immigrant) and Christine Matson. He had three older sisters: Alhilda (°1889), Clara (°1891) and May (°1893). George spent his whole life in Oakland living with his sister May and working at the Chevrolet automobile plant. He was called to arms on 1 September 1917.

George H. Johnson was killed in Waregem on 31 October at the beginning of the offensive at 07:30 hours. He was killed by machine gun fire: one bullet shattered his knee, another hit him in the stomach. He died of his wounds shortly afterwards. He was buried where he fell along the road in "Isolated Grave #5".

TOGSTAD Theodore
Private, Co. L, 362nd Infantry Regiment, 91st Division
KIA 31 October 1918
Plot B – Row 02 – Grave 02
Army Serial Number 2786757

Andrew (Andres) Togstad and Oline Larson (photo next page) emigrated to the U.S.A. from Norway and made their home in Pelican Rapids, MN. Theodore was born there on 31 December 1891. In search of options for independent farming they moved west and settled in Viking Township which was located about 4 miles north of Maddock, ND. It was a large family blessed with fourteen children: Severin, Lars (died in infancy), Elise, Lars (again), Anton, Christ, Lina, Annie, Andrew, Melvin, Theodore, David, Edwin and Ludvig. Oline was a fantastic hardworking lady. Not only bearing fourteen children of her own, she was also the local midwife in an area where no doctors were available for miles. It is estimated she helped over 300 mothers deliver their babies.

Theodore was called to arms on 24 May 1918 and received his basic training in Minnewaukan, ND. He received additional training with the 91st Division in Camp Lewis, WA and embarked for Europe on 6 July. He was killed by machinegun fire around 9 a.m. on 31 October. This happened close to Steenbrugge near the town of Anzegem while crossing a small stream during the advance. He was shot between the eyes and was killed instantly.

Edwin, Lars and Melvin were also serving in Europe. Lars was assigned to Co. K of the 362nd Regiment and was wounded on 29 September during the Meuse-Argonne offensive. As such he was unable to join his brother in Flanders. After the war, the American Legion Post #123 in Maddock, was named after Theodore.

From left to right: Eline, Lina and Annie.

Standing from left to right: Theodore, Edwin, David, Melvin, Ludvig.
Seated : Christ, Anton, Lars and Andrew.

The Togstad family have a generic record of serving their country. To mention only two: Norman, a son of Lars, was killed in Italy during World War II on 29 November 1943. He is interred at Sicily-Rome American Cemetery (Plot G Row 4 Grave 43). A great nephew of Theodore and grandson of Lars, Norman Williams, was killed in Vietnam in 1967.

STECH James M.

Private, Co. K, 148th Infantry Regiment, 37th Division
KIA 31 October 1918
Plot B – Row 02 – Grave 03
Army Serial Number 3746395

James (Jim) Michael Stech was the son of Joseph Stech and Catherine Plotz from Berwyn, IL. They had emigrated from Bohemia in 1882 and had five children: Joseph, James (°15 October 1895), Anna, George and Mary (photo: Catherine with her other four children). Joseph was a tailor and his daughters later followed in his footsteps and continued the profession. When James was called to register for the draft in 1917, he was living in Beaver Dam, WI, the city where Orine Trafka also originated from. He was sent to Camp Grant, IL for basic training and assigned to the 344th Infantry Regiment, 84th Black Hawk Division. From Camp Grant he wrote many letters to his mother in Bohemian, providing details of his training and living conditions in the camp.

Upon arrival in Europe he was assigned to the 148th Infantry Regiment. He was a passionate writer and wrote many letters home. On 17 October he wrote: " *We returned from the front yesterday to get some rest. We lost only a few men. The Germans were afraid of us and so we were able to advance every day. On the first day we advanced 17 miles and the following days we were always moving forward. I think that the war will be over soon and we'll be returning back to America in January.*" His last letter was dated 27 October, four days before being killed in Kruishoutem. "*I'm in good health and I hope that you too are all healthy. I like Belgium much better than France. It's very nice here and the soil is good for farming. When I get paid I think I'll be able to send you $ 50 so that you can buy coal for the winter. I wish I could tell you about everything I've seen here but I'm not allowed. I'll tell you all about it when the war is over. I have to finish my letter, I'm running out of time. Look after yourselves and write often. I haven't received any mail from you yet but I know it takes a long time to get here. Give my regards to my brothers and sisters. Your son Jim.........*" James was killed at 13:00 hours on 31 October while on a patrol in the trenches. He was buried at the top of Kruishoutem heights. His parents continued writing to him: the last letter being 3 December, more than a month after he was killed. Sometime later all their letters were returned stating "*verified deceased*".

Even after the armistice, communications were unreliable and slow. How great their joy must have been when they heard that the war was over, James was coming home. How even greater was their grief when they received the sad news.

James' mortal remains were reinterred in Waregem, plot C, grave 76 on 7 June 1919. His mother visited her son's grave at Flanders Field Cemetery on 7,8 and 9 July during the Gold Star Mothers Pilgrimage in 1931. She still only spoke Bohemian.

Gold Star Mothers at the French Army Monument, Compiègne near Paris.
Catherine is the 5th from right.

The grave of James Stech on Cemetery #1252.

ADMIRE Roger C.

Private, Co. G, 362nd Infantry Regiment, 91st Division
KIA 31 October 1918
Plot B – Row 02 – Grave 04
Army serial number 3444338

Roger Clay Admire was born in Chain of Rocks, MO on 28 March 1892. He was the son of Thomas Franklin Admire (left) and Jane (Jennie) Woodson. They had two other children: Ethel and Roy. Their fourth child (Ruby) died in 1900 at the age of four. Roger spent his youth in Ethlyn, MO. The family moved to St. Louis around 1910 and resided at 1342 Belt Avenue. (photo right insert: Roger as child)

Roger was drafted in St. Louis on 15 June 1918. He completed his boot camp with the School of Mines Training Detachment. He was later assigned to Co. B, 335th Infantry regiment, 84th (Lincoln) Division. This was a National Army Division mainly comprising of men from Illinois, Indiana and Kentucky. Shortly after their arrival in France (4 September 1918) the division was disbanded in Le Mans (F) and the men were reassigned to other divisions. Roger was assigned to Co. G of the 362nd Infantry Regiment, 91st Division.

He was killed on 31 October 1918, the first day of the attack around Waregem. He was hit by a shell at approximately half a mile west of Steenbrugge (Anzegem) and was buried on 3 November. He now rests in Plot B - Row 4 - Grave 2. Ill health prevented his mother joining one of the Gold Star Mothers Pilgrimages.

Photo next page: Roger with his sister Ethel.

BEDELL John C.
Private, Co. H, 106th Infantry Regiment, 27th Division
KIA 21 August 1918
Plot B – Row 02 – Grave 05
Army Serial Number 1208104

John C. Bedell was born in 1897 and joined the 14th Infantry Regiment New York National Guard in Brooklyn on 24 July 1917. This regiment together with the 23rd Infantry Regiment formed the base of the 106th Infantry Regiment, 27th Division.

John sailed for Europe on 10 May 1918. He was killed in action at the age of 21 and initially buried at Nine Elms British Cemetery in Poperinge. His emergency address was registered with his mother Mrs. Mabel Bedell, 185 Seventh Avenue, Brooklyn.

SPEAR George W.
Private 1st Class, Co C, 119th Infantry Regt., 30th Division
KIA 20 August 1918
Plot B – Row 02 – Grave 06
Army Serial Number 1317659

George Washington Spear was born in Clemmons, NC on 1 May 1894. He was the son of William Spear(s) and Rebecca Sheets. William and Rebecca had two other children: John and Rosa. George worked on the family farm.

George was assigned to the National Guard division from his home State. On 6 April 1918 he was requested to report to Winston-Salem, NC. After his basic training he was assigned to the 119th Infantry Regiment. On 7 August he was promoted to Private 1st Class. When he was sent to Europe, one of his treasured possessions was a bible. On the first page he had written: *"If anything should happen to me, return this bible to my mother."* This bible is now in the possession of a granddaughter of his brother John: Peggy Riddle. George has a memorial marker in the Lawrence Joel Memorial Coliseum in Winston-Salem (photo insert).

no photograph available

LOGAN William C.
Private, Co. E, 119th Infantry Regiment, 30th Division
KIA 26 July 1918
Plot B – Row 02 – Grave 07
Army Serial Number 1315579

William Claude Logan was born in Leipers Fork, TN on 8 January 1899. His parents, Willam Vance and Mary J. Logan, were farmers and had five more sons: George, Raymond, Frank, Thomas and Harvey.

He reported to the 2nd Infantry Regiment Tennessee National Guard in Nashville on 8 September 1917. He lied about his age claiming that he was 20. He received his basic training with the 65th Depot Brigade in Camp Sevier, SC.

On 26 July, only having been in the front line one day, Paul was part of a reconnaissance mission to locate enemy machinegun nests. He was killed instantly together with Sergeant Coleman McGraw, Private Leslie Stillman and Private Paul Stallings (Plot B – Row 02 - Grave 12) when an artillery shell fell close by. He and his comrades in arms were buried at Nine Elms British Cemetery in Poperinge. These men were the first of the division to be killed in action. William is one of the youngest men to be buried at Flanders Field.

ROSS Wendell A.
Private, Co. M, 119th Infantry Regiment, 30th Division
KIA 4 August 1918
Plot B – Row 02 – Grave 08
Army Serial Number 2161097

Wendell Alexander (Archie) Ross was born in Bellingham, MN on 21 February 1894. His parents were John (Canadian immigrant) and Margaret Bell Ross. He spent his youth on the family farm in Agassiz, MN and had four brothers: John Jr. (1892) Kenneth (1898) Guy (1901) Robert (1905) and three sisters Blanch (1891), Zella (1896) and Alta (1903). He was a respected and intelligent young man. In 1914 he moved to Appleton and sometime later married Bertha Olson. They had one son which he only saw a few times. Wendell Archie Ross Jr. who was born on 18 April 1918.

274

Wendell was called to arms in Benson, MN on 26 February 1918. After his training period in Camp Dodge, IA he was assigned to the 352nd Infantry Regiment, 88th Cloverleaf Division. Before this division was sent to Europe, Wendell was transferred to the 119th Infantry Regiment.

He was killed by a shell near Elzenwalle (Kemmel-Voormezele) on 4 August. According to an eyewitness account, he was killed instantly and never knew what hit him. He was the first man of his company to be killed and was buried in the British Nine Elms Cemetery in Poperinge (Cemetery 324) at XII.B.XIII on 6 August. This cemetery was located close to a field hospital where Wendell was initially taken.

Bertha remarried one year later. Wendell Jr. was raised by one of his father's aunts and uncle.

In reply to the letter of 2 October 1920 in regards to the permanent disposition of the remains of her late husband, Bertha replied that her wish was that the remains be repatriated to the USA. However on 11 January 1921, for reasons unknown, a second request by the War Department was sent to the widow. This time she replied: *"We wish to have his remains reburied in France. Am writing on behalf of his son – Wendell Archie Ross Jr."*

And so on 16 June 1922, Wendell received his final resting place at Flanders Field American Cemetery in Waregem. In the report of disinterment and reburial it stated that *"cross over grave only means of identification"*. This is contrary to the 1918 interment record where it was confirmed that identification tag was secured to the wooden marker and the duplicate buried with the body. Details on the extensive injuries to the left side of his body were also specified. Nonetheless there was no doubt whatsoever on the positive identification of his remains.

Katie Bradshaw (photo left) visited her great-grandfather's grave in September 2015. Lorinda Ross (photo right), a great granddaughter, visited Wendell's grave in October 2009. Photo insert: Wendell Ross Jr. served in North Africa during World War Two.

no photograph available

LINK Carl

Private, Co. D, 119th Infantry Regiment, 30th Division
KIA 24 July 1918
Plot B – Row 02 – Grave 09
Army Serial Number 1315359

Carl Link was born in Davie County, NC on 21 May 1895 (another source indicates August 1894). He was the son of Cicero Edward Link and Lillie Hartley who lived in Thomasville. They were blessed with seven children (five sons and two daughters: Roy, Carl, Mae, Charles, Webster, Agnes and Robert). Lillie passed away in 1908 and Edward remarried with Minnie Louella Leonard (photo insert) in 1910 with whom he had seven more children (three sons and four daughters: Gertha, Bertha, William, Ruby, Edward, Boyd and Annie). Minnie raised Lillie's children as if they were her own. She died at the age of 96.

Carl was called to register for the draft in 1917. His registration card indicates that he was illiterate. He was called to arms on 21 September 1917 and sent to Camp Jackson, Columbia, SC for his basic training. He was first assigned to the 321st Infantry Regiment, 81st Division and later transferred to the 119th Infantry Regiment, 30th Division. Before he was sent to Europe, Carl enrolled for a war insurance policy covering the amount of $10.000.

Two other men from Thomasville are also buried at Flanders Field Cemetery: Bennett Cornelius and Haymore Westmoreland.

A nephew of Carl was killed during World War II: Henry Link, son of Carl's younger brother Charles. Henry is buried at Brittany American cemetery in St. James, France (Plot F- Row 1 -Grave 13).

ARNETT John D.

1st Lieutenant, Medical Reserve Corps, attached British Army
KIA 16 April 1918
Plot B – Row 02 – Grave 10

John Deming Arnett was born in Millville, NJ in June 1888. His parents, John Arnett Sr. and Virginia Sherwood were farmers. He had three older brothers: Charles, George and Jesse, followed later by Ross, Ida and Fay. John was an exemplary student and after his graduation at Medina High School he applied for Buffalo Medical College where he spent his first three years studying to become a doctor. Following the footsteps of two brothers who had previously taken on the profession, he preferred completing his studies at Albany Medical College. The photo is his graduation picture of 1914.

On 6 January 1917 he married Florence Sayers from Albion. After the U.S. declaration of war he immediately volunteered for service and consequently was called to arms on 2 August as 1st Lieutenant in the Medical Reserve Corps. On 18 September 1917, after a short interlude in Washington DC , he was sent to Europe.

Upon arrival he was assigned to the British Royal Army Medical Corps in Portsmouth, UK, where he served for two months before being moved to Winchester. He was later transferred to the 5th General Hospital in Southsea where he tended the wounded arriving from the trenches in France. In his letters he described the types of wounds. In his letter of 28 December he wrote: *"The train enters the station with a large number of carriages, all of them marked with a red cross. Ambulances, stretcher bearers with blankets are waiting for the wounded. The doors open and all walking wounded leave the train and are escorted to a hospital. The more seriously wounded are carried to the ambulances. The Medical Officer performs a triage of medical and surgical cases. All the men are dirty. Their clothes are covered in mud and blood and their hair is long. However they are glad to be safe. Most of them ask for a light so they can smoke a cigarette before getting into the ambulance. I will never forget an Australian who said to me that he had seen many Americans in the field hospitals and that he was relieved to be admitted to an American hospital because he was sure he would be taken good care of. When the wounded arrive at the hospital they are first bathed. Then they must stay in bed for 48 hours. The majority of injured are gas victims (mustard gas, chlorine, etc.). Evidence is skin burns, infection of the eyes, loss of voice, heavy coughing, chest pains and bronchitis. The gas burns the mouth, throat and lungs. Most of them recover, but the recovery process is long. Those whose lungs are too badly infected don't make it. Shrapnel wounds are also very frequent, but one must try to imagine what the effects of a hot piece of iron can do when it enters the body at high velocity. Bullet wounds are rare because this injury is not considered serious enough to return to England for treatment. A few days ago I saw a man with a bullet entry wound to the left side of his nose, just under his eye with the exit wound just under his right ear. This man was on his way to the front.*

Other diseases are trench fever and trench foot. Trench fever is a kind of flu. With trench foot, the feet swell up to 2 or 3 times their normal size. This is extremely painful and sometimes toes need to be amputated. Shell shock is also very frequent. The shattering effects of exploding bombs causes changes in the blood circulation, cerebral function and the spine, which can damage the brain tissue. Symptoms are unconsciousness, splitting headaches and severe trembling of the whole body, lasting for months."

John landed in France on his first wedding anniversary, 6 January 1918, and was immediately sent to the front line where he was in charge of a dressing station with the British 99th Field Ambulance. His last letter home was written in a German pillbox which he had transformed into a dressing station, a short distance from the German trenches: *"The landscape is covered with shell holes as far as one can see. They are filled with water and above some of them hangs a green smog. The mud is very deep and we have to walk over "Duck-boards". I am in a pillbox we conquered from the Germans. The walls are 5 feet thick with a small hole as entrance. This pillbox is about 10 feet by 10 and 5 feet high. I feel quite safe in it. Each pillbox has a name: I saw Cascara farm, Fine Cot and Bigger Bush. During a calm period, I decided to drain some shell holes near the dressing station. I was shocked when, while I was digging, suddenly came across the head and shoulders of 5 Australian soldiers. There is no rest for the dead in this country."*

1st Lieutenant John Arnett was killed on 16 April 1918 at the Trappist Monastery at Mount Cats in Northern France. He was taking care of the wounded, assisted by the monks. In the book: *"From shell hole to château with Company I"* (recollections of a line officer of the 107th Inf. 27th Div.) one can read the following: *"Looking eastward from our tent we could see the spire of a church over the rising ground about a mile ahead of us. This was Steenvoorde. Further on, a few miles further, rose sharply on the skyline crowned with a group of buildings among which a shell would burst every few minutes was the famous Mont des Chats and it's Trappist Monastery, "Cat Hill" the British would call it......".*

For reasons unknown, his wife received a telegram from John on 20 April letting her know that he was in good health. This mystery has never been solved.

His widow remarried Alexander L. Strouse on 11 December 1922. This could have been the reason why his remains were left in Europe.

His mother visited his grave with the Gold Star Mothers Pilgrimage in 1931. The government had granted her medical assistance having undergone a major operation shortly before her departure.

John Sr. and Virginia Arnett.

Photo taken just before John's departure for Europe with his wife Florence standing right.
His brother Ross and his wife left.

PORCELLI Robert
Bugler, Co. H, 119th Infantry Regiment, 30th Division
KIA 17 July 1918
Plot B – Row 02 – Grave 11
Army Serial Number 1316095

Rafaelle (Robert) Porcelli was born in London, UK, on 19 March 1899. He was the son of Antonio Porcelli and Cecilia Firenzi from Viticuso, Italy. He emigrated to the U.S.A. accompanied by his father in 1912. They took residence in Fayetteville, NC. His mother, brother and sister remained in Italy. Antonio and Robert started their own business supplying ice. This way they hoped to earn enough money to bring the rest of the family over to the U.S.A.

He was only 16 years of age when he joined the Fayetteville National Guard (2nd North Carolina Infantry Regiment) and served during the punitive campaign along the Mexican border in 1916. Upon his return he remained in the military and was stationed at Camp Sevier, Greenville, SC. He was intelligent and respected by his friends and comrades in arms. He was promoted to Corporal but declined saying that he did not want to be higher in rank than his friends.

Robert Porcelli was killed on 17 July at 07.30 hours when a bursting shell sent him hurling in the air, landing head first on a steel lintel. The facial part of his skull was completely shattered. He is one of the youngest soldiers buried at Flanders Field Cemetery.

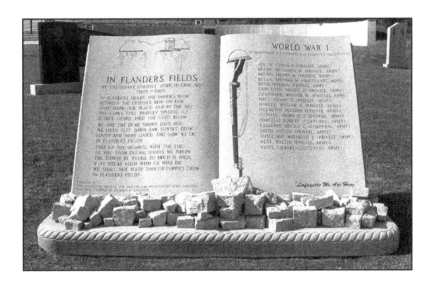

Memorial to all Cumberland County men who died in the line of duty during World War I.
Veterans Memorial Park, Hay and Robeson Streets, Fayetteville, NC.

STALLINGS Paul
Private, Co. G, 119th Infantry Regiment, 30th Division
KIA 26 July 1918
Plot B – Row 02 – Grave 12
Army Serial Number 1316023

William Paul Stallings was born in the Nicanor Section of Perquimans County, an area generally known as Long Swamp, NC, on 14 July 1895. His parents, William and Christian Virginia Stallings, were farmers and had five children: Olive, Paul, Leah, Fannie and Daniel. On 19 January 1917, Paul married Lillian Watson in Hertford, NC. A year later their daughter, Irma Pauline Stallings, was born on 22 February 1918. Photo insert right is Paul's wife Lillian with their daughter Irma Pauline.

On 3 October 1917, Paul was called to arms. At the time of enlistment he was working at the Rowntree Lumber Co., Belvidere. Completing his basic training he was assigned to the 316th Field Artillery Regiment of the 81st Division. This division was formed with conscripts from the Carolina's and Florida. Before sailing for Europe he was reassigned to the 30th Division. On 12 May he sailed for Europe out of Boston, MA on the Laomedon. Two weeks later he arrived in Calais, France.

On 26 July, only having been at the front one day, Paul was attached to a combat patrol training party with a mission to locate enemy machinegun nests. He was killed instantly during the advance in the front lines together with Sergeant Coleman McGraw, Private Leslie Stillman and Private William Logan (Plot B- Row 2 - Grave 07). He and his comrades in arms were buried at Nine Elms British Cemetery in Poperinge. These men were the first of the division to be killed in action.

282

Irma had three children, all still living today: Marie Sue Hart, Margaret Ann Hart and Henry Byran Hart IV. Paul only held Pauline (as he preferred to call her) on one occasion.

Paul was the only man who was killed from Perquimans County. The American Legion Post of the County in Hertford was named after him. Photo previous page left depicts his wooden marker on Cemetery 1252. Photo right on previous page is his granddaughter Margaret Hart from Bear, DE visiting his grave on Memorial Day 2016.

UMLAND Albert J.

Corporal, Co. G, 106th Infantry Regiment, 27th Division
DOW 9 August 1918
Plot B – Row 02 – Grave 13
Army Serial Number 1207806

Albert J. Umland was the son of John and Alice Umland from Brooklyn, NY. He was born in September 1893 and had an older sister Nellie. He enlisted with the 14th Infantry Regiment New York National Guard on 21 May 1917.

He was originally buried at Lyssenthoek Military Cemetery in Poperinge at XXXII.B.21. The family had first requested that his remains be repatriated to the USA but later revoked their initial request. The rank of Corporal is inscribed on his headstone notwithstanding the fact that according to his burial file he had achieved the rank of Sergeant.

His mother had agreed to take part in the Gold Star Mothers Pilgrimage of 1930 when her husband passed away. High blood pressure prevented her from taking the trip.

LEONARD William A.

Corporal, Co. I, 107th Infantry Regiment, 27th Division
KIA 14 July 1918
Plot B – Row 02 – Grave 14
Army Serial Number 1211449

William "Billy" Leonard was born in July 1890 as the son of John and Winifred Leonard from Flushing, NY. He had three brothers (Arthur, James and Eugene) and five sisters (Mary, Catherine, Winifred, Cecilia and Anita). William was City Editor of the Flushing Daily Times. He was a great idealist and so no one was surprised that, when the US declared war, he enlisted with the 7th Infantry Regiment New York National Guard on 11 June 1917.

He soon became member of the board of the Seventh Regiment Gazette. Everybody loved reading his articles. Even on serious matters there was always a sniff of humor to be found just around the corner. He could write about anything. He was very intelligent, a genius in journalism and everyone just fell for his irresistible charms.

On 14 July he volunteered for a dangerous mission *"just to see how they do it"*. Always itching for an interesting article. The mission was situated on Mount Scherpenberg. Together with a few men of the 26th Bn. Royal Fusiliers they were tasked to repair barbed wire in no man's land which had been damaged by artillery fire. No sooner had they left their trench, the British artillery opened fire towards the German lines which immediately triggered a counter artillery barrage. The British sergeant ordered the men back to their trench but before they could move an artillery shell burst in their midst. A British soldier was killed instantly and at the same time shell fragments had lodged into Billy's stomach. He was carried 100 yards back to safety but unfortunately Billy had already died. He was first buried at Wedge Wood Bank on the right flank of Mount Scherpenberg and shortly afterwards reinterred in a British cemetery in the village of Loker. He was once again disinterred on 5 June 1919 and temporarily laid to rest in the American Plot at Lyssenthoek cemetery. The Flushing Daily Times wrote: *"He fell advancing to meet the foe"*. William Leonard was the first soldier of his division to be killed in action.
Congressman Chas Pope Caldwell, a college chum, was greatly interested in this case and requested his remains be buried in a US cemetery as soon as possible.

The William A. Leonard American Legion Post 422 worked together with the New York Government Parks Service to dedicate a site in memory of William in 1934. Leonard Square is a sitting area located in the Queens neighborhood of Murray Hill on 155th Street, Northern Boulevard and Roosevelt Avenue. A bronze plaque on a standard octagon flagstaff with inscription: "In Memoriam Corporal Wm. A. Leonard – American Legion Post 422 – November 11, 1934".

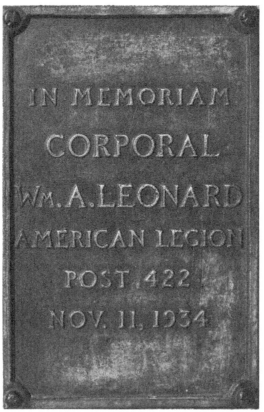

IN MEMORIAM
CORPORAL
WM. A. LEONARD
AMERICAN LEGION
POST 422
NOV. 11, 1934

Leonard Square and Memorial plaque

STRUCK Arthur J.
Private, Co. A, 106th MG Battalion, 27th Division
KIA 21 August 1918
Plot B – Row 02 – Grave 15
Army Serial Number 2672446

Arthur J. Struck was born in Manhattan, NY on 17 August 1895. He was the son of Jacob and Helen Struck. He had two sisters: Edna and Vivian. Jacob died in 1906 and Helen remarried John Froehlich and gave birth to another daughter Maybelle. The family lived in Richmond Hill, NY when Arthur was inducted on 5 April 1918. At that time he was employed as a clerk at the Commercial Exchange Bank. He had requested exemption of military service based on his chronicle hart problems. However this was not considered a valid reason.

He was struck by a shell fragment while standing watch at Company Headquarters and killed instantly. He was originally buried at Lyssenthoek Military Cemetery in Poperinghe at XXXII.C.7.

His mother visited Flanders Field Cemetery with the Gold Star Mothers Pilgrimage in 1930. She visited Arthur's grave on 29, 30 and 31 May.

Funeral at Lyssenthoek Military Cemetery.

55.

ROTOLLO Toney

Corporal, Co. I, 106th Infantry Regiment, 27th Division
KIA 2 September 1918
Plot B – Row 02 – Grave 16
Army Serial Number 1208408

Ton(e)y Rotollo, was born in Brooklyn in July 1897 and was the son of James and Louisa Rotollo. He enlisted with the 14th Infantry Regiment New York National Guard on 17 July 1917.

He was originally buried near Vierstraat (Isolated Grave #2 Kemmel). His remains were moved to Lyssenthoek Cemetery in Poperinge on 5 June 1919 and he found his final resting place in Waregem on 15 June 1922.

BRABENDER Theodore H.

Private, Co. F, 147th Infantry Regiment, 37th Division
KIA 11 November 1918
Plot B – Row 02 – Grave 17
Army Serial Number 2940982

Theodore Brabender was born in Hudson, NY on 11 May 1890. He was the son of Philip (born in Germany) and Bertha Brabender. He had one brother (Francis) and a sister (Flora). He attended school until 1908. He was employed as a plumber until 1916 at which time his father had purchased a farm in Stockport Center, NY. Theodore was put in charge and ran the farm. He continued running the farm until he was called to arms on 29 April 1918.

He received two months basic training with the 153rd Depot Brigade at Camp Dix, NJ. He was later reassigned to the 147th Infantry Regiment. On 7 June he embarked for Europe, disembarking at Brest, France. He served with the 37th Division throughout the European campaign but was killed in sight of the armistice on 11 November.

Theodore's name was also added to his mother's grave marker at the Hudson City cemetery, Hudson, NY.

VAN KIRK Edgar G.
Sergeant, Co. C, 112th Engineer Regiment, 37th Division
DOW 11 november 1918
Plot B – Row 02 – Grave 18
Army Serial Number 1538099

no photograph available

Edgar Glenn Van Kirk was born in Yellow Springs, OH in December 1889. He was the only son of Lawson Van Kirk and Martha Ann Elizabeth McCord. He had four sisters: Jesse, Lily, Fern and Ruth. He was an exemplary student and graduated as a civil engineer.

He reported to Camp Perry, OH on 9 June 1917 and joined the 1st Engineer Regiment Ohio National Guard, which later became the 112th Engineer Regiment. He was promoted to Sergeant on 1 June 1918.

He was wounded by a shell fragment on the last day of the war near the village of Zingem. He died at the 148th Field Hospital in Deinze and was buried in the communal cemetery by men of the 112th Sanitary Train. His remains were moved to Waregem and buried in plot A, grave 178 on 9 June 1919. A memorial marker was installed by his parents in the Washington Court House cemetery, Washington, OH (photo insert). His father was overwhelmed by grief and died in March 1919. Martha passed away in 1923. Fern had applied for permission to visit her brother's grave with the Gold Star Mothers Pilgrimage but her request was denied.

OLSON Thomas M.

Private, Co E, 148th Infantry Regiment, 37th Division
KIA 31 October 1918
Plot B – Row 02 – Grave 19
Army Serial Number 3749507

Thomas Meaer (Meier) Olson was born in Lenvik near Tromsö, Norway on 25 October 1893. He was the son of Ole Andreas Jensen and Sirianna Olsdattir. Thomas was a fisherman at the time he decided to emigrate to the USA with his twin brother Otto in 1913. His mother and five other brothers (Johan, Ole, Jens, Halvor and Karl) remained in Norway. Thomas and Otto settled in Madison (Windsor PA) where they were employed as agricultural laborers.

Thomas was called to arms on 24 July 1918 and reported to Camp Grant, IL where he received his basic training with the 161st Depot Brigade. Later he was assigned to the 344th Infantry Regiment, 86th Black Hawk Division. This division comprised mainly from men out of Illinois and Wisconsin. Upon arrival in Europe the division was disbanded and the men reassigned to other units. Thomas was attached to the 148th Infantry Regiment. Otto had been called to arms a month earlier and served with the 49th Field Artillery Regiment. Their emergency address was with a friend.

Thomas was killed by machine gun fire during his first engagement near the town of Olsene. He had been shot through the head and was buried where he fell. He had applied for US citizenship but his application had not yet been processed. His serial number is one digit different from that of Ole Olson (Plot D – Row 01 – Grave 13).

BARLOW William C.
Private, Co. F, 105th Engineer Regiment, 30th Division
KIA 27 August 1918
Plot B – Row 02 – Grave 20
Army serial number 1881232

William Cataloe Barlow, born near Brundidge, AL on 27 December 1888, is the only man from Alabama buried at Flanders Field. He was one of three children (Bryan °1887 and Essie °1890) born to Leroy Hamilton Barlow (°1849) and Russia Ducksworth Bryan (°1856). The family later moved to Dothan, where Leroy became a store manager.

However William, following the footsteps of his grandfather, became a farmer in Ashford. On 24 March 1918 he married Effie Palmer from Edison, GA. William had already been called to register for the draft in June 1917 but had applied for exemption based on his dependent parents. His request was denied. On 25 April, exactly one month and one day after he was married, he received his orders to report to Dothan. The next day he was on his way to the training camp in South Carolina. On 17 May William was assigned to Company F, 105th Engineer Regiment, 30th Division. Sailing on the SS Melita he arrived in Europe on 27 May 1918.

On 17 August, during the fighting around Voormezele, orders were received for the night of 24-25 Augustus in the 30th Division sector. It was scheduled to discharge 2517 gas cylinders towards the German lines on a front of about 600 yards. Due to adverse weather conditions this was postponed for three days. On 28 August at 02:25 hours, the wind direction was optimal for the attack and the gas cylinders were electronically discharged. As the gas was discharged, a downward current of air caught the edge of the cloud and blew it back on the members of the working party. The concentration to which these men were subjected was tremendous and resulted in 34 casualties of which three deaths. The latter due to the men trying to get out of the affected area, getting caught in barbed wire and so disarranging their masks. The three were Private Dave Lee from North Carolina (Plot B - Row 2 - Grave22), Corporal Ray Stroman from Indiana (Plot B - Row 2 - Grave 23) and William Barlow. He died a few minutes after arriving at a dressing station. Barlow, Lee and Stroman were buried at Hagle Dump British Military Cemetery in Poperinge.

In 1931, Russia Bryan Barlow (photo) visited her son's grave. Under exceptional circumstances she had received permission by the authorities for her daughter to accompany her. She departed New York on 25 June. Unfortunately during the outward journey Russia was slightly injured when a small ladder had fallen on her head. She was unconscious for a while and complained about headaches during the whole crossing. She claimed the incident was due to negligence on the part of the SS Roosevelt and filed an official complaint.

Although William's wife Effie also requested to visit her husband's grave this was denied as she had become ineligible due to the fact that she had remarried a certain Jasper Kirksey in 1930. Jasper was a successful cotton trader from Georgia. Effie died in Arlington, GA on 14 October 1969.

William's older brother Bryan (photo with William) graduated as Doctor in Medicine in 1916 and worked for an insurance company in Indiana. Bryan was killed in a vehicle accident in Minnesota in 1919. He had two small children and his wife was expecting a third. Bryan's son Robert was killed in action during World War II on 26 July 1942. He served with the 90th Bomber Squadron, 3rd Bomber Group, Heavy. He is memorialized on the Wall of Missing at the Manila American Cemetery in the Philippines.

William's father Leroy died on 5 May 1929. Russia survived him almost 25 years when she passed away in her 97th year on 26 March 1954 . William's younger sister Essie Dell remained unmarried. She was manager of a hat store but later sought employment in the same branch of work. She died in 1990 having reached 100 years of age and is buried next to her parents in Dothan. In 2007, a monument was erected to the memory of the fallen on which you can find William's name. The monument is located in the communal cemetery only 200 yards from where his parents and sister are buried.

LEDER Jack
Private 1st Class, Co. I, 106th Infantry Regiment, 27th Division
KIA 2 September 1918
Plot B – Row 02 – Grave 21
Army Serial Number 1208379

Jacob (Jack) Leder was the son of Nathan and Nellie Leder from Brooklyn, NY. They arrived in the USA from Austria-Hungary in 1895. Jacob was born in in Manhattan in February 1898. He was the second of eight children. He had four brothers (Carl, Abraham, Morris and Henry) and three sisters (Rosa, Rebecca and Lena). He worked in his father's bakery.
Jacob enlisted with the 47th Infantry Regiment New York National Guard on 3 June 1917. This was one of the regiments forming the 106th Infantry Regiment. At the time he was 19 years of age.

On 24 August he wrote home informing his parents that he was in the trenches *"showing the Germans how Americans can fight"*. Jack is just one of eight soldiers of the Jewish faith buried at Flanders Field under a Star of David. As so many others, he was killed during the battle at Vierstraat Ridge on 2 September. He was first buried at Hagle Dump British Cemetery on the outskirts of the village of Elverdinge.

Nellie, who was a member of the Gold Star Mothers of America, had set her mind on traveling to Europa to visit her son's grave with the Gold Star Mothers Pilgrimage. Unfortunately she passed away in 1929. Lena had requested to take her place but this was denied. The family had been saving up to visit Jack's grave for many years.

LEE Dave A.
Private, Co. F, 105th Engineer Regiment, 30th Division
KIA 27 August 1918
Plot B – Row 02 – Grave 22
Army Serial Number 1329779

David Albert Lee was the son of John Miller Lee and Sarah Agnes Feemster. He was born in Rock Hill, SC on 1 November 1887. Dave was the sixth child in row of nine sons and five daughters: Minnie, Rosalie, Robert, Walter, John, Dave, Nancy, Reuben, Claude, Mason, Mary, Samuel, Elijah and Clara. Robert and Walter were twin brothers as also Claude and Mason. At a certain point in time the family moved to North Carolina. David found employment and took residence in Charlotte, NC. He married Bessie McCall and on 4 October 1908 their son Alver Barlett was born. Dave joined the 1st Infantry Regiment North Carolina National Guard in Burlington on 22 June 1916.

On 17 August, during the fighting around Voormezele, orders were received for the night of 24-25 August in the 30th Division sector. It was scheduled to discharge 2517 gas cylinders towards the German lines on a front of about 600 yards. Due to adverse weather conditions this was postponed for three days. On 28 August at 02:25 hours, the wind direction was optimal for the attack and the gas cylinders were electronically discharged. As the gas was discharged, a downward current of air caught the edge of the cloud and blew it back on the members of the working party. The concentration to which these men were subjected was tremendous and resulted in 34 casualties of which three deaths. The latter due to the men trying to get out of the affected area, getting caught in barbed wire and so disarranging their masks. The three were Private William Barlow from Alabama (Plot B - Row 2 – Grave 20), Corporal Ray Stroman from Indiana (Plot B - Row 2 - Grave 23) and William Barlow. He died a few minutes after arriving at a dressing station. Lee, Barlow and Stroman were buried at Hagle Dump British Military Cemetery in Poperinge.

His mother hung Dave's photo above the hearth. No one was allowed to touch the photo or to mention his name. Bessie was later remarried to Robert Lowry. Claude and Mason also served in Europe in 1918. Mason was also attached to Co. F of the 105th Engineers Regiment. He must have had a firsthand experience of what happened to his brother. Claude and Mason returned unscathed from the war.

Dave has two grandchildren living somewhere in South Carolina but we were unable to locate them during our research.

STROMAN Ray A.
Corporal, Co. F, 105th Engineer Regiment, 30th Division
KIA 27 August 1918
Plot B – Row 02 – Grave 23
Army Serial Number 1985836

Ray Albert Stroman was born in Brushy Prairie, IN on 13 March 1895. It was a joyful day for his parents, Albert and Phoebe Stroman. The large family were unexpectedly blessed with twins, Roy being his twin brother. There were five other children in the family: two boys and three girls. Their father died at a young age and their mother together with the whole family moved to Topeka, IN in 1908. Ray and Roy were in every aspect model children. They remained inseparable and even both worked as chauffeurs for the same creamery, R.F. Miller & Co in Topeka. They were both selected for military service in 1917.

4 October 1917 was the first day that they ever became separated as they were sent to different training camps. Roy was trained as a mechanic but was honorably discharged on physical grounds. Ray was sent to Camp Taylor, KY and trained with the 159th Depot Brigade. Sometime later he was transferred to Camp Sevier, SC where he was assigned to the 105th Engineer Regiment of the 30th Division. He embarked for Europe on 28 May. Irma Peterson, his fiancé, promised to wait and marry him upon his return. He was an exemplary soldier and as such was soon promoted to Corporal.

Ray Stroman died under the same circumstances as William Barlow and Dave Lee who are all buried close together. He was also initially buried at the British Hagle Dump Cemetery in Elverdinge.

Roy died in 1979. He was 84. His whole life he had hoped to visit the grave of his twin brother. Unfortunately he never made it. Every Memorial Day he sat down and wept thinking of his brother.

Hagle Dump Cemetery

Roy and Ray as teenager

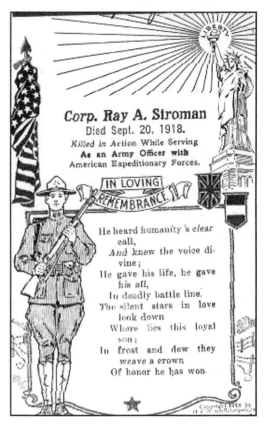

A memorial plaque (above) was attached to his parent's grave marker in the South Milford Indiana Cemetery.

298

URDAHL Christian
Private, Co. E, 148th Infantry Regiment, 37th Division
KIA 3 November 1918
Plot B – Row 03 – Grave 01
Army Serial Number 3749534

Kristian Urda(h)l was born in Gyland near Flekkefjord along the south coast of Norway on 15 March 1895. He was the son of Andreas Jesperson Urdal (1834-1915) and Anna Andreasdotter Lavstøll (1857-1906). There were fourteen children in this agricultural family: Helene, Jens, Tonette, Andreas, Anne Gurine (times three), Martin, Anders, Bertine, and Kristian are known. The other three children probably died in infancy. Kristian was the youngest. In the photo below Christian (aged 10) is standing second from right, between the two daughters of his sister Tonette who was married to a photographer. His father Andreas is third from left, mother Anna fourth from right.

Many people from this particular region departed for America hoping for a better future. This was also the case with Jens, Andreas, Anders and Kristian. Jens later returned to Gyland to run the family farm. It is unknown if the four brothers emigrated to the USA at the same time, however Kristian, according to the Ellis Island records, did arrive in 1915. He found work as an agricultural laborer in Burke, WI.

"Christ" was called to arms in Madison, WI on 2 July 1918. He was sent to Camp Grant, IL and attached to the 161st Depot Brigade. Less than one month later he was transferred to the 344th Infantry Regiment, 86th Black Hawk Division which was disbanded upon arrival in Europe. Christian was reassigned to the 148th Infantry Regiment.

He was killed on 3 November in Welden (near Oudenaarde) between 10:00 and 11:00 hours. He was hit just above the heart by a machine gun bullet, tried to reach his own lines but stumbled and collapsed before he was able to do so. He was disinterred and buried in Waregem on 11 June 1919. He had become a US naturalized citizen on 8 August 1918. His war insurance indemnity was paid out to his family in Norway.

no photograph available

TAGUE John A.
Corporal, Co. M, 148th Infantry Regiment, 37th Division
KIA 31 October 1918
Plot B – Row 03 – Grave 02
Army Serial Number 1530295

John Tague (°15 October 1894) was the son of Albert Tague and Harriet Young. He had two sisters: Ruth and Gertrude. Shortly after the US declaration of war, John enlisted with the Ohio National Guard (7th Infantry Regiment) on 4 May 1917. His emergency address was registered with his sister Ruth Tague McGreevy.

Around noon on 31 October, between the towns of Olsene and Kruishoutem, John was attempting to knock out an enemy machine gun nest when he was shot through the head and killed instantly. He was buried in Kruishoutem and his remains were reinterred in Waregem on 10 June 1919 (plot C, grave 42).

The American Legion Post #188 in New Lexington is named after him. There were no archives to be found on John at the American Legion Post and, until this investigation came to light, they were unaware of his permanent burial location.

no photograph available

MASTROMONACO Michele

Private 1st Class, Co. H, 361st Infantry Regiment, 91st Division
KIA 3 November 1918
Plot B – Row 03 – Grave 03
Army Serial Number 2257774

Michele Mastromonaco was born in Morrone Nel Sannio, Italy on 22 June 1895. He was the youngest in the family of Angelo Raffaele Mastromonaco (°1857) and Maria Rosa Mastandrea (°1858) who had four other children: Giovannantonio, Maria Luca (died aged five), Maria Louisa and Angelantonio. Michele departed from Italy with his brother Angelantonio and sister Maria Louisa, in September 1913. They sailed from Le Havre, France and arrived at Ellis Island on 7 November. Michele took residence in Seattle, WA where he found employment at the Pacific Coast Steel Company. Sometime later their parents also emigrated to the U.S.A.

Michele was called to arms and received his basic training at Camp Lewis, WA. He applied for his US citizenship on 31 May 1918. Shortly afterwards he sailed for Europe with the 91st Division. He was killed by a direct hit from a 1 pounder artillery shell which shattered the base of his skull and upper jaw.

Photo insert: Angelo and Maria

LORING David W. - D.S.C.
2nd Lieutenant, Co. C, 115th MG Battalion, 30th Division
DOW 24 August 1918
Plot B – Row 03 – Grave 04

David "Josh" Worth Loring was born in Sumter, SC on 20 March 1887. His parents were George Washington Loring and Nessfield Green. Three sisters (Carrie, Mary and Dorothy) died in infancy and so David was their only

surviving child. He was an exemplary student. In 1905 and 1906 he attended college at the University of South Carolina. His mother died In 1907. Shortly afterwards he joined the 2nd Infantry Regiment of the South Carolina National Guard. In 1914 he found

employment with the Atlantic Coast Line Railroad and moved to Wilmington, NC. There he met Viola Shaw and they married on 26 April 1916. On 15 January 1917, a baby boy was born but to their great disappointment and grief the child was not viable and died the following day.

Shortly after the US declaration of war he volunteered for service again and was soon appointed 2nd Lieutenant. However, sometime later he was rejected on medical grounds. Determined to serve his country he decided to undergo an operation and then reapply for military service as a Private. He was successful in his attempt and climbed the ranks to 2nd Lieutenant once again (29 December). After completing his basic training at Camp Sevier, SC, he was sent to Europe in May 1918.

Four of his letters were saved. On 15 July he wrote a remarkable letter to his father. He expressed his admiration of indirect fire and shells falling all around. He also wrote: "*I believe this 'hunting' over here for big game is more fun than hunting deer in Santee swamp at home.*"

His third letter, written to his aunt, dates from 6 August. Here he describes how his commanding officer was blocked in his dugout when a shell exploded, obstructing the entrance and how he was able to free him unscathed. He also described the continuing artillery attacks and shells falling close to their positions. He was always anxious to check on his men if any had been injured or worse. Being so concerned about the safety of his men was the cause of his death on 23 August. For his extraordinary bravery he was posthumously awarded the Distinguished Service Cross. The citation reads: *"For extraordinary heroism in action near Ypres, Belgium, August 23 1918. When his gun positions were rendered untenable by shell fire and his men ordered to seek shelter in dugouts, Lieutenant Loring left a place of safety for the purpose of seeing that all of his men were under cover, and was mortally wounded by a shell, dying on his way to the hospital."* He was taken to Remy Siding where he died two hours later. He was buried at Lyssenthoek Cemetery, the cemetery adjacent to the hospital, at XXXII. C. 9.

David's father died before the war. Viola remarried in 1925 to a certain Lars Peders, a captain of a steamboat. They had one child: Thomas. David's mother passed away in 1929.

A memorial marker was erected in David's memory in the cemetery of Sumter, NC. We assume this was requisitioned by his father shortly after the war

no photograph available

GRIFFITHS Arthur
Private, Co. L, 146th Infantry Regiment, 37th Division
KIA 2 November 1918
Plot B – Row 03 – Grave 05
Army Serial Number 1829294

Arthur Griffiths was born in Overhampton, England on 2 December 1894. The family (parents John and Mary, brother Joseph) emigrated to the U.S.A. in 1896. Once they had settled, Mary had two more children: Thomas and Edith. Joseph and Arthur found employment at a glass manufactory plant in Pittsburgh, PA.
He was called to arms and after his basic training at Camp Lee was assigned to the 146th Infantry Regiment. He was killed near the village of Heurne but buried in the village of Mullem (near Oudenaarde). His remains were interred in Waregem on 10 June 1919 (plot C, grave 28).

In reply to the query on the final disposition of Arthur's remains Mary replied: *"We would like to let his body where he was killed"*. She visited Flanders Field Cemetery with the Gold Star Mothers Pilgrimage on 24, 25 and 26 July 1933. At the time she was 61 years of age.

At the time of death Arthur had obtained his U.S. citizenship.

SCHAEFER Reinhold D.
Private, Co. G, 362nd Infantry Regiment, 91st Division
KIA 31 October 1918
Plot B – Row 03 – Grave 06
Army Serial Number 2786803

Reinhold Schaefer (or Rinehold Shafer, as he preferred to sign) was born in Lesterville, SD on 24 April 1895. He was the son of Johannes and Frederica Sayler Shaefer (photo insert). They had emigrated from Russia in 1878 and settled on a farm in South Dakota. They later moved to Underwood, ND in 1902. Reinhold was one of seventeen children: Sarah, Karl, Johanna, Jacob, Emil, Albert, Andrew, Anna, Rhinehold (Reinhold), Emanuel, Henry, Frieda, Gottlieb, Johannes, Jennie, William and Wanne.

On 5 June 1917, Reinhold was called to register for the draft in McClean County. He was inducted at Washburn and sent to Camp Lewis, WA for basic training on 24 May 1918 . At the time the 91st Division was formed, he was assigned to the 362nd Infantry Regiment.

Eyewitness statement by Corporal Carl Lorenz of the same Company: *"He was last seen near Bevere when going over the top on the morning of 31/10"*. Reinhold was killed instantly when a high explosive shell shattered his skull.

no photograph available

LANG Emil
Sergeant, Co. K, 362nd Infantry Regiment, 91st Division
KIA 31 October 1918
Plot B – Row 03 – Grave 07
Army Serial Number 2261440

Emil Lang was born in Long Island City, Queens, NY on 21 April 1891. He was the son of Ehrhard and Louise Lang (née Feuchter) from Elmsford, Westchester County, NY. He had three sisters (Louise, Clara and Anna) and a brother (William). From January through April 1917 Emil was employed as a dishwasher for the Northern Pacific Railroad Company. He moved to Lima, MT (date unknown) and here he was required to register for the draft.

He was called to arms on 3 October 1917 and assigned to the 166th Depot Brigade for basic training. He was an exemplary soldier and soon climbed the ranks to Sergeant.

Emil was shot through the head during the attack of 31 October. The fighting was so severe that one could not attempt to break cover to check on him if he was still alive. This incident occurred near Heirweg in Anzegem. He was buried in the temporary American cemetery in the Kleine Leiestraat (Little Lys street) in Anzegem, grave 17.

Carl and Carmen Johnson from Miami, Florida visited their great-uncle's grave on 12 July 2014.

no photograph available

CHRISTENSEN James T.
Private, Co. C, 106th Infantry Regiment, 27th Division
KIA 27 July 1918
Plot B – Row 03 – Grave 08
Army Serial Number 1206987

James "Christianson" was born in New York City on 19 July 1892. He was the son of Edward (born in Finland) and Annie (born in Ireland) Christianson. He had one brother Edward and a sister Anna.

James enlisted in Brooklyn, NY on 1 August 1917. He was killed in action and first buried at Lyssenthoek Military Cemetery. Edward's preference was that his brother's remains be repatriated to the U.S.A. Anna was adamant that his remains be left in Europe. As Anna was the sole beneficiary of James' war insurance policy, priority was given to her choice.

HILL Raymond D.
Private, Co. M, 106th Infantry Regiment, 27th Division
KIA 2 September 1918
Plot B – Row 03 – Grave 09
Army Serial Number 1209041

Raymond Duncan Hill was born in Brooklyn, NY on 7 April 1895 as son of Henry and Adelaide Hill (née Johnson) from Brooklyn, NY. They also had a daughter Marion. In 1917, Raymond worked as clerk for the Winchester Armor Co. in New Haven, CT. He registered for the draft on 5 June 1917 claiming exemption being a munitions worker. He enlisted with the 23rd Infantry Regiment, New York National Guard on 27 September 1917.

He was originally buried at Lyssenthoek Military Cemetery. His remains were interred in Waregem on 15 June 1922.
His mother could have joined the Gold Star Mothers Pilgrimage. However, as the government had rejected her request for her daughter to accompany her she decided to cancel her trip.

no photograph available

McCORMICK Walter J.
Private, Co. L, 106th Infantry Regiment, 27th Division
KIA 1 September 1918
Plot B – Row 03 – Grave 10
Army Serial Number 1208841

Walter McCormick was born in New York City in November 1897. His parents were Irish immigrants. He enlisted with the 23rd Infantry Regiment New York National Guard in Brooklyn on 23 July 1917.

He was originally buried in an isolated grave near Kemmel and on 4 June 1919 reinterred at Lyssenthoek Military Cemetery in Poperinge. In 1922, he received his final resting place at the Flanders Field Cemetery in Waregem. His mother, although only 59, was unable to take part in the Gold Star Mothers Pilgrimage as she was crippled from arthritis.

WERMALD James E.
Private 1st Class, Co. I, 106th Infantry Regiment, 27th Division
KIA 31 July 1918
Plot B – Row 03 – Grave 11
Army Serial Number 1208440

James Wermald originated from Brooklyn, NY. He was the son of Charles and Jennie Wermald both deceased.

He was first interred at Lyssenthoek Military Cemetery in Poperinge at XXXII.B.6. His sister, Mary Scott, who was point of contact in case of an emergency, requested that his remains be buried in Belgium: *"I don't want to disturb the body"*. She explained that this was his wish in the event of his death. She was willing to pay for the upkeep of the grave. She added that she could not endure to grieve a second time: *"He was all I had.*

RICE Robert B.
Private 1st Class, Co. G, 106th Infantry Regiment, 27th Division
KIA 2 September 1918
Plot B – Row 03 – Grave 12
Army Serial Number 1207877

Robert Rice was born in Waltonville, PA in May 1893. He was the son of Howard Rice and Mary Black from Dauphin, PA. He was the youngest in the family. There were four older boys (Roy, Howard, William and Charles) and two older girls (Laura and Ruth). William was a 1st Lieutenant with the 306th Machine Gun Battalion, 77th Division.

Robert enlisted in Brooklyn, NY on 2 May 1917 and was killed in the action near Vierstraat. He was buried where he fell (Isolated Grave #2 Kemmel). On 4 June 1919 he was reinterred at Lyssenthoek Military Cemetery in Poperinge and found his final resting place in Waregem on 15 June 1922.

VAN INGEN Richard W.
Private, Co. E, 106th Infantry Regiment, 27th Division
DOW 2 September 1918
Plot B – Row 03 – Grave 13
Army Serial Number 1207534

Richard Warner Van Ingen was born in Brooklyn, NY on 31 March 1894. He was the son of Anna Van Ingen and was married to Gladys. He was employed as an export clerk at the Williams & Higmore Co. on Broadway.
Richard enlisted on 24 September 1917. He was originally buried at Lyssenthoek Military Cemetery in Poperinge at XXXII.C.19. Anna initially requested that his remains be repatriated to the U.S.A. but changed her mind shortly afterwards. As she explained in her reply: *"remain at rest on the ground honored by his sacrifice"*.

When she received the official request to visit the grave in 1930, she enquired if her daughter would be allowed to accompany her. This request was denied and so Anna decided to accept and risk the trip to Flanders Field Cemetery. Gladys was not eligible for the Pilgrimage as she had remarried in 1921.

HARRINGTON James A.
Corporal, Co. K, 106th Infantry Regiment, 27th Division
KIA 2 September 1918
Plot B – Row 03 – Grave 14
Army Serial Number 1208505

James Harrington was born in November 1898. He was the son of Thomas and Ellen Harrington from Brooklyn, NY. He enlisted with the 14th Infantry Regiment New York National Guard, which later became the 106th Infantry Regiment, on 7 May 1917.

He was killed, as so many of his comrades, during the battle for Mount Kemmel. He was only 18 years of age. His remains were reinterred at Lyssenthoek Cemetery on 14 June 1919. His mother was invited to join the Gold Star Mothers Pilgrimage but replied "*not just at present*". Unfortunately she passed away on 31 May 1930. She was only 69 years of age.

Mount Kemmel 1919.

MASTERSON John
Private, Co. F, 106th Infantry Regiment, 27th Division
KIA 9 August 1918
Plot B – Row 03 – Grave 15
Army Serial Number 1207620

John Masterson was born in Derragh, County Longford, Ireland in 1894. His father Peter and mother Brigid Masterson (photo  right), had a small farm. They had five daughters (Brigid – John's twin sister, photo left) Ellen, Margaret, Annie and Catherine) and nine sons (John, Barney, Patrick, Kieran, Anthony, Joseph, Ta, Frank and Michael). Shortly before the outbreak of the war, John and his sister Ellen emigrated to the U.S.A. They took residence in Brooklyn, NY. John enlisted with the 14th Infantry Regiment New York National Guard, which later became the 106th Infantry Regiment, on 16 August 1917.

Barney also took part in the Great War. He served with the British Army. His arm was severely wounded and he was sent back home. These war wounds did not prevent him from taking active part in his strife for Irish independence in 1920-1921.

After the war, Ellen remained in the U.S.A. However Ill health and homesickness forced her to return to Ireland where she married and stayed for the rest of her life. The American dream had been shattered beyond recognition.

It was only in 2007, via a great-niece Breda Scully, that the family in Dublin learned that John was buried in Waregem. On Memorial Day 2016, Breda Scully, Eileen Clarke and her daughters Susan and Rachel visited their great-uncle's grave

JACOBS Samuel – Silver Star

Corporal, Co. G, 105th Infantry Regiment, 27th Division
DOW 2 September 1918
Plot B – Row 03 – Grave 16
Army Serial Number 1204553

Samuel Jacobs was born in New York City in 1889. His parents, Max and Rosie Jacobs, had four other children: Julius, Minnie, Juliet and Lillian. He enlisted with the 71st Infantry Regiment, which later became the 105th Infantry Regiment, New York National Guard, on 22 June 1916.

On 2 September at 16:30 hours, after the attack on Vierstraat, Samuel sought cover for his men at a location called Indus Farm, when an enemy shell fell close by. Shell fragments hit him in the chest and legs. He was rushed to a field dressing station but succumbed to his wounds later that day. He was initially buried at Lyssenthoek Military Cemetery in Poperinge at XXXII.C.24.

In 1929, Max received the government invitation enquiring if Rosie would like to join the Gold Star Mothers Pilgrimage in 1930 or later. Unfortunately Rosie had passed away in 1925. Max replied that he had never heard of a "Gold Star Mother" but was much flattered by the title.

Samuel received a Divisional Citation (in 1932 this became a separate medal "Silver Star").
"For great bravery and presence of mind in leading his men to a place of safety when the billets of his company were heavily shelled. In doing so he exposed himself and was severely wounded and later died. This near Dickebusch Lake, Belgium, September 1, 1918."

KANE Harry W.
Private, Co. G, 106th Infantry Regiment, 27th Division
KIA 2 September 1918
Plot B – Row 03 – Grave 17
Army Serial Number 1207929

Harry was born in Brooklyn, NY in 1900. He was the tenth of twelve children in the large family of Walter Kane and Mary Wixted. Walter and Mary were Irish immigrants. He was a Protestant from Belfast, she a Roman Catholic from Tipperary County.

Harry joined the 47th Infantry Regiment New York National Guard in 1916. When the 27th Division was formed he was assigned to the 106th Infantry Regiment and received his basic training in Spartanburg, SC. On 9 July he wrote a letter home explaining that he was optimistic, in good health and hoped to be back home by Christmas. He was killed by artillery fire during the fighting at Vierstraat. When his remains were disinterred to be moved to Flanders Field Cemetery in Waregem in 1922, it was determined that the cause of death was multiple fractures to the skull. He was only 18 when he died and so one of the younger men buried in the cemetery.

His mother died in 1915 and his father in 1922. The War Insurance was divided between the surviving brothers and sisters, each receiving $ 3.19 a month.

ANDERSON Frederick J. Jr.
Private, Co. D, 106th Infantry Regiment, 27th Division
DOW 26 July 1918
Plot B – Row 3 – Grave 18
Army serial number 1207185

Frederick Anderson was born in Bay Ridge, NY in June 1897. He worked beside his father as a reporter for The New York Evening Post. At the time of enlistment he lived with his parents at 4907, 11th Avenue, Brooklyn, NY. On 10 October 1917 he joined the forces at Fort Slocum, NY. Six days later he was assigned to Company D of the 106th Infantry Regiment, 27th Division.

When Frederick bade his father goodbye he said: *"I may pull through, but if it is necessary to give up my life in battle, just wear a smile. If I die, I will do so cheerfully for home and for America."* He arrived in Europe on 10 May 1918. He died of wounds received in action less than twenty-four hours after entering the front line near Mount Kemmel on 26 July 1918 and was buried on the spot. In 1919 his remains were temporarily buried at Lyssenthoek Military Cemetery in Poperinge.

no photograph available

ROVERE Vincent
Private, Co. C, 106th Infantry Regiment, 27th Division
DOW 28 July 1918
Plot B – Row 03 – Grave 19
Army Serial Number 2671994

Vincent Rovere was born in Ucrea, Messina, Italy, in February 1895. He emigrated to the U.S.A. with his parents and found residence in Astoria, Long Island, NY. He was inducted at Long Island City on 5 April 1918. He received his basic training with the 152nd Depot Brigade and three weeks later assigned to the 106th Infantry Regiment.

He was killed in action near Dickebusch Lake and initially buried at Lyssenthoek Military Cemetery in Poperinge.

American Plot at Lyssenthoek Military Cemetery in 1920

SHANNON Thomas J. E.

Sergeant, Co. E, 106th Infantry Regiment, 27th Division
DOW 1 September 1918
Plot B – Row 03 – Grave 20
Army Serial Number 1207341

Thomas Shannon was born on 7 September 1895. His parents (photo right), Thomas Joseph Shannon and Mary Elizabeth Nugent, had six children: John, Julia, Thomas, Charles, Walter, and Joseph. In 1900 the family took residence at 96th Street in Brooklyn. Tom was raised there and in 1909 found a job in the advertisement section of the Brooklyn Standard Union. Tom was known for his loyal commitment and his positive can do. One was always confident that he would achieve his goal no matter how difficult the assigned task was.

Tom enlisted with the 23rd Infantry Regiment New York National Guard on 20 April 1914 and spent three years serving along the Mexican border during the punitive campaign (Pancho Villa rebellion). He was promoted to Corporal on 23 July 1916 and became a Sergeant on 31 October of that same year. Tom was shot in the stomach on 1 September and succumbed to his wounds six hours later. He was buried in a field near Kemmel where other men of his division were interred. His remains were moved to Lyssenthoek Cemetery in Poperinge at XXXII.D.15. in 1919.

Initially Mary preferred that his remains be repatriated to the United States but his father wrote the letter with their final decision: *"remain where he is with his comrades"*.

Mary came to Flanders Field Cemetery with the 1930 Gold Star Mothers Pilgrimage. She departed the U.S.A. on 13 May on the SS Republic and visited Tom's grave on 29, 30 and 31 May. She was 66 years of age. When Thomas left for Europe he promised to marry Helen McGrath upon his return. Helen's grief was immense when she learned about his death. She wrote a beautiful and touching poem in memory of Tom.

I prayed for a pal that was staunch and true,
And I found him Tom, when I found you.
As the years seemed to grasp me the more I knew
That I had a pal and a sweetheart in you.

Then war was declared one April Day
And took you, Tom dear, away.
The thought of parting I did loathe
But God knew what was best for both.

But oh, what a change I now do see
To know that you have gone from me
Not for a day, a month or a year,
But forever and ever Tom dear.

I will not live, I will exist,
And memories of the past I'll ne'er resist.
To live in hopes your face to see
Where we meet again in Eternity.

Shortly afterwards Helen (photo above and left insert below) decided to take an active role in the war and she became one of the first females to join the Navy (Yeoman 1st Class). On 24 November 1920 she married Tom's brother Charles. Her whole life she wore a ring she had made from one of Tom's uniform buttons. Her daughter Patricia (Shannon) Odermatt (photo insert below right – died October 2016) always wore this ring.

Mary with other Gold Star Mothers on board the SS Republic.

315

no photograph available

WILLIAMS Ferdinand
Mechanic, Co. G, 106th Infantry Regiment, 27th Division
KIA 2 September 1918
Plot B – Row 03 – Grave 21
Army Serial Number 1207824

Ferdinand Williams was born in New York City on 18 July 1888. He was the son of Adolf and Lizzie Williams (German immigrants). He had three brothers (August, Adolf and Charles) and four sisters (Theresa, Lizzie, Lena and Annie). He enlisted with the 23rd Infantry Regiment New York National Guard in Brooklyn on 26 June 1916 and served along the Mexican border during the punitive campaign.

He was killed in action near Vierstraat and buried in "Isolated Grave #1, Felter Field Kemmel", where Thomas Shannon and William McCormick were also buried. His remains were moved to Lyssenthoek Cemetery in 1919 and buried at XXXII.D.5. There were two identification tags fixed to his marker and his collar indicated that he belonged to Company G. At the time of disinterment for positive identification it was found that his dental records didn't match. Under these circumstances, Lizzie decided that the remains be buried in Europe. Nonetheless, as the identification tags and company details on his collar were correct, he was buried at Flanders Field Cemetery as Ferdinand Williams.

CUDMORE John T.
Private 1st Class, Co. M, 106th Infantry Regiment, 27th Division
KIA 2 September 1918
Plot B – Row 03 – Grave 22
Army Serial Number 1208956

John T. Cudmore was born in Kilfinane, Ireland in December 1895. He was the son of Daniel and Ellen Cudmore (née Meany). The family had seven children. John emigrated to the U.S.A. and took residence with his cousin in Brooklyn. He enlisted at Van Cortlandt Park on 24 September 1917 and was assigned to the 23rd New York National Guard Regiment. He became Private 1st Class on 1 January 1918. Before his remains were interred at Flanders Field Cemetery he was buried at Lyssenthoek Military Cemetery in Poperinge.

O'HARE James A.

Private, Co. D, 106th Infantry Regiment, 27th Division
KIA 27 July 1918
Plot B – Row 03 – Grave 23
Army Serial Number 1207284

James O'Hare was born in Cohoes, NY on 16 February 1894. He was the son of John and Helen O'Hare. The family lived in Brooklyn. James graduated from High School and worked for an insurance company. On 29 November 1915 he volunteered with the 23rd Infantry Regiment and in 1916 served along the Mexican border during the punitive campaign. Two brothers also served : Joseph served in the same regiment and Thomas served with the 2nd Field Artillery, 8th Division. A fourth brother was too young to be eligible for military service.

Joseph also crossed the Atlantic with the 106th Infantry Regiment (Co H). It was he who wrote home informing that James had been severely wounded by shell fragments near Mount Kemmel and had died instantly. He also wrote that he visited his grave at Lyssenthoek Military Cemetery every day and that he had requisitioned a white marker. When the letter reached his parents they had still not been informed of his death by the military authorities. Thomas also served with the 27th Division in Europe. He belonged to the 105th Field Artillery Regiment which had not been assigned to Belgium.

Three O'Hare Brothers in U. S. Service;
They Come from Fighting Stock

JAMES A. O'HARE.

JOSEPH F. O'HARE.

THOMAS S. O'HARE.

MACLEISH Kenneth - NAVY CROSS
Lieutenant, US Navy
KIA 15 October 1918
Plot B – Row 04 – Grave 01

Kenneth MacLeish was born in Glencoe, IL on 19 September 1894. He was the son of Andrew and Martha (Hillard) MacLeish (photo insert right). The MacLeish's were a prominent and wealthy family. Photo below is their home *"Craigie Lea"* in Glencoe.

Kenneth attended Yale University where he was a member of the athletic and water polo team. He was scheduled to graduate in 1918.

Before the United States declared war, he was already part of a group of Yale undergraduates who were planning to form the Naval Flying Corps and then offer their services once the United States declared war on Germany. In March 1917 he enlisted in the Naval Reserve Flying Corps as an electrician, left college and moved to West Palm Beach, FL for training with seaplanes. He completed his training in

Huntington, NY and was commissioned and served as Officer Instructor at Langley Field, Norfolk, VA.

He sailed for Europe in October 1917 and was assigned as an instructor and later inspector at the Naval Assembly and Repair Bases in France, England and Scotland. However his heart was set on being a pilot and taking part in missions above enemy territory. In April 1918 he was finally assigned to the U.S. Naval Air Station in Dunkirk where most of his missions were with the British Royal Air Force attacking German submarine bases at Zeebrugge and Ostend. He received many favorable reports from his commanders and was promoted to Lieutenant. Early September he was requested to report back to Eastleigh in England where he became the First Flight Officer. He declined the offer of becoming a Squadron Commander as he claimed he could never endure or survive sitting behind a desk. Itching for action he also declined furlough to return to the U.S. for two weeks and applied with the 213th Squadron Royal Air Force based in Dunkirk, who were supporting the allies with their offensive in Flanders.

(Photo insert left: Kenneth far right). On 13 October, the day before he was killed in action , he was granted permission to join the squadron.

On the morning of 14 October he flew his first patrol over Flanders bringing down an enemy plane. In the afternoon he set out on a mission with eight other planes. Lieutenant MacLeish, Flight Commander Captain Green and a third, Lieutenant Allen, were flying together when they noticed two German planes below them. The first one was shot down by MacLeish, the second was brought down together with Allen. At this time, totally out of the blue, eight German planes dived down upon them. MacLeish was killed in the air and came down in Schore, Belgium. Allen went down in flames and of him or his plane, nothing was ever recovered.

Albert Roose, a wealthy architect and senator from the town of Gistel, was landlord of six farms. On 26 December 1918, together with two of his closest friends, he decided to check out his properties on the extent of war damages. All farms had evidently been destroyed. However when they arrived at the farm in Schore near Nieuwpoort, they found the remains of an American pilot close to a barn and remnants of his fallen plane close by. The body was found lying face upwards, the right arm extended horizontally, and the left arm thrown carelessly across his body. He was still wearing his gloves, coat buttoned, helmet on, and everything in his pockets was untouched. Among the personal belongings found were letters, photographs of the deceased and the details of his home address. It was Lieutenant

Kenneth MacLeish. Although the plane was riddled with machine gun bullets there was no evidence that Kenneth had received any body or head wounds. Alfred made arrangements for a casket and Kenneth's mortal remains were buried on the spot (see photo insert). The rest of his personal belongings were handed over to the British authorities. When word had reached the American Headquarters, they sent Lieutenant John Menzies, a Yale classmate of Kenneth, to inspect the gravesite and make an official report. For many years Alfred Roose also corresponded with the MacLeish family. When they visited Belgium they always stayed at Chateau de la Waere where Roose lived.

Lieutenant MacLeish, with the permission of his family, was originally buried on Roose's farm in Schore. As in the case of all isolated burials, the Graves Registration Service exhumed the remains in June 1919 and transferred them for burial to Lyssenthoek British Military Cemetery in Poperinge. He received his final resting place at Flanders Field Cemetery as being the only casualty serving with the Naval Squadron.

Kenneth wrote many letters home, to his friends and to his fiancée Priscilla Murdoch (photo insert). They were edited by Geoffrey L. Rossano in *"The Price of Honor: the World War One Letters of Naval Aviator Kenneth MacLeish"*.

When the church community in Glencoe built their Parish Hall, the assembly room was called "Kenneth MacLeish Hall". One source claims that the original wooden marker from the crash site is located under Kenneth's bronze statue.

The memory of Lieutenant MacLeish lived on. On 14 December 1919, his mother received a

telegram from the Secretary of the Navy: *"Have assigned name MacLeish to Destroyer No. 220 in honor of your son"* The DD-220 USS MacLeish (photo insert) was a vessel built by William Cramp & Sons in Philadelphia, PA and sponsored by Miss Ishbel

MacLeish, sister of Lieutenant Kenneth MacLeish. It was launched on 18 December 1919 and went into service on 2 August 1920 under Lieutenant Commander F.T. Berry. It completed many assignments of which China (Shanghai, 1925). In 1943 the MacLeish was assigned as escort during the allied offensive in North Africa. In January 1945 it was converted to AG-87 USS MacLeish and used as target ship for submarines in the Panama canal. It was decommissioned on 8 March 1946, officially cleared from the US Navy shipping list on 13 November, sold to Boston Metals Co. Baltimore and reduced to scrap metal.

Lt. Kenneth MacLeish was posthumously awarded the Navy Cross. This medal had been created within the Naval Service on 4 February 1919.

Although originally not inscribed on his permanent marker, this was corrected during a headstone re-engraving project in 2006.

The citation reads: *"The Navy Cross has been awarded to Lieutenant Kenneth MacLeish, as a pilot attached to the U. S. Naval Aviation Force, for distinguished and heroic service as pilot in the War Zone. Lieutenant MacLeish took part in attacks against the enemy, was shot down and killed during the Flanders campaign in October 1918"*.

Kenneth MacLeish also had two brothers serving with the American Expeditionary Forces in Europe. Norman Hillard MacLeish (who became famous after the war as an artist) was Second Lieutenant with the 53rd Field Artillery Regiment and in May 1919 was still with his unit in France. On 30 May, Memorial Day, he and a fellow officer were granted leave and traveled to Schore to place flowers on his brother's grave. Archibald

MacLeish (photo with his brother Kenneth), was Captain with the 146th Field Artillery

Regiment, but was better known as a poet. He became Chief Librarian of Congress and received the Pulitzer Prize twice in recognition of his literary works: "Conquistador" in 1932 and "Collected Poems" in 1952. He died in 1982 at the age of 90. He wrote at least three poems in memory of his brother Kenneth

Archibald was present during the dedication ceremony of Flanders Field American Cemetery on 8 August 1937 and on this occasion wrote the poem Memorial Rain.

MEMORIAL RAIN
For Kenneth MacLeish, 1894-1918

Ambassador Puser the ambassador
Reminds himself in French, felicitous tongue,
What these (young men no longer) like here for
In rows that once, and somewhere else, were young. . .

> All night in Brussels the wind had tugged at my door:
> I had heard the wind at my door and the trees strung
> Taut, and to me who had never been before
> In that country it was a strange wind, blowing
> Steadily, stiffening the walls, the floor,
> The roof of my room. I had not slept for knowing
> He too, dead, was a stranger in that land
> And felt beneath the earth in the wind's flowing
> A tightening of roots and would not understand,
> Remembering lake winds in Illinois,
> That Strange wind. I had felt his bones in the sand
> Listening.

... Reflects that these enjoy
Their country's gratitude, that deep repose,
That peace no pain can break, no hurt destroy,
That rest, that sleep. . .

> At Ghent the wind rose.
> There was a smell of rain and a heavy drag
> Of wind in the hedges but not as the wind blows
> Over fresh water when the waves lag
> Foaming and the willows huddle and it will rain;
> I felt him waiting.

. . Indicates the flag
Which (may he say) nestles in Flanders plain
This little field these happy, happy dead
Have made America. . .

In the ripe grain
The wind coiled glistening, darted, fled,
Dragging its heavy body: at Waereghem
The wind coiled in the grass above his head:
Waiting--listening. . .

. . .Dedicates to them
This earth their bones have hallowed, this last gift
A grateful country. . .

Under the dry grass stem
The words are blurred, are thickened, the words sift
Confused by the rasp of the wind, by the thin grating
Of ants under the grass, the minute shift
And tumble of dusty sand separating
From dusty sand. The roots of the grass strain,
Tighten, the earth is rigid, waits -- he is waiting --
And suddenly, and all at once, the rain!
The living scatter, they run into houses, the wind
Is trampled under the rain, shakes free, is again
Trampled. The rain gathers, running in thinned
Spurts of water that ravel in the dry sand,
Seeping in the sand under the grass roots, seeping
Between crack boards of the bones of a clenched hand:
The earth relaxes, loosens; he is sleeping,
He rests, he is quiet, he sleeps in a strange land.

TIO Frank E.

Private, Co. C, 148th Infantry Regiment, 37th Division
DOD 19 December 1918
Plot B – Row 04 – Grave 02
Army Serial Number 3751222

Frank Edward Tio originated from Hersey, WI. He was born in the agricultural family of John Tio and Anna Mae Hanson on 29 October 1892. They had five other children: Catherine, Mary, Emma, William and Marcus.

Tio was called to arms on 23 July 1918 in St. Croix, WI. He received his basic training with the 161st Depot Brigade. It was evident that there was an urgent need for fighting men in Europe. After only two weeks of training he was assigned to the 344th Infantry Regiment, 86th Division, and shipped to Europe. After the 86th Division was disbanded on 6 October, he was reassigned to the 148th Infantry Regiment. He died from meningitis, a common complication of the Spanish flu, on 19 December.

From left to right: Mary, Catherine, Marcus, Anna, William, Frank, Emma and John.

SNEDECOR Eliphalet Jr.
Corporal, Co. C, 106th MG Battalion, 27th Division
KIA 31 July 1918
Plot B – Row 04 – Grave 03
Army Serial Number 1216493

Eliphalet Snedecor originated from Flatbush, NY and was born on 21 July 1894. He was the son of Eliphalet Snedecor and Minnehaha Bedell. He had three sisters (Dorothy, Claire and Helen) and one brother (James). During the punitive campaign in 1916 and 1917, he was sent with his unit, the 1st Cavalry Regiment New York National Guard, to New Mexico and Arizona. During his training at Camp Wadsworth, Spartanburg, SC, the 1st Cavalry Regiment was disbanded and designated as the Machine Gun Battalion of the 106th Infantry Regiment. He was an intelligent young man and made many friends. Before he left for Europe in May 1918, he was engaged to Marion Strauch. Marion's brother, Edmund, was also killed in action on 22 October 1918 . He is interred at the Somme American Cemetery in Bony, France (Plot D – Row 22 – Grave 14). He had served with the 107th Infantry Regiment, 27th Division.

Eliphalet was first buried in the British La Clytte Military Cemetery and on 12 June 1919, before receiving his final resting place at Flanders Field, was reinterred at Lyssenthoek Military Cemetery in Poperinge at XXXII.E.25.

DILLON Festus
Private, Co. C, 363rd Infantry Regiment, 91st Division
DOD 20 October 1918
Plot B – Row 04 – Grave 04
Army Serial Number 3534779

Festus Dillon was born on 20 January 1896. He was the son of Franklin Dillon and Gilla Mannon residing in Scottown, OH. They had seven other children: Ruth, Frances, Floyd, Delsie, Osten, Lew and Mildred.

Festus was called to arms on 25 July 1918. After a short training period he was assigned to the 333rd Infantry Regiment, 84th Lincoln Division. Upon arrival in Europe he was transferred to the 363rd Infantry Regiment. Festus died of the Spanish flu on 20 October.

no photograph available

MUSCIETRO Giovanni
Private, Co. B, 305th Infantry Regiment, 77th Division
ACC 4 June 1918
Plot B – Row 04 – Grave 05
Army serial number 1677652

Giovanni Muscietro (also named John Masceto and/or Murciedero) was born in Fondichiaro, Italy around 1895. He emigrated to the U.S.A. and found employment in a tanning factory in Ballston Spa, NY. He was inducted on 23 February 1918 and served with the National Army division of New York: the 77th "Metropolitan" Division. He arrived in Europe on 16 April 1918.

On 2 June 1918 (at Moulle, Pas de Calais, France) Giovanni's platoon was being instructed on aiming and throwing hand grenades. Towards the end of the training session a grenade accidently exploded killing nine men instantly and wounding many more. Giovanni was one of the severely wounded and died in a British Army hospital two days later. He was initially buried at Bleue Maison British Military Cemetery in Eperlecques, France. George Ashe (Plot B – Row 04 – Grave 08) was also a victim of the same incident. They are the only two members of the 77th Division buried at Flanders Field.

Giovanni's name is memorialized on the Saratoga County World War I Memorial in New York. He had no family living in the U.S.A. and his emergency address was listed with his friend Alphonso Aufiero in Ballston Spa, NY.

no photograph available

PLIML Steve
Private 1st Class, Co. H, 145th Infantry Regiment, 37th Division
DOD 31 October 1918
Plot B – Row 04 – Grave 06
Army Serial Number 1518986

Steve Pliml was born in Bohemia in 1896. His mother Josefa (Josephine) was only 15 years of age. She emigrated to the USA with her husband Frank in 1911. Steve had two sisters (Gladys and Josephine) and two brothers (Jaroslav/Jerry and George). The family lived in Cleveland, OH where Steve joined the National Guard (5th Infantry Regiment) shortly after the U.S. declaration of war. Steve Pliml died of pneumonia (complication of the Spanish flu).

no photograph available

CASEY John
Corporal, Co. B, 106th Infantry Regiment, 27th Division
KIA 1 September 1918
Plot B – Row 04 – Grave 07
Army Serial Number 1206671

John Casey was born in Queens, NY on 5 September 1892. He lived with his father John and four sisters at 1863, Palmetto Street, Ridgewood, NY. He was working at the Edison Electric Company at the time he reported for duty with the 47th Infantry Regiment New York National Guard in May 1917. One battalion of the regiment was transferred to the 23rd Infantry Regiment which later formed the base of the 106th Infantry Regiment, 27th Division. John Casey was killed in action on 1 September. He was first buried by the British Army, together with twelve other casualties, near Kemmel. At the time of disinterment for processing and permanent reburial, it was determined that there was no 100% certainty that the remains were those of John Casey. As such, the official report in his burial file indicates: "presumably". It was also found that his rank was Corporal and not Private as inscribed on his headstone. His name is also memorialized on the War Memorial in Ridgewood NY.

ASHE George
Private, Co. B, 305th Infantry Regiment, 77th Division
ACC 3 June 1918
Plot B – Row 04 – Grave 08
Army serial number 1699210

George Ashe was born in in Homs (then Turkey, now Syria) on 18 November 1891. He lived in New York where he was registered for the draft. His registration card indicates that George was illiterate. He was called to arms on 25 February 1918 and attached to the National Army Division of New York, the 77th "Metropolitan" Division. He arrived in Europe on 16 April 1918.

On 2 June 1918 (at Moulle, Pas de Calais, France), George's platoon was being instructed on aiming and throwing hand grenades. Towards the end of the training session a grenade accidently exploded killing nine men instantly and wounding many more. Private Ashe was severely wounded and died in a British Army hospital the following day. (see also Giovanni Muscietro - Plot B-Row 04-Grave 05). On 12 June 1919 his remains were moved to Lyssenthoek British Military Cemetery in Poperinge. On 14 June 1922 he was permanently interred in Waregem.

no photograph available

RODER William A.
Private, 362nd Ambulance Co. 316th San.Train, 91st Division
DOD 29 October 1918
Plot B – Row 04 – Grave 09
Army Serial Number 2292038

William Arthur Roder was born in in Copenhagen, Denmark on 18 March 1896. He was the son of Axel and Anna Roder. He arrived in the U.S.A. on 28 August 1915. He found employment as an agricultural laborer in Seattle, WA. While at Camp Lewis he filed a petition for naturalization on 4 June 1918.

He died of pneumonia, a common complication of the Spanish flu, on 29 October and was buried in the communal cemetery in Roeselare (Grave #4) where a number of American soldiers were buried. At the time of death William Roder was still a Danish citizen.
His remains were moved to Flanders Field on 6 June 1919. Holger Wilfred Roder traveled from Copenhagen to visit his brother's grave in 1954. In the remarks column of the visitor's register he wrote: *"Thank the USA for the beautiful memorial for my dear brother"*.

American plot in Roeselare

BRISCO Floyd W.

Private 1st Class, Co. H, 145th Infantry Regiment, 37th Division
KIA 2 November 1918
Plot B – Row 04 – Grave 10
Army Serial Number 1518909

Floyd Whitcomb Brisco was born in Liberty, NY on 22 July 1898. He was the son of Joel Brisco and Ida May Jennison. He also had two sisters: Junietta and Chiquita. Floyd joined the Ohio National Guard in Cleveland on 28 May 1917. He was assigned to Company H of the 5th Regiment, which later became the 145th Infantry Regiment. He was promoted to Private 1st Class on 1 October 1917. Floyd Brisco was killed in action near the village of Eine on 2 November.

no photograph available

MORROW James

Private, Co. D, 145th Infantry Regiment, 37th Division
DOW 31 October 1918
Plot B – Row 04 – Grave 11
Army Serial Number 1852983

James Morrow was the son of James Morrow and Margaret Patton from Meenagowen, Donegal County, Ireland. He was born on 23 November 1892 and had two brothers and three sisters. In search of a better future he emigrated to the U.S.A. and took residence in Pittsburgh, PA. where he was employed as City Park gardener. His brother Ephram and sister Maggie had already moved to the U.S. earlier. From his registration card details (1917) we learned that he had signed a petition for U.S. citizenship. James was called to arms. He had an ideal profile; immigrant, unmarried, no children and no parents to care for.

He was hit by a small shell fragment in the neck at the start of the attack near Olsene. He refused treatment at a first aid post as he was adamant to continue the advance with his comrades. A few hours later he was wounded by another shell fragment. This time his wounds were far more serious and he was transported to Field Hospital #146 in Tielt. Unfortunately he died before reaching the hospital and was buried in the communal cemetery in Tielt.

STAFFORD John E.

Private, Co. E, 145th Infantry Regiment, 37th Division
KIA 31 October 1918
Plot B – Row 04 – Grave 12
Army Serial Number 1853112

John Edward Stafford, familiarly known as Ed, was born in Sharpsville, PA on 16 May 1889. He was the son of Reuben Stafford and Emma Firster. There were five other children in the family: Frank, Harry, James (John's twin brother), Jesse and Lucille. Emma died of pleurisy on 24 November 1902 leaving her husband to take care of the children of which four were quite young. At the time John was called to register for the draft in 1917, he was working at the Carnegie Steel Company in Greensville, PA.

John died of wounds, sustained in action by shell fragments, in Olsene during the first day of the attack. He was buried in the American plot of the communal cemetery in Tielt. Jesse was also serving with the A.E.F. in Europe. On the home front the family were enduring the aftermath of the Spanish flu. Two of his brothers had been very ill. Harry didn't survive and died just two weeks before John was killed in action.

Upon the request on the permanent disposition of remains his father had initially chosen for John to remain in Europe as he had received a photograph of the cemetery and was satisfied in the way it was maintained. However, in 1927 he had changed his mind and requested that John's remains be repatriated to the USA. Obviously his request came too late as the closing date for permanent disposition of remains was 1 April 1922.

Brian L. Stafford, a grandson of John's brother Jesse, was sworn in as 20th Director of the United States Secret Service on 4 March 1999. Brian had joined the Secret Service in 1971 and retired in 2003 after more than 30 years of service. During his tenure he had protected Presidents Richard Nixon, Gerald Ford, Jimmy Carter, Ronald Reagan, George W.H. Bush and Bill Clinton. He was also responsible for supervising several National Special Security Events including the 2002 Winter Olympics

DAY George W.
Private, Co. I, 363rd Infantry Regiment, 91st Division
KIA 24 October 1918
Plot B – Row 04 – Grave 13
Army Serial Number 3530788

George W. Day was born in Fairview, IN on 31 March 1891. He was a farmer, just like his parents William and Caroline Day (née Colen). He had two brothers (Charley and Ralph) and five sisters (Lavina, Mattie, Mable, Edith and Myrtle).

George was called to arms on 26 June 1918 and sent to Camp Sherman, Ohio for basic training with the 158th Depot Brigade. In September he sailed for Europe with the 84th Lincoln Division. This was a National Army division comprising of men from Illinois, Indiana and Kentucky. The division was disbanded upon arrival and George served as a replacement with the 363rd Infantry Regiment, 91st Division.

He was initially buried in the communal cemetery in the town of Oostnieuwkerke. His remains were interred in Waregem on 6 June 1919 (plot A - grave 115).

WHITE Merle J.
Private, HQ Co. 145th Infantry Regiment, 37th Division
KIA 4 November 1918
Plot B – Row 04 – Grave 14
Army Serial Number 1517220

Merle John White was born in South Bend, IN on 23 January 1896. As an infant he was orphaned and stayed at the Mishawaka orphanage where, at three years of age, he was adopted by John and Jane Berkey who ran a farm in Goshen, IN. He attended the Rensberger School and later the Goshen High School for two years. He joined the Indiana National Guard in February 1916 and served six months during the punitive campaign along the Mexican border. Shortly after the U.S. declaration of war on Germany he re-enlisted with the National Guard (21 August 1917). He was sent to Camp Sherman in Ohio and assigned to Headquarters Company of the 145th Infantry Regiment. From there he was sent to Camp Sheridan in Alabama and sailed for Europe from Virginia on 15 June.

On 2 September he wrote to his foster parents:
"Well, mother I am still among the living and intend to remain so, and I expect to return home safely. This may seem like a pretty broad assertion but I deem myself capable of competing with any Hun engaged in this terrible struggle for liberty. My return may be prolonged, but have patience, dear one, and it will be the sweeter homecoming when the "kid" does get there for I have an equal chance with them all. I am enclosing two of my division papers which will give you an idea of how the Sammies are going through the "Weine Hound" once called the "Kaiser's Pride". I fear that General Pershing is the only one that knows how this terrible struggle is going to end, but for myself there is only one way out, and that is another victory for the flag that has never known defeat".
Your devoted son,
Merle G. White
145th Infantry, A.P.O. 763, Am. Expeditionary Forces"

On 3 November, Merle was on duty as a line man in the Regiment Signal Platoon along the banks of the river Scheldt near Eine. He was searching for cover from enemy artillery fire and dug a large hole for shelter in the river bank. He was buried alive when a shell fell close by and suffocated before he could be set free. Another soldier, Private Robertson was also killed. His remains were repatriated to the U.S. in 1921. Private Merle J. White was an exemplary soldier. He was buried in the village of Herlegem.

Jane decided that his body remain buried in Europa. Merle carried a $5,000 life insurance policy in favor of his foster mother.

BOZENHART Ernest G. - D.S.C. + C.d.G. (F)
Private, Med. Det. 147th Infantry Regiment, 37th Division
DOW 1 November 1918
Plot B – Row 04 – Grave 15
Army Serial Number 1543504

Ernest Bozenhart was the son of George Botzenhardt (born in Germany and widower) from Toledo, OH. He was born in March 1898 and was the youngest of seven children: Anna, Clara, John, George Jr., Flora and Lucille. He was eighteen when he joined the Ohio National Guard on 21 June 1916 and served along the Mexican border during the punitive campaign. At the end of 1917 he was informed that he would be sent to the battlefields of France with the 37th National Guard Division. He changed his name to Bozenhart as Botzenhardt sounded too German. On 15 June he wrote a letter to his father enquiring if he had received the paperwork for his war insurance policy as he assumed that he would soon be sailing for France. He signed the letter with "Botzenhardt". The following week he was on his way to France.

Private Ernest Bozenhart was awarded the Distinguished Service Cross (DSC #6622) and the French Croix de Guerre (War Cross) for exceptional courage shown during the Argonne Offensive near Ivoiry, France on 29 September 1918. The French War Cross is not inscribed on his headstone.

DSC citation: *"For extraordinary heroism in action near Ivoiry, France, September 29, 1918. Making his way through heavy artillery and machinegun fire, he rendered valuable medical treatment to the wounded and assisted bringing the men to safety and forwarding them to a first aid station. In the performance of his duties he was shortly afterwards killed."*

In Belgium, Private Bozenhart was severely wounded by shell fragments while on his way to the front, setting up camp during the night of 30-31 October. He died of a complicated skull fracture at Field Hospital #146 in Tielt.

His brothers George and John served under their original name Botzendhardt. However they did not see active service in Europe. The war insurance indemnity was divided between brothers and sisters in 1931.

Ernest (seated right) with his brothers and Jeff Cameron from Utah at his great-uncle's grave

BARNES Charles P.
Private 1st Class, Co. C, 136th MG Battalion, 37th Division
KIA 4 November 1918
Plot B – Row 4 – Grave 16
Army serial number 2707294

Charles (Charlie) P. Barnes was the oldest of nine children. He was born in Nash County, NC on 25 February 1893. In the family his given middle name was "Murton". His parents, Joseph Francis Barnes, a train conductor, and Alice Jordan Williams had eight other children; Minnie, Osborne, Viola, Robert, Lewis, Lillie May, Marie and Kate.

Charles was called to register for the draft in March 1918. At that time he was a carpenter at Camp Lee, VA. His registration card indicates that he was tall and slim, had blue eyes and brown hair. He was called to arms on 3 May. He completed his basic training with the 155th

Depot Brigade, and his designated rank was Mechanic. After one month he was assigned as Private with the 136th Machine Gun Battalion, 37th Division. He was promoted to Private 1st Class on 7 October. He was killed in action one week before the armistice.

The son of his brother Robert, Robert Barnes Jr. (Gunner's Mate 3rd Class, U.S. Navy) was killed in action during World War II on 8 September 1945. His name is memorialized on the Wall of Missing at the Manila American Cemetery, Philippines.

no photograph available

PASH Alexander
Private, Co. A, 146th Infantry Regiment, 37th Division
DOD 3 November 1918
Plot B – Row 04 – Grave 17
Army Serial Number 2668711

Alexander Pash was born in Olyphant, PA on 27 December 1892. He was a miner in civilian life. He died of pneumonia, a common complication of the Spanish flu, at the American Evacuation Hospital (Mobile Hospital #9) in Staden and was buried in the graveyard close by. His sister Annie was the emergency contact as both parents had passed away. His remains were moved to Waregem on 5 June 1919.

no photograph available

AYK Jack
Private, Co. I, 361st Infantry Regiment, 91st Division
DOW 4 November 1918
Plot B – Row 4 – Grave 18
Army Serial number 2278223

Jacobus van Eyck was born on 19 February 1893. His parents were Francina and Anthonius Jacobus Van Eyck. He had already served seven years with the Dutch Navy before he emigrated to the U.S.A. Four months after his arrival he was already called to register for the draft. At the time he lived in Stockton, CA and worked in a sugar refinery in Manteca. His registration card indicates that he was medium built, had grey eyes, dark brown hair and being illiterate. Jack died of wounds and was buried in the American plot of the cemetery in Staden. As he had only been living in the U.S. for less than a year, he still retained his Dutch citizenship at the time of death.

MAXWELL Ernest E.
Private 1st Class, Co. G, 364th Infantry Regiment, 91st Division
DOD 20 October 1918
Plot B – Row 04 – Grave 19
Army Serial Number 2474576

Ernest Elmer Maxwell, born 1 August 1895 in McConnelsville, OH, was the son of George Maxwell and Alice Shriver. Alice passed away when Ernest was only three years of age. His father died In 1917, so Ernest lived with his grandmother, Eliza (Louisa) Maxwell.

He was called to arms on 26 May 1918. After basic training he was attached to the 333rd Infantry Regiment, 84th Lincoln Division. Upon arrival in France the division was disbanded on 3 October. On 7 October Ernest was reassigned and attached to the 91st Division. He died of the pneumonia on 20 October.

Ernest had a half-brother Haddie, who had already served four years in the military before the U.S. declaration of war. In 1917, he joined the Marines, was wounded in the arm and was sent back to the U.S.A. before the armistice.

EPLER David A.

Private, Co. I, 361st Infantry Regiment, 91st Division
KIA 2 November 1918
Plot B – Row 4 – Grave 20
Army Serial Number 2931929

David Allen Epler was born in Liberty, OH on 12 January 1893. He was the son of David Epler and Maybelle Thomas who were farmers living in Dalzell, OH. They had five other children: Myrtle Beatrice (°1890), Ollie May (°1891), John Homer (°1894), Mary E. (°1900) and Daniel (°1902). Insert right is a photograph of David in his teens.

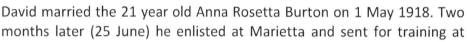

David married the 21 year old Anna Rosetta Burton on 1 May 1918. Two months later (25 June) he enlisted at Marietta and sent for training at Camp Sherman, Chillicothe, OH and Camp Mills, Long Island, NY. He embarked for Europe with Company E of the 335th Infantry Regiment, 84th "Lincoln" Division (conscripts from Illinois, Indiana and Kentucky). There was some confusion during the Atlantic crossing. It

was feared that that he was on the ship that was sunk off the British coast. The War Department personally informed his parents that he was alive and well. The division was disbanded one month after arrival in France (3 September) and David was reassigned and attached to Co. I of the 361st Infantry Regiment, 91st Division. He was killed in action in Oudenaarde while on guard duty. He was standing in a doorway when a high explosive shell struck front, killing him instantly. He was temporarily buried near the city prison and his remains were moved to Waregem on 6 September 1919.

It is unknown when his widow visited his grave with the Gold Star Mothers Pilgrimage.

CANTACESSO Trifone
Private 1st Class, Co. I, 361st Infantry Regiment, 91st Division
DOD 30 October 1918
Plot B – Row 04 – Grave 21
Army Serial Number 2277908

Trifone Cantacesso was born in Baro Baro, Italy on 19 January 1892. It is unknown when he emigrated to the U.S.A. but he settled in Dubuque, IA, where he had found a job. He was called to arms on 29 October 1917 and sent to Camp Lewis, WA, for basic training and consequently assigned to the 361st Infantry Regiment, 91st Division. His registration card indicates that Trifone was illiterate and that he had signed a petition to obtain U.S. citizenship.

He arrived in Europe on 6 July 1918. Trifone died on the eve of the last offensive of his division from complications of the Spanish flu. He was originally buried in Roeselare where Edward Longacre and William Roder were initially laid to rest.

His emergency address was with his parents Antonio and Adonio Volpe in Carbonaro, Italy.

no photograph available

VESEY Joseph
Corporal, Co. F, 145th Infantry Regiment, 37th Division
KIA 1 November 1918
Plot B – Row 04 – Grave 22
Army Serial Number 1518511

Joseph Vesey was the son of Martin and Bridget Vesey from Achill Island, Ireland. This is a small island off the west coast. Many members of his family still live there today. Joseph was born on 1 January 1893. In search of a better life he emigrated to the U.S.A. where he arrived on 24 April 1915. He immediately moved in with his aunt in Cleveland, OH. She had provided the funds for Joseph's Atlantic crossing. He worked as a streetcar conductor on the Detroit line.

"Joe" enlisted with the 5th Infantry Regiment, National Guard of Cleveland, OH on 24 August 1917. He achieved the rank of Corporal on 31 May 1918. Two weeks later he was on his way to Europe.

He was killed by fragments of a trench mortar shell at Eine and buried along the road to Gent on 14 November. His family initially requested that his remains be repatriated to Ireland. However, due to the instability of the country in 1922 caused by the civil war, repatriation to Ireland was temporarily cancelled. During the processing of remains and permanent reburial at Flanders Field on 14 June of that same year, a golden ring was found with the initials "JBV".

An interesting anecdote to the story of Joseph Vesey is the fact that Joseph made the crossing to the U.S.A. on the Lusitania in April 1915. As previously stated, he arrived in New York on 24 April. On 1 May the vessel sailed back to Europe with a considerable amount of ammunition on board. On 7 May at 14:10 hours, the Lusitania was sunk off the coast of Ireland by a German submarine. (U20 - Kommandant Schweiger). Within 18 minutes 1,119 lives (114 Americans) of the 1,924 passengers were lost. This incident resulted in many Americans reconsidering and choosing the side of the allies. As such, Joseph Vesey was a witness of the last crossing of the Lusitania.

In July 2005, Joe's grave received a visit from Ireland by his 85 year old nephew, also named Joseph. Joseph passed away in 2010.

MILLER Lew

Sergeant, HQ Co. 146th Infantry Regiment, 37th Division
DOD 1 November 1918
Plot B – Row 04 – Grave 23
Army Serial Number 1523557

Lew Wallace Miller was the only child of the Reverend John Frank (photo insert) and Marie Miller (née Baker) from Fostoria, OH. He was born in Dunkirk, OH and lived in the nearby town of Bucyrus. He graduated at the Bucyrus High School in 1915. He was very athletic (tennis and football), an actor and a musician (school conductor from 1913 through 1915). He was a very intelligent young man as he received the title of "Assistant Business Manager Bucyrian". The photo was taken from the 1915 High School annals. In the meantime he had joined the National Guard on 21 April 1914. After his graduation at the Bucyrus High School he attended the Otterbein College in Westerville, but in 1916 he was called to arms and sent to the Mexican border. After the U.S. declaration of war he was attached

THE REV. J. F. MILLER

to the Headquarters Company 8th Infantry Regiment Ohio National Guard, (which later became the 146th Infantry Regiment, 37th Division) and was sent to Camp Sheridan for additional training. With his exceptional musical talents he immediately became Jr. Musician, 3rd class. He was promoted to Corporal on 8 August 1917 and on 7 February 1918 became Band Sergeant. He arrived in Europe on 15 June 1918.

Lew was a boy who was highly respected by all and known to be passionate in his strife for freedom. He died of Broncho-pneumonia (a common complication of the Spanish flu) in the American Evacuation Hospital in Staden on 1 November. On 16 October, in a letter home he wrote that he was in good health. He was 24 years of age.

Mrs. Miller visited his grave with the Gold Star Mothers Pilgrimage in 1932. Due to her physical condition, an exception to policy was made for her husband to accompany her during the voyage. The Millers left France on 14 August for a side trip to England at their own expense. They rejoined the party in London on 18 August.

PLOT C

HORNER Bertram C.
Private 1st Class, 293rd Military Police Company
DOD 30 May 1919
Plot C – Row 01 – Grave 01
Army Serial Number 2219507

Bertram Cecil Horner was born in Saratoga Springs, MO on 20 September 1894. He was the son of Andrew Spencer Horner and Dona Roark (photo insert). Bertram was the oldest of five children: following Bertram were Marion Francis, Dallas Leroy, Louis Martin and Amos Earl. Andrew was killed in a lead and zinc mine cave-in west of Joplin in 1903. Dona remarried Albert Cooper and gave birth to two more daughters: Lillie and Nettie. Following the footsteps of his father, Bertram also worked as a miner and moved to North Miami, OK.

During the war he was attached to Co. D of the 104th Infantry Regiment, 35th Division. This National Guard division was engaged in the St. Mihiel and Meuse-Argonne offensives. He was wounded in October and admitted into hospital for a short period of time.

"Butch" Horner died in Antwerp from complications of the Spanish flu on 30 May 1919 and so the last man to die being interred at Flanders Field Cemetery. He is also the only man in the cemetery from Oklahoma and member of the 35th Division.

An unfortunate coincidence is that Bertram had a nephew (Dallas Leroy Horner Jr. – photo insert) who also lost his life in Antwerp during World War Two. His remains were repatriated and buried in the Grand Army of the Republic Cemetery, Miami, Ottawa County, Oklahoma on 6 August 1949.

CROSSLAND Bert S. – Belgian Croix de Guerre

Cook, Co. B, 316th Train HQ & Military Police, 91st Division
KIA 1 November 1918
Plot C – Row 01 – Grave 02
Army serial number 2274604

Bert Sydney Crossland was born in Connellsville, PA on 23 July 1891. He lived with his parents, Fuller and Nellie, in Torrance, CA and worked as a waiter at the Sarai Club in Los Angeles. Bert was medium built, had grey eyes and brown hair. His registration card indicates that he had made the request not to be called to arms as he was married. This of course to no avail. He was consequently called to arms on 20 September 1917 and on 8 November 1917 assigned to Co. B of the 316th Train Headquarters & Military Police. He arrived in Europe 14 July 1918 and for the duration of the war mostly served as a cook.

With the 91st Division he saw action on all fronts (St. Mihiel, Meuse-Argonne). During the Meuse-Argonne offensive he found himself in an awkward position. Together with five other men he was isolated from his unit for two days during a heavy artillery barrage.

He was killed in action in Waregem on 1 November 1918. For his courageous actions he was awarded the Belgian Croix de Guerre or War Cross. (Other sources wrongly indicate the French Croix de Guerre). The award is not recognized on his headstone. The citation reads: *"On the night of November 1st, 1918, in Waereghem, Belgium, during a heavy bombardment by enemy airplanes, he showed remarkable courage and devotion to duty, continuing with his duties until killed"*. He was buried in an isolated grave in Waregem and on 6 March 1919 his remains were moved to Cemetery #1252 (plot 1, grave #4).

Both in Los Angeles as in Torrance (population at the time only 750) Bert was loved by all. Ironically, of the 41 men from Torrance who had served in the war, Bert was the only man who didn't survive. He was married to the daughter of a wealthy chemist: Margaret Hodill. She could not cope with her immense grief and died six months later on 16 May 1919. She was only 20 years of age. Two days before her death she had received his Belgian War Cross. At the time of death, the War Cross was grasped tightly in her hands.
Six days after her death, Bert's brother passed away after a long illness.

Shortly after the war a large flagstaff was erected in memory of Bert Crossland.
In January 1920 the American Legion Post in Torrance was established and named after him.
His mother Nellie visited his grave with the Gold Star Mothers Pilgrimage in 1930.

.

RECORD George T.
Private, Co. G, 107th Infantry Regiment, 27th Division
KIA 13 August 1918
Plot C – Row 01 – Grave 03
Army Serial Number 1211146

George Tracy Record was born in Saratoga Springs, NY on 27 November 1893. He was the son of Chauncey Record and Minnie Gleason from Wayville, Stillwater, NY. They had one other son (Arthur) and two daughters (Dorcas and Marion). Chauncey's uncle Emery was a professional photographer, hence the many surviving photographs of George and his family. George found a job in Coopertown, NY and from there he enlisted for military service two days after the U.S. declared war on Germany. Arthur also volunteered and served with the Marines.

George from baby to adult

His parents received notice of his death from George's former work colleagues. They immediately contacted the military authorities. They replied that his name was not listed on any casualty list. Relieved as they were at the time, their joy was short-lived. Shortly afterwards, confirmation of death was received. He was the first man of Co. G killed in action and he was initially buried at Abeele Aerodrome Military Cemetery.

His name is memorialized (together with Giovanni Muscietro) on the Saratoga County Veterans Monument.

Photo left George – Photo right Arthur.

Family photo circa 1905: from left to right: Minnie, Chauncey, George, Arthur, Dorcas and Maria.

George during his training period in the trenches and laundry detail

DILEO Rocco
Private, Co. K, 148th Infantry Regiment, 37th Division
DOW 2 November 1918
Plot C – Row 01 – Grave 04
Army Serial Number 2413056

Rocco Dileo was born in Frigento, Italy on 2 April 1891. He emigrated with his older brother Guiseppe to the United States. They found residence in Little Ferry, NJ.

Rocco was called to arms on 26 February 1918 and after completing his basic training with the 153rd Depot Brigade in Camp Dix, NJ, he was assigned to the 308th Field Artillery Regiment of the 78th "Lightning" Division. This was a National Army Division with conscripts out of Delaware, New Jersey and New York. Rocco sailed to Europe with this division but one month later was reassigned to the 37th Division. He died of wounds received in action near the village of Heurne.

Guiseppe named one of his children Rocco in memory of his brother. Photo insert: Guiseppe with his wife Maria and Rocco in the background.

Sabino Dattolo (C-01-14) and Rocco were born on the same day, served with the same units and died on the same day.

WINSLOW Herbert L. – Silver Star

Corporal, Co. L, 107th Infantry Regiment, 27th Division
KIA 13 August 1918
Plot C – Row 01 – Grave 05
Army Serial Number 1211931

Herbert Winslow was born in Roseville, NJ in August 1895. He was the only child of Herbert Hall Winslow (photo insert) and Annie Lippincott. His father was a well-known play writer, actor and director. He wrote 56 plays of which 18 were performed on Broadway, approximately two hundred sketches and twelve film scenarios. He was mainly known for *Manon Lescaut* (1914), *The Decoy* (1916) and *The Millionaire Pirate* (1919). Herbert's mother was a successful opera singer performing under the name of Anita Armour in the U.S.A. and abroad. Her mother, Sara Lippincott (alias

Grace Greenwood), was a well-known writer, being an abolitionist and advocate for women's rights. Herbert was instructed at the Staunton Military Academy. However Herbert Jr. was not cut out for a military career. He had inherited the talents of his parents and grandmother: he became a film producer.

Although he had been living in Englewood, NJ for two years, Herbert joined the New York National Guard (7th Infantry Regiment). This regiment became the 107th Infantry Regiment of the 27th Division. He sailed for Europe on 10 May.

Herbert was responsible for the machine gun platoon of Co. L. On 13 August, he was sent to the front together with platoons Co. I and Co. L in the vicinity of Dikkebus (Ridgewood). They had just arrived when the Germans opened fire. Notwithstanding that the British units were forced to retreat, Herbert's platoon was successful in holding back the enemy during three consecutive attacks. Unfortunately Herbert was mortally wounded when a hand grenade exploded close by. For his courageous action he received a Divisional Citation (see also Di Giacomo A-1-21). He was the first of his company to be killed. His death was a tremendous shock to his company. He was liked by all as he had a reputation of being honest, faithful and warm hearted. His friend, Maitland Rice was a witness of his death and was at the point of collapse from grief. During that same battle Bryan Gallagher of the same company was also killed. They were both buried at the Abeele Aerodrome Military Cemetery.

The Winslow's were struck by immense grief. Herbert Sr. stopped writing for many years. He wrote his last play, *Reckless Romance*, in 1924 and died in 1930. Annie died lonely and in poverty at the age of 80. She had been left with Herbert's war insurance and her pension to survive.

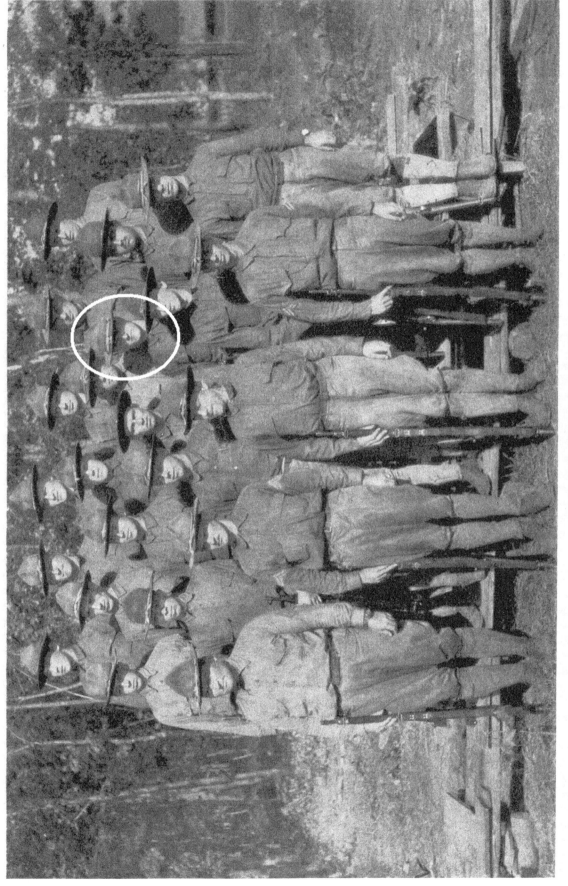

COMPANY "L"—THIRD PLATOON

First Row, left to right—Joseph A. Cox, William C. Higham, Edwin McGowan, Charles W. Hoblitzell, Warren M. Brown, Charles M. Allen.
Second Row, left to right—Ralph B. Tompkins, Walter Williams, Edward Paul, Charles R. Henderson, Joseph H. Kolb, John T. Woodside, Herbert L. Winslow, Maitland Rice.
Third Row, left to right—Wallace Hutchinson, George H. Jensen, Frank McHugh, Warren M. Nichols.
Fourth Row, left to right—Sergt. Edward Scott, Corp. Worthington S. Farley, Corp. Charles Glennen, Corp. Coit Ladd.

355

LIEBMANN Morris N. – Belgian Croix de Guerre
Lieutenant Colonel, 105th Infantry Regiment, 27th Division
KIA 6 August 1918
Plot C – Row 01 – Grave 06

Morris Nathaniel Liebmann was born in New York, NY on 13 July 1878. His father had emigrated to the U.S.A. from Frankfurt, Germany in 1866. Morris graduated from the University of Nebraska with a degree of Bachelor of Science in electrical engineering in June 1900. When the Spanish-American war broke out, Morris was a student at Nebraska and joined a Western Volunteer Regiment. After returning to New York in 1901, he joined the Foote-Pierson Company, a company specializing in fire-alarm and telegraph equipment. Liebmann soon became Chief Engineer and later Vice-President. He had also joined the 23rd New York National Guard as a private. Rising rapidly in rank, he became a corporal and later sergeant in 1904. In 1908 he was commissioned 1st Lieutenant and promoted to Captain in 1913. He served throughout the punitive campaign along the Mexican border in 1916. When the United States declared war, the 23rd Regiment became the 106th Infantry Regiment. On 3 May 1917 Morris was promoted to Lieutenant Colonel and transferred to the 105th Infantry Regiment as second in command. The Regiment sailed for Europe in May 1918.

Arriving in Belgium he became Commander of the 105th Infantry Regiment. During a routine inspection visit along the front, he was killed by a shell at Walker Farm (Dikkebus), which at

the time was headquarters of the 71st British Brigade. He had lost a leg and died almost instantly. He was buried at the British Abeele Aerodrome Military Cemetery on 18 August (Jewish marker photo insert). Morris Liebmann is the highest ranking officer from New York, the highest ranking Jewish officer of WWI and at the same time the highest ranking officer buried at Flanders Field Cemetery.

In 1921, the Belgian Government posthumously awarded Lieutenant Colonel Liebmann the Croix de Guerre (Belgian War Cross).

After the war the Foote-Pierson Company, Institute for Radio Engineers became the IEEE (Institute of Electrical and Electronic Engineers, Inc.). It is the world's leading professional association for the advancement of technology. In 1919, the IEEE Morris N. Liebmann Memorial Award was established by the Institute of Radio Engineers to perpetuate the memory of Lieutenant Colonel Morris N. Liebmann and was continued by the IEEE Board of Directors. It was superseded by the IEEE Daniel E. Noble Award in 2000.

Although no announcement had been made, Morris was engaged to marry Evelyn Van Horne after the war.

Walker Farm Then and Now

QUIRK Joseph J.
Private, Co. I, 363rd Infantry Regiment, 91st Division
DOW 1 November 1918
Plot C – Row 01 – Grave 07
Army Serial Number 3629597

Joseph Quirk was the son of Edward Quirk and Margaret Lahive (Irish immigrants) from Snow Shoe, PA. He was born on 13 July 1887, had two brothers: William and twin brother Patrick and three sisters: Elisabeth, Mary and Ella. William, Elisabeth and Mary died at a very young age. Joseph worked in the mines at the Lehigh Valley Coal Company. As an exemplary employee with leadership capabilities he was promoted to foreman at 22 years of age. He was called to arms on 29 June 1918 and received his basic training at Camp Lee, VA. He sailed for Europe at the end of August.

Joseph was wounded on 31 October during the initial attack in Waregem. He was first reported as missing but it was later confirmed that he had been taken to a French casualty clearing station on the outskirts of the village of Ooigem where he died the following day.

His brother Patrick, a foreman in the same mine, was also called to arms but survived the war. The Veterans of Foreign War Post #5644 in Snow Shoe, was named Quirk – Lauck - Kelly Post. His mother had planned to visit his grave with the Gold Star Mothers Pilgrimage in 1930. Unfortunately due to health issues she was unable to do so and sadly passed away on 26 December 1930.

BURNWORTH Willis L. – Silver Star

Sergeant, Co. H, 145th Infantry Regiment, 37th Division
DOW 1 November 1918
Plot C – Row 01 – Grave 08
Army Serial Number 1518883

Willis Lewis Burnworth was born in Bremen, OH on 6 June 1891. He was the son of A. Burnworth and Lavina Householder. He had four brothers: Charles, Newton, Edgar and Teddy, and four sisters: Goldie, Faye, Nellie and Viola. He was a member of the Methodist Church and attended the public schools of Rushcreek Township and the Bremen High School.

Willis worked as a farmer in Lancaster at the time he was called to arms on 30 May 1917. He was attached to the Ohio National Guard and received his basic training with Co. D of the 7th Infantry Regiment where he was promoted to Corporal on 10 October. When the 37th Division was formed, Willis was attached to Co. H of the 145th Infantry Regiment.

On 15 June he sailed from Hoboken, NJ on board the Leviathan (Vaterland)* and disembarked at Brest, France on 22 June. He served in the Baccarat, Avocourt, Meuse-Argonne and Pannes sector before arriving in Belgium. Here he was promoted to Sergeant on 25 October. For his actions on 31 October near the town of Olsene he received a Citation for Gallantry (in the 1930's this became the Silver Star – see Di Giacomo A-1-21). On this day he displayed exceptional coolness and courage in charging and capturing a strong machine gun nest. He was killed by concussion when an artillery shell fell close by.

He was buried where he fell close to the town of Olsene and on 6 July 1919 moved to Waregem. When his mother was asked on the final disposition of remains she replied:
"I want his remains be left over there since I am informed that they will be taken care of and remembered by a great nation for what he has done."

---

* USS Leviathan was originally the German passenger vessel "SS Vaterland" on the line Hamburg – New York. The vessel had only made a few Atlantic crossings when the German government decided to leave the ship at anchor in the harbor of Hoboken, NJ because of British control in the Atlantic. When the U.S.A. declared war in in 1917, the Vaterland was confiscated and used throughout the war for military transport to Europe.

HYDE Clarence A.

Private 1ˢᵗ Class, Co. D, 145ᵗʰ Infantry Regiment, 37ᵗʰ Division
KIA 1 November 1918
Plot C – Row 01 – Grave 09
Army Serial Number 1517919

Clarence Albert Hyde was born in Warren, OH on 22 December 1898. His parents were Washington George Oatley Hyde (a wealthy attorney – photo insert right) and Victoria Salina Pinkard. There were five other children in the family: Jessie, George, Charles, Edward and Lillian. Johnnie and Florence followed later but both died in infancy within a year.

Clarence volunteered with the National Guard in his home town Warren, OH on 26 May 1916 and was attached to the 5ᵗʰ Ohio Infantry Regiment. He was sent to Camp Sheridan, AL for his basic training. The 5ᵗʰ Ohio Infantry Regiment became part of the 145ᵗʰ Infantry Regiment, 37ᵗʰ Division.

On 7 October 1918 he wrote a letter to his friend Claude Perry with details of his experiences in the Argonne. He hoped his friend would never have to endure similar experiences. In the envelope he enclosed a button that he had torn from a German uniform. On 26 October he wrote home saying that he had taken part in four major attacks and that he never expected to survive. According to a witness statement by Private William Bergman of the same company, Clarence was killed on 31 October when he was hit by a shell killing him instantly. He was 19 years of age and so one of the youngest soldiers buried in Flanders Field.

His brother Edward was also serving in France with the 308ᵗʰ Ammunition Train, 83ʳᵈ National Army Division. They met during the Argonne offensive at the time Clarence was returning from the front lines. Edward gave him something to eat and a change of clothes. He wrote home that Clarence was in good health but that he looked a lot older than a few months earlier.

In December 1919, the American Legion Post #278 in Warren, OH was founded and named after him as he was the youngest soldier from Trumbull County killed during the war. On 12 February 1921, the "Ladies' Auxiliary" was established and his sister Lillian was elected commander.

Joe McGuane was also from Warren and is buried directly behind Clarence at Flanders Field.

no photograph available

WAJEIULA Jonas
Private, Co. I, 148th Infantry Regiment, 37th Division
KIA 1 November 1918
Plot C – Row 01 – Grave 10
Army Serial Number 1758082

Jonas (John) Wajciula (Waieiula) was born in Dankin, Lithuania (at the time former Russia) on 22 October 1893. His parents were Joseph Wajciula and Anna Wajciulene. He emigrated to the U.S.A. in July 1912 and found a job as a miner at the Staunton Coal Company in Livingston, IL. He had a brother Juozas (Joe) and a sister Annie, who also resided in the U.S.A. The name was spelled in many ways: Waijulus, Wajcinla, Waijulis, Wojzula, Waicaulis, Wajoenla, Wajcenea, Wajcuilis etc … Jonas wrote his name as Wajciula.

In 1917 he was called to register for the draft. His application for U.S. citizenship was ongoing: he had already received the documents and some sources claim that he had obtained his US citizenship in May 1918. He was called to arms on 30 April and after completing his basic training assigned to the 148th Infantry Regiment. He was killed on 1 November near the village of Kruishoutem and buried at the crossroads of Olsene and Kruishoutem together with twenty other American soldiers (photo below taken 2 November 1918). His remains were moved to Waregem on 7 June 1919 and buried in plot D, grave #139.

The American Legion Post in Livingston was named after him in 1924. The John "Waijulus" American Legion Post #377 lost its charter in 1963 but renewed in 1982. It was renamed the John J. Slifka Post in 1984.

no photograph available

ARPAIA Nicola S.
Private, Co. M, 148th Infantry Regiment, 37th Division
KIA 3 November 1918
Plot C – Row 1 – Grave 11
Army serial number 2833808

Nicola Arpaia was born in Irsina, Italy on 1 December 1890. His parents were Luca Arpaia and Cecilia Castelmezzano (stepmother). He had three sisters: Anna, Rachela and Maria. He emigrated to the U.S.A. in 1913. He obtained his U.S. citizenship in May 1918 and was employed by the Morgan and Randolph National Bio Co. at the time he was called to arms.

After his basic training he was assigned to Co. M of the 148th Infantry Regiment, 37th Division. He was killed in action on 3 November 1918 and buried together with other men of his division near the village of Kruishoutem. His remains were moved to Cemetery #1252 in Waregem and temporarily buried in plot D, grave #14. In 1922 he received his final resting place in Plot C – Row 1 – Grave 11.

His emergency address was registered with his friend Tony Savino in Chicago, who also originated from Irsina. In Irsina, a man bearing the same name was listed as missing after the war and memorialized on the town's war memorial. Research could not determine if they are referring to Nicola buried at Flanders Field.

MAXSON Clarence N.

Corporal, Co. L, 148th Infantry Regiment, 37th Division
KIA 1 November 1918
Plot C – Row 01 – Grave 12
Army Serial Number 1531074

Clarence Nathan Maxson was the son of Franklin Maxson and Julia Belle Davis (died 9 April 1917). He was born in Quincy, Logan County, OH on 15 May 1898. He had five half-brothers (Ira, David, Frank, Harry and Joe) from his father's first marriage with Ida J. Ball and two brothers from the second marriage (Herman and Lloyd). He was an exemplary student and attended the Rosewood High School. He moved with his parents to Sidney in 1916. He was very religious, loved music and was an excellent violinist.

In June 1916, at the age of 18, he volunteered for the Ohio National Guard and served along the Mexican border during the punitive campaign. After five months of basic training he served there with his brother Herman (Serial #1531044 – photo: Clarence and

Herman on duty in Mexico). They were assigned to Co. L of the 3rd Infantry Regiment Ohio National Guard (which later became the 148th Infantry Regiment, 37th Division). On 12 October 1917, Clarence was promoted to Private 1st Class and on 6 August 1918 to Corporal.

During his boot camp at Camp Sheridan he married Hazel Covault (photo insert) in Montgomery, AL on 18 April 1918. On that same day he became ill (Spanish flu) and was admitted into the base hospital. As he was placed in quarantine, Hazel was not allowed to visit him. She also caught the flu but quickly recovered thanks to the care she received from an Afro-American maid working at the hotel where she was staying. She dressed up as a nurse and with the help of one of Clarence's friends was able to smuggle herself into the base hospital to visit Clarence. The day he was discharged from hospital he received his reassignment orders.

He sailed for France on 22 June. He served with his brother in the Argonne. On 28 September his brother Herman was severely wounded. Clarence came to Belgium to take part in the last part of the Ypres-Lys offensive. On 30 October – two days before he was killed – he wrote his last will and testament. Details can be found on the next page. It is said that he was killed by a mine. He was buried at the crossroads between the villages of Olsene and Kruishoutem.

On 6 November one of Clarence's letters written to his wife a month earlier, was published in the Sidney Daily News.

My Darling Wife,
How are you by this time? Feeling fine and happy I hope. I am feeling fine. Received your letters a couple days ago and was glad to hear from you. This is the first chance I have had for over two weeks to write, but listen to the reason. We are just back from the front and was in a big drive and we sure did give them h----. I was under shell fire for six days and was in four different engagements so know what war means. Please don't worry for I am feeling fine…. In the third engagement Herman got wounded in the leg and arm by machine gun bullets so is not serious. Thank God we are still alive an I am able to keep the good work going. Your letter of September the fifth sure made me happy after going through what I did. Wish I could have been there to go with you to the fair. Maybe by next year I can be there to go with you. Here's hoping that I will be home before that. Well, I will have to close for this time. Hoping that you are well and that I may hear from you again soon.
Good bye,
Your husband, Corp. Clarence Maxson, Co. L, 148th Infantry, A.P.O. 763, American Ex. Forces."

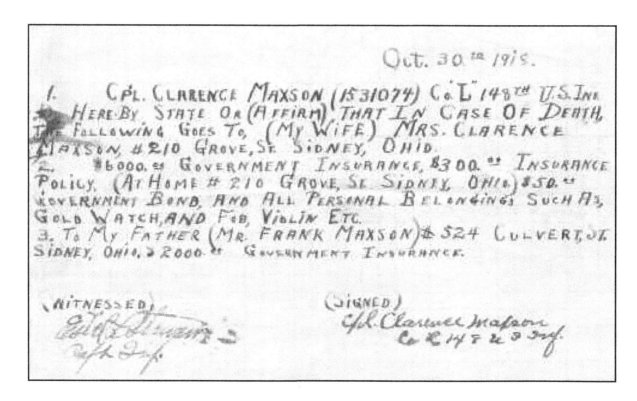

Oct. 30th 1918.

1. CPL. CLARENCE MAXSON (1531074) CoL 148rd U.S.Inf. HERE·BY STATE Or (AFFIRM) THAT IN CASE OF DEATH, THE FOLLOWING GOES TO, (MY WIFE) MRS. CLARENCE MAXSON, #210 GROVE, St. SIDNEY, OHIO.
2. $6000.00 GOVERNMENT INSURANCE, $300.00 INSURANCE POLICY, (AT HOME # 210 GROVE, St. SIDNEY, OHIO) $50.00 GOVERNMENT BOND, AND ALL PERSONAL BELONGINGS SUCH AS, GOLD WATCH, AND FOB, VIOLIN ETC.
3. To MY FATHER (MR. FRANK MAXSON) $524 CULVERT, St. SIDNEY, OHIO. $2000.00 GOVERNMENT INSURANCE.

(WITNESSED)

(SIGNED)
Cpl. Clarence Maxson
Co L 148 u s Inf.

The Memorial Service that was held for him back home concluded with: *"While his body lies in an unknown grave in France, we know that he died a Christian, a true soldier for Jesus Christ. As he helped to gain the mortal enemies of sic, death the victory for his country over her and hill by a living faith in his Redeemer. He shall have a share in the everlasting victory of Heaven. Darling Clarence, thou hast gone to rest, Help me, O Lord to say Thou Knowest best, Your noble life for your country was given, Your crown of glory was decked with the Stars of Heaven. You have crossed the golden sea, Where the waters roll to eternity. On that bright and shining shore. Troubles warfare are all o'er, Your noble life has won the crown, Your star of heaven will ne'er go down; It will shine forever on that heavenly shore, And there we'll meet where partings are no more."*

Franklin assumed that the remains of his son would be repatriated to the U.S. It was with great distress that he learned that Hazel had decided for his remains to be interred in Belgium. Photo insert is Clarence's wooden marker on Cemetery #1252.

no photograph available

HOLT Sherman C.
Private, Co. A, 147th Infantry Regiment, 37th Division
KIA 1 November 1918
Plot C – Row 01 – Grave 13
Army Serial Number 1758009

Sherman Charles Holt was born in Omaha, IL on 2 September 1892. He was the son of Solomon Holt and Martha Jean Taylor. He had two brothers (William Herchel and Larry Alvin) and four sisters (Ella, Flora, Liversa and Clara). He spent his whole life in Omaha. When he was called to arms in 1917, his registration card indicated that he claimed exemption based on having to take care of his father.

Sherman Holt was killed 1 km east of the village of Olsene on 31 October at 18:00 hours. He was digging in for the night when a shell fell close by and decapitated him. He was buried where he fell. He was moved to Waregem on 7 June 1919 and buried in plot D, grave 146 … or it was assumed. During the processing and final disposition of remains it was found that he was buried under the marker of Sabino Dattolo (in plot D, grave 144), who is now buried next to him. However there could be no doubt of identification as both of Sherman's ID tags were found on the remains.

no photograph available

DATTOLO Sabino
Private 1st Class, Co. K, 148th Infantry Regiment, 37th Division
KIA 2 November 1918
Plot C – Row 01 – Grave 14
Army Serial Number 2406411

Sabino Dattolo was born in Atripalda, Italy on 14 June 1892. He was the son of Carmela Tosca Dattolo. He emigrated to the U.S.A. in 1913 and found residence in Hackensack, NJ. He was called to register for the draft on 5 June 1917 and enlisted on 26 February 1918. He received his basic training with the 153rd Depot Brigade at Camp Dix, NJ. His emergency address was listed with his girlfriend Carmine Doeme.

On 14 September, shortly before the Meuse-Argonne offensive, he was promoted to Private 1st Class. He was killed near the village of Kruishoutem on 2 November and buried on 7 November. He was moved to Waregem on 6 July 1919.

Sabino and Rocco Dileo (C-1-4) were born on the same day, were attached to the same company and died on the same day.

WILLIAMS Henry
Sergeant, Co. I, 105th Infantry Regiment, 27th Division
KIA 1 September 1918
Plot C – Row 01 – Grave 15
Army Serial Number 1204979

Henry Williams was killed in action and first buried near the village of Dikkebus. The British later reburied him in the communal cemetery in the village of Voormezele. His remains were moved to Waregem on 8 November 1919 and interred at plot B, grave #195. On 15 March 1921 he was disinterred again and moved to plot D, grave 143. Both his parents had passed away and he had no other relatives. His emergency address was registered with his friend Warren Hulick, who was also the beneficiary of his war insurance policy. Warren decided that Henry's remains be permanently interred in Belgium. On 21 November 1923, Henry was finally laid to rest in Plot C.

STUBBS Roscoe H.
Private, Co. I, 117th Infantry Regiment, 30th Division
DOD 17 October 1918
Plot C – Row 01 – Grave 16
Army Serial Number 2154912

Roscoe Harold Stubbs was born in Pekin, IA on 25 January 1896. His parents were William and Kate Stubbs (née Lowenberg) both farmers. He had two brothers (John and Oliver) and two sisters (Ida and Maude). They had another child who died in infancy. The children spent a happy life on the farm in Hedrick, IA. Their father died in 1909 so Kathy was left to raise the children as a single parent.

He entered the service on 22 February and was sent for training to Camp Dodge, IA. He was attached to the 350th Infantry Regiment, 88th "Cloverleaf" Division. This division comprised of conscripts out of Illinois, Iowa, North Dakota and Minnesota. On 1 April he was transferred to Camp Sevier, SC and attached to Co. I of the 117th Infantry Regiment, 30th Division. He embarked for Europe via Camp Mills, NY. He disembarked in France on 24 May. He was wounded in the arm and taken prisoner on 7 October. His mother had first received word that he was missing in action. He died in Namur as prisoner of war from appendicitis on 17 October and buried in the communal cemetery (Cemetery #1836). It was not until

after 30 April 1920 that the authorities were made aware of the location of his remains in Namur. Shortly afterwards he was moved to Waregem and buried in in plot D, grave #136.

On 27 July 1932, his mother departed from Hedrick to Flanders Field with the Gold Star Mothers Pilgrimage. She was the only Gold Star Mother from Keokuk County traveling to Europe that year. She visited her son's grave on 11, 12 and 13 August.

The American Legion Post in Hedrick, IA was named after him. In 2015 Alan Stubbs visited the grave of his great-uncle.

CHERRY Edward H.

Private 1st Class, Co. K, 362nd Infantry Regiment, 91st Division
KIA 31 October 1918
Plot C – Row 01 – Grave 17
Army Serial Number 2936870

Edward Howard Cherry, son of John F. Cherry and Hester Matilda Porter, was born in Manila, IN on 28 October 1895. He was the youngest of the family. He had one brother John and two sisters, Minnie and Hazel.

Edward met Helen Hall and they had a son, James, born on 15 July 1916. They married the following year on 13 December 1917. He was employed as a mechanic in Indianapolis when he was called to arms on 24 June 1918 and sent for basic training to Camp Sherman, OH. He crossed the Atlantic with the 84th Lincoln Division in September. This was a National Army Division with conscripts from Illinois, Indiana and Kentucky. The division was disbanded upon arrival in Europe and Edward was reassigned to the 362nd Infantry Regiment, 91st Division.

Edward Cherry was shot through the head and chest by a sniper on 31 October near the village of Wortegem. He was killed instantly and buried in the Wortegem churchyard on 2 November.

no photograph available

JOHNSON Axel B.

Private, Co. G, 148th Infantry Regiment, 37th Division
KIA 1 November 1918
Plot C – Row 01 – Grave 18
Army Serial Number 3333873

Axel Bernhard Björk was born in Sweden. Nothing is known about his biological father. His mother, Matilda Kristina Johannisdottir married Johan Aron Björk in 1897 and he adopted Axel as his son. Johan and Matilda had five more children: three boys (Johan Gottfrid, Gunnar Fridolf and Carl Gustav) and two girls (Agnes and Emmi Regina). Axel emigrated to the U.S.A. on 8 November 1912 and found residence in Rossburg, MN with his aunt Amanda

Johnson. The name Björk, caused some difficulties in the U.S.A. so he first changed his name to Johanson and finally to Johnson. Axel was called to arms and sent to Europe. Before departure he took a war insurance policy to which his mother was made sole beneficiary.

He was attached to CO. K of the 344th Infantry Regiment, 86th Black Hawk Division. Upon

arrival in Europe the division was disbanded and Axel was reassigned to the 148th Infantry Regiment. He was killed near Kruishoutem on 1 November, circumstances of death unknown, and found in a ditch the next day. He was buried at the crossroads between Olsene and Kruishoutem by the divisional senior chaplain on 7 November. His remains were moved to Cemetery #1252 in 1919 and interred in plot D - grave 141. On 22 June 1922 he received his final resting place at Flanders Field Cemetery.

One of the men in this photograph is Axel Johnson. The postcard was provided courtesy of Mr. Elwood Swanson, Crystal, MN, who found it between his parent's personal belongings.

KINGDON Leon F.
Private, Co. L, 148th Infantry Regiment, 37th Division
KIA 1 November 1918
Plot C – Row 1 – Grave 19
Army Serial Number 2416954

Leon Kingdon was born in Stafford, NY on 7 October 1891. His parents were William (a Welsh immigrant) and Sarah Kingdon. He was the oldest of this farming family. He was followed by seven more children: four sons - Earl, Merton, Floyd and Lester – and three daughters– Bessie, Cary and Ruth. Photo insert is Leon on the right with one of his brothers during their teens. It is unknown when his father passed away but it must have been before 1910. Sarah was left behind to raise the

children as a single parent. Leon married Marie Louise Crouse from Batavia on 23 July 1917. They were blessed with a daughter Ruth Margaret in September 1918 (photo insert left). In the meantime Leon, inducted on 27 April, had been sent to Camp Dix, NJ for basic training.

He was killed on 1 November, shot through the heart by a machine gun bullet, and buried near Olsene. Seven months later his daughter Ruth Margaret passed away from a lung infection, most probably a complication of the Spanish flu. Marie later remarried a certain William Norton.

A memorial marker was erected in Leon's memory in the Stafford Rural Cemetery near Batavia. His mother Sarah (photo insert right) visited his grave with the Gold Star Mothers Pilgrimage in 1930. Due to health issues she had requested that her daughter, a nurse, would be allowed to accompany her during the trip. Her request was denied.

WHITE Ernest R.
Private, Co. D, 148th Infantry Regiment, 37th Division
KIA 31 October 1918
Plot C – Row 01 – Grave 20
Army Serial Number 2942593

E(a)rnest Richard White was born in Charleston, IL on 1 January 1894. He was the son of Thomas Marion White (1855-1917) and Eliza Williams (1858–1934) who were both farmers. They married in 1875 and were destined to have a difficult life. Thomas was an agricultural laborer. After living in Kentucky for a while they moved to Lena, IL (which to date has 400 inhabitants). They had nine children, six boys and three girls: Essie May (18 March 1877 -16 June 1887), Clarence H. (28 March 1880 - 17 September 1880), Bessie L. (09 August 1881 - 15 June 1887), Learline (26 April 1884 - 18 June 1887), James A. (29 August 1887 - 29 July 1962), Theodore (31 August 1890 – Summer 1979), his twin brother (31 August 1890 - 31 August 1890), Earnest and finally Fairel Reama (30 March 1900 – 04 February 1976). As one can see, Clarence died at 6 months of age. His three sisters died within four days during a measles epidemic and Theodore's twin brother only lived one day. So only four of their nine children survived into adulthood.

On the family photo from left to right: Eliza, James, Ernest, Theodore, Fairel and Thomas. The family endured many hardships during the upbringing of their children. Three of them served during World War I: Theodore, Ernest and Fairel. Ernest and Fairel served in Europe.

Ernest was called to arms on 29 April 1918 and reported for duty in Mattoon, IL. He sailed for Europe with Co. D of the 148th Infantry Regiment.

His legs above the knees were riddled with shell fragments. He smoked a cigarette and died fifteen minutes later. He was buried on the south side of the railroad in Olsene (Isolated Grave #4 Olsene) and his remains were moved to Waregem on 7 June 1919. Ernest was buried in plot D, grave #148.

Ernest wrote many letters home. His first letter was not dated. He asked his parents to be cautious and not to provide any details in writing on other military units crossing the Atlantic. He also mentioned he would write to his girlfriend Clara Lee in Charleston.

7 July 1918: he wrote that he had arrived safely "*somewhere in France*" and asked if they had received news on Fairel's whereabouts.

5 August 1918: Ernest wrote "*….I do not look for this to last much longer I hope not, for I am ready to come home any time but do not want to come until it is all over……..*" and "*I like my position that I now have. I am now one of the Runner boys………..*"

10 August 1918: "*Our boys had a clipping out of a paper the other day telling the names of the Coles County boys that weren't in the draft the 20th of June. There were sure a bunch of them. I haven't seen a Dutchman since I arrived in France only those that were taken prisoners. The experience I have had, about the only thing that seems natural out here besides our American boys is the sparrows. The owls even talk French………..*"

1 September 1918: "*We are back at the front lines again the same place we were before. I would much rather be in the front lines then to be back a ways for I do not mind it at all here. We boys were paid a few days ago, the first time since we reached France. The French money looks more like wallpaper than it does money….*" He was also concerned about his folks back home and the winter just around the corner: "*You had better buy coal enough for this winter before it gets cold weather. Maybe you and Overtons* (a neighbor) *can buy a car of coal together by doing that you can buy it cheaper.*"

29 October 1918: Two days before he was killed in action: "*Somewhere in Belgium – Dear Mother…We are still on the go and the dutch still going further for they have took to the Run march…….I got a letter from Clara she said she wished our boys were home and so do I.*" He was also concerned about his war insurance policy "*I don't know why you haven't gotten my insurance papers yet as the rest of the boys have got theirs but I will see about it soon. I will have to close as the mail is going out and will have to send it so am saying, From Son to Mother*"

IN MEMORY OF ERNEST WHITE
By Charles J. Gray

Sleep on, dear boy, beneath the sunny sky,
In quiet peaceful rest;
Thou taught us how a hero dies;
Thy memory is forever blest.

Thy golden star forever glows
To a light a land made free,
And from thy action flows
Choice gifts for all, for me.

A few brief days shall come and go,
And friends shall meet with you;
Then all shall fully know
You heroes as you pass in review.

Before the Prince of Peace,
And there receive your starry crown.
Take now your sweet release
For thou hast laid earth's burdens down.

His mother received $2,300 as compensation of Ernest's war insurance policy. With that money she bought a home in Charleston, where she retired. A memorial marker was also erected in memory of Ernest (photo insert) close to where she would be buried in Roselawn Cemetery in Charleston. On the marker one can read "Buried in France".

On 11 November 1921, the American Legion Post #93 in Charleston planted 26 trees in memory of the men from the County who were killed in action during the Great War. One in name of Ernest. On the Courthouse lawn in Charleston a War Memorial was also erected to those who lost their lives.

When his mother was asked what to do with his remains, she chose to leave Ernest in Europe because she had heard that many parents had received the wrong remains.

no photograph available

CRAWFORD Samuel W.
Private, Co. G, 146th Infantry Regiment, 37th Division
KIA 10 November 1918
Plot C – Row 01 – Grave 21
Army Serial Number 2705299

Samuel Wisler Crawford was born on 19 April 1894. He was employed as a clerk for a company in Philadelphia, PA. On his registration card he stipulated that he had his mother, Suzie Eichel, in his care. His father had passed away in 1901.

He was shot through the heart by a machinegun bullet the day before the armistice along the banks of the river Scheldt. This happened close to the village of Hermelgem. He was buried on the left bank of the river near the village of Zingem. His remains were moved to the communal cemetery of the village in March 1919 and to Waregem (plot B, grave #22) in 1921. Details in his NARA burial file indicate that Samuel was of the Jewish faith, yet he rests under a Latin Cross.

On the final disposition of remains, Suzie initially chose for repatriation but, as one of many, later changed her mind.

WISER Emil P.
Private, Ambulance Co. 112th Sanitary Train, 37th Division
KIA 31 October 1918
Plot C – Row 01 – Grave 22
Army Serial Number 2006688

Emil Paul Wiser was born in Lafayette, IN on 19 October 1891. His parents were Frank and Elizabeth Wiser. Frank was a watchmaker. The fact that they were Swiss immigrants may have played a role. Emil was an only child. He followed his father's footsteps and became a watchmaker. In a 1915 newspaper article Emil was cited as having won some property in the State lottery.

He was inducted on 26 April 1918 and sent for basic training to Camp Taylor, KY. He was attached to the 146th Ambulance Company, 112th Sanitary Train and served as a stretcher bearer. Sometime later he was transferred to Camp Sheridan, AL.

He was mortally wounded in the chest by a shell fragment on 31 October. He was originally buried near the town of Olsene, along the road to Deinze. His remains were moved to Waregem in 1919 and buried in plot B, grave #109.

His mother visited the family in Switzerland in 1921. She had requested the details on Emil's grave location with the Graves Registration. Her intentions were to place a private memorial marker on his grave. Of course this was denied (see Chapter 6 – American Graves Registration Service).

LANG Walter
Sergeant, Co. C, 147th Inf. Regiment, 37th Division
KIA 11 November 1918
Plot C – Row 01 – Grave 23
Army Serial Number 1525048

Walter Lang was the son of William Lang and Elizabeth Bisack from Cincinnati, OH. He was born in 1898 and had two brothers (William Jr. and Frederick) and one sister (Margaret).

Walter joined the Ohio National Guard on 6 April 1917, the day the US declared war on Germany. He was promoted to Private 1st Class on 15 July and Corporal on 6 June 1918. On 23 October he received his additional stripes as Sergeant. He was killed in action during the night of 10 and 11 November near the village of Zingem, a stone's throw from the river Scheldt. An important mission was assigned to him in bringing a message to the commander of Co D (cessation of hostilities?). He was killed by artillery fire on his way back to his unit. He was buried in the communal cemetery of Zingem and on 20 March 1919 his remains were moved to "New Syngem Belgian Cemetery". On 4 June of that same year he was moved to Waregem and buried in plot B, grave #21.

William and Frederick were also serving their country during the war. William was never assigned overseas but Frederick served with the 334th Infantry Regiment, 84th Division.

Elizabeth could not cope with the death of her son and died of grief in 1919. William and Frederick married two sisters: Marie and Rose Kallmeyer. In both cases there were no children. Walter Lang joined the service on the first day of the U.S. declaration of war and died on the last day of the war to end all wars.

McLAUGHLIN Joseph
Private 1st Class, Co. C, 107th Infantry Regt., 27th Division
KIA 16 August 1918
Plot C – Row 02 – Grave 01
Army Serial Number 1210224

Joseph McLaughlin was born in Kilwinning, Scotland on 7 November 1890. He was the son of John and Catherine McLaughlin (née Connelly – photo left). He

had three brothers (James, John and Bernard) and four sisters (Catherine, Susan, Annie and Elisabeth). Picture right is the family before Elisabeth was born. Joseph is the baby in his mother's arms. Joseph emigrated to the U.S.A. in 1911 and found residence in New York City. He was employed by the railroad as an engine driver.

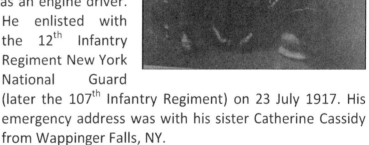

He enlisted with the 12th Infantry Regiment New York National Guard (later the 107th Infantry Regiment) on 23 July 1917. His emergency address was with his sister Catherine Cassidy from Wappinger Falls, NY.

He was originally buried at the Abeele Aerodrome Military Cemetery. The circumstances leading to his death are unknown but when he was disinterred for reburial in Waregem on 21 June 1922, it was found that he had a shattered skull.

On 26 September 2015, Gerry and Mary McDougall from Glasgow, Scotland, visited the grave of Gerry's great uncle.

no photograph available

GALLAGHER Bryan L.
Private, Co. I, 107th Infantry Regiment, 27th Division
KIA 13 August 1918
Plot C – Row 02 – Grave 02
Army Serial Number 409611

Bryan Gallagher was born in New York City in 1901. He was the son of Chas (Charles) Gallagher and Joanna Lawrence. Bryan had four brothers (George, Edwin, Charles and William) and three sisters (Nathalie, Mary and Margaret).

Bryan enlisted at Fort Slocum on 16 April 1918 and was attached to Co. I of the 107th Infantry Regiment on 23 April 1918 until death. He lied about his age claiming he was 20. He was killed when a mortar shell landed in his trench near Mount Kemmel. Herbert Winslow (C-01-05) was killed during the same incident. They were both buried at the Abeele Aerodrome Military Cemetery. When Bryan was disinterred for permanent burial in Waregem, a journal, cross and Roman Catholic related memorabilia were found in his pocket.

His mother visited Flanders Field Cemetery with the Gold Star Mothers Pilgrimage on 29, 30 and 31 May 1930. She was 55 years of age. She was very grateful for the trip and expressed her gratitude in a letter to the Government.

Bryan Gallagher and John Noonan (B-01-23) are the youngest soldiers buried in Flanders Field Cemetery. Both were under the age of 18 at the time of their death.

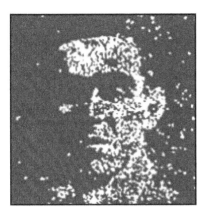

KELLY Lynn E.
Private 1st Class, Co C, 107th Infantry Regiment, 27th Division
KIA 17 August 1918
Plot C – Row 02 – Grave 03
Army Serial Number 1210210

Lynn Edward Kell(e)y was born in Bouckville, NY on 26 February 1891. He was the son of Michael and Jessie Kell(e)y. He enlisted with the 1st Infantry Regiment New York National Guard in Utica on 23 July 1917. Lynn had lived in Utica with his mother and sister Ethel since 1916. His father had passed away a number of years before and his mother remained single, taking care of the children. On his draft registration card we see that he was employed as a knitter at the Augusta Knitting Company in Utica.

Lynn Kelly sailed with the 107th Infantry Regiment to Europe. He became a Private 1st Class on 8 August. He was killed nine days later and initially buried at Abeele Aerodrome Military Cemetery. His remains were moved to Waregem on 20 June 1922.

KNOWN BUT TO GOD
Plot C – Row 02 – Grave 04

A keen – edged sword, a soldier's heart

Is greater than a poet's art

And greater than a poet's fame

A little grave that has no name

Francis Ledwidge (1887-1917)
Artillery Wood Cemetery – Boezinge, Belgium

ROBERTS Carl W.

Sergeant, Co M, 145th Infantry Regiment, 37th Division
KIA 4 November 1918
Plot C – Row 02 – Grave 05
Army Serial Number 1519876

Carl W. Roberts was born in Willoughby, OH on 18 August 1896. He was the only child of Cutler and Cora Alice Roberts (née Byers). His grandfather, Ransom Roberts was a veteran of the Civil War (insert right).

He attended Willoughby High School, was an active member in student associations and was also a keen athlete. At the time the United States declared war on Germany, Carl was employed at the "Standard Tire & Rubber Company ". He reported for duty with the Ohio National Guard on 7 May 1917.

On 12 September 1917 he married Gladys Lynn (insert right), who was pregnant with their daughter Mildred (born 8 December 1918) at the time Carl was killed in action.

Carl was attached to Co. M of the 145th Infantry Regiment, 37th Division. He was an exemplary soldier and after two months he had climbed the ranks to Sergeant. He was killed in action while trying to establish a bridgehead over the river Scheldt in Oudenaarde.

On 20 December 1918, an article on Carl was published in the Willoughby Republican making reference to the poem "In Flanders Field" by John McCrae in his honor. It is evident that the poem was rapidly becoming famous worldwide.

The American Legion Post #214 in Willoughby was named after him.

LEWIS Everett D.
Private, Co. M, 364th Infantry Regiment, 91st Division
DOW 2 November 1918
Plot C – Row 02 – Grave 06
Army Serial Number 2265679

Everett Denver Lewis was the son of Edward Lewis and Mollie Morris from Miller, MO. He was born in Oklahoma on 24 December 1888. He had one brother, Herman. Everett lived in Los Angeles, CA and worked as a carpenter at the time he was called to register for the draft in 1917.

He received his basic training at Camp Lewis, WA and participated in all of the 91st Division campaigns. During the fighting near Waregem he was hit in the left upper thigh by machinegun bullets. He was taken to Evacuation Hospital #5 in Staden but succumbed to his wounds shortly afterwards. His remains were moved to Waregem on 6 June 1919.

Mollie joined the Gold Star Mothers Pilgrimage and visited his grave on 7, 8, and 9 June 1931. His parents erected a memorial marker to the memory of Everett in the Miller cemetery.

Everett leaving for Camp Lewis (third from left)

no photograph available

TOCCOTELLI Tony
Private, HQ Co. 148th Infantry Regiment, 37th Division
KIA 31 October 1918
Plot C – Row 02 – Grave 07
Army Serial Number 1528159

Antonio (Tony) Toccotelli was born in Avezzono, Aquila province, Italy on 23 May 1893. He was the son of Frank and Maria Toccotelli. He emigrated to the United States on the SS Perugia, sailing from Naples and arriving in the U.S. on 16 February 1910. Tony was only 17 years of age.

At the time he was called to arms he was living in Bedford, OH. He enlisted on 18 September 1917 and received his basic training with the 158th Depot Brigade. He was later attached to Headquarters Company of the 148th Infantry Regiment.

He was buried in the American plot in Dentergem (grave #15). On 4 June 1919 he was moved to Waregem and buried in plot C, grave #148. During the permanent disposition and repatriation of remains program in 1922, a grave was found with marker Dominick Pasquatela. When the grave was opened the remains and Tony's ID tags were found. A thorough investigation followed and it was found that Domenico Pasquale (= correct name) had survived the war.

At the time of death he was still an Italian citizen. His emergency address was registered with his brother Frank in Italy.

CRAWFORD George
Private 1ˢᵗ Class, Co. E, 107ᵗʰ Infantry Regiment, 27ᵗʰ Division
KIA 16 August 1918
Plot C – Row 02 – Grave 08
Army Serial Number 1210632

George Crawford came from Newburgh, Orange County, NY. He was born on 18 September 1894. He reported for duty with the New York National Guard on 20 June 1916 and was attached to Co. E, 1ˢᵗ New York Infantry Regiment. He served with this unit during the punitive campaign along the Mexican border (Pancho Villa rebellion). When the A.E.F. was formed in 1917, the regiment became the 107ᵗʰ Infantry Regiment. George was promoted to Private 1ˢᵗ Class on 24 April 1918. The following month he sailed for Europe.

On 16 August he received orders to move forward to an advanced location together with three other men. He was killed by a direct hit from an artillery shell. The other men were severely wounded and one of them (Private Stephen McCaul) succumbed to his wounds two days later. The two other men were severely wounded. George was buried in the American plot at Abeele Aerodrome Military Cemetery.

no photograph available

McGUANE Joe V.
Corporal, Co. C, 135ᵗʰ MG Battalion, 37ᵗʰ Division
KIA 2 November 1918
Plot C – Row 02 – Grave 09
Army Serial Number 1516371

Joseph Vincent McGuane was born on 24 April 1896. He was the son of Thomas McGuane and Margaret (Maggie) Casey (both Irish immigrants) from Warren, OH. Joseph had one brother (John) and two sisters (Mary and Lizzie). "Joe" lived in Warren, OH and was employed by the Wells-Fargo Express Company. He reported to the Machine Gun Company, 10ᵗʰ Ohio National Guard in Youngstown on 4 June 1917.

One other soldier from Warren, OH, Clarence Hyde, is also interred at Flanders Field Cemetery (C – 01 - 09).

KASTEN Brook F.
Private, Co. L, 363rd Infantry Regiment, 91st Division
KIA 31 October 1918
Plot C – Row 02 – Grave 10
Army Serial Number 2780064

Brook Frank Kasten (°11 October 1890) was the son of Rudolf Kasten and Ardella (Della) Tinlin, farmers from Deerfield, MO. They had one other son (Rudolph) and one daughter (Rachel). Brook's grandfather was a German immigrant (1842) and had fought in the Civil War with the Missouri Militia. Brook's uncle Frank fought in the Spanish-American war. Brook found no future in Missouri and so moved to Los Angeles, CA where he found a job as a clerk with the Southern Pacific Company. In 1917 he was called to register for the draft and a few months later called to arms. As with most draftees from California, Brook was attached to the 91st Wild West Division.

Brook was mortally wounded by machinegun fire near Waregem on 31 October 1918. He was buried in the American plot 1673 (known in Waregem as Potegem 198) on 2 November. Twenty-five other American soldiers were temporarily buried at this location.

In reply to the query of the U.S. Government on the permanent disposition of remains, his parents replied: *"We prefer he would be buried in the soil where he gave his life for the people."*

His parents were very poor and the correspondence between them and the authorities in reference to the Gold Star Mothers Pilgrimage was very poignant. His mother could not take part as she had to take care of a handicapped brother. Della repeatedly pleaded for the possibility of receiving the monetary value of the trip to Europe be paid out to her in cash. This reflects the social hardships of the depression in the 1930's, when poverty and lack of social services were at the base of hardship and in many cases also lead to a point of starvation.

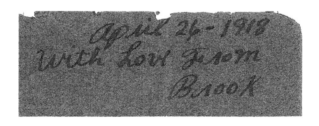

HERMAN Louis J.
Private 1st Class, Co. K, 108th Infantry Regiment, 27th Division
KIA 13 August 1918
Plot C – Row 02 – Grave 11
Army Serial Number 1215483

Louis Herman(n) was born on 2 July 1895. His parents were John Hermann and Maria Wilhelmine Kolbe, both of German origin. He had six sisters (Elsie, Dora, Helene, Ida, Amanda and Alice) and two brothers (Elmer and John Jr). On the photo insert, Louis is standing far right. This wealthy family lived in Martinsville, Niagara County, NY. This city was originally a settlement founded by German Lutherans. Most of them worked at the world renowned Wurlitzer Company. Due to his remarkable hearing abilities, Louis was hired as piano tuner. Louis was good looking and a ladies man. The number of photographs in the company of beautiful women are numerous.

As a member of Co. K of the 108th Infantry Regiment 27th Division he was sent to Europe. Photo insert next page was taken upon departure to the assembly point of embarkation.

There are two versions on his death. The first was published in a local newspaper: "*he was killed by an artillery shell when leaving his dugout.*" The second version being that his curiosity was his unfortunate fate. The men of his company claimed that he could have survived if he had kept his head below the trench parapet. He was shot through the head by a German sniper. He was initially buried at the British Abeele Aerodrome Military Cemetery (photo insert). After the war his friends returned his journal and the photo of his sister Ida which he had always kept with him.

no photograph available

NOVAK John
Private, Co. M, 106th Infantry Regiment, 27th Division
DOD 30 August 1918
Plot C – Row 02 – Grave 12
Army Serial Number 2039333

John Novak was born in Pittsburgh, PA on 24 June 1892. He was the son of Anthony and Pauline Novak (German-Polish immigrants). They had three daughters (Anna, Mary and Rose) and one son (Thomas). John married Mary Valinko in 1912 and within a year she gave birth to a boy, John Jr. Mary was born in Austria-Hungary and was only 15 years of age at the time of her marriage. They took residence in Passaic, NJ. John was working in Detroit, MI at the time he was called to register for the draft in 1917.

John Novak died of epileptic convulsions on 30 August. He was initially buried at the Abeele Aerodrome Military Cemetery near Poperinge.

Mary visited her husband's grave with the Gold Star Mothers Pilgrimage on 13 May 1930.

PETRO Stephen Jr.
Private, MG Co. 105th Infantry Regiment, 27th Division
KIA 12 August 1918
Plot C – Row 02 – Grave 13
Army Serial Number 2671660

Stephen Petro was born in Linoleumville, Staten Island, NY on 26 March 1891. He worked as a pipe fitter in New Jersey.

He was buried at the Abeele Aerodrome Military Cemetery on 13 August. When he was disinterred for permanent burial in Waregem it was determined that he had a fractured leg.

no photograph available

ANNANDALE Frederick N.
1st Lieutenant, Co. M, 148th Infantry Regiment, 37th Division
DOW 31 October 1918
Plot C – Row 02 – Grave 14

Frederick Napier Annandale was born in Stonehaven, Kincardineshire, Scotland on 16 November 1888. He was the son of Arthur Burnett Annandale (a renowned banker and wealthy landowner) and Martha Napier. He had three older brothers: Arthur Disney, James Scott and Charles James. Frederick emigrated to America around 1909. The first five years he worked as a clerk in a bank in Canada. In 1914 he moved to Sidney, OH and became an employee at Wagner House, a well-known hotel. He was praised for his dependability and efficiency. He hardly ever spoke of his life in Scotland. However it appears that he had gained some military experience while over there. At one time he said his only wish was to be able to return to his parents in Scotland as an American officer. He joined the Ohio National Guard on 19 June 1916. He was assigned to Co. L of the 3rd Infantry Regiment (photo next page – Frederick should be in the front row) and served along the Mexican border. In no time he was promoted to Corporal then Sergeant. In 1917, the 3rd Infantry Regiment became the 148th Infantry Regiment, 37th Division. Due to his military experience and above mentioned efficiency he was promoted to 2nd Lieutenant on 21 December 1917 and to 1st Lieutenant on 9 May 1918, first with Co. M of the same regiment and later to Headquarters Company.

He embarked for Europe on 22 June. In one of his letters sent from France to Alice Smith (his employer's daughter and in all probability his fiancée) he wrote about the adverse weather conditions in "that country". He also reported that he was proud in the manner in which the Americans stood their ground against the Germans. He had suffered from a gas attack but was back on duty within two days. He assumed that the "Dutch" had had enough of the war due to the American perseverance in battle.

1st Lieutenant Frederick Annandale died near the town of Olsene from wounds sustained in action on 31 October 1918. His friends described him as a gentleman officer.

His brother Charles James, who had immigrated to New Zealand, also served in the war. He was a bombardier with the 3rd Battery, New Zealand Artillery. He was killed in action in France during the Battle of the Somme on 16 September 1916. Charles is buried in the Caterpillar Valley Cemetery in Longueval at XIV.F.21 (photo insert).

393

WOLL Edward J.

Wagoner, Co. A, 104th MG Battalion, 27th Division
KIA 14 August 1918
Plot C – Row 02 – Grave 15
Army Serial Number 1200467

Wagoner Edward Joseph Woll, son of Michael and Katherine Woll was born in Brooklyn New York in 1898. He had one sister. Shortly after the U.S. declaration of war he joined the National Guard and was attached to Troop C, 1st New York Cavalry, which later became the 104th Machine Gun Battalion.

He was killed near Mount Scherpenberg on 14 August 1918. The circumstances of his death are described in the famous book *"Over there with O'Ryan's Roughnecks"* by Private 1st Class William F. Clarke: *"At 2:00 A.M we were relieved by a machine gun group from the 41st British Division. And I picked up our gun and tripod, ammunition belts and water cans to find our way back to platoon headquarters. When we reached the old farmhouse, our men had been relieved and had not waited for us. The boys in the trench of the Front Line let us through after a challenge. Finally we found the sunken road and arrived at Company Headquarters. There was something different. Several smashed limbers were laying around, three dead mules were lying outside Lieutenant Vanderbilt's dugout. Lieutenant Cummings and Battalion Adjutant Brodsky were there. Lieutenant Cashin was also there and gave us the story of what happened. Ambulances had removed the dead and wounded. All was quiet except the noise of the ration parties, when out of nowhere the whine of a large caliber shell was heard coming from the south. No one paid it much attention, the zest side of Scherpenberg was natural protection from a direct hit. Before it was too late to realize the danger, the shell exploded directly in front of and a little to our right of our Company's dugout. The casualties in our Company were four killed, two died of wounds, six wounded and four mules killed. The two limbers were shattered to kindling. There were Franklin Updike, Bill Higgins* (Plot C - Row 2 - Grave 17) *the crap shooter and one of the mule skinners, Eddie Woll, my pup tent mate, and Lee killed. "*

Wagoner Edward Joseph Woll was originally buried at the Abeele Aerodrome Military Cemetery (American Plot III) together with 81 other casualties of the 27th Division. Two graves further along the same row at Flanders Field cemetery is that of Wagoner William Ardiss Higgins Jr. who was killed during the same incident.

When in 1929 his mother received the letter inviting her to participate in the Gold Star Mothers Pilgrimages to Europe she declined due to her feeble health at the time. Later she changed her mind and was still able to join the 1930 passage to Europe. She visited her son's grave on 29 May 1930. She was 55 years of age.

no photograph available

BUSCEMO Salvatore

Private, Co. M, 105th Infantry Regiment, 27th Division
KIA 30 August 1918
Plot C – Row 02 – Grave 16
Army Serial Number 2672824

Salvatore Buscemo was born in Santa Croce, Italy on 3 April 1895. He was the son of Rafaelo Buscemo and lived in Brooklyn, NY. He had one brother, Antonio. They both worked as garment manufacturers at the Goldberg Button Co.

Salvatore and a corporal had been instructed to take position in a shell-hole out front of the line to act as observers near Dikkebus lake. Using a mirror as a periscope, the sun flashed in the mirror giving away their position and the Germans dropped several heavy shells killing them instantly. He was buried at the Abeele Aerodrome Military Cemetery and his remains were moved to Waregem on 20 June 1922.

no photograph available

HIGGINS William A. Jr.

Wagoner, Co. A, 104th MG Battalion, 27th Division
KIA 14 August 1918
Plot C – Row 02 – Grave 17
Army Serial Number 1200499

William Ardiss Higgins Jr. was born in Brooklyn, NY in 1896. He was the son of William Higgins Sr. and Linetta (Nettie) Strong. There were five other children in this wealthy family: Albert, Edmund, Robert, Louise and Mildred. William was an exemplary student attending his second year at the Rensselaer Polytechnic Institute, one of the oldest technological research universities in the U.S., when he decided to volunteer with the New York National Guard (1st Cavalry) on 22 May 1917. He was assigned as Wagoner with the 104th Machine Gun Battalion, 27th Division in April 1918.

He was killed on 14 August near Mount Scherpenberg during the same artillery incident as Edward Woll. Both were buried in the American plot at Abeele Aerodrome Military Cemetery before receiving permanent burial at Flanders Field.

His mother donated a stained glass window to the local church (Central Congregational Church) in memory of William. The details are that of Christ blessing a soldier with the words in gold: "*Thine O Lord, Is the Victory*".

In August 1932, Nettie (left) traveled to Europe with the Gold Star Mothers. Her daughter Mildred (right) accompanied her at her own expense. Mildred had already visited her brother's grave on two previous occasions in 1926.

To this day the family is still very influential in New York circles.

Mount Scherpenberg 1914 and 1918

William has a memorial marker in the family plot at Green-Wood Cemetery, Brooklyn.

WILLIAM ARDISS, JR
1897 — 1918

LIND Charles O.

Private, Co. I, 106th Infantry Regiment, 27th Division
KIA 31 August 1918
Plot C – Row 02 – Grave 18
Army Serial Number 1208247

Karl Olaf Lind was born in Sala, Sweden on 31 January 1894. His parents were August and Maria Lind. Upon arrival in the U.S. they took residence in Brooklyn, NY. Karl soon became "Charles" and he was a newspaper reporter for the Brooklyn Standard Union. He enlisted with the 14th Infantry Regiment New York National Guard on 7 June 1917. He had married just before he sailed for Europe.

Charles was wounded in the left leg and admitted into hospital for six weeks. After returning to his unit he wrote home on 25 August indicating that he had recuperated well and that he was glad to be back with his old friends.

He was buried at Abeele Aerodrome Military Cemetery and his remains were moved to Waregem on 21 June 1922. It had been his mother's wish that his remains be repatriated to the U.S.A., but in a letter she wrote about his wife: *"She remarried before he had turned cold in his grave."* This was apparently the reason why his wife had decided that his remains be left in Europe.

He had two brothers who were also serving their country: Eugene, who served with the Maryland National Guard during the punitive campaign along the Mexican border in 1916, was also stationed in Europe. Ellis Robert who had served as a career soldier in Panama was at that time in a camp in Louisiana.

Maria declined the invitation to the Gold Star Mothers Pilgrimages due to her ill health. She was 67 at the time.

The Lind family: August and Maria. To the rear from left to right: Eugene, Ellis Robert and Theodore. Charles is not in this photograph. It is thought that it was taken after the war.

no photograph available

WETMORE Albert A.

Corporal, Co. G, 105th Infantry Regiment, 27th Division
DOW 1 September 1918
Plot C – Row 02 – Grave 19
Army Serial Number 1204723

Albert Wetmore was born in November 1899. He was the son of Albert Wetmore and Harriet (Hattie) Titley from Port Leyden, NY. They had a daughter Bertha (°1893) and another son Clinton.

Albert enlisted with the local National Guard post in Gloversville, NY on 20 April 1917 (2nd Infantry Regiment – later became the 105th Infantry Regiment). He sailed for Europe on 7 May.

Albert was promoted to Corporal on 6 July 1918. On 1 September he was sent with his platoon on a reconnaissance mission trying to locate German machinegun nests. He was severely wounded while engaged. He was taken to a field hospital but succumbed to his wounds that same day. He was buried in the American plot at Abeele Aerodrome Military Cemetery (III.E.3).

Clinton was also called to arms but never served in Europe.

Hattie had registered to join the 1930 Gold Star Mothers Pilgrimage to Europe. However at the last minute she changed her mind as she feared the trip would be too emotional for her weak heart.

A memorial marker was erected by the family in Port Leyden cemetery, NY.

McGOWAN Henry.
Private, Co. I, 106th Infantry Regiment, 27th Division
KIA 29 August 1918
Plot C – Row 02 – Grave 20
Army Serial Number 1208386

Henry McGowan, son of William McGowan and Marguerite Murray, was raised by his aunt Elizabeth Kean in Brooklyn, NY. His parents died while he was still an infant. He had two brothers: George and Lester. Henry was employed as a clerk with the National Security Company in Manhattan. He enlisted with the 23rd Infantry Regiment New York National Guard on 17 September 1917. His brother George also served in Europe with the 21st Engineer Regiment (Light Train).

Henry was shot through the head by a German sniper ten minutes before going over the top. He was buried in the American plot at Abeele Aerodrome Military Cemetery. He was 21 years of age.

no photograph available

CAHILL Thomas F.
Sergeant, Co. L, 363rd Infantry Regiment, 91st Division
KIA 2 November 1918
Plot C – Row 02 – Grave 21
Army Serial Number 2265064

Thomas F. Cahill was born in Brosna, Kerry County, Ireland on 23 April 1888. He was the son of Patrick and Johanna Cahill. There were four other children: William, David, Katie and Nellie. Thomas arrived at Ellis Island on 13 April 1911 and continued his travels to San Francisco, CA where he was employed by the United Railroads. By 1917, his brothers William and David had joined him in San Francisco. His sisters Katie and Nellie found residence in Chicago, IL.

Thomas was the first to be inducted by the army in San Francisco. He was sent for basic training to Camp Lewis, WA on 5 September 1917. He was killed in Waregem on 2 November 1918 and was buried near the town center which was then known as American plot 1673 - Poteghem (plot 1, grave #8). His remains were transferred to Cemetery #1252 (which later became Flanders Field Cemetery) on 3 June 1919.

His mother wanted to visit his grave in 1937 and filed a request with the U.S. government. Of course to no avail as the last pilgrimage of the Gold Star Mothers was in 1933, these pilgrimages only being eligible for mothers and widows living in the U.S.A .

HUGILL Thomas W.
Corporal, Co. L, 363rd Infantry Regiment, 91st Division
KIA 31 October 1918
Plot C – Row 02 – Grave 22
Army Serial Number 2265069

Thomas Wilbur Hugill (°26 February 1893 in Stockton, CA) was the only son of Jonathan and Mary Rebecca Hugill (née Powell). He was still very young when de decided to take over a farm in Lodi, CA. In 1913 he had visited family in Liverpool with his mother. When he was called to register for the draft in June 1917, he specified that he was the sole caretaker of his mother, his father had passed away in 1897. Nonetheless he was called to arms on 19 September 1917 and sent to Camp Lewis, WA for basic training. Before leaving for Europe he subscribed to a war insurance policy of which his mother was to be the sole beneficiary.
Thomas had high moral standards and a strong Christian faith. He was highly respected by his fellow men and was soon promoted to Corporal. In his last letter home to his mother he wrote that he felt great, that there was no need to worry and that he was looking forward to seeing her again soon. As in all his letters, his last words were optimistic and reassuring.

On the first day of attack in Waregem he was sent with his platoon to spot and identify machinegun nests. While returning to give his report he was shot in the back, through the heart and killed instantaneously. He was buried close to the town center of Waregem.

His name is inscribed on the WWI Memorial in Lodi, together with eleven others who had been killed from the same town.

Mary Rebecca visited his grave with the Gold Star Mothers Pilgrimage in 1930 (insert left).

Thomas has a memorial marker in the Woodbridge Masonic cemetery in Lodi.

SELIG Merrill N.
Private, Co. I, 145th Infantry Regiment, 37th Division
DOW 1 November 1918
Plot C – Row 02 – Grave 23
Army Serial Number 1853194

Merrill Norwood Selig was born in Madison, IN on 9 March 1895. He was the son of George Selig (a German immigrant) and Margaret Stephanus. He had one sister (Fossie) and two brothers (Wilbur and Irwin). He was a very introvert, quiet boy. He left school at the age of fourteen and was employed by Tennly Shop as a button maker. Wilbur was assassinated in 1915 during a dispute over a women he had fallen in love with. In 1917 Merrill started work in an ammunition factory in Carnegie, Pa. Here he met Grace Scott and fell in love.

Merrill was called to arms and sent for basic training to Camp Lee, VA in February 1918. He was attached to the 145th Infantry Regiment and sailed for Europe on 27 July. His last letter home was dated 24 September while he was still in the Meuse-Argonne sector. He died of wounds received in action on 1 November and was buried near the town of Olsene along the road to the city of Gent (grave #18).

When his mother was informed of his death she claimed that she wasn't surprised as in the weeks before she had had a premonition of fear.

After the war their parents received the Bronze Medal of the city of Carnegie, PA. Their third son Irwin was electrocuted in 1919. On 4 June 1919, Merrill's remains were moved to Flanders Field cemetery and he received his final resting place on 21 June 1922. During the disinterment and identification process a gold signet ring was found on his finger with the initials "MNS". Inside the ring was inscribed "From Grace".

Margaret hesitated to visit her son's grave with the Gold Star Mothers Pilgrimage and in the end declined. As she said; she was far too nervous to embark on such a long trip.

Photo right: Mr. and Mrs. Stephanus visit the grave of their great-uncle in 2007.

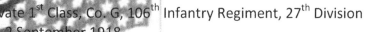

HARRIS Bernard J.
Private 1st Class, Co. G, 106th Infantry Regiment, 27th Division
KIA 2 September 1918
Plot C – Row 03 – Grave 01
Army Serial Number 1207852

Bernard Harris was born in Brooklyn, NY in October 1896. His mother was Margaret Harris, widow of Alexander Harris (photo insert). He had four sisters (Florence, Gertrude, Marrie and Hasel) and one brother (Eugene). He joined the 14th Infantry Regiment of the New York National Guard on 5 July 1917. On 17 October 1917, the 14th Infantry Regiment became the 106th Infantry Regiment. He sailed for Europe on the President Lincoln on 10 May 1918.

He was killed on 2 September, close to where the American monument is now located. Just before the family was notified of his death two of his sisters had passed away.

Bernard was buried near Vierstraat (Isolated Grave #9 Kemmel). His remains were moved to Lyssenthoek Cemetery in Poperinge (XXXII.D.76) on 6 May 1919. When Margaret received the letter requesting her decision on the final disposition of her son's remains, Eugene replied in her name: *"I wish to state in behalf of my mother and three sisters my brother remain left where he fell. Not for heartless reason do we think this, but we feel that he would not want to be moved from the place where he fought and died."*

On 19 July 1923, the renowned Father Francis Kelley, 27th Division senior chaplain, visited Flanders Field Cemetery. He noticed that Bernard was buried under a Star of David. Upon his request the marker was replaced with a Latin Cross.

Due to health issues, Margaret was unable to visit his grave with the Gold Star Mothers in 1930.

COCHRANE Richard.

Corporal, Co. I, 106th Infantry Regiment, 27th Division
KIA 31 July 1918
Plot C – Row 03 – Grave 02
Army Serial Number 1208261

Richard Cochrane was born in Ulster (Northern Ireland) in April 1890. His parents were Richard and Margaret Cochrane. He emigrated to the U.S.A. together with his brother James (°12 January 1888) and lived with their aunt in Brooklyn, NY.

Richard joined the National Guard on 4 June 1917. He was attached to the 23rd NY Infantry Regiment. (which later became the 106th Infantry Regiment). He was promoted to Corporal on 14 January.

James joined the Canadian Army in Toronto on 21 Augustus 1917. He served with the 15th Battalion, Canadian Infantry (Central Ontario Regiment).

Richard was killed during the battles around Mount Kemmel and was buried at Lyssenthoek Military Cemetery in Poperinge in XXXII.B.3. His remains were moved to Flanders Field on 17 June 1922.

One month later, on 1 September, his brother was also killed in action. He is buried in Queant Road Cemetery in Buissy, France (VII.E.34.)

DENELL Frank J.

Private, MG Co. 106th Infantry Regiment, 27th Division
ACC 9 August 1918
Plot C – Row 03 – Grave 03
Army Serial Number 2452659

Frank Jay DeNell was born in Washington D.C. on 28 October 1895. He was the son of John Nell and Minnie Carsten, a German immigrant (photo below right). He had one brother Albert, a half-brother Julian (whose father was a Cherokee Indian - photo below right) and two sisters: Essie and Viola. At the time of the U.S. declaration of war, Frank lived with his fiancée Ruth Schaeffer in Brooklyn, NY and worked as an automobile mechanic.

On all military documents reference Frank it indicates that he was "*negro*". Frank himself passed for white. When Frank was called to arms, he lied about his birthplace to hide the origins of his "race" (draft registration card shows that he was born in Winnipeg, Canada). This made sense if you consider the "Jim Crow" laws that were in effect at that time. Research performed by a family member shows that many generations ago their ancestors originated from West Africa.

Frank was killed by an accidental pistol shot. Ruth requested his remains be returned to the U.S.A. Minnie decided to leave him buried in Europe. He was initially interred at Lyssenthoek Military Cemetery in Poperinge and on 17 June 1922 moved to Waregem.

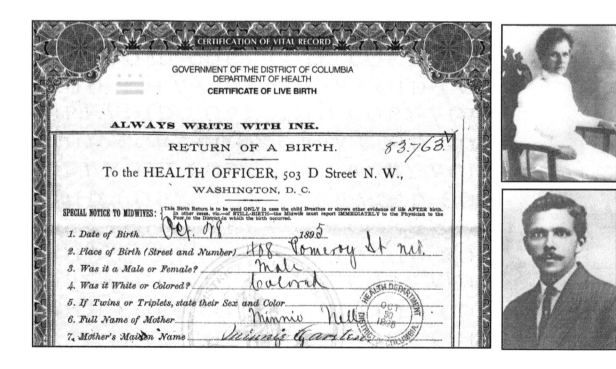

WELSH John

Private 1st Class, Co. I, 106th Infantry Regiment, 27th Division
KIA 31 July 1918
Plot C – Row 03 – Grave 04
Army Serial Number 1208327

John Welsh (°October 1899) was the son of Edward Welsh and Louisa Odell from Brooklyn, NY. He had five brothers (Joseph, Frank, Edward, William and George) and one sister (Catherine). John was employed by the Crane Shipyard Company at the time the U.S.A. declared war on Germany. He immediately volunteered with the 14th Infantry Regiment New York National Guard.

He wrote his last letter home on 4 July. John was only 19 at time of death. He was buried next to Richard Cochrane at Lyssenthoek Military Cemetery in Poperinge , XXXII.B.2.

TILLEY William E. Jr.

Private, Co. C, 106th MG Battalion, 27th Division
DOW 31 July 1918
Plot C – Row 03 – Grave 05
Army Serial Number 1216591

William Edgar Tilley Jr. was born in October 1896 in Roslyn, NY. His parents were William Tilley Sr. and Caroline Hutts. He had one brother (Eugean) and five sisters (Annie, Elizabeth, Hattie, Carine and Cornelia). William was an accountant in Manhattan when he joined the Coast Guard on 15 May. When the 27th Division was formed he was transferred to the 106th Machine Gun Battalion. His brother (Willard) Eugene also served in Europe with the 306th Infantry Regiment, 77th "Metropolitan" Division.

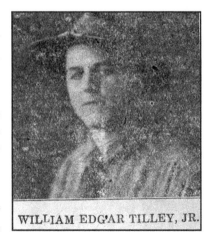

WILLIAM EDGAR TILLEY, JR.

He was mortally wounded by a trench mortar shell near Mount Kemmel on 31 July. He was taken to a Casualty Clearing Station but succumbed to his wounds two hours later. He was buried at Lyssenthoek Military Cemetery in Poperinge, XXXII.B.7.

BELCHER Richard J.

Sergeant, Co. I, 106th Infantry Regiment, 27th Division
KIA 1 September 1918
Plot C – Row 03 – Grave 06
Army Serial Number 1208232

Richard Belcher, son of Arthur Belcher and Anna Mae Hargrove, originated from Brooklyn, NY. He was born in October 1889 and had a brother Arthur and a sister, Katheryn. He was working as a steamfitter for his father at the time he joined the 14th Infantry Regiment New York National Guard as a mechanic in March 1914. He served during the punitive campaign along the Mexican border in 1916 and was awarded the sharpshooter's medal. He was promoted to Corporal on 9 May 1917 and Sergeant on 24 July 1917.

The Division was sent to Europe in May 1918. He was severely wounded on 10 August and taken to a Paris hospital for treatment. After two weeks he was able to return to his unit. He was killed in action on 1 September and buried near Kemmel. His remains were later moved to Lyssenthoek British Military Cemetery in Poperinge at XXXII.D.3.

MINZESHEIMER Irwin
Private, Co. G, 106th Infantry Regiment, 27th Division
KIA 2 September 1918
Plot C – Row 03 – Grave 07
Army Serial Number 1207958

Irwin Minzesheimer (°30 August 1899) was the son of Henry Minzesheimer. His mother died when Irwin was an infant and Henry remarried with Julia who took care of Irwin and his sister Jessie. Henry had three more children with Julia: Philip, Julie and Rose.

Irwin joined the 23rd Infantry Regiment New York National Guard in Brooklyn on 22 September 1917. He was only 19 years of age when he was killed and so one of the youngest men buried in the cemetery. He was originally buried in a mass grave near Vierstraat. In the grave, besides the remains of seven men who were repatriated in 1922, were the mortal remains of Hart, Harris, Kane and Rottolo. On 5 June 1919 they were moved to Lyssenthoek Cemetery in Poperinge. Irwin's temporary grave was at XXXII.D.22.

no photograph available

RIGSBEE Ike J.
Private 1st Class, Co. M, 120th Infantry Regiment, 30th Division
KIA 2 September 1918
Plot C – Row 03 – Grave 08
Army Serial Number 1322121

Isaac (Ike) Jake Rigsbee was born on 7 June 1895 in Durham, NC. He was the son of John Rigsbee and Mary Copley. He had one brother (Albert) and two sisters (Elizabeth and Alena). Ike was a mechanic at the Golden Belt Manufacturing Company in Durham. On 25 May 1917 he joined the North Carolina National Guard (3rd Infantry Regiment). At the time of enlistment he expressed a strong desire for a chance at the Huns, owing to the manner in which they had treated Belgians.

Witness statement on his death read: *" Me and him* were *sleeping in a dugout at Bedford Stables in Canal sector. A Sergeant had just come in to call us to stand to at 4:45 a.m. I had just gotten* up *when a shell came in and killed him instantly. The whole billet fell in on us both. He was dead before I could get on my feet."* He was buried the following day at Nine Elms British cemetery and his remains were moved to Waregem on 13 June 1919.

no photograph available

ROSCOE Joseph E.
Private, Co. I, 119th Infantry Regiment, 30th Division
KIA 31 August 1918
Plot C – Row 03 – Grave 09
Army Serial Number 1316329

Joseph Edgar Roscoe was born in Rockingham, NC on 21 July 1896. He was the son of Joseph (Joe) Roscoe. It is unknown who the mother was. At the time Joseph Sr. was young and single. When he brought a baby home he claimed to his parents that he was the father. He was also named Joseph. Joseph Sr. eventually married with Drucilla McBride and had five children: Harriett, Arthur, Annie, Grady and Robert. Drucilla took care of Joseph Jr. as if he had been her own. They lived in Osborne, NC, close to the border with South-Carolina.

Joseph Jr. married Sarah Ellen Smith on 1 April 1914. He was called to arms in Rockingham on 19 September 1917. He received his basic training at Camp Jackson, SC and assigned to the Supply Company of the 316th Field Artillery Regiment, 81st Division, being conscripts from Florida, and the Carolina's. He was later transferred to the 30th National Guard Division.

Joseph was killed during an enemy artillery barrage. He lost his right arm below the elbow and his right leg was shattered between knee and hip.

KNOWN BUT TO GOD
Plot C – Row 03 – Grave 10

I sometimes wonder as I sit
And write of battles past,
If we may not forget to soon
How long the scars will last.

Of awful sounds and gruesome sights,
The stench and cold and mud,
Which may, perhaps, more slowly heal
Than wounds marked up in blood.

I sometimes wonder if the boys,
Who fought so well for us,
Are just the same they were before,
They went through hell for us.

He fought in Flanders' Fields we say,
He served at St Mihiel:
Those places are all names to us –
Can we tell how they feel ?

Who knew the horror, stark and grim,
Who saw their comrades fall,
With fair young bodies bruised and torn,
With shot and shell and ball ?

Besides the bloody Marne we say,
He won the Croix de Guerre,
And while he fought his super-light,
We slept in safety here.

With thankful hearts we turn from war,
To paths of peace and yet,
While their scars last, I think perhaps,
We may to soon forget.

Mabel Haggard Henry (° 1879)

ECKARD Robert L.

Private, Co. D, 120th Infantry Regiment, 30th Division
KIA 29 August 1918
Plot C – Row 03 – Grave 11
Army Serial Number 1320170

Robert Lee Eckard (originally Echerd) was born on 11 May 1895 in Alexander County, NC. His parents were Newton Eckard and Mary Huffman, who owned a farm in Whittenburg along the Catawba river. Newton married three times. His first wife was Amanda Bolick who gave him four children (Rufus, David, Dallas and Carroll). His second marriage was with Mary Huffman (children: John, Laura, Della and Robert). She died in 1896 and Newton's third wife was Alice Starnes (children: Leona and Carol).

Robert was called to arms in Taylorsville on 9 October 1917. He was originally assigned to the 322nd Infantry Regiment, 81st (Wildcat) Division. This division was formed with conscripts out of Florida and the Carolina's. After basic training in Camp Jackson, SC, the division sailed for Europe in May 1918. Upon arrival Robert was almost immediately transferred to the 120th Infantry Regiment, 30th Division. On 29 August he was a assigned to a ration party when he lost all sense of direction and ran into a German patrol. They opened fire and Robert was shot in the abdomen by machinegun fire. He was killed instantly. He was initially buried at Nine Elms British Military Cemetery in Poperinge and moved to Waregem on 17 June 1922.

His father was the beneficiary to his war insurance policy however he died on 17 November of the same year from complications of the Spanish flu.

no photograph available

GODDARD Walter S.
Sergeant, Co. I, 119th Infantry Regiment, 30th Division
KIA 1 September 1918
Plot C – Row 03 – Grave 12
Army Serial Number 1316267

Walter Staton Goddard was born in Washington, Beaufort County, NC in July 1893 and lived in Hertford, Perquimans County. His parents were Noah Stanton Goddard and Fannie Fulford They had two older children: Hannah and Irvin. His father died in 1895, mother in 1917. Irvin passed away in 1918, Hannah in 1968. She never married so there are no descendants. The Goddard's were a prominent family: former slave traders, diamond traders in Liberia, Colonels, Admirals, lawyers, judges, etc. .... Irvin kept with the family tradition and became a lawyer and if Walter had had the opportunity he would most likely also have chosen the same profession. Walter was an exemplary student.

Walter volunteered with the 2nd Infantry Regiment of the North Carolina National Guard in Edenton on 20 June 1916. This regiment would become the base of the 119th Infantry Regiment. He was 25 years of age when he was shot in the face and killed instantly. His remains were moved to Waregem on 16 June 1922.

A grave marker in memory of Walter was erected in the Oakdale Cemetery, Washington, NC.

Grave marker erected in Oakdale Cemetery, City of Washington, Beaufort County, NC
(Photo courtesy of Ron Dailey)

414

WAYNE Harvey C.

Private, Co. D, 119th Infantry Regiment, 30th Division
KIA 21 July 1918
Plot C – Row 03 – Grave 13
Army Serial Number 1999150

Harvey Clinton Wayne was born on 9 March 1887. He was the son of Thomas Wayne and Victoria Brown from Custer IL. His father died in 1890 and his mother remarried on 4 January 1892 with William Danneberger. Harvey had a brother Samuel and two sisters: Maggie and Bertha. His mother conceived three more children with William Danneberger: Jessie, Bryan and Benjamin. Wayne's great grandmother was a half-sister of Abe Lincoln, sixteenth President of the U.S.A.

Harvey joined the service in Springfield, IL on 24 February 1918. He received his basic training at Camp Taylor, KY and Camp Sevier, SC. He was assigned to the 119th Infantry Regiment of the 30th Division. He sailed for Europe on 15 May.

He was originally buried as an unknown American soldier at Belgian Battery Corner Cemetery near Ypres (Cemetery #336, III.B.11). When his remains were moved to Nine Elms Cemetery (Cemetery #324) on 13 June 1919, it was determined that his identification tag was concealed on his body.

Photo left: Harvey with his half-sister Jessie Danneberger
Photo right: from left to right: nephew Glenn Griffin, sister Maggie Griffin, mother Victoria Danneberger and seated grandma Brown.

MENZKE Charles E.

Private, Co. K, 119th Infantry Regiment, 30th Division
KIA 26 August 1918
Plot C – Row 03 – Grave 14
Army Serial Number 1994300

Charles Emil Menzke was born on 2 August 1890. He was the son of Ernst and Lizzie Menzke. Ernst was a coal miner from Belleville IL. He emigrated to the U.S.A. from Germany in 1883. Charles had a sister Mary and two stepsisters; Lizzie and Lena. He worked as a molder at the local Commercial Foundry. When he was called to arms his father tried to persuade him to apply for exemption of military service. The reasoning behind this was that Charles' mother had passed away seven years earlier and his father, being a single parent had to take care of the family. Charles being an idealist, wanted to do his bit for the war effort and so neglected his father's wishes. He arrived at Camp Taylor, KY for basic training on 26 February. He was later transferred to Camp Sevier in Greenville, SC and was assigned to the 119th Infantry Regiment of the 30th Division.

He sailed for Europe and on 19 August he wrote home informing them that after sixteen days in the trenches he was now in the rear enjoying a couple of days of rest. He also mentioned that on 2 August he had celebrated his 27th birthday in the trenches.

On 26 August, Charles was killed in the trenches with three of his comrades during a German artillery barrage. They were advised to retreat from their observation post but Charles was determined to remain at post. He was buried at the British Nine Elms Cemetery.

In the Belleville Public Library, the Honor Roll where Charles' name is memorialized, is located at the end of the marble stairway.

Photo: Charles Menzke's grave at Nine Elms Cemetery in Poperinge.

417

KEHRLI Adolph
Private, Co. F, 148th Infantry Regiment, 37th Division
KIA 31 October 1918
Plot C – Row 03 – Grave 15
Army Serial Number 1907875

Adolph Kehrli was born in Cassadaga, NY on 21 July 1892. The large farming family of John Kehrli (a Swiss immigrant - photo) and Alwine Pappenfuss (a German immigrant) was blessed with thirteen children of which Adolph was the third in line. (John, Phillip, Adolph, Lena, Fred, Gertrude, William, Albert, Anna, Lester, Leslie, Gilbert and a girl who died in infancy of which her name is unknown). Adolph was called to arms on 27 September 1917. He registered in Ripley, NY, where his family lived. He was first assigned to the 307th Regiment Field Artillery, 78th Division. Two months later he was transferred to the 327th Infantry Regiment, 82nd Division where he served until 11 April. From there he was reassigned to the 157th Depot Brigade and finally, as of 26 May, served with the 148th Infantry Regiment until death.

Adolph was killed by machinegun fire near the town of Olsene on 31 October. He was buried where he fell and his remains were moved to Waregem on 3 June 1919.

1918 was a difficult year for the family. Alwine died in April and two brothers were also serving in Europe. They both survived the war: Philip (left) was a mechanic with the Air Service and Fred (right) served with the Marines.

KENNEDY John T.
Private, Co. F, 148th Infantry Regiment, 37th Division
DOW 4 November 1918
Plot C – Row 03 – Grave 16
Army Serial Number 1907644

John Thomas Kennedy was born in Enfield, CT on 25 June 1886. His parents, Edward and Martha Kennedy (née Bragington) were immigrants from Northern Ireland. They had four other children: two sons and two daughters. John was employed as a yarn spinner with Talcott Brothers in Talcottville, CT. He had previously served as an apprentice seaman with the Navy for two and a half months. He was called to arms on 4 October 1917 and reported for military duty in Rockville, CT. He started training with the 151st Depot Brigade and was later assigned to the 327th Infantry Regiment, 82nd Division. As in the case of Adolph Kehrli, he received further training with the 157th Depot Brigade before arriving at his final assignment with Co. F of the 148th Infantry Regiment.

John's left leg was riddled with bullets and he was taken to Field Hospital #146, located in Tielt, where he died of shock from hemorrhage. He was buried in Tielt and his remains were moved to Waregem on 6 June 1919.

no photograph available

YOUNG John B.
Private, Co. F, 145th Infantry Regiment, 37th Division
DOW 8 November 1918
Plot C – Row 03 – Grave 17
Army Serial Number 2442756

John Young was the son of Benjamin and Mary Elizabeth Young (née Benner) from Montgomery, PA. He was born on 16 August 1889 and had three brothers (Enos, Benjamin and Joseph) and three sisters (Suzie, Elizabeth and Edna). He was loved by all. He had promised to send money back home but unfortunately died before he could fulfill his promise. He succumbed to wounds received in action in the Evacuation Hospital in Staden and was buried in the American plot row 7, grave #94. His remains were moved to Waregem on 6 June 1919 and laid to rest in plot C, grave #83.

WALTERICK Claude L.
Private 1st Class, 148th Amb. Co. 112th San. Tn., 37th Division
DOW 31 October 1918
Plot C – Row 03 – Grave 18
Army Serial Number 1540528

Claude Walterick was the son of Edward Walterick from Terre Haute, IN. His mother, Edna Harter, died in 1900. He was born in September 1894 in North Baltimore, OH and spent his youth in Delphos, OH. He was a very special young man and active within many social circles. He joined the National Guard (Ambulance Company 1st Ohio National Guard) in Toledo together with his brother Charles on 29 May 1917.

Claude was killed on 31 October. He was dismembered during an enemy bombardment. He was going to be buried with fifteen others when someone informed the burial party that his brother

was stationed close by. His brother Charles was contacted and so the next day he was able to attend his brother's funeral. After the war a Veterans of Foreign Wars Post was jointly named after him: the VFW Walterick-Hemme Post #3035. In 2015 Keith E. Harman, Junior Vice-Commander-in Chief, V.F.W of the U.S.A. and member of the V.F.W. Post Walterick Hemme visited Claude's grave. Memorial at the Walterick-Hemme Post with the poem In Flanders Fields (photo insert left)

LONGACRE Edward
Sergeant, Battery C, 107th Field Artillery Regt., 28th Division
DOD 28 October 1918
Plot C – Row 03 – Grave 19
Army Serial Number 1250468

Edward Longacre, born 14 January 1880, was the son of Hannah Longacre from Norristown, PA, who also had a daughter Mary. His father William, a veteran of the Civil War, had died in 1899. Edward was married to Violet Longacre (née Faehl) and they had two children: John and Frank. He is one of two soldiers buried in the cemetery from the Pennsylvania National Guard Division. He was assigned, as Louis Ennis, to the 107th Field Artillery Regiment of the 28th (Keystone) Division. The artillery brigade of this division was attached to the 91st Division.

Edward died of heart failure in the village of Sleihage on 28 October and was buried in the town. Sometime later his remains were moved to the city of Roeselare, where ten other American soldiers were buried. (Trifone Cantacesso and William Roder being two of them). His remains were moved to Waregem In 1919.

no photograph available

BIANCHI Guiseppe
Private, Co. D, 148th Infantry Regiment, 37th Division
DOW 1 November 1918
Plot C – Row 03 – Grave 20
Army Serial Number 2943082

Guiseppe Bianchi was born in Petrella Tifernina, Province of Campobasso in Italy on 29 November 1887. At the time of enlistment (29 April 1918) he was living with his sister Consuela and her husband Michael de Matteo in Schenectady, NY. He had already served the military in Italy.

After completing his basic training he was assigned to the 148th Infantry Regiment, arriving in Europe in June 1918. He survived the battles of the Argonne unscathed. Guiseppe died of wounds sustained during the fighting near Heurne (Oudenaarde).

no photograph available

SPANO Guiseppi
Private, Co. E, 145th Infantry Regiment, 37th Division
DOW 4 November 1918
Plot C – Row 03 – Grave 21
Army Serial Number 2708320

Guiseppe "Joe" Spano, son of Giovanni and Brigida Spano, was born in Motta San Giovanni, Regio di Calabria, Italy, on 15 February 1893. He emigrated to the U.S.A. in October 1912 at the age of 19 and found a job in Detroit, Michigan.

Joe was called to arms and spent his first training period assigned to the 145th Infantry Regiment. On 29 April while still at Camp Lee, VA , he filed a petition for U.S. naturalization.

He was severely wounded at 06:00 hours on 4 November during a heavy artillery bombardment and rushed to the American Evacuation Hospital in Staden. He succumbed from his wounds shortly after and was buried in the American plot of the cemetery, row 8, grave #101. Details in his burial file reference date of death are contradictory. It mentions 4 and 9 November. His remains were moved to Waregem on 5 June 1919 and laid to rest in plot C, grave #95.

STOLZ Erman
1st Sergeant, Co. H, 148th Infantry Regiment, 37th Division
DOW 1 November 1918
Plot C – Row 03 – Grave 22
Army Serial Number 1530229

Erman (Irman) Stolz was born on 28 April 1895 and originated from Dayton, OH. He was the son of Samuel and Clara Stolz who had two other children: Wesley and Hattie. His parents had died before he was 11 years of age and so he was taken into care by his aunt and uncle George and Agnes Green. Erman was employed by the National Cash Register Company and was a member of the Dayton Fire Brigade. He joined the 3rd Infantry Regiment Ohio National Guard on 1 April 1916. He served during the punitive campaign along the Mexican border and upon his return was promoted to 1st Sergeant of Co. H on 22 June 1917. When he was sent to Europe he gave Maude Street, his girlfriend, as point of contact in case of an emergency.

In one of his last letters home he described how he had seen his friends fall to their death during battle. He also mentioned that he thought he would be home pretty soon. However on 30 October, after crossing the river Lys, he was severely wounded by shell fragments in his leg and abdominal area. He was first taken to a Casualty Clearing Station and then to the Evacuation Hospital in Staden. He died on 2 November at 14:30 (not on 1 November as indicated on his headstone). He had remained calm and courageous until the end.

Maude, who was a member of the Gold Star Mothers of America, would have loved to travel to Europe but health problems prevented her from doing so. She had opted for Erman's remains to be repatriated to the U.S. in 1922 but Wesley refused as direct bloodline had precedence in the final decision. His name is also memorialized on the WWI monument in Dayton.

MADARY Otto
Corporal, Co. L, 148th Infantry Regiment, 37th Division
KIA 1 November 1918
Plot C – Row 03 – Grave 23
Army Serial Number 1531112

Otto Madary was born in Fulton, IN on 13 January 1889, where he spent most of his youth. He was the son of Albert Madary and Susan Zabst who were farmers and they had four other children: John, William, Herbert and a daughter Mrs. Ida Mae Madary Sherbondy. Otto was a fireman with the Wabash Railroad in Toledo, OH. He was called to arms on 2 October 1917 and completed his basic training with the 158th Depot Brigade in Camp Sherman, OH. He was devoted to the cause and as an exemplary soldier was promoted to corporal before the Division sailed for Europe.

During the fighting along the banks of the river Scheldt in Heurne, Otto was hit by a shell fragment in the abdomen and died ten minutes later.

When his remains were moved to Waregem there was uncertainty of his true identity. It was a dubious case between the remains of Joseph Hajek and Otto. A ring with the initials O.M. was accepted as positive identification. The ring was sent to his sister who kept it in the original soiled condition for the rest of her life, this being the only tangible souvenir that remained of her brother.

HOWE George P. - D.S.C.

1st Lieutenant, Medical Reserve Corps
KIA 28 September 1917
Plot C – Row 04 – Grave 01

George Plummer Howe was born in Lawrence, MA on 11 December 1878. He was the son of Octavius Thorndike Howe and Elizabeth Plummer. George was an exemplary student and found his way to Harvard. He obtained his B.A. (Bachelor of Arts) in 1900 (photo right) and his M.D. (Doctor of Medicine) in 1904. For two years he worked as a physician and surgeon at the Boston City Hospital. In the Spring of 1906 he volunteered for the Anglo-American Arctic Expedition, led by Leffingwell – Mikkelsen. They were hoping to find a new continent north of the Mackenzie river. The expedition was a failure but they survived with the help of

an Eskimo community. It took George Howe sixteen months to get back to Massachusetts where he then took a position at the Lawrence General Hospital. At the same time he was a researcher for the Worcester State Mutual Life Insurance Co. He returned to Harvard in 1909 to study and teach anthropology and archeology (photo left dates from this period). He also lead an expedition to Yucatan. Two years later he married Marion Dudley Endicott and took on his former position as a physician in Boston. This time at the Carney and Boston City Hospital. He wrote many articles on diseases specific to Eskimo's and was co-author of "Conquering the Arctic Ice".

In 1917 "Peter" (as he was known to his friends) volunteered with the Medical Officers Reserve Corps. His first choice was to become an infantry combat soldier but being short-sighted he was rejected. Arriving in England he was attached to the British Army. George was sent to different posts. His first assignment was attending to German prisoners of war. Later he was assigned as surgeon to the 13th Battalion Royal Fusiliers and finally with the 10th Battalion Royal Fusiliers, 37th British Division. In one of his letters home he wrote that he preferred to stay with the British until the end of the war and that the Americans were not to be anxious of arriving too late: the Germans still had a lot of fight in them. He predicted the heaviest American battles for the summer of 1918. It is typical for our adventurous Howe that he wrote that he would never exchange his job in the front line for "the headship of a big base hospital".

George Howe was killed near *"Tower Hamlets"* (*Polygoon Wood*) by an artillery shell on 28 September 1917. He was buried at Goudeseune Farm near the Vierstraat crossroads. He received the Distinguished Service Cross for courage and devotion to duty on that day. Many laudatory comments were attributed to his unselfish personality. He is the only soldier buried at Flanders Field Cemetery who lost his life in 1917. His name is also memorialized at the Harvard WWI Memorial. He was the first American officer to be killed in combat.

The official citation of his DSC reads:

"During the operations of the Tower Hamlets Spur east of Ypres on 27th and 28th September 1917, this officer displayed the most conspicuous courage and devotion to duty in attending to the wounded of several different regiments under very heavy and continuous shell fire. He himself was wounded in the head early in the morning of the 28th, but refused to give in and continued to work at his Aid Post until killed by a shell when directing an officer, whose wounds he had dressed, to the Advanced Dressing Station. On many occasions during the period he was attached to the Division this gallant medical officer earned the respect and admiration of all ranks for his consummate coolness and utter contempt for danger under fire. His cheerfulness under trying conditions was proverbial."

Far left Leffingwell and next to him Ejnar Mikkelsen, the leaders of the Anglo-American Arctic Expedition. George P. Howe is second from right. This photo was taken during the outward bound voyage of the expedition on board the Duchess of Bedford.

no photograph available

HAGAN Joseph

Corporal, Co. K, 148th Infantry Regiment, 37th Division
KIA 2 November 1918
Plot C – Row 04 – Grave 02
Army Serial Number 2403831

Corporal Joseph Hagan was an immigrant from Castlecaulfield, County Tyrone, Northern Ireland. He was born on 1 August 1892. He arrived in the U.S.A. on 1 November 1910 aged nineteen, sailing on the Furnessia (photo) which had left Londonderry on 22 October. His brother Daniel already resided in New York. His immigration documents indicate that he had blond hair and blue eyes. He lived in Bridgeport,

CT together with Henry and Mary Hagan and was employee for a company specializing in metal constructions. Joseph was drafted in June 1917 and declared that he had already completed 11 months of military service with the Reserves. He was called to arms on 3 October 1917. His request for U.S. citizenship had already been submitted.

After his basic training Joseph was assigned to the 344th Infantry Regiment, 86th Black Hawk Division. Upon his arrival in Europe (10 June) he was reassigned to Co. K of the 148th Infantry Regiment, 37th Division. He was killed in Kruishoutem on 2 November and buried where he fell. His mother (Mary) received the news of his death in her home town Kincardine on Forth, Scotland.

His remains were moved to Waregem on 10 June 1919 and laid to rest in plot A, grave #129.

no photograph available

ROBINSON James L.
Corporal, Co. M, 364th Infantry Regiment, 91st Division
DOW 31 October 1918
Plot C – Row 04 – Grave 03
Army Serial Number 2780862

James Lee Robinson was born in Charles City, IA on 18 November 1889. He was the son of James Moses and Hanna Etta Robinson who had one other son Roy.

In 1917 James lived with his wife (name unknown) in Melba, ID, where they ran a small farm. He was called to register for the draft in June. Although he was married he did not file a request for exemption of military service. He had served two years as a fireman in the Navy. It came as a hard blow for his mother Etta, who had lost her husband James Moses due to the Spanish flu in March 1918, just six months before James was killed.

James was shot in the leg by machinegun fire and taken to the American Evacuation hospital in the village of Staden where he died shortly after arrival.

Hanna Etta came to Europe with the Gold Star Mothers Pilgrimage and visited Flanders Field Cemetery in 1930.

GOODMAN Roy L.
Private, Co. C, 361st Infantry Regiment, 91st Division
KIA 3 November 1918
Plot C – Row 04 – Grave 04
Army Serial Number 1997372

Roy Goodman was the son of Steven and Lottie Goodman who had three other sons : Arthur, Parkman and Orie. He was born in Eastview, KY in April 1895 but resided in Elizabethtown when he was called to arms on 23 February 1918.

He was originally a member of Co. F of the 335th Infantry Regiment, 84th (Lincoln) Division, a division comprising of conscripts from Kentucky, Illinois and Indiana. He arrived at Camp Taylor, KY for basic training on 23 February and sailed for Europe on 3 September. The division was disbanded upon arrival and Roy was reassigned to the 361st Infantry Regiment.

He was killed instantly on 3 November when shell fragments lodged in his shoulder and neck. This happened at the " *Nieuwe Bareel*" (New Barrel), 1 km southeast of the village of Moregem. He was buried in the village of Bevere after hostilities had ended on 12 November. His remains were moved to Waregem on 9 June 1919 (plot A, grave #190).

Lottie would have visited her son's grave in 1930, however health issues prevented her in doing so. She was 69 years of age.

Private Roy L. Goodman is memorialized on the Hardin County War Memorial (KY). His brother Parkman, serving with the Navy, survived the war.

REQUA Harry E.
Private, Co. M, 361st Infantry Regiment, 91st Division
KIA 2 November 1918
Plot C – Row 04 – Grave 05
Army Serial Number 2257431

Harry Ellsworth Requa was born in Austin, MN on 22 December 1895. He was the son of Samuel Requa and Celia Enright. Harry was the youngest of five boys (Walter, Frank, Benjamin, Howard and Harry) and two girls (Agnes and Olive). Two of the children (Olive and Benjamin) died in childhood. The family moved to Everett, WA, in 1900 where Samuel found a job with the Great Northern Railway Company. Harry and his brother opened a grocery store. However he was called to arms together with five other men from Everett on 17 September 1917 and traveled to Camp Lewis, WA for basic training. With the 91st Division, he was assigned to Co. M of the 361st Infantry Regiment. At the time Harry was ready to sail for Europe, his father had died as a result of the Spanish flu.

On 2 November Colonel Davis* wanted to check the German lines near Moregem. Harry was asked if he was willing to be part of the reconnaissance mission. He had taken on the task as runner while he was serving in the Argonne. Although at first he declined the request, he later changed his mind and joined the mission. Captain Howard Hughes, commander of Battalion A of the 361st was also part of the group. Colonel Davis ordered his chauffeur to drive towards a couple of buildings where they could take shelter. After a while, the three men left their shelter to get a better view of the enemy lines. They came in full view of the Germans. Artillery and machinegun fire opened up on them. The three men were unable to seek shelter in time and were killed instantly. They were buried in the Wortegem village churchyard.

*Colonel William Davis was the highest ranking officer killed in action on Belgian soil. His remains were repatriated to the US and interred at Arlington National Cemetery. Fort William Davis, a former U.S. Army Fort near Gatun, Panama, was named in his honor. (photo courtesy of his granddaughter Helen G. Davis)

KOCH Otto
Private 1st Class, Co. I, 105th Infantry Regiment, 27th Division
KIA 15 July1918
Plot C – Row 04 – Grave 06
Army Serial Number 1205085

Otto Koch was the son of Andrew and Elizabeth Koch from Glendale, Long Island, NY. He was born on 29 February 1896. He had two brothers (Herman and Henry) and six sisters (Elizabeth, Madeline, Caroline, Margret, Bertha and Mary). In 1916 he volunteered with the 71st Infantry Regiment New York National Guard, which later became the 105th Infantry Regiment.

In a letter home dated 19 July he wrote that he was expecting to be sent to the front pretty soon. He also described the Germans bombing the 105th camp and feeling relieved that there were no casualties.

Otto Koch was the second man of his Division to be killed in action. He was 24 years of age. He was originally buried at Lyssenthoek Military Cemetery in Poperinge (XXVII.L.22).

His mother visited Flanders Field Cemetery with the Gold Star Mothers Pilgrimage in 1930.

CAWEIN Raleigh D.
Private, Co. A, 105th Infantry Regiment, 27th Division
DOW 2 September 1918
Plot C – Row 04 – Grave 07
Army Serial Number 1203346

Raleigh Cawein was born on 16 April 1899. He was the son of John and Mary Elizabeth Cawein who were German immigrants. The family lived with their two other children, John and Beatrice, in the Bronx.

Raleigh was wounded to the head by shell fragments on 2 September 1918. He was taken to a Casualty Clearing Station but died one hour later. He was buried at Lyssenthoek Military Cemetery in Poperinge.

In reply to Raleigh's final disposition of remains his mother replied: *"Remains be permitted to rest where he fought and met death"*. She visited his grave with the Gold Star Mothers in 1930. He is one of the few soldiers buried being younger than 20 years of age.

HUFFMAN John D.

Sergeant, Co. A, 105th Engineer Train, 30th Division
KIA 16 July 1918
Plot C – Row 04 – Grave 08
Army Serial Number 1332530

John Davidson Huffman was born in Hickory, NC on 28 April 1891. He was the son of Davidson Cornelius Huffman and Harriet Malinda Miller. The family had seven other children: Vance, George, William, Mattie, Beulah, Paul and David.

John was a well-known guy in Hickory: good looking, courageous, respectful and he easily made friends. As junior he was an office runner for the Western Union and was praised by all. He later became a technician with the Hutton & Bourbonnais Company (a furniture factory). He had volunteered with the North Carolina National Guard in 1910 and on 28 July 1917 he was assigned to Co. A of the 1st North Carolina Infantry Regiment, which later became the 105th Engineers Regiment. On 15 April 1918 he was promoted to Sergeant. On 14 July, two days before his death, he wrote his last letter to his mother. It was evident that he was homesick. He concluded with: *"Give my love to everybody and keep lots for yourself"*.

Supply Sergeant John Huffman was killed instantly at his base camp during an air raid in the night of 16 - 17 July. During this attack six others were severely wounded of which two died from their wounds shortly afterwards. One of the severely wounded was Sergeant Herbert Champion who had refused treatment until all wounded had been brought to safety. For this he received the Distinguished Service Cross. Two others who were told to sleep in a tent at the beginning of the bombardment decided it was wiser to seek a safer place. John's commander, Lieutenant Cline, named John as the best mess officer in the United States Army. He was one of the first to be buried in the American plot at the British Nine Elms Cemetery (close to Robert Porcelli and Wiley Bissett). One of his brothers was also serving his country. Captain George Lee Huffman was one of the officers' training recruits at Camp Wadsworth.

In the Hickory Daily Record of 30 July, an article stated that John was the first Hickory man to be killed in action. On 7 August 1918, a poem was published which had been written in honor of his name.

434

Our Country we will save
Our enemies we'll brave
"They shall not pass"
With God Almighty's aid
On whom our hope is stayed
We'll make them all afraid,
"They shall not pass"

We stand for truth and right
Against this cruel might.
"They shall not pass",
High-sounding words they name
But brutish be their gain,
And oh, their deeds of shame,
"They shall not pass."

Though they be billions strong,
This still shall be our song:
"They shall not pass".
We fear no battlefield,
Jehovah as our Shield.
His sword we'll bravely wield,
"They shall not pass."

We'll pray, and work, and give,
That freedom still may live.
"They shall not pass"
We'll answer every call,
We'll pledge our lives, our all,
And though we stand for fall,
"They shall not pass."

The Lord still reigns on High,
And though we live or die,
"They shall not pass."
No blood is shed in vain
True honor to retain,
Our freedom shall remain
"They shall not pass."

Truth crushed to earth will rise,
And blood to Heaven cries:
"They shall not pass."
God's holy arm and strong
Avengeth every wrong,
And ours the victors' song:
"They shall not pass."

WHITE Charles S.
Private 1st Class, Co. G, 106th Infantry Regiment, 27th Division
KIA 2 September 1918
Plot C – Row 04 – Grave 09
Army Serial Number 1207804

Charles White was born in 1896. His parents were Samuel White and Ida Adriance from Brooklyn. They had three other children: Rutledge, Adrian and Helen. Charles was an exemplary student. He graduated at the Commercial High School in 1915.

He was killed in the vicinity of the village of Wijtschaete while in charge of a machinegun post. The account of his action: *"Charles led the machine gun detail brilliantly and bravely for five hours until three German snipers got him simultaneously. Two bullets went through his helmet into his skull and one went through his neck killing him instantly. He died with a smile on his face."*

He was originally buried in a grave with twelve others near Kemmel (among those were Toney Rotollo, Bernard Harris and Irwin Minzesheimer). In 1919 his remains were moved to Lyssenthoek Cemetery (XXXII.D.25). Ida visited his grave at Flanders Field Cemetery with the Gold Star Mothers Pilgrimage in 1930.

KIERNAN John A.
Corporal, Co. G, 106th Infantry Regiment, 27th Division
KIA 23 August 1918
Plot C – Row 04 – Grave 10
Army Serial Number 1207797

John Andrew Kiernan was the son of William and Mary Kiernan from Brooklyn, NY. They had seven children: Thomas, William, John (° June 1898), Helen, Frank, Anne and Claude. John enlisted with the 23rd Infantry Regiment New York National Guard on 19 June 1916. He was only 18 years of age. He served with this regiment during the punitive campaign along the Mexican border.

John was killed by a shell fragment during an enemy artillery barrage. On 25 August he was interred at Lyssenthoek Military Cemetery in Poperinge and his remains were moved to Waregem on 14 June 1922. During the identification process it was determined that both legs were missing.

Thomas and William were also serving their country. Thomas had joined the Navy and William was still in basic training at Camp Gordon when John was killed.

McGONIGLE Bernard T.
Private 1st Class, Co. E, 106th Infantry Regiment, 27th Division
KIA 28 August 1918
Plot C – Row 04 – Grave 11
Army Serial Number 1207492

Bernard Thomas McGonigle was the son of Daniel McGonigle from Brooklyn, NY. He was born in Brooklyn in May 1898. He joined the New York National Guard (23rd Infantry Regiment) on 19 September 1917.

The circumstances of his death are unknown. His mother was devastated by the news and died from grief four months later.

LUCAS Mike
Sergeant, Co. I, 145th Infantry Regiment, 37th Division
KIA 1 November 1918
Plot C – Row 04 – Grave 12
Army Serial Number 1519142

Mike Lucas (°May 1884) was the oldest in the family of Peter and Mary Lucas from Cleveland, OH. The other children were Julia, Anna, Margaret, Catherine, Susan and William. Mike volunteered with the local National guard on 21 June 1916 and served with his unit along the Mexican border. The group photo of Co. I, 5th Ohio Infantry Regiment (later to become the 145th Infantry Regiment) was taken at Fort Bliss, TX during the same period. After the U.S. declaration of war the unit received additional training with what was then part of the 37th Division. They arrived in France on 22 June 1918.

Mike was promoted to Corporal on 19 July and Sergeant on 27 October, four days before he was killed in action. At approximately 10:30 he was hit by a shell fragment while he was getting his platoon ready to cross the river Scheldt. He was buried in the communal cemetery in the village of Eine (grave #3). His remains were moved to Waregem on 10 June 1919.

Before he sailed for Europe, Mike married Julia Chepka. His family were unaware and only found out when they were informed that Julia was the beneficiary of Mike's war insurance policy. Julia never made contact with Mike's family and it is said that Mike married her because she was pregnant.

Mike is standing fourth from right

MAHONEY Patrick
Private, Co. B, 135th MG Battalion, 37th Division
KIA 2 November 1918
Plot C – Row 04 – Grave 13
Army Serial Number 370426

Patrick Mahoney was an Irish immigrant. He was the son of Bartholomew Mahoney and Nora Lisgoold from Middleton, Cork County. They had three other sons: Bartholomew, James and Michael.

An artillery shell had hit the building where Patrick and his platoon were taking shelter. The building collapsed and they were buried alive. (photo insert next page taken on site in 1919) He was known to be a man with a good heart, could be counted on to do his duty at all times and was greatly appreciated by the men of his company. He was buried in the communal cemetery in Eine on 14 November.

The family has not forgotten him. In 2009 he received a visit by his great nephew Neil Twoney from Dublin, Ireland (left) and in 2013 from his great niece Margaret O'Keefe from Cork (right).

no photograph available

JOHNSON Edward

Private, Co. E, 364th Infantry Regiment, 91st Division
DOD 4 November 1918
Plot C – Row 04 – Grave 14
Army Serial Number 3131114

Edward (actually Edwin) Johnson was born on 4 October 1893. He was the son of Frank and Marian (photo) Johnson from Sparta, WI. He had four brothers (Wesley, Otis, Harold and Marvean) and three sisters (Olive, Addie and Lilian).

He died at Staden Mobile Hospital of Broncho-pneumonia on 4 November and was originally buried in the temporary American cemetery near the hospital (row 5, grave #68). His remains were moved to Waregem in plot A, grave #123 on 6 June 1919.

PETERSON Henry F.

Private, Co. K, 363rd Infantry Regiment, 91st Division
DOW 3 November 1918
Plot C – Row 04 – Grave 15
Army Serial Number 2265016

Henry Fred Peterson was the son of Olaf (born in Sweden) and Winfred (born in Ireland) Peterson from Oakland, CA. He was born on 23 November 1889 and had two brothers (Edwin and John) and one sister (Minnie Freitas). Henry had worked in his father's saloon for twelve years when he was called to register for the draft in June 1917.

He was sent to Camp Lewis, WA for basic training before being attached to the Californian 363rd Infantry Regiment. He survived the Meuse-Argonne offensive. On 19 October he wrote a letter home informing that he was in good health and that there was absolutely nothing to complain about.
His brother John served with the 31st Infantry Regiment during the Siberian campaign.

BERNIK John

Private 1st Class, Co. L, 145th Infantry Regt., 37th Division
DOW 6 November 1918
Plot C – Row 04 – Grave 16
Army Serial Number 1519198

John Bernik was born in Lipto, Czechoslovakia (former Austria-Hungary) in January 1897. He emigrated to the U.S.A. with his mother Mary in 1912. His father John had taken residence as a farmer in Huntsburg, OH a few years earlier. At first he lived with his parents and his brothers Matthew, Adam and sister Marie. However he later moved to Cleveland seeking a better paid job in the local industry.

He volunteered with the 5th Ohio (National Guard) Infantry Regiment on 22 May 1917. This regiment was the base of the 145th Infantry Regiment, 37th Division. On 1 June 1918 he was promoted to Private 1st Class arriving in France one month later.

John survived the Argonne offensive but was severely wounded during the fighting near Kruishoutem: a bullet wound to the neck. He was transported to the Evacuation Hospital in Staden but died from his wounds a few days later. At the time of death he was still an Austrian citizen. He was buried in the American cemetery in Staden on 8 November and his remains were moved to

Waregem in 1922.

His mother visited his grave with the Gold Star Mothers Pilgrimage in 1932. She had also asked if she could visit her family in Czechoslovakia however this was denied.

ADAMS Frank Jr.
Private, Co. A, 148th Infantry Regiment, 37th Division
DOD 28 October 1918
Plot C – Row 04 – Grave 17
Army Serial Number 3752610

Frank Adams Jr. was born in Stevens Point, WI on 4 September 1891. He was the oldest child in the family of Frank Adams Sr. and Magdalena Shafranski (born in the Czech Republic – photo). He also had five sisters (Lottie, Frances, Mary, Helen and Pauline) and one brother (John). Two of the children died in infancy. Frank spent his whole youth in Stevens Point. He worked as a self-employed painter/decorator until he was called to arms on 24 July 1918.

The next day he was sent to Camp Grant in Rockford, IL, where he spent four weeks in basic training with the 161st Depot Brigade. He was then assigned to Co. L, 344th Infantry Regiment, 86th Black Hawk Division. Following a period of two weeks at Camp Mills, NY he sailed for Europe. The division was disbanded upon arrival and Frank was transferred to the 148th Infantry Regiment 37th Division on 7 October.

Frank Adams Jr. died three weeks later on 28 October from pneumonia, which was a common complication of the Spanish flu. In his last letter home he wrote that he was in good health.

DAVIS Samuel A. Jr. – Silver Star
Sergeant, Co F, 361st Infantry Regiment, 91st Division
KIA 1 November 1918
Plot C – Row 04 – Grave 18
Army Serial Number 2257467

Samuel Davis was born in Higbee, MO on 4 November 1889. His mother died when he was five years of age and he was raised by his aunt and uncle in Fayette, MO. In 1911 he moved west and found a job as an agricultural laborer in Cowlitz, WA. He was called to register for the draft on 5 June 1917. He requested exemption of military service claiming that he was physically unfit. To no avail. Notwithstanding his claim, Samuel was an exemplary soldier. In a very short time he climbed the ranks to Sergeant.

He was killed during an artillery barrage near the village of Moregem and was buried in the town of Bevere. His remains were moved to Waregem on 6 September 1919 (plot A, grave #192). Samuel received a Divisional Citation (cfr Di Giacomo A-1-21).

His grandmother Jabe Jones was the beneficiary of his war insurance policy.

SWAIN Russell B.
Private, San. Det., 106th Infantry Regiment, 27th Division
KIA 9 August 1918
Plot C – Row 04 – Grave 19
Army Serial Number 1209167

Russell Baker Swain was the son of Enoch and Annie Swain from Brooklyn, NY. (photo: Russel with his parents).

He was 18 when he volunteered with the 23rd Infantry Regiment, NY National Guard, but was rejected due to his impaired eyesight. His two brothers Enoch and Hobson were also serving and he didn't want to be left behind when they departed for Europe. Finally after pulling strings he was able to join. When the 106th Infantry Regiment was formed, Russell was assigned to the Hospital Corps, his two brothers with the Signal Corps (Enoch was serving with the Army Pigeon Corps).

On 9 August, his unit was caught in a heavy artillery barrage. The building where Russel sought shelter received a direct hit. He was killed instantly together with three other men of which one was Norman Stein. They were buried at Lyssenthoek Cemetery in Poperinge.
Enoch could never forget his brother. He was mentally torn. He later named his son Russell.

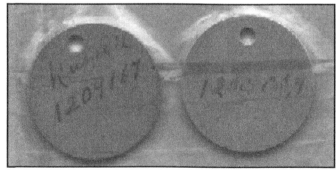

Right: Russel's ID tags
Left: Russel with the "3 sons in service" flag.

From left to right: Hobson, Russell and Enoch.   Russel's field Grave

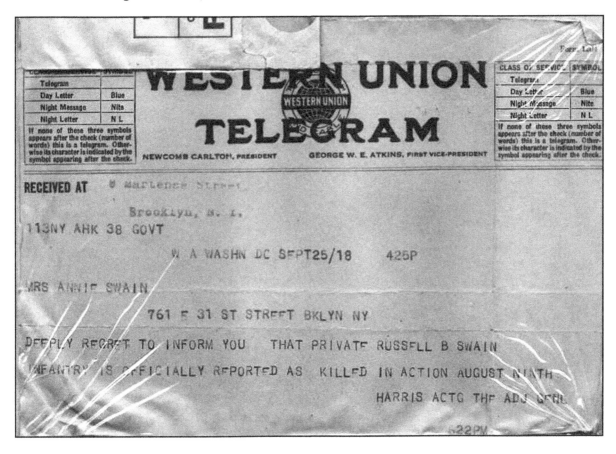

Telegram informing the death of Russel

STEIN Norman K.
Private 1st Class, San. Det., 106th Infantry Regt., 27th Division
KIA 9 August 1918
Plot C – Row 04 – Grave 20
Army Serial Number 1209165

Norman Stein was from Brooklyn, NY. He was originally serving with the 23rd NY National Guard Regiment. He was killed on 9 August when his shelter received a direct hit during an artillery barrage. Russell Swain was also one of the victims. They were buried at Lyssenthoek Military Cemetery in Poperinge. Enoch Swain wrote a letter to the Graves Registration asking if his son Russell could be buried next to Norman at the Flanders Field Cemetery. He had first contacted Norman's mother Anna who had initially chosen for repatriation. She immediately agreed to the proposal under these conditions and so now they are buried side by side.

Anna visited the Flanders Field Cemetery with the Gold Star Mothers Pilgrimage in 1930.

Norman Stein has a special marker. Not because he is one of the few Stars of David in the cemetery but because it's the only marker with an epitaph to the rear, These epitaphs were prominent with the British and so the option was also provided for American families. However, due to lack of interest it was discontinued after WWII.

The epitaph reads: "To eyes of men unwise they seem to die": which is derived from the Book of Solomon III, 1-3: "*The souls of the righteous are in the hands of God. In the sight of the unwise they seem to die and their departure is taken for misery and their going away from earth to be utter destruction, but they are in peace.*"

no photograph available

MAZZARELLA Angelo
Private, Co. I, 362nd Infantry Regiment, 91st Division
KIA 1 November 1918
Plot C – Row 04 – Grave 21
Army Serial Number 2665534

Angelo Mazarella was an Italian immigrant. He was born in Rome on 16 May 1890. His two year older brother Paul (Paolo) also resided in the U.S.A. Both took residence in Austin, WV where they worked as coal miners for the Austin Coal & Coke Company.

Angelo was called to arms on 30 April 1917 in Kittanning, PA. On 13 September 1918 he was assigned to the 91st Division. At 09:00 on October 31st, Co. I was ordered to go over the top. They were immediately spotted by the Germans who were hiding in the Spitaalsbossen. Within thirty minutes Frank Osborn, William Garner, James Miller and Angelo were killed. Angelo was killed by a direct hit. The witness statement indicates: *"He was blown to pieces"*. His remains were first buried in the village of Ooigem near a field hospital. This is probably the reason why the official date of death was incorrectly logged as being 1 November. In this case the date of death on his marker is also incorrect.

At the time of death Angelo was still an Italian citizen. His emergency address was registered with his father Pietro Mazzarella in Aquilo, Italy.

KIRSCH Basil A.
Private, Co. L, 364th Infantry Regiment, 91st Division
KIA 31 October 1918
Plot C – Row 04 – Grave 22
Army Serial Number 2783724

Basil Augustine Kirsch was born in in Nicktown, PA on 21 November 1892. He was the third born in the farming family of Augustin Kirsh and Barbara Parish. In total there were eleven children: Peter, Bonneface, Basil, Francesca, Agnes, Timothy, Augustine Paul, Irenaeus, Felix and Mary. The family moved west in 1901 and found residence in Stayton, Oregon.

The family in 1908 with 10 of their 11 children (Mary is absent). Basil is standing far left.

The farming business was too small and Basil purchased 320 acres in the southeast of Oregon. The war through a wrench in the works and Basil was unable to cultivate the land. He was called to arms to serve his country.

He was sent to Camp Lewis, WA for basic training. He passed his physical with flying colors. Even his teeth were beyond perfection. The physician had never seen such a perfect human body. At this time he enrolled for a war insurance policy for $10,000, his mother being the beneficiary. His brother Paul was also in Europe serving with the A.E.F. (photo insert). He served as a motorcycle messenger.

Basil was killed on the first day of the battle in Waregem. His company was in reserve and had received orders to move towards the front line when a artillery shell fell close by. He was buried near the crossroads where he fell in Waregem and on 10 June 1919 his remains were moved to Cemetery 1252, plot C, grave #31.

Barbara Kirsch visited the Flanders Field Cemetery with the Gold Star Mothers Pilgrimage in 1930. She kept a meaningful diary of the trip. On 18 June she wrote in her diary about the illness of Louis Landgraf's mother, one of the few fatalities during the Gold Star Mothers Pilgrimage. She also wrote that only seven mothers from Oregon made the trip. On 2 July 1930 she visited Flanders Field Cemetery: *"It is the most beautiful cemetery I have ever seen"*. On the morning of 3 July she returned and in the afternoon she visited the Ohio Bridge in Eine. On 4 July she made her final trip to Flanders Field. On 5 July the group returned to Paris, where they stayed and visited the touristic sites in the area until 10 July. The following day they embarked for their return trip to the U.S.A. She arrived back home on 25 July. Barbara died in 1940. Augustin in 1970: he was 105 years of age. Basil's land is still owned by the family to this day.

Jim and Catherine Kirsch, Basil's nephew and niece, visiting his grave in 2013.

Lawrence Kirsch, a son of Basil's brother Irenaeus (insert above left), was killed in WOII and is also buried in Belgium at the Henri-Chapelle Cemetery (Plot E-Row 2-Grave 6). Photo above: Dale and Lawrence visit their brother's grave. Below: at Basil's grave at Flanders Field in 2014.

LENTZ Peter
Private, Co. C, 347th MG Battalion, 91st Division
KIA 31 October 1918
Plot C – Row 04 – Grave 23
Army Serial Number 2256139

Peter Lentz was born in Menominee, MI on 28 February 1889. He was the son of Peter Lentz (born in Luxembourg) and Catherine Gauche (born in Messancy, Belgium). He had three brothers (Fred, William and Charles) and three sisters (Katherine, Margareth and Mary).

He moved to Washington State in search of employment and soon he found a job as a lumberman. When he was called to register for the draft, he requested exemption of military service based on his medical condition (rheumatism) but to no avail. He was called to arms and sent to Aberdeen.

"Pete" was killed on the first day of the battle near Waregem. He was killed at Steenbrugge (Anzegem) when a shell fell close by and fractured his skull.

PLOT D

DZIURZYNSKI John
Private 1st Class, Co. E, 148th Infantry Regiment, 37th Division
KIA 31 October 1918
Plot D – Row 01– Grave 01
Army Serial Number 1529573

Jan Dziura was born on 1 October 1886 in Wawrzenczyce, Poland (former Russia), approximately 35 km east of Cracow. He was the son of Pjotr Dziura and Marya Dziurzynska and had two brothers (Pjotr and Zegniud) and four sisters (Maryana, Aniela, Emilia and Stefa). He had served with the Russian Infantry for three years before he decided to seek a better future. He emigrated to the U.S.A. in July 1913. He embarked on the SS Finland in Antwerp, Belgium and arrived at Ellis Island on 2 August. He took residence in Cleveland, OH where he was proprietor of a barber shop.

John was called to arms on 4 October 1917. He received his basic training with the 158th Depot Brigade. Two weeks later he was assigned to Co. E of the 148th Infantry Regiment. He was killed near the village of Olsene on 31 October. There were no witness accounts. He was buried in the American plot of the communal cemetery on 3 November, grave 2. His remains were moved to Waregem on 3 June 1919 (plot D, grave #102). After the final disposition and repatriation of remains to the U.S.A. he received his final resting place on 23 June 1922.

His emergency address was with his brother Peter Dziurzynski in Hamtramck, MI.

ANDERSON Lionel A.

1st Lieutenant, Medical Reserve Corps, attached B.E.F.
DOD 18 February 1919
Plot D – Row 01 – Grave 02

Lionel Andrius Anderson was born in Peoria, IL on 11 April 1887. He was the son of a farming couple John W. (born in Sweden) and Nellie Anderson. He had two brothers: Robert and Forest. There was a fourth child in the family but no records were found. As a young family they moved to Prospect in Kansas. He attended the Baker University until 1910 and then in 1911 studied law at the Chicago University. In the annals of the Baker University (1910) he was described as *"A man without a country. For e'en though vanquished he argues still"* and as *"A man of high standing"*. In 1912 he attended the medical faculty of the University of Kansas in Lawrence until 1914. From there he continued his studies at the Washington University, St Louis, where he qualified as Doctor in Medicine in 1916. He became a surgeon at the Northern Pacific Railway Company in Glendive, MT and in St Paul, MN.
He was a member of the *Sigma Phi Epsilon* brotherhood and later a member of the Free Masons Lodge.

Lionel was promoted to 1st Lieutenant in the Medical Reserve Corps on 11 February 1918. His registration card indicated that he requested exemption except for the Medical Corps. He embarked for Europe on 1 June and upon arrival he was attached as a medical regimental officer to the British Medical Service. He served during major offensives in Belgium and northern France. Lt. Anderson died in the British Military hospital in Namen (Namur) - *Casualty Clearing Station #48* – from pneumonia, a common complication of the Spanish flu, on 18 February 1919. He was head of the X-ray department at the time of his death.

1st Lieutenant Lionel Anderson is the only man from Kansas interred at the cemetery and one of two who lost their lives in 1919.

MOEN Neil Merriam

Private, Co. E, 148th Infantry Regiment, 37th Division
KIA 31 October 1918
Plot D – Row 01 – Grave 03
Army Serial Number 3340807

Neil Merriam Moen was born in South Stillwater, Washington, MN on 14 August 1895. He was the son of Thron Moen and Mary Finsted (Norwegian immigrants) and he had three brothers (Ole, Marvin and Clarence) and one sister (Thelma). His main ambition was to become a farmer and he was persistent in trying to find a farmer who was willing to teach him the trade. He was also a devout Christian and took part in all activities organized by the local church community.

Neil moved to Stampede, ND where he had found another job on a farm. He was called to arms in June 1918 and after basic training in Camp Grant, IL was attached to Co. M of the 344th Infantry Regiment, 86th (Black Hawk) Division, a division with many servicemen from Illinois. The Division being disbanded upon arrival in Europe, Neil was reassigned to the 148th Infantry Regiment.

He was killed by machinegun fire and buried in the American mass grave along the road to Gent in the town of Olsene. His mother had signed up to visit his permanent gravesite at the Flanders Field Cemetery with the Gold Star Mothers Pilgrimage in 1930. Unfortunately she passed away on 24 February of that year.

THALMAN Chauncey C.
Private, MG Co. 363rd Infantry Regiment, 91st Division
KIA 31 October 1918
Plot D – Row 01 – Grave 04
Army Serial Number 2262927

Chauncey Clay Thalman was born in Rosalia, KS on 27 February 1891. His parents were Albert Henry Thalman and Retura (Tura) Alma Rannel (photo right). They had three other sons (William Edward, John Robert and Montgomery) and a daughter (Asa). Montgomery and Asa were twins but died very young. Chauncey spent his youth on his father's farm in Rosalia. At the age of 22 he moved with his brother John to Etiwanda, CA where

they were employed as laborers at one of the many orange orchards. For a while he also worked in the oil fields in Maricopa, CA but soon returned to the orange and lime plantations near Stockton, CA, the city where Jack Ayk (B-4-18) also originated from.

When the U.S. declared war on Germany, Chauncey volunteered for the coast artillery but was turned down because of his impaired vision. He was later called to arms and found fit for duty. He was sent for basic training to Camp Lewis where he arrived at the end of 1917. He survived the Meuse-Argonne offensive unscathed, however his best friend, Corporal Earl Woodward, was killed in action on 1 October (Plot H - Row 43 - Grave 9, Meuse Argonne American Cemetery, Romagne-Sous-Montfaucon, France).

Chauncey was killed in action in Waregem on 31 October. He was shot through the head by a German sniper. First aid was administered but one hour later he succumbed to his wounds. He was buried along the road between Nokere and Waregem, near the horse race track (Isolated Grave #1 Waregem). His remains were moved to Cemetery #1252 on 3 June 1919 and buried in plot D, grave #121.

Initially, John had decided that his brother's remains be repatriated to the U.S.A., but after being reassured by the Government that the graves in these overseas military cemeteries in Europe were going to be well cared for, revoked his earlier decision.

Machine Gun Company 363rd Infantry Regiment

Machine Gun Company 363rd Infantry Regiment during training

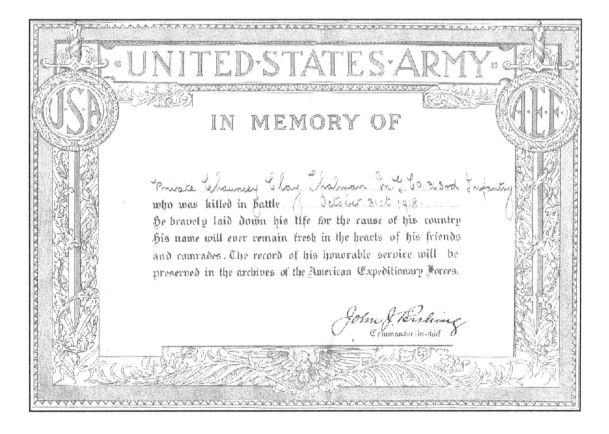

no photograph available

JAQUET Glenn H.
Private, Co. D, 136th MG Battalion, 37th Division
KIA 2 November 1918
Plot D – Row 01 – Grave 05
Army Serial Number 3341632

The Jaquet family originated from Alsace Lorraine, France. Glenn Herbert Jaquet was born in Loraine, Henry County, IL on 11 May 1893. He was the son of Frank Jaquet and Mary Obrecht and he had two older brothers and one younger sister: Clayton Frank, Raymond William and Myrtel Sarah. On 21 June 1917 he married Nettie Mowry (a schoolteacher). Glenn became an independent farmer in the vicinity of Geneseo, Henry County. They both worked very hard and were a happy couple until he was called to arms and sent to Camp Grant for basic training in July 1918.

He was attached to Co. L of the 344th Infantry Regiment, 86th (Black Hawk) Division, a division comprising mainly of conscripts from Illinois. This division was disbanded upon arrival in Europe and Glenn was reassigned to the 136th Machine Gun Battalion. In his last letter to his wife (18 October) he wrote that he had just been released from hospital where he had been admitted with the flu (Spanish flu) and was being transferred to a machine gun battalion. He concluded his letter with: *"Doesn't the talk of peace sound good?"* Unfortunately Glenn never lived long enough to experience peace again. He was killed by shell fire on 2 November and was buried in a residential garden west of the village of Heurne.

At the time of his death Nettie was pregnant and gave birth to a boy, Glen Herbert Jr., on 24 March 1919. Unfortunately the infant died within 5 days of birth. Nettie remarried In December 1920 with a certain Clarence Cross. The reason why she chose for Glenn's remains to be buried in Europe is evident. As in so many other similar cases, being the closest next of kin and having remarried, she was suppressing former grief and focusing on her new family. She never mentioned the fact of being previously married to her children. They only found out after her death. While going through her personal belongings they found the telegram announcing the death of Glenn being killed in action and other effects relating to Glenn Jr. No photograph of Glenn Jacquet was ever found.

Glenn's mother (photo insert) visited the Flanders Field cemetery with the Gold Star Mothers Pilgrimage in 1930. She was 65 years of age and very nervous to make the trip. This being understandable as she had never been beyond Illinois and now was faced to cross the Atlantic Ocean. With 230 other Gold Star Mothers she sailed for Europe on board the SS Roosevelt.
Glenn had never received a letter from home. He was killed before the first letters reached him. She had kept a box with the returned

letters and a lock of his hair during the voyage. Her feelings at the time were noted in her diary: *"I'd a thousand times rather have his body in a grave over here – than take this trip"*.

In 1931 she received a second invitation to make the trip which was obviously an administrative error. She replied to the invitation expressing her experiences of the previous year: *"from the depth of my heart, It was a wonderful privilege to visit my dear baby boy's grave. It was also a hard sad trip, but God gave me health and strength to go through with it."*

HESTERMAN Henry J.
Private, Co. A, 363rd Infantry Regiment, 91st Division
KIA 2 November 1918
Plot D – Row 01 – Grave 06
Army Serial Number 2286778

Henry John Hesterman was born in Lincoln, WI on 30 September 1890. His parents were German immigrants, Henry and Mary Hesterman (née Rehvinkel), later moved to Grangeville, ID. They also had three daughters: Henrietta, Frieda and Eva. Before he was called to arms he was engaged in the laundry business together with his brother-in-law Madison Meyer (Eva's husband), being proprietors of the Electric Laundry. He was a natural born businessman.

His parents received a letter dated 28 October. They felt so proud of their son's service overseas that the letter was read in many homes in the city. The letter was an account of his travels through Flanders: *"Dear Folks, --- Here I am again trying to write. I have a very comfortable place to write just now. I'm sure you would laugh if you could see me and what I'm calling a comfortable place. I've let down the back board of a dog wagon so it make a good desk and then I got a fine big German milk stool for a seat, so I'm at ease in fine style, under this thatched roof. When we are on the road it seems like we're in a town all the time as the country is so thickly settled and when we feel hungry at any time on our marches we can get a turnip or a carrot almost any time, and we see many odd things. Yesterday I saw a horse and a cow hitch up together to a wagon; another man was ploughing with his milk cow, and then at night sat down and milked her just the same. It is surely surprising how soon the people move back to their homes after they are retaken from the Germans. ... Some carry what few things they own on their backs, some have a small wagon, like this one I'm using as a writing desk, drawn by a large dog. And how glad they are to find that their places are not damaged and how quickly the repair and fix up those that have been damaged. We see a lot of breweries, sugar factories and places where they weave cloth and make mats from flax. The Germans retreated quite fast over this country we are no wand I guess it looked too good, even to them, to destroy. Well, I must get to work again so will have to quit now. I wish you would write soon and often, a letter helps.*"

Henry was killed in action while performing his duties as a stretcher bearer. His head was badly shattered. He was buried in a field across a creek southeast of Waregem. His remains were one of the first to be reburied in Cemetery #1252 (plot 1, grave #2). Later being reinterred in plot D, grave #153.

SILCOTT Clyde
Private, Co. C, 363rd Infantry Regiment, 91st Division
KIA 31 October 1918
Plot D – Row 01 – Grave 07
Army Serial Number 3533739

Clyde Silcott was born in Piketon, Pike County, OH on 5 July 1890. He was the son of Otto Spencer Silcott (an orphan) and Lavina Elizabeth Alexander (daughter of a wealthy family – photo insert). They had four other children: Annie Florence (°1879), Earl Thomas (°1881) Earnest Otto (°1888) and Malina (°1893).

Clyde was called to arms on 24 July 1918 in Waverly, OH. He received his basic training with the 158th Depot Brigade in Camp Sherman, OH through 10 August when he was assigned to the 333rd Infantry Regiment of the 84th Lincoln Division. This division was disbanded upon arrival in Europe and the men transferred to other divisions where heavy losses had been encountered.

On 2 September, Clyde was designated as a replacement to Co. C of the 363rd (California) Infantry Regiment, 91st Division.

He was killed by a HE (high explosive) shell while administering first aid to a wounded comrade. He was buried in Waregem near a creek (A.E.F. Cemetery Waregem #1, Grave #3). His brother Earnest named one of his children after him. Lavina (aged 78) had requested to visit Clyde's grave with the Gold Star Mothers Pilgrimage in 1932 but was unable to do so due to ill health.

CHIMIENTI Michele

Private 1st Class, Co. E, 316th Engineer Regt., 91st Division
ACC 1 November 1918
Plot D – Row 01 – Grave 08
Army Serial Number 2273521

Michele Chimienti was born on 9 March 1888. He was the son of Giovanni Chimienti and Angela Temasicchie, who also had two daughters. Their residence was at via Spiritu Santo 54 in Sannicando di Bari, Italy.

Michele emigrated to the USA around 1910 and after a while took residence in Benge, WA (photo insert taken about 1920). This was a small town situated 15 miles west of Lacrosse and 30 miles south of Ritzville with a population of approximately 100 in 1917. Michele was illiterate yet he became a foreman for the Spokane, Portland & Seattle Railway. This is no doubt the reason why he was attached to an Engineer Regiment of the 91st Division at the time he was called to arms on 6 October 1917.

The circumstances of his death are however questionable, as is his date of death. Officially the date of death is 1 November, other sources indicate 31 October. Circumstances of death range from killed in action to accident. However in his burial file held at the National Archives, the Graves Registration Form 114-A indicates the cause of death being suicide. At the time of death he had not yet obtained his U.S. citizenship although he had filed a petition for naturalization while at Camp Lewis on 29 May 1918.

Shortly after the war, a small memorial was erected by the De Zutter family in the grounds of Chateau Ter Elst in Waregem where Michele had lost his life. The memorial was lost over the years but was found again in 2002. The descendants of the De Zutter family renovated the memorial and during a short ceremony it was inaugurated again in 2003.

SCHOCH Clinton J.
Private, Co. E, 145th Infantry Regiment, 37th Division
KIA 4 November 1918
Plot D – Row 01 – Grave 09
Army Serial Number 2705066

Clinton Jacob Schoch was born on 10 January 1890. He was the oldest in the family of Enoch and Emma Schoch from Nazareth, PA. Clinton had four sisters (Minnie, Lottie, Carrie and Jennie) and three brothers (Floyd, Harvey and Willard).

He registered for the draft on 5 June 1917. He was killed by shell fire along the banks of the river Scheldt. He was buried in the village of Eine. His remains were disinterred and moved to Waregem on 11 June 1919.

no photograph available

BARLETT Leo R.
Private, Co. K, 361st Infantry Regiment, 91st Division
DOW 2 November 1918
Plot D – Row 01 – Grave 10
Army serial number 2477318

Leo Ralph Barlett was born in Gurneyville, OH on 26 November 1888. He lived in Jeffersonville, OH at the time he was called to arms on 26 May and received his basic training with the 158th Depot Brigade. On 17 July he was assigned to Co. A, 336th Infantry Regiment, 84th Division and sailed for Europe. Arriving in France the division was disbanded on 3 October and Leo was transferred to Co. K of the 361st Infantry Regiment, 91st Division on 5 October. His younger brother, Theo Raymond, was already in France serving with the 602nd Engineers. He had achieved the rank of Sergeant 1st Class.

Op 2 November 1918, Leo was hit in the back by shell fragments and succumbed to his wounds a few hours later.

PORTER George R.
Private 1st Class, Co. C, 348th MG Battalion, 91st Division
KIA 2 November 1918
Plot D – ROW 01 – Grave 11
Army Serial Number 3532752

George Rufus Porter was born on 22 February 1895. He lived with his parents Milton and Alice Porter (née Robinson) in Mount Sterling, OH. He was selected and called to arms in Circleville, OH on 23 July 1918.

George was sent to Camp Sherman in Ohio where he was assigned to the 333rd Infantry Regiment, 84th Lincoln Division. Upon arrival in Europe all the men of this division were reassigned and George arrived with Co. E of the 363rd Infantry Regiment. Two weeks later he was transferred to Co. C of the 348th Machine Gun Battalion, 91st Division.

Officially he was killed on 2 November. From the witness statement of Sgt. Sieman Manning of his company one can read that the date of death was 1 November. *"Porter was with us in a ditch as the area in front of us was being shelled. The company was on the move and he left us, cutting across a field to rejoin the company. A shell struck close to him. His head had been split open from front to rear and his brains scattered about."*

George Porter was buried in an isolated grave close to the village of Wortegem. His remains were moved to Waregem on 11 June 1919. The fact that he was buried in Wortegem confirms Sergeant Manning's witness statement on George's date of death. On that particular day the division was advancing through the village.

no photograph available

PLASKAWICKY Julius
Private, Co. D, 147th Infantry Regiment, 37th Division
KIA 31 October 1918
Plot D – Row 01 – Grave 12
Army Serial Number 1756172

Julchian Ploskawicki was born on 20 May 1895 in Kruhlica, now Poland, formerly part of Russia. In the summer of 1913 he emigrated to the U.S.A. and found employment at the Natural Gas Company in Buffalo, NY. Many Polish immigrants found a job with this company.

Julius was inducted on 28 April 1918 and arrived in Europe on 22 June. He was killed in the town of Olsene and initially buried in an isolated grave. His remains were reinterred in Waregem and laid to rest in plot A grave 95 on 10 June 1919. During the identification process it was determined that he had a fractured skull. Rosary beads were also found on his body.

His emergency address was with his cousin Ida Yagum where he lived during his stay in Buffalo, NY. At the time of death he was still a Russian citizen.

OLSON Ole
Private, Co. I, 148th Infantry Regiment, 37th Division
KIA 30 October 1918
Plot D – Row 01 – Grave 13
Army Serial Number 3749506

Ole Olson was born in Norway on 11 February 1891. He was the son of August Olson and Augusta Pedersdtr Nordby. He had two brothers and one sister: Peter (°1892), Karl (°1896) and Gunda (°1894). Augusta died from tuberculosis in 1901. August asked his brother Frantz and his wife Anne if they were prepared to raise Gunda. Frantz, Anne and Gunda emigrated to the U.S.A. in 1906. Searching for better prospects in life, Ole and his brother Peter followed in their footsteps and arrived in the U.S.A. in 1910. They lived with Gunda and Ole found a job as agricultural laborer in Christiana, WI. He obtained the U.S. citizenship on 8 August 1918.

He was drafted on 2 July and sent to Camp Grant in Illinois for basic training with the 161st Depot Brigade. From there he was assigned to the 344th Infantry Regiment, 86th Black Hawk Division. This division was mainly formed with draftees from Illinois. Upon arrival in Europe the division was disbanded and the men were sent as replacements to other divisions. Ole Olson was finally transferred and attached to Co. I of the 148th Infantry Regiment.

His emergency address was with his sister Gunda Larson, who lived in Cambridge, WI. When Peter had saved a considerable amount of money, he sent it to his brother Karl in Norway who in turn purchased the Gropen farm. He even changed his name from Olson to Gropen. Some years later, Peter returned to Norway where he remained for the rest of his life. He also changed his family name to Gropen, as his father August (photo insert left) had done before him.

Kare, Kari Elisabeth and Jon Einar Gropen from Rudshøgda, Norway visited their great uncle's grave on 7 May 2014.

Photos of Ole with sister Gunda (left) and friend Birger Larsen (right) who traveled to Wisconsin with him.

Ole just before his departure to Europe in 1918

RYDELL Axel T.

Private, Co. L, 362nd Infantry Regiment 91st Division
KIA 31 October 1918
Plot D – Row 01 – Grave 14
Army Serial Number 2286286

Axel Tolli Rydell was born in Moheda, Sweden on 6 April 1890. His parents were Anders Jonasson Rydell and Ingrid Cajsa Palmqvist (photo insert). He was the youngest of twelve.   (John, Carl, Anders, Lars, Mary, Carl Gustav II, Anna, Axel, Henrik, Oscar, Martha and Theolinda).

He emigrated to the U.S.A. on 1 August 1909 out of Copenhagen on the SS Adriatic and took residence near Dodson, MT. Four brothers and two sisters had emigrated before him. He obtained his U.S. citizenship on 23 September 1915. Axel married Ingeborg Nording in Minneapolis, MN on 26 April 1916 but the marriage didn't last and the following year they were divorced.

Axel Rydell was killed in action near the railroad station in the village of Anzegem. At 05:30 a.m. on the morning of the 31st, Axel and his company were waiting to go over the top during a heavy American barrage and German counter barrage. It was necessary to establish contact with the units of the second battalion on the left and Private Rydell was chosen as runner for the mission. He never returned. His remains were later found by another unit.

SUDBECK August
Private, MG Co. 363rd Infantry Regiment, 91st Division
KIA 31 October 1918
Plot D – Row 01 – Grave 15
Army Serial Number 3956254

August Südbeck, born 8 October 1889 in Bow Valley, NE, was the son of Stephen and Elizabeth Südbeck from Hartington, NE. He was part of a large family with six brothers (Edward, Peter, Leo, Anton, Herman and Paul) and three sisters (Elizabeth, Mary and Mathilda). It is assumed that his father was of German descent. August was very intelligent and had an excellent sense of humor. He took a job to pay for his higher education. At the time he was called to register for the draft he was a farm owner in Parkston, SD. His attempt to obtain exemption from military service due to his impaired vision was in vain. He was engaged at the time he was called to arms however they would never have the opportunity to see each other again.

After his basic training he was attached to Co. M of the 333rd Infantry Regiment, 84th (Lincoln) Division. The division was disbanded upon arrival in Europe and August was reassigned to the Machine Gun Company of the 363rd Infantry Regiment. On 31 October 1918, during his baptism of fire, he became disorientated and confused due to the heavy gun fire and was cut off from his unit. During his attempt to rejoin his company he was shot by a sniper.* He was buried in a field on a farm near Waregem, close to where the current horse race track is located. A letter was found on his remains with a hole pierced by the bullet that had killed him.

In reply to the request for repatriation or not, August's parents remained dubious and indecisive. Rumors had reached them on the uncertainty of identified remains however in this case there was no doubt. Details of his field grave, positive identification with ID tags on remains and wooden marker were undeniably correct. On 23 June 1923 his remains were interred at Flanders Field.

---

*This is just one of the many examples of the outcome of baptism of fire. Inexperience on the one hand but more importantly, as in this case, the element of cohesion that was lost due to the soldier's individual transfer from a unit where he was accustomed, trained, and had made comrades in arms, then arriving in a strange environment with the feeling of insecurity as a result. Although these facts were confirmed and reported to the War Department, no action was ever taken until the U.S. involvement in Afghanistan when it became mandatory that nothing less than a company with company commander could be transferred from one division to another.

Family photo: August standing second from left

Original grave - Cemetery #1252

" In Loving Remembrance "

475

McKINLEY Steven D.

Sergeant, Co. E, 145th Infantry Regiment, 37th Division
KIA 4 November 1918
Plot D – Row 01 – Grave 16
Army Serial Number 1518383

Stephen Douglas McKinley was the son of Stephen Douglas Sr. and Eva McKinley from Reading, MI. He was born on 29 May 1892 in Butler, Dekalb County, IN. He spent most of his life in Indiana. He only lived in Hicksville, OH one year before he joined the 2nd Infantry Regiment, Ohio National Guard on 28 May 1917. He married Stella (Maxwell) Burlingame on 9 July 1917. Steven spent eight months in Camp Sheridan, AL for his basic training.

He was promoted to Sergeant on 31 May 1918 and sailed for Europe two weeks later. Stella gave birth to their daughter Vivian on 29 August. However Steven would never see her.

Steven was killed in action on 4 November while leading his men into battle under heavy artillery and machinegun fire. He was shot by a German sniper and killed instantly. He was initially buried near the village of Kruishoutem. His remains were moved to Waregem on 11 June 1919. Tracy Clark (D-1-19), also from Hicksville, was killed on the same day.

Stella remarried in 1928 and so was not eligible to take part in the Gold Star Mothers Pilgrimage.

Steven and Stella

476

TOVSRUD Robert O.
Private, Co. D, 135th MG Battalion, 37th Division
KIA 31 October 1918
Plot D – Row 01 – Grave 17
Army Serial Number 3131582

Robert Oliver Tovsrud was born in Traill County, ND on 1 October 1894. He was the second child of nine in the Jens Gunderson and Anne Enderud family: Gina, Robert, Sina, Ella Gustava, Helga, Anna, Esther, Peter and Erick. Jens and Anne emigrated to the U.S.A. from Norway in 1892. In 1896 they took residence on a farm in Harlow, ND in an attempt to seek a more prosperous life. The farm was called "Tovsrude Farm" and from then onwards the family went through life with Tovsrud being their surname.

Robert took residence in Goldmedal (?), MT and in June 1917 was registered for military service. He was drafted on 28 May 1918 and sent for basic training to Camp Lewis, WA where he served with the 166th Depot Brigade. On 11 June he wrote that the whole camp was under quarantine due to an outbreak of measles. Military life in the camp suited him. He only dreaded washing his clothes. He also wrote that he wept frequently when he was thinking of the family back home and that he had completed his war insurance application indicating his father as beneficiary.

In June he was transferred to the 143rd Machine Gun Battalion of the 40th "Sunshine Division", a division mainly comprising of National Guard units from Arizona, California, Colorado, Nevada, New Mexico and Utah. He sailed for Europe on 8 August. Upon arrival in Europe the division became the 6th Depot Division and the men were transferred to other units. Robert was attached to the 135th Machine Gun Battalion. He was killed in action near the village of Kruishoutem (Isolated Grave #1 Cruyshautem). His remains were moved to Waregem and interred in plot A, grave 33 on 12 June 1919.

After the war the Veterans of Foreign Wars Post #757 in Harlow, ND was named after Robert. The photo of his marker in Cemetery #1252 was taken prior 1921.

PEIRCE William H.
Private, Co. C, 347th MG Battalion, 91st Division
DOW 30 October 1918
Plot D – Row 01 – Grave 18
Army Serial Number 2930632

William Henry Peirce was the son of William and Anna Peirce. He was born in Cincinnati, OH on 15 September 1889 and had three brothers: Albert, Joseph and Charles. At the time he was called to arms on 26 June 1918 he still lived in Cincinnati and was employed as printer at the Specialty Printing Company on Liberty street. He claimed exemption for military service on the grounds that he was the sole person taking care of his mother. He received his basic training with the 158th Depot Brigade and was later transferred to the Supply Company of the 336th Infantry Regiment, 84th Division.

Upon arrival in Europe the division was disbanded and the men were sent to serve as replacements to other units. William was attached with the 347th Machine Gun Battalion of the 91st Division. He was wounded on 30 October and died shortly after. His emergency address was with his brother Charles, who lived at the same address.

Joseph was also serving in Europe. He was attached to the 11th Infantry Regiment, 5th Division and was slightly wounded during the St. Mihiel offensive on 24 September 1918. After the war he was certified for 10% disability.

CLARK Tracy J.
Sergeant, Co. F, 145th Infantry Regiment, 37th Division
KIA 4 November 1918
Plot D – Row 01 – Grave 19
Army Serial Number 1518395

Tracy James Clark, son of Finley and Rilla Clark, was born in Hillsdale County, MI on 23 January 1893. He had one brother, Archie and a sister, Eva. In 1915 the family moved to Hicksville, OH.

Tracy enlisted with Co. E, 2nd Infantry Regiment of the Ohio National Guard on 30 May 1917. This was the company where all National Guardsmen of Hicksville were assembled. He received his basic training in Camp Sheridan, AL and was attached to Co. F of the 145th Infantry Regiment. He was promoted to Corporal on 8 December. He embarked for Europe on 15 June 1918 and arrived in France on 23 June. He fought and survived the Meuse-Argonne offensive unscathed. On 18 October, shortly before the division was sent to Flanders, he was promoted to Sergeant. On 8 November, his best friend Corporal Selve Hadsell, wrote home informing Tracy's parents on the circumstances of his death. Tracy was administering first aid when at a certain point he stood upright and was shot under the arm by a sniper. The wound was fatal and he succumbed to a massive hemorrhage before medical aid could be administered. Hadsell also mentioned that of the 250 men of his company only 100 had survived.

Tracy Clark was one of ten men from Hicksville who were killed in the war. Steven MC Kinley, Ellis Dull and Ralph Mabrey, all died on the same day. Steven McKinley is also interred at Flanders Field (D-1-16). A memorial marker for Tracy was placed in the Waldon Town cemetery in Michigan.

Left: Tracy Clark's wooden marker in Cemetery #1252

Below: memorial marker in Waldon Town Cemetery.

LABNO Stanislaw K.

Private, Co. C, 347th MG Battalion, 91st Division
KIA 30 oktober 1918
Plot D – Rij 01 – Graf 20
Army Serial Number 3951405

Stanislaw Labno was born in Skrzyszów, Tarnów, Poland on 10 November 1892. The village was located approximately 65 miles east of Cracow which at the time was Galicia and so part of Austria-Hungary. He was the son of Jon and Agnieska Labno who also had five other children: Stefania, Antoni, Zofia, Anna and Viktoria. The family was poor and they worked hard on a small plot of land for their own keep. Due to the financial situation, and as dowry's were needed for the four girls, Antoni emigrated to the U.S.A. in 1913. Also in 1913, Stanislaw obtained his own land. He had a plan for his small farm but to make his dream come true he also needed extra cash. So in 1914, he decided to follow his brother's footsteps. He lived with Antoni in Omaha, NE and at the time of his registration for the draft was employed as a pantry man at the Mandarin Café.

On the family photo you can see from left to right: Anna, Stanislaw, Agnieska, Zofia, Viktoria and Jon.

It was also in Omaha that he was requested to register for the draft on 5 June 1917. He was eventually called to arms in June of 1918 and completed his boot camp with the 163rd Depot Brigade in Camp Dodge, IA. At the same time he signed up for a war insurance covering $ 10.000 in the event of his death. A short time afterwards he was reassigned to the 84th Lincoln Division. As with all men of the 84th Division, upon their arrival in Europe they were reassigned as replacements to other divisions. This is how Stanislaw arrived with the 91st Division on 6 October. He was killed in action by shell fire during the first few hours of the fighting around Waregem and was buried in Anzegem (isolated grave #6). It had turned out to be his first and his last battle. At the time it was assumed that he still was a Polish citizen.

After the war a small monument was erected to his memory in Skrzyszów. However, this was destroyed by the Germans in World War II.

On Memorial Day 2009, Stanislaw's nephew, Zbigniew Gniadek from New York City, was present for the ceremony (photo insert next page).

no photograph available

CARPEN Joe
Private, Co. F, 145th Infantry Regiment, 37th Division
KIA 4 November 1918
Plot D – Row 01 – Grave 21
Army Serial Number 1518463

Joe Carpen (Karpin) was born in Willhonia (the village of Kortylis, Vohlyn Region) Russia in March 1889. He was married to Mary Carpen (née Marja Karpinska). He registered with the Ohio National Guard in Cleveland on 4 June 1917 and was attached to the 5th Infantry Regiment Ohio National Guard. This regiment later became the 145th Infantry Regiment. He arrived in Europa on 15 June 1918.

Joe was killed in action on 4 November. He was shot in the stomach by machinegun fire and killed instantly. He was buried near the village of Kruishoutem. His emergency address was registered with his brother Nick in Russia. After the war Marja returned to her family in Brest-Litovsk which is now Belarus, close to the Polish border.

FOSTER Alfred J.

Sergeant, MG Co. 363rd Infantry Regiment, 91st Division
KIA 31 October 1918
Plot D – Row 01 – Grave 22
Army Serial Number 2262829

Alfred John Foster was born on 1 September 1894 on his father's farm in Orland, Glenn County, CA. His parents, Joseph Foster and Marion Marks (née Marques), were born in the Azores (Portugal). Alfred was the fifth of 15 children (9 brothers and 5 sisters). He still lived in Orland at the time he was drafted. Alfred was the 5th on the draft list of Glenn County, but since the 4 men before him were exempted, he became the first one who really had to serve. He travelled by train from Willows, CA to Camp (now Fort) Lewis, WA, where the 91st (Wild West) Division was trained and formed. It wasn't long before he was promoted to corporal due to his "quiet efficiency", his cheerfulness, and for always being on standby to help his comrades.

His division disembarked at Cherbourg, France In July 1918. He fought in the battles of St. Mihiel and the Argonne where he was promoted to Sergeant on 1 October. According to his military records he was promoted for efficiency and dependability, particularly under fire. Sergeant Foster was killed by enemy machinegun fire when he became separated from his company near Waregem on 31 October. He was buried in a spot described as: *"a beautiful spot overlooking the Lys River".*

At 68 years of age, his mother visited the Flanders Field Cemetery during the Gold Star Mothers Pilgrimage in 1933. She said that she was not afraid of crossing the ocean, but that she was perturbed of the trip from California to New York, since she hardly spoke any English.

Alfred was part of Lt. James Boyd Jr 's Machine Gun Company of the 363rd Infantry Regiment. Lt. Boyd later became a judge in Glenn County. Upon his return, on July 4th 1919, he founded the "Alfred J. Foster American Legion Post #34." The farm, where Alfred and his parents cultivated the land, is now an orange plantation.

On 16 November 2003, a nephew, Dan Alfred Foster, son of Alfred's brother Benjamin, visited his uncle's grave.

MANGOGNA Charles
Private, Co. K, 106th Infantry Regiment, 27th Division
KIA 2 September 1918
Plot D – Row 01 – Grave 23
Army Serial Number 2671648

Charles Mangogna was the son of Vincenzo Mangogna from New York City. He was born on 29 December 1891 and had one brother, Peter. He was inducted on 5 April 1918 and after a short training period at Camp Upton, Long Island, NY, embarked for Europe with the 27th Division on 10 May.

Charles was killed in action in the vicinity of Vierstraat and York Road. According to an eyewitness from his company: *"At Dikkebus I heard that he had been wounded by machinegun bullets in the abdomen. He was lying in a shell hole when the Germans counterattacked stabbing with bayonet. He was dead when we found him. He was buried in this shell hole with Corporal Weiss and Corporal Cundy. He was Italian, very thin, dark complexion. I knew him six months. He was from Brooklyn."*

At the time his brother Peter did everything in his power to find out the details of his death. He published an article with photo in a newspaper hoping that men of his unit would recognize him and come forward with their story on what happened to Charles.

In June 1923, the Superintendent of the Flanders Field cemetery, John Pantilis, received a letter notifying him that remains of an American soldier had been found in the communal cemetery in the city of Kortrijk (Courtrai). John traveled to Kortrijk and met the man who had been ordered by the Germans to bury the American soldier. The grave had no marker but the civilian recalled the exact spot where he was interred. The Superintendent set the wheels in motion to obtain the identity of the soldier and was able to find a Belgian officer who was in charge for all the military cemeteries in the vicinity. Researching German documents they finally retrieved the pertinent details and identity of the American soldier: Charles Mangogna. Even details of birth, name of father and date of burial: 6 September. The mortal remains were disinterred and both identification tags were found with a silver crucifix. His remains were moved and permanently interred in Waregem on 26 August 1923.

CAMPARZI Mario
Private, Co. A, 364th Infantry Regiment, 91st Division
KIA 31 October 1918
Plot D – Row 02 – Grave 01
Army Serial Number 2266039

Mario Camparsi was an Italian immigrant. He was born in Dolce, Verona. He embarked in Le Havre, France and sailed on the La Provence. He arrived in the United States on 15 November 1913. Mario, aged 19, immediately joined his brother Angelo in Los Angeles, CA. He had emigrated to the States in March of that same year.

When the United States declared war on Germany, Mario was called to arms and served with Co. A of the 364th Infantry Regiment. While at Camp Lewis, WA, he filed a petition for naturalization on 29 May 1918. He was killed during the battles around Waregem on 31 October 1918. Mario is registered as Camparzi, although his birth certificate shows Camparsi.

no photograph available

FITZGERALD Wiliam C.
Private, Co. A, 364th Infantry Regiment, 91st Division
KIA 1 November 1918
Plot D – Row 02 – Grave 02
Army Serial Number 2266058

William Charles Fitzgerald was born on 11 September 1890. He was the son of Thomas Fitzgerald (born in Ireland) and Catherine O'Connor. His occupation was bookbinder. He also had three brothers (Thomas, James and John) and two sisters (Josephine and Mary). They lived on Golden State Avenue, San Francisco, CA.

"Fitz" was killed by enemy artillery. He was first buried near the town center of Waregem.

PHALEN John S.
Private, Co. F, 362nd Infantry Regiment, 91st Division
KIA 31 October 1918
Plot D – Row 02 – Grave 03
Army Serial Number 2000557

John Sylvester Phalen was born in Illinois on 27 September 1888. He was the son of William Phalen and Rose Ellen Burns (group insert left) from Jacksonville, IL. His grandfather John Phalen was an Irish immigrant from Tipperary. John had three sisters (Gertrude, Rose and Margaret) and four brothers

(James, William Jr, August and Stephen) of which two also served. August (group insert middle) was attached to the 2nd Indianhead Division, renowned for their heroic exploits in Belleau Wood (France). Lieutenant William Phalen (group insert right), remained stationed at Camp Greenleaf in Georgia throughout the war.

John was a traveling salesman for the Copper Clad Range Company in Jacksonville at the time he was called to arms. He left for Camp Taylor, KY on 24 February 1918 where he was promoted to Corporal on 22 May. He was later transferred to Camp Sherman, OH. He arrived in France with Co. B of the 335th Infantry Regiment, 84th Division (mainly conscripts from Illinois) on 27 September.

Upon arrival in France the division was disbanded and the men transferred to other divisions as replacements. John was attached to Co. F of the 362nd Infantry Regiment. He was killed in action during his baptism of fire on 31 October and buried near the village of Anzegem. His remains were transferred to Flanders Field on 3 June 1919.

When John was transferred to the 362nd he obviously joined these ranks again as Private as this is the rank indicated on his marker. His name is also memorialized on a monument in Central Park Plaza, Jacksonville which was dedicated to the memory of 64 other soldiers from Morgan County who gave their all during the Great War.

ARMY OF THE UNITED STATES OF AMERICA

To all who shall see these presents, greeting:

Know Ye, that reposing special trust and confidence in the fidelity and abilities of Private John Phalen I do hereby appoint him Corporal, Company "B", 335th Infantry of the National Army of the United States, to rank as such from the Twenty-second day of May one thousand nine hundred and Eighteen. He is therefore carefully and diligently to discharge the duty of Corporal by doing and performing all manner of things thereunto belonging. And I do strictly charge and require all noncommissioned Officers and Soldiers under his command to be obedient to his orders as Corporal And he is to observe and follow such orders and directions from time to time, as he shall receive from his Superior Officers and noncommissioned Officers set over him, according to the rules and discipline of War.

Given under my hand at Camp Zachary Taylor Kentucky this Twenty-seventh day of May in the year of our Lord one thousand nine hundred and Eighteen.

Major, 335th Infantry, Comdg

Form No. 153—A.G.O.
Ed. Aug. 16-17—500,000.

John S. Phalen – appointed to Corporal

FEELY Aloysius E.
Corporal, Co. I, 363rd Infantry Regiment, 91st Division
KIA 31 October 1918
Plot D – Row 02 – Grave 04
Army Serial Number 2264736

Aloysius Edward Feely was born in White Plains, NY on 2 September 1891. His parents were John Feely and Mary Hayes. He moved westward, and for ten years lived and worked as an electrician in San Francisco before moving to Fresno, CA. In his letters home to his parents and brothers (William, James, Joseph, Henry, and John) he wrote that the war would be over pretty soon as the Germans were being defeated time and time again.

Aloysius was killed in action before dawn on 31 October. He was shot by a sniper while cutting a way through barbed wire. He was initially buried in American Cemetery #1 Waereghem Grave #12 and moved to Flanders Field in June 1919.

491

ENNIS Louis H.
Private 1st Class, 107th Field Artillery Regt., 28th Division
KIA 30 October 1918
Plot D – Row 02 – Grave 05
Army Serial Number 1250572

Louis Henry Ennis was born in Mont Clare, PA on 15 August 1894. He was the son of Harry and Catherine Ennis from Phoenixville, PA. He had three brothers (Edward, Harry and George) and was married to Clara Maria Ennis. He was one of the star players of the Union Club Football Team in Phoenixville.

Louis enlisted with the Pennsylvania National Guard 5 June 1917. At the time he was employed as a laborer with the Phoenix Iron Co. He received his basic training at Camp Hancock, ND and was attached, as was Edward Longacre (C-3-19), to the 107th Field Artillery Regiment of the 28th (Keystone) Division. This Artillery Brigade was attached to the 91st Division during the Ypres-Lys offensive. Louis had the reputation of being a conscientious and reliable soldier.

When one of the other units in the Brigade suffered heavy losses due to a major gas attack, it was requested that a few experienced men be sent in as replacements. Louis was one of these men. He was killed by mortar shell fragments while on duty as a gas sentinel. He was buried within the grounds of a convent in Nieuwenhove near Waregem (Isolated Grave #1 Waereghem). His remains were moved to plot D, grave 52 at Cemetery #1252 on 3 June 1919.

His widow remarried, which could be the reason why his remains were permanently interred in Europe.

KICKA Paul

Private, Co. I, 145th Infantry Regiment, 37th Division
KIA 1 November 1918
Plot D – Row 02 – Grave 06
Army Serial Number 1519148

Pavol Kicka was born in Hromska, at the time part of Czechoslovakia, on 17 March 1893. He was the son of Pavol Kicka and Anna Tomcik. He had two sisters (Anna and Maria) and a much younger brother (Stefan). As so many other races, a great number of Slovaks emigrated to the U.S.A. Pavol was one of them. He moved in with his uncle, Adam Tomcik in Cleveland, OH and Americanized his name to Paul.

An estimated number of 600,000 Slovaks were already residing in the U.S.A. before the outbreak of the war. Many people fled the Austrian-Hungarian dictatorship. Paul didn't hesitate to join the 37th Division and travel back to Europe. He volunteered and joined the Ohio National Guard on 2 July 1917 and was attached to Co. I of the 145th Infantry Regiment.

He was killed near the town of Olsene at 09:00 on 1 November 1918. He was severely wounded above the hip while trying to locate a machinegun nest. He was buried in an isolated grave along the main road. His remains were moved to Waregem and laid to rest in plot D, grave #76 on 7 June 1919. His girlfriend (photo insert - not identified) was left behind in Cleveland, OH.

no photograph available

TRORANO Camillo
Private, Co. F, 145th Infantry Regiment, 37th Division
KIA 4 November 1918
Plot D – Row 02 – Grave 07
Army Serial Number 1518510

Camillo Troiano (note correct spelling) was born in Italy on 18 September 1894. He was the son of Antonio and Mariavincenza Troiano from Picciano, Province of Teramo. He emigrated to the U.S.A. and resided in New Castle, PA.

Camillo was killed by shell fire near the river Scheldt. He was buried south of the communal cemetery of the village of Eine. At the time of death he was still an Italian citizen. His remains were moved to Waregem on 10 July 1919. Before receiving his final resting place he was exhumed and reburied in plot D, grave #78.

no photograph available

CARUSO Ralph W.
Private, Co. H , 145th Infantry Regiment, 37th Division
KIA 4 November 1918
Plot D – Row 02 – Grave 08
Army Serial Number 1517241

Ralph William Caruso was born in Manila, Philippines, on 13 June 1889. He emigrated to the U.S.A. and took residence in Berea, OH. He enlisted with 5th Infantry Regiment Ohio National Guard on 29 July 1917 (5th Infantry Regiment later became the 145th Infantry Regiment). He wasn't very tall and was barely accepted for military service.

During the Meuse Argonne offensive, Ralph Caruso saved the life of Major John Southam, who later (1926) became Mayor of Berea. Ralph was one of many men who was killed under friendly fire. The official verdict was: *"Killed by shell from French artillery which fell short"*.
He was buried in the American plot of the communal village cemetery of Eine. When his remains were moved to Waregem he was identified as Samuel Kohler. However, Samuel Kohler survived the war which meant that the remains had to be exhumed again for positive identification. His emergency address was registered with his girlfriend, Eva Shire.

RAAB John F.
Private, Co. E, 145th Infantry Regiment, 37th Division
KIA 1 November 1918
Plot D – Row 02 – Grave 09
Army Serial Number 2705033

John Frank Raab was born in in Bethlehem, PA on 30 September 1888. His Registration Card indicates that he was employed as a town hall clerk (City Provisions). His parents, Henry Raab and Barbara Albert, were German immigrants. They had two other children: Anna and Stella (photo insert with Stella in 1902).

He was wounded by shell fire on the morning of 31 October and started back to the rear when another shell fell close by shattering his skull and killing him instantly. He was buried by his comrades near the town of Olsene on 1 November. The date on his marker is obviously a clerical error.

Barbara was a member of Party "H" of the Gold Star Mothers Pilgrimage visiting her son's grave on 2,3 and 4 July 1930 (photo next page).

no photograph available

SUTEA Mike
Private, Co. E, 145th Infantry Regiment, 37th Division
KIA 1 November 1918
Plot D – Row 02 – Grave 10
Army Serial Number 1518237

Mihai Sutea was just 15 years of age when he arrived at Ellis Island with his mother on 21 May 1914. His father, John, had traveled ahead and found residence in St. Joseph, MO. They had sailed out of Bremen (Germany) on the Kaiser Wilhelm der Grosse (William the Great). Mihai was born in Battonya, Hungary. Although Hungarian born he had Romanian roots and could have belonged to the gypsy race. He settled in Cleveland, OH and registered with the National Guard and was later attached to the 145th Infantry Regiment. He survived the Meuse-Argonne offensive unscathed. He was killed in action near the town of Olsene on 1 November and was buried in an isolated grave. From there his remains were moved to Waregem on 7 June 1919. He received his permanent burial location on 22 March 1920.

LAMBERT Wesley N.
Private 1st Class, Co. M, 364th Infantry Regt., 91st Division
KIA 30 October 1918
Plot D – Row 02 – Grave 11
Army Serial Number 2267962

Wesley Neil Lambert was the son of Neil Lambert and Eva Laura Parkinson. He was born in Riverside, CA on 5 November 1895 as the third of five children: Ray(mond), Gladys, Wesley, Harold and Guy. He was an idealistic and religious young man and became a prominent active member of the Methodist church in Riverside. After graduating from the Polytechnic High School in 1913, he was immediately employed by the local newspaper, Riverside Enterprise, as circulation manager. Wesley had already worked there as a newspaper boy during his schooldays and he enjoyed supporting the younger generation who were also employed there. Together with his mother and sister he organized camps along the banks of a lake near the San Bernardino mountains. Six months before he was called to arms he became manager of the advertising department. During this period he also became engaged to Celestine Friend.

Wesley was one of the first to reach Camp Lewis for basic training. In his last letter home he wrote that some days they had to march 18 to 20 hours and also sleep in the rain.
Nonetheless, he said he was having a fantastic time and that he was proud to serve with his friends to make this world a better place. He added that they were ready for the attack. His comrades in arms claimed that Wesley was always ready to give a helping hand, one of his life's many virtues. He was the spokesman for all the boys in Riverside. Also as a soldier he had many talents. He could handle a rifle and during his training always proofed himself to be the best, which evidently reflected on his exceptional psychical condition.

He was assigned to the 364th (California) Infantry Regiment of the 91st Division. On 30 October, the day before the attack, he was killed in the vicinity of Waregem *"facing Berlin"* (Riverside Enterprise, 20 November). A shell had fallen close by and shattered his skull. The day after his parents received the sad news of his death they received a letter from Wesley with a label for his Christmas box.

DOLL John A. – D.S.C . + Croix de Guerre (F)

Corporal, Co. E, 145th Infantry Regiment, 37th Division
KIA 1 November 1918
Plot D – Row 02 – Grave 12
Army Serial Number 2965378

Corporal John Albert Doll was born in York, Pennsylvania on 11 July 1889. His parents were Harry and Lizzie Doll (photo insert) and he had four brothers (Harry, Augustus, Moses and Earl) and five sisters (Lydia, Mabel, Eva, Irene and Minnie). At the time he was called to arms he worked in the dyeing industry.

He was attached to Co. E of the 145th Infantry Regiment, 37th Division. For his actions on 31 October he was awarded the Distinguished Service Cross * also the French Croix de Guerre (War Cross) with bronze palm and *"étoile de vermeil"* (gilt star). The Croix de Guerre was posthumously awarded to his mother on 6 August 1920.

Corporal Doll was killed by an artillery shell on 1 November. The day after his heroic deed, he was buried between the towns of Olsene and Kruishoutem. He had recently been promoted to Corporal but was still wearing his Private 1st Class uniform at the time he was killed. Consequently his headstone shows the rank of Private 1st Class (see Chapter VI, American Graves Registration Service, Adjutant General's final decision).

Lizzie had revoked her earlier decision for her son to be interred in Europe. As this request was made after the closing date for repatriation (1 April 1922), her request was denied. She was an active member of the American War Mothers and visited John's grave during the Gold Star Mothers Pilgrimage in 1930.

* Citation DSC: *"For extraordinary heroism in action near Olsene, Belgium, October 31st, 1918: While leading a squad forward, Private Doll suddenly found himself in the midst of an enemy barrage, but he exposed himself to the severe fire in trying to keep his men organized and continued the advance. He was killed while thus engaged."*

McDONOUGH Harry H.

Private 1st Class, Co. E, 145th Infantry Regt., 37th Division
KIA 1 November 1918
Plot D – Row 02 – Grave 13
Army Serial Number 1853041

Harry Hultz McDonough was born on 12 July 1888. He was the son of the farming family Hiram Hultz McDonough and Lillie McGraw from Cheswick, PA (insert right). There were a total of twelve children: Anna, Mary, Martha, Elizabeth, George, Harry, Frank, James, Elmer, Lilian, Ralph and Sara. Harry worked as a carpenter on the family farm.

Harry nor his brothers enjoyed farming and so in January 1907 Harry joined the Navy. He was eventually medically discharged in February 1915 as a result of a bad accident on the U.S.S. California which had forced him to spend more than two months in the Naval Hospital at Puget Sound, WA in 1908. He then worked for two years as a carpenter for his brother George who was founder of the McDonough Construction Company. When the U.S. declared war on Germany in 1917, Harry was called to register for the draft. On 26 February 1918 he received his orders and after a short training

period was attached to the 145th Infantry Regiment. Before he set sail for Europe he enrolled for a war insurance policy in which he named his mother as sole beneficiary.

Harry was killed instantly by shell fire near the town of Olsene and was buried near the railroad. His remains were moved to Waregem on 6 June 1919.

On 4 July 1930, Lillie visited Harry's grave with the Gold Star Mothers Pilgrimage (photo next page) She was aged 72. Harry's sister Lilian (left insert) also visited his grave in 1959.

WEBBER Raymond L.
Private, Co. E, 145th Infantry Regiment, 37th Division
KIA 1 November 1918
Plot D – Row 02 – Grave 14
Army Serial Number 2705096

Raymond Webber

Raymond Lloyd Webber was born in Lititz, PA on 5 March 1896. He was the youngest of twelve in the Franklin and Caroline Webber family (photo insert). The large family consisted of Frank Allison, Charles, James, Edwin, Kate, Minnie, Lydia, Frances, Elmer, Elson, Bertha and Erla. Caroline mainly spoke *"Penna Dutch"*.

Raymond was employed in Reading, PA as a paper bag maker. He soon became a foreman and it was from here that he was requested to register for the draft on 27 April 1918.

He wrote his last letter home on 6 October where he described his experiences on the Meuse-Argonne front: *"We certainly did go into the Fritzies and I did my share and feel like doing more"*.

Raymond met his death at 06:30 near the town of Olsene on 31 October. He was killed by shell fragments and was buried in a mass grave along the roadside (see photo Chapter VII, page 79).

His parents initially decided to have his remains repatriated to the United States but changed their mind soon after. Caroline would have joined the Gold Star Mothers Pilgrimage to Europe in 1932, but at the age of 80, her physician strongly advised against it.

Raymond is also memorialized at the cemetery in Lititz. The photograph of him on this page is the only photograph his parents possessed.

MAHAN Edward J.
Private, Co A, 148th Infantry Regiment, 37th Division
KIA 31 October 1918
Plot D – Row 02 – Grave 15
Army Serial Number 2966284

Edward J. Mahan was the son of Elmer and Mary Mahan from Philadelphia, PA . He had one sister named Mary. Elmer's father (Edward's grandfather) enlisted in the Spring of 1862 during the Civil War. He died of wounds on the battlefield in Chancellorsville, VA on 3 May 1863.

Edward was killed at 6 a.m. near Olsene on 31 October at about 250 yards after he crossed the railroad. A shell struck center of the road and a flying piece of shrapnel hit him cutting off the top of his head. He doubled forward on hands and knees. He was killed instantly.

YONKMAN Jacob
Private, Co. C, 148th Infantry Regiment, 37th Division
DOW 4 November 1918
Plot D – Row 02 – Grave 16
Army Serial Number 2822766

Jacob Yonkman was born in Chicago, IL on 22 September 1893. His parents were Gerrit Jonkman and Grietje (Grace) Mugg (Dutch immigrants). The family had ten children of which eight were still alive according to the 1910 census: John, Hendrick (Henry), Gertje (Gertrude), William, Gjork (Jacob), Ida, Isaac and Cise (Christopher). Jacob was an agricultural laborer at the time he was called to register for the draft in 1917. Subsequently he was called to arms on 25 May 1918.

He received his basic training with the 161st Depot Brigade in Camp Grant IL. He was then attached to Co. F, 344th Infantry Regiment, 86th (Black Hawk) Division, This National Army Division comprised of conscripts out of Illinois and Wisconsin. All personnel from this division were used as replacements upon their arrival in Europe on 3 October.

There were no witnesses to Jacob's death. He was buried near the crossroads between the towns of Olsene and Kruishoutem and his remains were moved to Waregem on 7 June 1919. There were some discrepancies during the identification process where letters addressed to Jacob were found on the remains of another soldier, Morris Hanson. Following A.G.R.S. procedures, positive identification was designated to the remains with corresponding identification tags. The mystery of the letters remain unsolved.

no photograph available

ANDERSON Herbert G.
Private, Co. I, 148th Infantry Regiment, 37th Division
KIA 1 November 1918
Plot D – Row 02 – Grave 17
Army serial number 3332157

Herbert Anderson (°29 April 1889) lived in Rockford, IL. He was the son of Herman (°1863) and Hulda Anderson (°1872), both born in Sweden. Herman emigrated to the U.S.A. in 1887. His second wife, Hulda followed him three years later. Herbert and his brother Walter (°January 1887) were offspring from Herman's first marriage. Herbert started his working career in a shoe factory where he had worked for 1 year. He then changed heart and worked for an agricultural machinery plant for 3 years before joining his father for 2 years performing manual labor in an iron foundry. At the time he was called to arms he had returned to the shoe factory where he had been working for 3 years.

He was killed by shell fire while advancing through a field near the village of Heurne on 1 November 1918 and buried in a field grave of an American plot between Olsene and Kruishoutem. His remains were moved to plot D, grave #127 in Cemetery #1252 on 7 June 1919, later receiving his permanent grave at the current location in the Flanders Field cemetery.

During this time his brother had joined the Navy. Their father died in 1926 and Hulda remarried to a certain Elon Omark in 1927. Hulda passed away in 1953.

SCHAU Otto C.
Private 1st Class, Co. K, 148th Infantry Regt. 37th Division
KIA 2 November 1918
Plot D – Row 02 – Grave 18
Army Serial Number 2403841

Otto Schau was the son of William and Eliza Schau (German immigrants). He was born in Brooklyn, NY in 1894 and had three brothers William Jr., Charles and Edward and one sister Dora. The family later moved to Hoboken, NJ. He was called to arms on 19 November 1917 and was sent to Camp Dix, NJ where he trained with the 153rd Depot Brigade. In June 1918 he was reassigned to the 148th Infantry Regiment.

He was killed on 2 November during an enemy artillery barrage. Shell fragments had shattered his skull. He was buried in an isolated grave near the town of Olsene. His remains were moved to Waregem on 7 June 1919.

LANDGRAF Louis F.
Private, Co. L, 148th Infantry Regiment, 37th Division
DOW 1 November 1918
Plot D – Row 02 – Grave 19
Army Serial Number 3340643

Louis Frederich Landgraf was born in Sheboygan, WI on 6 May 1894. He was the son of Frank and Johanna (Jennie) Landgraf (née Tietjen) who had five other children: Erma, Wilford, Franklin, Mildred and Lester. Frank and Johanna were German immigrants. Louis graduated from Business College and was employed as a printer at the Diamond Printing Company in Sheboygan. In 1915 the family moved to Two Dot, a small unincorporated community in west-central Wheatland County MO, where Louis became a signalman on the Chicago, Milwaukee and St. Paul Railway line.

When Louis was called to arms he requested to serve with the men from Wisconsin. This request was granted and instead of receiving his basic training at Camp Lewis, he was sent to Camp Grant and later to Camp Mills. He was attached to the 161st Depot Brigade and later reassigned to the 344th Infantry Regiment, 86th Black Hawk Division, a division with men from Illinois and Wisconsin. Upon their arrival in Europe all personnel became replacements to other divisions and Louis was assigned to the 37th Division. Two days before he died he wrote his last letter home. He was shot in the chest by machinegun fire and died instantly. He was buried near the town of Olsene and his remains were disinterred and moved to plot A, grave #128 in Waregem in June 1919.

Jennie visited the Flanders Field Cemetery with the Gold Star Mothers Pilgrimage in 1930. She was 69 years of age. At the time of departure she was feeling unwell (from the journal of Barabara Kirsh with whom she was traveling at the time). On her first visit to her son's grave on 4 July, due to immense grief and emotion, she suffered a slight heart attack. She would never completely recover. After she had returned home she wrote a letter of appreciation and thanks for the support and medical attention she was rendered. Also for the opportunity she was granted permission to visit a son and daughter in Wisconsin during her travels. Jennie died on 16 November of that same year.

509

ERB William L.
Captain, Co. L, 145th Infantry Regiment, 37th Division
KIA 4 November 1918
Plot D – Row 02 – Grave 20

William Ludwig Erb was born to the wealthy family of Lorenz (Lawrence) and Marie Erb (née Hasler) in Norwalk, OH on 23 February 1893. Lorenz and Marie emigrated to the U.S.A. from Germany in 1888. They had three other children: Otto, Eleanor and Carl. William lived with his wife Ella Bucholz in Cleveland. He applied for officers training with his brother Carl at Fort Harrison, IN. Shortly after the U.S. declared war on Germany he was called for active service. He achieved the rank of 2nd Lieutenant on 19 December 1917 and 1st Lieutenant in March of the following year. After his achievements during the Meuse-Argonne offensive he was promoted to Captain on 22 October. All through the war he served with the 145th Infantry Regiment. His brother Carl remained in the States serving as a 1st Lieutenant.

William had been wounded during the Meuse-Argonne offensive but was able to join his unit before they were transferred to Belgium. Company L was known as the "pump-off outfit" because they were always first out of the trenches. William was shot through the head on 4 November and was found lying next to a German machinegun nest with eight German dead. He was buried at the top of a ridge north-west of the village Kruishoutem. (American Cemetery Cruyshautem Grave #1). His remains were moved to plot A, grave #7 in Waregem on 4 June 1919.

Ella tried to visit William's grave in 1921. It could not be confirmed if she ever succeeded. When in 1920 she was asked to choose whether William's remains be repatriated or not she initially chose for repatriation. However when she heard about the permanent nature of the cemeteries in Europe and how well they were going to be taken care of, she revoked her decision. In a letter dated 3 March 1921 she requested the government to correct the rank on William's marker. On 5 April she received confirmation that the rank of Captain had been certified.

Ella remarried in 1925. Marie (photo insert) visited the Flanders Field Cemetery on 2,3 and 4 June during the Gold Star Mothers Pilgrimage of 1930. Ella had also applied for the trip but her request was denied as she had remarried. She tried her utmost to revoke this decision but to no avail.

Otto moved to Los Angeles, CA. Carl became an attorney and remained in Cleveland. Eleanor and her husband moved to Corpus Christi, FL. Lawrence and Marie later joined them but both died within three weeks of each other in 1939.

OSBORN Frank

Corporal, Co. I, 362nd Infantry Regiment, 91st Division
KIA 31 October 1918
Plot D – Row 02 – Grave 21
Army Serial Number 2261169

Frank Osborn was the son of Zack Preston Osborn and Hattie E. Baker. He was born in in Goldensfort (?), MN on 22 May 1893. He was second in a row of eleven children. Emily, Anna, Dora, Bertha, Nettie, Roy, Thomas, Delbert, Clarence, Mamie and Gertrude. The family moved to Deary, ID but Frank later moved to Bruce, MT seeking to purchase a farm. The war through a wrench in the works and he was called to arms on 18 September 1917. After completion of his basic training he was attached to the 362nd Infantry Regiment.

Frank was promoted to Corporal on 25 October although this is not recognized on his headstone (see Chapter VI - AGRS – final decision Adjutant General). Less than a week later he was killed in action during the battle for the Spitaalsbossen. Angelo Mazzarella (C-4-21), James Miller (A-3-11) and William Garner (D-3-20) were all killed during the same attack. Frank was buried near the village of Anzegem. Elsie Pierce (Emily's daughter) recalled how her grandmother wept when she received the notification of Frank's death.

Standing left to right: Roy, Anna, Bertha, Delbert, Thomas, Mamie, Dora and Nettie. Seated: Emily, father Zack Preston, mother Hattie and Gertrude.

Telegram announcing Frank's death.

First page of a letter dated 23 December 1918 sent to the family by his Captain, Thomas May.

My dear Mr Osborn,

I regret very much indeed to confirm the report announcing the death of your good son Corporal Frank Osborn.

Frank was killed October 31st near Steenhuize, Belgium. He was hit by a fragment from a large shell and lived for only about five minutes. His body was buried near the spot where he sacrificed his life for the cause of liberty.

Frank had a friend in every member of the company. His cheerful and faithful work had just won for him a promotion to corporal and he was a brave leader. He was an extremely steady and dependable soldier........

513

no photograph available

BRYAN Guy
Private, Co. K, 145th Infantry Regiment, 37th Division
DOW 1 November 1918
Plot D – Row 02 – Grave 22
Army Serial Number 2668600

Guy Bryan (°6 May 1892) was the oldest of eight children in the farming family of George W. and Anna E. Bryan from Robinson, PA. At the time he was called to arms he was employed as a laborer with the Watlieniz Iron Foundry.

Guy succumbed to wounds received in action on 1 November 1918. He was buried close to the main entrance of the communal cemetery in the town of Meulebeke.

After the war, a VFW Post was named after him but unfortunately does not exist anymore today. His mother visited his grave with the Gold Star Mothers Pilgrimage in 1930 (photo insert).

no photograph available

TAILOR James
Private, Co. D, 145th Infantry Regiment, 37th Division
KIA 1 November 1918
Plot D – Rij 02 – Graf 23
Army Serial Number 1852693

James Tailor was born in Rome, Italy on 21 January 1888. He emigrated to the U.S.A. from the town of Acquasanta Terme in the province of Ascoli. Acquasanta Terme was a neighboring village to Spelonga, where Francesco Schiavone (D-4-3) originated from. James had no relatives living in the U.S.A. At the time he was called to arms he was working as a candy maker (manufacturer).

He was killed when hit in the chest by shell fragments near the town of Olsene. According to witness statements this happened at 08:00 on 1 November. He was buried in a French military cemetery close to where he fell and on 10 June 1919 his remains were moved and interred in Waregem.

MOFFETT Charles A. – CdG(F) – Silver Star
Private 1st Class, Co. C, 112th Sanitary Train, 37th Division
KIA 4 November 1918
Plot D – Row 03 – Grave 01
Army Serial Number 1540359

Charles Asa Moffett was born in June 1897 and originated from Alderson, WV. He was the son of Thomas and Jean Moffett (née McConn) and had a brother named Frank. Both boys went through life using their middle name: Asa and Mather. Thomas left Jean and so she became a single parent raising her two boys. They moved to Ohio where it became obvious that Asa was an exemplary student. He attended high

school in Columbus and later joined the Ohio National Guard on 23 May 1917.

He was attached to Co. A of the 147th Infantry Regiment and later transferred to the 147th Ambulance Company of the 112th Sanitary Train. On 4 November Charles was attached to a first aid station close to the front line. On this day he was awarded a Divisional Citation with Silver Star (this was originally a small silver star worn on the ribbon of a service medal -see above- but in 1932 it was replaced by a separate medal). He was also awarded the French Croix de Guerre (War Cross) with palm for saving a comrade during a heavy artillery barrage. Later that day he helped three men seek shelter from a heavy artillery barrage. After the barrage had ceased they heard men scream for help and so left their place of shelter to administer first aid. At this point, another artillery shell fell close by and as they were running for shelter a shell fragment hit Asa in the back killing him instantly. Asa had

the reputation of being courageous, honest, highly conscientious and devoted to duty.

no photograph available

FERGUSON John R.

Corporal, Supply Co. 145th Infantry Regiment, 37th Division
DOD 21 November 1918
Plot D – Row 03 – Grave 02
Army Serial Number 1516993

John Russell Ferguson was born in Columbus, OH in 1892 and was the son of Frank and Louisa Ferguson. He had one brother (Earl) and two sisters (Helen and Edna). It is assumed that Louisa died giving birth to Edna.

John volunteered with the 5th Ohio National Guard Regiment in Cleveland on 20 June 1916. He participated in all battles of the division and remained unscathed. He was promoted to Corporal on 6 November. He died due to complications of influenza (Spanish flu) and was buried in the American plot near the Mobile Hospital in Staden.

MELICHAREK Gerald F.

Private, Co. B, 148th Infantry Regiment, 37th Division
KIA 2 November 1918
Plot D – Row 03 – Grave 03
Army Serial Number 3340717

Gerald Frank Melicharek was born in Chicago, IL on 8 March 1893. He was the son of Austrian immigrants Frank and Marie Melicharek (née Blecha) who later moved to Redlands in California to run a bakery. Gerald had two brothers (Frank Jr. and Erwin) and four sisters (Marie, Rose, Mildred and Edna). He was an exceptional athlete and good swimmer. The family later moved to Los Angeles, CA. Gerald had remained in Illinois where he was employed as a baker at a hotel.

He was called to arms, sent to Camp Grant and attached to Co. M of the 344th Infantry Regiment, 86th (Black Hawk) Division. Arriving in Europe as replacements, Gerald was attached to the 148th Infantry Regiment. The attack was launched on 31 October during a heavy enemy artillery barrage. Gerald was one of fifteen men killed in the barrage in the streets of the town Olsene. He was buried west of the Chateau (photo see Chapter 37th Division) along the main road between the towns of Olsene and Deinze on 1 November. Due to insufficient details at the time, an administrative decision was made by the A.G.R.S. showing 2 November as being Gerald's date of death.

CLOSTERMANN Albert M.
1st Lieutenant, Co. E, 362nd Infantry Regiment, 91st Division
KIA 3 November 1918
Plot D – Row 03 – Grave 04

Albert Clostermann was the son of George and Elisa Clostermann from Portland, OR. Albert was born in Hamburg, Germany and had one brother, Robert. Albert graduated from the Washington High School in Portland and before he enlisted was employed by the United States National Bank. He was well known as an excellent swimmer and took part in many athletic activities in various clubs of the city.

He registered with the Oregon National Guard (3rd Oregon Machine Gun Company – photo insert) and served along the Mexican border in 1916. Upon his return he attended the first officers training school at the Presidio, CA where he received his commission as 2nd Lieutenant. He sailed for Europe with Co. E of the 362nd Infantry Regiment. On 2 November 1917, while at Camp Lewis, he wrote a letter home in his mother tongue, German.

In a letter dated 29 July 1918 he writes: *"I had a very happy and pleasant trip across the ocean and landed safely in England. From England we went to France where we now are billeted in a small village….I am learning to speak a little French…"*
On 1 September: *"I'm getting along fine-am well and am being well taken care of. I am getting a little thinner. Our work is taking some of the extra fat off me and putting on more muscles………..I have already seen a good bit of France and I surely do like the Unites States best of all…"*
His last letter from Belgium dated 23 October was again in German: *"Most of the buildings have been destroyed and families are returning to the towns with the little possessions they can carry…..For my Christmas package I would like lots of candy………"*

At 05:00 on 3 November, near the village of Wortegem, Albert was preparing his men for the advance. He was severely wounded by shell fragments before the attack commenced and died shortly afterwards. Albert Clostermann was one of the youngest officers in the division.

His brother Robert built himself an impressive career. In the 1930's he became the German Consul in Portland. Sheri Clostermann Anderson (Robert's granddaughter) and her son Blake visited Albert's grave on 22 December 2008.

Above: Albert (second from right) along the Mexican border with the 3rd Oregon National Guard Regiment.

Below left: Albert's grave in Cemetery #1252 – right: Sheri Clostermann Anderson and her son Blake.

LIEBSCHER Frank W.

Private, Co. F, 361st Infantry Regiment, 91st Division
KIA 1 November 1918
Plot D – Row 03 – Grave 05
Army Serial Number 2785358

Frank Liebscher was born on 31 December 1892 in San Francisco, CA. His parents were Edward August and Caroline Wihelmine Liebscher (née Brodbeck). Besides Frank, there were seven siblings (Edward, William, Lucy, Alice, Clara, August and George) and three half siblings (Katherine, Sophie and Charles). Frank was a butcher and keen hunter. The wild game was sold in his father's store.

He received his basic training at Camp Lewis, WA. On 1 November he became the victim of enemy artillery fire. His legs were shattered from the impact and he was buried with six other victims southeast of the village of Moregem on the main road to Oudenaarde. At the time of death he had achieved the rank of corporal. This is not recognized on his headstone (see Chapter VI - A.G.R.S. – Adjutant General's final decision).

His mother Caroline visited her son's grave with the Gold Star Mothers Pilgrimage in 1930.

Photo next page: Frank with his brother George Washington Liebscher (1899-1995)

no photograph available

MEYERS Vernard J.
Private, MG Company, 361st Infantry Regt., 91st Division
KIA 3 November 1918
Plot D – Row 03 – Grave 06
Army Serial Number 2256591

Vernard J. Meyers was born in in Opportunity, WA on 26 January 1895. He lived there until he was called to arms. He was the son of John and Alice Meyers (née Rosslow) who were pioneer farmers in the area. They had one other son, Alpheus (Alphy). Vernard was employed by the Spokane Valley Land and Water Company in West Farms, WA. Alpheus was a real estate agent with the Lawyer Land Company.

"Dippy", as he was called, was killed instantly by shellfire near the village of Petegem at a location between two windmills on a farm which the Americans called *"Wedure Farm"*. He was buried in the village (Isolated Grave #4) and his remains were moved to Waregem (plot D, grave #46) on 9 June 1919.

His mother, in reply to the questionnaire in regards to the preference of disposition of the remains, replied: *"His body be left in Europe near where he fell if some of his comrades are left there too"* and she continued: *"This must sound like a strange wish coming from a mother, but this was Vernard's own wish."* Vernard had also asked a friend to make sure that if he died that he would be buried *"in a Field of Honor in France"*.

WHITNEY Roy A.
Private, Co. C, 361st Infantry Regiment, 91st Division
KIA 3 November 1918
Plot D – Row 03 – Grave 07
Army Serial Number 2293488

Roy Andrew Whitney was born in Elroy near Seneca, SD on 1 June 1896. His parents were Selwyn and Louise Whitney. He had four brothers: Ross Herman, Rollo Dayton, Louis Weeks and Claude Taylor. Around 1915, Roy and his brother Claude found a farm and cultivated the land in Ekalaka, MT. However, Roy was drafted and called to arms on 25 April 1918. He received his basic training at Camp Lewis, WA with the 166th Depot Brigade. He sailed for Europe with the 361st Infantry Regiment on 6 July 1918.

He was killed in action near the village of Petegem. When disinterred it was found that the facial portion of his skull, right arm and left leg had numerous fractures.

The American Legion Post in Seneca was named after him.

Roy Whitney's wooden marker on Cemetery #1252.

no photograph available

GUGLIARA Philip
Private, Co. H, 145th Infantry Regiment, 37th Division
DOW 3 November 1918
Plot D – Row 03 – Grave 08
Army Serial Number 1850340

Filippo Gugliara was born in Barrafranca, Province of Caltarisetta, Sicily on 19 April 1894. He was the son of Louis and Maria Gugliara (née Benferrara). He emigrated to the U.S.A. sailing out of Palermo on 30 April 1913. He arrived in the States on 15 May.

At the time Philip was called to register for the draft he was living in East Palestine, OH where he worked at the McGraw Litce Rubber Company. He enlisted on 19 March 1918 and received his basic training with the 155th Depot Brigade. He was attached to the 145th Infantry Regiment in May. At the time he was stationed at Camp Lee, he signed a petition for naturalization having lived in the States for more than five years. His emergency address was registered with his brother Joe in Boston, MA.

Philip was killed in action just one mile west of the village of Kruishoutem and was buried in an isolated grave. His remains were moved to plot A, grave #42 in Waregem on 12 June 1919.

no photograph available

BURCKELL David
Private, Co. C, 364th Infantry Regiment, 91st Division
KIA 31 October 1918
Plot D – Row 03 – Grave 09
Army Serial Number 2266419

David "Butch" Burckell was born in Santa Monica, CA on 27 March 1892. His mother was a single parent at the time when she married Henry Akin from Monrovia, CA. David had three stepbrothers (Henry, Raymond and John) and one stepsister (Elizabeth). His mother died young and he was raised by his grandparents Francisco and Angel Quiroz, (Mexican roots) who also lived in Santa Monica.

David had a large scar on his forehead which made him easily recognizable. He was killed near Waregem and temporarily buried in American Cemetery #1673 - Potegem in Waregem. His remains were moved to Cemetery #1252 on 3 June 1919.

CARLETILLO Nick
Private, Co. L, 363rd Infantry Regiment, 91st Division
KIA 31 October 1918
Plot D – Row 03 – Grave 10
Army Serial Number 2781046

Nicholas Carletillo was born in New York on 8 December 1889. His parents Dominick and Mary Carletillo (née Constantiano) had arrived in the United States a few years earlier. They soon moved from New York to California. Nick had two brothers (Louis and Johnnie) and two sisters (Minnie and Angeline).

Nick Carletillo lived in Los Angeles and was employed by Dramond Laundry Co. which at the time was located on 8th and Town Avenue. He was one of the first to be killed in action on 31 October during the fighting around Waregem. He was initially buried close to the town center in American Cemetery 1673 (with Burckell). His remains were later moved to Cemetery #1252, which later became Flanders Field, and buried in plot C, grave #173.

ALLEN Alonzo D.
Private, Co. L, 105th Infantry Regiment, 27th Division
KIA 31 July 1918
Plot D – Row 03 – Grave 11
Army serial number 1205482

Alonzo Allen was born in Lagrangeville, NY but lived with his aunt in Poughkeepsie, Dutchess County. His father (Alonzo Sr.) and mother had already passed away. He was employed by the Adams Express Company in Poughkeepsie. His grandfather was a veteran of the Civil War and so he became a member of the "Sons of Veterans". He was also a member of the "Loyal Order of Moose".

On 4 July 1917 he enlisted with the 10th Infantry Regiment National Guard. He was 27 years of age. As of 8 December this regiment became the foundation of the 105th Infantry Regiment, 27th Division. He sailed for Europe in May 1918. In his last letter to his aunt dated 15 May he wrote: *"I have arrived in France and will do my best"*.

On 31 July the 105th Infantry Regiment was heavily engaged around Mount Kemmel. Alonzo was on duty as stretcher bearer. It was dusk when Alonzo cautiously left his trench to administer first aid to a comrade. He was shot in the abdomen by a German sniper and died almost instantly. He was the first man in his company to be killed in action. It is said that he was found dead with a smile on his face.

Alonzo was loved by all. He was highly commended and respected by his commanders for his determination and sense of duty. He was initially buried in the Commonwealth Abeele Aerodrome Military Cemetery.

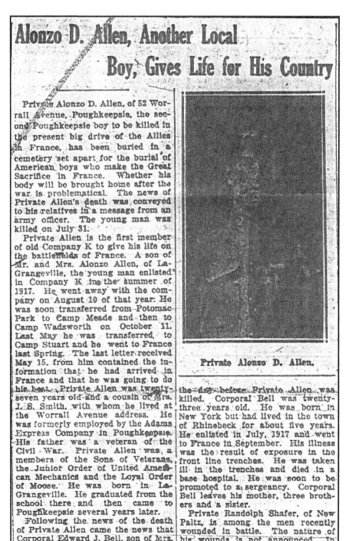

Alonzo D. Allen, Another Local Boy, Gives Life for His Country

Private Alonzo D. Allen, of 52 Worrall Avenue, Poughkeepsie, the second Poughkeepsie boy to be killed in the present big drive of the Allies in France, has been buried in a cemetery set apart for the burial of American boys who make the Great Sacrifice in France. Whether his body will be brought home after the war is problematical. The news of Private Allen's death was conveyed to his relatives in a message from an army officer. The young man was killed on July 31.

Private Allen is the first member of old Company K to give his life on the battlefields of France. A son of Mr. and Mrs. Alonzo Allen, of LaGrangeville, the young man enlisted in Company K in the summer of 1917. He went away with the company on August 10 of that year. He was soon transferred from Potomac Park to Camp Meade and then to Camp Wadsworth on October 11. Last May he was transferred to Camp Stuart and he went to France last Spring. The last letter received May 15, from him contained the information that he had arrived in France and that he was going to do his best. Private Allen was twenty-seven years old and a cousin of Mrs. L. S. Smith, with whom he lived at the Worrall Avenue address. He was formerly employed by the Adams Express Company in Poughkeepsie. His father was a veteran of the Civil War. Private Allen was a member of the Sons of Veterans, the Junior Order of United American Mechanics and the Loyal Order of Moose. He was born in LaGrangeville. He graduated from the school there and then came to Poughkeepsie several years later.

Following the news of the death of Private Allen came the news that Corporal Edward J. Bell, son of Mrs. Letetia Bell, of the town of Rhinebeck, had died in France. His death was caused by pneumonia. He died

the day before Private Allen was killed. Corporal Bell was twenty-three years old. He was born in New York but had lived in the town of Rhinebeck for about five years. He enlisted in July, 1917 and went to France in September. His illness was the result of exposure in the front line trenches. He was taken ill in the trenches and died in a base hospital. He was soon to be promoted to a sergeancy. Corporal Bell leaves his mother, three brothers and a sister.

Private Randolph Shafer, of New Paltz, is among the men recently wounded in battle. The nature of his wounds is not announced. In fact the war department reports that the severity of the wounds has not been determined.

Private Alonzo D. Allen.

ZELLERS George H.
1st Lieutenant, 20th Aero Squadron
KIA 30 July 1918
Plot D – Row 03 – Grave 12

George Herbert Zellers was born in Lebanon, PA on 19 January 1893. He was the son of the Rev. George and Mary Zellers from Morgantown, PA. He had three brothers, Clarence, John and Paul and two sisters, Florence and Amelia. His father was pastor at the St. Thomas Episcopal Church. George was more than an average student and he went to Lancaster where he attended the Franklin and Marshall College. Shortly before he enlisted in June 1917, he was an instructor at Hazleton High School where he taught science and biology.

The 20th Squadron was stationed in Boisdinghem near the Nieppe Forest close to Hazebrouck, France. On 30 July they received orders to carry out a reconnaissance mission along the German lines. Nine Bristols took off at dawn and were escorted by a second British squadron of S.E. 5's from Ypres. There were heavy clouds so visibility being poor most planes returned to base. Three Bristols (Lt. Hardcastle, Lt. Cowell and George) were lost in the clouds and continued their pursuit towards the German lines. They became an easy

target for fifteen Fokker planes cruising overhead. George's Bristol (F2b C904) was immediately hit by the leader of the German squadron Leutnant (Lieutenant) Franz Piechulek of Jasta 56 (photo insert). George wasn't wounded and made an attempt to stabilize his machine. He succeeded for a while but then the plane burst into flames and from 200 feet fell close to the allied lines in no man's land. George and his observer, Sergeant John Cormack were killed. Lieutenant Hardcastle was able to down Piechulek but he survived to fly again claiming his 14th victory in October. Hardcastle was sole survivor from this mission. Lieutenant J.J. Cowell (DCM, MM) was also shot down and buried at Longuenesse (St Omer) Souvenir Cemetery in northern France. George was initially buried near the town of Poperinge

To this very day a descendant of George Zellers Sr., is pastor at the St. Thomas Episcopal Church. A large number of family members are buried In Caernarvon Cemetery, Lancaster County. A memorial marker was erected in George's memory. His brother John, who died of Spanish flu in 1918, is buried next to the memorial.

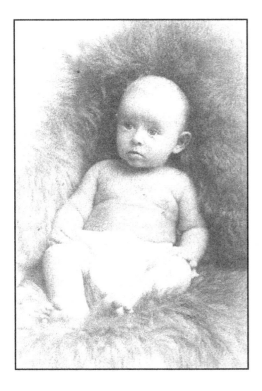

George as baby

George Sr. and Mary Zellers

George, Amy and Florence

Paul, Clarence, John and George

Memorial
Caernarvon Cemetery.

531

no photograph available

ERIKSEN Frederick F. – Silver Star

Private 1st Class, Co. A, 107th Infantry Regt. 27th Division
KIA 21 August 1918
Plot D – Row 03 – Grave 13
Army Serial Number 1209690

Frederick Frithiof Eriksen (Erickson) was the son of Jacob and Anna Eriksen. He was born in New York City on 26 February 1896. Jacob and Anna emigrated to the U.S.A. in May 1892 together with their two boys of which one was called Gottfried (Godfrey). The second boy must have died young as there was no mention of him in the 1910 census. Frederick also had an older sister Edith who had been born in 1895. His father died of insanity in 1925.

He enlisted on 17 July 1917 and served overseas as of 9 May 1918. He was awarded a Divisional Citation (Silver Star) for his actions on 14 August (this was originally a small silver star worn on the ribbon of a service medal -see above- but in 1932 it was replaced by a separate medal). He was killed a week later and buried at Abeele Aerodrome Military Cemetery. His emergency address was registered with his brother Gottfried.

One of Gottfried's sons, Robert, served in Europe during World War II. He was killed in action on 2 September 1944.

Frederick's Divisional Citation read: *Private, 1st Class, Frederick F. Eriksen (deceased), Company A. For disregard to danger in successfully advancing from the support to the front line, Dickebusch sector, near Mt. Kemmel, Belgium, August 14, 1918. This action occurred in broad daylight and this soldier covered a distance of about eight hundred yards over open ground, being fully exposed to enemy observation, machine gun and artillery fire.*

no photograph available

SEGALL Arthur R.
Private, Co. G, 145th Infantry Regiment, 37th Division
DOD 4 November 1918
Plot D – Row 03 – Grave 14
Army Serial Number 2708085

Aron (Arthur) Raphael Segall was born on 8 March 1893 in Chorzele, Poland, in a village that was part of Russia at that time. He was of the Jewish faith. Aron emigrated to the U.S.A. on 24 January 1914 and arrived on 5 February.

He was called to arms on 26 April 1918 and received his basic training with the 145th Infantry Regiment. While at Camp Virginia he submitted a petition for naturalization on 29 May. Arthur died from lobar pneumonia, a common complication of the Spanish flu, in the American Field Hospital in the town of Staden and was buried there that same day. Chackel, his father, requested that his remains be repatriated to Poland. His nephew, who Arthur had designated as point of contact in case of an emergency, requested that his remains be repatriated to the U.S.A. The reason why Arthur was finally buried in Waregem is unknown.

no photograph available

SMITH Andrew J.
Private, Co. C, 107th Infantry Regiment, 27th Division
KIA 17 August 1918
Plot D – Row 03 – Grave 15
Army Serial Number 405970

Arthur Charles Withers (°1883) was the son of Arthur and Catherine Withers from Brooklyn, NY. They had five other children: Margaret, George, James, Thomas and Etta. His wife Emma did not approve of Arthur joining the military so in 1917 he enlisted with the National Guard using an alias: Andrew J. Smith. To fulfill his legal obligations to his wife and two children, Catherine and Arthur Jr., Arthur signed up for a life insurance policy in the amount of $10,000. He also wrote them a farewell letter. Etta Weingart, his sister, was registered as point of contact in case of emergency.

On 16 August, the day before he was killed in action, he evidently had a change of heart and wrote a letter home indicating that he was in the front line and that anything could happen. However, it was 26 October before Etta was notified of his death.

He was initially buried at Abeele Aerodrome British Military Cemetery. Etta, who feared that her mother would die of grief, requested that his remains be returned to the U.S.A.. His wife, who legally was still the closest next of kin, decided that his remains be interred in Europa.

On the Eastern Parkway in Brooklyn, a number of trees were planted in memory of those soldiers from Brooklyn who had lost their lives. Each soldier was also honored with a memorial marker. Photo below is the marker dedicated to Arthur Withers.

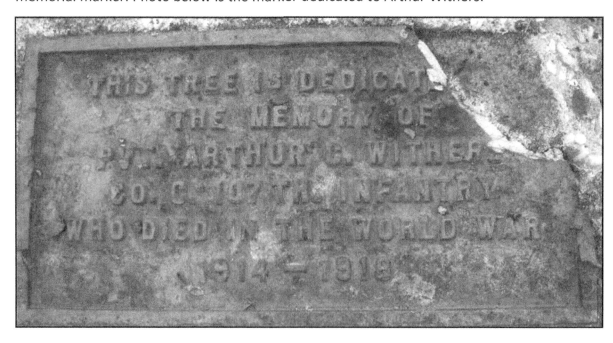

no photograph available

THOMPSON Stanley E.
Private, Co. B, 107th Infantry Regiment, 27th Division
KIA 13 August 1918
Plot D – Row 03 – Grave 16
Army Serial Number 1210039

Stanley E. Thompson was born in Madrid, NY on 12 April 1899. He was the son of Charles and Gertrude Thompson. He had an older sister Gladys and a younger brother Alton. He enlisted with the local National Guard at Ogdensburg NY on 17 April 1917.

He was killed during a mission for which he had volunteered. He was initially buried at Abeele Aerodrome Military Cemetery. He was 19 years of age. A memorial marker for Stanley was placed within the Thompson family plot in the Madrid Cemetery, Madrid, NY.

LUND John W.
Cook, Co. I, 363rd Infantry Regiment, 91st Division
KIA 1 November 1918
Plot D – Row 03 – Grave 17
Army Serial Number 2264679

John William Lund was born in Switzerland on 6 October 1893. He was the son of Hans and Anna Lund and lived in San Francisco, CA. Together with his brother-in-law, A. Ipsen, he ran the Boston Coffee House on 16th Street. He had three sisters: Lydia, Meta and Andrea.

John was a cook with Co. I of the 363rd Infantry Regiment, 91st Division. On the evening of 31 October he was at the head of a wagon train moving up to the front when a shell fragment hit him in the back. He was taken to the first aid station of the 316th Engineers where the doctor said that death was instantaneous. In this context, it is practically certain that his date of death was 31 October and not 1 November as indicated on his headstone.

BROWN Levin T.

Private 1st Class, Co. F, 148th Infantry Regt. 37th Division
KIA 31 October 1918
Plot D – Row 03 – Grave 18
Army Serial Number 2655381

Levin Brown was born in North Carolina on 7 April 1896 but lived in Normantown, Toombs County, GA. He was the son of Lovett Elbert Brown and Vandella Powell (a descendant of a Mayflower passenger). He had six brothers and three sisters: Archie Marvin (°1885), Elbert Duncan (°1888), John Gordon (°1889), Turner Dailey (°1891), Rufus Lee (°1894), Laura Belle (°1896, Levin's twin sister), Perry (°1898), Rosa Mae (°1901) and B. G. (°1907).

Due to his physical fitness, Levin was attached to Co. F of the 148th Infantry Regiment, 37th Division as a runner, hand carrying field messages from one post to another.
On 15 September he writes home: *"Will take this time to write you a few lines as it is Sunday and also as rest day it is very seldom we have a day off at all…….Have just been looking at an aeroplane battle as gunners fired over 100 shrapnel shots at it….."* The day before he died he wrote home expressing his feelings and that he had a premonition that he wouldn't survive. He was killed by machinegun fire while advancing with his platoon and buried in an American plot near the town of Olsene. His remains were moved to Waregem and buried in plot D, grave #71 on 3 June 1919.

Private 1st Class Levin Taylor Brown is the only man from Georgia buried at Flanders Field. His name is also inscribed on the War Memorial of Toombs County.

WHEELER Stanley B.

Mechanic, Co. F, 148th Infantry Regiment, 37th Division
KIA 31 October 1918
Plot D – Row 03 – Grave 19
Army Serial Number 1911466

Stanley Bowen Wheeler was born in Meriden, CT on 8 August 1888. He was the son of Edward Leslie Wheeler and Flora Bowan (died 9 May 1899). He had two brothers, Ernest and Lester. Stanley had learned the trade and was employed as a printer. He had worked for a while in a milk processing plant. At the time he was called to arms he was employed as a technician at the New England Westinghouse Company. He was engaged to Elsie Ellmers who lived in the same street.

He was called to arms on 4 October 1917. He completed his basic training with his brother Lester at Camp Devens, MA then at Camp Gordon, GA. Stanley was designated as bugle instructor with the 328th Infantry Regiment of the 82nd "All American" Division. Upon his arrival in Europe he remained bugle instructor and was reassigned to Co F of the 148th Infantry Regiment, consequently being separated from his brother. Between 26-30 September he took part in the battles of the Argonne. On 17 October he became Mechanic.

Stanley wrote his last letter home on 13 October. A few excerpts were printed on the first page of the Meriden Daily Journal on 29 November: *"I've been through a big battle and have come out without a scratch, except a few barbed wire scratches. It was a several days drive for us and we sure made history. We made one of the largest gains ever made in one day.*
There is a peace talk and I hope and pray it comes soon. We are all ready to go home. Would sure like to get home by spring to help with the planting etc.
Am on a quiet sector now, in woods, living like a woodchuck in a hole about six feet long, four feet wide and four feet deep, with logs laid over the top and dirt thrown on it. They are shrapnel proof. Fritz drops shells all around us but none very close.
It has been quite a time since I have written for we have been almost continually on the move, don't stay anywhere long. The day we came out of the drive twenty letters were awaiting me. I tell you they were mighty welcome.
I will be glad to get out of this country; it is the muddiest I ever struck. You pull up about ten pounds with each step, and perhaps, you can imagine how pleasant that is with sixty to seventy-five pounds of junk on your back.
Take it all in all, though we are getting on fine. The beating we are giving the Huns is encouraging and we all expect to finish it soon and get home to our loved ones."

On the morning of 31 October, Stanley was sent with a message to the 4th Platoon near Olsene. He was killed instantly by a machinegun bullet while returning after delivering the message. He was buried east of the town.

GARNER William L.

Private, Co. I, 362nd Infantry Regiment, 91st Division
KIA 3 November 1918
Plot D – Row 03 – Grave 20
Army Serial Number 3435858

William Lloyd Garner was born in Seward, NE on 19 July 1891. The large farming family consisted of James Alfred and Helen Garner (née Hageman) with their twelve other children:

Maggie, Martha, George, Fred, James, Newton, Jennie, Harry, Constance, Ella, Ruth and Edward. William was the eleventh in the row. A fourteenth child died shortly after birth.

William was called to arms on 14 June 1918 and was attached to Co. D of the 335th Infantry Regiment, 84th (Lincoln) Division. This division was formed with men from Illinois, Indiana and Kentucky and were used as replacements upon their arrival in Europe. William was attached to the 362nd Infantry Regiment, 91st Division. He was killed on 31 October (and not on 3 November as inscribed on his headstone) by the impact of an direct hit from an artillery shell. This occurred during the fighting in the wooded area of the Spitaalsbossen. With him, Frank Osborn, Angelo Mazzarella and James Miller, all attached to Co. I of the 362nd Infantry Regiment were killed.

.

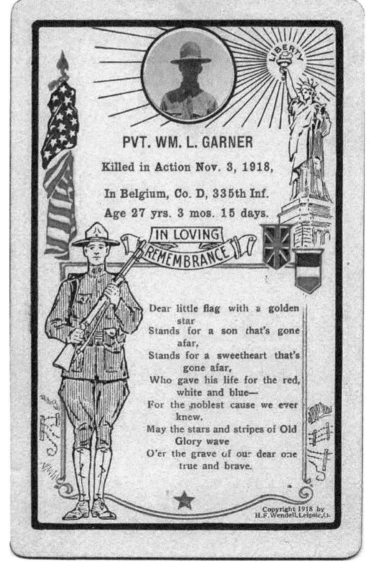

PVT. WM. L. GARNER

Killed in Action Nov. 3, 1918,

In Belgium, Co. D, 335th Inf.

Age 27 yrs. 3 mos. 15 days.

IN LOVING REMEMBRANCE

Dear little flag with a golden star
Stands for a son that's gone afar,
Stands for a sweetheart that's gone afar,
Who gave his life for the red, white and blue—
For the noblest cause we ever knew,
May the stars and stripes of Old Glory wave
O'er the grave of our dear one true and brave.

Copyright 1918 by
H. F. Wendell, Leipsic, O.

no photograph available

TALIBERTI Louis
Private, Co. F, 363rd Infantry Regiment, 91st Division
KIA 1 November 1918
Plot D – Row 03 – Grave 21
Army Serial Number 2287255

Louis (Lewis) Taliberti was born in California on 15 March 1895. His father, John, was an Italian immigrant. His mother Mary, a native of California, gave birth to her first child Carmelita when she was only fifteen. Her second born was Louis, followed by Rosa and John. At the age of nineteen she had already given birth to four children.

In 1917, Louis lived in Los Angeles where he worked as a store man for the Salt Lake Railroad. He was one of the first in the city to be called to military service. He received his basic training at Camp Lewis, WA where he was attached to Co. F of the 363rd Infantry Regiment. His registration card indicates that he was medium built, had dark brown eyes and black hair. He was killed in Waregem and buried in an isolated grave. His remains were moved to Cemetery #1252 on 4 June 1919.

In the 1918 obituaries, his name was spelled as Talibertie, Talliverti, Taliberti and Caliberti.

no photograph available

CONEDERA Umberto
Private, Co. F, 363rd Infantry Regiment, 91st Division
KIA 1 November 1918
Plot D – Row 03 – Grave 22
Army Serial Number 2779685

Umberto was born in Reventino, Catanzaro, Italy. After completing his military service in Italy, he emigrated to the U.S.A. in 1909 where he worked in the copper mines in Bingham, Utah. His petition for naturalization was ongoing at the time he was inducted on 25 April 1918. He embarked for Europe on 6 July 1918. His brother-in-law, Emilo Bier from Bingham was designated as point of contact in case of an emergency.
His friend Albert Comina is also buried at Flanders Field. They originated from the same region and worked in the same mine.

ELMO Nicola
Private, Co. H, 145th Infantry Regiment, 37th Division
DOW 4 November 1918
Plot D – Row 03 – Grave 23
Army Serial Number 1849078

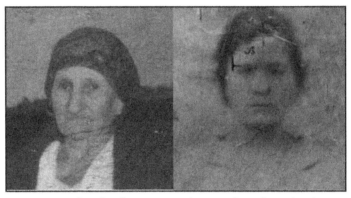

"Nicolino" Elmo was born in Acquaformosa, Calabria, Italy, on 20 May 1888. He was the son of Maria Vicchio. His father had already passed away. It is thought that this was the reason why Nicola, after completing his military service in Italy, emigrated to the U.S.A. in 1911. He arrived at Ellis Island on 22 March. He was married to Rosaria Barletta, photo left taken when she was 80, who had remained in Italy. They had one daughter, Maria Eva (photo right).

Nicola took residence in Trafford, PA, where he was employed by the Erie Railroad Company. His emergency address was registered with his brother Peter in Baltimore, MD.

On 31 October, near Olsene, he was wounded in the face and right leg by shell fragments. Although he was not severely wounded, his condition rapidly deteriorated and he died a few days later. He was initially buried near the village of Eine on 14 November and his remains moved to plot D, grave #33 in Cemetery #1252 on 9 June 1919. He received his permanent gravesite at Flanders Field on 22 June 1922. He was still an Italian citizen at the time of death.

Nicola's daughter Maria married Domenico Vicchio. She had five children but died during childbirth of her fifth.

His great-grandson, Nicola Cortese accompanied by his daughter Alessia, visited Nicola's grave during the Memorial Day ceremony in 2010. A few months prior to his visit he was not aware that Nicola was buried at Flanders Field. He wrote a moving poem for this occasion.

Nel Campo delle Fiandre.

Ho visto mia nonna
che ascoltava in silenzio,
il gemito dell'eroe e il lamento
dell'uomo morente.
Egli giace ora immemore sotto,
una coltre d'erba verde,
nel Campo delle Fiandre.
Oggi,domani,il suo nome rimarrà
scolpito tra le croci,
in lontana terra fiamminga.
Non c'è fiore più profumato,
non c'è amore così grande,
che possa ridare la voce al defunto.
Il tempo sommerge ogni ricordo.
È forse una Dea che muove
i fili sottili di questo strano mondo.
Perché,credetemi,niente è più
infinitamente distante:
come la vita e la morte.

Nicola   Cortese
Acquaformosa 18 ottobre 2009.

VANDERWAAL Albert T.

Private 1st Class, Co. A, 348th MG Battalion, 91st Division
KIA 1 November 1918
Plot D – Row 04 – Grave 01
Army Serial Number 2786674

Albert Vanderwaal was born in Marion, Clay County, IA on 14 August 1889. He was the son of Aart and Antonia (Nettie) Vanderwaal (née Tysling) from Erskine, MN. Both were born in the Netherlands but emigrated while still very young with their parents to the U.S.A. They had nine children: five sons (Arie, Herman, Henry, William and Albert) and four daughters (Minnie, Terra, Getrude and Izara). Albert was called to arms on 24 May 1918 and completed his basic training at Fort Yates, ND. At the time he owned a farm in Cannon Ball, ND.

He traveled by train to Camp Lewis, WA and less than one month later he was assigned to the 348th Machine Gun Battalion. He embarked for Europe on 6 July. Men were needed at the front rapidly and it was evident that many were inexperienced in battlefield tactics. On the other hand, Albert proofed himself to be an exemplary soldier and on 29 October, just three days before he met his death, he was promoted to Private 1st Class. He was killed by machinegun fire.

His brother Herman also served and climbed the ranks to Sergeant. He only arrived in Europe on 28 October, too late to be engaged at the front.

Back row from left to right: Arie, Gertrude, Herman, William, Minnie and Henry
Front row: Izora, Antonia, Aart and Laura. Albert center.

no photograph available

MATTHEWS Ira

Private, Co. M, 146th Infantry Regiment, 37th Division
KIA 3 November 1918
Plot D – Row 04 – Grave 02
Army serial number 1830561

Ira Matthews (°1 February 1894) was the son of Stewart and Susan Matthews from Beccaria, PA and had four brothers (Gilford, Elden, Lenwood and Edward) and five sisters (Ethel, Vida, Lois, Martha and Margaret). At the time he was called to arms he worked in a mine.

He was killed during an enemy artillery barrage on 3 November. His body was mutilated beyond recognition. He was buried in an isolated grave near the village of Kruishoutem and his remains were moved to Waregem on 11 June 1919.

His mother visited his grave with the Gold Star Mothers Pilgrimage in 1930.

no photograph available

SCHIAVONE Francesco

Private, Co. E, 145th Infantry Regiment, 37th Division
KIA 1 November 1918
Plot D – Row 04 – Grave 03
Army Serial Number 2705106

Francesco Schiavone was born in Pagis S. Vittorino, Teramo, Italy on 13 December 1894. He lived with his wife, Margherita, in Sperlonga, a hamlet near Arquata del Tronto on the province Ascoli Piceno. In search of better prospects he emigrated to the U.S.A. Margherita intended to follow him later. He took residence in Philadelphia, PA, where he found a job as a driver.

He was killed by shell fire (fractured skull) and was buried in an isolated grave near the town of Olsene on 1 November. His remains were moved to Waregem on 7 June 1919. At the time of death he was still an Italian citizen. Margherita remained in Italy all her life.

BORTLE Oscar R.
Private 1st Class, Co. B, 364th Infantry Regt., 91st Division
KIA 31 October 1918
Plot D –Row 04 – Grave 04
Army Serial Number 3126372

Oscar Robin Bortle was born in Whitewater, WI on 20 April 1888. He was the youngest in the family of Oscar D. Bortle Sr. and Eva McLean. He had two brothers (Lawrence and John) and one sister (Eva). The family moved to Minneapolis, MN in 1889. Oscar was an intelligent, eloquent and athletic young man. After attending the Emerson School in Minneapolis he graduated from the Central High School in 1907. He was an active member of the Plymouth Congregational Church and was employed by the Northwestern Fire and Marine Insurance Company for thirteen years before being called to arms. At that time he had already volunteered and been active with the Minnesota National Guard for several years where he had obtained the rank of Sergeant with the artillery. In 1917, Oscar was married to Donna Bonniwell (1888 - 1956).

He was inducted on 25 May 1918 and with just one month of basic training at Camp Lewis, embarked for Europe from Camp Merritt on the SS Olympic on 12 July. In a letter to Donna dated 22 October, he wrote about his experiences at the Meuse-Argonne front: "*I have been over the top and my feelings are indescribable. I think that only an infantry soldier can experience what war is all about. I can only say that it's horrendous: bombs, machineguns, snipers, …*" He continued explaining about hunger, rain and sleepless nights and thanked the good Lord that he had survived the offensive unscathed.

Oscar was killed in the Spitaelsbosschen (woods), close to where the Flanders Field cemetery is now located, on 31 October. He was shot through the head during the advance, charging a German machinegun nest. He was given a shallow grave where he fell and later moved to an American plot in the center of Waregem (Poteghem cemetery #1673 – plot 1, grave #15). Notification of his death was only received after the Armistice. His remains were reinterred in plot C, grave #162 in Cemetery #1252 on 2 June 1919.

Donna never remarried and lived with her parents in Los Angeles. She visited her husband's grave with the Gold Star Mothers Pilgrimage in July 1930 (photo insert).

DURAND Anthony P.

Private, Co. I, 148th Infantry Regiment, 37th Division
DOW 2 November 1918
Plot D – Rij 04 – Graf 05
Army Serial Number 1762583

Anthony Philip Durand was born in Romelfing, Lorraine, France (then Germany) on 23 October 1887. His parents Philip Durand (1859-1928), Marie Blaising (1859-1934) and their two children (his brother Emil was a year older) emigrated to the U.S.A. in 1890. They took residence in Albany, NY. Seven more children were born in the U.S.A.: George, Mary, Madeline, Loretta, Philip, Rose and Gertrude. At the time he was called to arms, Anthony was a liquor dealer in Albany, NY.

Anthony was inducted on 5 April 1918 and attached to the 153rd Depot Brigade for his basic training. On 10 June he was transferred to the 148th Infantry Regiment, 37th Division. Shortly afterwards he sailed for Europe. In a letter home dated 25 October 1918 he wrote that he expected the war would be over within a month.

During the disinterment process there was a discrepancy on Anthony's grave location. In 1919 he was registered as being buried in plot A, grave 35. He was found to be buried in grave 36 under the marker of Ira Matthews (D-4-2).

At left, Anthony P. Durand, one of the Albany boys killed in the World war; center, the grave in Flanders Field, which his mother, Mrs. Marie Durand of 313 Madison avenue, at right, will visit this summer.

His mother visited Flanders Field with the Gold Star Mothers Pilgrimage in 1930. As an exception to rule, she had been granted permission to leave the group for five days, visiting her family in Alsace-Lorraine. She hadn't seen them in forty years. She remembered the French-Prussian war and the annexation to Germany very clearly. Also being victims of discrimination due to them speaking the French language.

Above right: Anthony with two friends.
Below: Relatives Celeste and Rita Durand at Anthony's grave on Memorial Day 2005.

CASAJUS John B.
Corporal, Co. L, 363rd Infantry Regiment, 91st Division
KIA 31 October 1918
Plot D – Row 04 – Grave 06
Army Serial Number 2263108

John (Jean) Baptist Casajus lived in Ryde near Sacramento, CA, a town which is now practically deserted. He was born in Lescun, department Pyrénées Atlantiques, France on 4 March 1889. His mother still resided there in 1918. He married Marie Sybil Charamuga (born 18 March 1897 in Azores, Portugal – photo insert) on 17 June 1917 and he also had four brothers and one sister, Marie Casajus Chaix, who lived in Oakland. John was one of the first to be inducted from Ryde and sent to Camp Lewis on 6 October 1917. In June 1918, after eight months training, he was  sent to France with Company L of the 363rd Infantry Regiment, 91st Division. He wrote his last letter to his wife on 9 October 1918. He described the fighting on the Meuse-Argonne front and had his doubts if he would ever survive the war.

"Well. It is War.".
"It is the first time I have been under fire and it makes a fellow feel queer wondering where the next shell will fall. Well, it is war and I can expect nothing else.
The whole regiment is proud of having contributed to sending back the divisions of the Prussian Guard, famous for their tenacity. Next time we go into action we hope to still do better.
"Saw work of Germans"
"Ought to see all those small towns in ruins. Miles after miles of territory laid waste. France will have some work rebuilding all her towns. I am satisfied to say that the Germans are getting hell at the present time. They stood only eight days in 1914 in some French villages, but before they left they took gasoline and sprinkled the towns and set them on fire. A fellow can hardly believe it but it is true."
"Many find resting place"
"If it is God's will, I hope to see you all again. Otherwise I may find a resting place somewhere in France. Meantime be merry and do not worry about the fate that may wait me, as I am not the only one over here. Many American mothers have dear ones fighting on this soil in France."

His brother Henry fought with the French Army and was stationed just 50 miles from John, however they never met. Henry is buried in the communal cemetery in Lescun. John is also memorialized on two monuments in the village where he was born. His widow applied for a passport in 1922 and visited her parents in June of that year. She died aged 57 on 5 May 1954 in Hazill Hill, Guysborough, Canada.

no photograph available

KARAS Charles P.
Private, Co. L, 363rd Infantry Regiment, 91st Division
KIA 31 October 1918
Plot D – Row 04 – Grave 07
Army Serial Number 2265168

Charles Paraskevas Karas was an orthodox Christian and born in Pamphylla on the island of Lesbos, Greece as Eustratios Paraskevas Karakontis on 15 October 1889. He was the son of Paraskevas Karakontis and Kokkoni Koutri. He had one brother, Panagiotis (°1887) and two sisters, Basiliki (°1886) and Ropodi (°1895). He lost his father at a young age so his mother had difficulties in raising her four children. Eustratios emigrated to the U.S.A. in 1910 where his name was Americanized to Charles Karas. He found a job in Camino, El Dorado County, CA as a lumber piler at R.E. Danahar Company. He was an American citizen at the time he was called to arms, however Greek was still his mother tongue. Before embarking for Europe he signed up for a war insurance policy with his mother as beneficiary.

He was killed by machine gun fire near Waregem on 31 October and was buried in the American plot American Cemetery# 1673 Poteghem plot 1, grave #21. His remains were moved to plot C, grave #154 in Cemetery #1252 on 2 June 1919. He received his final resting place at Flanders Field In 1922.

In November 1933, Charles' war insurance indemnity amounting to $ 4,093.40 was paid out to his brother and sister as his mother had passed away in 1931.

no photograph available

BEVINS Thomas F.
Private, Co. E, 119th Infantry Regiment, 30th Division
KIA 20 August 1918
Plot D – Row 04 – Grave 08
Army Serial Number 2158340

Thomas Francis Bevins was born in Windham, IA on 24 September 1889. He was the third child of Thomas H. Bevins and Catherine Susan McCabe (photo insert). The family had five other children: John Edward (°1882), Daniel James (°1883), Josie Anna (°1892), Anna Agnes (°1894) and Hubert Ambrose (°1897). The family moved to Van Horne, IA in 1911. His father died in the fall of 1914. In the meantime Thomas had become a successful farmer. Thomas was notified that he

was on the short list to be called to arms towards the end of 1917 and so in October he decided to sell his farm lock, stock and barrel. With the profits they invested in a family home in Van Horne.

On 26 February he left Benton County to join the 119th Infantry Regiment. Thomas often wrote home. On 2 April he wrote from Camp Dodge: "*..I am subject to transfer most any time. We expect the whole company to move soon. I like it fine so far, it's hard work drilling the way they are pushing us…*" Before embarking for Europe they assembled at Camp Merritt, NJ and on 8 May he wrote: " *…Having the time of my life. But after this next move I think it won't be so pleasant….I won't be sorry for the trip if I get home OK again, even with the hardships we are sure to see, and we will see it, even if we don't get home to tell about it. But it don't worry me a bit…*" Thomas embarked on the SS Haverford (British ship) on 10 May out of Philadelphia and sailed for Nova Scotia, Canada. From there they sailed in convoy and arrived in Liverpool, England on 27 May. Upon disembarking the men immediately traveled by train to Dover where they made the crossing to France, arriving on 29 May.

The month of June was spent training with the British. General John J. Pershing visited the division on 30 June, praising the troops on their physical fitness. On 13 July Thomas wrote: *"...They have a fine crop here of grain and potatoes, also garden stuff. I never saw finer wheat....I hope the crops at home are good this year....Don't worry about me for I have never felt better, and have plenty to eat..."* Mid July, the division was sent to the front. On 1 August he writes: *"I thought I would drop you a few lines to let you know that I am well and feeling fine. I just came out of the front line last night and we had a good lunch while up there, our company loss was small. I was out twice on patrol in no man's land but we did not get a Bosch".*

On 16 August the 119th Infantry Regiment received orders to relieve a British unit near Assan farm in the village of Dickebush (photo insert)
Four days later Thomas was killed by shell fire. On the 18th he had sent a letter to his brother saying all was well. However on the same day he wrote home saying that he was at peace with God in the event he should be killed. He was initially buried at Hagle Dump British Cemetery in Poperinge. The news of his death only reached the family mid-September. At that time his mother was in hospital recovering from a major operation so the devastating news was kept from her. When she was later informed, all she could say was that she was proud that Thomas had served his country. She died on 19 March 1919.

One year after Thomas' death, the American Legion Post #148 in Van Horne was named after him.

Initially the family requested that Thomas' remains be repatriated to the United States but as in so many cases they revoked their decision. On 17 May 1920 the Graves Registration Service received a letter from his brother Daniel requesting his remains be interred in Europe. Thomas received his final resting place at Flanders Field Cemetery on 19 June 1922.

Hubert was also called to arms on 3 August 1918 and served with the U.S. Navy. In September he contracted the Spanish flu but survived. His oldest son was born in 1926 and named Thomas Francis Bevins.

STALTER Charles F.
Private, HQ Company, 148th Infantry Regt. 37th Division
KIA 31 October 1918
Plot D – Row 04 – Grave 09
Army Serial Number 2415061

Charles Frederick Stalter was the son of Jeremiah (Jerry) and Anna Elizabeth Stalter (née Van Horn) from Park Ridge, NJ. He was born in Montvale, NJ on 21 August 1888. Jerry died when Charles was one year old and Anna remarried with Stephen Beecher Stalter who was fourteen years younger than Anna and possibly a brother of Jerry. Stephen as a stepfather was only thirteen years older than Charles. Anna had seven children: Clarence, Carrie, Nicholas, Loretta, Charles, Norman and Elsie. Charles was a factory laborer in Park Ridge at the time he was called to register for the draft in 1917. He was inducted on 1 April 1918 and sent to Hackensack, NJ.

He received his basic training with the 153rd Depot Brigade and on 10 June attached to the Headquarters Company of the 148th Infantry Regiment. He was killed at the start of the attack near the town of Olsene when a shell exploded close by. He had a shattered skull and fractured left arm. He was buried along the road to Gent.

Anna requested that his remains be interred in Europe: *"Please let the boy rest where he fell"*. Health issues prevented her from joining one of the Gold Star Mothers Pilgrimages to Flanders Field.

no photograph available

TALLON Martin
Bugler, Co. H, 145th Infantry Regiment, 37th Division
DOW 3 November 1918
Plot D – Row 04 – Grave 10
Army Serial Number 1518904

The correct background information on Martin Tallon (°March 1884 in Ohio) from St. Louis, MO, remains a mystery. He had joined the military under the alias John Cain. Information obtained from the National Archives indicates his parents being Richard and Eliza Tallon and his brothers Joseph, Richard, John Tallon and sister Lida Cain. The Missouri State Archives indicate James Cain from Louisville, KY as being the father. The most reasonable theory is that Tallon is his real name as this can be retrieved in census records. In the 1900 census, Martin is registered with his brother John in a penitentiary for youth delinquents in Missouri.

He volunteered on 24 July 1917 with the 5th Regiment National Guard in Cleveland, OH under the alias John Cain. On 15 June 1918 he embarked for Europe with the 145th Infantry Regiment. In July he was designated as Bugler.

Martin was shot in the head and left leg and moved behind the lines to the American hospital in the village of Staden but later succumbed to his injuries. His remains were moved to plot A, grave #53 in Waregem on 6 June 1919. In 1921, a letter from his sister Lida Cain Thompson was received by the authorities where she requested that her brother's remains be interred in Europe under the name Martin Tallon.

American Plot Staden

DEMARIA John A.
Private, Co. M, 147th Infantry Regiment, 37th Division
DOW 1 November 1918
Plot D – Row 04 – Grave 11
Army Serial Number 2943054

John Anthony DeMaria was born in Buffalo, NY on 22 January 1893. His parents were Felix and Maria DeMaria. John was the first to be born in the U.S.A. Their parents had emigrated to the U.S.A. from Italy the previous year with their oldest son Thomas. The others were Joseph, Carmella, Angeline, Michael, Anna and Frank. Two of them died in infancy. John became a bowling alley manager and on 31 December 1917 married the three year older Mae Bennett who already had a child. He was inducted and after a brief training period was sent to Europe with the 147th Infantry Regiment.

He was wounded in the neck and right leg by machinegun fire on 1 November and succumbed to his wounds on the way to the American hospital in the village of Staden. He was buried in the American plot. His remains were moved to plot A, grave #74 in Waregem on 6 June 1919.

Mae remarried in 1921 and requested the remains of her husband be interred in Europe. His mother had already passed away and so his sister Angela had requested permission to visit John's grave during the Gold Star Mothers Pilgrimage in 1930. Her request was denied.

no photograph available

WOJCIECHOWSKI Frank
Corporal, Co. G, 145th Infantry Regiment, 37th Division
DOW 4 November 1918
Plot D – Row 04 – Grave 12
Army Serial Number 1518748

Frank Wojciechowski was born in Sint-Petersburg, Russia in January 1898. It is unknown when he emigrated to the U.S.A. He had a cousin, Anna Sadowski, who lived in Cleveland, OH. He was inducted on 24 November 1917 and mustered in the Ohio National Guard. He was promoted to Corporal on 12 June 1918. His emergency address was registered with his mother Anna at 10615 Crestwood Avenue, Cleveland, OH.

He died in the American hospital in Staden from wounds received in action. Following her religious beliefs his mother requested that his remains be buried where he fell. He received his final resting place at Flanders Field on 20 June 1922.

IVERSON John
Private, Co. B, 148th Infantry Regiment, 37th Division
KIA 1 November 1918
Plot D – Row 04 – Grave 13
Army Serial Number 2076366

John Iverson was born in Stavanger, Norway on 13 February 1891. He was the only son of Thomas and Johanna Iverson (née Topness). The family emigrated to the U.S.A. and took residence in Whalan, MN. John found work as an agricultural laborer. His registration card indicates that he had completed six months of military service with the artillery at Fort Riley, Kansas.

John was called to arms in Preston, MN on 24 June 1918 and after his basic training was attached to Co. E, 344th Infantry Regiment, 86th Black Hawk Division. Upon arrival in Europe the division was disbanded and the men attached as replacements to other divisions. John was reassigned to the 148th Infantry Regiment. He was one of fifteen men killed in action during an enemy barrage.

At the time of death he was still a Norwegian citizen. He was initially buried in the town of Olsene along the road to Gent with thirty other American soldiers. When he was moved to Waregem in 1919, there were issues in regards to his serial number during the identification process. One of the ID tags indicated the number 3747402. This number had been issued to a certain John Hurless, who never served in Europe.

FRUTH Norbeth L.

Private, Co. L, 148th Infantry Regiment, 37th Division
DOW 2 November 1918
Plot D – Row 04 – Grave 14
Army Serial Number 3337043

Norbeth (Norbert) Louis Fruth was born in St. Wendel Township, MN on 19 January 1895. In the farming family of Leonard Fruth and Sophie Fruth (née Iten). There were two other children: an older sister Ida and younger brother Edmund. The family experienced many setbacks. His mother passed away the day before his fifth birthday and his sister Ida died in 1909. Photo insert is Nortbeth at the age of five. He was a keen hunter and loved fishing. In 1915 he moved in with the Lietz family in St. Joseph where he was employed as an agricultural laborer.

Norbeth was an optimist and had no problem joining the military. His military service was practically identical to that of William Fossum (A-2-15). They were both inducted at the end of June and sent to Camp Grant, IL for basic training with 161st Depot Brigade and then attached to Co. D, 344th Infantry Regiment 86th Division. Norbeth and William Fossum were attached as replacements to the 37th Division.

He was wounded by shell fragments when his unit advanced through a field near the village of Heurne. When his comrades checked on him he mumbled: *"I guess they got me."* He succumbed to his wounds on 2 November and was buried the following day in the American cemetery in the town of Staden. His father received notification of his death two weeks after the Armistice on 24 November. His remains were moved to Waregem in June 1919. Norbeth is also memorialized on a private monument in the St. Joseph cemetery.

The Fruth family originated from Bayern, Germany and continued to have strong bonds with the community in that area. It was ironic to read in an obituary the announcement of Norbeth's death written in the early Goth language of a German newspaper.

St. Joseph. 1918-8-4

Letzten Sonntagabend traf hier die Nachricht ein, daß Norbert, Sohn der Familie Leonard Fruth, die zu dieser Gemeinde gehört, in einer Schlacht auf französischem Boden sein Leben für die Ehre des Vaterlandes opferte. Der Verstorbene stand im 23. Lebensjahre. Im Monat Mai folgte er dem Rufe zur Fahne, und kurze Zeit nachher machte er mit seiner Kompagnie die Reise übers Wasser nach Frankreich, wo er des Heldentodes starb. Den trauernden Eltern entbietet der „Nordstern" sein tiefempfundenes Beileid. — Hochw. P. Victor Rassier, O. S. B., von der St. Be-

no photograph available

NOVICH Joe
Private, Co. C, 145th Infantry Regiment, 37th Division
KIA 11 November 1918
Plot D – Row 04 – Grave 15
Army Serial Number 1517734

Joe Novich was born in Selecha, Russia on 11 December 1893. He was the son of Nik Novik and Anna Issacovna Novikova. He worked as a miner for the United Coal Co. in Meadow Lands, PA. He was drafted on 3 June 1917 and at the time of induction signed a Petition for Naturalization on 28 May 1918.

He died of wounds (fractured skull) received in action at the evacuation hospital in the town of Staden on the last day of the war and was buried in row 8 grave #103. His remains were moved to Waregem on 6 June 1919 and they were laid to rest in plot A grave #67. He received his current grave location at Flanders Field on 20 June 1922.

MARCH George S.

Private, Co. B, 347th MG Battalion, 91st Division
DOW 3 November 1918
Plot D – Row 04 – Grave 16
Army Serial Number 2783196

Private George Steven March was born in California on 23 August 1893. He was the second son of John and Alice March (née Kesner) from Orosi, CA. He had three brothers (Walter, Leroy and Henry) and four sisters (Louisa, Mabel, Mary and Irene). His Draft Registration Card indicates that his mother was dependent on him. He became head of the household when his father abandoned the family. He worked as an agricultural laborer at the time he was called

to arms and received his basic training at Camp Lewis, WA. He was later attached to the 347th Machine Gun Battalion.

He was wounded to his right hand during the Meuse-Argonne offensive and after a short admission into hospital was released to join his company for their transfer to Flanders. An eyewitness statement provided by Corporal Claud Owens: *"Private George S. March was in a house near Audenarde, Belgium, when a H.E. shell struck the building. A fragment of the shell struck Pvt. March in the abdomen. He was immediately taken to a First Aid Station and then to the Evacuation Hospital where he died."*

His mother was preparing his Christmas package when she received the sad news of his death.

From left to right: two youngest sisters with George. Irene, who died aged 19 in 1919 and Mary who died aged 21 in 1920. His brother Henry (insert right) also served in the military.

BELL Forrest L.

2nd Lieutenant, Co. L, 119th Infantry Regiment, 30th Division
KIA 31 August 1918
Plot D – Row 04 – Grave 17

Forrest Lambert Bell was born in Corder, MO on 19 February 1896. He was the only son of Robert Frank and Clara C. Bell (née Peacock) who were farmers. He attended school in Corder and was known to be a dedicated, cheerful and dutiful young man. He graduated High School In 1913. While attending the State University of Columbia, war was declared and Forrest left college for what it was and volunteered on 6 May 1917. He was sent for three months officers training to Fort Riley and from there to Fort Sheridan, IL where he became the youngest officer receiving his commission. He was attached to the 305th Infantry Regiment, 77th New York Division. On 27 December, after a short period of home leave, he was sent to Europe where he arrived on 11 January. Forrest was later reassigned to the 119th Infantry Regiment.

2nd Lieutenant Forrest Bell was killed on 31 August 1918. He was the first man from Corder to lose his life. He was buried at Nine Elms British Military Cemetery on 2 September XII.F.10. He received his final resting place at Flanders Field Cemetery on 17 June 1922. His parents later received his sword, knife and Purple Heart medal.

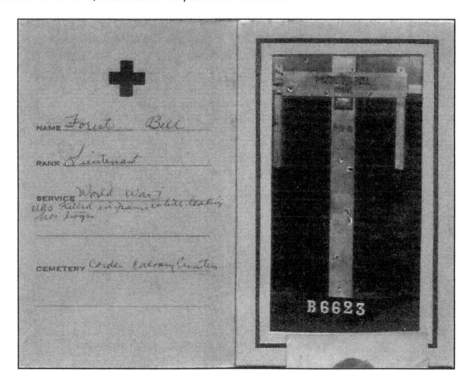

DOSTER Halley F.
Private 1st Class, Co. I, 145th Infantry Regt. 37th Division
DOW 12 November 1918
Plot D – Row 04 – Grave 18
Army Serial Number 1519216

Halley Frank Doster was born in Oakwood, OH on 29 October 1891. Halley was raised in Broughton, County Paulding (a wealthy town at the time but now only counts 150 inhabitants). He was the son of Milton and Celina R. Doster. There were seven brothers; Erna, Loy, Julius, Edgar, Foster, Carl and Lester and one sister, Essa. In 1910, Halley was living in Jackson with Essa and her husband Jesse Flint.

Halley worked in grain silos when he decided to enlist with the National Guard on 21 May 1917. He was attached to Co. I of the 145th Infantry Regiment on 27 October. According to Ohio Military Men 1917-1918, Halley became Private 1st Class on 1 June 1918. Two weeks later he was in France. He survived the Meuse-Argonne offensive unscathed. He was wounded towards the end of the war and succumbed to his wounds on 12 November, one day after the Armistice. He is buried at Flanders Field as a Private instead of Private 1st Class.

His twenty year old brother Julius was a Sergeant with the National Guard, also with Co. I, 145th Infantry Regiment. He was slightly wounded on 13 October 1918 but survived the war. He received his honorary discharge on 22 April 1919.

WOLD John

Private, Co. K, 148th Infantry Regiment, 37th Division
KIA 1 November 1918
Plot D – Row 04 – Grave 19
Army Serial Number 3339551

John Wold was born as John Kommandantvold in Røros, Norway on 26 August 1891. His parents were Nils and Gertrjud Marie Kommandantvold. He had three brothers: Reinholt (°1886), Simen (°1891) and Magnus (°1897).
Photo left insert seated from left to right: Magnus, Gertrjud Marie, an aunt and Simen. Standing left to right: Reinholt, Nils and Jon. Photo right: John as baby.

Reinholt had emigrated to the U.S.A. in 1904 and in 1910 returned to Norway on a permanent basis. John emigrated via Canada to the U.S.A. in 1911 and took residence in Glenwood, MN. He was employed in the painting business of Kornelius Moan, who also was an immigrant from the same town in Norway. He described John as being a serious, reliable and dedicated employee. He had quickly integrated himself in the community, had many friends and became very active in social life. The photo (insert right) was taken during this period. John is standing far right.

John was inducted on 28 June and sent for basic training to Camp Grant. He was assigned to the 344th Infantry Regiment, 86th Black Hawk Division. In a letter dated 5 October he informed Kornelius Moan that he had safely arrived in France via England. The crossing was smooth and they had not encountered

any German submarines. Shortly after his arrival in Europe he was sent as a replacement to the 148th Infantry Regiment.

On the eve of 4 November, John and the other men of his unit had taken their new positions on the right bank of the river Scheldt and had dug in for the night. At this point John was wounded when shell fragments hit him in the face. It was only when an order was passed on from man to man that they noticed that John was not responding. He was buried in the village of Nederename near Oudenaarde. At the time he was disinterred for identification it was determined that no ID tags were on the body and so he was buried in Waregem as "Unknown 2808", first in plot B, grave #95 and later in plot C, grave #143. It was only during the permanent burial at Flanders Field Cemetery on 1 July 1922, when a letter addressed to John was found in his pocket so that a formal identification could be made.

Photo left from left to right: Magnus, Simen, John and Reinholt
Photo right: visit of Rune Ask, great-nephew to John Wold, on 29 July 2014.

MIKULA Steve
Private, Co. D, 364th Infantry Regiment, 91st Division
KIA 1 November 1918
Plot D – Row 04 – Grave 20
Army Serial Number 3530240

Steve Mikula was the son of Jacob and Mary Mikula. He was born in Manistee, MI on 15 October 1894. Steve had five brothers and six sisters. The whole family moved to South Bend, IN in 1903.

Steve was called to arms on 27 June 1918. He received his basic training with the 158th Depot Brigade at Camp Sherman, OH. After his training he was assigned to the 333rd Infantry Regiment, 84th Lincoln Division, a division with men from Illinois, Indiana and Kentucky. He embarked for Europe on 2 September and upon arrival Steve was sent as a replacement to the 364th Infantry Regiment. His brother (Joseph) was also serving in Europe.

He was killed near Waregem by a shell on 1 November and buried where he fell (Isolated Grave #2 Anzegem). His remains were moved to Waregem (plot C, grave #141) on 4 June 1919. Mary had initially requested that his remains be interred in Europe. However when she realized how many men from South Bend were being repatriated she revoked her decision. Unfortunately her decision came too late as repatriation was no longer possible after 1 April 1922.

McGEE Matthew B.
Corporal, Co. B, 145th Infantry Regiment, 37th Division
KIA 4 November 1918
Plot D – Row 04 – Grave 21
Army Serial Number 2712883

Matthew Bernard McGee was born in Maryland on 23 July 1887. He was the son of Patrick and Elizabeth McGee (Irish immigrants). There were three other boys (John, Thomas and James) and two girls (Mary and Maggie). From Baltimore he was requested to register for the draft in 1917. He was inducted on 27 April 1918 and trained with the 145th Depot Brigade. He was assigned to the 145th Infantry Regiment on 30 May.
He was killed by friendly fire during an artillery barrage near the village of Eine on 4 November and buried where he fell. His remains were moved to Waregem on 4 June 1919.

KNOWN BUT TO GOD
Plot D – Row 04 – Grave 22

They shall grow not old,

As we that are left grow old:

Age shall not weary them,

Nor the years condemn,

At the going down of the sun

And in the morning

We will remember them.

Laurence Binyon (1869-1943)

no photograph available

MLODORZENIEC Joseph
Private, Co. A, 135th MG Battalion, 37th Division
KIA 31 October 1918
Plot D – Row 04 – Grave 23
Army Serial Number 1814615

Joseph Mlodorzeniec was the son of Maryanna Mlodorzeniec from Chrusta, Poland. When he emigrated to the U.S.A. he took residence in Philadelphia, PA.

He was killed instantly in Olsene due to concussion from a bursting shell. There was also a wound at the back and left side of his head. He was buried one mile west of the town of Kruishoutem.

WALL OF MISSING

BAVIS Carey D.
Corporal, Co. M, 148th Infantry Regiment, 37th Division
DOW 10 November 1918
Wall of Missing
Serial number 1531273

Carey Bavis, son of Clement L. and Clara Bavis (née Ball) was born near New Harmony, OH on 28 July 1897. Carey and his sister Hila were still young when their father died, leaving Clara to raise the children on her own.

Carey Davis joined the service in Georgetown, OH on 23 July 1917 and received his basic training at Camp Sheridan, AL with Co. M of the 1st Ohio National Guard Regiment, which became the 148th Infantry Regiment on 26 October 1917. He achieved the rank of Private 1st Class on 1 October and Corporal on 1 June 1918. He married Bess May Tracy a few days before he sailed for Europe.

He arrived in Europe on 22 June. During the Meuse-Argonne offensive he became overwhelmed during a gas attack on 30 September and spent three days recovering in a Field Hospital. During the Flanders offensive he was shot by machinegun fire along the river Scheldt on 3 November. He succumbed to his wounds on 10 November, the day before the Armistice. He was buried in an isolated grave near the village of Nederename on 11 November.

During exhumation and reburial at Flanders Field in 1919, there was confusion around the identity of three men: Joseph Hajek, Otto Madary and Carey Bavis. All now are buried in the cemetery as "Known but to God". Their names inscribed on the Wall of Missing. His burial file at NARA referred to a report from 1925 indicating the assumption of Bavis being buried in plot A – row 4 – grave 18.

After the war, the American Legion Post #180 in Georgetown was named after him. Bess had remained a widow for more than thirty years when she finally remarried.

BEATTIE Joseph W.
Sergeant, Co. K, 106th Infantry Regiment, 27th Division
DOW 1 September 1918
Wall of Missing
Army serial number 1208491

Joseph Beattie lived in Brooklyn, NY and was born on 2 October 1897. He was the son of Walter and Eleanor (Ellen) Beattie who were immigrants from Northern-Ireland. He had three sisters: Mary, Florence and Lillian. Joseph had received his education at the St. Peters Academy and was also Deputy Chairman of the Sacred Heart Club. He enlisted with the 23rd Infantry Regiment New York National Guard on 8 May 1916. He served along the Mexican border during the Pancho Villa uprising. He was promoted to Corporal on 14 March 1918 and Sergeant on 27 June 1918.

Joseph had the reputation of being a courageous man. He had been confined to sickbay but when on 1 September he heard that his company was being sent to the front, he immediately joined his company. An act of courage which proved to be fatal for him on this day. He received a Divisional citation (cfr. Di Giacomo A-1-21). *"Although excused on medical grounds, the sergeant volunteered to go up the lines hearing that his company was in the fight at Dickebush, September 1, 1918. Showed high courage in his work. Was helping Sergeant Monahan of his Company, who had been gassed, to the rear, when struck by a whizz-bang; died of wounds."* (helping: was administering first aid)
Fatally wounded he was moved to a hospital in the rear where he died a few hours later. He was buried near the village of Kemmel.

Before receiving any official notification, his mother had already received word of his death. His best friend, Joseph Juliano, had informed the account of his friend's death to another member of the *Sacred Heart Club*. Joseph Juliano had been slightly wounded. When Beattie heard that his friend had been wounded he was relieved to find him in an ambulance. He took a few photographs out of his pocket and said to his friend: *"Here Joe, if I don't come back send one to your girl, May, because she loves me just as much as I love her, and send the rest home"*. Joe Juliano: *"Don't talk like a darned fool. You will come back alright."*
That was the last time Joe Juliano saw him. He later stated: *"He died like a hero. He tried to save the lives of four other unfortunate fellows who were gassed, but it seems to me he had no luck at all. He gave his live but saved two of the men."*
It is unclear what happened when his remains were moved from Kemmel to the Lyssenthoek Military Cemetery in Poperinge. Upon arrival at Lyssenthoek cemetery, there was confusion on the identification of four men from Company K: Beattie, Wiss, Mandak and Cundy. As no

positive identification could be established, they were all buried as "unknowns", first at Lyssenthoek Cemetery and later at Flanders Field.

A number of trees were planted in memory of the fallen from Brooklyn on the Eastern Parkway. They also received a memorial marker, one was dedicated to Joseph Beattie.

BENOIT Maurice H.

Private, Co. K, 106th Infantry Regiment, 27th Division
KIA 30 August 1918
Wall of Missing
Army Serial Number 1208550

Maurice H. Benoit was born in Brooklyn on 1 May 1900 and lived with his sister Nathalie, father Henry and stepmother Ida at 1004 Bergen Street. He was inducted on 2 August 1917 and attached to the 23rd Infantry Regiment New York National Guard.

He was shot through the heart near Vierstraat. He was only 18. Initially it was assumed that he was buried at La Clytte Military Cemetery near the village of Reningelst, however when exhumed the body of a British soldier was found. It is also uncertain about his date of death. One source indicates 30 August, another 2 September. Henry engaged his Congressman and lawyers to write letters

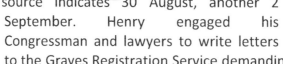

to the Graves Registration Service demanding they find the remains of his son. All in vain.

Ida (photo insert) took part in the 1930 Gold Star Mothers Pilgrimage to Europe. It was a long and painful voyage. Ida suffered from her nerves and her condition deteriorated so fast that she had to be admitted into the American Hospital in Paris.

BONAWITZ Edward
Private, Co. M, 145th Infantry Regiment, 37th Division
KIA 4 November 1918
Wall of Missing
Army Serial Number 2966074

Edward Bonawitz was born in Plymouth PA on 23 July 1886. His parents were Frank and Ellen Bonawitz (née Shaver). He had two sisters (Susan and Rosa Mae) and two brothers (Clarence and Frank). Aged thirteen he was already working as a miner for D.V.H. Coal Company in Larksville. He was still working there at the time he was called to arms on 29 April 1918. After a short training period with the 155th Depot Brigade he was transferred to the 145th Infantry Regiment.

He was killed in action on 4 November when shell fragments shattered his legs. His last words were: *"Give me a cigarette"*. He was buried on the spot near the village of Heurne in the same grave as Clarence Petersen and Louis Kohler. Their remains were later moved to Waregem but it was impossible to make individual identification of the bodies. A wallet was found with the initial "B" on one set of remains but the Graves Registration Service found this insufficient to determine a positive identification of Bonawitz. All three men lay buried at Flanders Field as "Known but to God".

CHESTON Galloway G.
1st Lieutenant, 206th Squadron Royal Air Force
KIA 29 July 1918
Wall of Missing

Galloway Grinnell Cheston was born in West River, MD on 3 May 1896. His parents were prominent and wealthy people. His father, Galloway Cheston was a judge and passed away in 1905 at the age of sixty. His mother, Galloway's second wife and twenty-five years younger, was Henrietta Seymore McCulloch. Galloway had two older sisters; Kitty (1884) and Bessie (1886) His forefathers had made a fortune, not only in the cotton trade, tobacco and grain, but also in the slave trade.

Galloway attended the Reserve Officers Training Corps at Fort Myer on 25 June 1917, his intentions of becoming a pilot. He also took courses at the School of Military Aeronautics at Cornell University. He was sent to England in September where he completed his training with the 9th Aviation Instruction Center in March 1918. He was assigned to the 206th Squadron Royal Flying Corps (The Royal Air Force only being formed in April 1918).

On 25 July 1918 he won his first and only victory. Four days later Galloway and his DH9 B7668 were downed near the village of Geluveld by Lt. F. Ritter von Röth* of Jasta 16 (photo insert). Corporal J.W. Parcey, Galloway's co-pilot, survived the crash and became prisoner of war.

*Friederich von Röth had been severely injured as an artillery officer. After spending 2 years in hospital he was discharged and transferred to the air service. He turned out to be an excellent fighter pilot with 28 victories of which 20 balloons (all in 1918). After the war, not being able to cope with the humiliation that Germany had lost, he became depressed and finally committed suicide.

COMBS Edgar H.
Private 1st Class, Co. C, 120th Infantry Regt. 30th Division
KIA 31 August 1918
Wall of Missing
Army Serial Number 1319847

Edgar Harrison Combs was born in Wilkes County, NC in 1897. He was the son of Lucy Ellen "Duck" Combs (photo insert) who raised her three children as a single parent: Bruce, Thomas and Edgar. It is unknown who Edgar's father was, but Lucy later married a William Rufus Call on 25 January 1910. She died on 26 February 1917. Edgar had joined the North Carolina National Guard in September 1916 and was attached to Co. C of the 3rd Infantry Regiment. He achieved the rank of Private 1st Class on 25 July 1917. His regiment later became part of the 120th Infantry Regiment, 30th Division. About this time he met Ennis Johnson with whom he had made many plans. Before he sailed for Europe he registered for a war insurance policy amounting to $10,000.

"Big Boy Combs", as he was known to his friends being 6 ft. 7 in. and weighing 188 Lbs. sailed for Europe on 12 May 1918. On 28 August, three days before he was killed, Edgar wrote a letter to his brother Bruce. He explained that he was doing fine and asked him to send some chewing tobacco. He also asked Bruce and Thomas to write often as he had not

received any news from them since his arrival in Europe. He was killed when struck by a bullet in the heart and right temple. There was no record on location of burial. He was also never listed as missing in action.

Inspection of Co. C   (Edgar second from left)   Edgar with Ennis Johnson

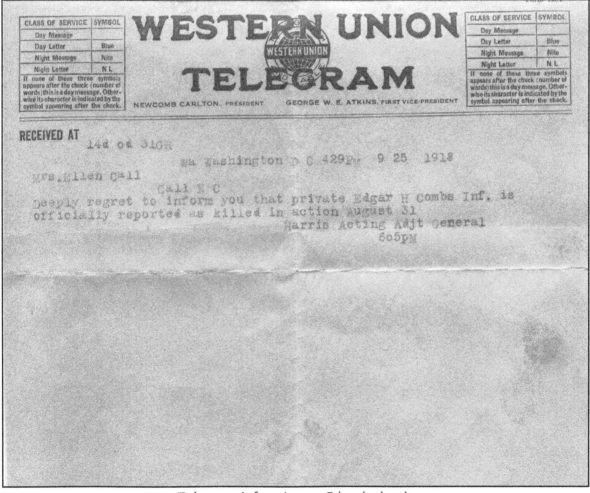

Telegram informing on Edgar's death.

no photograph available

CORNELIUS Bennett

Private, Co. L, 120th Infantry Regiment, 30th Division
KIA 31 August 1918
Wall of Missing
Army Serial Number 1321847

Bennett Cornelius was born in Randolph County, NC on 20 March 1899. He was the son of Benjamin and Louisa Cornelius (née Hunt) who also had three daughters: Mollie, Bertha and Allie. Sometime later the family moved to Thomasville, Davidson County, where shortly after his eighteenth birthday Bennett joined the 3rd Infantry Regiment of the North Carolina National Guard on 27 June 1917. On 1 November 1917 he was promoted to Private 1st Class (not inscribed). At that time he was employed in the cotton industry.

His unit had been sent to an advanced observation post in no man's land near Lankhof Farm, close to Ypres, where they had been dug in for four days. On 31 August, one of the men had made an attempt to relay a message to their Company HQ but failed. Bennett immediately volunteered. He was shot in the stomach by a sniper while thus engaged and died almost instantly. He was only 19.

Obituaries on Bennett and a number of other men from Thomasville were published in The Lexington Dispatch on 9 October. Two of these men are also interred at Flanders Field: Haymore Westmoreland and Carl Link. All three were part of Co L, or the *"Thomasville Company"* as they were known. In said article Bennett Cornelius was listed as Corporal.

His mother (left insert with Mollie) did not make it to Europe with the Gold Star Mothers Pilgrimage due to ill health.

A grave marker to the memory of Bennett was erected in the family plot of Mount Zion Methodist Church Cemetery in Trinity.

no photograph available

CRAVEN William S. – Croix de Guerre (F)

Cook, Ambulance Service Section 577
KIA 25 April 1918
Wall of Missing
Army Serial Number 8854

William Sheldon Craven was born in Meriden, CT on 10 June 1891. He was the son of Ezekiel and Jeanette Craven. He had a younger brother and sister: Mildred and James.

He is one of the few regular career soldiers buried at Flanders Field. He enlisted in Columbus, OH on 24 June 1916 and received medical training in Houston, TX and Deming, NM. He was assigned to the 577th Section of the Ambulance Service in August 1917. He arrived in Europe in December and served as a cook with the French Army.

He was killed with two other American soldiers near the village of Boeschepe on 25 April. Civilian eyewitness account stated that they were driving through the village when an artillery shell fell close by and killed them instantly. They were buried in the communal cemetery. In 1921 their remains were disinterred by the French. One man could not be identified and as all French unknowns were transported to the village of Gravelines. It is plausible that William is buried in the French Ossuary in Gravelines. It is assumed that lack of communication is the reason why his remains were never found, consequently being listed as missing in action. William was awarded the French *"Croix de Guerre"* (War Cross).

James also served in the military but was never sent to Europe. He received his honorary discharge on 26 May 1919 achieving the rank of Sergeant. Jeanette ordered a permanent marker in William's memory which was placed in the cemetery where she lived. She preferred to believe that he was buried there. Her impaired eyesight prevented her from making the trip to Europe with the Gold Star Mothers Pilgrimage.

In addition, William's name is also inscribed on his parent's grave marker at Westville Cemetery, New Haven, CT.

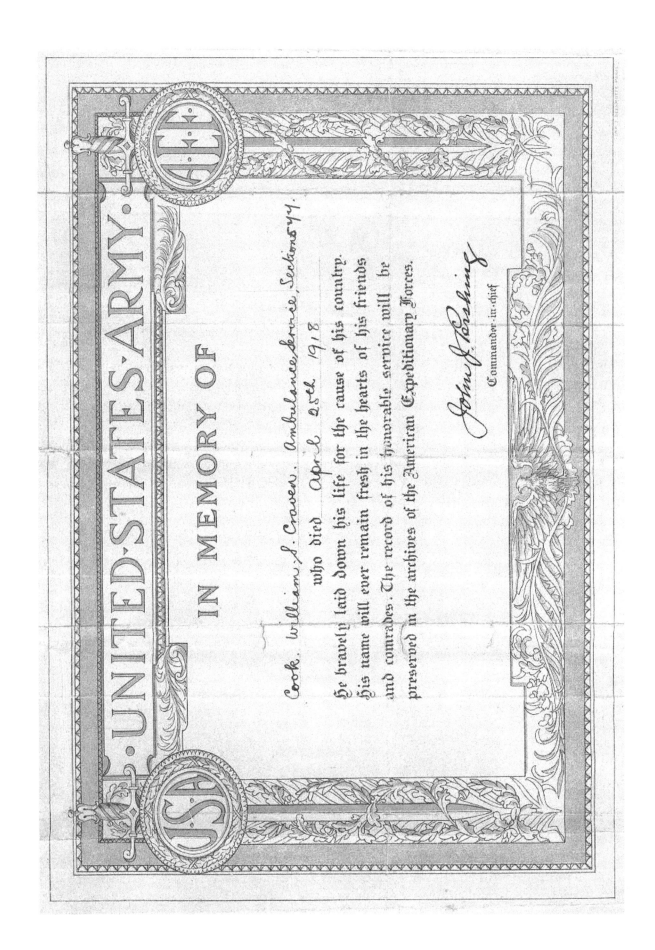

578

CREECH Wesley J.

Private, Co. C, 120th Infantry Regiment, 30th Division
KIA 31 August 1918
Wall of Missing
Army Serial Number 1319895

Wesley Jackson Creech was born on a secluded farm near Hallsboro, NC on 15 March 1887. His parents were Henry Marshall and Martha Elizabeth Creech (née Byrd). They had eight children. The family photo (insert) was taken in 1902. Back row left to right: John, William and Wesley. Front row: Hicks, Sims, Sara, Lewis, the parents and Lucinda far right. The family lived in primitive

circumstances as most farmers did in those days. There were no utilities and water came from a well. The most important crop was cotton. When his father died in 1909, Martha was left to raise all her children. Wesley was extremely talented in music and could play a variety of instruments. (banjo, mandolin, violin, ...) He was also member of the local hoedowns and square dance parties (photo insert below – Wesley in the middle).

Wesley moved to Bolton where he was employed as a lumber inspector for the Waccamaw Company. He met Carzetta Williamson, fell in love and they were married in 1917. Sometime later he was called to arms and requested to report to Whiteville, NC by 1 October. In the meantime Carzetta had become pregnant. Wesley was assigned to the Machine Gun Company of the 322nd Infantry Regiment, 81st (Wildcat) Division. This division was formed with conscripts from Florida and the Carolina's. After basic training at Camp Jackson, SC the division sailed for Europe in May of 1918. Wesley's daughter, Marie, was born on 14 March. Unfortunately he did not see her very often. The last time was a month prior to his departure for Europe when Marie was two months old. Wesley wrote more than 25 letters to his wife and little girl. The contents revealed his eagerness to get back home. His letters started with *"Dear wife and baby"* or *"My dear ones"* and ended *"Kiss baby for me"* or *"I hope you and dear little Marie are well"*. His faith and trust in God was also evident. *"I am so tired of this. If it is God's will, I hope it won't be so long. I have no idea how long it will be. Of course, some are going to be left over here, but I trust I can be one of the lucky ones. We pray to God to be with us. I'm trying to make the best of it. How glad I would be if I was in Bolton."*

Upon his arrival in Europe, Wesley was reassigned as a replacement to the 30th Division. Wesley wrote his last letters on 24 and 26 August, a few days before he was killed in action. It was if he had a premonition that this was going to be his farewell letter. As in his previous letters he wrote how much he missed his wife and little girl, how much he longed for home. But then his tone changed, he hoped that God would be with him in his hour of need, but he was also doubting the fact that he would ever see them again. To his daughter he wrote: *"Be a good girl"* and *"If I never see you and Marie any more in this life, I hope to meet you in a Better Place"*. The letter ended with *"Goodbye"*.

Wesley was shot through the head by a sniper and was killed instantly. The ground they had taken during the advance could not be held so there was no time to give Wesley a suitable grave. According to his burial file at the National Archives, it is thought he had been buried as an unknown in the Perth British Cemetery (China Wall) in the village of Zillebeke near Ypres (Ieper), later being reinterred in the American plot at Lyssenthoek Military Cemetery, Poperinge. In that case, in all probability, he is buried at Flanders Field Cemetery as "Known but to God".

His obituary appeared in a local newspaper in September, already citing the famous poem by John McCrae *"In Flanders Fields"*.

Carzetta was left with her five month old daughter (photo insert). She remarried in 1922 with Oliver Davis and conceived four more children. Marie inherited her father's musical talents. She became an exceptional pianist, teaching music for many years. She married Roland Otto Jones and had two children: Wesley (named after her father) and

Mary. Mary, in turn, inherited her grandfather's talents and still plays the church organ to this day.

As Carzetta had remarried she was no longer entitled to make the pilgrimage to Europe with the Gold Star Mothers. Wesley's mother would have but her feeble health prevented her from doing so. She was 71 at the time.

Wesley's memory is still kept alive within the family. Not only his grandson but a nephew was also named after him. Wesley Creech was stationed in England as member of a B17 bomber crew during World War II.

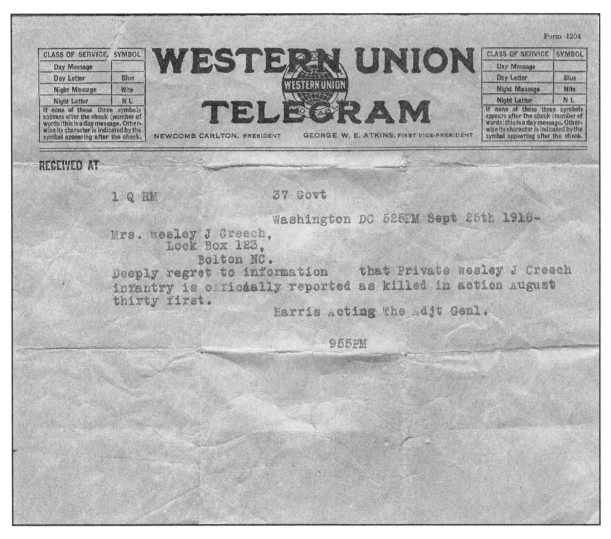

Marie aged 2   Marie as a young woman   Card sent by Wesley from Ypres

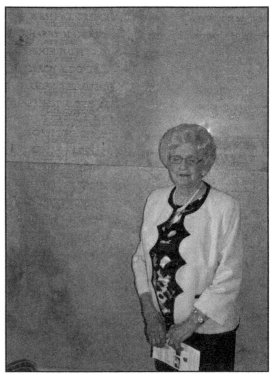

Photo left: From left to right: granddaughter Mary Jones Alsup, daughter Marie, wife Carzetta and mother Martha. Photo right: Mary Frances Alsup in front of the Wall of Missing where her grandfather's name is inscribed, Memorial Day 2015.

CUNDY Harry M.
Private 1st Class, Co. K, 106th Infantry Regt. 27th Division
KIA 1 September 1918
Wall of Missing
Army Serial Number 1208498

Harry Monroe Cundy was born in Plainfield, NJ in 1898. His parents were Henry and Lillie Cundy. They had one other son (Thomas) and two daughters (Ella and Mildred). The family moved to Brooklyn, NY where Harry attended school later finding a job in the automobile industry. He entered the service with the 23rd Infantry Regiment New York National Guard on 26 June 1916 and consequently served along the Mexican border. In 1917 the 106th Infantry Regiment was formed from the 23rd NY National Guard Infantry Regiment. They were sent for basic training at Camp Wadsworth, Spartanburg, SC. Harry was loved by all and he became a popular entertainer. He took part in the musical *"You know me, Al"*. On 1 February he was promoted to Private 1st Class, sailing for Europe on 10 May.

There is some lack of clarity about the date of Harry's death. His mother still hadn't received an official notification of his death by 14 October. His friend, Corporal George Holmes, had informed her that Harry had been killed on 11 August during the third attack of the day near Vierstraat. His last words were: *"Tell mother not to worry, I died for my country."* His official date and cause of death was *"Shot through the head on 1 September"*.

He had a known field grave at the crossroads of Vierstraat and York Road, where others of his unit had been buried. Four of them could not be positively identified: Harry, Joseph Beattie, Mathias Mandak and Frank Wiss. All were buried at Flanders Field Cemetery as *"Known but to God"*.

On the Eastern Parkway in Brooklyn, trees were planted in memory of those soldiers killed from Brooklyn. They also received a memorial marker, one of them dedicated to Harry Cundy.

DALEY Hugh
Private 1st Class, Co. L, 107th Infantry Regt. 27th Division
KIA 20 August 1918
Wall of Missing
Army Serial Number 1211885

Hugh Daley was born in August 1886. He was the oldest of six children. His parents were James and Ellen Daley from Newburgh, NY (where George Crawford also originated from). He had four brothers (William, Samuel, Thomas and Andrew) and one sister (Margaret). James and Ellen were Irish immigrants.

"Hughie" was a veteran. For some time he had served as a regular soldier before enlisting with the 1st Infantry Regiment of the New York National Guard on 25 January 1916. In between military service he had worked in a cigar factory and in a weaving mill. Samuel had also enlisted with the National Guard and sailed with the same company to Europe.

Hugh was stationed in an advanced observation post somewhere in no man's land near the village of Dikkebus when he was taken prisoner during a night skirmish with the enemy. He was listed as missing but on 20 August officially registered as killed in action.

DOYLE Leroy A.
Private, Co. M, 106th Infantry Regiment, 27th Division
KIA 2 September 1918
Wall of Missing
Army Serial Number 1209017

Leroy Alonzo Doyle was born in Cementon, NY on 22 November 1898. The city was named after a large cement factory which provided work for the majority of its inhabitants. Leroy's parents Simon Doyle (a veteran of the Civil War) and Anna Miller were married when Anna was only fifteen years of age. The family had thirteen children of which at least four boys and one girl died very young. Anna also had a miscarriage when she was struck by lightning. At the time she died, only 4 children were still living. Leroy was the eleventh in row. On the family photo, Leroy is the baby sitting on his mother's lap.

Leroy enlisted with the 10th Infantry Regiment New York National Guard in Catskill on 8 May 1917 and with the forming of the 27th Division was assigned to the 106th Infantry Regiment. Training and transfer to Europe occurred without any problems.

His nephew Clarence Gardner (photo insert page 580), with whom he had grown up and joined the service together, was with Leroy at the time that he was mortally wounded. This happened just a few hundred meters from where the monument dedicated to the 27th and 30th Division now stands. Clarence was also wounded (machine gun fire) and had suffered from gas intoxication. It was thought that he was also killed in action as they found both his identity tags. Simon and Anna, who had raised Clarence, received a letter from a nurse that Clarence was alive and being treated in a hospital. Sometime later they received an official government telegram, apparently unaware of his hospitalization, indicating that he had been killed in action.

A Graves Registration document found in the burial file of Clement Yates indicated that three men of Company M were listed as missing. Two had been killed in France on 29 September, one on 2 September. At that time the Division was still in Belgium. There was only one unknown from Company M who was buried at Lyssenthoek Military Cemetery. Why the link wasn't laid with Leroy's remains a mystery as all the information found was on one and the same document. It also appears that in 1919, many researchers didn't know that France and Belgium were different countries (as on some documents Belgium was indicated as a department of France) nor did they compare files to check on possible similarities. If they had, they would have discovered that Leroy was buried at Lyssenthoek in XXXII.C.XXX.

That is why he is one of the missing now buried with a marker " Known But to God". We can even assume that he is one of the four unknowns in row 4 of Plot A between Clement Yates and William Doherty.

Prvt. Lerey A. Doyle

Born Nov. 22, 1898.
Died Sept. 2, 1918.
Killed in Action While Serving
As an Infantryman with
American Expeditionary Forces.

IN LOVING REMEMBRANCE

He heard humanity's clear
call,
And knew the voice di-
vine;
He gave his life, he gave
his all,
In deadly battle line.
The silent stars in love
look down
Where lies this loyal
son;
In frost and dew they
weave a crown
Of honor he has won.

Copyright 1918 by
H.F. Wendell, Leipsic, O.

He is also remembered on the WW1 Memorial in Catskill. He was only 19 and so one of the youngest soldiers buried at Flanders Field.

Clarence returned home where in January 1918 a little girl had been born. Leroy's mother waited for Clarence as she preferred him to give a name . The girl was named Helen. In 2005, Helen's daughter, Regina Zimmermann and her husband Bill visited Flanders Field Cemetery and the battlefield around Ypres where Leroy had been killed (photo insert below). Upon their return they sent an application to the authorities in New York to obtain the New York Medal, an award that Leroy should have received posthumously after the war. This was presented to them by a Senator of New York. Leroy was also enrolled in the National Purple Heart Hall of Honor. However they were unable to obtain the Victory Medal.

ELROSE Ralph J. Jr.

Private, Co. L, 106th Infantry Regiment, 27th Division
KIA 31 August 1918
Wall of Missing
Army Serial Number 1208790

Ralph Elrose (left insert at 5 years of age) was born in Brooklyn, NY on 18 October 1894. It is unknown who his real mother was except for the fact that she was an actress. His father remarried with the much younger Emily (photo insert right) and they had eight children: Daniel, Louis, Tessy, Laura, Rose, Mary, Frances and Emily (who died young). Emily raised Ralph as if he was her own son. Ralph was employed as a bookbinder with Brown, Lent and Pett in New York City.

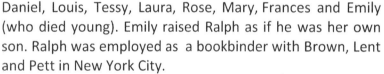

He enlisted with the 23rd Infantry Regiment of the New York National Guard on 24 June 1917. He was shot near the village of Dikkebus on 31 August at 18:00 hours. (and not 28 August as indicated in some official records). As there was no time for burial during the attack, he was pulled in a shell hole before the rest of his unit continued the advance. After the battle his remains were never found.

When Emily heard about the 1930 Gold Star Mothers Pilgrimage to Europe she immediately enquired on the procedures to take part. Her request was initially denied as at the time mothers and widows of MIA (Missing in Action) were not entitled to join the pilgrimages. In 1931 the regulations were modified and so Emily was able to make the trip to Flanders Field Cemetery. She sailed on the SS Republic and shared her cabin with the mother of Samuel Hochfelder (also memorialized on the Wall of Missing). As she could not express her grief at a grave site she laid flowers at the grave of a "Known but to God" (photo following page). Upon her return in New York she wrote two letters to the Government expressing her gratitude for all the courtesies extended to her during the trip.

Daniel and Louis also served in Europe during World War II.

Emily (far left front row) during a group visit to the American monument in Oudenaarde

GIROUX Ernest A. – D.S.C. + Croix de Guerre (F)

1st Lieutenant, 103rd Aero Squadron
KIA 22 August 1918
Wall of Missing

Ernest Armand Giroux was born in Roxbury, MA on 4 December 1895. He was the son of Ernest and Jessie Stuart. Ernest had two brothers, Silvan and Archie.

His passport was issued on 16 April 1917 and he sailed for France on the 21st. He proceeded to the front as a Sergeant in the Camion Transport Section #526. (photo insert). He entered the American Aviation service on 15 August writing, *"It is now time that every American take part in as belligerent work as he is fitted for."* He was commissioned First Lieutenant on 20 November 1917 and joined the 103rd Pursuit Squadron (formerly the Lafayette Escadrille). He was engaged in a dog fight on 22 May 1918 and shot down near Laventie (Northern France). He was buried in Estaires, northeast of Béthune and posthumously awarded the Distinguished Service Cross and French Croix de Guerre for his courage and self-sacrifice.

His D.S.C. citation read: *"Lieutenant Giroux while on patrol with four other scout planes attacked an enemy formation of eight monoplanes. Two companions were forced to retire. Despite numerical superiority Lieutenant Giroux continued the attack, endeavoring to protect his leader, until finally forced down and killed."*
His *Croix de Guerre* citation said: *"He did not hesitate to attack within their lines……."*

Ernest made many friends. Those who knew him said: *"Ernest had had a rare personality that attracted all men to him whether they shared his likes and dislikes or not."* Lieutenant Colonel William Thaw said: *"In the short time he had been with us we had all come to consider him as a good pal and to admire him for his energetic courage."*

Ernest's motivation and reasoning on why he entered the war was astounding. *"I feel no rancor towards the enemy. In a way I cannot help but pity them."* On the other hand he grew to hate all that the German military represented. *"I have seen prisoners, stoop-shouldered, broken in spirit, not knowing what the whole thing means, men driven by the war gods behind them, by the war gods who are to blame, and deserve no mercy."*

To his mother he wrote: *"This is our war....and you are doing your part....A war in which one mother's son is no better than any other mother's son. We are only doing our little part. You have always been the best of mothers and we want you to continue and be the bravest of mothers in this sacrifice."*

Ernest was downed by the German ace of Jasta 18, Hans Müller (12 victories – photo insert). He came down in flames near the road between Bailleul and Armentières close to the hamlet of La Croche. Although his gravesite had been clearly mapped, his remains were never found. After the war, Archie had contacted Müller in an attempt to obtain more details and so hopefully find Ernest's gravesite. Müller claimed that Ernest had been buried northeast of Estaires and not southeast as initially documented. All searches were in vain and Archie returned to the U.S.A.

Lt. Müller later changed his name to "Garrelt" and died from a brain tumor in 1964.

Jessie had planned to visit Flanders Field cemetery with the Gold Star Mothers Pilgrimage in 1933. Unfortunately she was admitted into hospital and so had to cancel the trip.

GRIDER John McGavock

1st Lieutenant, 85th Aero Squadron
KIA 22 August 1918
Wall of Missing

The family roots of the Grider family can be found in Germany. "Kreuter" being their original family name. When they emigrated to the U.S.A. in 1777 their family name became "Grider", named after the town Grider in Arkansas, where the family was living at the time.

John McGavock Grider was born in Sans Souci, AR on 28 May 1892. His parents were William and Sue Grider and they owned a cotton plantation along the banks of the Mississippi named "*Sans Souci* (French meaning "no worries"). Around the beginning on the 20th century the family moved to Memphis where John attended the Memphis University. At the age of 17 he married a Memphis girl, Marguerite Samuels on 29 March 1909. When the U.S.A. declared war in 1917 they had two children but were already divorced. Although father of two small sons, Grider volunteered with the Aviation Section of the Signal Corps and left his children in the care of his sister Georgia who was also registered as point of contact in case of an emergency.

In September of the same year he sailed for Europe, destination Italy. During the voyage, orders were changed and he finally arrived in England staying in Oxford. John was not happy at all: " *Not going to Italy after all. Got to go to ground school. Orders all bawled up in Paris. Someone has made a major error. All our mail is in Italy, all our money in Lire. Our letters of credit are drawn on Banks in Rome and I've wasted two weeks studying Italian.*"

In this university city he trained with the second Oxford Detachment. Afterwards Grider, together with two friends, Springs and Callahan (the "three musketeers" as they were called, - photo insert), trained to become fighter pilots in different areas in England. On 1 April, Grider was promoted to 1st Lieutenant with the 85th Aero Squadron, attached British Air Service, with base at Petite Synthe (near Dunkirk), France. Major William Bishop VC, his great idol, was also a member of this squadron.

On 8 June the squadron was engaged in offensive patrols near St. Omer between Nieppe and Ieper. On 17 June the three musketeers made their first kill. The following day they were also engaged in a dog fight and the German plane was seen to crash along the "Menin Road". Grider was never seen again. Sometime later a German pilot dropt a message with the details that Lt. Grider had been KIA. A witness statement declared that this happened between Armentières and Houplines. His remains were never found.

In the official report by the US War Department: *"Lieutenant Grider in one machine and another officer in another machine chased a German two-seater back of the German lines and after downing the two-seater started back to the allied lines against strong wind and through anti-aircraft fire. Grider was in the rear, was seen several times following but finally lost sight of. It was not thought that he was downed by anti-aircraft fire. It was thought that he had to land on account of engine trouble, or lost back of the German lines."* He had a good reputation as a fighter and had 4 official German planes to his credit in six weeks.

A diary was found between his belongings. In 1926, his friend Elliott Springs (photo insert) published his diary in book form: *"War Birds, Diary of an Unknown Aviator"*. It was also published in Liberty Magazine as a series. From the entries in his diary one can only determine how much he hated the war. Over himself he wrote: *"I didn't live very well, but I'm determined to die well"*. The last day – 17 June – his last entry describes the cunningness of the Germans. He ends ironically with the statement: *"This is certainly a nice friendly war."*

No date
"War is a horrible thing, a grotesque comedy. And it is so useless. This war won't prove anything. All we'll do when we win is to substitute one sort of Dictator for another. In the meantime we have destroyed our best resources. Human life, the most precious thing in the world, has become the cheapest." He continues: *"To me the most contemptible cur in the world is the man who lets political influence be used to keep him away from the front. For he lets another man die in his place. The worst thing about this war is that it takes the best. If it lasts long enough the world will be populated by cowards and weaklings and their children. And the whole thing is so useless, so unnecessary, so terrible! Even those who live through it will never be fit for anything else."*

One sister, Josephine Grider Jacobs, also wrote a book based on his journal: *"Marse John goes to war"* (1933).

His sister Georgia Grider Williamson wrote a letter to the War Office on 28 December 1929: *"I see in the papers that the U.S. Government is offering a trip abroad to the Gold Star Mothers who lost their loved ones in the World War. I had no son in the war but my brother named me as his next of kin and left his children in my care when he went abroad.........The circumstances I have just mentioned make me particularly anxious to make a trip to the French battlefields in an effort to discover trace of my missing brother. His mother is dead and there is no one to go....Hoping that you will permit me to make this trip with the other women who will embark on a similar mission........."* Her request was denied.

Grider Memorial Park is located on the Grider plantation south of Osceola and was named for Lieutenant McGavock Grider of the Royal Flying Corps, killed near Armentieres, France The park is a ten acre wooded grove, outlined sharply against the flat treeless fields that surround it.

Grider Army Air Field was a World War II Army Air Corps training facility located in Jefferson County. Named posthumously in honor of World War I pilot John McGavock Grider of Osceola (Mississippi County), it opened on March 22, 1941

Grider Airfield, Pine Bluff, Jefferson County, serves as the only jet capable airport in southeast Arkansas and is a designated reliever for Little Rock National Airport. Grider Field provides a bad-weather alternative for pilots going to Warren, Fordyce, Star City, and Monticello.

John McGavock's sons followed in their father's footsteps. John McGavock Jr. (°1910 in Sans Souci) was a Lieutenant in the Pacific and commander of a destroyer during WWII. He was awarded the Bronze Star with Oak Leaf Cluster. He died on 6 November 1984.

George William Grider (° 1 October 1912 in Memphis TN) graduated at the U.S. Naval Academy, Annapolis, MD on 4 June 1936 . Following a successful carrier as captain of the submarine USS Flasher during World War II and credited for sinking the most Japanese tankers during the war (Navy Cross, Silver Star and Presidential Citation), he retired after a

heart attack in September 1947. Afterwards he attended the University of Virginia where he successfully became a lawyer.

He wrote his war memoirs together with Lydel Sims titled "War Fish", in the same sense as "War Birds", and was published in 1958. In 1964 he was chosen as Democrat Representative for the 89th Congress for the State of Tennessee. In 1967 he lost his seat but continued to work in Memphis as a lawyer until his retirement. George William Grider died on 20 March 1991. He was 78.

no photograph available

HAJEK Joseph
Private, Co. L, 148th Infantry Regiment, 37th Division
DOW 1 November 1918
Wall of Missing
Army Serial Number 2832374

Joseph Hajek was born in Serabov, Bohemia on 18 March 1893. He was the son of Frank and Rose Hajek, who emigrated to the U.S.A. and settled in Pennsylvania. They had five other children: Marie, Bessie, John, Frank and Anna. Joseph was employed as a mechanic at the Westinghouse Electric Co.

Joseph was inducted on 27 May 1918 and received his basic training with the 161st Depot Brigade at Camp Grant, IL. After a brief training period he was attached to Co D, 344th Infantry Regiment, 86th (Black Hawk) Division. On 3 October, shortly after their arrival in Europe, the division was disbanded and the men sent as replacements to other divisions.

Joseph died of wounds caused by the impact of a mortar shell. Shell fragments had lodged in the kidney area. Due to the ongoing attack on the opposite bank of the river Scheldt, they were unable to bring him behind the lines to a casualty clearing station. He succumbed to his wounds four hours later. He was buried with his identification tags in Isolated Grave #4 near the village of Nederename. In 1919 his remains, together with those of Otto Madary and Carey Bavis, were moved to Waregem.

There was confusion during the exhumation process and transportation to Cemetery #1252 in Waregem. Somehow the identification tags did not correspond with the remains of Carey Bavis and Joseph Hajek. As a result, Joseph Hajek is buried at Flanders Field Cemetery as "Known but to God".

Studying the Bavis file and comparing it with a 1925 report, there is a strong possibility that Joseph is buried in Plot A – Row 03 – Grave 03.

HART Daniel A.
Private 1st Class, Co. B, 106th Infantry Regt., 27th Division
KIA 1 September 1918
Wall of Missing
Army Serial Number 1206701

Daniel Hart (°1893) was the son of Daniel and Elizabeth Hart from Brooklyn, NY. His father was a Lieutenant at the Bath Beach Police Station in Brooklyn. Daniel was a company clerk at the time he volunteered with the 14th Infantry Regiment of the New York National Guard on 9 June 1916. He served with the "14th" along the Mexican border during the Pancho Villa uprising.

His parents wished for his remains to be repatriated to the U.S. Unfortunately Daniel could not be positively identified. He was supposedly buried at Lyssenthoek Military Cemetery. In that case he would be one of the men buried as Known but to God. His mother visited the Flanders Field cemetery in 1931. She was 62 years of age.

HOCHFELDER Samuel J.
Private, Co. L, 106th Infantry Regiment, 27th Division
KIA 28 August 1918
Wall of Missing
Army Serial Number 1208812

Samuel Hochfelder was born in January 1899. He was the son of Louis and Rose Hochfelder, Jewish - Hungarian immigrants. They had five children: Helen, Tessie, Samuel, Julia and Edith. The family lived in the Bronx, NY. Samuel volunteered with the 23rd Infantry Regiment New York National Guard on 7 June 1917.

On Sunday 1 September at 10 a.m., he became the victim of a "direct hit". He was mutilated beyond recognition. As the attack was ongoing there was no time for burial and his comrades pulled him in a shell crater. His remains were never recovered. He was only 19 years of age and so one of the youngest men memorialized at the cemetery.

His mother was scheduled to take part in the Gold Star Mothers Pilgrimage in July 1931 but due to a sudden illness was unable to participate. Fortunately she was able to reschedule and take part the following year. She was 58 years of age at the time.

HOLTZMAN Sol
Private 1st Class, Co. F, 148th Infantry Regt. 37th Division
KIA 4 November 1918
Wall of Missing
Army Serial Number 1757684

Sol Holtzman was born in Shaki (Sakiai), formerly Russia now Lithuania, on 15 March 1888. The majority of the population in Shaki was of the Jewish faith. It is unknown when he emigrated to the United States but at the time war was declared he was living with his two brothers and sisters in Rochester, NY. Until 1915 he had a clothes store in Penn Yan, NY but then returned to his family in Rochester to start another business.

Sol was 30 years of age when he was called to arms on 28 April 1918. He received his basic training with the 153rd Depot Brigade and later attached to the 148th Infantry Regiment at Camp Lee, VA. He was promoted to Private 1st Class on 28 October 1918. A letter by Lieutenant Wesley Morris Jr. described the circumstances of his death: *"Company F was entrenched in a railroad cut near the town of Heuvel when the German heavy artillery, located near Gent, laid a heavy barrage on our lines. During this barrage a shell struck near the shelter of Private Holtzman, killing him instantly and wounding a comrade who was near him. He must of died of shock because I could not find a mark on him when I went to him. His grave is located near the town of Heuvel. Private Holtzman was always ready for any duty. His specialty was rifle grenades and he had no equal in our company. My boys are more than comrades of mine. I was talking to Private Holtzman on the afternoon of November 4th. He expressed a desire to visit his parents before returning to the United States after the war. I am proud to have had him as one of my company. No man ever served his country more faithfully."*

Photo insert: photo's of Sol's Rochester and New York WW1 medals.

JETT Richard L.
Captain, Medical Reserve Corps – Attached B. E. F.
KIA 13 April 1918
Wall of Missing

Richard Lawrence Jett was born in Jett, Woodford County, KY on 15 February 1885. He was the youngest in the family of William and Sarah Jett (née Coleman) and lived in Duckers (also known as Jett Station). He had three brothers and three sisters. Richard was an exemplary student and loved by all. Of *"Kid"* (as he was called being the youngest) was said: *"to know him is to love him",* as he had the gift of doing and saying the right thing at all times. He attended the Jefferson Medical College of Thomas Jefferson University, Philadelphia and graduated in 1907. He practiced at the Babies Dispensary and Hospital in Cleveland, OH. One said of him: *"Friendly, humble Dick, whose greatest pride was to bring each baby into this world without them experiencing the slightest fear."*

Richard was working as a doctor In 1914 when war was declared on Germany. He applied for a passport on 13 February 1915 and volunteered to serve with the allies. Serving as a surgeon during the British-Serbian campaign he was awarded the Order of Saint Sava (of which only nineteen were awarded during the war) and the Serbian Red Cross medal.

When the U.S.A. declared war, he was called into active service with the A.E.F. as a Captain in the Army Medical Corps on 24 May 1917. He sailed for France on 16 June 1917.

He was killed somewhere between the towns of Bailleul and Nieppe, France, while serving with the 102nd Field Ambulance which was attached to the 22nd Northumberland Fusiliers (B.E.F.). His remains were never found.

His foreign awards are not listed next to his name on the Wall of Missing. He is also the only known individual memorialized at Flanders Field whose family received the Victory Medal.

Following page:
Photo 1: Richard in the four stages of his life.
Photo 2: Richard (standing fifth from left) on leave somewhere in France.

no photograph available

KOHLER Louis
Private, Co. K, 148th Infantry Regiment, 37th Division
KIA 4 November 1918
Wall of Missing
Army Serial Number 1765223

Louis Kohler was born in Hackensack, NJ on 28 March 1889. He was the son of Mary Kohler Beyer from Meriden, CT, who had emigrated from Germany at a very young age. Louis worked as an agricultural laborer on a farm in New Brunswick, NJ.

He was called to arms on 3 April and received his basic training with the 153rd Depot Brigade at Camp Dix, NJ. On 23 April he was attached to the 310th Infantry Regiment, 78th (Lightning) Division. This division was formed with conscripts from New Jersey, New York and Delaware. Just before he sailed for Europe he was reassigned to the 148th Infantry Regiment.

He fought at the Argonne where he was listed as missing on 27 September. He was later found in a field hospital on 1 October being treated on the effects of gas. He returned to his unit on 18 October just in time to make the transfer to Belgium. He died of wounds on 4 November and was buried near the village of Heurne the following day. His emergency address was listed with Fred Baird, a friend, and strangely enough not with his mother who also lived in New Brunswick.

Louis, William Mundes, Albert Schultz and William McVerry were moved to Waregem in 1919. During the identification process there was evidently a mix up with identity discs and William Mundes was the only one they were able to positively identify on the account of the specific details of his injuries. Louis Kohler, Albert Schulz and William McVerry are buried at Flanders Field cemetery as "Known but to God".

Mary was 67 years of age when she visited Flanders Field cemetery with the Gold Star Mothers Pilgrimage in 1932 (photo insert).

LAING Harvey E.
Private, Co. L, 106th Infantry Regiment, 27th Division
KIA 3 September 1918
Wall of Missing
Army Serial Number 2038147

Harvey E. Laing was born in Saginaw, MI on 6 July 1886. He was the son of John H. Laing (a Scottish immigrant) and Alice A. Parks. He had one sister, Grace. Harvey lived in Saginaw all his life. At the time he was called to arms on 30 March 1918 he was working as a packer at the Central Warehouse Co. (see draft registration card)

He commenced his basic training with the 160th Depot Brigade. On 5 April he was transferred to the Replacement Training Organization at Camp Gordon, GA followed by the 10th Provisional Company, which was part of the 102nd Ammunition Train of the 27th Division on 6 June. His final transfer on 5 August brought him to Co. L. He was killed instantly by shell fragments near the village of Wijtschaete on 1 September. He was mutilated beyond recognition. The official date of death of 3 September was made by administrative deliberation.

Harvey is also memorialized on the World War I monument in Saginaw.

no photograph available

LARSON John L.
Private 1st Class Co. K, 106th Infantry Regt. 27th Division
KIA 2 September 1918
Wall of Missing
Army Serial Number 1208594

John Leonard Larson was born in New York in 1898. He was the son of John and Ina Larson, who were Swedish immigrants. He had one brother: Clarence (°1899), and four sisters; Florence (°1900), Anna (°1904), Selma (°1906) and Ruth (°1909). The family lived in Brooklyn, NY.

John enlisted with the 14th Infantry Regiment New York National Guard on 4 May 1917. He was barely 19 years of age. He was killed near Vierstraat. Many men of the 106th were killed and went missing in the vicinity on this day. Some were found and identified, others were never found. Many names on the Wall of Missing were serving with this regiment.

Florence named her oldest son after him.

LEHMANN Peter
Private, Co. E, 106th Infantry Regiment, 27th Division
KIA 2 September 1918
Wall of Missing
Army Serial Number 1207486

Peter Lehmann was born in December 1895. He was the son of Frederick and Emma Lehmann from Brooklyn, NY. Besides Peter there were three children; Sophia, William and Pauline. He enlisted with the 23rd Infantry Regiment, New York National Guard on 19 July 1917.

In his last letter home he wrote that he had been wounded during the attack and at the same time his fountain pen had broken. He was killed as so many others during the fighting near Vierstraat.

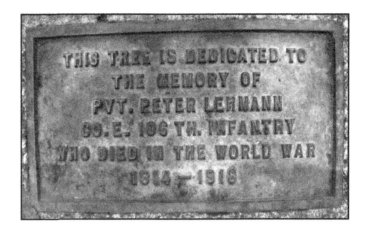

On the Eastern Parkway in Brooklyn, trees were planted in memory of those soldiers killed from Brooklyn. They also received a memorial marker, one of them was dedicated to Peter Lehmann.

McGEEHIN Richard J.
Corporal, Co. I, 106th Infantry Regiment, 27th Division
KIA 2 September 1918
Wall of Missing
Army Serial Number 1208304

Richard McGeehin was from Brooklyn, NY and was born in 1878. His parents were Richard and Bridget McGeehin (née Curley). He had one brother, John and four sisters, Elizabeth, Catherine Ellen (Kitty), Mary and Anna Rose. His father was a veteran of the Civil War and had served with the 14th Infantry Regiment of Brooklyn at Gettysburg.

The story of Richard McGeehin is one of many unsolved mysteries. He enlisted on 2 May 1898 at the age of 19 and was mustered in the 47th Infantry New York National Guard a few weeks later. He went missing between 15 and 22 July. On trial he was sentenced to 14 days hard labor, leaving the service in March the following year. He had no current address in Brooklyn and was 40 years of age at the time he was killed. When the U.S. declared war on Germany, Richard re-enlisted with the 47th Infantry Regiment NY National Guard on 26 June 1917. His emergency address was listed with James Keenan (brother-in-law) in Brooklyn.
Richard was married but no details on his spouse were found in the files at the National Archives besides the fact that she had remarried.

He had a registered field grave with others killed from his unit at the crossroads between Vierstraat and York Road. It is unknown how he went missing.

McLAUGHLIN Joseph F.

Private, Co. D, 105th Infantry Regiment, 27th Division
KIA 2 September 1918
Wall of Missing
Army Serial Number 1204061

Joseph *"Joe"* McLaughlin was the son of Patrick McLaughlin. He was born in Schenectady, NY in July 1899. He had two brothers, Stephen and Eugene and two sisters Harriet (photo insert in uniform) and Sarah. The family later moved to Troy, NY. He was a well-known basketball and baseball player in Troy. He enlisted with the 2nd Infantry Regiment New York National Guard on 27 May 1917 .

Joseph was a machine gunner. He was shot through the head and killed instantly. He is one of the youngest soldiers memorialized at Flanders Field.

McMAHON Clarence

Mechanic, Co. M, 145th Inf. Regiment, 37th Division
KIA 2 November 1918
Wall of Missing
Army Serial Number 1519993

Clarence McMahon was born in Canton, IL in 1894. His parents were John and Laura McMahon (née Anderson) and he had two older brothers: Leo and Frank. For six years he worked as a machine operator. However, as a talented musician he moved to Cincinnati, OH where he attended the Academy of Music for piano in 1916. It was from here that he registered for military service with the National Guard on 7 July 1917. He received his basic training with the 62nd Depot Brigade and in October he was attached to the 145th Infantry Regiment as a mechanic.

He was killed near the village of Kruishoutem. His remains were reinterred in plot B, grave #50 in Waregem in 1919. During the identification process for repatriation in 1922, the grave contained no remains. He could also not be identified with other unknown remains.

no photograph available

McMAHON William

Private, Co. C, 106th Infantry Regiment, 27th Division
KIA 31 August 1918
Wall of Missing
Army Serial Number 2671370

William McMahon was an immigrant from Tullamore, Ireland. He arrived at Ellis Island on 26 September 1909. He was called to arms on 6 April 1918 and received his basic training with the 3rd Company, 12th Provisional Battalion, 152nd Depot Brigade. Less than one month later he was attached to the 106th Infantry Regiment.

The circumstances of William's death are unknown. Although he is memorialized on the Wall of Missing he is buried in the cemetery as "Known but to God". Details in his burial file shows that he was buried at Lyssenthoek Cemetery in Poperinge. During the exhumation process the following was noted; *"Bodies of unknowns in graves 5,17,29,30 Lyssenthoek exhumed 12 August 1920. No possible means of ID as 3 of 4 have no head."*

His great nephew, Frank McMahon, visited the cemetery with his son Tom on Memorial Day 2013 (photo insert)

no photograph available

McVERRY William
Private, Co. K, 148th Infantry Regiment, 37th Division
KIA 4 November 1918
Wall of Missing
Army Serial Number 2414618

William McVerry was born in Washington DC on 12 November 1893. He was the son of Owen and Mary Jane McVerry, Irish immigrants living in Upper Marlboro, MD. William had four brothers (James, Owen, Michael and John) and three sisters (Annie, Anna and Mary).

At the time William was called to register for the draft he lived in Kent, DE. He was called to arms on 31 March 1918 and received his basic training with the 153rd Depot Brigade. He was attached to the 148th Infantry Regiment on 10 June.

William was killed near the village of Heurne on 4 November and buried the following day in Nederzwalm-Hermelgem. One of his identification tags had been nailed to the temporary marker as per standard operating procedures but after the war no remains were found in his grave. His parents had indicated their preference for repatriation and burial at Arlington National Cemetery. He is the only soldier from Delaware memorialized at the cemetery.

His mother visited the Flanders Field Cemetery with the Gold Star Mothers Pilgrimage in 1931. She was driven by car from Washington DC to NY where she joined "Party H" sailing for Europe on 24 June. She had continuing health issues caused by nerves before visiting the cemetery. Her first visit was on 7 July. Her medical file indicated that she wept bitterly after her visit. Her condition gradually improved and on 25 July Mary was back home.

MAGNUSON Albert G.
Private, Co. L, 148th Infantry Regiment, 37th Division
KIA 2 November 1918
Wall of Missing
Army Serial Number 3337081

Albert Sven Gustav Magnuson (photo late teens-early twenties) was the son of Gustav Nathaniel and Augusta Magnuson (née Swensdotter–photo insert right), who were Swedish immigrants. He was born in Minneapolis, MN on 22 October 1892 and grew up on an 80-acre dairy farm in Rossburg, Aitkin County, MN. He had five sisters: Edith °1890, Florence °1895, Hazel °1898, Myrtle °1900 and Beatrice °1905 and one brother Bernard °1902. (photo insert left taken about 1900 – Albert standing far left).

Albert was drafted with 76 other men from Aitkin County in June 1918. His first day of military service was 26 June 1918. He received his basic training with the 161st Depot Brigade in Camp Grant, IL and later assigned to the 344th Infantry Regiment, 86th (Black Hawk) Division. Soon after their arrival in Europe the division was disbanded and all men reassigned as replacements to other divisions. Albert was attached to the 148th Infantry Regiment, 37th Division on 6 October 1918 and moved into Belgium on the 18th. On 29 October the Division moved to the front in preparation for the attack which started at 05:30 on October 31ˢᵗ.

Albert was probably killed by shell fire while crossing the river Scheldt. His remains were never found. Witness statements by different men of his company basically all confirm the same.

One account by Sergeant Lon Huffman from Lewistown, OH dated 25 January 1926 stated: " ...he was killed crossing the Escaut (Scheldt) river in Belgium on Nov. 2, 1918. He was hit by shrapnel from a German 77 gun. I know nothing concerning his burial place as the burial detail had not reported it to the company."

Herold A. Jorgenson from La Crosse, WI, who was with Albert from the time they were training at Camp Grant, stated: "……He was a nice quiet fellow or in other words sensible and I had many a good talk with him. About the 5ᵗʰ or 6ᵗʰ of November I met some boys in a little town in Belgium who had been transferred in the same company as Magnuson and told me that Magnuson had been drowned going across some bridge which had been hit by a bomb or shell."

Magnuson family home, Rossburg, MN early 20ᵗʰ century – Albert is third from left.
(all photographs courtesy of James Earl Green, Wauwatosa, Wisconsin, USA)

MANDAK Matias
Cook, Co. K, 106th Infantry Regiment, 27th Division
KIA 2 September 1918
Wall of Missing
Army Serial Number 1208482

Matias Mandak was born in Miloňovice, a part of Bohemia, now Czech Republic, on 10 March 1888. His mother was Jana Mandak. He was 23 years of age when he emigrated to the USA in 1908. His sister Mary and brother Joseph emigrated at the same time. He found a job as machinist in Bay Shore, NY. He joined the 23rd Infantry Regiment, New York National Guard on 29 June 1917. During his basic training at Camp Wadsworth he was admitted into hospital with measles in January 1918.

He was killed in action near Kemmel (Ypres) and buried where he fell. Both his identification tags were found in his burial file at the National Archives. Although his name is memorialized on the Wall of the Missing, there is the possibility that he is buried in Flanders Field American Cemetery as a soldier "Known but to God".

MICHAEL John J.
Private 1st Class, Co. K, 106th Infantry Regt. 27th Division
KIA 2 September 1918
Wall of Missing
Army Serial Number 1208518

John Jacob Michael (actually Michel) was the son of Stephen and Elizabeth Michel (German immigrants) from New York City. He was born in April 1895 and had an older brother (Ludwig) and two younger sisters (Mathilda and Magdaline). At 23, he enlisted with the 23rd Infantry Regiment New York National Guard (Brooklyn) on 23 May 1917.

He was killed by a direct hit near Kemmel. The incident is described in O'Ryan's History of the 27th Division: *"he was blown to pieces in a dugout explosion"*.

His mother took part with the Gold Star Mothers Pilgrimage in 1931 with an unusual request. As her son was missing she requested to visit the grave of an unknown soldier at the American cemetery in Suresnes near Paris. She also requested permission to visit family and relatives in Ludwigshafen near Mannheim, Germany at her own expense. Permission was granted on both accounts.

MORGAN Harold S. - Military Cross (B.E.F.)
1st Lieutenant, Medical Reserve Corps
Attached British Expeditionary Force
KIA 12 April 1918
Wall of Missing

Harold Sydney Morgan was born on 2 May 1890 in Winton, PA. He was the son of Davy Morgan and Ellen Shaefer (Welsh immigrants) who had five children (photo): standing from left to right: Jeannette and Mabel. Victor, Gwladys and Harold below. Harold was a doctor and had graduated from Stanford Medical as one of the first of his class. He was selected by Wilfred Grenfell to help with his

missions in Labrador. Grenfell was a well-known missionary doctor who set up hospitals, orphanages and other social services. Afterwards, Harold worked at the Bellevue Hospital in New York City. He was engaged to Margaret Sanborn (inset photograph) from Redlands, CA. Shortly afterwards, his address was in Vancouver Barracks, WA, where he is mentioned on the Honor Roll. Additionally he is also mentioned on the Honor Roll in San Diego, CA. He was the first man from this city to be killed in action. The High School of San Diego is named after him: the Harold Sydney Morgan Memorial High School.

Before the U.S. declaration of war, Harold was serving with the Medical Reserve Corps. His active service began on August 9, 1917. He set foot in France in November 1917 and was instructed to report to the British 36th (Ulster) Division. He was assigned to an Advanced Dressing Station two kilometers behind the front. By the end of the year, he was already a Battalion Medical Officer with the 9th Royal Irish Rifles.

On March 21st, his unit became heavily involved in the fighting around St Quentin (Seraucourt-le-Grand). Around him he saw how three battalions were almost completely disseminated. It was during these battles that he was awarded the British Military Cross for conspicuous bravery: *"For conspicuous gallantry and devotion to duty during the retirement from Grand Seraucourt, on the morning of March 22nd. This officer was retiring behind the rear-guard, and on approaching Artemps, was told that some wounded were still lying in Grand Seraucourt. Although he knew that the enemy was already on the outskirts of the village, he returned at once with some stretcher bearers and succeeded in bringing out the wounded. He thus at the commencement of the operations set a splendid example to his stretcher bearers of devotion and courage."*

In 1919, Harold Hays*, a Major in the Medical Corps, A.E.F., wrote a book about his war experiences titled " *Cheerio* ". He dedicated the book to Harold Morgan, who had been his best friend and with whom he had shared many gruesome experiences from November 1917 through 1918. He described Harold as being a big cheerful man, always smiling with red cheeks. The book contains a letter from Harold to Hays. The letter was written on March 19th, two days before the battles of Seraucourt-le-Grand. Morgan wrote that he was pleased about the appointment of Major Hays. "*The Germans are very quiet*" he wrote, and he hoped that one week later he would be on leave in England. He was glad that he had been assigned to the field and not to a Base Hospital in the rear. However, Harold never went on leave. Instead he volunteered to replace a fellow doctor, who was suffering from shell shock.

On 12 April, the 9th Royal Irish Rifles were fighting in the village of Messines, Belgium. Harold and two stretcher bearers were tending the wounded on the battlefield when a shell exploded close by. A shell fragment had lodged in Harold's back. While one of the stretcher bearers administered first aid a second blast completely buried the other. Harold was now fatally wounded and died shortly afterwards. He was killed just one month before his 29th birthday. Syd was buried north of the road from Messines to Wulvergem.

After the war his remains were not found, or at least they were not positively identified. There were remains of an unknown (X2933) which was suspected to be Harold's but there was no 100% certainty. The family could not accept this and his sisters Gwladys and Jeanette travelled to Europe in August 1922. They searched for his grave in vain. In January 1923, disappointed and weary, they returned to the United States.

OTT Ferdinand W.

Private, Co. B, 106th Infantry Regiment, 27th Division
KIA 2 September 1918
Wall of Missing
Army Serial Number 1206822

Ferdinand Wilhelm Ott was born in Michigan in August 1897. He was the son of Robert and Johanna Ott (née Weisinger), German immigrants. The family moved to Brooklyn and Ferdinand joined the 23rd Infantry Regiment New York National Guard on 2 September 1917. He had previously served with the Navy and had received an honorary discharge. He was killed one year to the day after joining the service. His brother, Sergeant Charles Ott, also served with the 51st Pioneer Infantry, Army of Occupation, in Germany in 1919.

PETERSEN Clarence W.

Private, Co. M, 148th Infantry Regiment, 37th Division
DOW 4 November 1918
Wall of Missing
Army Serial Number 3333809

Clarence William Petersen was born in Minneapolis, MN on 14 October 1888. He was the son of Peter and Larzina Anna Petersen (née Larsen), who were Norwegian immigrants. He had two sisters (Tillie and Bessie) and two brothers (Gustav and Walter). At the time he registered for the draft he was employed as a photo engraver with the Twin City Engraving Company. In 1912 Peter built his own home where Clarence also lived (photo insert) until he married Carrie Gibbons from Boone, IA on 30 June 1913.

Clarence was called to arms on 22 June 1918 and received his basic training with the 161st Depot Brigade at Camp Grant in Rockford, IL. He was then transferred to the 344th Infantry Regiment, 86th Division. Upon arrival in Europe the division was disbanded and Clarence was sent as a replacement with the 148th Infantry Regiment.

Corporal Hollister Sage of Co. M, 148th Infantry provided the following eye witness account: *"It was on the night of November 4th and I was detailed to report to the 145th Infantry. On my way I heard a voice and upon investigating discovered it was Clarence Petersen in a trench with a broken leg. As I could not stop to take him back I promised to stop on the way back. I gave him a canteen of water and started my errand but was taken prisoner by the Germans but lucky enough to escape. Could not get back to Clarence as Germans had taken up the position. He was still alive when last seen by me but in weak condition."*

1916 to 1918 were dramatic years for the family. Carrie passed away in 1916 and was buried with Clarence's parents. His mother Anna died In 1917 and then Clarence in 1918. Peter requested that his remains be repatriated to the U.S.A. It is unknown why the remains of Clarence were never recovered. According to the Minnesota Gold Star Roll database, he was killed near the hamlet of "Raasbosch" and buried on the spot.

The American Legion erected a cenotaph in memory of Clarence at the Victory Memorial Drive in Minneapolis, MN. (photo below)

POSNANSKY Morris
Private 1st Class, Co. B, 106th Infantry Regt. 27th Division
KIA 2 September 1918
Wall of Missing
Army Serial Number 2671641

Morris Posnansky was born in Petrograd, Russia on 5 March 1895. His parents were Abraham and Rosa Posnansky. He had one brother, Max and one sister, Rebecca. The family emigrated to the U.S.A. in 1906 and Morris was employed as a tailor in New York City. He was inducted on 5 April 1918 and received his basic training with the 152nd Depot Brigade, later serving as a tailor with the 106th Infantry Regiment.

A statement made by James Williams who was serving in the same unit: *"He was killed at Dikkebus on 2 September before he went into the lines. He used to be a tailor in our company. I didn't see him killed but some of the boys told me about it. He was hit by machine gun fire and shrapnel and died a few minutes later. I don't know where he was buried "*

It is uncertain if his remains were ever found amongst the number of unknowns disinterred. One record indicated that during a deduction process it was assumed that Morris had been interred at Lyssenthoek with grave location XXXII.D.23. However, a positive identification could never be made as his head was missing.

His mother Jennie declined the invitation for the Gold Star Mothers Pilgrimage on grounds of saving money for the government as she had no marker to visit. On the other hand she was willing to accept the pilgrimage if she could stop off in Dublin, Ireland for the marriage of her son who was studying medicine at the University of Dublin. Other documents found indicated their request being for 14 days in Dublin and 5 days in Leipzig, Germany. It is unknown if the Government approved or declined her request.

SCHULTZ Albert E. W.

Private, Co. K, 148th Infantry Regiment, 37th Division
KIA 1 November 1918
Wall of Missing
Army Serial Number 3747848.

Albert Ernest William Schultz was the son of August and Augusta Schultz (née Hammelman) from Lewis, WI. He was born in Stillwater, MN on 6 April 1892. He had three half-brothers and a half-sister from his father's previous marriage (William, Frank, Joseph and Pearl). When his father married Augusta they had seven more children: five boys (Albert, August, Alfred, Henry and Theodore) and two girls (Emily and Agnes). Albert was a bashful, sensitive and a quiet man who had never left home and worked as an agricultural laborer on the family farm. He wept bitterly when on 23 June he had to leave home to join the forces. After one month  of basic training at Camp Grant, IL, he was attached to the 344th Infantry Regiment, 86th Black Hawk Division. Upon arrival in Europe the division was disbanded and Albert was sent as a replacement with the 148th Infantry Regiment.

There was no eye witness account of Albert's death and no grave was ever found after hostilities ended. There were no chaplain's nor searchers reports available and sketches and communal lists did not show his name. Soldiers killed on 1 November from the same unit were originally buried in isolated graves and then reburied in cemetery 1252. Dental information compared with the unknowns did not check favorably. His mother could not get over the loss of her son. Replying to the invitation to join the Gold Star Mothers Pilgrimage she replied: "....I do not think I could stand the trip but would like to know if it would be possible to get a picture of the grave of said deceased or a picture of the entire cemetery." The government replied that it would be possible but that a fee would most likely be charged.

Polk County (where Albert originated from) provides an illustration on the causes of death within the American army. 63 men never returned from the war, 43 of them died from complications of the Spanish flu.

SEERY William F.
Private 1st Class, Co. L, 106th Infantry Regt. 27th Division
KIA 28 August 1918
Wall of Missing
Army Serial Number 1208754

William Seery was born in Manhattan, NY in September 1896. He was in Federal Service in 1916 at the time war was declared. He enlisted with the 14th Infantry Regiment New York National Guard on 30 April 1917 and was transferred to Company L, 106th Infantry on 18 October. His point of contact in case of an emergency was with his father, Peter S. Seery in Brooklyn, New York. He also had a sister, Mrs J. Garbarin, living in Keyport, NJ.

The following witness statement was provided by Sergeant Lyman Ceely of same company which indicates that William was killed on 31 August versus 28 August as inscribed on the Wall of Missing: *"William Seery was killed in action on Saturday 31 August 1918 about 7 P.M. by a direct hit that mutilated his body beyond recognition. This happened close to where Ralph Elrose was killed. Likewise no burial or grave to my knowledge for reasons as explained above"*

His burial file at NARA indicated *"blown to pieces by artillery"*. As such it can be safely ascertained that no remains were ever found.

There was initially some confusion and mystery around another Private 1st Class William F. Seery (Army Serial number: 1216389) who also served overseas with the 106th Machine Gun Battalion from 10 May 1918 through 18 March 1919. However he received his honorary discharge on 2 April 1919. There is also a mystery connected to a Private John W. Seery (Army Serial nr: 12100924) of the 107th Infantry who was killed in action near Guillemont Farm (Somme, France) and who at the time had a known grave (photo insert right). In his case there is no further record of burial or listing as missing.

SILCOX Jessie L.

Private, Co. M, 363rd Infantry Regiment, 91st Division
DOW 2 November 1918
Wall of Missing
Army Serial Number 3172735

Jessie Lee Silcox was born in Stratton, Dickenson County, VA on 4 September 1893. His parents were Joseph and Laura Silcox (née Ball). Besides Jessie there were twelve other children: Lorenzo, James, William, Joseph, Charles, Henry, Crawford, Rufus, Winfield, Luther, Nancy and Elihu.

Jessie was called to arms in Clintwood, VA on 24 May 1918 and received his basic training at Camp Lee, VA with the 155th Depot Brigade attached to the 303rd Infantry Regiment, 76th Division. He sailed for Europe on the USS Madawaska on 6 August and disembarked at Brest, France on the 21st. Upon arrival in Europe the division was disbanded and Jesse was first reassigned to Headquarters Company of the 91st Division and later to the 363rd Infantry Regiment.

During the first day of the attack he was a member of a thirteen troop detail on a scouting mission enquiring with a local farmer where the Germans were located. The following day the farmer found the bodies of five Americans together with a number of Germans on his land. He buried them on the spot. The five Americans were George Bulaich, Alva Diver, Edward Smith, Orlindo Giunchi and a fifth unidentified man from Company M. As Jessie is the only man from Company M, 91st Division memorialized on the Wall of Missing, the only possible explanation is that they could not positively identify him as both identification tags had been

removed from the body. (They were found in his burial file at the National Archives). Another plausible explanation is that there was confusion during transportation from the isolated grave to the cemetery. Being attached as a replacement to the 91st Division he was also new and unfamiliar with his comrades in arms. As the four other victims are buried in plot A, row 4 there is a strong possibility that Jessie is buried in the same row as "Known but to God".

The Veterans of Foreign Wars Post in Clinchco, VA was named after him.

Jessie is standing far left. We can also see two of his nephews: David Silcox standing second from right and kneeling far right in the second row Leonard White (KIA 31 October 1918, interred at the Meuse Argonne Cemetery Plot C – Row 42 – Grave 14.)

SIMS Robert
Private, Co. E, 106th Infantry Regiment, 27th Division
KIA 2 September 1918
Wall of Missing
Army Serial Number 1207421

Robert Sims was the son of Simon and Annie Simmowitsky from Brooklyn, immigrants from Lithuania. He was born in New York City in December 1898. He had two brothers (George and Anton) and one sister (Annie). Annie died shortly after 1910 and Simon remarried. They had two more children (Elon Helen and Veronika). Simon Sr. passed away in 1915. Everyone in the family had a good job (accountants) or had graduated from business school. At the time the United States declared war on Germany, Robert was employed as a clerk and had married Adele Sims. It is plausible that he was a member of the Jewish faith.

Robert enlisted with the 47th Infantry Regiment New York National Guard on 13 June 1916. He wrote many letters home illustrating the difficulties he and his friends encountered. In his last letter he wrote that he couldn't wait to be confronted with the "Huns". He was killed near Vierstraat on 2 September. There were no witnesses and there was no record of burial.

SPIDLE Murray K.
1st Lieutenant, 17th Aero Squadron
KIA 3 August 1918
Wall of Missing

1st Lieutenant Murray Kenneth Spidle was born in Wilmot, OH on 28 August 1897 and later took residence in Massillon, OH. He was the only child of Leroy Clarence and Martha Spidle. In high school and college he was famous for his sporting abilities (football and athletics) and his eloquence during debating and discussion groups. He was also a member of the school choir.

Lieutenant Spidle entered the service from Mt. Union College, Alliance on 14 May 1917. He was first sent for training at Fort Harrison and it was from here that he volunteered for the aero service. On 15 August 1917 he was sent to Toronto, Canada and later Ft. Worth for extensive training. He was commissioned 1st Lieutenant on 11 January 1918 while attached to the 28th Aero Squadron. On 13 January he was transferred to the 17th (U.S. Pursuit) Aero Squadron.

He wrote many letters home depicting his eagerness for more action. He was frustrated of being stationed in a quiet sector. In his letter of 28 June 1918 he wrote: *"....I don't remember whether I told you about the Chinamen or not. They have a big flock of them here as a labor battalion and one night Fritz hit their billets with a bomb and killed a few of them and they retaliated by going over to the Hun prison camp and cutting the throats of an equal number they had killed. These Chinks are a very happy crowd........."*
On 30 June he wrote: *"My patrol went up 18,000 ft. and you can imagine how cold it is up there. We sighted one Hun formation of a whole squadron and as there were only five of us we let them pass by. We seldom see any stray Huns or small formation in this particular part of the line. We would take a formation three to one or something of that order but there were thirty at least in this gang so we let them pass. They bombed us pretty heavy the night before last and almost destroyed a nearby squadron. We got even with them yesterday."* In a third letter dated 5 July: *"Monday night my roomie and I went to the movies and just as we*

stepped outside we heard the siren and the hum of a Mercedes coming in the distance. All at once the motors stopped and I said to Desson "You and I are pretty lucky tonight as we are safe in town while the poor boys at the drome are getting theirs." Well I no sooner got that out my mouth when we heard the hiss of a bomb coming down. We jumped into a doorway as we heard the little old pill go "wonk" just up the street."

In one of his last letters he wrote how his plane had been damaged during a dogfight. The four letters were, ironically, published in the Evening Independent on Saturday 3 August

1918, the day he was killed in action. That day he went missing during a patrol with his squadron. Leonard Desson, his roommate and best friend wrote home to his parents: "*...he was last seen diving after a German plane with his Sopwith Camel E5159. From that time he had not been seen. We all figure his chances of being shot down were very small, as all through the fight none of the "Huns" was seen to open fire. We think that in diving his engine would not pick up again and he was forced to land.*" Apparently somewhere in the Diksmuide area he was flying too low and was hit by artillery fire. However Luitenant L. Beckmann (photo insert) of Jasta 56 claimed his victory on Murray and reported that he had seen him at 09:45 hours near Stadenberg, 2 km south of the town of Roeselare, and had shot him down. Although there were doubts within the allied lines, Luitenant Beckmann received official recognition of the kill. Murray nor his plane were ever found.

1st Lieutenant Murray K. Spidle was known for his courage and complete ignorance of fear. He had been shot down five times but kept on flying. He is memorialized on the Wall of Missing. Another pilot from his squadron also lies buried at Flanders Field Cemetery: George Glenn (Plot A - Row 03 - Grave 15).

The football team, Murray seated third from left.

no photograph available

WHALEY Austin R.
Private 1st Class, Co. L, 119th Infantry Regt. 30th Division
KIA 31 August 1918
Wall of Missing
Army Serial Number 1316763

Austin Rudie Whaley was born in March 1899. He lived with his parents William Whaley and Julia "Sophie" Garland (photo insert) in Model, TN. He had a sister Josephine who was three years older. William left Julia between 1900 and 1910 and Julia remarried Spurling Sills and gave birth to another daughter, Viola.

Austin was inducted with the 2nd Infantry Regiment of the National Guard in Dover, TN on 14 July 1917 and sailed for Europe on 12 May 1918. Eyewitness account of Private Joseph Moore, Co. L, 119th Infantry stated: *He was killed instantly by machine gun fire while attacking the Germans at Voormezele on 31 August 1918 and buried at Nine Elms "* He was only 19 years of age.

WISS Frank J.
Corporal, Co. K, 106th Infantry Regiment, 27th Division
KIA 1 September 1918
Wall of Missing
Army Serial Number 1208536

Frank (Franz) Joseph Wiss was born on 14 December 1890. He was the son of Emanuel and Marie Wiss, Swiss immigrants, from Brooklyn. They also had two daughters, Irma and Emily. He worked as a clerk for a local brewery at the time he enlisted with the 23rd Infantry Regiment of the New York National Guard on 30 July 1917. He served overseas from 10 May 1918 and was promoted to Corporal on 7 June.

Frank was originally buried at the crossroads of Vierstraat and York Road. His remains were moved to Lyssenthoek Cemetery however a positive identification could not be established as the case was with Joseph Beattie, Matias Mandak and Harry Cundy. These four men are definitely interred at Flanders Field Cemetery as "Known but to God".

Marie became severely depressed after receiving the notification of his death and was bedridden for many months. She was debating to join the Gold Star Mothers Pilgrimage to Europe in 1931. Marie was fully aware that her son had no known grave but she wanted to see his name on the Wall of Missing. Unfortunately she had a heart condition and felt unsafe to make the trip alone. Her request for her two daughters to accompany her was denied.

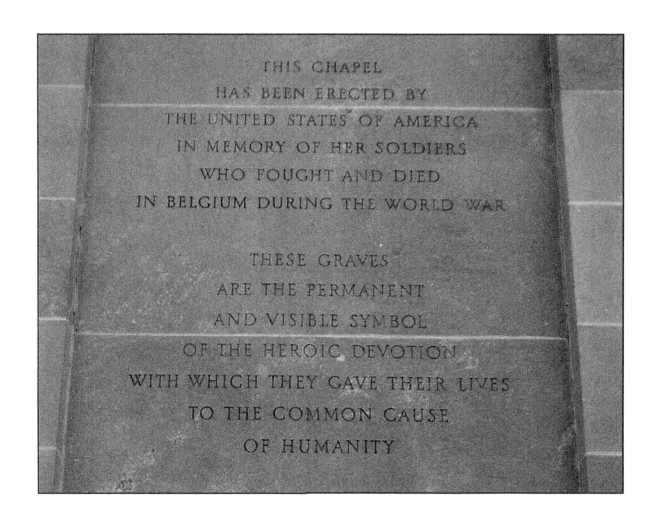

LYSSENTHOEK MILITARY CEMETERY

BEATTIE David S.
Sergeant HQ. Co, 105th Infantry Regiment, 27th Division
KIA 31 August 1918
C.W.G.C. Lyssenthoek Mil. Cemetery - Poperinge XXXII.G.15
Army serial number 1202774

David Stanley Beattie (°1896) was the only child of David Sr. and Isabel Beattie, 22 Hawthorne Avenue, Troy, NY. He graduated as one of the most popular students at Troy High School. He was manager and player of the school football team and also the school correspondent for the Troy Times. As a member of the debating society he was considered an excellent speaker. David Beattie was employed by the Manufacturers' Bank before enlisting with the National Guard.

He enlisted on 7 March 1916 and was mustered into Company A of the 2nd New York Infantry Regiment and sent to the Mexican border during the Pancho Villa uprising. There again he was admired for his pluck and fortitude shown on long hikes and his other assigned tasks. When the United States declared war on Germany he was sent for further training at Camp Wadsworth in Spartanburg, SC and attached to the 105th Infantry Regiment, 27th Division. On 6 May 1918 he was promoted to sergeant .

Sergeant David Beattie met his death on 31 August. An eyewitness report by Sergeant Myron Fayes of HQ Company stated: *"Sgt. Beattie met his death while on duty in a forward observation post in the Dickebusch Sector, Belgium. I had just called his attention to a party of Huns on a path near our field of vision and handed over the telescope to him when a high explosive shell burst directly in front of our post. A fragment of the shell cut through the top of the high parapet of the post and struck Sgt. Beattie over the left temple. He died less than an hour later in the First Aid Station, never regaining consciousness."* He was buried at Lyssenthoek Military Cemetery in Poperinge. In reply to the request on the choice of final disposition of remains their parents insisted that his remains not be disturbed. *"After much thought I have decided that our son remain where he now lies."* David is buried with a standard Commonwealth marker. His epitaph reads: *"He Lived By Faith – He Still Lives"*.

KING Harry A.
Private 1st Class, Troop F, 3rd Cavalry Regiment
DOD 20 September 1918
C.W.G.C. Lyssenthoek Mil. Cemetery - Poperinge XXXII.A.11
Army Serial Number 209559

Harry King was the son of John and Susan King from Stoke-on-Trent, England. He had four brothers (Ernest, George, Reginald and Lewis) and three sisters (Eva, Alice and Elian).

Four brothers emigrated to the U.S.A. in search of a better life. Only Lewis remained behind. Ernest was already in America in 1908. Harry, Reginald and George followed his footsteps in April 1914, the same year their father died. However when war broke out in Europe a few months later, "Reggy" decided to return to England to join the British Forces.

Harry King enlisted on 6 May 1917 and sailed with the 3rd Cavalry Regiment, A.E.F. in November 1917. This unit was crucial in transporting supplies, weapons and ammunition to the front.
Harry died of broncho pneumonia, which was one of the common complications of the Spanish flu, at Bourbonne les Bains, Haute-Marne, France on 20 September 1918.

Harry's mother initially requested that his remains be repatriated to Checkley in England where he would have been buried next to his father. Reginald (left insert) who had been serving with the Royal Army Service Corps had died of wounds the previous year on 17 October 1917 and was buried at C.W.G.C. Lyssenthoek British Military Cemetery in Poperinge (XXI.H.17). As the British Government didn't allow repatriation of remains, Susan, as an alternative option, requested Harry's remains be buried next to his brother at Lyssenthoek.

Harry's remains had already been processed and buried at the Meuse-Argonne American Cemetery in Romagne-sous-Montfaucon, France. Her request being granted, the A.G.R.S. exhumed Harry's remains on 21 October 1921 and reinterred Harry close to his brother at Lyssenthoek Cemetery (XXXII.A.11) on 2 December. He is the only American soldier from World War I who served with the Cavalry and buried in Belgium.

George (left) and Lewis (right) were also serving in the military. After America declared war, George joined the Canadian army. He survived unscathed, settled in New York City and as a tailor started his own business.

Gunner Lewis King had also joined the Canadian Army in 1916. He was attached to the Army Service Corps – Motor Transport and was later transferred to the Tank Corps. He also survived the war unscathed.

Below left, Harry's grave marker with the epitaph: *"The Best Of Sons And Brothers Also His Brother Reggie Buried Here Nearby"*. Reginald's epitaph reads: *"Thy Way Not Mine Oh Lord"*.

PIGUE James A.
1st Lieutenant Co. A, 117th Infantry Regiment, 30th Division
KIA 18 July 1918
C.W.G.C. Lyssenthoek Mil. Cemetery - Poperinge XXXII.E.09

Lieutenant James Aaron Pigue was born in Nashville, TN in October 1884 and was the only son of Edward and Fannie Pigue. They were devoted followers of the Baptist Church.

"Jim" was a charming young man who had set his mind on becoming a career soldier. He attended the Virginia Military Institute from 1901 to 1902. In 1904 he joined the U.S. Marine Corps and was sent for training to the Naval Academy in Annapolis. He was one of six men chosen by William C. Gorgas to accompany him on a special mission in the Panama canal zone. They were charged to find ways to improve the sanitary conditions for the people who were working there. They were able to eliminate all outbreaks of yellow fever in the region. His commanding officers were so impressed with James that he earned the "Panama Campaign badge". A year later he returned to the U.S.A. and was commissioned Lieutenant. The next four years he served on different assignments on both land and sea. One of his missions took him to the North Atlantic (Scout with the Atlantic Fleet) and another to the Mediterranean region. He received an honorary discharge with the Marine Corps in 1909 and was awarded two medals for exemplary service. He returned to civilian life in Nashville. His mother had passed away in 1912 and so leaving Jim and his father to cope on their own.

Jim was a patriot in heart and soul and believed in loyalty and duty to his country. When the rebellion broke out along the Mexican border in 1916, Jim immediately returned to service and was attached to the 1st Tennessee National Guard Regiment. He soon achieved the rank of 2nd Lieutenant. The regiment was sent to Texas where he was commissioned 1st Lieutenant, again receiving two medals for exemplary service. While in Texas he met and fell in love with Jane Weller. He married her much to the displeasure and against the will of his father. His father's premonitions would later turn out to be true.
After Mexico he returned with his regiment to Nashville and left the service to become a civilian again with his newly wed wife. It would turn out to be a short term engagement.

When the U.S.A. declared war on Germany in 1917, Jim immediately registered for service with the 1st Tennessee National Guard Regiment and was soon called for active service. He was sent with his regiment to Camp Sevier in Greenville, SC. Here his regiment became an artillery regiment. Jim preferred the infantry and requested a transfer. He was attached to the 3rd Tennessee National Guard Regiment which formed the base of the 117th Infantry Regiment of the 30th Division.

On 4 May 1918, he sailed for Europe leaving his wife and son, who he would never know. Upon arrival in Belgium the regiment was attached to the British Second Army. This Second Army had a shortage of officers and so while the rest of the 117th was engaged in training, Jim would be sent to command British or Australian artillery brigades. He had returned to his regiment on 15 July and was given command of a battalion. The following day the regiment was sent to the front where they took full responsibility of the "East Poperinghe Line". On 18 July Jim was shot through the heart by a sniper while on duty at an observation post. He was the first man of the Old Hickory Division killed in the war.

Everyone who knew him praised Jim for his courage and devotion to duty. Six days before he died he wrote a letter to his wife: *"We can't all be heroes and wear medals and get our names in the dispatches. But we can do our full duty and wear our medals on our heart."* Although his father disapproved of his marriage to Jane, he was very proud of the fact that *"my boy's heart was in the service of his country"*. When notification of his death was received, a church service was held in the local First Baptist Church which turned out to be too small for the occasion.

Jim was first buried at Gwalia British Cemetery but reinterred in the American plot at Lyssenthoek Cemetery in June 1919.

Jane and her baby returned to Ranger in Texas. When she received the request on final disposition of remains in 1920, she replied that Jim's remains not be disturbed under any circumstances. Jane remarried shortly after and neglected all future paperwork enquiries from the War Department. In order to complete the administrative formalities the Army contacted Jim's father.

Edward Pigue took the matter in his own hands and decided to sail for Europe to see his son's final resting place with his own eyes. He visited his son's grave with a delegation of the Imperial War Graves Commission in July 1921 and they assured him that the British Government would take care of the grave in perpetuity. Edward then made the final decision to leave his son's remains undisturbed. His epitaph reads: *"Gave His Life For Humanity"*.

James has a special memorial and life size statue in Mt. Olivet cemetery in Nashville TN. Facing him on his left you will find an image of his mother and on the right side that of his paternal grandmother.

At the foot of the memorial the inscription that says all: "We can't all be heroes and wear medals and get our names in the dispatches. But we can do our full duty and wear our medals on our hearts."

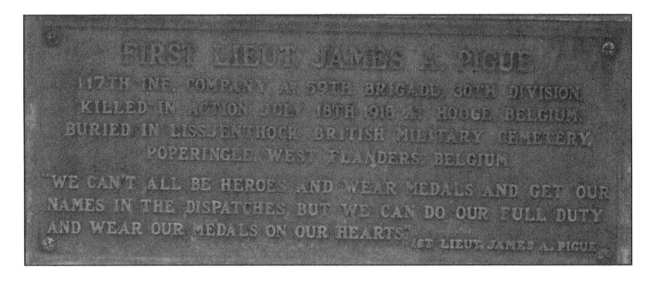

SELECTED BIBLIOGRAPHY

CHAPTER 1: THE BEGINNING

ANDRIESSEN, J.H.J. *De Andere Waarheid.(The Other Truth)* The French-British approach, p.23-27. Conflict in the Balkans, p. 42. Amsterdam: De Bataafsche Leeuw, 1998.

BROGAN, Hugh. *Longman History of the United States of America.* Chapter 19: The Progressive Adventure 1897-1914, p.448-452. New York. Harper Collins Publishers, 1986.

CHURCHILL, Winston. *The World Crisis 1911-1918.* Volume I, Chapter 1: Bismarck's precautions, p. 5-13. Chapter 2: The Admiralty Program 1909, p.23-26. Chapter 3: Crisis of Agadir 1911, p. 28-49. New York: Barnes & Noble, 1993.

FAY, Sidney Bradshaw. *Before Sarajevo-The Origins of the World War.* New York: Vol.1, Free Press, consulted on 12 June 2008, http://yamaguchy.netfirms.com/7897401/fay/origin_html

GEORGE, David Lloyd. *War Memoirs of David Lloyd George.* Volume I, Chapter I: The Brewing of the Storm, p. 1-47. London: Odhams Press, 1938.

JAMES, Lawrence. *The Rise and Fall of the British Empire.* Chapter 10: The Edwardian Empire and the People, p. 320-325. Chapter 11: The Empire and the Coming War, p. 334-349. New York: St. Martin's Press, 1994.

PIRENNE Henri. *Histoire de Belgique, Vol. 4.* Chapitre IV: A la veille de la guerre, p. 239-240. Bruxelles : La Renaissance du Livre, 1931.

TREVELYAN, George Macauley. *British History in the Nineteenth Century and After (1782-1919).* Chapter XXIII: The Franco-Prussian War, p. 360-362. Epilogue 1902-1919, Chapter III, The Ententes with France and Russia, p. 457-469. New York: Green & Co., 1937.

STRAUBING, Harold Elk, Editor. *The Last Magnificent War. Rare Journalistic and Eyewitness Accounts of World War I.* Introduction, xi. Part I: War's Crystal Ball, Germany and the Next War, General Friederich von Bernhardi (translated by Allen H. Powles), p. 3-17. New York: Paragon House, 1989.

TUCHMAN, Barbara. *The Canons of August.* Chapter 1: The Funeral, p. 11-18. Chapter 3: In the Shadow of Sedan, p. 39-40. Amsterdam: Agon BV., 1989.

CHAPTER 2: 1914 - 1917

BAKER, Ray Stannard. *Woodrow Wilson Life and Letters. Vol. 3. Governor 1910-1913.* Chapter VII: The Campaign of 1912, p. 390-412. Chapter VIII: The President Elect - Choosing his Cabinet, p. 437-443. London: William Heinemann Ltd., 1932.

BAKER, Ray Stannard. *Woodrow Wilson Life and Letters. Vol.6. Facing War 1915-1917.* Chapter V: Crisis in Wilson's Leadership, p. 118-176. Chapter VI: Facing Europe, p. 177-230. Chapter VII: Wilson's Campaign and Election in 1916, p. 231-301. Chapter VIII: Growth of Entanglement in the war, p. 302-347. Chapter IX: Renewed struggles for peace, p. 348-411. Chapter X: Appeal to the people of the waring Nations, p. 412-446. Chapter XI: The break with Germany, p. 447-485. Chapter XII: Accepting the inevitable - The Decision: War, p. 486-517. London: William Heinemann Ltd., 1932.

BROGAN, H. *Longman History of the United States of America.* Chapter 17: The Billion-Dollar Country 1865-1900: Immigration, p. 413-414. Chapter 19: The Progressive Adventure, p. 456. Chapter 20: The Education of Woodrow Wilson 1914-1921, p. 481-491. London: Longman Group Ltd., 1987.

CENTER OF MILITARY HISTORY. *American Armies and Battlefields in Europe.* Chapter I: The War before the entry of the United States, p. 1-9. Washington DC: ABMC, US Government Printing Office, 1992.

CHURCHILL, Winston. *The World Crisis 1911-1918.* Volume II, Chapter IX: The Intervention of the United States, p. 1120-1127. New York: Barnes & Noble, 1993.

GIBSON & WARD. *Courage Remembered. The History of the Commonwealth War Graves Commission.* Chapter 17: Miscellany - Cross of Sacrifice at Arlington National Cemetery, VA, USA, p. 208. London, HMSO., 1989.

JANSEN, Axel. *Individuelle Bewährung im Krieg - Amerikaner in Europa 1914-1917.* Kapitel 1: Einleitung - Der europäische Krieg verstärkt Spannungen in den USA, p. 11-12. Kapitel 9: Das amerikanischer Engagement in Deutschland, England und Belgien, p. 222-226. Kapitel 11: Die Kriegsfreiwilligen als "amerikanische Avantgarde", p. 283-299. Frankfurt: Campus Verlag, 2003.

O'LEARY, Cecilia Elizabeth. *To Die For.* Chapter 12: "My Country Right or Wrong" World War I and the Paradox of American Patriotism, p. 225. Princeton, NJ: Princeton University Press, 1999.

POHANKA, Brian. *Visit to the Western Front.* Part 1: Belloy-en-Santerre and NW. http://www.famouspoetsandpoems.com-/poets/alan_seeger/photo.

STRAUBING, Harold Elk, Editor. *The Last Magnificent War. Rare Journalistic and Eyewitness Accounts of World War I.* Part I: War's Crystal Ball - Germany and the Next War, General Friederich von Bernhardi (translated by Allen H. Powles). Part III: Propaganda - How We advertized America, George Creel, p. 109-125 . New York: Paragon House, 1989.

WILSON, Andrew. *A President's Love Affair with the Lake District, Woodrow Wilson's Second Home.* Chapter 9: President of Peace forced into War, p. 47-49. Windermere, Cumbria, UK: Lakeland Press Publisher, 1996.

CHAPTER 3: 1917 - 1918

CENTER OF MILITARY HISTORY UNITED STATES ARMY. *American Armies and Battlefields in Europe.* Chapter I: Organization of the American Expeditionary Forces and formation of its Combat Army, p. 15-19. Chapter XIV: Cumulative arrivals of American military personnel for the A.E.F., p. 502. Washington DC: The US Government Printing Office,1992.

CENTER OF MILITARY HISTORY: Historical Division Department of the Army. *United States Army in the World War 1917-1919.* AG. GHQ. AEF: 1841: Letter - "Proposal concerning transfer of American citizens from British Armies to the American Army", p. 37 and p. 47. Washington DC: US Government Printing Office, 1948.

COMMONWEALTH WAR GRAVES COMMISSION. *Report on the Commonwealth War Dead in Belgium with Home Town in the U.S.A.* Maidenhead UK: Records of the Commonwealth War Graves Commission, 1998.

GEORGE, David Lloyd. *War Memoirs of David Lloyd George.* Volume II, Chapter LXXIV: The Military Position - The Allied Strategy for 1918, p. 1628. Chapter LXXXI: The American Armies in France - Pershing suspicious of Allies, p. 1806. London: Odhams Press, 1938.

HOLMES, Oliver Wendell. *Never or Now: American War Ballads and Lyrics, a collection of the Colonial Wars, The Revolution, The War of 1812-15, the War with Mexico and the Civil War, Volume II.* p. 28. edited by George Cary Eggleston, New York: G.P. Putnam's Sons, The Knickerbocker Press, 1889.

THIELEMANS, Marie-Rose. *Albert I: Carnets et Correspondence de Guerre 1914 -1918.* (Albert I: Journal and Correspondence 1914-1918) 10 décembre 1917: Visite du général Pétain accompagné du général Anthoine, p. 332. Londres, 10 juillet 1918: Compte rendu d'un entretien avec les membres du War Committee, p. 483. La Panne, 14 aout 1918: Lettre au général Pershing, p. 493-494. Paris: éditions Duculot, 1991.

VANDEWEYER, Luc. *De Eerste Wereldoorlog Koning Albert en zijn Soldaten* (The First World War King Albert and his Soldiers) Chapter 15 : The Allied Offensive in Flanders, p.357 ; Chapter 16 : Armistice and Peace Treaty, p.372 ; Antwerp, Standaard Uitgeverij, 2005.

CHAPTER 4: THE FOUR DIVISIONS

27th Division

AMERICAN BATTLE MONUMENTS COMMISSION. *27th Division Summary of Operations in the World War*. I: Organization and Service from Arrival in the A.E.F. until 24 July, p. 3. Dickebusch Lake and Scherpenberg, Ypres-Lys Offensive 19 August-3 September 1918, p. 5-11. Casualties, p. 12. Washington DC: US Government Printing Office, 1944.

CENTER OF MILITARY HISTORY UNITED STATES ARMY. *American Armies and Battlefields in Europe*. Chapter VI: American Battlefields North of Paris, p. 402-405. Washington DC: ABMC, US Government Printing Office, 1992.

CLARK, William F. *Over there with O'Ryan's Roughnecks*. Chapter VI: Action on the Ypres-Kemmel Front, p. 45-68. Photo Major-General John F. Ryan, p.72. Seattle, WA: Superior Publishing Co., 1968.

EGGERS, John H. *The 27th Division, the story of its sacrifices and achievements*. Engagements in Belgium, Map Dickebusch and Vierstraat, p. 28-31. New York: Eggers Co.

HARRIS Stephen L. *Duty, Honor, Privilege - New York's Silk Stocking Regiment*. Chapter 6: His heart, I know, is back in God's Country. Corporal Billy Leonard, p. 135-143. Dulles, VA: Brassey's Inc., 2001.

LELAND, Claude C. Captain. *From Shell Hole to Chateau with Company I*. Chapter II: Moving Up - Corporal Bill Leonard, p. 77. Chapter III: Baptism of Fire, p. 110-143. New York: The Society of Ninth Company Veterans, 1950.

MITCHELL, Harry T. *Company "L" 107th Infantry, 54th Brigade, 27th Division*. p. 23-26, (1917-1919)

O'RYAN, John F. Major General. *The Story of the 27th Division*. Chapter XIII: Service with the Second British Army, p. 195 & p. 212. Chapter XIV: Battle of Vierstraat Ridge, p. 225-242. New York: Wynkoop Hallenbeck Crawford Co., 1921.

SCHUYLER, Philip V.R. *Sergeant. C Company, 106th Machine Gun Battalion, 27th Division*. New York: published by the company, 1919.

SWETLAND, Maurice & Lilli. *These Men*. On the Belgian Front, p. 125-139. Harrisburg, PA: The Military Service Pub. Co., 1940.
US Army Signal Corps, #SC-18706, RG111, NARA, College Park, MD.

WAR VETERANS ASSOCIATION. *History of Company "E" 107th Infantry, 54th Brigade, 27th Division*. War: p. 93-101. New York City, Published by the Association, 1921.

YOCKELSON, Mitchell A. *Borrowed Soldiers, Americans under British Command, 1918.* Chapter 13: Ypres, p. 98. Chapter 14: Aftermath of Battle, p. 108. Oklahoma, University of Oklahoma Press: Norman, 2008.

30th Division

AMERICAN BATTLE MONUMENTS COMMISSION. *30th Division Summary of Operations in the World War.* Canal Sector and Ypres-Lys Offensive, p. 6-9. Casualties, p. 10. Washington DC: The US Government Printing Office, 1944.

CENTER OF MILITARY HISTORY UNITED STATES ARMY. *American Armies and Battlefields in Europe.* Chapter VI: American Battlefields North of Paris, p. 402-405. Washington DC: ABMC, US Government Printing Office, 1992.

History of the 113th Field Artillery, 30th Division. Brief History, p. 203. Raleigh , NC, The History Committee of 113th F.A.

History of the 119th Infantry, 60th Brigade, 30th Division, USA. Organization of 119th Infantry, p. 1. Training Period Overseas, p. 7-18. Occupation and Operations in the Canal Sector up to and including September 4th, 1918, p. 21-33. Casualties, p. 59. Wilmington, NC: Wilmington Chamber of Commerce publishing in honor of Colonel John Van B. Metts.

LAWRENCE, Joseph D. *Fighting Soldier - The AEF in 1918.* Chapter II: Ypres - Dirty Bucket Camp, p. 16-17. Chapter III: Lost in No Mans Land - Allied gas attack, p. 44-45. Denver: Colorado Ass. Press, 1985.

MURPHY, Elmer and THOMAS, Robert. *The 30th Division in the World War.* Chapter X: Training with the British - Second Period of Training, p. 70-74. Chapter XI: The Canal Sector p. 75-79. Ypres-Lys Offensive - The Gas Attack, p.81. Voormezele Captured, p. 83. Appendices: Voormezele 1 September 1918, p. 157. Lepanto, AR: Old Hickory Publishing Company, 1936.

OHIONA AUTHORS: *Elsie Janis.* Consulted on 15 August 2008, http://www.ohioana-authors.org/

SPENCER, E.W. *The History of Gas Attacks upon the American Expeditionary Forces during the World War.* Cylinder Attack - 27 August 1918, p. 621-623. Historical Section, U.S. Army Medical Research Institute of Chemical Defense. MD. Aberdeen Proving Ground.
With special thanks to Dr. Benjamin A. Hill, Lt. Col., U.S. Army Physician Scientist. U.S. Army Medical Research Institute of Chemical Defense. Aberdeen Proving Ground, MD.

SULLIVAN, Willard and TUCKER, Harry. *The History of the 105th Regiment of Engineers.* Chapter VI: Training and Work in the Ypres and Canal Sectors with the British, p. 43-65.

Chapter VII: Occupation of the Canal Sector and the Battle of Voormezele, Ypres-Lys Offensive, August 17th to September 3rd, 1918, p. 66-89. Chapter XV: Honor Roll, p. 277-278. New York, George H. Doran Company.

With the 114th Machine Gun Battalion 1917-1919. Operations Thirtieth Division, p. 137.

WALKER, John. GRAHAM, William and FAUNTLEROY, Thomas. *Official History of the 120th Infantry – 3rd North Carolina – 30th Div.* Chapter IV: Training with the British, p. 10-12. Chapter V: Canal Sector, p. 14-15. Chapter VI: Transfer of Regiment, p.17-18. Lynchburg, VA: J.P. Bell Co.

WILLIAMS, John Francis II. *Experiences in the Great War.* The Raid, p. 21-25. The Trenches, p. 26-29. Palm Beach, CA: privately printed.

YOCKELSON, Mitchell A. *Borrowed Soldiers, Americans under British Command, 1918.* Chapter 13: Ypres, p. 98. Chapter 14: Aftermath of Battle, p. 108. Oklahoma, University of Oklahoma Press: Norman, 2008.

The 37th (Buckeye) and 91st (Wild West) Divisions in Flanders (Prologue)

ARCHIVE: Centrum voor Historische Documentatie van de Krijgsmacht (Military Documents Center) , Kwartier Koningin Elisabeth, Block 6Bis, 1140 Brussel.

DWIGHT, Robert. *Diary of Private Robert Dwight.* Consulted on 3 August 2009, http://home.stny.rr.com/wmcpherson/notebookpages.html

HISTORICAL DIVISION DEPARTMENT OF THE ARMY. *United States Army in the World War 1917-1919.* Military Operations of the A.E.F. - Telegram No. 4779: Message Centre 1st Army, p. 327. Washington DC., 1948.

PETERSEN, W.E. *"Over the Top" The Diary of an American Doughboy in World War I.* Courtesy Mr. Filip Santens, Vichte, Belgium.

VERMEULEN, Edward. *Nalatenschap. (Inheritance)* From his Journal, p. 93. Roeselare, Boekhandel Roeland, 1964.

VUYLSTEKE, Gustave. *Mijn Oorlogsdagboek, Meulebeke tijdens 1914-'18. (My War Journal, Meulebeke during 1914-'18)* p. 247 and 253. Tielt: De Roede van Tielt, 2000.

37th Division

AMERICAN BATTLE MONUMENTS COMMISSION. *37th Division Summary of Operations in the World War.* Ypres-Lys Offensive October 25 - November 11, p. 20-31. Casualties, p. 31. Washington DC: The US Government Printing Office., 1944.

ARCHIVE FLANDERS FIELD AMERICAN CEMETERY

CADWALLADER, William. *Major Conelly's Front Line Fighters, 1st Bn, 148th Inf. 37th Div.* Chapter 14: Over the Top Again: Olsene 30 October 1918, p. 44. Chapter 15: Hugs and Kisses from the Belgians - Division occupies the crest of Chruyshautem, p. 47. Chapter 16: Crossing the Escaut River, p. 50-56. Chapter 17: Shirt Readings, p. 57. Cleveland, OH: The Connelly Co., 1919.

CENTER OF MILITARY HISTORY UNITED STATES ARMY. *American Armies and Battlefields in Europe.* Chapter VI: American Battlefields North of Paris, p. 395-397. Washington DC: ABMC, US Government Printing Office, 1992.

COLE, Ralph Dayton & HOWELLS, W.C. *The Thirty-Seventh Division in the World War 1917-1918.* Columbus, OH: 37th Division Veterans Association, 1929. Volume I, Chapter I: Training in Europe, p. 79. Volume II, Chapter XIV: Our Vigilance must not relax, p. 369, Field Orders No. 41, p. 396, Field Orders No. 44, p. 411.

GENERAL STAFF AEF, G-2. *Histories of Two Hundred and Fifty-one Divisions of the German Army 1914-1918.* Compiled from Records of the Intelligence Section, Chaumont, France 1919: p. 171, 229 & 334. Washington DC, The US Government Printing Office, 1920.

HISTORICAL DIVISION DEPARTMENT OF THE ARMY. *United States Army in the World War 1917-1919.* Washington DC, The US Government Printing Office, 1948.
Field Orders No. 32, 17/10/1918, Entrainment 37th Division, p. 336.
Field Orders No. 33, 25/10/1918, Enlargement of Divisional Zone, p. 347.
Field Orders No. 34, 27/10/1918, Movement 37th Division, p. 351.
Intelligence Memorandum No. 5, 29/10/1918, Enemy Order of Battle, p. 362-363.
Field Orders No. 36, 30/10/1918, Attack Order for 37th Division, p. 368.
237-20.1: Summary of Intelligence October 30/31 October, p. 378.
Special Orders No. 44, French XXX Corps, 03/11/1918, Exploitation of Gains on Escaut, p. 400
237-32.1: Report of Operations in the Flanders Offensive October 31 - November 4, 1918 inclusive, p. 406-411.
Special Order No. 470, 07/11/1918, Preparations for Attack, p. 424.
Annex to Field Orders No. 43, HQ 37th Div. 09/11/1918, Information of the Enemy, p. 438-440.
G-3, GHQ, AEF, Report of Operations, Crossing of the Escaut River at Syngem, November 9/11, 1918, p. 457-460.
Map nr. 89, Resume of Operations, p. 463.

IRELAND, M.W. Surgeon General Major General. *The Medical Department of the United States in the World War: Volume XIII, Field Operations, Section V, Chapter XXXVI, Ypres-Lys (Flanders) Operation, 37*th *and 91*st *Divisions*. p. 871-872. Washington DC: The US Government Printing Office. Consulted on 10 August 2009. http://history.amedd.army.mil/booksdocs-/wwi/fieldoperations/chapter36.html.

JOHNSON, Ray Neil. *Heaven, Hell or Hoboken*. Illustration by Don Palmer, US Army Military Institute, 940.36/613, p. 140.

KÖHLER Victor, Major. *Das Kürassier-Regiment von Seydlitz (Magdeburgisches) Nr. 7, Seine Geschichte, 1918. – Abwehrschlacht in Flandern von 2 oktoberen / 3 november. - Kampf bei Cruyshautem am 31 oktoberen 1918*, p. 488-492.

NYS, E. *Letter to the author from the Annals of the Holy Family Convent, Tielt, 24 March 1984*.

US ARMY MILITARY HISTORY INSTITUTE. *Roster and Story of Company A, 112*th *U.S. Engineers in France and Belgium, 1918-1919*, p.12-19.

U.S.S. Huntingdon. *"Catapult"* Volume 3, Nr. 19, March 20, 1919: Homeward Bound. p. 15-16.

VAN ROSSEM, Franky. photo archives.

91st Division

91st DIVISION PUBLICATION COMMITTEE. *Story of the 91*st *Division*. Chapter 1: Organization and Arrival Overseas, p. 1-8. Chapter VI: Account of four days of fighting in Belgium, October 31 - November 3, p. 64. San Mateo, Ca., 1919.

AMERICAN BATTLE MONUMENTS COMMISSION. *American Armies and Battlefields in Europe.* Chapter XIV: Interesting facts concerning the A.E.F. - American Divisions sent to Europe. p. 515. Washington DC: The US Government Printing Office, 1992.

AMERICAN BATTLE MONUMENTS COMMISSION. *91*st *Division Summary of Operations in the World War.* Organization and Service, p. 1, p. 23. Washington DC: The US Government Printing Office, 1944.

BOGAERT Jef. *Oorlog in de Gaverstreke. (War in the Gaver area)* p. 169-275. Waregem, Historical and Genealogical Society" De Gaverstreke", 2000.

BURTON, Harold. *600 Days Service: a history of the 361*st *Infantry Regiment*. Chapter VIII: To the Belgian Front, p. 124-136. Chapter IX: The Capture of Audenarde, p. 141-154. Chapter X:

Second Phase of the Lys-Scheldt Offensive, p. 160-164. Portland, OR, James, Kerns, & Abbott Co., 1919.

Co."C" 316*th* *Field Signal Battalion*. San Francisco, CA, Ingrim-Rutledge Company, 1919.

Confidential Memorandum A.E.F. Copy Nr. 33, Field Orders June 30 - December 26, 1918.

DEWEER, Jean-Pierre Dr. *De Slag aan de Schelde 1918.(Battle of the Scheldt),* Oudenaarde, Sanderus, 1988.

GENERAL STAFF AEF. *Histories of Two Hundred and Fifty-one Divisions of the German Army 1914-1918.* Compiled by the Intelligence Section, Chaumont, France, 1919, p. 485, p.665. Washington DC, The US Government Printing Office.

GRAUPNER, Adolphus Earhart. *War Book of "E" Company, 364*th* Infantry*, Archives U.S. Military Institute, Carlisle Barracks, PA., 1920.

HISTORICAL DIVISION DEPARTMENT OF THE ARMY. *United States Army in the World War 1917-1919.* Washington DC, The US Government Printing Office, 1948.
Field Orders No. 16, 15/10/1918, Transfer of 91st Division, p. 330.
Special Orders No. 439, 15/10/1918, Attachment of 53rd Artillery Brigade, p. 344.
Field Orders No. 19, 24/10/1918, Extension of Area Assigned to the Division, p. 346.
Field Orders No. 21, 30/10/1918, Attack Orders, p. 370-371.
Map Zone of Action 91st Division, October 31 – 11 November 1918, p. 463.
291-20.8: Summary: Impressions of the Day, 31 October 1918, p. 381.
General Orders No. 26, 08/11/1918, Plans for Crossing Escaut, p. 429-430.
Field Orders No. 27, Amendment to Field Order 26, 08/11/1918, p. 434.
Field Orders No. 33, Hostilities Suspended, 11/11/1918, p. 457.

HISTORYLINK.org: The Free Online Encyclopedia of Washington State History. *Fort Lewis Cultural Resources Program, Essay 8455.* Consulted on 28 September 2009, http://www.historylink.org/index.cfm?DisplayPage=output.cfm&file_id=8455. *Infantry in Battle.* Chapter VI: Time and Space, p. 86-88. Washington D.C., The Infantry Journal Inc., 1939.

IRELAND, M.W. Surgeon General Major. *The Medical Department of the United States in the World War: Volume XIII, Field Operations, Section V, Chapter XXXVI, Ypres-Lys (Flanders) Operation, 37*th* and 91*st* Divisions*. p. 870-874. Plate LII. Washington DC, The US Government Printing Office. Consulted on 10 August 2009. http://history.amedd.army.mil-/booksdocs/wwi/fieldoperations/chapter36.html.

JOHNSTON, William Major General + 26 etchings by E. Kufferath and Emile Leroi: *Pages of Glory and History: The 91*st* Division in the Argonne and Flanders*. p. 56. Paris - New York - San Francisco, City of Paris, 1918.

*Journal of Operations of the 364*th* Infantry* A.E.F. Archives U.S. Military Institute, Carlisle Barracks, PA.

NATIONAL ARCHIVES AND RECORDS ADMINISTRATION, College Park, MD: Confidential Memorandum A.E.F., Copy Nr. 33, Field Orders June 30-December 26, 1918, Folder # 2.

Field Messages 181st Infantry Brigade, Records Group 120, Entry 291-32.16.
Personnel Notes, Commissioned Officers 91st Division. Confidential Memorandum, Appendix Nr. 6, RG1241, Box 11.

Guide to German War Diaries from Reichsarchiv Source., Heersarchiv, Potsdam, Germany, RG 165-320, Box 171, 179.

History of the 316th Engineers, 1919. RG 120-1241, Box 16-17.

NIELSEN, William. Private . *Diary, Masonic Ambulance Corps (364th Ambulance Co.),* p. 15. Archives U.S. Army Military History Institute, Carlisle Barracks, PA.

Pennsylvania in the World War. History of the 28th Division, Vol. II. States Publications Society, 1921.

PRICE, William Gray. *Activities and Citations of the 53rd Artillery Brigade, 28th Division.* Archives U.S. Military Institute, Carlisle Barracks, PA .

WAREGEM CITY ARCHIVES, Aerial photograph Spitaelsbossen, 26 October 1918.

TIBBONS, Mirton L & SOLVE, Milton T. *Nine Months Overseas being a h*istory *of "H" Company, 361st Infantry.* Archives U.S. Military Institute, Carlisle Barracks, PA., 1919.

WILSON, Bryant & TOOZE, Lamar. First Lieutenants. *With the 364th Infantry in America, France & Belgium.* Nota General Cameron aan Pershing, p. 86. Chapter VIII: Routing the Boche from Spitaals Bosschen, p. 102-126. New York*:* The Knickerbocker Press, 1919.

WIKIPEDIA: the free encyclopedia. Consulted on 28 September 2009
http://en.wikipedia.org/wiki/File:Scene_at_Camp_Lewis,_Washington.jpg

CHAPTER 5: THE POEM "IN FLANDERS FIELD"

Archives Flanders Field American Cemetery

GUELPH Museums, *A Timeline of the Life of John McCrae,* Reference No. M968.354.1.2x consulted on 6 February 2015.

HELMER, Alex. photo, consulted on 5 December 2009,
http://www.greatwar.nl/poppies/alexishelmer.html

MICHAEL, Moina Belle (1869-1944), *Biography,* consulted on 5 December 2009,
http://www.greatwar.co.uk/people/moina-belle-michael-biography.htm

RUGGENBERG, Rob. *The Making of "In Flanders Fields"* consulted on 5 December 2009, http://www.greatwar.nl/frames/default-poppies.html

VERLEYEN, Herwig. *In Flanders Fields, the Story of John McCrae, his Poem and the Poppy,* Veurne, De Klaproos, 1995.

CHAPTER 6: AMERICAN GRAVES REGISTRATION SERVICE

BUDREAU, Lisa. *The Politics of Remembrance: The Gold Star Mothers Pilgrimage and America's Fading Memory of the Great War - Repatriation and the Graves Registration Service.* The Journal of Military History, Volume 72, Nr. 2, p. 374-381, April 2008.

BUDREAU, Lisa. *Bodies of War.* .Chapter 5: A Problem of Policy, p. 49. Chapter 13: Sacred Space and Strife, p. 118-119, New York, New York University Press, 2009.

HAYES, Ralph. *The Care of the Fallen.* A Report to the Secretary of War on American Military Dead Overseas. Washington DC, The US Government Printing Office, 1920.

HISTORY OF THE AMERICAN GRAVES REGISTRATION SERVICE. Quarter Master Corps in Europe (The Library Office of the Quartermaster General, Washington DC). Cemeterial Division, Office of the Quarter Master General:
- History AGRS, Vol. I
    Chapter V, Policies American dead on German soil, p. 94
    Chapter X, Operations in Mid-Europe, p. 183-184
- History AGRS, Vol. II
    Chapter II, General Policies, p. 29, p. 62, p. 76-79
    Chapter III, Port Activities, p. 80
- History AGRS, Vol. III
    Chapter VI, Evacuation of Cemeteries, p. 31-62
SLEDGE, Michael. *Soldier Dead. How we Recover, Identify, Bury and Honor our Military Fallen.* Chapter 4: Identification-Discrepancies, Errors, Issues. p. 119. Chapter V: Return of the Dead, p. 135-136, p. 148 & p. 161-164. New York, Columbia University Press, 2005.

STEVERLYNCK, Family, Belgium – photo field grave in the village of Vichte.

WAR DEPARTMENT General Staff, Special Report Statistics Branch. *Location of Graves and Disposition of Bodies of American Soldiers who Died Overseas.* Concentration and Removal of Bodies, p. 5. War Department, WGPO., 1920.

CHAPTER 7: FLANDERS FIELD AMERICAN CEMETERY # 1252

HISTORY OF THE AMERICAN GRAVES REGISTRATION SERVICE . Vol. III, Chapter VI: Evacuation of Cemeteries, p, 31-62. Washington D.C., Library Office Quartermaster General.

MINISTERE DES AFFAIRES ETRANGERES, Paris, Quai d'Orsay., ARCHIVES DIPLOMATIQUES. AMERIQUE 1918-1929. Séries : Correspondence Politique et Commerciale. B-Amerique. Sous séries: Etats – Unis Période 1918-1940, Volume 19, Dossier 171 : *Armée, Cimetières, cérémonies, monuments militaires Americains en France, Janvier 1922 - Mai 1924 : $5,000 for Flanders Field (Waregem) by Joint Resolution 263, Public Res. #44, 67 Congress,.*

CITY ARCHIVES Waregem.

CITY ARCHIVES Roeselare, Woodrow Wilson visit, photo's.

TETON Christian, 75011 Paris, photo grave Kearney, correspondence C. Sims, 30 March 2005.

CHAPTER 8: AMERICAN BATTLE MONUMENTS COMMISSION

ARCHIVE - Flanders Field American Cemetery

ARCHIVES - THE AMERICAN BATTLE MONUMENTS COMMISSION, European Reg., Paris, France.

GIBSON & WARD. *Courage Remembered. The History of the Commonwealth War Graves Commission,* Chapter 15: The Memorials, p. 156. London, HMSO., 1989.

GROSSMAN, Elizabeth. *Architecture for a Public Client: The Monuments and Chapels of the American Battle Monuments Commission.* Journal of the Society of Architectural Historians, 14 May 1984. Volume XLIII, Nr. 2, p. 119-143.

LONGWORTH, Philip. *The Unending Vigil.* Chapter 4: Commemorating the Missing, p. 102-105. London UK, Leo Cooper/Secker & Warburg, 1985.

NATIONAL ARCHIVES AND RECORDS ADMINISTRATION, College Park, MD. World War I Cemetery Files, Journal 12 July 1940, RG 117, Box 49.

NORTH, Thomas. *One Soldiers Job.* unpublished manuscript, Secretary American Battle Monuments Commission 1946-1968, p. 5.

STEERE & BOARDMAN (1957), *Final Disposition of World War II Dead 1945-1951.* Chapter XI: Repatriation from the European Theater, p. 341-366. QMC Historical Studies, Office of the Quartermaster General, 1957.

Temple of Winds. Consulted on 10 October 2009,
http://www2.brevard.edu/hinklehl/Temple%20of%20the%20winds%20pics.htm

CHAPTER 9: MEMORIAL DAY

AMERICAN OVERSEAS MEMORIAL DAY ASSOCIATION, Belgian Branch, www.aomda.org.

ARCHIVE Flanders Field American Cemetery

ARCHIVES of THE AMERICAN BATTLE MONUMENTS COMMISSION, European Region, Paris, France. www.abmc.gov.

HISTORICAL DIVISION DEPARTMENT OF THE ARMY. *United States Army in the World War 1917-1919.* Military Operations of the American Expeditionary Forces, Bulletin Nr. 37: Observance of Memorial Day, p. 259. Washington DC, 1948.

History of the American Graves Registration Service. Volume I, Chapter VII: Memorial Day 1920, p. 127-137.

NICHOLSON, Harold. *King George the Fifth, His Life and Reign,* p. 427, London, Constable & Co., 1952.

PEDLOW, Gregory. *The American Overseas Memorial Day Association of Belgium, 1923-2003.* 80 Years of Honoring America's Fallen from the Two World Wars.

CITY ARCHIVES Waregem, Memorial Day photo's 1923-1970.

UNITED STATES DEPARTMENT OF VETERANS AFFAIRS. *Memorial Day History.* Consulted on 11 September 2009: http://www1.va.gov/opa/speceven/memday/history.asp#hist

CHAPTER 10: GOLD STAR MOTHERS PILGRIMAGES

AMERICAN LEGION MAGAZINE (May 1927). *Second American Expeditionary Force.*

AMERICAN LEGION WEEKLY (9 September 1921). *Unpardonable.*

BUDREAU, Lisa. *The Politics of Remembrance: The Gold Star Mothers Pilgrimage and America's Fading Memory of the Great War - Repatriation and the Graves Registration Service.* The Journal of Military History, Volume 72, Nr. 2, p. 377-378. April 2008. "Gold Star Mothers Honored", p. 394, p. 421.

FENELON, Holly. Historian Gold Star Mother's Association, letter to the author with authentic pilgrimage documentation, 20 November 2001.

GRAHAM, John W. *The Gold Star Mother Pilgrimages of the 1930's.* Chapter 1: What were the Gold Star Pilgrimages?

CHICAGO DAILY NEWS, photo Gold Star Mothers in Grant Park, Chicago 1918, , negatives collection, DN 0070373, Chicago Historical Society, 2004.

HISTORY OF THE AMERICAN GRAVES REGISTRATION SERVICE. Quarter Master Corps in Europe. The Library Office of the Quartermaster General, Washington DC. Volume II, Chapter 2, General Policies, p. 26.

INDIANA HISTORICAL COMMISSION. *Indiana World War Records - Gold Star Honor Roll 1914 – 1918.* Indianapolis, IN: Wayne Printing Company, 1921.

NATIONAL ARCHIVES AND RECORDS ADMINISTRATION, College Park, MD. Cemeterial Files, RG 92, Box 26, Party K, 1931 - Burial Files, RG 92, soldiers Flanders Field cemetery.

SMITH, George Bartlett. *The Life of the Right Honourable William Ewart Gladstone 1809-1898.* London, Cassell, Petter, Galpin & Co.

CHAPTER 11: THE SOLDIERS OF FLANDERS FIELD

ADAMS Frank – p. 443
TEPP Gail, Stevens Point, WI, USA.
GRACZYKOWSKI Scott J., Saint Paul, MN, USA .
NATIONAL ARCHIVES AND RECORDS ADMINISTRATION, College Park, MD, USA.

ADAMS Ralph – p. 247
COUROS, Jim. East Meredith, NY, USA.
ANCESTRY.com – De Clerck family tree.
HAUSEE, HOWE & DOYLE. *Soldiers of the Great War.* Washington D.C.: Soldiers Record Publishing Association, 1920.
CENTRAL LIBRARY, Rochester and Monroe County, Local History and Genealogy Division/LN, Rochester, NY.

ADMIRE Roger – p. 271
ADMIRE Cliff, Richmond, IL, USA.
HILL Dorothy M., Washington, MO, USA.
PERRINE Jordan, Normandy Park, WA,USA.
MELDRUM T. *A History of the 362nd Infantry.* Ogden, UT: A.L. Scoville Press, 1920.
ANCESTRY.com – Admire Family Tree
NATIONAL ARCHIVES AND RECORDS ADMINISTRATION, College Park, MD, USA

ALLEN Alonzo – p. 529
POUGHKEEPSIE JOURNAL, August 13, 1918, Poughkeepsie, NY, USA.
POUGHKEPSIE SUNDAY COURIER, August 19, 1918, Poughkeepsie, NY, USA.
LUCAS Lynn, ADRIANCE MEMORIAL LIBRARY, Poughkeepsie, NY, USA.
LAUGHNER Niles W. WWI COLLECTION, Keene, NH, USA.
GANDY Jim, NY STATE MILITARY MUSEUM, Saratoga Springs, NY, USA.
A short History and Illustrated Roster of the 105th Infantry United States Army, 1917 (1918). Philadelphia, PA: Edward Stern & Co., Inc.

ANDERSON Frederick Jr. – p. 312
A short History and Illustrated Roster of the 106th Infantry United States Army, 1917 (1918).
Philadelphia, PA: Edward Stern & Co., Inc.
NATIONAL ARCHIVES AND RECORDS ADMINISTRATION, College Park, MD, USA.
ANCESTRY.com – New York Abstracts of World War I Military Service 1917-1919

ANDERSON Herbert – p. 506
FITZGERALD Becky, Erlanders Home Museum, Rockford, IL, USA.
NATIONAL ARCHIVES AND RECORDS ADMINISTRATION, College Park, MD, USA

ANDERSON Lionel – p. 457
JORDAN Paul, Douglas Genealogical and County History Society Lawrence, KS, USA.
NEELEY Kathleen, Lawrence, KS, USA.
UNIVERSITY ARCHIVES, KENNETH SPENCER RESEARCH LIBRARY, Lawrence, KS, USA.
ANCESTRY.com – 1900 U.S. Federal Census and 1910 U.S. Federal Census.

ANNANDALE Frederick – p. 392
ANNANDALE Barry M., Christchurch, New Zealand.
KOONS Steve, Dayton, OH, USA.
OHIO ADJUDANTS GENERAL'S DEPARTMENT. *The official Roster Ohio Soldiers, Sailors and Marines in the World War 1917-1918.* Columbus, OH: F.J. Heer Printing, 1926.

ARNETT John – p. 277
RUSTEY Mark, Orleans County Genealogical Society, NY, USA.
HARTMAN-POGGI Sherry MLS, Associate Professor Albany Medical College, Delmar, NY, USA.
ROBINSON Dee, Reference Librarian, Swan Library, Albion, NY.
THE ORLEANS REPUBLICAN, 23 January 1918.
THE ORLEANS REPUBLICAN, 3 April 1918.
THE ORLEANS REPUBLICAN, 1 May 1918.
PERSONAL NARRATIVES (1950). *From shell hole to chateau with Company I" (recollections of an officer of the 107th Inf. 27th Div.)* Society of 9th Co. Veterans, 7th Reg. N.Y.N.G, NY.
ANCESTRY.com – Arnett Family Tree
ANCESTRY.com – New York Abstracts of World War I Military Service 1917-1919

ARPAIA Nicola – p. 363
ARPAIA Luigi, Irsina, Italy.
SEPIC Chris, Tarboro, NC, USA.
NATIONAL ARCHIVES AND RECORDS ADMINISTRATION, College Park, MD, USA.
ANCESTRY.com - U.S. World War I Draft Registration Cards 1917-1918

ASHE George – p. 329
HAUSEE, HOWE & DOYLE. *Soldiers of the Great War.* Soldiers Record Publishing Association, Washington D.C., USA, 1920.
KNOMICEK Helena, Mount Vernon, NY, USA.
NATIONAL ARCHIVES AND RECORDS ADMINISTRATION, College Park, MD, USA.
ANCESTRY.com - U.S. World War I Draft Registration Cards 1917-1918

AYERS Frederick – p. 207
KNOMICEK Helena, Mount Vernon, NY, USA
NATIONAL ARCHIVES AND RECORDS ADMINISTRATION, College Park, MD, USA.
ANCESTRY.com - U.S. World War I Draft Registration Cards 1917-1918
NEW YORK War Veterans Service Data 1913-1919

AYK Jack – p. 338
NATIONAL ARCHIVES AND RECORDS ADMINISTRATION, College Park, MD, USA.

BALL Clayton – p. 238
SIMON Scott & BALL Deborah, Clarksville, TN, USA.
VFW Post # 2341, Albion, PA, USA.
GRUBER Betty, Albion, PA, USA .
ANCESTRY.com – 1910 U.S. Federal Census

BARLETT Leo – p. 468
HALTERMAN Eddie, Jeffersonville, OH, USA.
NATIONAL ARCHIVES AND RECORDS ADMINISTRATION, College Park, MD, USA.

BARLOW William – p. 292
PETERSON Darren, Dothan, AL, USA.
SULLIVAN Willard P. & TUCKER Harry. *The History of the 105th Regiment of of Engineers.*
New York: George H. Doran CO., 1919.
ANCESTRY.com – Campbell Family Tree - 1910 US Federal Census and U.S. World War I Draft
Registration Cards 1917-1918
SPENCER, E.W. *The History of Gas Attacks upon the American Expeditionary Forces during
the World War.* Cylinder Attack pages 621-623

BARNES Charles – p. 336
THOMPSON Tracy, Rocky Mount, NC, USA.
WHEELESS Mark, Raleigh, NC, USA.
PRYOR Vonnie, Winston-Salem, NC, USA.
FLEMING Monika, Tarboro, NC, USA.
ANCESTRY.com - U.S. World War I Draft Registration Cards 1917-1918

BASTL Tony – p. 144
BASTL KAEMPEN Dee, West Mont, Illinois, USA.
BROESTL Jane, Westlake, OH, USA.
POTTER Alfred, Des Plaines, Illinois, USA.

BAVIS Carey – p. 570
POBST Bonnie, Las Vegas, NV, USA.
TARVIN Gary, Georgetown, OH, USA.
CASE Marvin, Georgetown, OH, USA.
NICHOLS Bob, Georgetown, Ohio, USA.
HELTON Dorothy, Georgetown, OH, USA.
NATIONAL ARCHIVES AND RECORDS ADMINISTRATION, College Park, MD, USA.

BEATTIE David – p. 631
KARREMER Larry, Troy Public Library, Troy, NY,USA.
NATIONAL ARCHIVES AND RECORDS ADMINISTRATION, College Park, MD, USA.
ANCESTRY.com – New York Abstracts of World War I Military Service 1917-1919

BEATTIE Joseph – p. 571
BROOKLYN DAILY EAGLE, Brooklyn Public Library - Brooklyn Collection, Brooklyn, NY, USA.
A short History and Illustrated Roster of the 106th Infantry United States Army, 1917.
Philadelphia, PA: Edward Stern & Co., Inc., 1918.
NATIONAL ARCHIVES AND RECORDS ADMINISTRATION, College Park, MD, USA.
ANCESTRY.com – New York Abstracts of World War I Military Service 1917-1919
FINDAGRAVE.com : Eastern Parkway Brooklyn WWI Tree Memorials

BEDELL John – p. 273
A short History and Illustrated Roster of the 106th Infantry United States Army, 1917.
Philadelphia, PA: Edward Stern & Co., Inc., 1918
NATIONAL ARCHIVES AND RECORDS ADMINISTRATION, College Park, MD, USA.
ANCESTRY.com – New York Abstracts of World War I Military Service 1917-1919

BELCHER Richard – p. 409
A short History and Illustrated Roster of the 106th Infantry United States Army, 1917.
Philadelphia, PA: Edward Stern & Co., Inc., 1918.
THE NEW YORK TRIBUNE, November 24, 1918, New York City, NY, USA.
NATIONAL ARCHIVES AND RECORDS ADMINISTRATION, College Park, MD, USA.
ANCESTRY.com – Belcher Family Tree, U.S. World War I Draft Registration Cards 1917-1918
and New York Abstracts of World War I Military Service 1917-1919

BELL Forest – p. 562
WAHRENBROCK Lucille, Story City, IA, USA.
THE CORDER JOURNAL, October 3, 1918, Corder, MO, USA.
ANCESTRY.com - U.S. World War I Draft Registration Cards 1917-1918

BENOIT Maurice – p. 572
A short History and Illustrated Roster of the 106th Infantry United States Army, 1917.
Philadelphia, PA: Edward Stern & Co., Inc., 1918.
BROOKLYN DAILY EAGLE, Brooklyn Public Library - Brooklyn Collection, Brooklyn, NY, USA.
NATIONAL ARCHIVES AND RECORDS ADMINISTRATION, College Park, MD, USA.

BERNIK John – p. 442
KOVACH Dorothy, Orwell, OH, USA.
SCHOONOVER Virginia, Bonita Springs, FL, USA.
BERNICK John, CO,USA.
NATIONAL ARCHIVES AND RECORDS ADMINISTRATION, College Park, MD, USA.

BEVINS Thomas – p. 550
BEVINS Dan, Bernardsville, NJ, USA.
HANSEN Charlene, Cedar Rapids, IA, USA.
LONG Marthe, Vinton, IA, USA.

BEYERS Bernard – p. 190
HOLTHAUS Pat, Pana, IL, USA.
SCHMIDT Shelly, Wheaton, IL, USA.
CARNEGIE-SCHUYLER LIBRARY, Pana, IL, USA.
NATIONAL ARCHIVES AND RECORDS ADMINISTRATION, College Park, MD, USA.
ANCESTRY.com – 1900 U.S. Federal Census

BIANCHI Guiseppe – p. 421
NATIONAL ARCHIVES AND RECORDS ADMINISTRATION, College Park, MD, USA.
MACKEY, Patty RECORD, Anderson, SC, USA.
ANCESTRY.com – New York Abstracts of World War I Military Service 1917-1919

BISSETT Wiley Clifton – p. 263
BISSETT Lawrence, South Charleston, VA, USA
PETERSON Darren, Dothan, AL, USA.
MACKEY, Patty. RECORD, Anderson, SC, USA
NEW BERN SUN JOURNAL 25 July 1918, 26 July 1918, 27 July 1918, 31 July 1918, 1 August 1918. New Bern, NC, USA .
MORNING NEW BERNIAN, 26 July 1918, 31 July 1918, 3 August 1918, 7 August 1918. New Bern, NC, USA.

BONAWITZ Edward – p. 573
VOLENCE Lois, Reading, PA, USA
NATIONAL ARCHIVES AND RECORDS ADMINISTRATION, College Park, MD, USA.
HAUSEE, HOWE & DOYLE . *Soldiers of the Great War*. Washington D.C.: Soldiers Record Publishing Association, 1920.
ANCESTRY.com - U.S. World War I Draft Registration Cards 1917-1918

BORTLE Oscar – p. 545
THOMPSON James E., Minneapolis, MN, USA.
SCHUMAN Claudia, Minneapolis, MN, USA.
GRACZYKOWSKI Scott T. J., Saint Paul, MN, USA.
PETERSON Darren, Dothan, AL, USA.

BOZENHART Ernest – p. 335
WELLS Karen, Grand Rapids, Missouri, USA.
HEMINGER Mark, OH, USA.
TOLEDO-LUCAS COUNTY PUBLIC LIBRARY, Toledo, OH, USA.
OHIO ADJUDANTS GENERAL'S DEPARTMENT. *The official Roster Ohio Soldiers, Sailors and Marines in the World War 1917-1918*. Columbus, OH: F.J. Heer Printing Co., 1926.
COLE R. and HOWELLS W. *The Thirty-Seventh Division in the World War 1917-1918,* Volume II, 37th Division Veterans Association, Columbus, Ohio, 1929, page 673.

BRABENDER Theodore – p. 289
MILBERT Charles, Delmar, NY, USA.
PICKETT Grance S., Columbia County Hist. Society, Kinderhook, NY, USA.
NATIONAL ARCHIVES AND RECORDS ADMINISTRATION, College Park, MD, USA.
ANCESTRY.com – 1900 U.S. Federal Census
FINDAGRAVE.com – Hudson City Cemetery, NY, Memorial Nr: 106490354 created by Jim Morris.

BRIGGS Lewis - p. 140
PAINESVILLE TELEGRAPH, Spec. Edition, July 3, 1919, Painesville, OH, USA
ANCESTRY.com – 1910 Census

BRINDZA Frank – p. 255
GRACZYKOWSKI Scott T. J., Saint Paul, MN, USA.
NATIONAL ARCHIVES AND RECORDS ADMINISTRATION, College Park, MD, USA.

BRISCO Floyd – p. 331
MCHENRY Chris, Lawrenceburg, IN, USA.
MACKEY, Patty RECORD, Anderson, SC, USA.
OHIO ADJUDANTS GENERAL'S DEPARTMENT. *The official Roster Ohio Soldiers, Sailors and Marines in the World War 1917-1918.* Columbus, OH: F.J. Heer Printing Co., 1926.

BROKAW Charles – p. 176
CALIFORNIA STATE LIBRARY, Sacramento, CA, USA.
KLEMM Scott J., Highland, CA, USA.
BROKAW Dennis, San Diego, CA, USA.
BROKAW Russ, Racine, WI, USA.
STEMAN Tom, Western Reserve University, Cleveland, OH, USA.
DE LA ROSA Romana, Colton Public Library, Colton, CA, USA.
COLTON COURIER, November 29, 1918, Colton, CA, USA.
WESTERN RESERVE UNIVERSITY, Cleveland, OH, USA.

BROWN Levin – p. 536
CHEATWOOD Marsha, Nunez, GA, USA.
MOHSIN Dee, TX, USA.
TAPLEY Ray, Atlanta, GA, USA.
NATIONAL ARCHIVES AND RECORDS ADMINISTRATION, College Park, MD, USA.

BRYAN Guy – p. 515
ST. CLAIR VAUGHN Theresa, Houston, TX, USA.
NATIONAL ARCHIVES AND RECORDS ADMINISTRATION, College Park, MD, USA.
ANCESTRY.com - U.S. World War I Draft Registration Cards 1917-1918

BULAICH George – p. 215
NATIONAL ARCHIVES AND RECORDS ADMINISTRATION, College Park, MD, USA.
WHITTLE Syd, El Dorado Hills, California
U.S. Naturalization Records 1795-1972 – World Archives Project

BURCKELL David – p. 527
RIX W., librarian Santa Monica Public Library, Santa Monica, California, USA.
KNOBLOCK Betty, Marina Del Rey, CA, USA.
NATIONAL ARCHIVES AND RECORDS ADMINISTRATION, College Park, MD, USA

BURNWORTH Willis – p. 359
SNIDER VAN A. *Fairfield County in the World War*. Lancaster, OH: Mallory Printing Co., 1926.
OHIO ADJUDANTS GENERAL'S DEPARTMENT. *The official Roster Ohio Soldiers, Sailors and Marines in the World War 1917-1918*. Columbus, OH: F.J. Heer Printing Co., 1926.
NATIONAL ARCHIVES AND RECORDS ADMINISTRATION, College Park, MD, USA.

BUSCEMO Salvatore – p. 395
NATIONAL ARCHIVES AND RECORDS ADMINISTRATION, College Park, MD, USA.
ANCESTRY.com – New York Abstracts of World War I Military Service 1917-1919

CAHILL Thomas – p. 400
KANBARA Mitzi, San Francisco Public Library, San Francisco, CA, USA.
THE SAN FRANCISCO EXAMINER, 11 December 1918, San Francisco, CA, USA.
MACKEY, Patty RECORD, Anderson, SC, USA.
NATIONAL ARCHIVES AND RECORDS ADMINISTRATION, College Park, MD, USA.
ANCESTRY.com - U.S. World War I Draft Registration Cards 1917-1918.

CAMPARZI Mario – p. 488
PETERSON Darren, Dothan, AL, USA.
CALIFORNIA STATE LIBRARY, Sacramento, CA, USA.
www.ellisisland.org consulted on 25 May 2007

CANTACESSO Trifone – p. 342
STATE HISTORICAL SOCIETY OF IOWA, Des Moines, IA, USA.

CARLETILLO Nick – p. 528
PETERSON Darren, Dothan, AL, USA.
CALIFORNIA STATE LIBRARY, Sacramento, CA, USA.
NATIONAL ARCHIVES AND RECORDS ADMINISTRATION, College Park, MD, USA.
HATHCOCK Barbara Jean, Columbus, OH, USA.
ANCESTRY.com - U.S. World War I Draft Registration Cards 1917-1918

CARPEN Joe – p. 485
OHIO ADJUDANTS GENERAL'S DEPARTMENT. *The official Roster Ohio Soldiers, Sailors and Marines in the World War 1917-1918*. Columbus, OH: F.J. Heer Printing Co., 1926.
MACKEY, Patty RECORD, Anderson, SC, USA.
NATIONAL ARCHIVES AND RECORDS ADMINISTRATION, College Park, MD, USA.

CARUSO Ralph – p. 495
OHIO ADJUDANTS GENERAL'S DEPARTMENT. *The official Roster Ohio Soldiers, Sailors and Marines in the World War 1917-1918*. Columbus, OH: F.J. Heer Printing Co., 1926.
MACKEY, Patty RECORD, Anderson, SC, USA.

NATIONAL ARCHIVES AND RECORDS ADMINISTRATION, College Park, MD, USA.
ANCESTRY.com - U.S. World War I Draft Registration Cards 1917-1918

CASAJUS John – p. 548
ROBINSON William, Rio Vista, California, USA.
BROCA Andrée, Lons, France.
SACRAMENTO Bee, 14 December 1914, Sacramento, California, USA.
MOREBECK Nancy, Vacaville, CA, USA.
SCOTT James, Sacramento, California, USA.
ANCESTRY.com - U.S. World War I Draft Registration Cards 1917-1918, California World War
I Death Announcements, 1920 U.S. Federal Census, U.S. Passport Applications 1795-1925.

CASEY John – p. 329
A short History and Illustrated Roster of the 106th Infantry United States Army, 1917.
Philadelphia, PA: Edward Stern & Co., Inc.
http://www.bklyn-genealogy-info.com/Military/WW1/C.html consulted on 2 May 2005.
NATIONAL ARCHIVES AND RECORDS ADMINISTRATION, College Park, MD, USA.

CAWEIN Raleigh – p. 433
A short History and Illustrated Roster of the 105th Infantry United States Army, 1917.
Philadelphia, PA: Edward Stern & Co., Inc., 1918.
GANDY Jim, NY STATE MILITARY MUSEUM, Saratoga Springs, NY, USA.
LAUGHNER Niles W. WWI COLLECTION, Keene, NH, USA.
NATIONAL ARCHIVES AND RECORDS ADMINISTRATION, College Park, MD, USA.

CHERRY Edward – p. 370
SHENEMAN Franklin, South Bend, IN, USA.
SHELBY COUNTY PUBLIC LIBRARY, Shelbyville, IN, USA.
GORDON Bob, Shelbyville, IN, USA.
MORSE Irvin, Mishawaka, IN, USA.
PETERSON Darren, Dothan, AL, USA.
PERRINE Jordan, Normandy Park, WA,USA.
MELDRUM T. (1920). *A History of the 362nd Infantry.* Ogden, UT: A.L. Scoville Press.
INDIANA HISTORICAL COMMISSION. *Indiana World War Records Gold Star Honor Roll 1914-1918.* Indianapolis: Fort Wayne Printing Co., 1921.
ANCESTRY.com – 1900 U.S. Federal Census

CHESTON Galloway – p. 573
RUSSO Jean, Annapolis, MD, USA.
KORMANN Jef, Enoch Pratt Free Library, Baltimore, MD, USA.
PROFFEN Elisabeth, Maryland Historical Society Library, Baltimore, MD, USA.
MCINTIRE Robert Harry (1979). *Annapolis Maryland Families.* Baltimore, MD: Gateway
Press.
http://www.theaerodrome.com consulted on 02/03/2007.
ANCESTRY.com – 1900 U.S. Federal Census - U.S. World War I Draft Registration Cards
1917-1918 - Maryland in the World War 1917-1919, Military and Naval Service Records.

CHIMIENTI Michele – p. 466
DE ZUTTER Charles, Waregem, Belgium.
CLINESMITH Karin, Benge, WA, USA.
SPRAGUE Charles A. *History of Adams County in the World War.* Ritzville, WA: The Journal Times, 1920
NATIONAL ARCHIVES AND RECORDS ADMINISTRATION, College Park, MD, USA.
ANCESTRY.com - U.S. World War I Draft Registration Cards 1917-1918 and U.S. Naturalization Records 1795-1972 – World Archives Project

CHRISTENSEN James – p. 306
GRACZYKOWSKI Scott J., Saint Paul, MN, USA.
NATIONAL ARCHIVES AND RECORDS ADMINISTRATION, College Park, MD, USA.
ANCESTRY.com – New York Abstracts of World War I Military Service 1917-1919

CHRISTY Angelo – p. 161
Fayette County Genealogy Society, Uniontown, PA, USA.
MACKEY, Patty RECORD, Anderson, SC, USA.
NATIONAL ARCHIVES AND RECORDS ADMINISTRATION, College Park, MD, USA.
ANCESTRY.com - U.S. World War I Draft Registration Cards 1917-1918

CLARK Harold – p. 139
LIGHT Harold & Emma, Sheldon, IL, USA.
CORKE Denise, Watseka, IL, USA.
RIEGEL Dorothy, Bonfield, IL, USA.

CLARK Tracy – p. 481
SNIDER Phil, Hicksville, OH.
KLINE Diane, Hicksville, OH.
OHIO ADJUDANTS GENERAL'S DEPARTMENT. *The official Roster Ohio Soldiers, Sailors and Marines in the World War 1917-1918.* Columbus, OH: F.J. Heer Printing Co., 1926.
ANCESTRY.com – 1910 U.S. Federal Census

CLEAR Francis – p. 259
DOUGHERTY Lisa, Castleton, NY, USA.
GANDY Jim, NY STATE MILITARY MUSEUM, Saratoga Springs, NY, USA.
LAUGHNER Niles W. WWI COLLECTION, Keene, NH, USA.
Glens Falls Post Star, 24 September 1918, Glens Falls, NY, USA.
Glens Falls Post Star, 8 April 1988, Glens Falls, NY, USA

CLOSTERMANN Albert – p. 519
CLOSTERMANN - ANDERSON Sheri, Portland, OR, USA.
HAUSEE, HOWE & DOYLE. *Soldiers of the Great War.* Washington D.C.: Soldiers Record Publishing Association, 1920.
MELDRUM T. *A History of the 362nd Infantry.* Ogden, UT: A.L. Scoville Press, 1920.

COCHRANE Richard – p. 405
REID Edith, Staines, Middlesex, UK.
ANCESTRY.com – New York Abstracts of World War I Military Service 1917-1919

COMBS Edgar – p. 574
CHURCH Vanessa, North Wilkesboro, NC, USA..
MOORE Len, Wilkesboro, NC, USA.
NATIONAL ARCHIVES AND RECORDS ADMINISTRATION, College Park, MD, USA

COMINA Albert – p. 249
RIVA John, Quebec, Canada.
Salt Lake City Public Library, Salt Lake city, UT, USA.
NATIONAL ARCHIVES AND RECORDS ADMINISTRATION, College Park, MD, USA
ANCESTRY.com - U.S. World War I Draft Registration Cards 1917-1918

CONDON Edward – p. 131
NATIONAL ARCHIVES AND RECORDS ADMINISTRATION, College Park, MD, USA.
ANCESTRY.com – 1910 Census

CONEDERA Alberto – p. 540
RIVA John, Quebec, Canada.
ANCESTRY.com - U.S. World War I Draft Registration Cards 1917-1918

CORNELIUS Bennett – p. 576
PRYOR Vonnie, Winston-Salem, NC, USA.
MILLER Wisdom, Thomasville, NC, USA.
SNIDER Dewey, Lexington, NC, USA.
NATIONAL ARCHIVES AND RECORDS ADMINISTRATION, College Park, MD, USA
ANCESTRY.com – 1910 U.S. Federal Census
FINDAGRAVE.com – Mount Zion Methodist Church Cemetery, Trinity, Randolph County, NC.
Memorial nr.: 11741776 created by Armantia.

CRAVEN William – p. 577
NATIONAL ARCHIVES AND RECORDS ADMINISTRATION, College Park, MD, USA.
New Haven Colony Historical Society, New Haven, CT, USA.
FINDAGRAVE.com – Westville Cemetery, Newhaven, CT. Memorial nr.: 31054364 created by
Mona Rhone

CRAWFORD George – p. 386
DUNPHY Edward P. *Newburgh in the World War. Newburgh*, NY: Newburgh World War Pub.
Co., 1924.
FORRESTER Rita, Newburgh, NY, USA.
WHITE Reg, Patterson, NY, USA.
ANCESTRY.com – New York Abstracts of World War I Military Service 1917-1919

CRAWFORD Samuel – p. 376
NATIONAL ARCHIVES AND RECORDS ADMINISTRATION, College Park, MD, USA.

CREECH Wesley – p. 579
ALSUP - JONES Mary, Lake Waccamaw, NC, USA.
JONES Wesley, Wilmington, NC.
JONES James F., Boone, NC.
DUNCAN Tom, Shalotte, NC, USA.
PRYOR Vonnie, Winston-Salem, NC, USA.
NATIONAL ARCHIVES AND RECORDS ADMINISTRATION, College Park, MD, USA
ANCESTRY.com - U.S. World War I Draft Registration Cards 1917-1918

CROSSLAND Bert S. – p. 347
NEWELL George, Com. American Legion Post 170 Bert S. Crossland. Torrance, CA, USA.
KNOBLOCK Betty, Marina del Rey, California, USA.
LOS ANGELES WESTSIDE GENEALOGICAL SOC., Marina del Rey, CA, USA.
McCOMAS Lucille, Torrance Historical Society, Torrance, California, USA.
THE LOS ANGELES TIMES, 2 December 1918, Los Angeles, USA.
BELGIAN ARMY, Central Military Registration Office, Brussels, Belgium.
NATIONAL ARCHIVES AND RECORDS ADMINISTRATION, College Park, MD, USA

CUDMORE John – p. 318
A short History and Illustrated Roster of the 106th Infantry United States Army, 1917.
Philadelphia, PA: Edward Stern & Co., Inc., 1918.
NATIONAL ARCHIVES AND RECORDS ADMINISTRATION, College Park, MD, USA.
ANCESTRY.com – New York Abstracts of World War I Military Service 1917-1919
WHITE Reg, Patterson, NY, USA.
www.ellisisland.org consulted on 02 May 2005

CUNDY Harry – p. 583
CUNDY Agnes, Lockwood, NY, USA.
A short History and Illustrated Roster of the 106th Infantry United States Army, 1917 (1918).
Philadelphia, PA: Edward Stern & Co., Inc.
NATIONAL ARCHIVES AND RECORDS ADMINISTRATION, College Park, MD, USA.
WHITE Reg, Patterson, NY, USA.
THE BROOKLYN STANDARD UNION, 14 October 1918, Brooklyn, NY, USA.
FINDAGRAVE.com : Eastern Parkway Brooklyn WWI Tree Memorials

DAGLIS Tony – p. 199
CARLSON Ken, Rhode Island State Archives, Providence, RI, USA.
NATIONAL ARCHIVES AND RECORDS ADMINISTRATION, College Park, MD, USA.

DALEY Hugh – p. 584
FORRESTER Rita, Newburgh, NY, USA.
WHITE Reg, Patterson, NY, USA.
DUNPHY Edward P. *Newburgh in the World War. Newburgh*, NY: Newburgh World War Pub.
Co., 1924.
NATIONAL ARCHIVES AND RECORDS ADMINISTRATION, College Park, MD, USA.
ANCESTRY.com – 1910 U.S. Federal Census

DATTOLO Sabino – p. 367
NATIONAL ARCHIVES AND RECORDS ADMINISTRATION, College Park, MD, USA.

DAVIS Samuel – p. 445
DAVIS Denny, Fayette, MO, USA.
FAYETTE DEMOCRAT LEADER, 18 December 1918, Fayette, MO, USA.
NATIONAL ARCHIVES AND RECORDS ADMINISTRATION, College Park, MD, USA.

DAY George – p. 333
NATIONAL ARCHIVES AND RECORDS ADMINISTRATION, College Park, MD, USA.
INDIANA HISTORICAL COMMISSION. *Indiana World War Records Gold Star Honor Roll 1914-1918*. Indianapolis: Fort Wayne Printing Co., 1921.

DECKARD Isaiah – p. 166
DECKARD Ron, Jacksonville, FL, USA.
DECKARD Edward, Monroe, LA, USA.
ADMIRE Jim, Broomfield, CO, USA.
HAUSEE, HOWE & DOYLE. *Soldiers of the Great War*. Washington D.C.: Soldiers Record Publishing Association, 1921.

DE FOREST Walter – p. 253
TROY Mike, Carmel, NY, USA.
A short History and Illustrated Roster of the 105th Infantry United States Army, 1917. Philadelphia, PA: Edward Stern & Co., Inc., 1918.
GANDY Jim, NY STATE MILITARY MUSEUM, Saratoga Springs, NY, USA.
LAUGHNER Niles W. WWI COLLECTION, Keene, NH, USA.
SUTLIFFE Robert Stewart. *Seventy-First New York In The World War*. New York: J.J. Little & Ives Co., 1922.
PUTNAM COUNTY COURIER, 4 October 1918, Putnam, NY, USA.
ANCESTRY.com – New York, Record of Award Medal, 1920-1991

DE MARCO Louis – p. 258
NATIONAL ARCHIVES AND RECORDS ADMINISTRATION, College Park, MD, USA.
ANCESTRY.com - U.S. World War I Draft Registration Cards 1917-1918

DEMARIA John – p. 555
SAMBROTTO Joan, West Seneca, NY, USA.
BUFFALO DAILY COURIER, 30 November 1917, Buffalo, NY, USA.
NATIONAL ARCHIVES AND RECORDS ADMINISTRATION, College Park, MD, USA.
ANCESTRY.com - U.S. World War I Draft Registration Cards 1917-1918

DENELL Frank – p. 406
MILLER Chris, Livingston, MT, USA.
LEE Karrie, MD, USA.
MACKEY, Patty RECORD, Anderson, SC, USA.
NATIONAL ARCHIVES AND RECORDS ADMINISTRATION, College Park, MD, USA.

ANCESTRY.com - U.S. World War I Draft Registration Cards 1917-1918 and New York Abstracts of World War I Military Service 1917-1919

DI GIACOMO Pasquale – p. 153
PETERSON Darren, Dothan, AL, USA.
COLE, Ralph Dayton & HOWELLS, W.C. *The Thirty-Seventh Division in the World War 1917-1918.* Columbus, OH: 37th Division Veterans Association, 1929, Citation page 673
OHIO ADJUDANTS GENERAL'S DEPARTMENT. *The official Roster Ohio Soldiers, Sailors and Marines in the World War 1917-1918.* Columbus, OH: F.J. Heer Printing Co., 1926.
AKRON TIMES, 11 January 1919, Akron, OH, USA.
AKRON-SUMMIT COUNTY PUBLIC LIBRARY, Akron, OH, USA.

DILEO Rocco – p. 352
DILEO Rocco Mrs, Glen Cove, NY, USA.
DILEO Joseph, Davie, FL, USA.
NATIONAL ARCHIVES AND RECORDS ADMINISTRATION, College Park, MD, USA.

DILLON Festus – p. 327
POWERS Lena, Proctorville, OH, USA.
DILLON Henry, Lincoln, CA, USA.
COUNTS Mary, Ironton, OH, USA.

DILUGI Patrick – p. 178
DI LUIGI Ferruccio, Heusden-Zolder, Belgium
MACKEY, Patty RECORD, Anderson, SC, USA.
www.ellisisland.org consulted on 9 September 2005.
NATIONAL ARCHIVES AND RECORDS ADMINISTRATION, College Park, MD, USA.

DINGEE Harry – p. 167
TARRYTOWN DAILY NEWS, 25 November 1918, Tarrytown, NY,USA.
WELTZHEIMER Kris, Tarrytown, NY, USA.
SUTHERLAND Jeanne, Briarcliff Manor, NY, USA
NATIONAL ARCHIVES AND RECORDS ADMINISTRATION, College Park, MD, USA.
OHIO ADJUDANTS GENERAL'S DEPARTMENT. *The official Roster Ohio Soldiers, Sailors and Marines in the World War 1917-1918.* Columbus, OH: F.J. Heer Printing Co., 1926.

DIVER Alva – p. 232
MORRIS NELSON Sallie Lou, San Benito, TX, USA.
SHENEMAN Franklin, South Bend, Indiana, USA.
MACKEY, Patty RECORD, Anderson, SC, USA.
HECKARD Evelyn, Logansport, IN, USA.
GITCHELL Susan, Elma, WA, USA.
INDIANA HISTORICAL COMMISSION . *Indiana World War Records Gold Star Honor Roll 1914-1918.* Indianapolis: Fort Wayne Printing Co., 1921.
ANCESTRY.com – 1900 U.S. Federal Census

DOHERTY William – p. 223
BROOKLYN STANDARD UNION, November 1918, Brooklyn, NY, USA.
A short History and Illustrated Roster of the 106th Infantry United States Army, 1917. Philadelphia, PA: Edward Stern & Co., Inc., 1918.
BROOKLYN DAILY EAGLE, Brooklyn Public Library - Brooklyn Collection, Brooklyn, NY, USA.

DOLL John – p. 500
SCHRAVEN Vicky, Weaverville, NC, USA.
YORK COUNTY HERITAGE TRUST, York, PA, USA.
YORK GAZETTE, 7 August 1920, York, PA, USA.
NATIONAL ARCHIVES AND RECORDS ADMINISTRATION, College Park, MD, USA
COLE R. and HOWELLS W. *The Thirty-Seventh Division in the World War 1917-1918,* Volume II, 37th Division Veterans Association, Columbus, Ohio, 1929, pages 679-680.

DOSTER Halley – p. 563
DOSTER Sue, Fort Wayne, IN, USA.
HARTWIG Mary, Paulding, OH, USA.
DENSMORE Methel, Melrose, OH, USA.

DOYLE Leroy – p. 585
ZIMMERMAN Regina & Bill, Catskill, NY, USA.
ENGELIN Helen, Cementon - Smith's Landing, NY, USA.
HAGUE Beth, Catskill, NY, USA.
ANCESTRY.com – New York Abstracts of World War I Military Service 1917-1919 and New York World War I Veterans Service Data 1913-1919

DROBICHEVSKI Mitro – p. 199
NATIONAL ARCHIVES AND RECORDS ADMINISTRATION, College Park, MD, USA.

DURAND Anthony – p. 546
DURAND - FRANCIS Celeste, Pensacola, FL, USA.
DURAND Rita, Pensacola, FL, USA.
ANCESTRY.com - U.S. World War I Draft Registration Cards 1917-1918

DZIURZYNSKI John – p. 456
OHIO ADJUDANTS GENERAL'S DEPARTMENT. *The official Roster Ohio Soldiers, Sailors and Marines in the World War 1917-1918.* Columbus, OH: F.J. Heer Printing Co., 1926.
HAUSEE, HOWE & DOYLE (1920). *Soldiers of the Great War.* Washington D.C.: Soldiers Record Publishing Association.
NATIONAL ARCHIVES AND RECORDS ADMINISTRATION, College Park, MD, USA.

ECKARD Robert – p. 413
POOLE Herb, Statesville, NC, USA.
PRYOR Vonnie, Winston-Salem, NC, USA.
HOYLE Gary, Taylorsville, NC, USA.
NATIONAL ARCHIVES AND RECORDS ADMINISTRATION, College Park, MD, USA.
ANCESTRY.com – Han/Hahn Adam Echert Family Tree

<u>ELMO Nicola – p. 541</u>
CORTESE Nicolino, Acquaformosa, Italy.
DANZA Domenico, Acquaformosa, Italy.
NATIONAL ARCHIVES AND RECORDS ADMINISTRATION, College Park, MD, USA.
ANCESTRY.com - U.S. World War I Draft Registration Cards 1917-1918.

<u>ELROSE Ralph – p. 588</u>
IMPELLIZERI Joe Ralph, Salem, CT, USA.
POLIZZI Frances, Melbourne, FL, USA.
NATIONAL ARCHIVES AND RECORDS ADMINISTRATION, College Park, MD, USA.
ANCESTRY.com – 1900 U.S. Federal Census - U.S. World War I Draft Registration Cards 1917-
1918 and New York Abstracts of World War I Military Service 1917-1919.

<u>ENNIS Louis – p. 492</u>
STAVRIDES Dorothy, Phoenixville, PA, USA.
LINDLEY Dan, Phoenixville, PA, USA.
JOHNSON Faith, The President's Lodge, Wolfson College, Cambridge, UK.
GARBER David S. *Service with Battery "C", 107th Artillery Brigade, 28th Division A.E.F.*
Philadelphia, PA: Innes & Sons, 1919..
*Pennsylvania in the World War, an Illustrated History of the Twenty-Eighth Division, Volume
II,* States Publications Society, Pittsburgh-Chicago, 1921
NATIONAL ARCHIVES AND RECORDS ADMINISTRATION, College Park, MD, USA.
ANCESTRY.com - U.S. World War I Draft Registration Cards 1917-1918

<u>EPLER David – p. 340</u>
EPLER Evelyn, Zanesville, OH, USA.
EPLER HANA Linda, Mount Vernon, OH, USA.
WASHINGTON COUNTY PUBLIC LIBRARY, Marietta, OH, USA.
NATIONAL ARCHIVES AND RECORDS ADMINISTRATION, College Park, MD, USA.
ANCESTRY.com – 1900 U.S. Federal Census

<u>ERB William – p. 510</u>
MACKEY Patty RECORD, Anderson, SC, USA.
KROSEL Christine, Cleveland, OH, USA.
BROESTL Jane, Cleveland, OH, USA
OHIO ADJUDANTS GENERAL'S DEPARTMENT. *The official Roster Ohio Soldiers, Sailors and
Marines in the World War 1917-1918.* Columbus, OH: F.J. Heer Printing Co., 1926.
TIMMAN, Henry, Norwalk OH, USA.
NORWALK REFLECTOR HERALD, Norwalk, OH, 28 December 1918 and 3 January 1919
WORK Donna, Homewood, IL, USA
CLAIRHOUT, Godfried, Tielt, Belgium
NATIONAL ARCHIVES AND RECORDS ADMINISTRATION, College Park, MD, USA.
ANCESTRY.com – Erb Family Tree and 1910 U.S. Federal Census

ERIKSEN Frederick – p. 532
FELDBIN Mark, New York City, NY, USA.
MACKEY, Patty RECORD, Anderson, SC, USA.
NATIONAL ARCHIVES AND RECORDS ADMINISTRATION, College Park, MD, USA.
ANCESTRY.com – New York Abstracts of World War I Military Service 1917-1919

FEELY Aloysius – p. 491
CALIFORNIA STATE LIBRARY, Sacramento, CA, USA.
NATIONAL ARCHIVES AND RECORDS ADMINISTRATION, College Park, MD, USA.

FERGUSON John – p. 518
OHIO ADJUDANTS GENERAL'S DEPARTMENT. *The official Roster Ohio Soldiers, Sailors and Marines in the World War 1917-1918*. Columbus, OH: F.J. Heer Printing Co., 1926.
NATIONAL ARCHIVES AND RECORDS ADMINISTRATION, College Park, MD, USA.

FERRARO Francesco – p. 145
NATIONAL ARCHIVES AND RECORDS ADMINISTRATION, College Park, MD, USA.
ANCESTRY.com - U.S. World War I Draft Registration Cards 1917-1918

FITZGERALD William – p. 488
NATIONAL ARCHIVES AND RECORDS ADMINISTRATION, College Park, MD, USA.

FLYNN Charles - p. 131
HAUSEE, HOWE & DOYLE. *Soldiers of the Great War*. Washington D.C.: Soldiers Record Publishing Association, 1920.
NATIONAL ARCHIVES AND RECORDS ADMINISTRATION, College Park, MD, USA.
MACKEY, Patty RECORD, Anderson, SC, USA.
FORTIN Archie – p. 165
FORTIN Brian, North Caldwell, NJ, USA.
PETERSON Darren, Dothan, AL, USA.
NATIONAL ARCHIVES AND RECORDS ADMINISTRATION, College Park, MD, USA.
ANCESTRY.com - U.S. World War I Draft Registration Cards 1917-1918

FOSSUM William – p. 170
FOSSUM Warren & HOWARD, Dassel, MN, USA.
GREEN James, Wauwatosa, WI, USA.
DASSEL AREA HISTORICAL SOCIETY, Dassel, MN, USA
ANCESTRY.com – Fossum family tree
ANCESTRY.com - U.S. World War I Draft Registration Cards 1917-1918

FOSTER Alfred – p. 486
FOSTER Dan Alfred, Half Moon Bay, CA, USA.
LA DOUCER William, Willows, California, USA.
KONU Emily A., Orland Free Library, Orland, CA, USA.
HAUSEE, HOWE & DOYLE. *Soldiers of the Great War*. Washington D.C.: Soldiers Record Publishing Association, 1920.
NATIONAL ARCHIVES AND RECORDS ADMINISTRATION, College Park, MD, USA.

FRUTH Norbeth – p. 558
RUDD Winifred, La Crosse, WI.
GRACZYKOWSKI Scott J., Saint Paul, MN, USA.
GREEN James, Wauwatosa, WI, USA.
THIELMANN Clarence J., St Cloud, MN, USA.
ANCESTRY.com – U.S. World War I Draft Registration Cards 1917-1918

GALLAGHER Bryan – p. 380
WHITE Reg, Patterson, NY, USA
MACKEY, Patty RECORD, Anderson, SC, USA.
NATIONAL ARCHIVES AND RECORDS ADMINISTRATION, College Park, MD, USA.
ANCESTRY.com – New York Abstracts of World War I Military Service 1917-1919 –
1910 and 1915 U.S. Federal Census

GARNER William – p. 539
WHITE Patricia, MARITTO,CA, USA.
PERRINE Jordan, Normandy Park, WA,USA.
MELDRUM T. *A History of the 362nd Infantry.* Ogden, UT: A.L. Scoville Press, 1920.
ANCESTRY.com – Sandall Family Tree and U.S. World War I Draft Registration Cards 1917-1918.

GARWOOD Roy – p. 146
GARWOOD - CRANDAL Tammy, Salisbury, NC, USA.
PRYOR Vonnie, Winston-Salem, NC, USA.
ROUSE Deborah H., Salisbury, NC, USA.
ANCESTRY.com – Garwood Family Tree
Maryland in the World War 1917-1919, Military and Naval Service Records. Baltimore, MD, USA: Maryland War Records Commission, 1933.

GIROUX Ernest – p. 590
History of the American Field Service in France. Boston, MA: Boston & New York Houghton Mifflin Company, 1920.
BOSTON DAILY GLOBE, 27 June 1918, Boston, MA, USA.
DEVINE John J. Jr., Boston Public Library, Boston, MA, USA.
www.theaerodrome.com consulted on 2 March 2007.
NATIONAL ARCHIVES AND RECORDS ADMINISTRATION, College Park, MD, USA.
ANCESTRY.com – Giroux-Wartinbee Family Tree – 1910 U.S. Federal Census – U.S. Passport Applications 1795-1925.
https://centennialbook.afs.org/Celebrations/WWIDrivers/1742 consulted on 3 March 2015.

GIUNCHI Orlindo – p. 213
GIUNCHI Luana, Lucca, Italy.
BROWER Maria E., Nevada City, CA, USA.
www.ellisisland.org consulted on 14 September 2005.

GLENN George – p. 201
REED Otill Lowell & ROLAND George. *The Camel Drivers-The 17th Aero Squadron in World War I.*. Atglen, PA: Schiffer Publishing Ltd., 2000.
Memorandum AEF-US Air Service, Paris dated 22 April 1919.
War Department Record HMS 1-217 dated 29 July 1922.
PETERSON Darren, Dothan, AL, USA.

GODDARD Walter – p. 414
MACKEY, Patty RECORD, Anderson, SC, USA.
DAILEY, Ron - photo grave marker Oakdale Cemetery, Washington, NC

GOMSEY Isaac – p. 168
BARTIZAL Judy, Hudson, WI, USA.
PETERSON Darren, Dothan, AL, USA.
U.S. Naturalization Records 1795-1972 – World Archives Project

GOODMAN Roy – p. 430
HAUSEE, HOWE & DOYLE. *Soldiers of the Great War*. Washington D.C.: Soldiers Record Publishing Association, 1920.
HART Larry, Athens, Il, USA.
BOGERT Pen, Louisville, Kentucky, USA.
NATIONAL ARCHIVES AND RECORDS ADMINISTRATION, College Park, MD, USA.

GRIDER John McGavock – p. 593
NATIONAL ARCHIVES AND RECORDS ADMINISTRATION, College Park, MD, USA.
American Red Cross correspondence dated 10/12/1918 and 07/01/ 1919.
War Department correspondence dated 20/01/1919.
Letter dated 28/12/1921 from Mrs. Georgia Grider-Williams to the War Department.
GRIDER Terry, Pine Bluff, AR, USA.
War Birds, Diary of an unknown soldier. London: John Hamilton Ltd., 1926.
ANCESTRY.com - U.S. World War I Draft Registration Cards 1917-1918
www.mcagov.com/history/GriderPark consulted on 28 January 2015
www.warfish.com/george (George William Grider) consulted on 28 January 2015.
www.afamilytree.net/Griderprivacy/johnmcgavockgrider consulted on 28 January 2015.

GRIFFITHS Arthur – p. 303
MACKEY, Patty RECORD, Anderson, SC, USA.
NATIONAL ARCHIVES AND RECORDS ADMINISTRATION, College Park, MD, USA.
ANCESTRY.com – 1910 U.S. Federal Census

GROVE Walter – p. 162
MILLER Mel, York, PA, USA.
BROUCKE Carine, Waregem, Belgium
HAUSEE, HOWE & DOYLE. *Soldiers of the Great War*. Washington D.C.: Soldiers Record Publishing Association, 1920.
ANCESTRY.com – 1900 U.S. Federal Census

GRZYWACZ Steve – p. 160
NATIONAL ARCHIVES AND RECORDS ADMINISTRATION, College Park, MD, USA.
MACKEY, Patty RECORD, Anderson, SC, USA.

GUARINO Antonio – p. 193
GUARINO Salvatore, Desio (Mi), Italy.
GUARINO Lorenzo, Lissone (Mi), Italy.
GUARINO Annarita, Santa Lucia di Serino (Av), Italy.
NATIONAL ARCHIVES AND RECORDS ADMINISTRATION, College Park, MD, USA.

GUGLIARA Philip – p. 527
OHIO ADJUDANTS GENERAL'S DEPARTMENT. *The official Roster Ohio Soldiers, Sailors and Marines in the World War 1917-1918.* Columbus, OH: F.J. Heer Printing Co., 1926.
MACKEY, Patty RECORD, Anderson, SC, USA.
http://www.trumanlibrary.org/photographs/65-4071.jpg consulted on 7 March 2009.
NATIONAL ARCHIVES AND RECORDS ADMINISTRATION, College Park, MD, USA.
ANCESTRY.com - U.S. World War I Draft Registration Cards 1917-1918

GUSLER Paul – p. 173
GUSLER-DAUD Patricia, Delray Beach, FL, USA.
NATIONAL ARCHIVES AND RECORDS ADMINISTRATION, College Park, MD, USA.
ANCESTRY.com – 1900 U.S. Federal Census

GUTH Fred – p. 251
LERCH - GUTH Virginia, Chattanooga, TN, USA.
LOUALLEN Amanda, Dayton, TN, USA.
ANCESTRY.com – Tennessee Northrup family tree

HAGAN Joseph – p. 428
BARROW Dennis, Fairfield, CT, USA.
MACKEY, Patty RECORD, Anderson, SC, USA.
NATIONAL ARCHIVES AND RECORDS ADMINISTRATION, College Park, MD, USA.

HAJEK Joseph – p. 598
VOLENCE Lois, Reading, PA, USA.
NATIONAL ARCHIVES AND RECORDS ADMINISTRATION, College Park, MD, USA.
ANCESTRY.com - U.S. World War I Draft Registration Cards 1917-1918

HAMM Anthony – p. 209
HAMM Joe, Orlando, FL, USA
GANDY Jim, NY STATE MILITARY MUSEUM, Saratoga Springs, NY, USA.
THE NEW YORK TRIBUNE, December 1, 1918, New York City, NY, USA.
A short History and Illustrated Roster of the 105th Infantry United States Army, 1917. Philadelphia, PA: Edward Stern & Co., Inc, 1918.
NATIONAL ARCHIVES AND RECORDS ADMINISTRATION, College Park, MD, USA.
ANCESTRY.com – New York Abstracts of World War I Military Service 1917-1919

HARRINGTON James – p. 309
A short History and Illustrated Roster of the 106th Infantry United States Army, 1917.
Philadelphia, PA: Edward Stern & Co., Inc., 1918.
BROOKLYN DAILY EAGLE, Brooklyn Public Library - Brooklyn Collection, Brooklyn, NY, USA.
ANCESTRY.com – New York Abstracts of World War I Military Service 1917-1919

HARRIS Bernard – p. 404
A short History and Illustrated Roster of the 106th Infantry United States Army, 1917.
Philadelphia, PA: Edward Stern & Co., Inc., 1918.
BROOKLYN DAILY EAGLE, Brooklyn Public Library - Brooklyn Collection, Brooklyn, NY, USA.
NATIONAL ARCHIVES AND RECORDS ADMINISTRATION, College Park, MD, USA.
ANCESTRY.com – 1910 U.S. Federal Census

HART Daniel – p. 599
A short History and Illustrated Roster of the 106th Infantry United States Army, 1917 (1918).
Philadelphia, PA: Edward Stern & Co., Inc., 1918.
NATIONAL ARCHIVES AND RECORDS ADMINISTRATION, College Park, MD, USA.
BROOKLYN DAILY EAGLE, Brooklyn Public Library - Brooklyn Collection, Brooklyn, NY, USA.
ANCESTRY.com – New York Abstracts of World War I Military Service 1917-1919

HARVEY Alfred – p. 257
BERTELSON James, Commissay, France.
RAMSEY Tami, Dublin, VA, USA.
FISHER Ann, Radford Public Library, Radford, VA, USA.

HASSETT John – p. 159
NATIONAL ARCHIVES AND RECORDS ADMINISTRATION, College Park, MD, USA.
MACKEY, Patty RECORD, Anderson, SC, USA.
PERRINE Jordan, Normandy Park, WA,USA.
MELDRUM T. *A History of the 362nd Infantry.* Ogden, UT: A.L. Scoville Press, 1920.

HENLEY Alex – p. 250
HILDERBRAND Gordon, Wasco, OR, USA.
BOSWELL Priscilla, Lynnwood, WA, USA.
ANCESTRY.com – Ontario, Canada Births 1869-1913, Birth Certificate ONMS929 135-0142
ANCESTRY.com – 1910 U.S. Federal Census

HERMAN Louis – p. 389
METZLOFF Carl & Emma, Tonawanda, NY, USA.
BOHRK Betty, New Port Beach, CA, USA.
WOOD Ernestine, Lockport, NY, USA.
ANCESTRY.com – New York Abstracts of World War I Military Service 1917-1919

HESTERMAN Henry – p. 464
SAMS - ANGLEN Carol, Boise, ID, USA.
GRACZYKOWSKI Scott J., Saint Paul, MN, USA.
CORNETT Chris, Grangeville, ID, USA.

GITCHEL Susan, Elma, WA, USA.
FULLER Bonnie, Boise, ID, USA.
THE GRANGEVILLE GLOBE, 5 December 1918, " Local People Bereft of Only Son "
NATIONAL ARCHIVES AND RECORDS ADMINISTRATION, College Park, MD, USA.

HICKTON William – p. 208
A *short History and Illustrated Roster of the 106th Infantry United States Army, 1917.*
Philadelphia, PA: Edward Stern & Co., Inc., 1918.
NATIONAL ARCHIVES AND RECORDS ADMINISTRATION, College Park, MD, USA.
BROOKLYN DAILY EAGLE, Brooklyn Public Library - Brooklyn Collection, Brooklyn, NY, USA.
ANCESTRY.com - U.S. World War I Draft Registration Cards 1917-1918

HIGGINS William – p. 395
NATIONAL ARCHIVES AND RECORDS ADMINISTRATION, College Park, MD, USA.
MACKEY, Patty RECORD, Anderson, SC, USA.
BROOKLYN STANDARD UNION, 19 October 1918, Brooklyn, NY, USA.
ANCESTRY.com – New York Abstracts of World War I Military Service 1917-1919
FINDAGRAVE.com – Green-Wood Cemetery, Brooklyn, NY. Memorial nr.: 130092579
created by Bob Collins

HILL Raymond – p. 306
A *short History and Illustrated Roster of the 106th Infantry United States Army, 1917.*
Philadelphia, PA: Edward Stern & Co., Inc., 1918.
NATIONAL ARCHIVES AND RECORDS ADMINISTRATION, College Park, MD, USA.
BROOKLYN DAILY EAGLE, Brooklyn Public Library - Brooklyn Collection, Brooklyn, NY.
ANCESTRY.com - Beck Family Tree - U.S. World War I Draft Registration Cards 1917-1918
and New York Abstracts of World War I Military Service 1917-1919.

HOCHFELDER Samuel – p. 599
STEING Renee, Dix Hills (Long Island), NY, USA. *A short History and Illustrated Roster of the
106th Infantry United States Army, 1917.* Philadelphia, PA: Edward Stern & Co., Inc., 1918.
NATIONAL ARCHIVES AND RECORDS ADMINISTRATION, College Park, MD, USA.
ANCESTRY.com – New York Abstracts of World War I Military Service 1917-1919

HOLT Sherman – p. 367
VOLENCE Lois, Reading, PA, USA.
NATIONAL ARCHIVES AND RECORDS ADMINISTRATION, College Park, MD, USA.
ANCESTRY.com – 1900 U.S. Federal Census

HOLTZMAN Sol – p. 600
COORUS James, East Meredith, NY, USA.
HAND Joannie, Penn Yann, NY.
WILSON Dawn, Sierra Vista, AZ.
LOCAL HISTORY AND GENEALOGY DIVISION, Central Library of Rochester and Monroe
County, Rochester, NY, USA.
NERSINGER Carol, Rochester Public Library, Rochester, NY, USA.

HORNER Bertram – p. 345
HORNER Senior & Marilyn, Welch, OK, USA.
HORNER Fredalene, Cassville, MO, USA.
PULLEY Bettie, North Miami, OK, USA.
MACKEY, Patty RECORD, Anderson, SC, USA.
NATIONAL ARCHIVES AND RECORDS ADMINISTRATION, College Park, MD, USA.

HORRELL Andrew – p. 152
BREWER Kenneth, Saint Louis, Missouri, USA.
GARDNER Lynn, Edwardsville, Illinois, USA.
NATIONAL ARCHIVES AND RECORDS ADMINISTRATION, College Park, MD, USA.
ANCESTRY.com - U.S. World War I Draft Registration Cards 1917-1918

HOWE George P. – p. 425
CHAPIN W.A.R., *The Lost Legion: The Story of the Fifteen Hundred American Doctors who served with the B.E.F. in the Great War*, p. 42, Press of the Loring-Axtell Co., Springfield, MA, 1926.
RAUER Michael, *Yanks in the King's Forces: American Physicians serving with the British Expeditionary Force during World War I*, p. 35, Office of Medical History, OSG, US Army.
FEELEY Patricia, BOSTON PUBLIC LIBRARY, Boston, Massachusetts, USA.
Harvard College Class of 1900 Secretary's fifth report, privately printed by the Plimton Press, Norwood, MA, USA.
MURPHY Eva, STATE LIBRARY OF MASSACHUSETTS, Boston, MA, USA.
ANCESTRY.com – U.S. Passport Applications 1795-1925

HUFFMAN John – p. 434
WETMORE Kim & FLOYD Alex, Catawba county Library, Newton, NC, USA.
DEAL Jane, Hickory Public Library, Hickory, NC, USA.
PRYOR Vonnie, Winston-Salem, NC, USA.
HUFFMAN Carol, Hickory, NC, USA.
PETERSON Darren, Dothan, AL, USA.
HAUSEE, HOWE & DOYLE. *Soldiers of the Great War*. Washington D.C.: Soldiers Record Publishing Association, 1920.

HUGILL Thomas – p. 401
LODI PUBLIC LIBRARY, Lodi, California, USA.
MASTELL Debbie, Lodi, California, USA.
CALIFORNIA STATE LIBRARY, Sacramento, California, USA.
NATIONAL ARCHIVES AND RECORDS ADMINISTRATION, College Park, MD, USA.
ANCESTRY.com – Hugill Family Tree

HUOVINEN Jacob – p. 166
HEIKKINEN Raili, Kajaani, Finland.
GREEN James, Wauwatosa, WI, USA.
NATIONAL ARCHIVES AND RECORDS ADMINISTRATION, College Park, MD, USA.
ANCESTRY.com - U.S. World War I Draft Registration Cards 1917-1918

HYDE Clarence – p. 360
MYERS Linda, Phoenix, AZ, USA.
DOUGLASS Bill, Newton Falls, OH, USA.
RIDER Debbie, Warren, Ohio, USA.
ANCESTRY.com – Swensen Family Tree

HYLAND William – p. 254
BUCHOLZ Deborah, Gloversville, NY, USA.
GANDY Jim, NY STATE MILITARY MUSEUM, Saratoga Springs, NY, USA.
LAUGHNER Niles W. WWI COLLECTION, Keene, NH, USA.
MORRISON James, Gloversville, NY, USA.

IVERSON John – p. 556
HAUSEE, HOWE & DOYLE. *Soldiers of the Great War*. Soldiers Record Publishing Association,
Washington D.C., USA, 1920.
GREEN James, Wauwatosa, WI, USA.
TOPNESS Borghild, USA
ANCESTRY.com - U.S. World War I Draft Registration Cards 1917-1918

JACOBS Samuel – p. 311
GANDY Jim, NY STATE MILITARY MUSEUM, Saratoga Springs, NY, USA.
LAUGHNER Niles W. WWI COLLECTION, Keene, NH, USA.
A short History and Illustrated Roster of the 105th Infantry United States Army, 1917.
Philadelphia, PA: Edward Stern & Co., Inc., 1918.
ANCESTRY.com – New York Abstracts of World War I Military Service 1917-1919

JAQUET Glenn – p. 463
FLATT Linda, Geneseo Public Library, Geneseo,IL, USA.
JAQUET MILLER Sandra, Rock Falls, IL, USA.
NATIONAL ARCHIVES AND RECORDS ADMINISTRATION, College Park, MD, USA.

JETT Richard – p. 601
ROBERTSON Susan, Lexington, KY, USA.
ROBERTSON Richard Conrad, Lexington, KY, USA.
BARRETT DARNELL Elizabeth, Lexington, KY, USA.
BOGERT Pen, Louisville, KY, USA.
NATIONAL ARCHIVES AND RECORDS ADMINISTRATION, College Park, MD, USA.
ANCESTRY.com – U.S. Passport Applications 1795-1925

JOHNSON Axel – p. 370
ANDERSON Ruth, Minnesota Historical Society, Saint Paul, MN, USA.
SWANSON Elwood, Crystal, MN, USA.
GREEN James, USA.
NATIONAL ARCHIVES AND RECORDS ADMINISTRATION, College Park, MD, USA.
WIDAR Gosta, Svenljunga, Sweden.

JOHNSON Edward – p. 441
GREENWOOD Leonard, La Crescent, MN, USA.
MACKEY, Patty RECORD, Anderson, SC, USA.
NATIONAL ARCHIVES AND RECORDS ADMINISTRATION, College Park, MD, USA.

JOHNSON George – p. 266
HANSON Keith, Olathe, KS, USA.
NATIONAL ARCHIVES AND RECORDS ADMINISTRATION, College Park, MD, USA.

JORGENSEN Louis – p. 189
TOMAHAWK LEADER, December 12, 1918, Tomahawk, WI, USA.
TEAL Kay, Tomahawk Public Library, Tomahawk, WI, USA.
NATIONAL ARCHIVES AND RECORDS ADMINISTRATION, College Park, MD, USA.

KANE Harry – p. 312
DUFFY Mary Ellen, Cutchogue, NY, USA.
A short History and Illustrated Roster of the 106th Infantry United States Army, 1917.
Philadelphia, PA: Edward Stern & Co., Inc., 1918.
BROOKLYN DAILY EAGLE, Brooklyn Public Library - Brooklyn Collection, Brooklyn, NY, USA.
NATIONAL ARCHIVES AND RECORDS ADMINISTRATION, College Park, MD, USA.

KARAS Charles – p. 549
DAMERVAL Carol, Placerville, CA, USA.
CALIFORNIA STATE LIBRARY, Sacramento, CA, USA.
NATIONAL ARCHIVES AND RECORDS ADMINISTRATION, College Park, MD, USA.
ANCESTRY.com - U.S. World War I Draft Registration Cards 1917-1918

KASTEN Brook – p. 387
KASTEN GARTON Katherine, Bronaugh, MO, USA.
BROPHY Patrick, Bushwaker Museum, Nevada, MO, USA.
BANKS MCQUEEN Jean, Vernon County Hist. Society, Nevada, MO, USA .
NATIONAL ARCHIVES AND RECORDS ADMINISTRATION, College Park, MD, USA.
ANCESTRY.com – T. Lobmeyer-Lozoya Family Tree and 1910 U.S. Federal Census

KEARNEY Thomas – p. 137
KEARNEY Mike, Carrollton, TX, USA.
MEMPHIS COMMERCIAL APPEAL, September 18, 1918, Memphis, TN, USA.
LAPOINTE Patricia, Memphis, TN, USA.

KEHRLI Adolph – p. 418
PELL Richard Mrs., Ripley, NY, USA.
SEDLMAYER Walt, Chautauqua County Genealogical Society, Fredonia, NY, USA.
NATIONAL ARCHIVES AND RECORDS ADMINISTRATION, College Park, MD, USA.
ANCESTRY.com – New York Abstracts of World War I Military Service 1917-1919

KELLY Lynn – p. 381
DESANCTIS Edward, Oneida Historical Society, Utica, NY, USA.
MACKEY, Patty RECORD, Anderson, SC, USA.
NATIONAL ARCHIVES AND RECORDS ADMINISTRATION, College Park, MD, USA.
ANCESTRY.com – U.S. World War I Draft Registration Cards 1917-1918 and
New York Abstracts of World War I Military Service 1917-1919

KENNEDY John – p. 419
ABBOTT Ardiss S., Vernon Historical Society, Vernon, CT, USA.
DIXON Bernice, Vernon, CT, USA.
NATIONAL ARCHIVES AND RECORDS ADMINISTRATION, College Park, MD, USA.
ANCESTRY.com - U.S. World War I Draft Registration Cards 1917-1918

KICKA Paul – p. 493
GAYNOR Mary J., Barberton, OH, USA.
ELLIOT Michael, Akron, OH, USA.
NATIONAL ARCHIVES AND RECORDS ADMINISTRATION, College Park, MD, USA
ANCESTRY.com - U.S. World War I Draft Registration Cards 1917-1918

KIERNAN John – p. 436
FANNIN Tom, Brooklyn, NY, USA.
A short History and Illustrated Roster of the 106th Infantry United States Army, 1917.
Philadelphia, PA: Edward Stern & Co., Inc., 1918.
NATIONAL ARCHIVES AND RECORDS ADMINISTRATION, College Park, MD, USA.
ANCESTRY.com – New York Abstracts of World War I Military Service 1917-1919

KINDER Ira – p. 164
PIACENTI Jim, Ladd, IL, USA.
OSBORN Lois, Princeton, IL, USA.
LANGE Pam, Princeton, IL, USA.
ANCESTRY.com – 1900 U.S. Federal Census

KING Harry – p. 632
THE SENTINEL NEWSPAPER, 17 October 1917, Staffordshire, UK.
NATIONAL ARCHIVES AND RECORDS ADMINISTRATION, College Park, MD, USA.
COMMONWEALTH WAR GRAVES COMMISSION, Berkshire, UK.
ANCESTRY.com – New York Abstracts of World War I Military Service 1917-1919

KINGDON Leon – p. 371
KERSHENSKI Kathleen, Batavia, NY, USA.
ZEITS Evelyn, Varysburg, NY, USA.
OWEN James, Batavia, NY, USA.
HAUSEE, HOWE & DOYLE. *Soldiers of the Great War*. Washington D.C.: Soldiers Record
Publishing Association, 1920.
NATIONAL ARCHIVES AND RECORDS ADMINISTRATION, College Park, MD, USA.

KIRSCH Basil – p. 451
KIRSCH Steve & Kathy, Stayton, OR, USA.
KIRSCH Dale & Mary, Gates, OR, USA.
SZEKERES Rick, Newport, PA, USA.
DUNN Meridee, Hope, ID, USA.
NATIONAL ARCHIVES AND RECORDS ADMINISTRATION, College Park, MD, USA.

KISTNER Ray – p. 196
BURGESS Pam, Poland, Ohio, USA.
SKONECKI Leonard, Fostoria, OH, USA.
JUSTICE Penny, Fostoria, OH, USA.
MANN Richard, Fostoria, OH, USA.
THE FOSTORIA DAILY REVIEW, 4 December, 1918, Fostoria, OH, USA.
TIFFIN DAILY TRIBUNE, 5 December 1918, Tiffin, OH
MACKEY, Patty RECORD, Anderson, SC, USA.
NATIONAL ARCHIVES AND RECORDS ADMINISTRATION, College Park, MD, USA.

KLINGENSMITH Russel – p. 236
NATIONAL ARCHIVES AND RECORDS ADMINISTRATION, College Park, MD, USA.
MACKEY, Patty RECORD, Anderson, SC, USA.

KNOWLES Frank – p. 157
TIMM Elaine, Niagara Falls, NY, USA.
PALASZYNSKI Diane, Niagara Falls Public Library, Niagara, NY, USA.
RIVERS Marcia, Lockport, NY, USA.
NIAGARA FALLS GAZETTE, 28 September 1918, Niagara Falls, NY, USA.
NIAGARA FALLS GAZETTE, 9 October 1918, Niagara Falls, NY, USA.
NATIONAL ARCHIVES AND RECORDS ADMINISTRATION, College Park, MD, USA.
ANCESTRY.com – 1900 U.S. Federal Census

KOCH Otto – p. 432
GANDY Jim, NY STATE MILITARY MUSEUM, Saratoga Springs, NY, USA.
A short History and Illustrated Roster of the 105th Infantry United States Army, 1917.
Philadelphia, PA: Edward Stern & Co., Inc., 1918.
LAUGHNER Niles W. WWI COLLECTION, Keene, NH, USA
NATIONAL ARCHIVES AND RECORDS ADMINISTRATION, College Park, MD, USA.

KOHLER Louis – p. 604
NATIONAL ARCHIVES AND RECORDS ADMINISTRATION, College Park, MD, USA.

LABNO Stanislaw – p. 483
GNIADEK Zbigniew, New York City, NY, USA.
NATIONAL ARCHIVES AND RECORDS ADMINISTRATION, College Park, MD, USA.
ANCESTRY.com - U.S. World War I Draft Registration Cards 1917-1918

LAING Harvey – p. 605
BARNES Doris, Marlette, MI, USA.
GRACZYKOWSKI Scott J., Saint Paul, Minnesota, USA.
FELTON Mary, Saginaw, MI, USA.
BOHINSKY Patrick, Saginaw, Michigan, USA.
NATIONAL ARCHIVES AND RECORDS ADMINISTRATION, College Park, MD, USA.

LAMBERT Wesley – p. 499
HAUSEE, HOWE & DOYLE. *Soldiers of the Great War*. Washington D.C.: Soldiers Record Publishing Association, 1920.
THE RIVERSIDE ENTREPRISE, Riverside, CA, USA.
RIVERSIDE PUBLIC LIBRARY, Riverside, Ca, USA.
CALIFORNIA STATE LIBRARY, Sacramento, CA, USA.
NATIONAL ARCHIVES AND RECORDS ADMINISTRATION, College Park, MD, USA.
ANCESTRY.com - U.S. World War I Draft Registration Cards 1917-1918

LANDGRAF Louis – p. 508
GRACZYKOWSKI Scott J., Saint Paul, MN, USA.
GREEN James, USA.
NATIONAL ARCHIVES AND RECORDS ADMINISTRATION, College Park, MD, USA.
ANCESTRY.com – 1910 U.S. Federal Census and World War I Draft Registration Cards 1917-1918

LANG Emil – p. 305
PERRINE Jordan, Normandy Park, WA,USA.
MELDRUM T. *A History of the 362nd Infantry*. Ogden, UT: A.L. Scoville Press, 1920.
NATIONAL ARCHIVES AND RECORDS ADMINISTRATION, College Park, MD, USA.
ANCESTRY.com – Johnson9 Family Tree

LANG Walter – p. 377
OHIO ADJUDANTS GENERAL'S DEPARTMENT. *The official Roster Ohio Soldiers, Sailors and Marines in the World War 1917-1918*. Columbus, OH: F.J. Heer Printing Co., 1926.
NATIONAL ARCHIVES AND RECORDS ADMINISTRATION, College Park, MD, USA.

LARSON John – p. 606
NATIONAL ARCHIVES AND RECORDS ADMINISTRATION, College Park, MD, USA.
ANCESTRY.com – Larson Family Tree – 1910 US Federal Census – 1915 New York State Census - New York Abstracts of World War I Military Service 1917-1919.

LEDER Jack – p. 294
BROOKLYN DAILY EAGLE, Brooklyn Public Library - Brooklyn Collection, Brooklyn, NY, USA.
MACKEY, Patty RECORD, Anderson, SC, USA.
BROOKLYN STANDARD UNION, 14 October, Brooklyn, NY, USA
NATIONAL ARCHIVES AND RECORDS ADMINISTRATION, College Park, MD, USA
ANCESTRY.com – New York Abstracts of World War I Military Service 1917-1919

LEE Dave – p. 295
TIERNEY Key, Graham, NY, USA.
KOBRIN Lisa, Burlington, NC, USA.
PRYOR Vonnie, Winston-Salem, NC, USA.
PETERSON Darren, Dothan, AL, USA.
SULLIVAN WILLARD P. & TUCKER HARRY. *The History of the 105th Regiment of of Engineers.*
NY: George H Doran CO., 1919.
SPENCER, E.W. *The History of Gas Attacks upon the American Expeditionary Forces during the World War.* Cylinder Attack pages 621-623

LEHMANN Peter – p. 606
A short History and Illustrated Roster of the 106th Infantry United States Army, 1917.
Philadelphia, PA: Edward Stern & Co., Inc., 1918.
BROOKLYN DAILY EAGLE, Brooklyn Public Library - Brooklyn Collection, Brooklyn, NY, USA.
NATIONAL ARCHIVES AND RECORDS ADMINISTRATION, College Park, MD, USA.
ANCESTRY.com – New York State Census 1915
FINDAGRAVE.com : Eastern Parkway Brooklyn WWI Tree Memorials

LENTZ Peter – p. 455
GRUN Bruce, Aberdeen, WA, USA.
CALLOW Janet, Marinette, MI, USA.
NATIONAL ARCHIVES AND RECORDS ADMINISTRATION, College Park, MD, USA.

LEONARD William – p. 284
WHITE Reg, Patterson, NY, USA.
HARRIS Stephen L. *Duty, Honor, Privilege.* Dulles, VA: Potomac Books Inc., 2001.
NATIONAL ARCHIVES AND RECORDS ADMINISTRATION, College Park, MD, USA.
ANCESTRY.com – New York Abstracts of World War I Military Service 1917-
1919http://www.nycgovparks.org/parks/leonard-square/history

LEWIS Everett – p. 383
REUSTLE Judy, Springfield, Missouri, USA.
LANDERS Bill, Cape Cod, Ma, USA.
DAUGHTREY G., Lawrence Historical Society, Mount Vernon, MO, USA.
WEST Dale, Longview, Texas, USA.
GRANICY Armitta and Robin Granicy-Sergent, Lancaster California
THE CHIEFTAIN, 7 November 1918
ANCESTRY.com – 1910 Census

LIEBMANN Morris – p. 356
SUTLIFFE, Robert S. *71st New York in the World War.* NY City: J.J. Little & Ives Co., 1922.
THE CORNHUSKER. *Alumni killed in WWI, Vol.13,* Univ. of Nebraska, Omaha, NE, USA, 1919.
www.lee,org/about/awards consulted on 14 November 2005.
CLARKE William F. *Over there with O'Ryan's Roughnecks.* Seattle, WA: Superior Publishing Company, 1968. Page 44.
SIMON Emil J. *Life of Colonel Morris N. Liebmann,* Proceedings of the IRE (Institute Radio Engineers), page 438-439

O'RYAN, John F., *The Story of the 27th Division,* Wynkoop Hallenberg Crawford Co., New York, 1922, pages 219-221.

NEW YORK TIMES, 6 June 1921, *Belgium Decorates Heroes of the 27th*.

A Short History and Illustrated Roster of the 105th Infantry, Edward Stern & Co., Philadelphia, PA, photograph of Colonel Liebmann and burial in Belgium.

ANCESTRY.com – New York Abstracts of World War I Military Service 1917-1919

NEW YORK Military Service Cards 1816-1979

LIEBSCHER Frank – p. 522

LIEBSCHER Mervin, Reno, NE, USA.

HAUSEE, HOWE & DOYLE. *Soldiers of the Great War*. Washington D.C.: Soldiers Record Publishing Association, 1920.

SAN FRANCISCO CHRONICLE, 18 December, 1918, San Francisco, CA, USA.

NATIONAL ARCHIVES AND RECORDS ADMINISTRATION, College Park, MD, USA.

ANCESTRY.com – Frische-Liebscher Family Tree

LIND Charles – p. 398

LIND Richard, Memphis, TN, USA.

BROOKLYN DAILY EAGLE, Brooklyn Public Library - Brooklyn Collection, Brooklyn, NY, USA.

NATIONAL ARCHIVES AND RECORDS ADMINISTRATION, College Park, MD, USA

ANCESTRY.com – New York Abstracts of World War I Military Service 1917-1919

LINK Carl – p. 276

LINK Mary, Lexington, NC, USA.

CHASTAIN Christine, Lexington, NC, USA.

SNIDER Dewey, Lexington, NC, USA

PRYOR Vonnie, Winston-Salem, NC, USA.

GREEN Hugh, Lexington NC, USA.

NATIONAL ARCHIVES AND RECORDS ADMINISTRATION, College Park, MD, USA.

LISTER Edward – p. 154

NELSON Angela, Montpelier, ID, USA.

LISTER Darlene, Lancaster, CA, USA.

ANCESTRY.com - U.S. World War I Draft Registration Cards 1917-1918

HAUSEE, HOWE & DOYLE. *Soldiers of the Great War*. Washington D.C.: Soldiers Record Publishing Association, 1920.

NATIONAL ARCHIVES AND RECORDS ADMINISTRATION, College Park, MD, USA.

LOGAN William – p. 274

DOUGLASS Dorris, Franklin, TN, USA.

NATIONAL ARCHIVES AND RECORDS ADMINISTRATION, College Park, MD, USA.

LONGACRE Edward – p. 421

NATIONAL ARCHIVES AND RECORDS ADMINISTRATION, College Park, MD, USA.

JOHNSON Faith, The President's Lodge, Wolfson College, Cambridge, UK.

GARBER David S. *Service with Battery "C", 107th Artillery Brigade, 28th Division A.E.F.* Philadelphia, PA: Innes & Sons, 1919

Pennsylvania in the World War, an Illustrated History of the Twenty-Eighth Division, Volume II, States Publications Society, Pittsburgh-Chicago, 1921.

LORING David – p. 302
GIRARDEAU Edward Mr. & Mrs., Aiken, SC, USA.
MURPHY Elmer and THOMAS Robert. *The Thirtieth Division in the World War"* Old Hickory Publishing Company, Lepanto, Arkansas, 1936, page 255.

LUCAS Mike – p. 438
SCIGULINSKY - VARGO Alice, Brecksville, OH, USA.
TKACZ Eleanor, Brook Park, Ohio, USA.
NATIONAL ARCHIVES AND RECORDS ADMINISTRATION, College Park, MD, USA.

LUND John – p. 535
CALIFORNIA STATE LIBRARY, Sacramento, CA, USA.
NATIONAL ARCHIVES AND RECORDS ADMINISTRATION, College Park, MD, USA.
ANCESTRY.com - U.S. World War I Draft Registration Cards 1917-1918

LYONS Wilbert – p. 183
A short History and Illustrated Roster of the 106th Infantry United States Army, 1917. Philadelphia, PA: Edward Stern & Co., Inc., 1918.
NATIONAL ARCHIVES AND RECORDS ADMINISTRATION, College Park, MD, USA.
ANCESTRY.com – New York Abstracts of World War I Military Service 1917-1919

MACLEISH Kenneth – p. 320
PASELTINER Ellen, Wilmette, Illinois, USA.
The Price of Honor, The World War I Letters of Naval Aviator Kenneth MacLeish. Edited by Geoffrey L. Rossano. Annapolis, MD: Navy Institute Press, 1991.
GRACZYKOWSKI Scott J., Saint Paul, MN, USA.
NATIONAL ARCHIVES AND RECORDS ADMINISTRATION, College park, MD, USA.

MADARY Otto – p. 424
INDIANA HISTORICAL COMMISSION. *Indiana World War Records Gold Star Honor Roll 1914-1918.* Indianapolis: Fort Wayne Printing Co., 1921.
SHENEMAN Franklin, South Bend, Indiana, USA.
VAN TRUMP Harold. *Fulton county in the World War. Rochester, IN:* Fulton County Council of Defense,1920.
OHIO ADJUDANTS GENERAL'S DEPARTMENT. *The official Roster Ohio Soldiers, Sailors and Marines in the World War 1917-1918.* Columbus, OH: F.J. Heer Printing Co., 1926.
FRANKS Gary, Perrysburg, OH.

MAGNUSON Albert – p. 611
GREEN James, *" The Magnuson who Died in World War One"* Wauwatosa, WI, USA, 2012

MAHAN Edward – p. 505
HAUSEE, HOWE & DOYLE. *Soldiers of the Great War*. Washington D.C.: Soldiers Record Publishing Association, 1920.
NATIONAL ARCHIVES AND RECORDS ADMINISTRATION, College Park, MD, USA.

MAHONEY Patrick – p. 439
TWONEY Neil, Blackrock, Dublin, Ireland.
O'KEEFFE Margaret, Cork City, Ireland
NATIONAL ARCHIVES AND RECORDS ADMINISTRATION, College Park, MD, USA.

MANDAK Matias – p. 614
WICKS PERRY S. *War Record of the Town of Islip, Long Island, NY, World War 1917-1918*. Islip, NY: Town of Islip publishing, 1921.
A short History and Illustrated Roster of the 106th Infantry United States Army, 1917. Philadelphia, PA: Edward Stern & Co., Inc., 1918.
NATIONAL ARCHIVES AND RECORDS ADMINISTRATION, College Park, MD, USA.
ANCESTRY.com - U.S. World War I Draft Registration Cards 1917-1918 and   New York Abstracts of World War I Military Service 1917-1919

MANGOGNA Charles – p. 487
NATIONAL ARCHIVES AND RECORDS ADMINISTRATION, College Park, MD, USA.
ANCESTRY.com – New York Abstracts of World War I Military Service 1917-1919

MARCH George – p. 561
HAUSEE, HOWE & DOYLE. *Soldiers of the Great War*. Washington D.C.: Soldiers Record Publishing Association, 1920.
PATTEE Dallas, Cutler, CA, USA.
STAILEY Mabel, Exeter, CA, USA
DUNCIL Phyllis, Lemoore, CA, USA
THIJS Krista, Zandhoven, Belgium
NATIONAL ARCHIVES AND RECORDS ADMINISTRATION, College Park, MD, USA.
ANCESTRY.com - U.S. World War I Draft Registration Cards 1917-1918

MASTERSON John – p.310
GAYNOR Breda, Dublin, Ireland.
A short History and Illustrated Roster of the 106th Infantry United States Army, 1917. Philadelphia, PA: Edward Stern & Co., Inc., 1918.
NATIONAL ARCHIVES AND RECORDS ADMINISTRATION, College Park, MD, USA.
ANCESTRY.com – New York Abstracts of World War I Military Service 1917-1919

MASTROMONACO Michele – p. 301
CALUSARDO John, Seattle, WA, USA.
NATIONAL ARCHIVES AND RECORDS ADMINISTRATION, College Park, MD, USA.

MATTHEWS Ira – p. 544
MACKEY, Patty RECORD, Anderson, SC, USA.
NATIONAL ARCHIVES AND RECORDS ADMINISTRATION, College Park, MD, USA.

MAXSON Clarence – p. 364
KEMP Jane, Sidney, OH, USA.
KOONS Steve, Dayton, OH, USA.
ADAMS Barbara, Sydney, OH, USA.
NATIONAL ARCHIVES AND RECORDS ADMINISTRATION, College Park, MD, USA.

MAXWELL Ernest – p. 339
WAGNER Melissa, MORGAN COUNTY LIBR., Mc Connelsville, OH, USA.
WHITE - REED Chris, McConnelsville, OH, USA.
OHIO ADJUDANTS GENERAL'S DEPARTMENT. *The official Roster Ohio Soldiers, Sailors and Marines in the World War 1917-1918*. Columbus, OH: F.J. Heer Printing Co., 1926.
GREEN Sara, Athens, OH, USA.
WASHINGTON COUNTY PUBLIC LIBRARY, Marietta, OH, USA.

MAZZARELLA Angelo – p. 450
PERRINE Jordan, Normandy Park, WA,USA.
MELDRUM T. *A History of the 362nd Infantry.* Ogden, UT: A.L. Scoville Press, 1920.
NATIONAL ARCHIVES AND RECORDS ADMINISTRATION, College Park, MD, USA.

McCORMICK Walter – p. 307
NATIONAL ARCHIVES AND RECORDS ADMINISTRATION, College Park, MD, USA.
ANCESTRY.com – New York Abstracts of World War I Military Service 1917-1919

McDONOUGH Harry – p. 502
ALLEN Judith, Springdale, PA, USA.
NATIONAL ARCHIVES AND RECORDS ADMINISTRATION, College Park, MD, USA.
ANCESTRY.com - U.S. World War I Draft Registration Cards 1917-1918
U.S.S. CALIFORNIA, Letter No. 174-b-08 dated 27 April 1908

McGEE Matthew – p. 567
HAUSEE, HOWE & DOYLE. *Soldiers of the Great War.* Washington D.C.: Soldiers Record Publishing Association, 1920.
MACCUBBIN Kathleen, Towson, MD, USA.
ORNDOFF Anthony J., Baltimore Historical Society, Baltimore, MD, USA.
BONSTEEL Don, Enoch Pratt Free Library, Baltimore, MD, USA.
NATIONAL ARCHIVES AND RECORDS ADMINISTRATION, College Park, MD, USA.
ANCESTRY.com - U.S. World War I Draft Registration Cards 1917-1918

McGEEHIN Richard – p. 607
GRACZYKOWSKI Scott J., Saint Paul, MN, USA.
MACKEY, Patty RECORD, Anderson, SC, USA.
NATIONAL ARCHIVES AND RECORDS ADMINISTRATION, College Park, MD, USA.
ANCESTRY.com – New York, Spanish-American War Military and Naval Service Records 1898-1902 – US Federal Census 1880 and 1910 - New York Abstracts of World War I Military Service 1917-1919.

McGONIGLE Bernard – p. 437
A short History and Illustrated Roster of the 106th Infantry United States Army, 1917.
Philadelphia, PA: Edward Stern & Co., Inc., 1918.
NATIONAL ARCHIVES AND RECORDS ADMINISTRATION, College Park, MD, USA.

McGOWAN Henry – p. 400
A short History and Illustrated Roster of the 106th Infantry United States Army, 1917.
Philadelphia, PA: Edward Stern & Co., Inc., 1918.
BROOKLYN STANDARD UNION, 3 October 1918, Brooklyn, NY, USA
NATIONAL ARCHIVES AND RECORDS ADMINISTRATION, College Park, MD, USA.
ANCESTRY.com – New York Abstracts of World War I Military Service 1917-1919

McGRATH Joseph – p. 259
GANDY Jim, NY STATE MILITARY MUSEUM, Saratoga Springs, NY, USA.
A short History and Illustrated Roster of the 105th Infantry United States Army, 1917.
Philadelphia, PA: Edward Stern & Co., Inc., 1918.
NATIONAL ARCHIVES AND RECORDS ADMINISTRATION, College Park, MD, USA.
ANCESTRY.com - U.S. World War I Draft Registration Cards 1917-1918

McGUANE Joe – p. 386
RIDER Debbie, Warren, Ohio, USA.
MACKEY, Patty RECORD, Anderson, SC, USA.
OHIO ADJUDANTS GENERAL'S DEPARTMENT . *The official Roster Ohio Soldiers, Sailors and Marines in the World War 1917-1918.* Columbus, OH: F.J. Heer Printing Co., 1926.

McKINLEY Steven – p. 476
SNIDER Phil & Matthew, Hicksville, OH, USA.
KLINE Dianne, Hicksville, OH, USA.
OHIO ADJUDANTS GENERAL'S DEPARTMENT. *The official Roster Ohio Soldiers, Sailors and Marines in the World War 1917-1918.* Columbus, OH: F.J. Heer Printing Co., 1926.
NATIONAL ARCHIVES AND RECORDS ADMINISTRATION, College Park, MD, USA.

McLAUGHLIN Joseph – p. 379
MACKEY, Patty RECORD, Anderson, SC, USA.
NATIONAL ARCHIVES AND RECORDS ADMINISTRATION, College Park, MD, USA.
ANCESTRY.com – New York Abstracts of World War I Military Service 1917-1919

McLAUGHLIN Joseph – p. 608
NATIONAL ARCHIVES AND RECORDS ADMINISTRATION, College Park, MD, USA.
KAMMERER Larry, TROY PUBLIC LIBRARY, Troy, NY, USA.
ANCESTRY.com – New York Abstracts of World War I Military Service 1917-1919

McMAHON Clarence – p. 608
OHIO ADJUDANTS GENERAL'S DEPARTMENT. *The official Roster Ohio Soldiers, Sailors and Marines in the World War 1917-1918.* Columbus, OH: F.J. Heer Printing Co., 1926.
NATIONAL ARCHIVES AND RECORDS ADMINISTRATION, College Park, MD, USA.

McMAHON Walter – p. 260
WHITE Reg, Patterson, NY, USA.
NATIONAL ARCHIVES AND RECORDS ADMINISTRATION, College Park, MD, USA.
ANCESTRY.com – New York Abstracts of World War I Military Service 1917-1919

McMAHON William – p. 609
NATIONAL ARCHIVES AND RECORDS ADMINISTRATION, College Park, MD, USA.

McVERRY William – p. 610
ROBERTS Kenneth A, Dover, DE, USA.
GRACZYKOWSKI Scott J., Saint Paul, MN, USA.
VOLENCE Lois, Reading, PA, USA.
ANCESTRY.com - U.S. World War I Draft Registration Cards 1917-1918

McWALTERS James – p. 253
NATIONAL ARCHIVES AND RECORDS ADMINISTRATION, College Park, MD, USA.

MEKONIS William – p. 145
NATIONAL ARCHIVES AND RECORDS ADMINISTRATION, College Park, MD, USA.

MELICHAREK Gerald – p. 518
HAUSEE, HOWE & DOYLE. *Soldiers of the Great War*. Washington D.C.: Soldiers Record
Publishing Association, 1920.
LOS ANGELES HERALD, 11 December 1918, Los Angeles, CA, USA.
NATIONAL ARCHIVES AND RECORDS ADMINISTRATION, College Park, MD, USA.
ANCESTRY.com – 1910 U.S. Federal Census
CALIFORNIA WAR HISTORY COMMITTEE - California WWI Soldier Service Cards and Photos,
1917-1918.

MENZKE Charles – p. 416
LAROBARDIER Charly, Belleville, IL, USA.
BELLEVILLE PUBLIC LIBRARY, Belleville, IL, USA.
NATIONAL ARCHIVES AND RECORDS ADMINISTRATION, College Park, MD, USA.
ANCESTRY.com - U.S. World War I Draft Registration Cards 1917-1918 and 1900 U.S.
Federal Census

MEYERS Vernard – p. 524
SPOKANE CHRONICLE, 28 November 1918, Spokane, WA, USA
NATIONAL ARCHIVES AND RECORDS ADMINISTRATION, College Park, MD, USA.

MICHAEL John – p. 614
HAUSEE, HOWE & DOYLE. *Soldiers of the Great War*. Washington D.C.: Soldiers Record
Publishing Association, 1920.
GRACZYKOWSKI Scott J., Saint Paul, MN, USA.
NATIONAL ARCHIVES AND RECORDS ADMINISTRATION, College Park, MD, USA.
ANCESTRY.com – New York Abstracts of World War I Military Service 1917-1919

MIKULA Steve – p. 567
INDIANA HISTORICAL COMMISSION. *Indiana World War Records Gold Star Honor Roll 1914-1918*. Indianapolis: Fort Wayne Printing Co., 1921.
SOUTH BEND TRIBUNE, 17 January 1919, South Bend, IN, USA.

MILLER James – p. 197
BURNS Thea, Columbus, OH, USA.
THOMPSON Clarence, Hemlock, OH, USA.
PERRINE Jordan, Normandy Park, WA, USA.
MELDRUM T. *A History of the 362nd Infantry.* Ogden, UT: A.L. Scoville Press, 1920.
NATIONAL ARCHIVES AND RECORDS ADMINISTRATION, College Park, MD, USA.

MILLER Lew – p. 344
FRUTH Deana, Bucyrus, OH, USA.
JUSTICE Penny, Fostoria, OH, USA.
OHIO ADJUDANTS GENERAL'S DEPARTMENT. *The official Roster Ohio Soldiers, Sailors and Marines in the World War 1917-1918.* Columbus, OH: F.J. Heer Printing Co., 1926.
NATIONAL ARCHIVES AND RECORDS ADMINISTRATION, College Park, MD, USA.

MINZESHEIMER Irwin – p. 410
A short History and Illustrated Roster of the 106th Infantry United States Army, 1917. Philadelphia, PA: Edward Stern & Co., Inc., 1918.
NATIONAL ARCHIVES AND RECORDS ADMINISTRATION, College Park, MD, USA.
ANCESTRY.com – 1915 New York State Census and New York Abstracts of World War I Military Service 1917-1919.

MIX Arthur – p. 136
MIX - HAWKINS Muriel, West Des Moines, IA, USA.

MLEKO Stanley – p. 142
OHIO ADJUDANTS GENERAL'S DEPARTMENT . *The official Roster Ohio Soldiers, Sailors and Marines in the World War 1917-1918.* Columbus, OH: F.J. Heer Printing Co., 1926.
www.ellisisland.org consulted 20 December 2007.

MLODORZENIEC Joseph – p. 569
NATIONAL ARCHIVES AND RECORDS ADMINISTRATION, College Park, MD, USA.

MOEN Neil – p. 459
PETERSON Brent T., Stillwater, MN, USA.
KLINNERT Yvonne, Stillwater, MN, USA.
ANDERSON Ruth, Minnesota Historical Society, Saint Paul, MN, USA.
NATIONAL ARCHIVES AND RECORDS ADMINISTRATION, College Park, MD, USA.
ANCESTRY.com –1910 U.S. Federal Census and World War I Draft Registration Cards 1917-1918

MOFFETT Charles – p. 516
BANKS Jay, Union, WV, USA.
MACKEY, Patty RECORD, Anderson, SC, USA.
OHIO ADJUDANTS GENERAL'S DEPARTMENT. *The official Roster Ohio Soldiers, Sailors and Marines in the World War 1917-1918.* Columbus, OH: F.J. Heer Printing Co., 1926.
KINO Janet, Denmark.
WEST VIRGINIA NEWS, 18 January 1919, Ronceverte, WV, USA.
NATIONAL ARCHIVES AND RECORDS ADMINISTRATION, College Park, MD, USA.

MOHLER Allen – p. 246
SHUPE John, Lebanon, OH, USA.
OHIO ADJUDANTS GENERAL'S DEPARTMENT . *The official Roster Ohio Soldiers, Sailors and Marines in the World War 1917-1918.* Columbus, OH: F.J. Heer Printing Co., 1926.
ANCESTRY.com – 1910 U.S. Federal Census

MONK Robert – p. 158
MONK Flower, West Union, IL, USA.
PERRINE Jordan, Normandy Park, WA,USA.
MELDRUM T. *A History of the 362nd Infantry.* Ogden, UT: A.L. Scoville Press., 1920.
NATIONAL ARCHIVES AND RECORDS ADMINISTRATION, College Park, MD, USA.
ANCESTRY.com – 1900 U.S. Federal Census

MOOREHOUSE Harold – p. 172
OHIO ADJUDANTS GENERAL'S DEPARTMENT. *The official Roster Ohio Soldiers, Sailors and Marines in the World War 1917-1918.* Columbus, OH: F.J. Heer Printing Co., 1926.
NATIONAL ARCHIVES AND RECORDS ADMINISTRATION, College Park, MD, USA.
NORRIS Milton R., Canfield, Ohio, USA.
HAHN William, Ravenna, Ohio, USA.
NATIONAL ARCHIVES AND RECORDS ADMINISTRATION, College Park, MD, USA
ANCESTRY.com – 1910 Census

MORGAN Harold – p. 615
CHAPIN W.A.R., *The Lost Legion: The Story of the Fifteen Hundred American Doctors who served with the B.E.F. in the Great War,* Press of the Loring-Axtell Co., Springfield, MA, 1926.
RAUER Michael, *Yanks in the King's Forces: American Physicians serving with the British Expeditionary Force during World War I,* pp 33-34, Office of Medical History, OSG, US Army.
SEITZ Susan, Petaluma, CA, USA.
BATES Barbara, Flagstaff, AZ, USA.
MACKEY, Patty RECORD, Anderson, SC, USA.
GRACZYKOWSKI Scott J., Saint Paul, MN, USA.
RICHARDS Anthony, Imperial War Museum, London, UK
NATIONAL ARCHIVES AND RECORDS ADMINISTRATION, College Park, MD, USA.
ANCESTRY.com – New York Abstracts of World War I Military Service 1917-1919 – California WWI Soldier Service Cards and Photos 1917-18.

MORROW James – p. 331
NATIONAL ARCHIVES AND RECORDS ADMINISTRATION, College Park, MD, USA.
ANCESTRY.com - U.S. World War I Draft Registration Cards 1917-1918

MUNCH Emil – p. 206
KRAUS Joanne, Cambria, CA, USA.
NATIONAL ARCHIVES AND RECORDS ADMINISTRATION, College Park, MD, USA.
ANCESTRY.com - U.S. World War I Draft Registration Cards 1917-1918

MUNDES William – p. 228
KRAUS Joanne, Cambria, CA, USA.
NATIONAL ARCHIVES AND RECORDS ADMINISTRATION, College Park, MD, USA.
NEW JERSEY SERVICE RECORDS, NJ, USA.

MUSCIETRO Giovanni – p. 328
DOUGHERTY Lisa, Saratoga Springs, NY, USA.
NATIONAL ARCHIVES AND RECORDS ADMINISTRATION, College Park, MD, USA.
ANCESTRY.com – New York Abstracts of World War I Military Service 1917-1919

NEUHAUS Norman – p. 147
GRACZYKOWSKI Scott J., Saint Paul, MN, USA.
NATIONAL ARCHIVES AND RECORDS ADMINISTRATION, College Park, MD, USA.
FRANKS Gary, Perrysburg, OH, USA.
JOHNSON Eric, Milwaukee, WI, USA.

NILSEN Karl – p. 155
OYVIND Helle, *Hafrsfjord,* Norway.
NATIONAL ARCHIVES AND RECORDS ADMINISTRATION, College Park, MD, USA.
ANCESTRY.com - U.S. World War I Draft Registration Cards 1917-1918
U.S. Naturalization Records 1795-1972 – World Archives Project

NOONAN John – p. 265
GOODMAN Lori, Pittsford, NY, USA.
NATIONAL ARCHIVES AND RECORDS ADMINISTRATION, College Park, MD, USA.
ANCESTRY.com – New York Abstracts of World War I Military Service 1917-1919

NOVAK John – p. 391
GRACZYKOWSKI Scott J., Saint Paul, MN, USA.
MACKEY, Patty RECORD, Anderson, SC, USA.
NATIONAL ARCHIVES AND RECORDS ADMINISTRATION, College Park, MD, USA.

NOVICH Joe – p. 560
NATIONAL ARCHIVES AND RECORDS ADMINISTRATION, College Park, MD, USA.
ANCESTRY.com - U.S. World War I Draft Registration Cards 1917-1918 and U.S.
Naturalization Records 1795-1972 (World Archives Project)

O'CONNOR Clement – p. 142
CALLOW Janette, Marinett, WI, USA.
NATIONAL ARCHIVES AND RECORDS ADMINISTRATION, College Park, MD, USA.
ANCESTRY-com – 1910 Census

O'HARE James – p. 319
BROOKLYN DAILY EAGLE, Brooklyn Public Library - Brooklyn Collection, Brooklyn, NY, USA.
NATIONAL ARCHIVES AND RECORDS ADMINISTRATION, College Park, MD, USA.

OLSON Ole – p. 471
MATHISON Linda, Cambridge, WI, USA.
MATHISON Florence, Cambridge, WI, USA.
MACKEY, Patty RECORD, Anderson, SC, USA.
NATIONAL ARCHIVES AND RECORDS ADMINISTRATION, College Park, MD, USA.
GROPEN Kare and Kari, Rudshøgda, Norway

OLSON Thomas – p. 291
NYSTED PLETTEN Inger Hanne, Kvaløysletta, Norway.
SUN PRAIRIE COUNTRYMAN, 5 December, Sun Prairie, WI, USA.
NORDERHAUG Abbie, Madison, WI, USA.
NATIONAL ARCHIVES AND RECORDS ADMINISTRATION, College Park, MD, USA.

OSBORN Frank – p. 512
JOHNSTON Glenna, Orofino, Idaho, USA
PIERCE Elsie, Moscow, Idaho, USA
MELDRUM T. *A History of the 362nd Infantry.* Ogden, UT: A.L. Scoville Press, 1920.
ANCESTRY.com – Wagner Family Tree

OTT Ferdinand – p. 618
BROOKLYN STANDARD UNION, 18 October 1918, Brooklyn, NY, USA.
HAUSEE, HOWE & DOYLE . *Soldiers of the Great War.* Washington D.C.: Soldiers Record Publishing Association, 1920.
MELDRUM T. (1920). *A History of the 362nd Infantry.* Ogden, UT: A.L. Scoville Press.
NATIONAL ARCHIVES AND RECORDS ADMINISTRATION, College Park, MD, USA.
ANCESTRY.com - New York Abstracts of World War I Military Service 1917-1919

PASH Alexander – p. 338
NATIONAL ARCHIVES AND RECORDS ADMINISTRATION, College Park, MD, USA.

PEIRCE William – p. 480
OHIO ADJUDANTS GENERAL'S DEPARTMENT . *The official Roster Ohio Soldiers, Sailors and Marines in the World War 1917-1918.* Columbus, OH: F.J. Heer Printing Co., 1926.
MACKEY, Patty RECORD, Anderson, SC, USA.
MIDWEEK PICTORIAL. Our Nation's Roll of Honor

PERONE John – p. 143
CASTELLANO Eleanor, Marble, MN, USA.
NATIONAL ARCHIVES AND RECORDS ADMINISTRATION, College Park, MD, USA.
ANCESTRY.com – U.S. World War I Draft Registration Cards 1917-1918

PETERSEN Clarence – p. 618
GRACZYKOWSKI Scott J., Saint Paul, MN, USA.
ANDERSON Ruth, Minnesota Historical Society, Saint Paul, MN, USA.
MINNESOTA WAR RECORDS COMMISSION, Minneapolis, MN.
FINDAGRAVE.com – Victory Memorial Drive, Minneapolis, Hennepin County, MN, Memorial
nr.: 120603341 created by mordecaarr

PETERSON Henry – p. 441
PETERSON Darren, Dothan, AL, USA.
NATIONAL ARCHIVES AND RECORDS ADMINISTRATION, College Park, MD, USA.

PETRO Stephen – p. 391
HAUSEE, HOWE & DOYLE. *Soldiers of the Great War*. Washington D.C.: Soldiers Record
Publishing Association, 1920.
NATIONAL ARCHIVES AND RECORDS ADMINISTRATION, College Park, MD, USA.
ANCESTRY.com - U.S. World War I Draft Registration Cards 1917-1918

PHALEN John – p. 489
PHALEN James & Pat, Jacksonville, IL, USA.
ASHMORE Chris, Jacksonville, IL, USA.
NATIONAL ARCHIVES AND RECORDS ADMINISTRATION, College Park, MD, USA.

PIGUE James – p. 634
NATIONAL ARCHIVES AND RECORDS ADMINISTRATION, College Park, MD, USA.
KAPLAN Carol, Nashville, TN, USA.
GILMORE LONG Rose. *Davidson County Women in the World War 1914-1919*. Nashville, TN:
Foster & Parke, 1921.
LENTZ Susan, Nashville Landmarks Examiner: *WWI Soldier stands guard over family plot at
Mt. Olivet,* 24 October 2009.
ANCESTRY.com – Bailey Family Tree
PLASKAWICKY Julius – p. 470
NATIONAL ARCHIVES AND RECORDS ADMINISTRATION, College Park, MD, USA.
ANCESTRY.com – New York Abstracts of World War I Military Service 1917-1919

PLIML Steve – p. 328
OHIO ADJUDANTS GENERAL'S DEPARTMENT. *The official Roster Ohio Soldiers, Sailors and
Marines in the World War 1917-1918.* Columbus, OH: F.J. Heer Printing Co., 1926.
NATIONAL ARCHIVES AND RECORDS ADMINISTRATION, College Park, MD, USA.

PORCELLI Robert – p. 281
PETERSON Darren, Dothan, AL, USA.
PRYOR Vonnie, Winston-Salem, NC, USA.
FAYETTEVILLE OBSERVER, 7 August 1918, Fayetteville, NC, USA.
FAYETTEVILLE OBSERVER, 14 August 1918, Fayetteville, NC, USA.

PORTER George – p. 469
WALDEN Julia, London, OH, USA.
HAUSEE, HOWE & DOYLE. *Soldiers of the Great War*. Washington D.C.: Soldiers Record
Publishing Association, 1920.
OHIO ADJUDANTS GENERAL'S DEPARTMENT. *The official Roster Ohio Soldiers, Sailors and
Marines in the World War 1917-1918.* Columbus, OH: F.J. Heer Printing Co., 1926.
WASHINGTON COUNTY PUBLIC LIBRARY, Marietta, Ohio, USA.
ANCESTRY.com – Magrum Family Tree and 1900 U.S. Federal Census.

POSNANSKY Morris – p. 620
HAUSEE, HOWE & DOYLE. *Soldiers of the Great War*. Washington D.C.: Soldiers Record
Publishing Association, 1920.
NATIONAL ARCHIVES AND RECORDS ADMINISTRATION, College Park, MD, USA.
ANCESTRY.com – 1910 U.S. Federal Census and New York Abstracts of World War I Military
Service 1917-1919.

QUIGLEY Arthur – p 257
A short History and Illustrated Roster of the 106th Infantry United States Army, 1917.
Philadelphia, PA: Edward Stern & Co., Inc., 1918.
NATIONAL ARCHIVES AND RECORDS ADMINISTRATION, College Park, MD, USA.
BROOKLYN DAILY EAGLE, Brooklyn Public Library - Brooklyn Collection, Brooklyn, NY, USA.
ANCESTRY.com – New York City Births 1891-1902 and 1900 U.S. Federal Census

QUIRK Joseph – p. 358
CHAMBERS Cordess III, Snow Shoe, PA,USA.
THE CENTRE DEMOCRAT, 12 December 1918, State College, PA, USA.
NATIONAL ARCHIVES AND RECORDS ADMINISTRATION, College Park, MD, USA.

RAAB John – p. 496
ANDERKO Elaine, Bethlehem, PA, USA.
NATIONAL ARCHIVES AND RECORDS ADMINISTRATION, College Park, MD, USA.
ANCESTRY.com - U.S. World War I Draft Registration Cards 1917-1918

READY Joseph – p. 172
OHIO ADJUDANTS GENERAL'S DEPARTMENT . *The official Roster Ohio Soldiers, Sailors and
Marines in the World War 1917-1918.* Columbus, OH: F.J. Heer Printing Co., 1926.
READY Su, Cincinnati, OH, USA.
NATIONAL ARCHIVES AND RECORDS ADMINISTRATION, College Park, MD, USA.
ANCESTRY.com – 1900 U.S. Federal Census

RECORD George – p. 349
ZETTERSTROM Alice, Saratoga Springs, NY, USA.
MACKEY, Patty RECORD, Anderson, SC, USA.
THE SARATOGIAN, 24 September 1918, Saratoga Springs, NY, USA.
NATIONAL ARCHIVES AND RECORDS ADMINISTRATION, College Park, MD, USA
ANCESTRY.com – New York Abstracts of World War I Military Service 1917-1919

REQUA Harry – p. 431
MASON William H. *The Part Played in the Great War by the Soldiers, Sailors, Marines and Patriotic Civilians of Snohomish County.* Everett, WA, Mason Publishing Co., Inc., 1926.
REQUA Amos C. REV. (1985). *Family of Requa.* Peekskill, NY: unknown, USA.
RIDDLE Margaret, Everett WA, USA.

RICE Robert – p. 308
A short History and Illustrated Roster of the 106th Infantry United States Army, 1917. Philadelphia, PA: Edward Stern & Co., Inc., 1918.
HAUSEE, HOWE & DOYLE . *Soldiers of the Great War.* Washington D.C.: Soldiers Record Publishing Association, 1920.
NATIONAL ARCHIVES AND RECORDS ADMINISTRATION, College Park, MD, USA.
ANCESTRY.com – New York Abstracts of World War I Military Service 1917-1919

RIGSBEE Ike – p. 410
PRYOR Vonnie, Winston-Salem, NC, USA.
GREENSBORO Daily News (Greensboro, NC) – 26 September 1918
NATIONAL ARCHIVES AND RECORDS ADMINISTRATION, College Park, MD, USA.

ROBERTS Carl – p. 382
HAUSEE, HOWE & DOYLE. *Soldiers of the Great War.* Washington D.C., 1920
OHIO ADJUDANTS GENERAL'S DEPARTMENT. *The official Roster Ohio Soldiers, Sailors and Marines in the World War 1917-1918.* Columbus, OH: F.J. Heer Printing Co., 1926.
PAINESVILLE TELEGRAPH, 3 July 1919, Painesville, OH, USA.
BINKLEY Patricia, West Covina, California
ROBINSON James – p. 429
DUNN Janis, Nampa, ID, USA.
NATIONAL ARCHIVES AND RECORDS ADMINISTRATION, College Park, MD, USA.

RODER William – p. 330
NATIONAL ARCHIVES AND RECORDS ADMINISTRATION, College Park, MD, USA.
FLANDERS FIELD AMERICAN CEMETERY Archives
U.S. Naturalization Records 1795-1972 – World Archives Project

ROSCOE Joseph – p. 411
THOMAS H. LEATH LIBRARY, Rockingham, NC, USA.
NATIONAL ARCHIVES AND RECORDS ADMINISTRATION, College Park, MD, USA.
ANCESTRY.com - U.S. World War I Draft Registration Cards 1917-1918

ROSS Karl – p. 240
EMERSON Michael Sgt., San Francisco, CA, USA.
AMERICAN LEGION POST KARL ROSS, Stockton, CA, USA.
STOCKTON DAILY EVENING RECORD, 30 Nov. 1918, Stockton, CA, USA.
GAMPP Ute, Lodi, CA, USA.
GRETCHEN Louden, Stockton, CA, USA.
ANCESTRY.com - California World War I Death Announcements 1918-1921
WAR DEPARTMENT: *Congressional Medal of Honor, the Distinguished Service Cross and the Distinguished Service Medal,* Compiled by the Office of the Adjutant General of the Army, Washington GPO, 1920, page 574

ROSS Wendell – p. 274
ROSS Lori, St Louis Park, MN, USA.
NATIONAL ARCHIVES AND RECORDS ADMINISTRATION, College Park, MD, USA.
ANCESTRY.com – 1910 U.S. Federal Census

ROTOLLO Toney – p. 289
HAUSEE, HOWE & DOYLE. *Soldiers of the Great War.* Washington D.C.: Soldiers Record Publishing Association., 1920.
BROOKLYN STANDARD UNION, 4 December 1918, Brooklyn, NY, USA.
A short History and Illustrated Roster of the 106th Infantry United States Army, 1917. Philadelphia, PA: Edward Stern & Co., Inc., 1918.
NATIONAL ARCHIVES AND RECORDS ADMINISTRATION, College Park, MD, USA.
ANCESTRY.com – New York Abstracts of World War I Military Service 1917-1919

ROVERE Vincent – p. 313
NATIONAL ARCHIVES AND RECORDS ADMINISTRATION, College Park, MD, USA.
ANCESTRY.com – New York Abstracts of World War I Military Service 1917-1919

RYDELL Axel – p. 473
RYDELL Dennis, Kempner, TX, USA.
OLSON Conny, Fargo, ND, USA.
PERRINE Jordan, Normandy Park, WA, USA.
MELDRUM T. *A History of the 362nd Infantry.* Ogden, UT: A.L. Scoville Press, 1920.
NATIONAL ARCHIVES AND RECORDS ADMINISTRATION, College Park, MD, USA.
ANCESTRY.com – Minnesota Marriages Index 1849-1950

SCELZO Anthony – p. 234
A short History and Illustrated Roster of the 106th Infantry United States Army, 1917. Philadelphia, PA: Edward Stern & Co., Inc., 1918.
BROOKLYN DAILY EAGLE, Brooklyn Public Library - Brooklyn Collection, Brooklyn, NY, USA.
NATIONAL ARCHIVES AND RECORDS ADMINISTRATION, College Park, MD, USA.

SCHAEFER Reinhold – p. 304
MERKEL Vivian, Washburn, ND, USA.
SCHELL Diane, Underwood, ND, USA.
KING Darren, York, PA, USA.

NATIONAL ARCHIVES AND RECORDS ADMINISTRATION, College Park, MD, USA.
ANCESTRY.com – Kern-Schafer Family Tree
Roster of Men and Women who served in the Army, Naval Service including the Marine Corps of the United States or its Allies from the State of North Dakota in the World War 1917-1918, Volume 4. Rich to Zygmond.

SCHAIRER James – p. 243
RAUGH Jill, Benton Harbor, MI, USA.
FRIE Cindy, Benton Harbor MI, USA.
HAUSEE, HOWE & DOYLE. *Soldiers of the Great War.* Washington D.C.: Soldiers Record Publishing Association, 1920.
OHIO ADJUDANTS GENERAL'S DEPARTMENT. *The official Roster Ohio Soldiers, Sailors and Marines in the World War 1917-1918.* Columbus, OH: F.J. Heer Printing Co., 1926.
THE HERALD PRESS, February 1, 1919, St Joseph, MI, USA.
THE HERALD PRESS, 17 November 1934, St Joseph, MI, USA.
COLE R. and HOWELLS W. The Thirty-seventh Division in the World War 1917-1918, Vol. II, the 37th Division Veterans Association, Columbus, OH, page 677.
WAR DEPARTMENT: *Congressional Medal of Honor, the Distinguished Service Cross and the Distinguished Service Medal,* Compiled by the Office of the Adjutant General of the Army, Washington GPO, 1920, page 576.

SCHAU Otto – p. 507
HAUSEE, HOWE & DOYLE. *Soldiers of the Great War.* Washington D.C.: Soldiers Record Publishing Association, 1920.
NATIONAL ARCHIVES AND RECORDS ADMINISTRATION, College Park, MD, USA.
ANCESTRY.com – 1910 U.S. Federal Census

SCHIAVONE Francesco – p. 544
GRACZYKOWSKI Scott J., Saint Paul, MN, USA.
NATIONAL ARCHIVES AND RECORDS ADMINISTRATION, College Park, MD, USA.
ANCESTRY.com - U.S. World War I Draft Registration Cards 1917-1918

SCHMITT Max – p. 186
SAGLIBENE Nancy, Buffalo, NY, USA.
NATIONAL ARCHIVES AND RECORDS ADMINISTRATION, College Park, MD, USA.
ANCESTRY.com – 1900 U.S. Federal Census

SCHNELL Paul – p. 148
HISER Jane & Ben, Piqua, OH, USA.
FURROW Sherry, Piqua, OH, USA.
WASHINGTON COUNTY PUBLIC LIBRARY, Marietta, OH, USA.
PIQUA DAILY CALL, 2 December 1918, Piqua, OH, USA.
CRON Rachel, Piqua, OH, USA.

SCHOCH Clinton – p. 468
HAUSEE, HOWE & DOYLE . *Soldiers of the Great War.* Washington D.C.: Soldiers Record Publishing Association, 1920.

SNODGRASS PILLA Lynn, Nazareth, PA, USA.
NATIONAL ARCHIVES AND RECORDS ADMINISTRATION, College Park, MD, USA.
ANCESTRY.com - U.S. World War I Draft Registration Cards 1917-1918

SCHULTZ Albert – p. 621
SCHULTZ - ANDERSON Lois, Grantsburg, WI, USA.
GREEN James, Wauwatosa, WI, USA.
GRACZYKOWSKI Scott J., Saint Paul, MN, USA.
LARSON Cheryl, Eden Prairie, MN, USA.

SEERY William – p. 623
A short History and Illustrated Roster of the 106th Infantry United States Army, 1917.
Philadelphia, PA: Edward Stern & Co., Inc., 1918.
MACKEY, Patty RECORD, Anderson, SC, USA.
NATIONAL ARCHIVES AND RECORDS ADMINISTRATION, College Park, MD, USA.
ANCESTRY.com – New York Abstracts of World War I Military Service 1917-1919
O'RYAN, John F., *The Story of the 27th Division,* Wynkoop Hallenberg Crawford Co., New York, 1922, Volume 2, page 1086.

SEGALL Arthur – p. 533
www.ellisisland.org consulted on 3 March 2005.
NATIONAL ARCHIVES AND RECORDS ADMINISTRATION, College Park, MD, USA

SELIG Merrill – p. 402
SELIG John, Lexington, IN, USA
SELIG SMALL Virginia, Mentor, OH, USA.
SELIG Steve, New River, AZ, USA.
SHENEMAN Franklin, South Bend, IN, USA.
COTTMANN GEORGE S. *Jefferson County in the World War.* Madison, IN: Jefferson County Historical Society, 1920.
BARNES Janice, Madison, IN, USA.
THE MADISON COURIER, 3 March 1919, Madison, IN, USA.
NATIONAL ARCHIVES AND RECORDS ADMINISTRATION, College Park, MD, USA.
ANCESTRY.com - U.S. World War I Draft Registration Cards 1917-1918

SHANNON Thomas – p. 314
SHANNON - ODERMATT Patricia, Rockville Centre NY, USA.
SHANNON - JEFFERSON Maureen, Cape Coral, FL, USA.
A short History and Illustrated Roster of the 106th Infantry United States Army, 1917.
Philadelphia, PA: Edward Stern & Co., Inc., 1918.
ANCESTRY.com – New York Abstracts of World War I Military Service 1917-1919

SILCOTT Clyde – p. 465
SILCOTT Ernest O., Piketon, OH, USA.
ADKINS Tom, Waverly, OH, USA.
GARNET A. WILSON PUBLIC LIBRARY OF PIKE COUNTY, Waverly, OH USA.
BREINING David A. *The Pike County War Book.* Unknown: Scholl Printing, 1919.

NATIONAL ARCHIVES AND RECORDS ADMINISTRATION, College Park, MD, USA.
ANCESTRY.com - 1900 United States Federal Census

SILCOX Jessie – p. 624
SILCOX Oscar C., Clincho, VA, USA.
PUCKETT Alma, Clincho, VA, USA.
RAKES-FISHER Ginger, Bakersfield, CA, USA.
SUTHERLAND Elihu J. *Dickenson County in War Time*. Publisher unknown.
NATIONAL ARCHIVES AND RECORDS ADMINISTRATION, College Park, MD, USA.

SIMS Robert – p. 625
A short History and Illustrated Roster of the 106th Infantry United States Army, 1917.
Philadelphia, PA: Edward Stern & Co., Inc.,1918.
MACKEY, Patty RECORD, Anderson, SC, USA.
NATIONAL ARCHIVES AND RECORDS ADMINISTRATION, College Park, MD, USA.
BROOKLYN DAILY EAGLE, Brooklyn Public Library - Brooklyn Collection, Brooklyn, NY, USA.
ANCESTRY.com – New York Abstracts of World War I Military Service 1917-1919.

SMEDLEY Clarence – p. 195
HACKETT Cathy, Springfield, Ohio, USA.
SANDERS Scott, Yellow Springs, OH, USA.
SPRINGFIELD DAILY NEWS, 28 November 1918, Springfield, OH, USA.
NATIONAL ARCHIVES AND RECORDS ADMINISTRATION, College Park, MD, USA.

SMITH Andrew – p. 534
MACKEY, Patty RECORD, Anderson, SC, USA.
NATIONAL ARCHIVES AND RECORDS ADMINISTRATION, College Park, MD, USA.
BROOKLYN DAILY EAGLE, Brooklyn Public Library - Brooklyn Collection, Brooklyn, NY, USA.

SMITH Edward – p. 231
SEARCY Susan, Nevada State Library and Archives, Carson City, NV.

SNEDECOR Eliphalet – p. 327
HILDEBRANDT DUSENBURY Marjorie, USA.
MACKEY, Patty RECORD, Anderson, SC, USA.
BROOKLYN DAILY EAGLE, Brooklyn Public Library - Brooklyn Collection, Brooklyn, NY, USA.
NATIONAL ARCHIVES AND RECORDS ADMINISTRATION, College Park, MD, USA.
ANCESTRY.com – New York Abstracts of World War I Military Service 1917-1919

SONVILLE Ernest – p. 175
MILLS John, Seattle, WA, USA.
GITCHEL Susan, Elma, WA, USA.
MACKEY, Patty RECORD, Anderson, SC, USA.
GRACZYKOWSKI Scott J., Saint Paul, MN, USA.
NATIONAL ARCHIVES AND RECORDS ADMINISTRATION, College Park, MD, USA.
ANCESTRY.com – 1900 U.S. Federal Census
ANCESTRY.com - U.S. World War I Draft Registration Cards 1917-1918

SPANO Guiseppi– p. 422
NATIONAL ARCHIVES AND RECORDS ADMINISTRATION, College Park, MD, USA.
MACKEY, Patty RECORD, Anderson, SC, USA.

SPEAR George – p. 273
RIDDLE Peggy, Advance, NC, USA.
PRYOR Vonnie, Winston-Salem, NC, USA.
BREWER Ed, Clemmons, NC, USA.
TOOLE Christine, Clemmons, NC, USA.
BLUM Nicole, Winston-Salem, NC, USA.

SPIDLE Murray – p. 626
EVENING INDEPENDANT, 3 August 1918, Massillon, OH, USA.
EVENING INDEPENDANT, 19 August 1918, Massillon, OH, USA.
ROLAND G. & REED O.L. *The Camel Drivers - The 17th Aero Squadron in World War I.*
Lancaster, PA: Shiffer Publishing Ltd., 1921.
ADKINS Jean, Massillon, OH, USA.
PETERSON Darren, Dothan, AL, USA.
www.theaereodrome.com consulted on 1 March 2007.

STAFFORD John – p. 332
KITCH Tom, Columbus, OH, USA.
HOMER Patricia, Greenville, PA, USA.
PETERSON Darren, Dothan, AL, USA
STAFFORD Brian, Vienna, VA, USA
THE RECORD-ARGUS, Greenville, PA, 28 Nov. 1902/30 Nov. 1918/11 June 1919
NATIONAL ARCHIVES AND RECORDS ADMINISTRATION, College Park, MD, USA.
ANCESTRY.com - U.S. World War I Draft Registration Cards 1917-1918

STALLINGS Paul – p. 282
HART Margaret, Bear, DE, USA.
STALLINGS John, Belvidere, NC, USA.
SKINNER Charles, Hertford, NC.
AMERICAN LEGION POST W. P. STALLINGS, Post 126, Hertford, NC, USA.
ANCESTRY.com - U.S. World War I Draft Registration Cards 1917-1918

STALTER Charles – p. 552
NEW JERSEY STATE ARCHIVES, Department of State, Trenton, NJ, USA.
NATIONAL ARCHIVES AND RECORDS ADMINISTRATION, College Park, MD, USA.
ANCESTRY.com – Stalter/Nagel Family Tree, 1910 U.S. Federal Census and U.S. World War I
Draft Registration Cards 1917-1918

STECH James – p. 269
KRAKORA-LOOBY Janice, Lake Forest, IL, USA.
MACKEY, Patty RECORD, Anderson, SC, USA.
VOLENCE Lois, Reading, PA, USA.
NATIONAL ARCHIVES AND RECORDS ADMINISTRATION, College Park, MD, USA.

STEIN Norman – p. 449
A short History and Illustrated Roster of the 106th Infantry United States Army, 1917.
Philadelphia, PA: Edward Stern & Co., Inc., 1918.
NATIONAL ARCHIVES AND RECORDS ADMINISTRATION, College Park, MD, USA.

STOLZ Herman – p. 423
KOONS Steve, Dayton, OH, USA.
DAYTON DAILY NEWS, 27 November 1918, Dayton, OH, USA.
NATIONAL ARCHIVES AND RECORDS ADMINISTRATION, College Park, MD, USA.

STROMAN Ray – p. 297
HAYES Catheleen, Ligonier, IN USA.
STROMAN Albert, Goshen, IN, USA.
STROMAN Darol, Kendalville, IN, USA.
SHENEMAN Franklin, South Bend, IN, USA.
WISLER Amanda, LaGrange, IN, USA.
SULLIVAN Willard P. & TUCKER Harry. *The History of the 105th Regiment of Engineers.* NY: George H Doran CO., 1919.
INDIANA HISTORICAL COMMISSION. *Indiana World War Records Gold Star Honor Roll 1914-1918.* Indianapolis, IN: Fort Wayne Printing Co., 1921.
ANCESTRY.com - U.S. World War I Draft Registration Cards 1917-1918

STRUCK Arthur – p. 287
MACKEY, Patty RECORD, Anderson, SC, USA.
NATIONAL ARCHIVES AND RECORDS ADMINISTRATION, College Park, MD, USA.
ANCESTRY.com - U.S. World War I Draft Registration Cards 1917-1918 and New York
Abstracts of World War I Military Service 1917-1919.

STUBBS Roscoe – p. 369
STUBBS Alan, Ottumwa, IA, USA.
GRACZYKOWSKI Scott J., Saint Paul, MN, USA.
KEOKUK HISTORICAL SOCIETY, Sigourney, IA, USA.
MARTIN Carl A., Veterans Affairs Commission, Sigourney, IA, USA.
STAATS David, Ottumwa, IA, USA.
MILLER Robert, Delta, IA, USA.
BAKEHOUSE Glen & Lois, Sigourney, IA USA.
NATIONAL ARCHIVES AND RECORDS ADMINISTRATION, College Park, MD, USA.
ANCESTRY.com – McDowell Ryan Family Tree and 1910 US Federal Census.

SUDBECK August – p. 474
SUDBECK Vernon, Hartington, NE, USA.
SUDBECK Donavin, Hartington, NE, USA.
NATIONAL ARCHIVES AND RECORDS ADMINISTRATION, College Park, MD, USA.
GRACZYKOWSKI Scott J., Saint Paul, MN, USA.
HAUSEE, HOWE & DOYLE. *Soldiers of the Great War.* Washington D.C.: Soldiers Record Publishing Association, 1920.

SUTEA Mike – p. 498
NATIONAL ARCHIVES AND RECORDS ADMINISTRATION, College Park, MD, USA.
OHIO ADJUDANTS GENERAL'S DEPARTMENT. *The official Roster Ohio Soldiers, Sailors and Marines in the World War 1917-1918.* Columbus, OH: F.J. Heer Printing Co., 1926.

SWAIN Russell– p. 446
SCHILLING Chip, Syracuse, NY, USA.
SWAIN Alan, Orange Park, FL, USA.
BROOKLYN DAILY EAGLE, Brooklyn Public Library - Brooklyn Collection, Brooklyn, NY, USA.
NATIONAL ARCHIVES AND RECORDS ADMINISTRATION, College Park, MD, USA.

TAGUE John – p. 300
TAGUE Tom, Southgate, MI, USA.
OHIO ADJUDANTS GENERAL'S DEPARTMENT. *The official Roster Ohio Soldiers, Sailors and Marines in the World War 1917-1918.* Columbus, OH: F.J. Heer Printing Co., 1926.
NATIONAL ARCHIVES AND RECORDS ADMINISTRATION, College Park, MD, USA.

TAILOR James – p. 515
MACKEY, Patty RECORD, Anderson, SC, USA.
NATIONAL ARCHIVES AND RECORDS ADMINISTRATION, College Park, MD, USA.
ANCESTRY.com - U.S. World War I Draft Registration Cards 1917-1918

TALIBERTI Louis – p. 540
LOS ANGELES WESTSIDE GENEALOGICAL SOCIETY, Marina del Rey, CA, USA.
CALIFORNIA STATE LIBRARY, Sacramento, CA, USA.
ANCESTRY.com – 1900 U.S. Federal Census

TALLON Martin – p. 554
MISSOURI STATE ARCHIVES, Jefferson City, MO, USA.
NATIONAL ARCHIVES AND RECORDS ADMINISTRATION, College Park, MD, USA.
MACKEY, Patty RECORD, Anderson, SC, USA.

TENNEY Levi – p. 202
TENNEY Malcolm Jr. M.D., Staunton, VA, USA.
NEW JERSEY STATE ARCHIVES, EPSTEIN BETTE, Trenton, NJ, USA.
NATIONAL ARCHIVES AND RECORDS ADMINISTRATION, College Park, MD, USA.

THALMAN Chauncey – p. 460
BURGE Conny, Aurora, CA, USA.
BURGE EUNICE, Arriba, CO, USA.
NATIONAL ARCHIVES AND RECORDS ADMINISTRATION, College Park, MD, USA.
SEPIC Chris, Tarboro, NC, USA.
GRACZYKOWSKI Scott J., Saint Paul, MN, USA.
ANCESTRY.com – Lambert Family Tree

THOMPSON John – p. 132
NATIONAL ARCHIVES AND RECORDS ADMINISTRATION, College Park, MD, USA.
OHIO ADJUDANTS GENERAL'S DEPARTMENT. *The official Roster Ohio Soldiers, Sailors and Marines in the World War 1917-1918*. Columbus, OH: F.J. Heer Printing Co., 1926.

THOMPSON Stanley – p. 535
DAY-SCHULZ Sara, Madrid, NY, USA.
NATIONAL ARCHIVES AND RECORDS ADMINISTRATION, College Park, MD, USA.
ANCESTRY.com – New York Abstracts of World War I Military Service 1917-1919
FINDAGRAVE.com – Madrid Cemetery, St. Lawrence County, NY. Memorial nr.: 30251106 created by Northern Neighbors

TILLEY William – p. 408
BOYLE Eleanor, Roslyn, NY, USA.
HAUSEE, HOWE & DOYLE . *Soldiers of the Great War*. Washington D.C.: Soldiers Record Publishing Association, 1920.
NATIONAL ARCHIVES AND RECORDS ADMINISTRATION, College Park, MD, USA.
ANCESTRY.com – U.S. World War I Draft Registration Cards 1917-1918 and New York Abstracts of World War I Military Service 1917-1919

TIO Frank – p. 326
TIO Clarence, Eau Claire, WI, USA.
GRACZYKOWSKI Scott J., Saint Paul, MN, USA.

TOCCOTELLI Tony – p. 385
OHIO ADJUDANTS GENERAL'S DEPARTMENT. *The official Roster Ohio Soldiers, Sailors and Marines in the World War 1917-1918*. Columbus, OH: F.J. Heer Printing Co., 1926.
NATIONAL ARCHIVES AND RECORDS ADMINISTRATION, College Park, MD, USA.

TODD Theodore – p. 261
THE NEW YORK TRIBUNE, October 27, 1918, New York City, NY, USA.
DUNN Meridee, Hope, ID, USA.
HOOPER, Caryl, Port Washington, NY, U.S.A.
NATIONAL ARCHIVES AND RECORDS ADMINISTRATION, College Park, MD, USA.
ANCESTRY.com – New York Abstracts of World War I Military Service 1917-1919
ANCESTRY.com – Outcault Family Tree and 1900 US Federal Census

TOGSTAD Theodore – p. 266
WILLIAMS Rodger, Maddock, ND, USA.
TOGSTAD Gary, Vincennes, IN, USA.
TOGSTAD Harris, Maddock, ND, USA.
HARTMAN Patrice, Regent, ND, USA.
PERRINE Jordan, Normandy Park, WA, USA.
MELDRUM T. *A History of the 362nd Infantry*. Ogden, UT: A.L. Scoville Press, 1920.
ANCESTRY.com - U.S. World War I Draft Registration Cards 1917-1918 and 1900 US Federal Census.

TOVSRUD Robert – p. 478
JACOBSEN Jean, Moorhead, MN, USA.
HERMANSON Jon, COMM. R. TOVSRUD VFW POST # 757, Harlow, ND, USA.
HARTMAN Patrice, Regent, ND, USA.
NATIONAL ARCHIVES AND RECORDS ADMINISTRATION, College Park, MD, USA.
ANCESTRY.com – 1910 U.S. Federal Census and World War I Draft Registration Cards 1917-1918

TRAFKA Orine – p. 133
LEHR Mary, Algoma, WI, USA.
NATIONAL ARCHIVES AND RECORDS ADMINISTRATION, College Park, MD, USA.

TRORANO Camillo – p. 495
NATIONAL ARCHIVES AND RECORDS ADMINISTRATION, College Park, MD, USA.

UMLAND Albert – p. 283
A short History and Illustrated Roster of the 106th Infantry United States Army, 1917.
Philadelphia, PA: Edward Stern & Co., Inc., 1918.
NATIONAL ARCHIVES AND RECORDS ADMINISTRATION, College Park, MD, USA.
ANCESTRY.com – New York Abstracts of World War I Military Service 1917-1919

UNKNOWN SOLDIERS
picture copyright http://www.thepoppyman.com

URDAHL Christian – p. 299
URDAL Jens, Flekkefjord, Norway.
GRACZYKOWSKI Scott J., Saint Paul, MN, USA.
NATIONAL ARCHIVES AND RECORDS ADMINISTRATION, College Park, MD, USA.
ANCESTRY.com – US Naturalization Record Indexes 1791-1992

VANDERWAAL Albert – p. 543
VANDERWAAL Robert, Erskine, MN, USA.
BJORGEN Brian, Seattle, WA USA.
BAKKE Margit, Flom, MN, USA.
CROOKSTON PUBLIC LIBRARY, Crookston, MN, USA.
EAST GRAND FORKS CAMPBELL LIBRARY, East Grand Forks, MN, USA.
WENTSEL Claude E. *Polk County, Minnesota in the World War 1917-1918-1919*. Ada, MN,
Wentsel Claude E., 1922.
ANCESTRY.com – 1900 U.S. Federal Census

VAN INGEN Richard – p. 308
A short History and Illustrated Roster of the 106th Infantry United States Army, 1917.
Philadelphia, PA: Edward Stern & Co., Inc., 1918.
NATIONAL ARCHIVES AND RECORDS ADMINISTRATION, College Park, MD, USA.
ANCESTRY.com - U.S. World War I Draft Registration Cards 1917-1918 and New York
Abstracts of World War I Military Service 1917-1919

VAN KIRK Edgar – p. 290
SANDERS Scott, Yellow Springs, OH, USA
OHIO ADJUDANTS GENERAL'S DEPARTMENT. *The official Roster Ohio Soldiers, Sailors and Marines in the World War 1917-1918.* Columbus, OH: F.J. Heer Printing Co., 1926.
NATIONAL ARCHIVES AND RECORDS ADMINISTRATION, College Park, MD, USA.
ANCESTRY.com – 1900 US Federal Census and Family Tree
FINDAGRAVE.com – Washington Court House Cemetery, OH. Memorial nr.: 88764360 created by Chris and Sally Baughn

VESEY Joseph – p. 343
OHIO ADJUDANTS GENERAL'S DEPARTMENT. *The official Roster Ohio Soldiers, Sailors and Marines in the World War 1917-1918.* Columbus, OH: F.J. Heer Printing Co., 1926.
McHUGH Anthony, Pollagh, Keel, Achill, County Mayo, Ireland.
www.ellisisland.org cnsulted on 3 March 2005.
HERZOG Bodo, *60 Jahre Deutsche Uboote 1906-1966,* J.E. Lehmanns Verlag, Munchen, 1968, page 119.
ANCESTRY.com - U.S. World War I Draft Registration Cards 1917-1918

VOLZ Harry – p. 141
SMITH Jean, Baraboo, WI, USA.
GRACZYKOWSKI Scott J., Saint Paul, MN, USA.
NATIONAL ARCHIVES AND RECORDS ADMINISTRATION, College Park, MD, USA.

WAJEIULA Jonas – p. 362
RUHMANN Elizabeth, Livingston, IL, USA.
NATIONAL ARCHIVES AND RECORDS ADMINISTRATION, College Park, MD, USA.
VAN DEN EEDEN Chuck, Lombard, IL, USA.
HITCH Barbara, Livingston, IL, USA.

WALTERICK Claude – p. 420
SCHUCK Richard, Delphos, OH, USA.
VFW WALTERICK-HEMME POST 3035, Delphos, OH, USA.
OHIO ADJUDANTS GENERAL'S DEPARTMENT. *The official Roster Ohio Soldiers, Sailors and Marines in the World War 1917-1918.* Columbus, OH: F.J. Heer Printing Co., 1926.

WATTELET Leonard – p. 179
WOOD David & Kay, Long Beach, CA, USA.
BOLAND Gordon & Gail, Bartlesville, OR, USA.
WATTELET Jean, Waziers, France.
NATIONAL ARCHIVES AND RECORDS ADMINISTRATION, College Park, MD, USA.

WAYNE Harvey – p. 415
DANNENBERGER Margaret, Rochester, IL, USA.
SANGAMON COUNTY GENEALOGICAL SOCIETY, Springfield, IL, USA.
NATIONAL ARCHIVES AND RECORDS ADMINISTRATION, College Park, MD, USA
ANCESTRY.com - U.S. World War I Draft Registration Cards 1917-1918

WEBBER Raymond – p. 504
ZIMMERMAN Mary, Ephrata, PA, USA.
BRUBAKER Paul, Ephrata, PA, USA.
SITES Julie, Manheim, PA, USA.
MOYER Karl, Lancaster, PA, USA.
NATIONAL ARCHIVES AND RECORDS ADMINISTRATION, College Park, MD, USA

WELSH John – p. 408
A short History and Illustrated Roster of the 106th Infantry United States Army, 1917.
Philadelphia, PA: Edward Stern & Co., Inc., 1918.
BROOKLYN DAILY EAGLE, Brooklyn Public Library - Brooklyn Collection, Brooklyn, NY, USA.
NATIONAL ARCHIVES AND RECORDS ADMINISTRATION, College Park, MD, USA

WERMALD James – p. 307
A short History and Illustrated Roster of the 106th Infantry United States Army, 1917.
Philadelphia, PA: Edward Stern & Co., Inc., 1918.
NATIONAL ARCHIVES AND RECORDS ADMINISTRATION, College Park, MD, USA.

WESTMORELAND Haymore – p. 204
LOGGINS Doris, High Point, NC, USA.

WETMORE Albert – p. 399
WETMORE Kevin J., Cheshire, CT, USA.
MACKEY, Patty RECORD, Anderson, SC, USA.
NATIONAL ARCHIVES AND RECORDS ADMINISTRATION, College Park, MD, USA.
ANCESTRY.com – New York Abstracts of World War I Military Service 1917-1919

WHALEY Austin – p. 629
SILLS Ruth, Dover, TN, USA.
FORD Pam, Dover, TN, USA.
GRACZYKOWSKI Scott J., Saint Paul, MN, USA.
NATIONAL ARCHIVES AND RECORDS ADMINISTRATION, College Park, MD, USA.

WHEELER Stanley – p. 538
CHURCH Allan, The Record Journal, Meriden, Connecticut, USA.
FRANCO Janis, Meriden Public Library, Meriden, Connecticut, USA.
THE MERIDEN DAILY JOURNAL, 29 November 1918, Meriden, CT, USA.
HAUSEE, HOWE & DOYLE. *Soldiers of the Great War.* Washington D.C.: Soldiers Record
Publishing Association, 1920.
NATIONAL ARCHIVES AND RECORDS ADMINISTRATION, College Park, MD, USA.
STATE OF CONNECTICUT – Military Service Record for Stanley Bowen Wheeler

WHITE Charles – p. 436
A short History and Illustrated Roster of the 106th Infantry United States Army, 1917.
Philadelphia, PA: Edward Stern & Co., Inc., 1918.
BROOKLYN DAILY EAGLE, Brooklyn Public Library - Brooklyn Collection, Brooklyn, NY, USA.
NATIONAL ARCHIVES AND RECORDS ADMINISTRATION, College Park, MD, USA.

WHITE Ernest – p. 372
WEAVER WHITE Ruth & Max, Charleston, IL, USA.
WHITE James A., Mattoon, IL, USA.
HOMANN WHITE Patty, Mattoon, IL, USA.
NATIONAL ARCHIVES AND RECORDS ADMINISTRATION, College Park, MD, USA.

WHITE Merle – p. 334
SHENEMAN Franklin, South Bend, Indiana, USA.
INDIANA HISTORICAL COMMISSION. *Indiana World War Records Gold Star Honor Roll 1914-1918*. Indianapolis: Fort Wayne Printing Co., 1921.
MORSE Irvin, Mishawaka, IN, USA.
ZORNOW Diana, Bristol, IN, USA.
NATIONAL ARCHIVES AND RECORDS ADMINISTRATION, College Park, MD, USA.

WHITNEY Roy – p. 525
ZEIGLER Wayne, Seneca, MT, USA.
NATIONAL ARCHIVES AND RECORDS ADMINISTRATION, College Park, MD, USA.
ANCESTRY.com - U.S. World War I Draft Registration Cards 1917-1918

WIESNEWSKI John – p. 200
NATIONAL ARCHIVES AND RECORDS ADMINISTRATION, College Park, MD, USA.
HAUSEE, HOWE & DOYLE. *Soldiers of the Great War*. Washington D.C.: Soldiers Record Publishing Association, 1920.
ANCESTRY.com – New York Abstracts of World War I Military Service 1917-1919
ANCESTRY.com - U.S. World War I Draft Registration Cards 1917-1918

WIGNEL Frank – p. 161
OHIO ADJUDANTS GENERAL'S DEPARTMENT. *The official Roster Ohio Soldiers, Sailors and Marines in the World War 1917-1918*. Columbus, OH: F.J. Heer Printing Co., 1926.
NATIONAL ARCHIVES AND RECORDS ADMINISTRATION, College Park, MD, USA.
ANCESTRY.com - U.S. World War I Draft Registration Cards 1917-1918

WILDFIER Joseph – p. 160
WILDFIRE FINGADO Pam, Saint Mary's, PA, USA.
NATIONAL ARCHIVES AND RECORDS ADMINISTRATION, College Park, MD, USA.

WILKENSON Reuben – p. 216
WILKINSON Patrick, Santa Cruz, CA, USA.
NELSON Robert L, American Legion Post 64, Santa Cruz, CA, USA.
GENEALOGICAL SOCIETY, Santa Cruz, California, USA.
SANTA CRUZ SENTINEL, 3 December 1918, Santa Cruz, CA, USA.

WILLIAMS Ferdinand – p. 318
NATIONAL ARCHIVES AND RECORDS ADMINISTRATION, College Park, MD, USA.
ANCESTRY.com – New York Abstracts of World War I Military Service 1917-1919

WILLIAMS Henry – p. 368
NATIONAL ARCHIVES AND RECORDS ADMINISTRATION, College Park, MD, USA.
GANDY Jim, NY STATE MILITARY MUSEUM, Saratoga Springs, NY, USA.
A short History and Illustrated Roster of the 105th Infantry United States Army, 1917.
Philadelphia, PA: Edward Stern & Co., Inc., 1918.

WILLIAMS Ringius – p. 182
A short History and Illustrated Roster of the 106th Infantry United States Army, 1917.
Philadelphia, PA: Edward Stern & Co., Inc., 1918.
BROOKLYN DAILY EAGLE, Brooklyn Public Library - Brooklyn Collection, Brooklyn, NY, USA.
ANCESTRY.com - New York Abstracts of World War I Military Service 1917-1919

WILLIAMS Sherman – p. 226
SPRADLIN Freddie, Torrance, CA, USA.
BLUEFIELD DAILY TELEGRAPH, 26 November 1918, Bluefield, WV, USA.
ANCESTRY.com – 1910 U.S. Federal Census

WILSON John – p. 149
GRACZYKOWSKI Scott J., Saint Paul, MN, USA.
NATIONAL ARCHIVES AND RECORDS ADMINISTRATION, College Park, MD, USA.
ANCESTRY.com – 1900 U.S. Federal Census
ANCESTRY.com – Minnesota Births and Christenings Index 1840-1980
WILSON, Weldon, St. Cloud, MN
MAHIEU Geert, Esen-Diksmuide, Belgium

WINSLOW Herbert – p. 353
TAUBERT S., Comm. J. Daley VFW Post # 200, Hastings-on-Hudson, NY, USA.
OLLSON Muriel, Hastings-On- Hudson, NY, USA.
HASTINGS HISTORICAL SOCIETY, Hastings-on-Hudson, NY, USA.
WHITE Reg, Patterson, NY, USA.
NATIONAL ARCHIVES AND RECORDS ADMINISTRATION, College Park, MD, USA.

WISER Emil – p. 376
SHENEMAN Franklin, South Bend, IN, USA.
INDIANA HISTORICAL COMMISSION. *Indiana World War Records Gold Star Honor Roll 1914-1918.* Indianapolis: Fort Wayne Printing Co., 1921.
NATIONAL ARCHIVES AND RECORDS ADMINISTRATION, College Park, MD, USA.

WISS Frank – p. 629
GRACZYKOWSKI Scott J., Saint Paul, MN, USA.
BROOKLYN DAILY EAGLE, Brooklyn Public Library - Brooklyn Collection, Brooklyn, NY, USA.
ROTHENBURG Mark, Patchoque-Medford Library, NY
BAUWENS Danny, Belgium
A short History and Illustrated Roster of the 106th Infantry United States Army, 1917.
Philadelphia, PA: Edward Stern & Co., Inc., 1918.
NATIONAL ARCHIVES AND RECORDS ADMINISTRATION, College Park, MD, USA.
ANCESTRY.com – New York Abstracts of World War I Military Service 1917-1919.

WOJCIECHOWSKI Frank – p. 555
OHIO ADJUDANTS GENERAL'S DEPARTMENT. *The official Roster Ohio Soldiers, Sailors and Marines in the World War 1917-1918.* Columbus, OH: F.J. Heer Printing Co., 1926.
NATIONAL ARCHIVES AND RECORDS ADMINISTRATION, College Park, MD, USA.

WOLD John – p. 564
ANDERSON Ruth, Minnesota Historical Society, Saint Paul, MN, USA.
PETERSON Merlin, Glenwood MN, USA.
RANDALL Leslie, Glenwood, MN, USA.
RUNE Ask, Baerums Verk, Oslo, Norway
VANDERDONCKT Philippe, Ronse, Belgium
ANCESTRY.com - U.S. World War I Draft Registration Cards 1917-1918

WOLL Edward – p. 394
CLARKE William F. *Over there with O'Ryan's Roughnecks.* Seattle, Wa: Superior Publishing Company, 1968.
NATIONAL ARCHIVES AND RECORDS ADMINISTRATION, College Park, MD, USA.

YATES Clement – p. 219
A short History and Illustrated Roster of the 106th Infantry United States Army, 1917. Philadelphia, PA: Edward Stern & Co., Inc., 1918.
NATIONAL ARCHIVES AND RECORDS ADMINISTRATION, College Park, MD, USA.

YONKMAN Jacob – p. 505
Fighting Men of Illinois. Publishers Subscription Company, IL, USA, 1918.
VOLENCE Lois, Reading, PA, USA.
MACKEY, Patty RECORD, Anderson, SC, USA.
NATIONAL ARCHIVES AND RECORDS ADMINISTRATION, College Park, MD, USA.

YOUNG John – p. 419
NATIONAL ARCHIVES AND RECORDS ADMINISTRATION, College Park, MD, USA
YOUNG Nancy, Mount Laurel, PA.
HEYNDERYCX Femke, Gent, Belgium

ZAISS Adolph – p. 245
NATIONAL ARCHIVES AND RECORDS ADMINISTRATION, College Park, MD, USA.
GRACZYKOWSKI Scott J., Saint Paul, MN, USA.
PANUM Philip, Denver, CO, USA.
ANCESTRY.com - U.S. World War I Draft Registration Cards 1917-1918

ZELLERS George – p. 530
HART Eleanor,(Reverend) Morgantown, PA, USA.
MOYER Karl, Lancaster, PA, USA.
HISTORICAL SOCIETY OF BERKS COUNTY, Reading, PA, USA.
NATIONAL ARCHIVES AND RECORDS ADMINISTRATION, College Park, MD, USA.
ANCESTRY.com – 1910 U.S. Federal Census and World War I Draft Registration Cards 1917-1918

LIST OF ABBREVIATIONS

STATES

AL	ALABAMA		MT	MONTANA
AK	ALASKA		NE	NEBRASKA
AR	ARKANSAS		NC	NORTH CAROLINA
AZ	ARIZONA		ND	NORTH DAKOTA
CA	CALIFORNIA		NH	NEW HAMPSHIRE
CO	COLORADO		NJ	NEW JERSEY
CT	CONNECTICUT		NM	NEW MEXICO
DC	DISTRICT OF COLUMBIA		NV	NEVADA
DE	DELAWARE		NY	NEW YORK
FL	FLORIDA		OH	OHIO
GA	GEORGIA		OK	OKLAHOMA
HI	HAWAII		OR	OREGON
IA	IOWA		PA	PENNSYLVANIA
ID	IDAHO		RI	RHODE ISLAND
IL	ILLINOIS		SC	SOUTH CAROLINA
IN	INDIANA		SD	SOUTH DAKOTA
KS	KANSAS		TN	TENNESSEE
KY	KENTUCKY		TX	TEXAS
LA	LOUISIANA		UT	UTAH
MA	MASSACHUSETTS		VT	VERMONT
MD	MARYLAND		VA	VIRGINIA
ME	MAINE		WA	WASHINGTON
MI	MICHIGAN		WI	WISCONSIN
MN	MINNESOTA		WV	WEST VIRGINIA
MO	MISSOURI		WY	WYOMING
MS	MISSISSIPPI			

CAUSES OF DEATH

ACC	Accident
DIS	Died of disease
DOW	Died of wounds
KIA	Killed in action

CPSIA information can be obtained
at www.ICGtesting.com
Printed in the USA
BVOW05s0838190517

484529BV00007B/8/P